Celebrating the Saints

Celebrating the Saints

Devotional Readings for Saints' Days

compiled and introduced by Robert Atwell
and Christopher L. Webber

MOREHOUSE PUBLISHING

Morehouse Publishing
P.O. Box 1321
Harrisburg, PA 17105

Morehouse Publishing is a division of The Morehouse Group.

We have made every effort to trace and identify sources correctly and to secure the necessary permission for printing. If we have made any errors in this text, we apologize sincerely. Please notify Morehouse Publishing if any corrections are to be made in subsequent printings.

First Published 1998 by The Canterbury Press Norwich, (a publishing imprint of Hymns Ancient & Modern Limited a registered charity), St. Mary's Works, St. Mary's Plain, Norwich, Norfolk, NR3 3BH, U.K.

Cover design by Corey Kent.

Library of Congress Cataloguing-in-Publication Data
Celebrating the saints: devotional readings for Saints' days / compiled by Robert Atwell and Christopher L. Webber.

p. cm.
First published 1998.
Includes bibliographical references and index.
ISBN 0-8192-1883-9

1. Church year meditations. 2. Christian saints--Meditations. 3. Devotional calendars--Church of England. I Atwell, Robert. II. Webber, Christopher L..

BV30-C437 2001
242'.37—dc21

00-053386
Rev.

Printed in the United States of America
01 02 03 04 05 06 07 08 09   9 8 7 6 5 4 3 2 1

CONTENTS

Introduction i

January 1

February 49

March 79

April 119

May 147

June 177

July 213

August 247

September 285

October 331

November 379

December 435

Abbreviations 477

Notes and Sources 478

Index of Saints' Days 496

Biographical Notes 503

Acknowledgements 509

Authors' Notes

Sources of extracts, translations and notes are listed at the end of the book, together with biographical sketches of authors not already covered by their inclusion in the Saints' Calendar. To keep extracts within reasonable limits while maintaining their sense, sentences or paragraphs have sometimes been omitted or transposed. Occasionally these omissions are noted by ellipses, but normally the text has been left free of marks so as not to distract the reader. Any abridgement, paraphrase, or alteration of a text is recorded in the notes.

Major feast days, and some individual commemorations, are supplied with a choice of readings. In the case of major feast days the readings have been chosen to reflect the spectrum of Patristic, Medieval, Reformation, (and occasionally contemporary) spirituality.

The vast majority of extracts do not exceed 500 words. Where a longer extract is reproduced, square brackets indicate sections that may be omitted if, for example, reading in church necessitates shortening the extract.

Robert Atwell and Christopher L. Webber

Preface

For many years I served in a parish where every day began with a celebration of the Eucharist. We always commemorated those whose names are found in *Lesser Feasts or Fasts* so that their names become very familiar. Often I would look in my library for additional material about them for a homily. Nonetheless, I had never read a sermon by Absalom Jones or seen the letters sent by the Martyrs of Memphis or read the thoughts of Queen Emma of Hawaii on the subject of prayer. Preparing an American edition of *Celebrating the Saints* has given me an opportunity to get better acquainted with some of these members of the communion of saints and I am grateful for that.

I am also grateful to all those who have helped me find these materials: Laura Moore at the General Theological Seminary Library; Jennifer Peters at the National Archives of the Episcopal Church; Mary H. Miller of the Episcopal Peace Fellowship; the Rev. Charles R. Henery, professor of church history at Nashotah House; Stuart Ching, historiographer of the Diocese of Honolulu; Stan Upchurch, historiographer of the Diocese of Oklahoma; Anne Armour and Mary Anne Hill of the School of Theology of the University of the South; the Rev. Louise Kalemkerian, and Frank Peterson of Christ Church Canaan. Without their help, and such conveniences as the Internet, a fax machine, and a computer, it would have been impossible to assemble this material so quickly and easily.

I have often compared All Saints Day to a family reunion at the end of the year at which we remember those of the family no longer physically present and the difference they have made in our common life. Those celebrations will be richer for me as a result of the deeper acquaintance I now have with this "great cloud of witnesses."

Christopher L. Webber

We thank thee for thy mercies of blood, for thy redemption by
    blood. For the blood of thy martyrs and saints
shall enrich the earth, shall create the holy places.
For wherever a saint has dwelt, wherever a martyr has given
    his blood for the blood of Christ,
There is holy ground, and the sanctity shall not depart from it
Though armies trample over it, though sightseers come with
    guide-books looking over it;
From where the western seas gnaw at the coast of Iona,
To the death in the desert, the prayer in forgotten places by the
    broken imperial column,
From such ground springs that which forever renews the earth
Though it is forever denied.

T. S. Eliot, *Murder in the Cathedral*

INTRODUCTION

What would you go to the stake for? An eminent theologian once said to me that there were only two doctrines for which he would be prepared to die: the doctrine of original sin and the doctrine of the communion of saints. It seemed an eccentric choice, and still does, but over the years I have also had cause to ponder its wisdom.

To some both doctrines seem outmoded—theological whales marooned on Dover beach in the roar of the retreating tide of faith. Certainly, neither exactly dovetails with ideas of progress, or with the values and aspirations of a post-modern society. The doctrine of original sin, for example, speaks of an inherent disposition within humankind to put self at the center, often with disastrous and destructive results. It points to our clay feet. It exposes the shadow-side of our corporate memory: the trenches of the First World War, Auschwitz, Hiroshima, the Soviet death camps, the rape of the Amazonian rain-forests—things we would rather forget. In so doing the doctrine pulls humanity back from the indulgence of illusion, forcing us to a more realistic appraisal of history.

It is easy to caricature such talk as depressing and defeatist. In reality, however, it is full of hope because it does not pander to self-deception. Furthermore, although it demands we take responsibility for our actions, both individually and corporately, it also sets limits on culpability. To put it simply: "It's not all your fault." None of us begins life with a clean slate. We are the inheritors not only of genes, but also through our early nurturing of attitudes, patterns of behavior, and family baggage; and later, as adults, of the history and memories of communities and nations. Our capacity to act freely is impaired: we are constrained.

It would indeed be intolerably depressing if this were all, if the picture Christians painted were of a graceless world. However, the gospel of redemption insists that we do not have to be the victims of our genes, our mistakes, our sins, or the failings of earlier generations. The way of the cross invites movement, journey, transformation; but it is a journey into truth, not in spite of it. In this respect the doctrine of the communion of saints emerges from the ashes of human failure as a testament of glory. It is the theological counterpoise to the doctrine of original sin because it articulates a vision of the ultimate triumph of grace in a fallen world.

For the Christian, the history of God's saving purposes is supremely a *personal* history focused in the life, death and resurrection of Jesus Christ. The communion of saints, in the broadest sense of the term, is the company of those who have willed that their own life-stories be shaped and transformed by this event. They are, in Gregory Dix's immortal phrase,[1] the *plebs sancta Dei*—the holy common people of God—a pilgrim people journeying to their promised land. Over the centuries, the Church has come to recognize particular individuals within this company—those who by custom are specifically called "saints"—in and through whom God's purposes of love, mercy, peace, and justice have been specially revealed. The church's Calendar of Saints designates some of them to be companions on our journey, holding them up to successive generations of Christians as icons of hope that invite our prayerful reflection.

In the stories of individual saints it is as if the intense white light of the gospel has passed through a prism and been refracted into its constituent colors, making visible the spectrum of God's call to holiness. As we ponder their lives we glimpse little by little the face of the Christ who is coming to gather up all things in himself. The saints celebrate the vocation of the whole people of God to share in his very being. But this is cause for discomfort as well as joy because the doctrine of the communion of saints thereby confronts us with the realities of judgement and mortality. It challenges us to resurrection *now,* to abundant living *now*, but defines the way as being only via the cross, a dying and rising with Christ. The lives of the saints through the ages question human priorities, particularly those who see death as necessary defeat, and staying alive as an end in itself. The saints redefine life and death by placing both within the purposes of God for creation. In the words of Athanasius of Alexandria, writing in the fourth century:

> Death is a pilgrimage, a lifetime's pilgrimage which none of us must shirk. It is a pilgrimage from decay to imperishable life, from mortality to immortality, from anxiety to tranquillity of mind. Do not be afraid of the word death: rather rejoice in the blessings which follow a happy death. After all, what is death but the burial of sin and the harvest of goodness?[2]

Historical Background

This perspective is evident from the way that the primitive church commemorated its martyrs on the anniversary not of their births, but of their deaths—their *dies natalis* or *natalicia*—literally their birthdays to eternal life. From the outset, Christians remembered before God their contemporaries who had died for the faith and in faith, and the stories of their witness and the circumstances of their deaths were recorded and circulated.[3] With such commemorations the liturgical year of the church began to take shape. Our forebears had a strong sense of the mutual and reciprocal nature of prayer between the living and the departed. The account of the martyrdom of Polycarp around 155 is just such a case in point. It is probably the oldest authentic narrative of a Christian martyrdom outside the New Testament. The Christians of Smyrna wrote to other churches sharing the news of his courageous death, and how:

> When it was all over we gathered up his bones, more precious to us than jewels, finer than pure gold, and we laid them to rest in a place we had already set aside. There, the Lord permitting, we shall gather and celebrate with great gladness and joy the day of his martyrdom as a birthday. It will serve as a commemoration of all who have gone before us, and training and preparing those of us for whom a crown may be in store.[4]

Accounts such as this helped to form the mind and memory of the church. As Tertullian observed at the beginning of the third century, "the blood of the martyrs is the seed-bed of the Church." It was customary for their *passions*, as they were called, to be read aloud during the celebration of the Eucharist on the anniversary of their deaths, either in church or at the place of their burial. To eat and drink the Eucharist was to be sharing in the same heavenly banquet that the martyrs now enjoyed in glory. Their annual commemoration must have been an extremely moving event in the life of a Christian community. It precipitated within the consciousness of the Church a powerful sense of solidarity, of a belonging in Christ that transcended death. This awareness is something recent generations seem largely to have lost—at least in the West.

With the toleration of Christianity at the beginning of the fourth century, the concept of martyrdom itself begins to shift and broaden. Preaching to the people of Milan, Ambrose can state:

> Just as there are many kinds of persecution, so there are many forms of martyrdom. You are a witness to Christ every day of your life.... A witness is one who testifies to the precepts of the Lord Jesus and supports his deposition by deeds. Many are martyrs of Christ and confess the Lord Jesus each day in secret. This kind of martyrdom and faithful witnessing to Christ was known to the apostle Paul, who said: "Our boast is this, the testimony of our conscience."[5]

It was not long, therefore, before it became customary for certain outstanding Christians who had not been martyred to be also commemorated liturgically. Martin of Tours (d. 397) seems to have been the first person so commemorated. Here was a man whose life and example pointed people to Christ in such a profound way that he was considered worthy of wide veneration. In time, bishops, confessors and teachers of the faith, monks, nuns, and missionaries all came to be honored alongside the martyrs. As Augustine commented in one of his sermons:

> The holy martyrs imitated Christ even to the point of shedding their blood in emulation of his passion. But it was not only the martyrs who imitated him. When they passed into eternity, the bridge was not broken down, nor did the fountain dry up after they drank from it. Indeed, the garden of the Lord contains not only the roses of martyrdom but also the lilies of virginity, the ivy of marriage, and the violets of widowhood. So no one, my dear friends, need despair of his or her vocation.[6]

It is abundantly clear that Ambrose, Augustine, and their fellow bishops were always careful to distinguish between the worship offered to God and the veneration due to his saints. Augustine, for example, states unequivocally that:

> We, the Christian community, assemble to celebrate the memory of the martyrs with ritual solemnity because we want to be inspired to follow their example, share in their merits, and be helped by their prayers. Yet we erect no altars to any of the martyrs, even in the martyrs' burial chapels themselves.... What is offered is offered always to God who crowned the martyrs.... We venerate them with the same veneration of love and fellowship that we give to the saints of God still with us. But the veneration strictly called "worship" or *latria,* that is, the special homage belonging only to the divinity, is something we give and teach others to give to God alone.[7]

If such a fine distinction was clear in the mind of Augustine and his contemporaries, it became increasingly less clear in the minds of ordinary people in the centuries that followed; there was a blurring of theological subtleties. By the time of the Middle Ages, saints were being venerated chiefly as workers of miracles. Their earthly remains were believed to effect their presence,[8] their very physicality providing powerful access to the courts of heaven. The medieval church (at least in the West) had divided up the faithful departed into those *for* whom it was appropriate to pray, and those *to* whom it was appropriate to turn for aid and prayer.[9] It was inevitable that the popular veneration of images, pilgrimages, and the extravagant cult of individual saints, together with certain "abuses" associated with the doctrine of purgatory, should have provoked a cry for reform.

Like their continental counterparts (and indeed the later Roman Catholic reformers at the Council of Trent) the English Reformers were concerned to eliminate abuses, and above all to restore Christ to his pre-eminent position as sole mediator between God and man. But the Reformers went further: the dead were not to be categorized, and saints were to be commemorated not for their intercession or miracles, but for the holiness of their lives and for the example they offer the living. This emphasis is evident, for example, in the First Prayer Book of 1549:

> And here we do give unto thee most high praise, and hearty thanks, for the wonderful grace and virtue, declared in all thy saints, from the beginning of the world: and chiefly in the glorious and most Blessed Virgin Mary, mother of thy Son Jesus Christ our Lord and God, and in the holy Patriarchs, Prophets, Apostles and Martyrs, whose examples, O Lord, and steadfastness in thy faith, and keeping thy holy commandments, grant us to follow. We commend unto thy mercy, O Lord, all other thy servants which are departed hence from us, with the sign of faith, and now do rest in the sleep of peace: Grant unto them, we beseech thee, thy mercy, and everlasting peace, and that, at the day of the general resurrection, we and all they which be of the mystical body of thy Son, may altogether be set on his right hand.

This was the theological position that came to obtain within the Church of England as it emerged from the controversies of the sixteenth century. What is remarkable is that unique among the reformed churches, the Church of England (initially under the influence of Archbishop Thomas Cranmer, and later under Archbishop Matthew Parker during the reign of Elizabeth I) retained a calendar of saints, and required that some of them at least be commemorated by a special collect and readings.[10] This strong liturgical framework shaped definitively the worship and theology of Anglicanism. Among some of the Reformers, notably Hugh Latimer, Bishop of Worcester, there also emerged a return to a more primitive idea of reciprocal prayer uniting the mystical body of Christ. For example, writing on the saints and the faithful departed in 1533 he stated that:

> As touching the saints in heaven, they be not our mediators by way of redemption; for so Christ alone is our mediator and their both: so that the blood of martyrs hath nothing to do by way of redemption; the blood of Christ is enough for a thousand worlds. But by way of intercession, so

saints in heaven may be mediators, and pray for us: as I think they do when we call not upon them; for they be charitable, and need no spurs ... They be members of the mystical body of Christ as we be, and in more surety than we be. They love us charitably. Charity is not idle; if it be, it worketh and sheweth itself: and therefore I say, they wish us well, and pray for us.[11]

Of course, this was not the universal opinion of the Reformers. However, it was certainly the predominant view of the Caroline Divines and the generation that succeeded them. Thomas Traherne (1636-74), for example, could write movingly of the communion of saints, calling the saints "storehouses of God's holy word" and "living conduit-pipes of the Holy Ghost."[12] It was this broader vision that was obtained among many nineteenth century Episcopalians, and not just the Tractarians. Bishop Westcott, for example, writing of the communion of saints, says:

If the outward were the measure of the Church of Christ, we might well despair. But side by side with us, when we fondly think like Elijah or Elijah's servant that we stand alone, are countless multitudes whom we know not, angels whom we have no power to discern, children of God whom we have not learnt to recognize. We have come to the kingdom of God, peopled with armies of angels and men working for us and with us because they are working for God. And though we cannot grasp the fullness of the truth, and free ourselves from the fetters of sense, yet we can, in the light of the Incarnation, feel the fact of this unseen fellowship; we can feel that heaven has been re-opened to us by Christ.[13]

Rediscovering the Saints

Today the controversies that so exercised the minds of our sixteenth century forebears seem remote. Most people are agnostic about what specialized knowledge (if any) individual saints might have of the living. And yet, perhaps because of the fragmentation of society, people are also increasingly aware of the need both to find and to give concrete expression to a sense of solidarity in Christ. Christians across a wide spectrum of theological opinion are once again talking of the saints not simply in terms of fellowship, but of *communion.* There is a renewed emphasis upon an understanding of the Christian life as a participation in the life of the Trinity—a communion with God and one another in Christ, empowered by the Holy Spirit. And the currency of such participation is prayer in which the whole Church shares, living and departed, commending one another to the mercy of God.

The most recent revision of its Calendar of Saints by the Episcopal Church (to which this anthology corresponds) is more *inclusive* than anything that has gone before. While honoring the great heroes that laid the foundations of Christianity, its compass is more contemporary in feel and certainly more international. Until comparatively recently, one could have been forgiven for thinking that there were no more saints after 1500!

The new calendar is also more *catholic* in the technical sense of that word. At a time when destructive nationalistic movements seem to be in the ascendant right across the world, a more international calendar may encourage Christians to a wider vision of the church and the purposes of God in his world. Certainly in our schools and colleges, the religious and social education of children of different faiths and from different cultures can be greatly helped through learning about the lives of one another's heroes and saints. Children (and adults for that matter) often learn more through stories than through concepts. To this end, I hope that this book, with its biographical sketches and readings, will be a valuable resource for teachers.

The new calendar is also much more *ecumenical.* The inclusion of great Christian figures from other communions, including those who died for their convictions, provides not only opportunities for exploring something of the richness of other traditions, but also opportunities for prayer and indeed penitence. Their stories challenge us to a fresh examination of our perceptions about the past. We need to learn how fellow Christians from whom we have been historically and theologically separated for generations understand the tragedy as well as the glory of Christian history. As Mark Santer has written:

> There is a connection between our self-identification as members of particular communities and the stories we tell about the past. It is by the things we remember, and the way we remember them, and by the things we fail to remember, that we identify ourselves as belonging to this or that group. What we remember, or do not remember, molds our reactions and our behavior towards others at a level deeper than that of conscious reflection.[14]

This anthology is offered as a contribution to enable this ecumenical encounter to continue and deepen. It is offered as a contribution to the process of healing the corporate memory of the Church. The literature it includes spans almost two thousand years. It contains extracts from the lives of saints and the accounts of martyrdoms—and not just of those who died in the first three centuries, but of women and men right up to our own time from different countries and cultures who gave their lives for Christ. There are extracts from sermons, hymns, theological treatises, letters, journals, prayers, and poems. It is a rich treasury worthy of study and reflection. As Bishop Jeremy Taylor, writing in the seventeenth century, advised: "To distinguish festival days from common, let it not be lessening the devotion of ordinary days, but enlarge upon the holy day."[15] This book has been assembled to assist in the process of "enlargement".

The saints offer each generation exciting and contrasting models of how to follow Christ. They constitute very individual stars in a wide galaxy, and their sheer variety and vitality affirms the worthwhileness of the Christian endeavor. They teach us something profound about God's call to holiness, about being a Christian in the world today, about being a human being. Thomas Merton once wrote:

> Unlike the animals and the trees, it is not enough for us to be what our nature intends. It is not enough for us to be individuals. For us, holiness is more than humanity. If we are never anything but men and women, never anything but people, we will not be saints and we will not be able to offer to God the worship of our imitation, which is sanctity.It is true to say that for me sanctity consists in being *myself* and for you sanctity consists in being *yourself* and that, in the last analysis, your sanctity will never be mine and mine will never be yours, except in the communism of charity and grace. For me to be a saint means to be myself. Therefore the problem of sanctity and salvation is in fact the problem of finding out who I am and of discovering my true self.[16]

The saints, though diverse, are united in their witness to the crucified and risen Christ. Like John the Baptist, their lives point consistently away from themselves and toward Christ: "He must grow greater, and I must grow smaller." It is to be hoped that in making their lives and writings accessible to a wider public, we in our generation may be renewed in our discipleship, and recover a more dynamic sense of our participation in the body of Christ.

Robert Atwell

1 Gregory Dix, *The Shape of the Liturgy,* London, 1945, p. 744.

2 Athanasius, *On the Blessing of Death,* 4, 15.

3 In all probability, the custom of commemorating martyrs was something that Christians inherited from Judaism. Since at least the time of the Maccabean Revolt, martyrs were very important in the life and thought of Jewish communities.

4 *Martyrdom of Polycarp,* 9.

5 Ambrose, *Commentary on Psalm 118,* 20, 479.

6 Augustine, *Sermon* 304.

7 Augustine, *Against Faustus,* 20, 21.

8 The inscription on the tomb of Saint Martin of Tours is a good example: 'Here lies Martin the bishop, of holy memory, whose soul is in the hand of God; but he is fully here, present and made plain in miracles of every kind.' See Peter Brown, *The Cult of the Saints,* London, 1981, pp. 4ff.

9 This tendency was emerging even in the time of Augustine. He wrote: 'At the table of the Lord we do not commemorate the martyrs in the same way as we commemorate others who rest in peace, in order to pray for them also. We commemorate them rather so that they may pray for us, that we may follow closely in their footsteps; for they have reached the fullness of that love of which our Lord spoke when he said: 'Greater love has no one than to lay down his life for his friends.' *Homilies on Saint John's Gospel,* 84, 2.

10 The 1549 English Prayer Book drastically pruned the number of Saints' Days to those with scriptural warrant. The 1552 Prayer Book relaxed this rule somewhat, adding commemorations of George, Laurence, Clement of Rome and Lammas Day. In 1561 Elizabeth I issued a royal decree which added a further fifty-eight Feasts to the Calendar, and yet more were added in the revisions of 1604 and 1662. None of these additional Saints' Days, however, were provided with propers to enable their liturgical observance.

11 Hugh Latimer, 'Articles Untruly, Falsely, Uncharitably Imputed to me by Dr. Powell of Salisbury', *Sermons and Remains of Bishop Hugh Latimer,* Cambridge, 1844, pp. 234 & 236.

12 Thomas Traherne, *Poems, Centuries and Three Thanksgivings,* ed. Anne Ridler, Oxford, 1966.

13 B. F. Westcott, *Christus Consummator,* London, 1886, p. 58.

14 Mark Santer, 'The Reconciliation of Memories,' in *Their Lord and Ours,* ed. Mark Santer, London, 1982, p.160.

15 Jeremy Taylor, *The Rule and Exercises of Holy Living,* VI.

16 Thomas Merton, *Seeds of Contemplation,* London, 1961, pp. 245.

JANUARY

January 1

The Holy Name of Our Lord Jesus Christ

The celebration of this scriptural festival marks three events: first, the naming of the infant Jesus; secondly, the performance of the rite of circumcision as a sign of the covenant between God and Abraham "and his children for ever"—thus Christ's keeping of the Law; thirdly and traditionally, it is honored as the first shedding of the Christ's blood. The name Jesus means literally "Yahweh saves." Theologically, it may be linked to the question asked by Moses of God: "What is your name?" "I am who I am" was the reply; hence the significance of Jesus' own words: "Before Abraham was, I am." The feast has been observed in the Church since at least the sixth century.

A Reading from the treatise *On Contemplating God*
by William of St. Thierry

O God, you alone are the Lord. To be ruled by you is for us salvation. For us to serve you is nothing else but to be saved by you!

But how is it that we are saved by you, O Lord, from whom salvation comes and whose blessing is upon your people, if it is not in receiving from you the gift of loving you and being loved by you? That, Lord, is why you willed that the Son of your right hand, the "man whom you made so strong for yourself," should be called Jesus, that is to say, Savior, "for he will save his people from their sins." There is no other in whom is salvation except him who taught us to love himself when he first loved us, even to death on the cross. By loving us and holding us so dear he stirred us up to love himself, who first had loved us to the end.

You who first loved us did this, precisely this. You first loved us so that we might love you. And that was not because you needed to be loved by us, but because we could not be what you created us to be, except by loving you. Having then "in many ways and on various occasions spoken to our fathers by the prophets, now in these last days you have spoken to us in the Son," your Word, by whom the heavens were established, and all the power of them by the breath of his mouth. For you to speak thus in your Son was an open declaration, a "setting in the sun" as it were, of how much and in what sort of way you loved us, in that you spared not your own Son, but delivered him up for us all. Yes, and he himself loved us and gave himself for us.

This, Lord, is your word to us; this is your all-powerful message: he who, "while all things kept silence" (that is, were in the depths of error), "came from the royal throne," the stern opponent of error and the gentle apostle of love. And everything he did and everything he said on earth, even the insults, the spitting, the buffeting, the cross and the grave, all that was nothing but yourself speaking to us in the Son, appealing to us by your love, and stirring up our love for you.

alternative reading

A Reading from a sermon of Mark Frank

This name "which is above every name" has all things in it, and brings all things with it. It speaks more in five letters than we can do in five thousand words. It speaks more in it than we can speak today; and yet we intend today to speak of nothing else, nothing but Jesus, nothing but Jesus.

Before his birth the angel announced that this child, born of Mary, would be great: "he shall be called Son of the Highest, and the Lord God shall give him the throne of his father David." The angel thus intimates that this was a name of the highest majesty and glory. And what can we say upon it, less than burst out with the psalmist into a holy exclamation, "O Lord our Governor, O Lord our Jesus, how excellent is thy name in all the world!" It is all "clothed with majesty and honor;" it is "decked with light;" it comes riding to us "upon the wings of the wind"; the Holy Spirit breathes it full upon us, covering heaven and earth with its glory.

But it is a name of grace and mercy, as well as majesty and glory. For "there is no other name under heaven given by which we can be saved," but the name of Jesus. In his name we live, and in that name we die. As Saint Ambrose has written: "Jesus is all things to us if we will." Therefore I will have nothing else but him; and I have all if I have him.

The "looking unto Jesus" which the apostle advises, will keep us from being weary or fainting under our crosses; for this name was set upon the cross over our Savior's head. This same Jesus at the end fixes and fastens all. The love of God in Jesus will never leave us, never forsake us; come what can, it sweetens all.

Is there any one sad?—let him take Jesus into his heart, and he will take heart presently, and his joy will return upon him. Is any one fallen into a sin?—let him call heartily upon this name, and it will raise him up. Is any one troubled with hardness of heart, or dullness of spirit, or dejection of mind, or drowsiness in doing well?—in the meditation of this name, Jesus, all vanish and fly away. Our days would look dark and heavy, which were not lightened with the name of the "Sun of Righteousness"; our nights but sad and dolesome, which we entered not with this sweet name, when we lay down without commending ourselves to God in it.

So then let us remember to begin and end all in Jesus. The New Testament, the covenant of our salvation, begins so, "the generation of Jesus"; and "Come Lord Jesus," so it ends. May we all end so too, and when we are going hence, commend our spirits into his hands; and when he comes, may he receive them to sing praises and alleluias to his blessed name amidst the saints and angels in his glorious kingdom for ever.

January 2

Seraphim of Sarov

Monk and Spiritual Guide, 1833

Born in 1759 at Kursk in Russia, Seraphim entered the Monastery of our Lady at Sarov near Moscow when he was twenty years old. He lived as a solitary for more than thirty years but his gifts as a staretz, *or spiritual guide, became more widely known until he found himself sharing his gift of healing spirit, soul and body with the thousands who made the pilgrimage to his monastery. The "Jesus Prayer" formed the heart of his own devotional life and he stressed the need for all Christians to have an unceasing communion with the person of Jesus. He died on this day in 1833 and is revered in the Russian Orthodox Church as "an icon of Orthodox Spirituality."*

A Reading from a conversation of Seraphim of Sarov with Nicholas Motovilov concerning aims of the Christian life

It was Thursday. The day was gloomy. Snow lay deep on the ground and snowflakes were falling thickly from the sky when Father Seraphim began his conversation with me in the plot near his hermitage over against the river Sarovka, on the hill which slopes down to the river-bank. He sat me on the stump of a tree which he had just felled, and himself squatted before me.

"Prayer, fasting, watching," he said, "and all other Christian acts, however good they may be, do not alone constitute the aim of our Christian life, although they serve as the indispensable means of reaching this aim. The true aim of our Christian life is to acquire the Holy Spirit of God.

"We must begin by a right faith in our Lord Jesus Christ, the Son of God, who came into the world to save sinners, and by winning for ourselves the grace of the Holy Spirit who brings into our hearts the kingdom of God and lays for us the path to win the blessings of the future life.

"Every virtuous act done for Christ's sake gives us the grace of the Holy Spirit, but most of all is this given through prayer; for prayer is somehow always in our hands as an instrument for acquiring the grace of the Spirit. You wish, for instance, to go to church and there is no church near or the service is over; or you wish to give to the poor and there is none by you or you have nothing to give; you wish to perform some other virtuous act for Christ's sake and the strength or the opportunity is lacking. But this in no way affects prayer; prayer is always possible for everyone, rich and poor, noble and simple, strong and weak, healthy and suffering, righteous and sinful. Great is the power of prayer; most of all does it bring the Spirit of God and easiest of all is it to exercise.

"Prayer is given to us in order to converse with our good and life-giving God and Savior; but even here we must pray only until the Holy Spirit descends on us in measures of his heavenly grace known to him. When he comes to visit us, we must cease to pray. How can we pray to God, 'Come and abide in us, cleanse us from all evil, and save our souls, O gracious Lord,' when he has already come to us to save us who trust in him and call on his holy name in truth, that humbly and with love we may receive him, the Comforter, in the chamber of our souls, hungering and thirsting for his coming?

"Acquire therefore, my son, the grace of the Holy Spirit by all the virtues in Christ; trade in those that are most profitable to you. Thus, if prayer and watching give you more of God's grace, pray and watch; if fasting gives much of God's Spirit, then fast; if almsgiving gives more, give alms. Be always as a candle, burning with earthly fire, lighting other candles for the illumination of darkened places, but without its own light ever being diminished. For if this is the reality of earthly fire, what shall we say of the fire of the grace of God's Holy Spirit?"

January 2

Vedanayagam Samuel Azariah

Bishop in South India and Evangelist, 1945

Samuel Azariah was born in 1874 in a small village in South India, his father, Thomas Vedanayagam, being a simple village priest, and his mother, Ellen, having a deep love and understanding of the Scriptures. Samuel became a YMCA evangelist while still only nineteen, and secretary of the organization throughout South India a few years later. He saw that, for the church in India to grow and attract ordinary Indians, it had to have an indigenous leadership and reduce the strong western influences and almost totally white leadership that pervaded it. He was ordained priest at the age of thirty-five and bishop just three years later, his work moving from primary evangelism to forwarding his desire for more Indian clergy and the need to raise their educational standards. He was an avid ecumenist and was one of the first to see the importance to mission of a united church. He died on January 1, 1945, just two years before the creation of a united church of South India.

A Reading from *An Ecumenical Venture: The History of Nandyal Diocese in Andhra Pradesh* by Constance Millington

Azariah had two great priorities in his work: evangelism and the desire for Christian unity.

He understood evangelism to be the acid test of Christianity. When asked what he would preach about in a village that had never heard of Christ, Azariah answered without hesitation: "The resurrection." From a convert he demanded the full acceptance of Christianity which would include baptism and which could therefore include separation from family and caste. He claimed that Christianity took its origin in the death and resurrection of Jesus Christ and the outburst of supernatural power that this society manifested in the world.

Azariah recognized that because four-fifths of Indian people live in villages, for the Church to be an indigenous one it must be a rural Church. He was constantly in the villages, inspiring and guiding the teachers, clergy and congregations. He blamed the missionaries for not training people in evangelism, and thought their teaching had been mission centered instead of Church centered, and he pleaded with missionaries to build up the Indian Church. Much of the Christian outreach in his area was among the outcast people. Gradually as Christianity spread among the villages, the social situation began to change, the Christian outcasts gaining a new self-respect as they realized their worth in the eyes of God.

Azariah considered that one of the factors that hampered evangelism, and possibly the deepening of the spiritual life of the convert, was the western appearance of the Church in both its buildings and its services. As early as 1912 he had visions of a cathedral for the diocese to be built in the eastern style, where all Christians could feel spiritually at home regardless of their religious background and race. Building was delayed because of the Great War in Europe, but finally his dream was realized when the cathedral of The Most Glorious Epiphany was consecrated on January 6, 1936. The building is a beautiful structure embodying ideas from Christian, Hindu and Moslem architecture. Its dignity and spaciousness create a very different effect from that of the nineteenth and twentieth century Gothic churches and furnishings scattered elsewhere in India.

If evangelization of India was Azariah's first priority, the second was that of Church unity. He saw the two as inter-related. He believed that a united Church was in accordance with the will of God, "that we may all be one," and he also believed that a united church would be more effective for evangelism. Addressing the Lambeth Conference in 1930 he pleaded:

> In India we wonder if you have sufficiently contemplated the grievous sin of perpetuating your divisions and denominational bitterness in these your daughter churches. We want you to take us seriously when we say that the problem of union is one of life and death to us. Do not, we plead with you, do not give us your aid to keep us separate, but lead us to union so that you and we may go forward together and fulfill the prayer, "That we may all be one."

January 6

The Epiphany of Our Lord Jesus Christ

The subtitle in the English Book of Common Prayer *of this, one of the principal feasts of the Church, is "The Manifestation of Christ to the Gentiles." This emphasizes that, from the moment of the Incarnation, the good news of Jesus Christ is for all: Jew and Gentile, the wise and the simple, male and female. Nothing in the Greek text of the Gospels indicates that the Magi were all male or even three in number, and the idea that they were kings is a much later, non-scriptural tradition. The date chosen to celebrate this feast is related to the choice of the Winter Solstice for the celebration of the Nativity of Christ: the northern European pre-Christian tradition celebrated the birth of the Sun on December 25 whereas the Mediterranean and East customarily observed January 6 as the Solstice. As often happens, the two dates merged into a beginning and an end of the same celebration. The Western Church adopted "the twelve days of Christmas" climaxing on the eve of Epiphany, or "Twelfth Night." The implication by the fifth century was that this was the night on which the Magi arrived. The complications of dating became even more confused with the changing in the West from the Julian to the Gregorian Calendar, the Eastern Church refusing to adopt the change. So this day remains the chief day of celebrating the Incarnation in Orthodox Churches.*

A Reading from a sermon of Peter Chrysologos

In the mystery of our Lord's incarnation there were clear indications of his eternal Godhead. Yet the great events we celebrate today disclose and reveal in different ways the fact that God himself took a human body. Mortals, enshrouded always in darkness, must not be left in ignorance, and so be deprived of what they can understand and retain only by grace.

In choosing to be born for us, God chose to be known by us. He therefore reveals himself in this way, in order that this great sacrament of his love may not be an occasion for us of great misunderstanding.

Today the Magi find, crying in a manger, the one they have followed as he shone in the sky. Today the Magi see clearly, in swaddling clothes, the one they have long awaited as he lay hidden among the stars. Today the Magi gaze in deep wonder at what they see: heaven on earth, earth in heaven, humankind in God, God in human flesh, one whom the whole universe cannot contain now enclosed in a tiny body. As they look, they believe and do not question, as their symbolic gifts bear witness: incense for God, gold for a king, myrrh for one who is to die.

So the Gentiles, who were the last, become the first: the faith of the Magi is the firstfruits of the belief of the Gentiles.

Today Christ enters the Jordan to wash away the sin of the world. John himself testifies that this is why he has come: "Behold the Lamb of God, behold him who takes away the sins of the world." Today a servant lays his hand on the Lord, a man lays his hand on God. John lays his hand on Christ, not to forgive but to receive forgiveness.

Today, as the psalmist prophesied: "The voice of the Lord is heard - above the waters." What does the voice say? "This is my beloved Son, in whom I am well pleased."

Today the Holy Spirit hovers over the waters in the likeness of a dove. A dove announced to Noah that the flood had disappeared from the earth; so now a dove is to reveal that the world's shipwreck is at an end for ever. The sign is no longer an olive-shoot of the old stock: instead, the Spirit pours out on Christ's head the full richness of a new anointing by the Father, to fulfill what the psalmist had prophesied: "Therefore God, your God, has anointed you with the oil of gladness above your fellows."

Today Christ works the first of his signs from heaven by turning water into wine. But water has still to be changed into the sacrament of his blood, so that Christ may offer spiritual drink from the chalice of his body, to fulfill the psalmist's prophecy: "How excellent is my chalice, warming my spirit."

alternative reading

A Reading from a hymn of Ephrem of Syria

Who, being a mortal, can tell about the Reviver of all,
Who left the height of his majesty and came down to smallness?
You, who magnify all by being born, magnify my weak mind
    that I may tell about your birth,
    not to investigate your majesty,
    but to proclaim your grace.
Blessed is he who is both hidden and revealed in his actions!

It is a great wonder that the Son, who dwelt entirely in a body,
inhabited it entirely, and it sufficed for him.
Although limitless, he dwelt in it.
His will was entirely in him; but his totality was not in him.
Who is sufficient to proclaim that
although he dwelt entirely in a body,
still he dwelt entirely in the universe?
Blessed is the Unlimited who was limited!

Your majesty is hidden from us; your grace is revealed before us.
I will be silent, my Lord, about your majesty,
but I will speak about your grace.
Your grace made you a babe;
your grace made you a human being.
Your majesty contracted and stretched out.
Blessed is the power that became small and became great!

The Magi rejoiced from afar; the scribes proclaimed from nearby.
The prophet showed his erudition, and Herod his fury.
The scribes showed interpretations; the Magi showed offerings.
It is a wonder that to one babe the kinspeople
rushed with their swords,
but strangers with their offerings.
Blessed is your birth that stirred up the universe!

alternative reading

A Reading from a sermon of Lancelot Andrewes preached before King James I at Whitehall in 1620

What place more proper for him who is "the living bread that came down from heaven," to give life to the world, than Bethlehem, the least and lowest of all the houses of Judah. This natural birth-place of his sheweth his spiritual nature. Christ's birth fell in the sharpest season, in the deep of winter. As humility his place, so affliction his time. The time and place fit well.

And there came from the East wise men, Gentiles; and that concerns us, for so are we. Christ's birth is made manifest to them by the star of heaven. It is the Gentiles' star, and so ours too. We may set our course by it, to seek and find, and worship him as well as they. So we come in, for "God hath also to the Gentiles set open a door of faith," and that he would do this, and call us in, there was some small star-light from the beginning. This he promised by the Patriarchs, shadowed forth in the figures of the Law and the Temple and the Tabernacle, and foresung in the Psalms, and it is this day fulfilled.

These wise men are come and we with them. Not only in their own names, but in ours did they make their entry; came and sought after, and found and worshipped, their Savior and ours, the Savior of the whole world. A little wicket there was left open, whereat divers Gentiles did come in, but only one or two. But now the great gate set wide opens this day for all—for these here with their camels and dromedaries to enter, and all their carriage. Christ is not only for russet cloaks, shepherds and such; but even grandees, great states such as these came too; and when they came were welcome to him. For they were sent for and invited by this star, their star properly.

They came a long journey, and they came an uneasy journey. They came now, at the worst season of the year. And all but to do worship at Christ's birth. They stayed not their coming till the opening of the year, till they might have better weather and way, and have longer days, and so more seasonable and fit to travel in. So desirous were they to come with the first, and to be there as soon as possibly they might; broke through all these difficulties, and behold, they did come.

And we, what excuse shall we have if we come not? If so short and easy a way we come not, as from our chambers hither? And these wise men were never a whit less wise for so coming; nay, to come to Christ is one of the wisest parts that ever these wise men did. And if we believe this, that this was their wisdom, if they and we be wise in one Spirit, by the same principles, we will follow the same star, tread the same way, and so come at last whither they are happily gone before us.

[In the old ritual of the Church we find that on the cover of the canister wherein was the sacrament of his body, there was a star engraven, to shew us that now the star leads us thither, to his body there. So what shall I say now, but according as St. John saith, and the star, and the wise men say "Come." And he whose star it is, and to whom the wise men came, saith "Come." And let them that are disposed "Come." And let whosoever will, take of the "Bread of Life which came down from heaven" this day into Bethlehem, the house of bread. Of which bread the Church is this day the house, the true Bethlehem, and all the Bethlehem we have now left to come to for the Bread of Life—of that life which we hope for in heaven. And this our nearest coming that here we can come, till we shall by another coming "Come" unto him in his heavenly kingdom.]

alternative reading

A Reading from a poem by William Blake

The Divine Image

To Mercy, Pity, Peace, and Love
All pray in their distress;
And to these virtues of delight
Return their thankfulness.

For Mercy, Pity, Peace, and Love
Is God, our father dear,
And Mercy, Pity, Peace, and Love
Is Man, his child and care.

For Mercy has a human heart,
Pity a human face,
And Love, the human form divine,
And Peace, the human dress.

Then every man, of every clime,
That prays in his distress,
Prays to the human form divine,
Love, Mercy, Pity, Peace.

And all must love the human form,
In Heathen, Turk, or Jew;
Where Mercy, Love, and Pity dwell
There God is dwelling too.

A Reading from a poem by T. S. Eliot

Journey of the Magi

"A cold coming we had of it,
Just the worst time of the year
For a journey, and such a long journey:
The ways deep and the weather sharp,
The very dead of winter."
And the camels galled, sore-footed, refractory,
Lying down in the melting snow.
There were times we regretted
The summer palaces on slopes, the terraces,
And the silken girls bringing sherbet.
Then the camel men cursing and grumbling
And running away, and wanting their liquor and women,
And the night-fires going out, and the lack of shelters,
And the cities hostile and the towns unfriendly
And the villages dirty and charging high prices:
A hard time we had of it.
At the end we preferred to travel at night,
Sleeping in snatches,
With the voices singing in our ears, saying
That this was all folly.

Then at dawn we came down to a temperate valley,
Wet, below the snow line, smelling of vegetation,
With a running stream and a water-mill beating the darkness,
And three trees on the low sky.
And an old white horse galloped away in the meadow.
Then we came to a tavern with vine-leaves over the lintel,
Six hands at an open door dicing for pieces of silver,
And feet kicking the empty wine-skins.
But there was no information, so we continued
And arrived at evening, not a moment too soon
Finding the place; it was (you may say) satisfactory.

All this was a long time ago, I remember,
And I would do it again, but set down
This set down
This: were we led all that way for

Birth or Death? There was a Birth, certainly,
We had evidence and no doubt. I had seen birth and death,
But had thought they were different; this Birth was
Hard and bitter agony for us, like Death, our death.
We returned to our places, these Kingdoms,
But no longer at ease here, in the old dispensation,
With an alien people clutching their gods.
I should be glad of another death.

January 9

Julia Chester Emery
1922

Born in 1852, the story of Julia Chester Emery is a critical chapter in the evolution of the ministry of women in the Episcopal Church. The General Convention of the church decided in 1871 that the time had come to organize a Woman's Auxiliary and Julia Emery's older sister was given the task. Four year's later, however, she married (those were the days when women chose marriage or a career) and recommended her younger sister, then twenty-three years old, to succeed her. "Julia is young," she said, "but she can do it." Indeed she could. For the next forty years she was the general secretary of the Woman's Auxiliary, helping to establish branches in every diocese and missionary district. In a day when the Auxiliary often provided as much support for mission work as the official church budget, Miss Emery traveled around the world to see firsthand what that work was. She organized the church Periodical Club to provide literature to missionaries at home and abroad and the United Thank Offering to increase the financial resources available. More important, she helped provide a place where women could acquire leadership skills and move from roles in the "auxiliary" to leadership in every aspect of the church's work in the span of one hundred years.

A Reading from a tribute to Julia Chester Emery
by her co-worker, Grace Lindley

One thinks of her large, clear outlook and planning. She always seemed to keep the end in view, never becoming so engrossed in details as to lose sight of the reason why sharing in the mission of the church is the supreme duty and privilege of every member of the church. That is why the one who built up the Woman's Auxiliary never allowed us to become engrossed in the organization, but made the wonderful organization only a means through which the church's daughters might serve the church. So we think not so much of her love of the Auxiliary, but of her deep love of the church.

Having said that, one thinks of the keynote of her character and all her work—absolute, entire consecration. She gave herself so absolutely and completely to the Christ and his church that her whole life was a beautiful one of love and service. As a natural result, it was a life of energy. Fortunately, she had wonderful health, and she gave all her time and strength to the work. A remark made by one of the women missionaries in China brings a smile. After Miss Emery's energetic visitation of the missions, this missionary wrote: "The only thing that troubled us was the fear that she wouldn't think we worked hard enough, for we couldn't keep up with her!" But the missionary need not have worried; there never was any criticism. In all the years I have never heard one word of criticism of anyone, and many words of approval and commendation. Her reports mentioned this and that person, this and that branch doing such good work, introducing a new plan, and she was continually referring questioners to persons who could help them. I cannot imagine that a jealous thought ever entered her mind; in fact, I can't think she ever thought of herself, but only of the work and of others.

One more characteristic must be mentioned, because we shall want to remember it—her willingness for change and new ways of development. Those of us who heard her closing speech at the Triennial in St. Louis, made the morning when she had definitely decided to resign, will remember how she told us change should mean new life, and that we should go forward gladly. One of the newspapers spoke of her resigning in 1916 on account of "failing health," but it was for no such reason. She resigned because she felt the next generation should have the privilege of carrying on the work. In these last years of change and adjustment, she encouraged us to try new ways.

A letter came from a troubled member of the Auxiliary begging us to make no changes in the Auxiliary, at least as long as Miss Emery was there to be hurt by them. I sent the request to Miss Emery, telling her that my answer had been that she was the most progressive, not to say radical, one of us all!

January 10

William Laud
Archbishop of Canterbury, 1645

William Laud was appointed Archbishop of Canterbury by his friend and ecclesiastical ally, Charles I, in 1633. The aim of both Archbishop and monarch was to counter the reforming Puritan movement, which emphasized personal and ecclesial austerity as a means of sustaining conversion. Laud was a High Churchman who felt that the majesty of God should be reflected in the liturgy of the church and rigorously set about ensuring that its ministers should practice what he preached. His relentless approach left no room for variance of practice—but neither did the Puritans, and the latter had the upper hand in Parliament and eventually impeached him in 1640 and imprisoned him in the Tower of London. His friend the King did not—or could not—come to his aid and he was beheaded on this day in 1645.

A Reading from the last words of William Laud, Archbishop of Canterbury, preached in a sermon from the scaffold on Tower Hill, before he was beheaded, January 10, 1645

Good People, you'll pardon my old memory, and upon so sad occasions as I am come to this place, to make use of my papers, I dare not trust myself otherwise. This is a very uncomfortable place to preach in, and yet I shall begin with a text of Scripture, in the twelfth of the Hebrews: "Let us run with patience the race that is set before us, looking unto Jesus the author and finisher of our faith, who for the joy that was set before him, endured the cross, despising the shame, and is set down at the right hand of the throne of God."

I have been long in my race, and how I have looked unto Jesus the author and finisher of my faith, is best known to him: I am now come to the end of my race, and here I find the cross, a death of shame, but the shame must be despised, or there is no coming to the right hand of God; Jesus despised the shame for me, and God forbid but I should despise the shame for him; I am going apace, as you see, toward the Red Sea, and my feet are upon the very brink of it, an argument, I hope, that God is bringing me to the Land of Promise, for that was the way by which of old he led his people; but before they came to the sea, he instituted a Passover for them, a lamb it was, but it was to be eaten with very sour herbs, as in the twelfth of Exodus.

I shall obey, and labor to digest the sour herbs, as well as the lamb, and I shall remember that it is the Lord's Passover; I shall not think of the herbs, nor be angry with the hands which gathered them, but look up only to him who instituted the one, and governeth the other. For men can have no more power over me, than that which is given them from above. I am not in love with this passage through the Red Sea, for I have the weakness and infirmity of flesh and blood in me, and I have prayed as my Saviour taught me, and exampled me, that this cup of red wine might pass away from me. But since it is not that my will may, his will be done; and I shall most willingly drink of this cup as deep as he pleases, and enter into this sea, ay and pass through it in the way that he shall be pleased to lead me.

And I pray God bless all this people, and open their eyes, that they may see the right way; for if it fall out that the blind lead the blind, doubtless they will both into the ditch. For myself, I am (and I acknowledge it in all humility) a most grievous sinner in many ways, by thought, word and deed, and therefore I cannot doubt but that God hath mercy in store for me a poor penitent, as well as for other sinners. I have, upon this sad occasion, ransacked every corner of my heart, and yet I thank God, I have not found any of my sins that are there, any sins now deserving death by any known law of this kingdom. And yet thereby I charge nothing upon my judges.

And though I am not only the first archbishop, but the first man that ever died in this way, yet some of my predecessors have gone this way, though not by this means. Many examples great and good, and they teach me patience, for I hope my cause in heaven will look of another dye than the color that is put upon it here upon earth.

I will not enlarge myself any further. I have done. I forgive all the world, all and every of those bitter enemies, or others whatsoever they have been which have any ways prosecuted me in this kind, and I humbly desire to be forgiven first of God, and then of every man, whether I have offended him or no, if he do but conceive that I have. Lord, do thou forgive me, and I beg forgiveness of him, and so I heartily desire you to join with me in prayer.

January 11

Mary Slessor

Missionary in West Africa, 1915

Mary Slessor was born into a working-class, Presbyterian family in Aberdeen, Scotland, in 1848. As a child in Dundee, she was enthralled by stories of missions in Africa. For years, she read diligently as she worked in the mills, and eventually, in 1875, she was accepted as a teacher for the mission in Calabar, Nigeria. Her fluency in the local language, physical resilience and lack of pretension endeared her to those to whom she ministered. She adopted unwanted children, particularly twins who would otherwise, according to local superstition, have been put to death. She was influential in organizing trade and in settling disputes, contributing much to the development of the Okoyong people with whom she later settled. She died, still in Africa, on this day in 1915.

A Reading from *Far Above Rubies*
by Richard Symonds

Partly as a result of her lack of formal education, particularly in Presbyterian theology, Mary Slessor took a broad-minded view of local beliefs and customs when she arrived in Calabar, and as a result acquired an unusual understanding of them. The local people, she was often to insist, were not irreligious; they believed in God but were troubled by their belief in evil spirits.

She rapidly acquired a remarkable fluency in the Efik language. In the afternoons, when teaching was finished, it was her duty to visit women in the town, dosing ailments, instructing in housecraft and needlework, vaccinating against smallpox, and counseling. She was also sent to visit the Mission Stations, travelling by river and on foot through the forest, and found the rural people more congenial than the more sophisticated population of the town.

The European lifestyle of her fellow missionaries irked her, and she longed to work among "the untouched multitudes." Accordingly she asked to be posted further inland among the Okoyong, a Bantu tribe who had no direct contact with Europeans. Now commenced her practice of living entirely on local food, at first because this enabled her to send part of her salary home to Scotland, and later because it brought her closer to Africans. From there she supervised schools, dispensed medicines, trained teachers and visited villages to preach. She became an intrepid traveler. It was here that she began to adopt the children who were later to accompany her everywhere, even to Scotland when she went on leave. Most of them were twins, who were always considered as offspring of evil spirits and abandoned, if not murdered. Others were orphans of slave mothers who had died.

Refreshed by home leave in 1907, Mary returned with two European helpers who took over her station and enabled her to move once more in order to set up a women's industrial training center. Long experience had convinced her that the problems of the women were economic. They had no status except as dependents, and were exploited by men as laborers. If they were not attached to some man, they could be insulted or injured with impunity. She saw the solution as the establishment of centers where unattached women could support themselves by farming and industrial work.

Mary Slessor's religion is quite as interesting as the work which it inspired. Although she recollected that as a girl "hell fire" had driven her into the kingdom, she found it a kingdom of love and tenderness and mercy, and never sought to bring anyone into it by shock. "Fear is not worship," she said, "nor does it honor God."

In her own lifetime she became something of a legend. In spite of terrible illness and pain, her radiance and thankfulness for the privilege of her work remained until the end. She died in 1915, surrounded by adopted children. Her last words were in Efik as she prayed: "O God, release me soon."

January 12

Aelred

Abbot of Rievaulx, 1167

Aelred was born at Hexham in 1109. His father was a priest and he entered the Cistercian Order at Rievaulx in about 1133, after spending some years in the court of King David of Scotland. He became Abbot of Revesby in 1143 and returned to Rievaulx four years later to become abbot and there to spend the remainder of his life. He was profoundly influential through his spiritual writings, which he began at the request of Bernard of Clairvaux, the two having a similar approach to the spiritual life. Because of this, Aelred was often called "The Bernard of the North." He died on this day at Rievaulx in 1167.

A Reading from the *Pastoral Prayers*
of Aelred of Rievaulx

A Special Prayer for Wisdom

These things, my Hope,
I need for my own sake.
But there are others that I need
not only for myself, but for the sake of those
to whom you bid me be a power for good,
rather than merely a superior.

There was a wise king once, who asked
that wisdom might be given him to rule your people.
His prayer found favor in your eyes,
you did hearken thereto;
and at that time you had not met the cross,
nor shown your people that amazing love.
But now, sweet Lord, behold before your face
your own peculiar people,
whose eyes are ever on your cross,
and who themselves are signed with it.

You have entrusted to your sinful servant
the task of ruling them.
My God, you know what a fool I am,
my weakness is not hidden from your sight.
Therefore, sweet Lord, I ask you not for gold,
I ask you not for silver, nor for jewels,
but only that you would give me wisdom,
that I may know to rule your people well.

O fount of wisdom, send her from your throne of might,
to be with me, to work with me,
to act in me, to speak in me,
to order all my thoughts and words and deeds and plans
according to your will,
and to the glory of your name,
to further their advance and my salvation.

A Reading from the treatise *On Spiritual Friendship*
by Aelred of Rievaulx

What happiness, what security, what joy to have someone to whom you dare to speak on terms of equality as to another self; one to whom you need have no fear to confess your failings; one to whom you can unblushingly make known progress you have made in the spiritual life; one to whom you can entrust all the secrets of your heart and before whom you can place all your plans! What, therefore, is more pleasant than so to unite to oneself the spirit of another and of two to form one, that no boasting is thereafter to be feared, no suspicion to be dreaded, no correction of one by the other to cause pain, no praise on the part of one to bring a charge of adulation from the other.

"A friend," says the Wise Man, "is the medicine of life." Excellent, indeed, is that saying. For medicine is not more powerful or more efficacious for our wounds in all our temporal needs than the possession of a friend who meets every misfortune joyfully, so that, as the Apostle says, shoulder to shoulder, they "bear one another's burdens." Even more—each one carries his own injuries even more lightly than that of his friend. Friendship, therefore, heightens the joys of prosperity and mitigates the sorrows of adversity by dividing and sharing them. Hence, the best medicine in life is a friend.

Even the philosophers took pleasure in the thought: not even water, nor the sun, nor fire do we use in more instances than a friend. In every action, in every pursuit, in certainty, in doubt, in every event and fortune of whatever sort, in private and in public, in every deliberation, at home and abroad, everywhere friendship is found to be appreciated, a friend a necessity, a friend's service a thing of utility.

Friendship is a stage bordering upon that perfection which consists in the love and knowledge of God, so that from being a friend of our neighbors, we become the friend of God, according to the words of the Savior in the gospel: "I will not now call you servants, but my friends."

January 13

Hilary
Bishop of Poitiers, Teacher of the Faith, 367

Hilary was born at Poitiers in about the year 315; his family, though pagan, gave him an excellent education and he was proficient in Latin and Greek. After extensive personal study, he tells us that he was baptized at the age of thirty. He was elected bishop of the city in the year 350 and immediately became caught up in the Arian controversy, himself asserting that mortals of this world were created to practice moral virtues, thus reflecting the One in whose image they are made, the eternal and creative first cause, God; and that Jesus Christ, the incarnate Son of God, is of one substance with the Father. His learning and oratory led to his title of "Athanasius of the West". He was known as a gentle, kind friend to all, even though his writings seemed severe at times. He died in the year 367.

A Reading from the treatise *On the Trinity*
by Hilary of Poitiers

When I began to search for the meaning of life, I was at first attracted by the pursuit of wealth and leisure. As most people discover there is little satisfaction in such things, and a life oriented to the gratification of greed or killing time is unworthy of our humanity. We have been given life in order to achieve something worthwhile, to make good use of our talents, for life itself points us to eternity. How otherwise could one regard as a gift from God this life which is painful, fraught with anxiety, and which starts in infancy with a blank mind and ends in the rambling conversations of the old? It is my belief that human beings, prompted by our very nature, have always sought to raise our sights through the teaching and practice of the virtues such as patience, chastity and forgiveness, in the conviction that a good life is secured only through good deeds and good thoughts. Could the immortal God have given us life with no other horizon but death? Could the Giver of good inspire us with a sense of life only to have it overshadowed by the fear of death?

Thus I sought to know the God and Father who has given us this great gift of life, to whom I felt I owed my existence, in whose service was honor, and on whom my hopes were fixed. I was inflamed by a passionate desire to apprehend or know this God.

Some religions teach that there are a variety of deities, with male gods and female gods, and people trace an entire lineage of them one from another. Other religions teach that there are powerful deities and less powerful ones, each with different characteristics. Yet others claim that there is no God at all and worship nature instead, which they say came into being purely by chance vibrations and collisions. Most people, however, admit that God exists, but feel that he is ignorant or indifferent to the lot of humanity.

I was reflecting on these various ideas when I chanced upon the books that, according to Jewish tradition, were written by Moses and the prophets. In them I discovered that God the creator bears witness to himself in these words: "I am who I am." I was amazed by the perfection of this insight which puts into intelligent language the incomprehensible knowledge of God. Nothing better suggests God as Being. "The God who is" can have neither end nor beginning.

I came to see that there is no space without God: space does not exist apart from God. God is in heaven, in hell, and beyond the seas. God lives in everything and enfolds everything. God embraces all that is, and is embraced by the universe: confined to no part within it, he encompasses all that exists.

My soul drew joy from contemplating the mystery of God's wisdom, his sheer majesty, and I worshipped the eternity and immeasurable greatness of my Father and creator. But I longed also to behold his beauty. And here my mind was baffled, overcome by its own limitations, but I discovered in these words of the prophet a magnificent statement about God: "From the greatness and beauty of created things comes a corresponding perception of their creator."

I then went on to learn the truths taught by the apostle in the fourth Gospel. I learned more about God than I had expected. I understood that my creator was God born of God. I learned that the Word was God and was with God from the beginning. I came to know the light of the world. I understood that the Word was made flesh and dwelt among us and that those who welcomed him became children of God—not by a birth in flesh but in faith.

In all this my soul had discovered a hope bigger than I had ever imagined possible. It is a gift of God offered to everyone. My soul joyfully received the revelation of this mystery because by means of my flesh I was drawing near to God; by means of my faith I was called to a new birth. I was given freedom and empowered to receive a new birth from on high.

January 15

Martin Luther King, Jr.

Pastor and Civil Rights Leader, 1968

In December 1955, a black woman, Rosa Parks, was arrested for refusing to give up her seat to a white man and move to the back of a bus in Montgomery, Alabama. The subsequent boycott of the bus lines by the black community focused national attention on the issue of equality under the law and brought Martin Luther King, Jr., the new pastor of a church in that community, into a leadership role in the developing civil rights movement. Born in 1929, King became the most eloquent voice of the civil rights era in America. Appealing to the highest principles of American democracy, his outlook was undergirded by a strong Christian faith, and deeply influenced by the passive resistance techniques of Mohandas Gandhi. His speech at the great Civil Rights Rally in Washington on August 28, 1963, gave unforgettable expression to the ideals that served ultimately to unite Americans of both races in a common cause. Threatened constantly, jailed often, stabbed once almost fatally, he was killed by an assassin's bullet on April 4, 1968.

A Reading from a speech by Martin Luther King, Jr.

I am not unmindful that some of you have come here out of excessive trials and tribulation. Some of you have come fresh from narrow jail cells. Some of you have come from areas where your quest for freedom left you battered by the storms of persecution and staggered by the winds of police brutality. You have been the veterans of creative suffering. Continue to work with the faith that unearned suffering is redemptive.

Go back to Mississippi; go back to Alabama; go back to South Carolina; go back to Georgia; go back to Louisiana; go back to the slums and ghettos of the northern cities, knowing that somehow this situation can and will be changed. Let us not wallow in the valley of despair.

So I say to you, my friends, that even though we must face the difficulties of today and tomorrow, I still have a dream. It is a dream deeply rooted in the American dream that one day this nation will rise up and live out the true meaning of its creed—we hold these truths to be self-evident, that all men are created equal.

I have a dream that one day on the red hills of Georgia, sons of former slaves and sons of former slave-owners will be able to sit down together at the table of brotherhood.

I have a dream that one day, even the state of Mississippi, a state sweltering with the heat of injustice, sweltering with the heat of oppression, will be transformed into an oasis of freedom and justice.

I have a dream my four little children will one day live in a nation where they will not be judged by the color of their skin but by content of their character. I have a dream today!

I have a dream that one day, down in Alabama, with its vicious racists, with its governor having his lips dripping with the words of interposition and nullification, that one day, right there in Alabama, little black boys and black girls will be able to join hands with little white boys and white girls as sisters and brothers. I have a dream today!

I have a dream that one day every valley shall be exalted, every hill and mountain shall be made low, the rough places shall be made plain, and the crooked places shall be made straight and the glory of the Lord will be revealed and all flesh shall see it together.

This is our hope. This is the faith that I go back to the South with.

With this faith we will be able to hew out of the mountain of despair a stone of hope. With this faith we will be able to transform the jangling discords of our nation into a beautiful symphony of brotherhood.

With this faith we will be able to work together, to pray together, to struggle together, to go to jail together, to stand up for freedom together, knowing that we will be free one day. This will be the day when all of God's children will be able to sing with new meaning—"my country 'tis of thee; sweet land of liberty; of thee I sing; land where my fathers died, land of the pilgrim's pride; from every mountain side, let freedom ring"—and if America is to be a great nation, this must become true.

So let freedom ring from the prodigious hilltops of New Hampshire.

Let freedom ring from the mighty mountains of New York.

Let freedom ring from the heightening Alleghenies of Pennsylvania.

Let freedom ring from the snowcapped Rockies of Colorado.

Let freedom ring from the curvaceous slopes of California.

But not only that.

Let freedom ring from Stone Mountain of Georgia.

Let freedom ring from Lookout Mountain of Tennessee.

Let freedom ring from every hill and molehill of Mississippi, from every mountainside, let freedom ring.

And when we allow freedom to ring, when we let it ring from every village and hamlet, from every state and city, we will be able to speed up that day when all of God's children—black men and white men, Jews and Gentiles, Catholics and Protestants—will be able to join hands and to sing in the words of the old Negro spiritual—"Free at last, free at last; thank God Almighty, we are free at last."

January 17

Antony
Abbot in Egypt, 356

Born about the year 251, Antony heard the gospel message: "If you would be perfect, go, sell your possessions, and give the money to the poor, and you will have treasure in heaven; then come, follow me." He was twenty years old and rich, following the death of his parents, but he did as the gospel instructed and went to live in the desert, living an austere life of manual work, charity and prayer. His many spiritual struggles left him both wise and sensible and he became a spiritual guide for many who flocked to him. His simple rule of personal discipline and prayer was taken up and spread throughout Christendom. He died peacefully in the desert in the year 356 at the great age of 105, asking that he be buried secretly, so that his person might be hidden in death as in life.

A Reading from *The Life of Antony*
by Athanasius of Alexandria

Antony was an Egyptian by race. His parents were well born and prosperous, and since they were Christians, he also was reared in Christian manner. Following their death he was left alone with one young sister. He was about eighteen or even twenty years old, and he was responsible both for the home and his sister. Six months had not passed since the death of his parents when, going to the Lord's house as usual and gathering his thoughts, he considered while he walked how the apostles, forsaking everything, followed their Savior, and how in the Acts of Apostles some sold what they possessed and took the proceeds and placed them at the feet of the apostles for distribution among those in need, and what great hope is stored up for such people in heaven.

He went into the church pondering these things, and just then it happened that the gospel was being read, and he heard the Lord saying to the rich young man: "If you would be perfect, go sell what you possess and give to the poor, and you will have treasure in heaven." It was as if by God's design he held the saints in his recollection, and as if the passage were read on his account. Immediately Antony went out from the Lord's house and gave to the townspeople the possessions he had from his forebears (three hundred very beautiful *arourae* of land) so that they would not disturb him or his sister in the least. And selling all the rest that was portable, when he had collected sufficient money, he donated it to the poor, keeping back a few things for his sister.

But when, entering the Lord's house once more, he heard in the gospel the Lord saying: "Do not be anxious about tomorrow," he could not remain any longer, but going out he gave those remaining possessions also to the needy. Placing his sister in the charge of respected and trusted virgins, and giving her over to the convent for rearing, he devoted himself from then on to the discipline rather than to the household, giving heed to himself and patiently training himself. There were not yet many monasteries in Egypt, and no monk knew at all the great desert, but each of those wishing to give attention to his life disciplined himself in isolation, not far from his own village. At first Antony also began by remaining in places proximate to his village. And going forth from there, if he heard of some zealous person anywhere, he searched him out like the wise bee.

He worked with his hands, having heard that "he who is idle, let him not eat." He spent what he made partly on bread, and partly on those in need. He prayed constantly, since he learned also that it is necessary to pray unceasingly in private. For he paid such close attention to what was read that nothing from Scripture did he fail to take in—rather he grasped everything, and in him the memory took the place of books.

Living his life in this way, Antony was loved by all. People used to call him "God-loved", and some hailed him as "son", and others as "brother".

January 18

The Confession of Saint Peter the Apostle

The "confession of Saint Peter," the acknowledgment of Jesus as Christ and Son of God, is the turning point in the Gospels. As the Gospels tell the story, Jesus, at a certain point, asked the disciples who they believed him to be. Peter confessed, "You are the Christ, the Son of the Living God." Before that point, Jesus had carried on a ministry of teaching and healing in Galilee, but when one of the disciples had understood, however imperfectly, who Jesus was and could state it, Jesus could go to Jerusalem to be accepted or rejected in the capital city. Peter, however, is also remembered as a man who was both impulsive and wavering in his faith. He would step out of the boat to walk on the sea, but then be overcome with doubt. He would promise never to deny Jesus and then do so three times. An early legend tells us that he was on his way out of Rome to avoid death when Jesus met him and asked him where he was going ("Quo vadis?"), *and that Peter then turned back to be crucified. The story was known at least by the third century and, whether factually true, remains an excellent picture of the man known to the early church.*

A Reading from the Acts of the Holy Apostles
Peter and Paul

Then Nero, having summoned Agrippa the propraetor, said to him: "It is necessary that men introducing mischievous religious observances should die. Therefore I order them to take iron clubs, and to be killed in the sea-fight." Agrippa the propraetor said: "Most sacred emperor, what you have ordered is not fitting for these men, since Paul seems innocent beside Peter." Nero said: "By what fate, then, shall they die?" Agrippa answered and said: "As seems to me, it is just that Paul's head should be cut off, and that Peter should be raised on a cross." Nero said: "You have most excellently judged."

Then both Peter and Paul were led away from the presence of Nero. And Paul was beheaded on the Ostesian road.

And Peter, having come to the cross, said: "Since my Lord Jesus Christ, who came down from the heaven upon the earth, was raised upon the cross upright, and he has deigned to call to heaven me, who am of the earth, my cross ought to be fixed head downmost, so as to direct my feet toward heaven; for I am not worthy to be crucified like my Lord." Then, having reversed the cross, they nailed his feet up.

And the multitude was assembled reviling Caesar, and wishing to kill him. But Peter restrained them, saying: "A few days ago, being exhorted by the brethren, I was going away; and my Lord Jesus Christ met me, and having adored him, I said, 'Lord, where are you going?' And he said to me, 'I am going to Rome to be crucified.' And I said to him, 'Lord, were you not crucified once for all?' And the Lord answering, said, 'I saw you fleeing from death, and I wish to be crucified instead of you.' And I said, 'Lord, I go; I fulfill your command.' And he said to me, "Fear not, for I am with you.' On this account, then, children, do not hinder my going; for already my feet are going on the road to heaven. Do not grieve, therefore, but rather rejoice with me, for today I receive the fruit of my labors." And thus speaking, he said: "I thank you, good Shepherd, that the sheep that you have entrusted to me sympathize with me; I ask, then, that with me they may have a part in your Kingdom." And having thus spoken, he gave up the ghost.

And after these things, all having assembled with glory and singing of praise, they put them in the place built for them. And the consummation of the holy glorious Apostles Peter and Paul was on the twenty-ninth of the month of June in Christ Jesus our Lord, to whom be glory and strength.

January 19

Wulfstan

Bishop of Worcester, 1095

Born in about the year 1009, Wulfstan's first twenty-five years after his ordination were spent in the monastery at Worcester. Against his will, he was elected Bishop of Worcester in 1062, but went on to prove an able administrator and pastor. He carefully and gently nurtured both church and state through the transition from Saxon to Norman rule. He died at Worcester on this day in the year 1095.

A Reading from *The Life of Saint Wulfstan* by William of Malmesbury

Having been consecrated a bishop, Wulfstan immediately turned his mind to works of piety; indeed, the very next day he dedicated a church to Blessed Bede. It was fitting that he should have begun his episcopal ministry by dedicating a church to one whose name stands first in English scholarship. That day Wulfstan watered the people with so flowing a sermon that no one doubted that he was inspired by the Holy Spirit with the same powerful eloquence that had once moved the tongue of Bede. And not only on this occasion but throughout his life, the fame of Wulfstan's preaching meant that wherever he was to dedicate a church, large crowds of people gathered to hear him.

He loved preaching, and always spoke about Christ, resolutely setting Christ before his hearers so that even the most reluctant might hear his name. In his personal discipline, in vigils and in fasting, he was no less rigorous. His prayers assaulted heaven, so that of him and others like him, the Lord rightly said: "The kingdom of heaven has suffered violence, and the violent take it by force."

Wulfstan maintained a balanced life, never relinquishing his two-fold calling. Although bishop, he remained obedient to the discipline of the monastic life: as a monk, his way of life revealed the authority of a bishop. His integrity singled him out from his contemporaries. To any who came to him for counsel, he was full of wisdom and accessible. If a discernment had to be made, he was impartial in his assessments and swift to give his decision. When he was put in the role of judge, he would always err on the side of mercy. He would never seek the patronage of the rich or reject the poor for their poverty. He was unmoved by flattery and disliked the flatterer. He would never distort the claims of justice out of fear of the powerful, nor pay them any honor they did not merit. When he was praised for a good deed, Wulfstan praised the grace of God that had made it possible; and thus he never succumbed to pride.

If ever Wulfstan was ridiculed, he forgave those who ridiculed him, secure in a good conscience, but this occurred seldom since he cherished each person in his care as if his own child, with the result that all loved him as their father. His heart was always glad and his face bright because even in this life he was already tasting in hope of the waters of the wells of heaven; indeed, now he is drinking long draughts.

Although he never neglected the interior life of his soul, he was never slack or lazy in dealing with the exterior duties that required his attention. He built many churches in the diocese, beginning each project with zeal, and completing each nobly. Foremost among these was the cathedral church of Worcester which Wulfstan erected from its foundation to its final stone. The number of monks in the cathedral monastery increased and he brought them under the *Rule* of the Order.

Yours, O Lord, are the graces that we praise in Wulfstan, seeing that all our life is yours.

January 20

Fabian

Bishop and Martyr of Rome, 250

When the Bishop of Rome died in the year 236, an assembly was held to choose someone to succeed him. Fabian, who was a stranger in Rome, was standing in the crowd when suddenly a dove alighted on him. The gathering, seeing it as evidence of the choice of the Holy Spirit, set up a cry of "He is worthy!" As it turned out, it was a good choice. Fabian was an excellent administrator and carried through a program of reform while resisting heresy and showing honor to those before him. It was Fabian who appointed the seven deacons who became an integral part of the structure of the Roman Church and Fabian who established the custom of venerating the shrines of the martyrs in the catacombs. He also brought back to Rome the body of one of his predecessors who had died in exile. In the year 249, the Emperor Decian ordered the first persecution of the church throughout the empire and Fabian was among the first to die, setting an example for others to follow.

A Reading from the First Epistle of Fabian

To all the ministers of the church catholic: We beg it of your love in paternal blessing, that the holy church may now find the good will of your love in all things and obtain the comforts of your favor whenever there is necessity. And as the goodness of your zeal affords us the assurance that we ought to distrust it in nothing, but rather commit those things in all confidence to you as to wise sons of our church; so, small importance being attached to opportune occasions, your virtue ought to exert itself the more strenuously in labors and keep off reproaches by all possible means, and with all zeal. We exhort you also, according to the word of the apostle, to be "steadfast and immoveable, always abounding in the work of the Lord; forasmuch as you know that your labor is not vain in the Lord." And in another place: "Watch and pray, and stand fast in the faith. Quit you like men, and be strong. Let all things be done with charity. Beware of all who hold a faith and doctrine different from that which the apostles and their successors have held and taught, lest (which may God forbid) going after him you fall into the toils of Satan, and be bound with his fetters. Therefore with most earnest prayers we beg it of your brotherly love, that you may deem it fit to remember our insignificance in your holy prayers, beseeching and entreating the Lord of heaven that we, as well as our holy mother the church of Christ, redeemed with his precious blood, may be delivered from the toils of Satan, who lies in wait for us, and from troublesome and wicked men, and that the word of God may have free course and be glorified, and that the evil doctrine of them, and of all who teach things contrary to the truth, may be overthrown and perish. We beseech you also to be zealous in praying in your pious supplications, that our God and Lord Jesus Christ, who will have all men to be saved, and no one to perish, may, by his vast omnipotence, cause their hearts to turn again to sound doctrine and to the catholic faith, in order that they may be recovered from the toils of the devil who are held captive by him, and be united with the children of our mother the church. Be mindful also of your brethren, and have pity upon them, and labor for them by all means in your power, that they be not lost, but be saved to the Lord by your prayers and other efforts of your goodness. So act therefore in these matters that you may prove yourselves obedient and faithful children of the holy church of God, and that you may obtain the recompense of reward.

Let every one of you, sustained by this apostolic representation, act according to his strength, and study in brotherly love and in godly piety to keep his own manners correct, and to help each other, and to abide in charity, and to keep himself in the will of God unceasingly, in order that we may praise the Lord together, and give him thanks always without wearying. Farewell in the Lord, dearly beloved, and with the Lord's help strive to fulfill to the best of your ability the things before mentioned.

January 21

Agnes

Child-Martyr at Rome, 304

The reason Agnes is one of the most well-known and widely-venerated of the early Roman martyrs is perhaps because of the expression of mature resilience and sheer bravery in a thirteen-year-old girl. Agnes is reputed to have refused an arranged marriage because of her total dedication to Christ and stated that she preferred even death of the body to the death of her consecrated virginity. The growing veneration for the state of consecrated virginity at this time, combined with the last, major Roman persecution under the emperor Diocletian, climaxing in the shedding of an innocent child's blood, placed her at the forefront of veneration almost from the moment the persecution ended. She is believed to have died in the year 304 and her feast has ever since been celebrated on this day.

A Reading from the treatise *On Virginity*
by Ambrose, Bishop of Milan

Today is the birthday of Saint Agnes. She is said to have suffered martyrdom at the age of twelve. The cruelty which did not spare even so young a child serves only to demonstrate more clearly the power of faith which found witness in one so young.

There was not even room in her little body for a wound. Though she could barely receive the sword's point, she could overcome it. Girls of her age tend to wilt under the slightest frown from a parent. Pricked by a needle, they cry as if given a mortal wound. But Agnes showed no fear of the blood-stained hands of her executioners. She was undaunted by the weight of clanging chains. She offered her whole body to the sword of the raging soldiers. Too young to have any acquaintanceship with death, she nevertheless stood ready before it. Dragged against her will to the altar of sacrifice, she was ready to stretch out her hands to Christ in the midst of the flames, making the triumphant sign of Christ the victor on the altars of sacrilege. She was even prepared to put her neck and hands into iron bands—though none of them was small enough to enclose her tiny limbs.

Is this a new kind of martyrdom? The girl was too young to be punished, yet old enough to wear a martyr's crown; too young for the contest, but mature enough to gain victory. Her tender years put her at a disadvantage, but she won the trial of virtue. If she had been a bride, she could not have hastened to her wedding night as much as she, a virgin, went with joyful steps to the place of her execution, her head adorned with Christ himself rather than plaits, with a garland woven of virtues instead of flowers.

Everyone was weeping, but she herself shed no tears. The crowds marveled at her spendthrift attitude to life, discarding it untasted, but as if she had lived it to the full. All were astonished that one not yet of legal age, could give testimony to God. It was her final achievement that people believed that she must have received the inner resource for such testimony from God, for humanly speaking it was impossible. They reasoned that what is beyond the power of nature can only come from its creator.

You can imagine with what threats the executioner tried to frighten her; what promises were made to seduce her; indeed, how many people there were who would have been prepared to marry her! But she answered, "It would insult my Spouse if I were to give myself to another. I will be his who first chose me for himself. Executioner, why do you delay? If eyes that I do not want, desire this body, then let it perish."

She stood still, praying, and offered her neck. You could see the executioner trembling as though he were himself condemned. His right hand began to shake, and his face drained of color aware of her danger, though the child herself showed no fear. In one victim then, we are given a twofold witness in martyrdom, to modesty and to religion. Agnes preserved her virginity and gained a martyr's crown.

January 22

Vincent of Saragossa

Deacon, first Martyr of Spain, 304

Vincent was born in Saragossa in Aragon in the latter part of the third century and was ordained to the diaconate by Valerian, his bishop in that city. When the Diocletian persecutions began, both men were brought before the Roman governor but, because Valerian stammered badly, he relied on Vincent to speak for them both. Vincent spoke eloquently for both his bishop and his Church, proclaiming the good news of Jesus Christ and condemning paganism. He so angered the governor that he was immediately condemned to a painful death, reputedly on the gridiron. Thus he lived and gave his life in the tradition of Stephen, the first martyr and also a deacon; he died in the year 304 and his feast has been celebrated on this day since the persecutions ended in 312.

A Reading from a sermon of Augustine

With the eyes of faith we have just beheld an amazing sight, the sight of Vincent conquering far and wide. He conquered through the words he spoke and the punishment he received; he conquered in his confession of faith and in the sufferings he endured; he conquered when they burnt his flesh in the fire and threatened him with drowning; finally, he conquered even as he was being tortured and in death itself.

Whoever gave such endurance to one of his soldiers, if not the one who first shed his own blood for them? Of such it is said in the psalms: "You, O Lord, are my hope, my trust, from my youth."

A great struggle procures great glory: not human or worldly glory, but that which is divine and eternal. It is faith which contends, and when faith contends no one can overcome the flesh. For although our flesh may be torn and mutilated, who can ever perish when we have been redeemed by the blood of Christ? A wealthy person cannot bear to part with his wealth, so how can Christ ever be made to let go of those whom he has bought with his own blood? Vincent's death stands as a tribute not to the glory of man but to the glory of God.

From God comes all endurance. True endurance is holy, religious and upright. Christian endurance is a gift of God. There are thieves who bear torture with great endurance, not yielding, and overcoming their torturer; but afterwards they will be punished by eternal fire. It is the reason for death which distinguishes the endurance of the martyr from that of the hardened criminal. The punishment may be the same, but the reasons are different.

Vincent would have used in his prayers the very words from the psalms we have just sung: "Judge me, O God, defend my cause against an ungodly people." There was no doubt about his cause because he struggled for truth, for justice, for God, for Christ, for the faith, for the unity of the Church, for undivided love.

January 23

Phillips Brooks

Bishop of Massachusetts, 1893

Phillips Brooks has been called the greatest preacher in the history of American Christianity and it is certain that no other preacher made so great an impact on his time. Born in Boston in the year 1835, he returned to Boston as rector of Trinity Church and a new building had to be erected to accommodate the crowds that came. Brooks read his sermons at breakneck speed, seldom looking up, but his eloquent use of language speaks to us still. "Preaching," he once said, "is the communication of truth through personality," and it is clear that for Brooks life and preaching were of one piece. A parishioner found him one day in the apartment of an elderly woman, scrubbing the floor on his knees. Though he was elected Bishop of Massachusetts at the end of his life, it was preaching that was his gift and for which he is still remembered—that, and the hymn, "O Little Town of Bethlehem," which he wrote and which has become a fixture in the traditional music of Christmas.

A Reading from *The Light of the World and Other Sermons* by Phillips Brooks

The mystery of man! How Christ believed in that! Oh, my dear friends, he who does not believe in that cannot enter into the full glory of the Incarnation, cannot really believe in Christ. Where the mysterious reach of manhood touches the divine, there Christ appears. No mere development of human nature outgoing any other reach that it has made, yet still not incapable of being matched, perhaps of being overcome; not that, not that—unique and separate forever—but possible, because of this same mystery of man in which the least of us has share. To him who knows the hither edges of that mystery in his own life, the story of how in, on, at its depths it should be able to receive and to contain divinity cannot seem incredible; may I not say, cannot seem strange?

Men talk about the Christhood, and say, "How strange it is! Strange that Christ should have been—strange that Christ should have suffered for mankind." I cannot see that so we most magnify him or bring him nearest to us. Once feel the mystery of man and is it strange? Once think it possible that God should fill a humanity with himself, once see humanity capable of being filled with God, and can you conceive of his not doing it? Must there not be an Incarnation? Do you not instantly begin to search earth for the holy steps? Once think it possible that Christ can, and are you not sure that Christ must give himself for our redemption? So only, when it seems inevitable and natural, does the Christhood become our pattern. Then only does it shine on the mountain-top up toward which we can feel the low lines of our low life aspiring. The Son of God is also the Son of Man. Then in us, the sons of men, there is the key to the secret of his being and his work. Know Christ that you may know yourself. But, oh, also know yourself that you may know Christ!

I think to every Christian there come times when all the strangeness disappears from the divine humanity which stands radiant at the center of his faith. He finds it hard to believe in himself and in his brethren perhaps; but that Christ should and should be Christ appears the one reasonable, natural, certain thing in all the universe. In him all broken lines unite; in him all scattered sounds are gathered into harmony; and out of the consummate certainty of him, the soul comes back to find the certainty of common things which the lower faith holds, which advancing faith loses, and then finds again in Christ.

How every truth attains to its enlargement and reality in this great truth—that the soul of man carries the highest possibilities within itself, and that what Christ does for it is to kindle and call forth these possibilities to actual experience. We do not understand the church until we understand this truth. Seen in its light the Christian church is nothing in the world except the promise and prophecy and picture of what the world in its idea is and always has been, and in its completion must visibly become. It is the primary crystalization of humanity.

alternative reading

A Reading from a hymn of Phillips Brooks

O little town of Bethlehem, how still we see thee lie!
Above thy deep and dreamless sleep the silent stars go by;
yet in thy dark streets shineth the everlasting Light;
the hopes and fears of all the years are met in thee tonight.

For Christ is born of Mary; and gathered all above,
while mortals sleep, the angels keep their watch
of wondering love.
O morning stars, together proclaim the holy birth!
and praises sing to God the King and peace to men on earth.

How silently, how silently, the wondrous gift is given!
So God imparts to human hearts the blessings of his heaven.
No ear may hear his coming, but in this world of sin,
where meek souls will receive him, still the dear Christ enters in.

Where children pure and happy pray to the blessed Child,
where misery cries out to thee, Son of the mother mild;
where charity stands watching and faith holds wide the door,
the dark night wakes, the glory breaks, and Christmas
comes once more.

O holy Child of Bethlehem, descend to us, we pray;
cast out our sin and enter in, be born in us today.
We hear the Christmas angels the great glad tidings tell;
O come to us, abide with us, our Lord Emmanuel!

January 24

Francis de Sales

Bishop of Geneva, Teacher of the Faith, 1622

Francis de Sales was born in 1567 in the castle at Sales in Savoy. He was educated in Paris and Padua, first as a legal advocate, and then as a priest. His preaching against Calvinism began in 1593 to win back the Chablais to Roman Catholicism. In 1599 he was appointed Bishop-Coadjutor of Geneva, and moved to Annecy from where he administered the diocese when he became the diocesan bishop in 1602. It was not until 1799 that Roman Catholic worship was officially permitted again in Geneva. In his preaching and writings, particularly his book Introduction to the Devout Life, *Francis concentrated on putting prayer and meditation within the reach of all Christians. He died at Lyons on December 28, 1622 and his body was translated to Annecy on this day in 1623.*

A Reading from *Introduction to the Devout Life*
by Francis de Sales

The world ridicules devotion in life, caricaturing devout people as peevish, gloomy and sullen, and insinuating that religion makes a person melancholy and unsociable. But the Holy Spirit, speaking through the mouths of the saints, and indeed through our Savior himself, assures us that a devout life is wholesome, pleasant and happy.

The world observes how devout people fast, pray and suffer reproach; how they nurse the sick, give alms to the poor, restrain their temper and do similar deeds which in themselves and viewed in isolation, are hard and painful. But the world fails to discern the interior devotion which renders these actions agreeable, sweet and pleasant.

Look at the bees: they suck the bitter juice from thyme and convert it into honey because that is their nature. Devout souls, it is true, do experience bitterness in works of self-discipline, but they are engaged in a process that converts such bitterness into a delicious sweetness. Sour green fruits are sweetened by sugar, bringing a ripeness to what had been unwholesome to the palate. In the same way, true devotion is a spiritual sugar which takes away the bitterness of self-discipline. It counteracts the poor person's discontent and the rich person's smugness; the loneliness of the oppressed and the conceit of the successful; the sadness of one who lives alone and the dissipation of the one who is at the center of society. In a word its gift is an equanimity and balance which refreshes the soul.

In creation God has commanded the plants to bring forth fruit, each according to its kind. Similarly, he commands all Christians, who are the living plants of his church, to bring forth the fruits of devotion according to each person's ability and vocation. The practice of devotion will need to be adapted to the capabilities, jobs and duties of each individual. For example, it is not appropriate for a bishop to be leading the solitary life of a Carthusian; or for the father of a family to be refusing to put aside money as if he were a Franciscan; or for a tradesman to spend the entire day in church as if he were a religious; or for someone in religious vows to be endlessly interrupted by the needs of his neighbor as a bishop must be. Such a pattern of life and devotion is incompatible and ridiculous.

True devotion, however, harms no one; on the contrary, it brings a person to wholeness. If our devotional life is not compatible with our lawful vocation then it is manifestly false. Aristotle says that the bee extracts honey from flowers without ever injuring them, leaving them as fresh and as whole as it finds them. True devotion does better still; it not only does no harm to our vocation and employment, it adorns and beautifies them.

January 25

The Conversion of Saint Paul the Apostle

The conversion of the anti-Christian zealot, Saul, to the Apostle Paul is clearly related in the Acts of the Apostles, but it has to be remembered that this was a beginning of a process. Saul took some time to become Paul and to begin to understand the dimensions of his call to preach—to Jew and to Gentile—the saving power of Jesus, the Son of God. It was a whole life's journey for him. In his Letter to the Church in Galatia, Paul writes: "God set me apart before I was born and called me through his grace. Three years after [the Damascus Road conversion], I went up to Jerusalem." The preparation for this moment of his conversion was his whole life. This feast has been celebrated in the Church since the sixth century but became universal in the twelfth century.

A Reading from a homily *"In Praise of Saint Paul"* by John Chrysostom

Paul, more than anyone else, shows us what humanity really is, in what our nobility consists, and of what virtue this particular animal is capable. Each day Paul aimed ever higher; each day he rose up with greater ardor and faced with new eagerness the dangers that threatened him. He summed up his attitude in the words: "I forget what is behind me and push on to what lies ahead." When he saw death imminent, he bade others share his joy: "Rejoice and be glad with me." And when danger, injustice and abuse threatened, he said: "I am content with weakness, mistreatment and persecution." These he called the weapons of righteousness, thus telling us that he derived immense profit from them.

Thus, amid the traps set for him by his enemies, with exultant heart he turned their every attack into a victory for himself; constantly beaten, abused and cursed, he boasted of it as though he were celebrating a triumphal procession and taking trophies home, and offered thanks to God for it all: "Thanks be to God who is always victorious in us!" This is why he was far more eager for the shameful abuse that his zeal in preaching brought upon him than we are for the most pleasing honors, more eager for death than we are for life, for poverty than we are for wealth; he yearned for toil far more than others yearn for rest after toil. The one thing he feared, indeed dreaded, was to offend God; nothing else could sway him. Therefore, the only thing he really wanted was always to please God.

The most important thing of all to Paul, however, was that he knew himself to be loved by Christ. Enjoying this love, he considered himself happier than anyone else; were he without it, it would be no satisfaction to be the friend of principalities and powers. He preferred to be loved and be the least of all, or even to be among the damned, than be without that love and be among the great and honored.

To be separated from that love was, in his eyes, the greatest and most extraordinary of torments; the pain of that loss would alone have been hell, and endless, unbearable torture. So too, in being loved by Christ he thought of himself as possessing life, the world, the angels, present and future, the kingdom, the promise and countless blessings. Apart from that love nothing saddened or delighted him; for nothing earthly did he regard as bitter or sweet.

Paul set no store by the things that fill our visible world, any more than one sets value on the withered grass of the field. As for tyrannical rulers or the people enraged against him, he paid them no more heed than gnats. Death itself and pain and whatever torments might come were but child's play to Paul, provided that thereby he might bear some burden for the sake of Christ.

I urge you, therefore, not only to admire, but also to follow his example of virtue. For in this way we will be able to share in the same crown of glory.

alternative reading

A Reading from a sermon of Augustine

Today we heard in our reading from the Acts of the Apostles how the apostle Paul from being a persecutor of Christians, became the great preacher of Christ. The encouragement we draw from his conversion, to which he himself testifies in his letters—indeed, he says, it was for this reason that he was pardoned by God for his sins, for the rage and violence with which he had dragged Christians to their death, for the way he became an agent of the fury of the Jews, not only in the stoning of the holy martyr Stephen but in delivering up and bringing many for punishment—is that none of us should ever despair of ourselves. Even if, like Paul, we have committed terrible sins, become ensnared in great crimes, we should never think ourselves beyond the reach of Christ's pardon who, hanging on the cross, prayed for his persecutors, saying: "Father, forgive them, for they know not what they do."

From a persecutor Paul was changed into a preacher and teacher of the nations. As he says when writing to Timothy, "I was a blasphemer, a persecutor, and a man of violence: but I received mercy so that in me, as the foremost, Jesus Christ might display the utmost patience, making me an example to those who would come to believe in him for eternal life." For by the grace of God we are healed of our sins in which we lay languishing. The medicine which heals our souls is God's alone because though the soul can wound itself, it is unable to heal itself.

With regard to our bodies, though it lies within our power to let ourselves become ill, it is not equally within our power to recover. If we push ourselves too hard or live self-indulgently, if we pursue a lifestyle incompatible with good health and abuse our bodies, one day we will fall ill and not be able to recover our health. In such circumstances we call for the help of a doctor. So also with the soul. That we should fall into sin that leads to death, exchanging mortality for immortality, allowing ourselves to be seduced by the devil, was all within our power. But healing is the prerogative of God alone.

It is to the afflicted and troubled that Christ the doctor comes, saying: "The healthy have no need of the doctor, but those who are sick. I have not come to call the righteous, but sinners." Christ is calling sinners to peace, he is calling the sick to health.

January 26

Timothy and Titus

Companions of Saint Paul

On the day following the Conversion of Saint Paul, the church remembers his two companions, Timothy and Titus, whom he describes as "partners and fellow-workers in God's service," and to whom the so-called "Pastoral Epistles" are dedicated. Timothy, we are told, was a native of Lystra in Asia Minor, who had a Jewish mother and a Greek father, while Titus was wholly Greek. It was because of Titus that Paul stood out against compulsory circumcision but, to avoid suspicion from other Jews, Paul insisted that Timothy be circumcised. Christian tradition associates Timothy with the Christian community at Ephesus, and Titus with the care of the Christian community in Crete where he is honored as the first bishop of Gortyna. Both men are honored in the Church for their devotion and faithfulness to the gospel.

A Reading from a homily of John Chrysostom

Why did Paul write a second letter to Timothy? In his previous letter he had said that "I hope to come to see you shortly," but it is clear that this meeting did not take place. So instead of visiting him in person, Paul now consoles Timothy by letter—perhaps Timothy was grieving for Paul's absence, oppressed by the responsibilities of government which had been committed to him? For we should remember that even great people, when placed at the helm and charged with steering the course of the Church, can be overwhelmed, as it were, by the waves of duties that confront them. This was certainly the case when the gospel began first to be preached, when the ground was unplowed, and people were unresponsive and hostile. There were also many false teachings emanating from Jewish teachers which needed to be confronted.

Paul addresses Timothy not merely as his son, but as his "beloved son." Paul had called the Galatians his children, at the same time adding how he found himself once again "in labor over them." But here he bears particular witness to the virtue of Timothy by calling him beloved. Where love does not arise spontaneously with nature, it must come from an appreciation of worth. Our natural children are loved by us both on account of their worth and from the sheer force of nature; but when the children of faith are so loved, it can be for no other reason than their intrinsic worth. And this was especially the case with Paul who never acted from partiality.

Paul reminds Timothy "to rekindle the gift of God that is within you through the laying on of my hands." One can guess from these words how dispirited and dejected Paul must have believed Timothy to be at this time. Paul's words remind us that much zeal is required to stir up the gift of God in us. Just as a fire requires fuel, so grace requires our glad and willing consent if it is to be fervent. For it lies within our power to kindle or extinguish the grace of God within each of us. That is why Paul admonishes us: "Do not quench the Spirit." The Spirit is quenched by sloth and carelessness, but kept alive by being watchful and diligent.

As Paul goes on to say: "God did not give us a spirit of fear, but rather a spirit of power and of love and of self-discipline." In other words, we have not received the Spirit that we should not need to make any effort in life, but rather that we may speak with boldness. Many people are dominated by a spirit of fear, as is evident from the countless histories of wars. But to us God has given a spirit of power and of love for himself.

This is the work of grace, and yet not only of grace: we too have a part to play. For the same Spirit that makes us cry out "Abba, Father!" inspires us with love both for God and for our neighbor that we may love one another. Love arises from this power, and from not being afraid; for nothing is so sure to dissolve love as fear and the suspicion of betrayal.

January 27

John Chrysostom
Bishop of Constantinople, 407

John was born in Antioch, the third city of the Roman Empire, about the year 347. He was a brilliant preacher, which earned him in the sixth century the surname "Chrysostom," literally "golden-mouthed." He is honored as one of the four Greek Doctors of the church. Against his wish he was made Patriarch of Constantinople in 398. He set about reforming the church and exposing corruption among the clergy and in the Imperial administration. "Mules bear fortunes and Christ dies of hunger at your gate," he is alleged to have cried out. He fell foul of the Empress Eudoxia, and in spite of the support of Pope Innocent I of Rome, was sent into exile twice, finally dying of exhaustion and starvation in September 407, with the words "Glory be to God for everything" on his lips. The reading is taken from the last sermon he delivered before leaving Constantinople for exile.

A Reading from the homily preached by John Chrysostom in Constantinople before he went into exile

The waves have risen and the surging sea is dangerous, but we do not fear drowning for we stand upon the rock. Let the sea surge! It cannot destroy the rock. Let the waves rise! They cannot sink the boat of Jesus. Tell me, what are we to fear? Is it death? But "for me life is Christ, and death is gain." So tell me, is it exile? "The earth is the Lord's and all that it contains." Is it the confiscation of property? "We brought nothing into the world and it is certain we can take nothing out of it." I have nothing but contempt for the threats of this world; its treasures I ridicule. I am not afraid of poverty, I do not crave after wealth, I am not afraid of death, and I do not seek to live except it be of help to you. So I simply mention my present circumstances and call on you, my dear people, to remain steadfast in your love.

Do you not hear the Lord saying, "Where two or three are gathered together in my name, there I am among them?" Where will he be absent, for where will there not be two or three bound together by love? I have his pledge, so I do not have to rely on my own strength. I cling to his promise: it is my staff, my security, it is my peaceful harbor. Even though the entire world be in turmoil, I cling to his promise and read it. It is my rampart and my shield. What promise is this? "I am with you always, even to the end of time."

Christ is with me, whom then shall I fear? Let the waves rise up against me, the seas, the wrath of rulers: these things to me are mere cobwebs. And if you, my dear people, had not held me back I would have left this very day. I always say, "Lord, your will be done;" not what this person or that person wishes, but as you wish. This is my fortress, this is my immovable rock, this is my firm staff. If God wishes this to be, then so be it. If he wishes me to be here, I thank him. Wherever he wants me to be, I thank him. Wherever I am, there are you also; where you are, there am I too; we are one body. And the body cannot be separated from its head, nor the head from the rest of the body. We may be separated by space, but we are united by love. Not even death can sever us. For even if my body dies, my soul will live on, and my soul will remember you, my people.

You are my fellow-citizens, my fathers, my brothers, my children, my limbs, my body, my light, and yes, dearer to me than light. For what can the rays of the sun give me when compared with the gift of your love? Its rays are useful to me in this present life, but your love is weaving for me a crown for the life that is to come.

January 28

Thomas Aquinas

Priest and Friar, 1274

Thomas Aquinas has been described as the greatest thinker and teacher of the medieval church. Born at Rocca Secca, near Aquino, in Italy, Thomas was educated first by the Benedictines at Monte Cassino, and then at the University of Naples. Against his family's wishes, he joined the mendicant Dominican Order of Preachers. His profound, theological wisdom and capacity to impart this, as well in homilies as in hymns, along with his gentleness of spirit in dealing with all, earned him the title "the Angelic Doctor." He died on March 7, 1274, en route to the Council of Lyons, and his feast has been celebrated on this day since 1970.

A Reading from the foreword and beginning of the *Summa Theologiae* of Thomas Aquinas

Since it is the duty of a teacher of catholic truth not only to build up those who are mature in their faith, but also to shape those who are just beginning—as the apostle Paul himself records, "As infants in Christ, I fed you with milk, not solid food, because you were not ready for it"—so the declared purpose of this work is to convey the things that pertain to the Christian religion in a way that is readily accessible to beginners.

We have noticed that newcomers are invariably put off reflecting more deeply upon their faith by various writings, intimidated partly by the swarm of pointless questions, articles, and arguments, but also because essential information is being communicated under the constraints of textual commentary or academic debate rather than sound educational methods, and because repetition breeds boredom and muddled thinking.

Eager, therefore, to avoid these and similar pitfalls, and trusting in the help of God, we shall try in this work to examine the claims of Christian teaching, and to be precise and clear in our language, as far as the matter under discussion allows.

It is clear that Christian teaching employs human reason, not so as to prove anything because that would undermine the merit of believing, but rather in order to elucidate the implications of its thought. We should note that just as grace never scraps our human nature, but instead brings it to perfection, so in the same way our natural ability to reason should assist faith as the natural loving inclination of our will yields to charity.

January 30

Charles

King and Martyr, 1649

Born in 1600, the second son of King James I, Charles became heir apparent when he was twelve on the death of his elder brother. He succeeded to the throne in 1625, where he came up against the increasing power of an antagonistic Parliament. Combined with the religious Puritanism which was prevalent, this made Charles staunch in his resistance of the power of either force in the land. He frequently dismissed sittings of Parliament and tried to enforce High-Church

Anglican practice on all, throughout both the kingdoms of England and Scotland. Opposition resulted in civil war. After Charles' imprisonment and trial, he was put to death on this day in 1649. Although some see him as a victim of his own pride, his faith and willingness to suffer and die for what he believed in are not in doubt.

A Reading from a letter of Charles I to his son, the Prince of Wales, and delivered into the hands of his chaplain, the Bishop of London, just before his execution on January 30, 1649

With God I would have you begin and end, who is King of Kings, the sovereign disposer of the kingdoms of the world, who pulleth down one and setteth up another. The best government and highest sovereignty you can attain to is to be subject to him, that the scepter of his word and spirit may rule in your heart. The true glory of princes consists in advancing God's glory, in the maintenance of true religion and the Church's good; also in the dispensation of civil power, with justice and honor to the public peace.

Piety will make you prosperous, at least it will keep you from becoming miserable; nor is he much a loser that loseth all, yet saveth his own soul at last. To which center of true happiness, God (I trust) hath and will graciously direct all these black lines of affliction which he hath been pleased to draw on me, and by which he hath (I hope) drawn me nearer to himself. You have already tasted of that cup whereof I have liberally drunk; which I look upon as God's physic, having that in healthfulness which it wants in pleasure.

Above all, I would have you, as I hope you are already, well grounded and settled in your religion, the best profession of which I have ever esteemed that of the Church of England, in which you have been educated; yet I would have your own judgement and reason now sealed to that sacred bond which education hath written, that it may be judiciously your own religion, and not other men's custom or tradition which you profess.

Let nothing seem little or despicable to you in matters which concern religion and the Church's peace, so as to neglect a speedy reforming and effectually suppressing errors and schisms. What may seem at first but as a hand-breadth, by seditious spirits, as by strong winds, are soon made a cover and darken the whole heaven.

Never charge your head with such a crown as shall, by its heaviness, oppress the whole body, the weakness of whose parts cannot return anything of strength, honor, or safety to the head, but a necessary debilitation and ruin. Your prerogative is best showed and exercised in remitting rather than exacting the rigor of the laws; there being nothing worse than legal tyranny.

In these two points of preservation of established religion and laws, I may (without vanity) turn the reproach of my sufferings, as to the world's censure, into the honor of a kind of martyrdom, as to the testimony of my conscience—the troublers of my kingdoms having nothing else to object against me but this, that I prefer religion and laws established before those alterations they propounded. And so indeed I do, and ever shall, till I am convinced by better arguments than what hitherto have been chiefly used against me—tumults, armies, and prisons.

I know God can—I hope he will—restore me to my rights. I cannot despair, either of his mercy, or my people's love and pity. At worst, I trust I shall but go before you to a better kingdom, which God hath prepared for me, and me for it, through my Savior Jesus Christ, to whose mercy I commend you, and all mine.

Farewell, till we meet, if not on earth, yet in heaven.

January 31

John Bosco

Priest, Founder of the Salesian Teaching Order, 1888

Born in 1815 to a peasant family, John Bosco spent most of his life in the Turin area of Italy. He had a particular call to help young men and pioneered new educational methods, for example, in rejecting corporal punishment. His work with homeless youth received the admiration even of anticlerical politicians and his promotion of vocational training, including evening classes and industrial schools, became a pattern for others to follow. To extend the work, he founded in 1859 a religious community, the Pious Society of Saint Francis de Sales, usually known as the Salesians. It grew rapidly and was well-established in several countries by the time of his death on this day in 1888.

A Reading from a letter of John Bosco

If we want to be thought of as those who have the real happiness of our pupils at heart, and who help each to fulfill his role in life, you must never forget that you are taking the place of parents who love their children. I have always worked, studied, and exercised my priesthood out of love for them. And not I alone, but the whole Salesian Order.

How often in my long career has this great truth come home to me! It is so much easier to get angry than to be patient, to threaten a boy rather than to persuade him. I would even say that usually it is so much more convenient for our own impatience and pride to punish them rather than to correct them patiently with firmness and gentleness.

I recommend to you the love Saint Paul had for his new converts. When he found them inattentive and unresponsive to his love, that same love led him to tears and prayers.

Be careful not to give anyone reason to think that you act under the impulse of anger. It is difficult to keep calm when administering punishment. But it is very necessary if you are not to give the impression that you are simply asserting your authority or giving vent to your anger. Let us look on those over whom we have a certain authority, as sons. Let us be determined to be at their service, even as Jesus came to obey and not to command. We should be ashamed to give the least impression of domineering. We should only exercise authority in order the better to serve the boys.

That was how Jesus treated his apostles. He put up with their ignorance and dullness and their lack of faith. His attitude toward sinners was full of kindness and loving friendship. This astonished some and scandalized others, but to others it gave enough hope to ask forgiveness from God.

Given that the boys in our charge are to be seen as our sons, we must put aside all anger when we correct their faults, or at least restrain it so much that it is almost completely suppressed. There must be no angry outburst, no look of contempt, no hurtful words. Instead, like true parents, really intent on their children's welfare and growth, show them compassion now, and always hold out hope for the future.

FEBRUARY

February 1

Brigid

Abbess of Kildare, *c.*525

Brigid (also known as Bride) was born in the latter part of the fifth century, of humble origin just five miles from Kildare. She was to become first a nun in the monastery there and later its abbess. She is believed to have been baptized by Saint Patrick and the stories of her portray a woman of great compassion who, like many Celtic saints, had a particular affinity with animals and the natural world. Her life was written in the middle of the seventh century and is the earliest life of an Irish saint. She is said to have been consecrated a bishop by Bishop Ibor, because of her resemblance to the Virgin Mary, but this may have been put abroad to support the claim of the primacy of the Abbey of Kildare. By her prayers and miracles, she is reputed to have influenced strongly the formation of the Church throughout Ireland, where she is, with Patrick, the patron saint. She died in about the year 525.

A Reading from *The Life of Saint Brigid* by Cogitosus

Holy Brigid, whom God had chosen beforehand to be conformed and predestined to his image, was born of Christian parents. As the chosen of God, she was indeed a girl of great modesty, who as she grew in years grew also in serenity.

Once a lone wild boar that was being hunted charged out of the forest, and in the course of its panicked flight careered into a herd of pigs that belonged to the most blessed Brigid. She noticed its presence and she blessed it. Immediately the creature lost its sense of fear and settled down quietly among the herd of pigs. See, my friends, how even the wild beasts and animals could not resist either her bidding or her will, but served her docilely and humbly.

On another occasion the blessed Brigid felt a tenderness for some ducks that she saw swimming on the water and occasionally taking wing. She bid them fly to her, and a great flock of them flew toward her, without any fear, as if they were humans under obedience to her. She touched them with her hand and embraced them tenderly. She then released them and they flew into the sky. And as they did so she praised God the Creator of all living things, to whom all life is subject, and for the service of whom all life is gift.

From these and many other episodes that demonstrated her power, it is certain that blessed Brigid could command the affections of wild animals, cattle and the birds of the air.

February 2

The Presentation of Our Lord Jesus Christ in the Temple

This day marks the completion of forty days since the birth of Jesus, when Mary and Joseph took the child to the Temple in Jerusalem. The requirement in Levitical law was for Mary to be "cleansed," the completion of her purification following the birth of a male child. Until that day, she could touch no holy thing nor enter the sanctuary. Yet on seeing the holy family, Simeon praised God and acclaimed the infant as "the light to enlighten the nations," and the prophet Anna gave thanks and proclaimed him her redeemer. The image of Christ as the light has led to the celebration of light countering darkness, with candles often taking a central place in the observance of this festival.

A Reading from a sermon of Sophronius of Jerusalem

Let us all hasten to meet Christ, we who honor and venerate the divine mystery we celebrate today. Everyone should be eager to join the procession to share in this meeting. Let no one refuse to carry a light. Our bright shining candles are a sign of the divine splendor of the one who comes to expel the dark shadows of evil and to make the whole universe radiant with the brilliance of his eternal light. Our candles also show how bright our souls should be when we go to meet Christ.

The God-bearer, the most pure Virgin, carried the true Light in her arms and brought him to help those who lay in darkness. In the same way, we too should carry a light for all to see and reflect the radiance of the true light as we hasten to meet him.

Indeed, this is the mystery we celebrate today, that the Light has come and has shone upon a world enveloped in shadow; the Dayspring from on high has visited us and given light to those who were sitting in darkness. This is our feast, and we join in procession with lighted candles to show both that the light has shone upon us and to signify the glory that is yet to come to us through him. So let us hasten all together to meet our God.

The true light has come, "the light that enlightens every person who is born into this world." Let all of us, beloved, be enlightened and be radiant with its light. Let none of us remain a stranger to this brightness; let no one who is filled remain in the darkness. Let us be shining ourselves as we go together to meet and to receive with the aged Simeon the light whose brilliance is eternal. Rejoicing with Simeon, let us sing a hymn of thanksgiving to God, the Origin and Father of the Light, who sent the true Light to dispel the darkness and to give us all a share in his splendor.

Through Simeon's eyes we too have seen the salvation of God that he has prepared for all the nations, and has revealed the glory of us who are the new Israel. As Simeon was released from the bonds of this life when he had seen Christ, so we too were at once freed from our old state of sinfulness. By faith we too embraced Christ, the salvation of God the Father, as he came to us from Bethlehem. Gentiles before, we have now become the people of God. Our eyes have seen God made flesh, and because we have seen him present among us and have cradled him in our minds, we are called the new Israel. Never let us forget this presence; every year let us keep this feast in his honor.

alternative reading

A Reading from a hymn of Ephrem of Syria

Praise to you, Son of the Most High, who has put on our body.

Into the holy temple Simeon carried the Christ-child
and sang a lullaby to him:
"You have come, Compassionate One,
having pity on my old age, making my bones enter
into Sheol in peace. By you I will be raised
out of the grave into paradise."
Anna embraced the child; she placed her mouth
upon his lips, and then the Spirit rested

upon her lips, like Isaiah
whose mouth was silent until a coal drew near
to his lips and opened his mouth.
Anna was aglow with the spirit of his mouth.
She sang him a lullaby:
"Royal Son,
despised son, being silent, you hear;
hidden, you see; concealed, you know;
God-man, glory to your name."

Even the barren heard and came running with their provisions.
The Magi are coming with their treasures.
The barren are coming with their provisions.
Provisions and treasures were heaped up suddenly among the poor.

The barren woman Elizabeth cried out as she was accustomed,
"Who has granted to me, blessed woman,
to see your Babe by whom heaven and earth are filled?
Blessed is your fruit
that brought forth the cluster on a barren vine."

Praise to you, Son of the Most High, who has put on our body.

alternative reading

A Reading from a sermon of Guerric of Igny

Today as we bear in our hands lighted candles, how can we not fail to remember that venerable old man Simeon who on this day held the child Jesus in his arms—the Word who was latent in a body, as light is latent in a wax candle—and declared him to be "the light to enlighten the nations?" Indeed, Simeon was himself a bright and shining lamp bearing witness to the Light. Under the guidance of the Spirit which filled him, he came into the temple precisely in order that, "receiving your loving kindness, O God, in the midst of your temple," he might proclaim Jesus to be that loving kindness and the light of your people.

Behold then, the candle alight in Simeon's hands. You must light your own candles by enkindling them at his, those lamps which the Lord commanded you to bear in your hands. So come to him and be enlightened that you do not so much bear lamps as become them, shining within yourselves and radiating light to your neighbors. May there be a lamp in your heart, in your hand and in your mouth: let the lamp in your heart shine for yourself, the lamp in your hand and mouth shine for your neighbors. The lamp in your heart is a reverence for God inspired by faith; the lamp in your hand is the example of a good life; and the lamp in your mouth is the words of consolation you speak.

We have to shine not only before others by our good works and by what we say, but also before the angels in our prayer, and before God by the intentions of our hearts. In the presence of the angels our lamps will shine with unsullied reverence when we sing the psalms attentively in their sight or pray fervently; before God our lamp is single-minded resolve to please him alone to whom we have entrusted ourselves.

My friends, in order to light all these lamps for yourselves, I beg you to approach the source of light and become enlightened—I mean Jesus himself who shines in Simeon's hands to enlighten your faith, who shines on your works, who inspires your speech, who makes your prayer fervent and purifies the intentions of your heart. Then, when the lamp of this mortal life is extinguished, there will appear for you who had so many lamps shining within you the light of unquenchable life, and it will shine for you at the evening of your life like the brightness of the noonday sun. And though you may think your light is quenched in death, you will rise like the daystar and your darkness be made bright as noon. As Scripture says, "No longer will you need the light of sun to shine upon you by day, or the light of the moon by night; but the Lord will be an everlasting light for you." For the light of the new Jerusalem is the Lamb. To him be glory and praise for ever.

February 3

Anskar

Archbishop of Hamburg
Missionary to Denmark and Sweden, 865

Anskar was a native of Picardy. At the age of four, following his mother's death, he was entrusted to the care of the monastery of Corbie near Amiens where, at the age of thirteen, he was professed as a monk. Following the conversion of King Harold of Denmark to Christianity in 826, Anskar was sent to Schleswig and attempted to start a Christian school there. His first attempt to Christianize the Danes failed and he went on to Sweden, where he is reputed to have built the first Christian church. In the year 832 he was consecrated Archbishop of Hamburg, but in 845 the town was sacked by Vikings and he transferred the See to Bremen. He continued to work among the Danes, preaching widely throughout Scandinavia. He was much-loved for his work with the poor and in mitigating the slave trade. Praised for his good deeds, he is said to have replied: "If I were counted worthy to stand before God, I would ask him one single thing, that of by grace becoming a good human being." Anskar is the patron saint of Denmark. He died at Candlemastide in the year 865.

A Reading from *The Life of Saint Anskar*
by his disciple Rimbert

When the emperor wanted to send back Harold to his native land and regain the crown with his help, he looked for a holy and pious man who would accompany the king, and teach both him and his people the doctrine of salvation in order to be converted and made steadfast in faith. The Abbot of Corbie informed him that he knew of a monk in his monastery who was ablaze for the holy faith and wanted to suffer much for the name of God.

Later, a delegation from Sweden arrived with a message for the emperor Louis. They said that among their people there were many who wanted to embrace the Christian faith; even the king himself was favorable to the thought of receiving Christian priests if the emperor would most graciously send some wise preachers. Again the name of Anskar was mentioned. The man of God clearly understood the task entrusted to him. He became ablaze with the love of God, and saw it as a great joy to be allowed to work for the salvation of souls.

How blessed, how worthy of all praise and commendation, was Anskar! He imitated the greatest of the saints and was endowed with unnumbered virtues. He was holy in thought and chaste in body and, like the virgins, followed the Lamb wherever he went. As a confessor of Christ he remains for ever, and shall occupy a glorious place among those who have confessed Christ. In the new creation he will sit with the apostles on their lofty seat of judgement, judging the world which he had turned his back on. He will receive with the martyrs the crown of justice and the divinely promised palm of martyrdom.

For it is clear that there are two kinds of martyrdom: one occurs when the church is at peace and is hidden from sight; the other occurs during times of persecution and is visible to all. Anskar desired both kinds of martyrdom, but in the end only attained one. For day after day, with tears, vigils, fasts, disciplining the flesh and mortifying his bodily desires, he offered up to God a sacrifice on the altar of his heart, and in so doing attained a martyrdom as far as is possible in a time of peace.

He was indeed a martyr because, as the apostle Paul says, the world was crucified to him and he to the world. He was a martyr because, amid the temptations of the evil one, the enticements of the flesh, the persecutions of the heathen, and the opposition of Christians, he persevered to the end of his life unperturbed, immovable, and unconquerable as a confessor of Christ. He was indeed a martyr because the word "martyr" means "witness," and he was a witness of God's word and of the name of Christ.

Therefore, just as Anskar was in all things an imitator of Christ, so we should strive to be imitators of him. In so doing Anskar will live with us on earth to the end of the world, and we will be worthy to live with him in heaven when our present life is over. He will live with us on earth if the holiness of his life and the remembrance of his teaching recall him to us. We too shall live with him in heaven if we follow his example, if with all our strength and desire we long for him to whom Anskar has gone before us, Jesus Christ our Lord.

February 4

Cornelius the Centurion

A crucial task facing the first Christians was to understand who they were: another variation on Judaism or something with a radically different mission. The conversion and baptism of a centurion, or Roman officer, called Cornelius was a major turning point in that process of definition. The story is told in detail in the Book of Acts, chapters 10-11. Both Peter, the leader of the apostles, and Cornelius, the Gentile, respond to visions that bring them together and lead Peter to exclaim, "I truly understand that God shows no partiality, but in every nation anyone who fears him and does what is right is acceptable to him." Cornelius and his household then were baptized and became the first Gentile members of the new Christian church. According to tradition, Cornelius later became the second Bishop of Caesarea.

A Reading from a catechetical lecture of
Cyril of Alexandria

How great a dignity the Lord confers on you in your transfer from the order of catechumens to that of believers, is expressed for you by the apostle Paul when he says, "God is faithful, by whom you were called to the fellowship of his Son Jesus Christ." Called by a God who is faithful, you receive this epithet as well, and so are the recipient of a great dignity. For as God has the titles good, righteous, almighty, creator of the universe, so also he has the title faithful. Think therefore to what a dignity you are promoted in now coming to share one of the divine titles!

Now the one and only faith that you are to take and preserve in the way of learning and professing it is that which is now being committed to you by the church as confirmed throughout the Scriptures. For seeing that not everyone can read the Scriptures, some because they lack the learning and others because, for one reason or another, they find no opportunity to get to know them, we gain possession of the whole doctrine of the Christian faith in a few articles, and that to prevent any soul from being lost through not learning the faith.

This doctrine I want you to commit to memory word for word and say it over to one another as much as you can, not writing it out on paper but using memory to engrave it on your heart. But take care lest, in giving your whole mind to this, you should, by any chance, let any catechumen overhear what you have had committed to you. I want you to retain this provision for your way as long as your life shall last, and not to receive any other faith than this henceforth: not even if I were to change my mind and say something that contradicted what you are now being taught; no, nor if a dark angel were to disguise himself as an angel of light and made to lead you astray. "For though we, or an angel from heaven, preach any other gospel unto you than that you have received, let him be accursed." And at this stage listen to the exact form of words and memorize this faith, leaving it to the appropriate season for each of the articles which it contains to be built up from Holy Scripture. For these articles of our faith were not composed out of human opinion, but are the principal points collected out of the whole of Scripture to complete a single doctrinal formulation of the faith. And in like manner as the mustard seed contains numbers of branches-to-be within its tiny grain, so also this creed embraces in a few phrases all the religious knowledge contained in the Old and New Testaments together.

Look now, brethren, and "hold the traditions" that are now being imparted to you, and "write them on the table of your hearts."

Preserve them with godly fear, lest the Enemy spoil any of you through your conceit, or some heretic misrepresent any of the things you have had delivered to you. Faith, you see, is like cash paid over the counter (which is what I have now done), but God requires you to account for what you have had: as the Apostle says, "I charge you before God, who quickens all things, and before Jesus Christ, who before Pontius Pilate witnessed a good confession that you keep without spot, until the appearing of our Lord Jesus Christ" this faith committed to you. A treasure of life has now been committed to you, and at his coming the Master looks for the deposit, "which in his times he shall show, who is the blessed and only Potentate, the King of kings and Lord of lords, who only hath immortality, dwelling in the light that no man can approach unto, whom no man has seen or can see, to whom be honor and glory world without end." Amen.

February 5

The Martyrs of Japan

Almost fifty years after Francis Xavier had arrived in Japan as its first Christian apostle, the presence of several thousand baptized Christians in the land became a subject of suspicion to the ruler Hideyoshi, who soon began a period of persecution. Twenty-six men and women, religious and lay, were first mutilated then crucified near Nagasaki in 1597, the most famous of whom was Paul Miki. After their martyrdom, their blood-stained clothes were kept and held in reverence by their fellow Christians. The period of persecution continued for another thirty-five years, many new witness-martyrs being added to their number.

A Reading from a contemporary account of the martyrdom
of Paul Miki and his companions in Japan
during February 1597

The crosses were set in place. Father Pasio and Father Rodriguez took turns encouraging the victims. Their steadfast behavior was wonderful to see. The Father Bursar stood motionless, his eyes turned heavenward. Brother Martin gave thanks to God's goodness by singing psalms. Again and again he repeated, "Into your hands, Lord, I entrust my life." Brother Francisco Blanco also thanked God in a loud voice. Brother Gonsalvo in a very loud voice kept saying the Our Father and the Hail Mary.

Our brother Paul Miki saw himself standing now in the noblest pulpit he had ever filled. To this congregation he began by proclaiming that he was a Japanese and a Jesuit, and that he was dying for preaching the gospel. He gave thanks to God for this wonderful blessing, and he ended with these words:

> As I come to this supreme moment of my life, I am sure none of you would suppose I want to deceive you. And so I tell you plainly: there is no route to salvation except the one that Christians follow. My religion teaches me to pardon my enemies and all who have offended me. I do gladly pardon the emperor and all who have brought about my death, and I beg them to seek Christian baptism.

Then he looked at his comrades and began to encourage them in their final struggle. Joy glowed in all their faces, and in that of Luis most of all. When a Christian in the crowd called out to him that he would soon be in heaven, his hands and his whole body strained upward with such joy that every eye was fixed upon him.

Antonio, hanging at Luis' side, looked toward heaven and called upon the holy names of Jesus and Mary. He began to sing a psalm, "O Praise the Lord, all you children!" He had learned this at the catechetical school in Nagasaki, for among the tasks given to the children there had been included the learning of some psalms such as these.

The others kept repeating, "Jesus, Mary!" Their faces were serene. Some of them even took to urging the people standing by to live worthy Christian lives. In these and other ways they showed their readiness to die.

Then, according to Japanese custom, four executioners began to unsheathe their spears. At this dreadful sight, all the Christians cried out, "Jesus, Mary!" And a storm of anguished weeping then arose to batter the very skies. The executioners killed them one by one—one thrust of the spear, then a second blow. It was over in a very short time.

A Reading from *The Epitome of the Divine Institutes*
by Lactantius

Things may be said with justice in this world. But who will hear them when those who exercise authority get angry and feel threatened by the exercise of personal liberty? In religion alone has liberty placed her dwelling. Here is an area of life which above all others should be a matter of free will: no one should be put under compulsion to worship that which he does not wish to.

Thus, if some through fear of threats, or overwhelmed by pain when under torture, agree to offer detestable sacrifices, you should know that they are not doing so of their own free will. They will not do voluntarily what they are made to do under compulsion. As soon as the opportunity arises and their liberty is restored, they will flee to God, and with prayers and tears beseech his mercy for what they have had to endure; and pardon is never denied them. What then do those who mutilate the body but who cannot change the will, hope to accomplish by their actions?

If others, terrified neither by threats nor by torture, are prepared to maintain their faith and forfeit their life, against such people cruelty exerts all its strength, contriving unspeakable tortures, unbearable pain, just because it is known that death for the sake of God is deemed glorious, and that victory consists in rising above torment and in laying down one's life for faith and religion. Against such people the torturers go into competition: they will not risk allowing their victims to die; instead they devise new and subtle cruelties to compel the human spirit to submit to bodily pain. Should they fail, they pause, applying to the wounds they have inflicted every care, knowing that pain from repeated torture is worse when wounds are raw. In these ways they ply their trade against the innocent. They consider themselves pious, just and even religious (for with such rites they believe their gods will be pleased) and denigrate their victims as impious and wild people. What perversity this is!

It is said that those who revile the religious observances of the state which have been handed down by their ancestors, are rightly and deservedly punished. But what if those ancestors were fools in adopting empty religious rites? Are we Christians to be prohibited from pursuing a true and better course? Why should we abandon our liberty and become enslaved and addicted to what is false? Allow us to be wise and to seek after truth. If it suits the authorities to defend the practice of ancestral religion, then why, for example, are the Egyptians exempt who worship cattle and creatures of every kind as gods? Why are actors in the theatre allowed to ridicule the gods? Why is someone honored because he has mocked the gods with a display of wit? Why are philosophers listened to when they argue that there are no gods, or that if they do exist, that they have no care or interest in human affairs, or that there is no providential ordering to the world?

Of all the human race it would seem that the only ones who are judged irreligious are Christians who follow after the truth of God.

February 10

Scholastica

Sister of Benedict, Abbess of Plombariola, *c.*543

Scholastica is a more shadowy figure than her famous brother, Benedict. She too was born at Nursia, central Italy, around the year 480. At an early age she chose to consecrate herself to God, but probably continued to live at home. Only after Benedict moved to Monte Cassino did she settle at Plombariola nearby, joining or maybe founding a nunnery under his direction. As abbess she sought to follow his Rule, *and met him each year at a house near his monastery where they would praise God together and discuss spiritual matters. She died in about the year 543. Benedict had a vision of her soul rising up to heaven and, collecting her body, he had her buried in the tomb prepared for himself. Scholastica soon became a figure for veneration by all nuns who followed Benedict's* Rule.

A Reading from the *Dialogues* of Gregory the Great

Saint Benedict's sister, Scholastica, who had been consecrated to almighty God in early childhood, used to visit her brother once a year. On these occasions he would go down to meet her in a house belonging to the monastery, a short distance from the entrance.

For this particular visit he joined her there with a few of his disciples and they spent the whole day singing God's praises and conversing about the spiritual life. When darkness was setting in, they took their meal together and continued their conversation at table until it was quite late. Then the holy nun said to him "Please do not leave me tonight; let us keep on talking about the joys of heaven till morning."

"What are you saying, sister?" he replied. "You know I cannot stay away from the monastery." At her brother's refusal, Scholastica folded her hands on the table and rested her head upon them in earnest prayer. When she looked up again, there was a sudden burst of lightning and thunder, accompanied by such a downpour that Benedict and his companions were unable to set foot outside the door.

Realizing that he could not return to the monastery in this terrible storm, Benedict complained bitterly. "God forgive you, sister," he said, "What have you done?" Scholastica simply answered, "When I appealed to you, you would not listen to me. So I turned to my God and he heard my prayer. Leave now if you can. Leave me here and go back to your monastery."

This, of course, he could not do. He had no choice now but to stay, in spite of his unwillingness. They spent the entire night together and both of them derived great profit from the holy converse they had about the interior life. We need not be surprised that in this instance the woman proved mightier than her brother. Do we not read in St. John that God is love? Surely it is no more than right that her influence was greater than his, since hers was the greater love.

Three days later as he stood in his room looking up toward the sky, the man of God beheld his sister's soul leaving her body and entering the court of heaven in the form of a dove. Overjoyed at her eternal glory, he gave thanks to almighty God in hymns of praise. Then Benedict sent some of his brethren to bring her body to the monastery and bury it in the tomb he had prepared for himself. The bodies of these two were now to share a common resting place just as in life their souls had always been one in God.

February 13

Absalom Jones

Priest, 1818

Born in Delaware in slavery in the year 1746, Absalom Jones educated himself and purchased first his wife's freedom and then his own. He served as lay minister for the black congregation of a Methodist Church in Philadelphia until the growth of black membership alarmed the white congregation so much that in 1792 they decided that blacks would be directed to sit in the upstairs gallery. Rather than obey this directive, however, the black members walked out and organized a Free African Society. In the flowing year an epidemic of yellow fever hit Philadelphia and so many died that there was no one left to bury the dead. When the mayor issued a call for volunteers, Absalom Jones offered to organize the workers needed and over the following months he and others went from house to house locating the sick and burying the dead. Jones himself became sick but recovered and continued the work. The following year, he and his associates built a church and applied to the Episcopal Diocese of Pennsylvania for membership. The Diocese accepted the congregation as St. Thomas Church in 1794 and Absalom Jones was ordained a deacon the next year and a priest in 1802, the first African American to serve in that capacity in the Episcopal Church.

A Reading from a sermon preached by the Reverend Absalom Jones to celebrate the abolition of the African slave trade by the Congress of the United States in 1808

The history of the world shows us that the deliverance of the children of Israel from their bondage is not the only instance in which it has pleased God to appear in behalf of oppressed and distressed nations as the deliverer of the innocent and of those who call upon his name. He is as unchangeable in his nature and character as he is in his wisdom and power. The great and blessed event, which we have this day met to celebrate, is a striking proof that the God of heaven and earth is the same yesterday, and today, and forever. Yes, my brethren, the nations from which most of us have descended, and the country in which some of us were born, have been visited by the tender mercy of the Common Father of the human race. He has seen the affliction of our countrymen, with an eye of pity. He has seen ships fitted out from different ports in Europe and America, and freighted with trinkets to be exchanged for the bodies and souls of men. He has seen the anguish which has taken place, when parents have been torn from their children and children from their parents and conveyed, with their hands and feet bound in fetters, on board of ships prepared to receive them. He has seen them thrust in crowds into the holds of those ships, where many of them have perished from the want of air. He has seen such of them as have escaped from that noxious place of confinement leap into the ocean with a faint hope of swimming back to their native shore, or a determination to seek an early retreat from their impending misery in a watery grave. He has seen them exposed for sale, like horses and cattle, upon the wharves; or, like bales of goods, in warehouses of West India and American seaports. He has seen the pangs of separation between members of the same family. He has seen them driven into the sugar, the rice, and the tobacco fields, and compelled to work in spite of the habits of ease which they derived from the natural fertility of their own country in the open air, beneath a burning sun, with scarcely as much clothing upon them as modesty required. He has seen them faint beneath the pressure of their labors. He has seen them return to their smoky huts in the evening, with nothing to satisfy their hunger but a scanty allowance of roots; and these, cultivated for themselves, on that day only, which God ordained as a day of rest for man and beast. He has seen the neglect with which their masters have treated their immortal souls; not only in withholding religious instruction from them but, in some instances, depriving them of access to the means of obtaining it. He has seen all the different modes of torture, by means of the ship, the screw, the pincers, and the red-hot iron, which have been exercised upon their bodies by inhuman overseers—overseers, did I say? Yes, but not by these only. Our God has seen masters and mistresses, educated in fashionable life, sometimes take the instruments of torture into their own hands and, deaf to the cries and shrieks of their agonizing slaves, exceed even their overseers in cruelty. Inhuman wretches! Though you have been deaf to their cries and shrieks, they have been heard in heaven. The ears of Jehovah have been constantly open to them. He has heard the prayers that have ascended from the hearts of his people; and he has, as in the case of his ancient and chosen people the Jews, *come down to deliver* our suffering countrymen from the hands of their oppressors.

February 14

Cyril and Methodius

Apostles to the Slavs, Patrons of Europe, 869 & 885

Constantine (his later monastic name was Cyril) and his older brother Methodius were born in Salonika and educated in Constantinople. At the invitation of its Prince, and with the authority of the Patriarch of Constantinople, the brothers went in 863 to Moravia (the modern Czech Republic and Slovenia) to reform the church on Byzantine lines. They conceived their mandate in broad terms because they had no desire to impose on the people foreign usages as earlier Frankish clergy had imposed Latin usages. Instead they sought to promote a truly indigenous Christianity. To this end Cyril, who was an outstanding scholar and linguist, created an alphabet for the Slavic language which still bears his name (Cyrillic) and set about translating the Scriptures and other liturgical texts into the language (now known as Old Slavonic). In the course of their work they negotiated controversy and opposition with tact and pastoral skill. Cyril died on this day in the year 869, while the brothers were in Rome, there to obtain papal support for their evangelistic work. Methodius returned to Moravia as bishop where he completed the translation of the Bible and continued his missionary work. He died in what is now Hungary in the year 885.

Today Cyril and Methodius are honored not only as the "Apostles to the Slavs," and along with Saint Benedict as "Patrons of Europe," but also as forerunners of an authentic ecumenism between the two great branches of Christendom.

A Reading from the Old Slavonic *Life of Constantine (Cyril)*

Constantine, already burdened by many hardships, became ill. At one point during his extended illness, he experienced a vision of God and began to sing this verse from the psalms: "My spirit rejoices and my heart exults for we shall go into the house of the Lord." Afterwards he remained dressed in the vestments that were to be venerated later, and he rejoiced for an entire day, saying: "From now on, I am not the servant of the emperor or of any man on earth, but of almighty God alone. Before, I was dead, but now I am alive, and I shall live for ever. Amen." The following day he assumed the monastic habit and took the religious name Cyril. He lived the life of a monk for fifty days.

When the time came for him to set out from this world to the peace of the heavenly homeland, he prayed to God with his hands outstretched and his eyes filled with tears: "O Lord, my God, you have created the choirs of angels and spiritual powers; you have stretched forth the heavens and established the earth, creating all that exists from nothing. You hear those who obey your will and keep your commands in holy fear. Hear my prayer now and protect your faithful people, for you have established me as their unsuitable and unworthy servant.

"Keep them free from harm and all the worldly cunning of those who blaspheme you. Build up your church and gather all into unity. Make your people known for the unity and profession of their faith. Inspire the hearts of your people with your Word and your teaching. You called us to preach the gospel of your Christ and to encourage them to lives and works pleasing to you.

"I now return to you your people, your gift to me. Direct them with your powerful right hand and protect them under the shadow of your wings. May all praise and glorify your name, the Father, Son, and Holy Spirit. Amen."

Once he had exchanged the gift of peace with everyone, he said: "Blessed be God, who did not hand us over to our invisible enemy, but freed us from his snare and delivered us from perdition." He then fell asleep in the Lord at the age of forty-two.

February 14

Valentine

Martyr at Rome, *c.*269

Valentine was a priest or a bishop of Terni who was martyred at Rome under the Emperor Claudius. The association of his commemoration with lovers seems to have originated either from the traditional day in medieval belief when birds mated, or more likely, from a link with the pagan Lupercalia festival in Rome, which occurred on the Ides of February. For Christians, the day marks an acknowledgement of an all-loving God who blesses those who love one another, as Jesus implored his own disciples to do.

A Reading from a letter of Cyprian of Carthage

God is watching us as we go into battle and engage in the combat of faith. His angels are watching us, and so is Christ himself. How great is the dignity of that glory, how great the happiness of fighting knowing that we have God as our protector, and Christ as our judge when he crowns us with the wreath of victory!

Let us be ready for battle then, my friends, engaging with all our strength, our minds prepared, our faith sound, armed with true determination. Let the army of God march to where the battle sounds. The apostle Paul has described to us the armor of God; so let us take up these arms, confident in the spiritual and heavenly protection they offer, that on the evil day we may be able to withstand the assaults of the devil and beat them back.

Let us put on the breastplate of righteousness, that our hearts may be fortified and safe against the darts of the enemy. As for shoes, let our feet be wearing the teaching of the gospel, so that when we start trampling on the head of the serpent, crushing his head, he will be unable to bite back and overpower us.

Bravely let us carry the great shield of faith into battle, so that with its protection we can parry whatever the enemy may hurl at us.

Let us also protect our head with the helmet of salvation, that our ears may be closed to delusive commands that would only lead us to destruction, our eyes shielded from the sight of graven images, our foreheads fortified to protect the sign of God we bear, and our mouths emboldened that in victory we may confess Christ is Lord.

Finally, let us take up in our right hand the sword of the Spirit, that it may repudiate false sacrifices. It is the same right hand that in the Eucharist receives the body of the Lord that will one day also embrace the Lord himself, receiving from him a heavenly crown.

My beloved friends, let these things take hold of our hearts. Let this be our daily preparation for battle, our nightly meditation, so that if the day of persecution overtake us, as soldiers of Christ we will be ready, well-equipped in his precepts, and unafraid of the battle, but prepared for a crown.

alternative reading

A Reading from the poetry of George Herbert

Love

Love bade me welcome: yet my soul drew back,
Guilty of dust and sin.
But quick-ey'd Love, observing me grow slack
From my first entrance in,
Drew nearer to me, sweetly questioning,
If I lack'd any thing.

A guest, I answer'd, worthy to be here:
Love said, You shall be he.
I the unkind, ungrateful? Ah my dear,
I cannot look on thee.
Love took my hand, and smiling did reply,
Who made the eyes but I?

Truth Lord, but I have marr'd them: let my shame
Go where it doth deserve.
And know you not, says Love, who bore the blame?
My dear, then I will serve.
You must sit down, says Love, and taste my meat:
So I did sit and eat.

February 15

Thomas Bray

Priest and Missionary, 1730

Born at Marton in Shropshire in 1656, Thomas Bray was educated at Oxford and subsequently ordained. He was chosen by the Bishop of London to assist with the work of organizing the Church in Maryland in the U.S.A. During an extended delay in his setting out due to legal complications, he managed to organize a system of free parochial libraries, initially for use in America but later also instituted in England. This led to his founding the "Society for the Promotion of Christian Knowledge" (SPCK) in 1698. He finally set sail for Maryland in 1699. Though well received by the governor, Bray found that he could better promote his purposes from England. On his return to Europe, he also founded the "Society for the Propagation of the Gospel" (SPG). He died on this day in the year 1730.

A Reading from a sermon preached by Thomas Bray
at Saint Paul's Cathedral, December 19, 1697

Proportionately as the assistances given "to many to righteousness" shall be extensive and lasting, in the same measure we must suppose the degrees of glory will be allotted to such piety. It will, therefore, follow that those pious persons will most effectually consult their future happiness and provide best for an exalted glory, who shall expend most in fixing libraries of necessary and useful books in Divinity, in order to the instruction both of minister and people.

Such indeed cannot be said, by so doing, to hazard their persons in the converting of mankind, and may not be entitled thereby to the reward of martyrs and confessors. But however, they may be much more instrumental in "turning many to righteousness" even than those who actually labor in the work itself, because that, in effect, it will be they who preach, catechise, and instruct those parts of the world as well in future as in the present age. It is they who will be the fountain; we shall be only the conduit-pipes through which the waters of life will be conveyed to the people. And therefore, except we shall bestir ourselves very much, they will far outstrip us in the pursuit of eternal glory.

In short, those who shall make such a lasting provision for the instruction and conversion of any considerable part of mankind may, in so doing, be very well looked upon as a sort of apostle to those parts of the world. And if so, we may conclude a great deal concerning the degrees of glory wherewith such shall be recompensed, from that promise of our Savior to his apostles: "Verily, I say unto you, when the Son of Man shall sit on the throne of his glory, ye also shall sit upon the twelve thrones, judging the twelve tribes of Israel." For though we are not to conclude from these words that any besides the twelve shall be exalted to the highest degrees of happiness, yet from hence we may clearly gather that, proportionately as persons shall approach nearest to the apostles in evangelizing mankind, they shall be placed nearer and nearer to them upon the several ascents to the highest stations in the kingdom of heaven.

February 17

Janani Luwum

Archbishop of Uganda, Martyr, 1977

Janani Luwum was born in 1922 at Acholi in Uganda. His childhood and youth were spent as a goatherd but he quickly showed an ability to learn and absorb knowledge when given the opportunity. Soon after he became a teacher, he was converted to Christianity and was eventually ordained in 1956, becoming Bishop of Northern Uganda in 1969 and Archbishop of Uganda in 1974. Idi Amin had come to power in Uganda in 1971 as the result of a military coup and his undemocratic and harsh rule was the subject of much criticism by the Church and others. After Amin received a letter from the bishops protesting at the virtual institution of state murder, Janani and two of Amin's own government ministers were stated as having been found dead following a car accident. It emerged quickly that they had in fact died on the implicit instructions of the President. Janani's enthusiasm for the good news of Jesus, combined with his willingness to sacrifice even his own life for what he believed in, led him to his martyrdom on this day in 1977.

A Reading from *Janani* by Margaret Ford

During 1976 the preaching of both churches, Anglican and Roman Catholic, became more direct. "Uganda is killing Uganda," Janani told the men at the police barracks at Nsambya during an official visit at the end of August. "We look to you to uphold the laws of our land. Do not abuse this privilege." Afterwards some thanked the archbishop for speaking so openly, and showing them so clearly their responsibility. But others were afraid his words would annoy the President, whose anger might fall on them.

Janani continued to attend government functions. "Even the President needs friends," he would say. "We must love the President. We must pray for him. He is a child of God." He feared no one but God who was the center of his life. But his wish that the church of Uganda should have a guiding influence upon the government misled some people, who complained that he lived a comfortable life and was on the government side. When the Archbishop met one of his critics in December, he made clear the truth. In words that proved prophetic, he told him: "I do not know for how long I shall be occupying this chair. I live as though there will be no tomorrow. I face daily being picked up by the soldiers. While the opportunity is there, I preach the gospel with all my might, and my conscience is clear before God that I have not sided with the present government, which is utterly self-seeking. I have been threatened many times. Whenever I have the opportunity, I have told the President the things the churches disapprove of. God is my witness."

alternative reading

A Reading from a homily of Pope Paul VI on the occasion of the canonization of the Ugandan Martyrs, October 18, 1964

Every time we utter the word "martyr" in the sense it has acquired in Christian hagiography, we should bring to our mind's eye a drama evoking horror and wonder. Horror, because of the injustice which unlooses such a drama with the instruments of power and cruelty; horror, again, because of the blood which is shed and of the death so unfeelingly inflicted; wonder, then, because of the simple strength which submits without struggle or physical resistance to torment, happy and proud to witness to the unconquerable truth of a faith which has fused itself with life.

Life, however, dies, faith lives on. We see brute as opposed to moral force; the first knowing in its very success defeat; the second, triumph in failure! Martyrdom, then, is a drama: an appalling drama, let it be said, but one rich in teaching. The unjust and evil violence which it brings about tends almost to be forgotten, while in the memory of centuries the gentleness which makes the offering of self a sacrifice, a holocaust, remains with all its luster and attractiveness; a supreme act of love and faithfulness with regard to Christ; an example and a witnessing, and enduring message to contemporary and future generations alike. Such is martyrdom: such has been the glory of the church through the centuries, and which we commemorate today.

February 18

Martin Luther

Reformer, 1546

Martin Luther was born in 1483 at Eisleben in Saxony and educated at the cathedral school in Magdeburg and the university in Erfurt. He joined an order of Augustinian hermits there and was ordained priest in 1507, becoming a lecturer in the University of Wittenberg. He became Vicar of his Order in 1515, having charge of a dozen monasteries. His Christian faith began to take on a new shape, with his increasing dissatisfaction with the worship and order of the church. He became convinced that the Gospels taught that humanity is saved by faith and not by works, finding support in the writings of Saint Augustine of Hippo. He refuted the teaching of the Letter of James, calling it "an epistle of straw." Martin sought to debate the whole matter by posting ninety-five theses or propositions on the door of the Castle church in Wittenberg on this day in the year 1517. The hierarchy chose to see it as a direct attack on the church, which forced Martin into open rebellion. The Protestant Reformation spread throughout Germany and then Europe, many seeing it as liberation from a church that held them in fear rather than love. Martin Luther died in the year 1546, having effected a renaissance in the church, both Protestant and Catholic.

A Reading from Martin Luther's preface to the first volume of Latin writings, published in 1545

Meanwhile in that year [1541] I had already returned to interpret the Psalter anew. I had confidence in the fact that I was more skillful, after I had lectured in the university on Saint Paul's Epistles to the Romans, to the Galatians, and the one to the Hebrews. I had indeed been captivated with an extraordinary ardor for understanding Paul in the Epistle to the Romans. But up till then it was not the cold blood about the heart, but a single word in chapter one, "In it the righteousness of God is revealed," that had stood in my way. For I hated that word "righteousness of God," which, according to the use and custom of all the teachers, I had been taught to understand philosophically regarding the formal or active righteousness, as they called it, with which God is righteous and punishes the unrighteous sinner.

Though I lived as a monk without reproach, I felt that I was a sinner before God with an extremely disturbed conscience. I could not believe that he was placated by my satisfaction. I did not love, yes, I hated the righteous God who punishes sinners, and secretly, if not blasphemously, certainly murmuring greatly, I was angry with God, and said, "As if it were not enough that miserable sinners should be eternally lost through original sin, crushed by every kind of calamity which the law of the decalogue lays on them, without having God add pain to pain by the gospel threatening us with his righteousness and wrath!" Thus I raged with a fierce and troubled conscience. Nevertheless, I beat importunately upon Paul at that place, most ardently desiring to know what he meant.

At last, by the mercy of God, meditating day and night, I gave heed to the context of the words, namely, "In it the righteousness of God is revealed, as it is written, 'He who through faith is righteous shall live.' " There I began to understand that the righteousness of God is that by which the righteous lives by a gift of God, namely by faith. And this is the meaning: the righteousness of God is revealed by the gospel, namely, the passive righteousness with which the merciful God justifies us by faith, as it is written, "He who through faith is righteous shall live." Here I felt as if I was altogether born again and had entered paradise itself through open gates. The whole face of scripture appeared to me in a new light. Thereupon I ran through the scriptures from memory. I also found in other terms the same analogy as the "work of God" (that is, what God does in us), the "power of God," with which he makes us strong, the "wisdom of God," with which he makes us wise, the "strength of God," the "salvation of God," and the "glory of God."

And now, where I had once hated the phrase "the righteousness of God," so much, I began now to love and extol it as the sweetest of words, so that this passage in Paul became the very gate of paradise for me.

February 23

Polycarp

Bishop and Martyr of Smyrna, *c.* 156

Honored as one of the first Christian martyrs, Polycarp had been Bishop of Smyrna on the Adriatic coast of Asia Minor for more than forty years when the persecution of Christians began. He was arrested and given the option to renounce his faith and save his life, but refused. He was burnt at the stake. His remains were gathered together and buried outside the city; thus began the practice of celebrating the Eucharist over his burial place on the anniversary of his death. This custom also developed at the martyrs' tombs in the Roman catacombs. Polycarp died about 156 A.D..

A Reading from a contemporary account of the martyrdom of Polycarp, Bishop of Smyrna

Polycarp was led before the proconsul. He questioned him saying, "Take the oath, and I will let you go. Curse your Christ!" Polycarp replied, "I have served him for eighty-six years, and he has done me no wrong. How can I blaspheme my king who saved me?" But the proconsul persisted, saying: "Swear by the spirit of Caesar!" But Polycarp answered, "If you are really so foolish as to think that I would do such a thing, and if you pretend that you do not know who I am, then hear this plainly: I am a Christian."

When the fire was ready, Polycarp took off his outer garments, loosened his belt, and even removed his sandals. The irons with which the fire was equipped were fastened around him; but when they tried to nail him to the stake as well, he said, "Let me be. The One who gives me the strength to endure the flames will give me the strength to stay in them without you making sure of it with nails." So they did not nail him, but only tied him up. Bound like that, his arms behind his back, he looked like a noble ram, selected from some great flock, a burnt offering, acceptable and made ready for God. Looking up to heaven, he said:

> O Lord God almighty, Father of your beloved and blessed child Jesus Christ, through whom we have received knowledge of you, the God of angels and powers, and of all creation, of all the generations of righteous who live in your sight, I bless you for counting me worthy of this day and of this hour, so that I might be numbered among your martyrs and share the cup of your Christ, and so rise again to eternal life in body and soul in the immortality of the Holy Spirit. May I be received today into the company of your martyrs as a rich and acceptable sacrifice, in the way you have prepared and revealed, and have now brought to completion, for you are a God of truth in whom no falsehood can exist. So I praise you for all that you have done. I bless you through our eternal high priest in heaven, your beloved child, Jesus Christ, through whom be glory to you, together with him and the Holy Spirit, now and for ever. Amen.

As soon as he said "Amen" and completed his prayer, the officers in charge lit the fire. A huge sheet of flame burst out, but those of us privileged to witness it, and who have been spared to tell the tale, saw an amazing sight. For the fire took on the shape of a great vault, like a ship's sail unfurling and billowing out in the wind, the flames forming a wall around the body of the martyr. Indeed, the body did not look like burning flesh, but like bread that is baking, or like gold and silver being refined in a furnace. There was also a pervasive sweet smell in the air as of incense or some precious spice.

Finally, when they realized that his body was slow to be destroyed by the fire, they ordered an executioner to reach in and stab Polycarp to death. And as he did so, a dove flew out, and much blood poured out, dousing the flames.

When it was all over we gathered up his bones, more precious to us than jewels, finer than pure gold, and we laid them to rest in a place we had already set aside. There, the Lord permitting, we shall gather and celebrate with great gladness and joy the day of his martyrdom as a birthday. It will serve as a commemoration of all who have gone before us, and training and preparing those of us for whom a crown may be in store.

February 24

Saint Matthias the Apostle

After the betrayal of Jesus by Judas Iscariot, the apostles brought their number back to twelve by choosing Matthias to replace him. He was chosen by lot from among the disciples. According to Luke, the author of the Acts of the Apostles, the number of apostles had to be restored so that they might "sit on thrones judging the twelve tribes of Israel." It was conditional that they had to have been with Jesus during his earthly ministry and witnesses to the resurrection. The point of being chosen by lot, rather than by some democratic method, indicated the election or choosing by God, rather than by mortals.

A Reading from a homily of John Chrysostom

Peter was an impetuous man, and yet it was to him that Christ entrusted his flock; and therefore, as the first of the apostles, it was he who enjoyed the privilege of speaking first.

"Friends, the Scripture must be fulfilled, which the Holy Spirit through David foretold concerning Judas, who became a guide to those who arrested Jesus." Observe how Peter never acts imperiously, but always seeks a common mind. He is seeking to console the disciples about what has just happened; because let there be no mistake, the action of Judas had devastated the disciples. And yet note the moderation of Peter's language. He does not ridicule Judas, or label him "wretch" or "criminal," he simply states the facts.

"We must choose someone from among those who accompanied us to take his place." Peter allowed the whole body of believers to choose, and so secured honor for the person elected, as well as avoiding any ill-feeling that might have arisen against himself. For occasions such as these invariably have evil repercussions. Did Peter himself then not have the right to choose? What was his motive in acting as he did? I think it is because he did not want to be charged with favoritism. Besides which, he still had not received the Spirit.

"They put forward two names, Joseph called Barsabbas, who was surnamed Justus, and Matthias." Note that Peter did not himself select either of the two candidates who were put forward; and although it was he who had made the suggestion, he points out that it was not his own idea, but rather in fulfillment of an ancient prophecy. In other words, Peter is concerned to interpret, not to give orders.

He was also anxious that they should be eyewitnesses. Even though the Spirit was about to come, Peter was very particular on this point: "from among those who accompanied us during all the time that the Lord Jesus went in and out among us." What was important for Peter was that they had lived with the Lord, rather than simply being one of the crowds who followed him. And then he said, "One of these must become with us a witness to his resurrection." This is important. Peter did not say, "a witness to his other acts," but specifically, "a witness to his resurrection." A witness would be more credible if he could say that this man with whom I ate and drank, and who was crucified, has risen again."

"All prayed together and said, 'Lord, you know everyone's heart: show us which of the two you have chosen.' " You, not we. It was right for them to say that God knew the hearts of all, for the choice indeed was to be made by God and no one else. They spoke confidently in the assurance that one would be chosen. They did not even say "choose," but "show," show whom you have chosen, since they knew that all things had been preordained by God. "And they cast lots, and the lot fell upon Matthias."

My friends, let us imitate the apostles. And here I wish to speak to those among you who are ambitious for preferment. If you believe that an episcopal election is in the hands of God, do not be displeased at its outcome. If you are, it is with God that you are displeased: it is with God you are exasperated. For God has made his choice, and God knows how to dispose things for the best. Quite often you will feel yourself more qualified than another candidate; but perhaps you were not the right person. Or again, you may be irreproachable in your life, your behavior may be exemplary; but in the church, something more is wanted. One person is suitable for this post, another for that.

Finally, let me say why such events in the life of the church have become the subject of competition. It is because those of us who are called to the episcopate are more concerned with our own status in which we then take our repose, than in devoting ourselves to the care and leadership of our brothers and sisters.

February 27

George Herbert
Priest and Poet, 1633

Born in 1593 into the aristocratic Pembroke family, George Herbert went up to Cambridge in 1614, eventually becoming a Fellow of Trinity College. At the age of twenty-five, he became Public Orator in the University and then a Member of Parliament, apparently destined for a life at court. To everyone's surprise, he decided to be ordained and, after spending a time with his friend Nicholas Ferrar at Little Gidding, he was made deacon in 1626. He married in 1629, was priested in 1630 and given the care of souls of the parish of Bemerton, near Salisbury, where he spent the rest of his short life. He wrote prolifically, his hymns still being popular throughout the English-speaking world. His treatise The Country Parson *on the priestly life, and his poetry, especially* The Temple, *earned Herbert a leading place in English literature. He never neglected the care of the souls of Bemerton, however, and encouraged attendance at the weekday recitation of the daily office, calling to mind the words of his hymn, "Seven whole days, not one in seven, I will praise thee." He died on this day in the year 1633.*

A Reading from *The Country Parson*
by George Herbert

The Country Parson, when he is to read divine services, composeth himself to all possible reverence; lifting up his heart and hands and eyes, and using all other gestures which may express a hearty and unfeigned devotion. This he doth, first, as being truly touched and amazed with the majesty of God before whom he then presents himself; yet not as himself alone, but as presenting with himself the whole congregation whose sins he then bears, and brings with his own to the heavenly altar to be bathed and washed in the sacred laver of Christ's blood.

Secondly, as this is the true reason of his inward fear, so he is content to express this outwardly to the utmost of his power; that being first affected himself, he may affect also his people, knowing that no sermon moves them so much to a reverence, which they forget again, when they come to pray, as a devout behavior in the very act of praying. Accordingly his voice is humble, his words treatable, and slow; yet not so slow neither as to let the fervency of the supplicant hang and die between speaking, but with a grave liveliness between fear and zeal, pausing yet pressing, he performs his duty.

Besides his example, he having often instructed his people how to carry themselves in divine service, exacts of them all possible reverence, by no means enduring either talking, or sleeping, or gazing, or leaning, or half-kneeling, or any undutiful behavior in them, but causing them, when they sit or stand or kneel, to do all in a straight and steady posture as attending to what is done in the church, and everyone, man and child, answering aloud both *Amen*, and all other answers which are on the Clerk's and people's part to answer; which were also to be done not in a huddling or slobbering fashion, gaping, or scratching the head, or spitting even in the midst of their answer, but gently and pausably, thinking what they say; so that while they answer, *As it was in the beginning, is now, and ever shall be etc*. they meditate as they speak, that God hath ever had his people that have glorified him as well as now, and that he shall have so for ever. And the like in other answers. This is what the apostle calls "a reasonable service" when we speak not as parrots without reason, or offer up such sacrifices as they did of old which was of beasts devoid of reason; but when we use our reason, and apply our powers to the service of him that gives them.

If there be any of the gentry or nobility of the parish who sometimes make it a piece of state not to come at the beginning of the service with their poor neighbors, but at mid-prayers, both to their own loss and of theirs also who gaze upon them when they come in, and neglect the present service of God, he by no means suffers it, but after divers gentle admonitions, if they persevere, he causes them to be presented: or if the poor churchwardens be affrighted with their greatness, notwithstanding his instruction that they ought not to be so, but even to let the world sink, so they do their duty; he presents them himself, only protesting to them that not any ill will draws him to it, but the debt and obligation of his calling being to obey God rather than men.

alternative reading

Aaron

Holiness on the head,
Light and perfections on the breast,
Harmonious bells below, raising the dead
To lead them unto life and rest:
Thus are true Aarons drest.

Profaneness in my head,
Defects and darkness in my breast,
A noise of passions ringing me for dead
Unto a place where is no rest:
Poor priest thus am I drest.

Only another head
I have, another heart and breast,
Another music, making live not dead,
Without whom I could have no rest:
In him I am well drest.

Christ is my only head,
My alone only heart and breast,
My only music, striking me ev'n dead;
That to the old man I may rest:
And be in him new drest.

So holy in my head,
Perfect and light in my dear breast,
My doctrine tuned by Christ, (who is not dead,
But lives in me while I do rest):
Come, people; Aaron's drest.

MARCH

March 1

David

Bishop of Menevia, Wales, *c.*589

David, or Dewi, was a monk and a bishop in the sixth century. He was reputed to be an exemplar of the ascetic, spiritual life but was also highly regarded for his kindness and compassion to others, particularly the poor and the sick. He is believed to have founded the monastery at Menevia, now St. David's, and also at least a dozen other monasteries. He is said to have based his Rule for his monasteries on that of the Egyptian desert monks, with a strong emphasis on hard work, abstinence from alcohol and a refraining from unnecessary speech. He died about the year 589 and has been regarded as the patron saint of Wales since at least the twelfth century.

A Reading from *The Life of Saint David*
by Rhigyfarch the Wise

Although our Lord has loved and known his own before ever he created the world, yet there are some whom he makes known beforehand by many tokens and revelations. Consequently, that saint who was named David in his baptism but Dewi by the common people, was not only foretold by authentic prophecies of angels thirty years before his birth, but was also proclaimed as one who was enriched with mystic gifts and endowments.

During his life, throughout our land, the brethren built monasteries: everywhere are heard evidences of churches; everywhere voices are raised to heaven in prayer; everywhere the virtues are constantly brought back to the bosom of the Church; everywhere charitable offerings are with open hands distributed to the needy. To all the holy Bishop Dewi was the supreme overseer, the supreme protector, the supreme preacher, from whom all received their standard and pattern of living virtuously. He was brought to a ripe old age and was extolled as the leader of the entire British race and the ornament of his country.

When the day of his departure drew near, an angel spoke with him, saying: "Make ready, and gird yourself; for on the first day of March our Lord Jesus Christ, accompanied by a great host of angels, will come to meet you." From that hour onward until the day of his death, he remained in the church, preaching.

When the third day of the week arrived, at cock crow, the monastery was filled with choirs of angels, and was melodious with heavenly singing, and filled with the most delightful fragrance. At the hour of matins, while the monks were singing hymns at divine service, our Lord Jesus Christ deigned to bestow his presence for the consolation of the father, as he had promised. On seeing him, and entirely rejoicing in spirit, he said: "Take me with you." With these words, and with Christ as his companion, David gave up his life to God; and attended by the escort of angels, he sought the portals of heaven.

And so his body, borne on the arms of holy brethren, and accompanied by a great concourse, was with all honor committed to the earth, and buried in the grounds of his own monastery: but his soul, set free from the bounds of this transitory life, is crowned throughout endless ages.

March 2

Chad

Bishop of Lichfield, 672

Chad was born in Northumbria, the youngest of four sons, all of whom became both priests and monks. They entered the monastery on the isle of Lindisfarne and were taught by Saint Aidan. Chad's brother Cedd had founded the abbey at Lastingham and, on his brother's death, Chad was elected abbot. During the confusion in ecclesiastical discipline between the Celtic-oriented Anglo-Saxon hierarchy and the pressure from Rome for conformity, Chad became Bishop of York for a time. He graciously stepped back with the arrival in Britain of Theodore, who doubted the validity of indigenous consecrations. This was eventually rectified and Chad became Bishop of Mercia, a huge diocese, the center of which he moved from Repton to Lichfield. Chad traveled extensively and became much loved for his wisdom and gentleness in otherwise difficult situations. The plague was prevalent at this time and Chad died on this day in the year 672.

A Reading from *A History of the English Church and People* by the Venerable Bede

King Alhfrith sent the priest Wilfrid to the king of the Gauls to be consecrated bishop for himself and his people. He was detained overseas for a considerable time on account of his consecration, and King Oswy sent to Canterbury to be consecrated Bishop of York, a holy man, modest in his ways, learned in the Scriptures, and zealous in carrying out their teaching. This was a priest named Chad, a brother of the most reverend Bishop Cedd, who at that time was Abbot of the monastery of Lastingham.

On arriving in Canterbury, they found that Archbishop Deusdedit had died and that no successor had as yet been appointed in his place. They therefore went to the province of the West Saxons where Wine was bishop. He consecrated Chad with the assistance of two bishops of the British.

When he became bishop, Chad immediately devoted himself to maintaining the truth and purity of the Church, and set himself to practice humility and temperance, and to study. After the example of the apostles, he traveled on foot and not on horseback when he went to preach the gospel, whether in cities or country districts, in towns, villages, or strongholds; for he was one of Aidan's disciples and always sought to instruct his people in the ways and customs of his master Aidan and his own brother Cedd.

Later, however, when Theodore of Tarsus was consecrated Archbishop of Canterbury, he was asked to judge between Wilfrid and Chad. When he informed Bishop Chad that his consecration was irregular, the latter replied with the greatest humility: "If you believe that my consecration as bishop was irregular, I willingly resign the office; for I have never thought myself worthy of it. Although unworthy, I accepted it solely under obedience." At this humble reply, Theodore assured him that there was no need for him to give up his office, and himself completed his consecration according to catholic rites.

At that time King Wulfere of Mercia desired Archbishop Theodore to supply him and his people with a bishop. Theodore therefore suggested to King Oswy that Chad might become their bishop. Chad was by this time living in retirement at his monastery at Lastingham, Wilfrid ruling the bishopric of York. Theodore ordered Chad to ride a horse when he was faced with a long journey; but Chad was hesitant, having long been accustomed to ministering on foot. The archbishop knew Chad to be a man of great holiness, and as if to persuade him to take his advice, helped Chad into the saddle with his own hands.

Thus it was that Chad received the bishopric of the Mercians. He established his episcopal seat in the town of Lichfield where he also died and was buried, and where the succeeding bishops of the province have their see to this day.

March 3

John and Charles Wesley
Evangelists, Hymn Writers, 1791 & 1788

Born respectively in 1703 and 1707 at Epworth Rectory in Lincolnshire, John and Charles Wesley were the sons of an Anglican clergyman and a Puritan mother. Ordained as priests of the Church of England, the two brothers were deeply affected by German pietism and set out to revive the English church by a strict "Method" of religious faith and practice. The type of evangelism practiced by the Wesleys was fiercely opposed by many in the Church of England and eventually the movement separated itself and developed into the Methodist Church. John and Charles, however, always opposed such a separation and died as members of the Church of England. John, a gifted administrator with a magnetic personality, is noted chiefly for his preaching and his constant evangelistic travels, averaging eight thousand miles a year. Charles, a gentler and more attractive personality in many ways, is remembered especially for the more than 5,500 hymns he wrote. Among the best known of Charles Wesley's hymns are "Hark! The Herald Angels Sing," "Love Divine, All Loves Excelling," and "Lo! He Comes, With Clouds Descending." John died on March 2, 1791, and Charles on March 29, 1788.

A Reading from the Journal of John Wesley's travels in Cornwall

Eleventh Journey, 1755

Having spent two days comfortably, and I hope usefully, on Monday the 25th I rode over the mountains, close by the sea, to Looe, a town near half as large as Islington, which sends four Members to the Parliament! And each county in North Wales sends one! At Fowey, a little company met us, and conducted us to Luxulyan. Between six and seven I preached in what was once the courtyard of a rich and honorable man; but he and all his family are in the dust, and his very memory is almost perished. The congregation was large and deeply serious; but it was still larger on Tuesday evening, and several seemed to be cut to the heart. On Wednesday they flocked from all parts. And with what eagerness did they receive the word! Surely many of these last will be first.

Thursday, August 28.
I preached at St. Mewan. I do not remember ever to have seen the yard in which I stood quite full before but it would not now contain the congregation: many were obliged to stand without the gate. At five in the morning I preached at St. Austell to more than our room could contain. In the evening I was at St. Ewe. One or two felt the edge of God's sword and sank to the ground, and indeed it seemed as if God would suffer none to escape him—as if he both heard and answered our prayer:

Dart into all the melting flame
Of love, and make the mountains flow.

Saturday, August 30.
As I was tiding through Truro one stopped my horse and insisted on my alighting. Presently two or three more of Mr. Walker's society came in, and we seemed to have been acquainted with each other many years; but I was constrained to break from them. About five I found the congregation waiting in a broad, convenient part of the street in Redruth. I was extremely weary, and our friends were so glad to see me that none once thought of asking me to eat or drink; but my weariness vanished when I began to speak. Surely God is in this place also.

Sunday, August 31.
Understanding there were many present who did once run well, I preached at eight (the rain ceasing just in time) on "How shall I give thee up, Ephraim?" (Hosea 2:8). Many endeavored, but in vain, to hide their tears. I was agreeably surprised at church to hear the prayers read, not only with deliberation, but with uncommon propriety. At one the congregation was nearly double to what it was in the morning, and all were still as night. Surely these are patient hearers. God grant they may be fruitful ones.

At five I preached in Owennap to several thousands, but not one of them light or inattentive. After I had done the storm arose, and the rain poured down till about four in the morning. Then the sky cleared, and many of them that feared God gladly assembled before him.

Monday, September 1.
I preached at Penryn to abundantly more than the house could contain.

Tuesday, September 2.
We went to Falmouth. The town is not now what it was ten years since. All is quiet from one end to the other. I had thoughts of preaching on the hill near the church, but the violent wind made it impracticable, so I was obliged to stay in our own room. The people could hear in the yard likewise, and the adjoining houses, and all were deeply attentive.

Wednesday, September 3.
At four Mrs. M. came into my room, all in tears, and told me she had seen, as it were, our Lord standing by her, calling her by her name, and had ever since been filled with joy unspeakable. Soon after came her sister, in almost the same condition, and afterwards her niece, who likewise quickly melted into tears and refused to be comforted. Which of these will endure to the end? Now at least, God is among them.

alternative reading

A Reading from a hymn of Charles Wesley
based on Jacob's wrestling with the angel
in the Book of Genesis

Wrestling Jacob

Come, O thou Traveler unknown
Whom still I hold, but cannot see,
My company before is gone,
And I am left alone with thee,
With thee all night I mean to stay,
And wrestle till the break of day.

I need not tell thee who I am,
My misery, or sin declare,
Thyself hast called me by my name,
Look on thy hands, and read it there.
But who, I ask thee, who art thou?
Tell me thy name, and tell me now.

In vain thou strugglest to get free,
I never will unloose my hold:
Art thou the Man that died for me?
The secret of thy love unfold.
Wrestling I will not let thee go,
Till I thy name, thy nature know.

Yield to me now—for I am weak;
But confident in self-despair:
Speak to my heart, in blessings speak,
Be conquered by my instant prayer,
Speak, or thou never hence shalt move,
And tell me, if thy name is Love.

'Tis Love, 'tis Love! Thou diedst for me,
I hear thy whisper in my heart.
The morning breaks, the shadows flee:
Pure Universal Love thou art;
To me, to all, thy bowels move,
Thy nature, and thy name, is Love.

March 7

Perpetua, Felicity, and their Companions

Martyrs at Carthage, 203

The moving, contemporary account of these early third-century, African martyrs proved to be of great significance in the life of the early Church. Vibia Perpetua was a young, married noblewoman of Carthage, and Felicity was her personal slave. Saturas was possibly a priest and there were two other men, Saturninus and Revocatus, the latter also a slave. Felicity was pregnant. It seems most of them were catechumens when arrested and only baptized later in prison. They were condemned as Christians by the Roman authorities and dispatched to the public arena, there to be mauled by wild animals. The contemporary account of their deaths was much circulated secretly throughout the Christian congregations and brought renown to their courage and encouragement to their fellow Christians in the face of adversity. They were martyred for their faith on this day in the year 203.

A Reading from a contemporary account of the martyrdom of Perpetua, Felicity and their companions at Carthage in the year 203

If ancient examples of faith, which testify to the grace of God and give us encouragement, are honored and recorded for posterity in writing, so that by reading them the deeds of God are glorified and others are strengthened, why should we not in our generation also set down new witnesses which serve these ends. One day their example will also be ancient and important to our children, if at this present time, because of the reverence we accord to antiquity, they seem less weighty to us.

When the day of their victory dawned, the martyrs marched from the prison to the amphitheater, their faces joyful yet dignified, as if they were on their way to heaven. If they trembled at all, it was for joy, not fear. Perpetua took up the rear of the procession. She looked noble, a true wife of Christ and beloved of God, her piercing gaze causing spectators to avert their eyes. With them also went Felicity, rejoicing that her baby had been born safely that she might now fight with beasts, one flow of blood to be succeeded by another, ready to exchange her midwife for a gladiator that she might undergo the labor of a second baptism.

The women were stripped naked, placed in nets and were brought into the arena to face a mad heifer. Even the crowd was horrified seeing in one net a delicate young girl, and in the other a woman, fresh from child-birth, her full breasts still dripping with milk. So the women were recalled and dressed in loose clothing. Perpetua was thrown to the animal first, falling on her back. She stood up and saw that Felicity had been crushed to the ground. She went and gave her hand to help her up; and so they stood, side by side.

Now that the cruelty of the mob had been appeased, they were recalled to the Gate of Life. There Perpetua was supported by a certain Rusticus, a catechumen at the time, who was keeping close to her. She called her brother to her and the catechumen, and spoke to them both saying: "Stand firm in your faith, and love one another. Do not let our suffering be a stumbling-block to you."

As the show was ending, her brother was thrown to a leopard, and with one bite was so drenched with blood that as he came back the crowd shouted out (in witness to his second baptism) "Well washed! Well washed!" Indeed he was saved who had been washed in this way. Then he became unconscious, and was thrown with the rest into the place where they have their throats cut.

But the mob demanded that the Christians be brought back into the open so that they could watch the sword being plunged into their bodies, and so be party to the spectacle of their murder. The martyrs rose unbidden to where the mob wanted them, after first kissing one another, that they might seal their martyrdom with the kiss of peace. Each received the sword without resistance and in silence. Perpetua, however, had yet to taste more pain. She screamed as she was struck on the bone; then she herself had to guide the fumbling hand of the novice gladiator to her throat. Perhaps so great a woman who was feared by the unclean spirit, could not otherwise be killed, unless she herself gave her consent.

O most courageous and blessed martyrs! Truly are you called and chosen for the glory of Jesus Christ our Lord! All you who seek to magnify, honor and adore the glory of Christ, should read the story of these new witnesses, who no less than the ancient witnesses, have been raised up for the Church's edification; for these new manifestations of virtue testify that the same Holy Spirit is working among us now.

March 8

Edward King

Bishop of Lincoln, 1910

Born in London in 1829, Edward King, both as a priest and then as a bishop, was revered for the holiness of his life and the wisdom of his counsel. He was Chaplain, then Principal, of Cuddesdon Theological College, followed by a dozen years as a professor of theology in Oxford, during which time he exercised a great influence on a generation of ordinands. In 1885, he was consecrated Bishop of Lincoln, a position he held until his death. His advocacy of catholic principles in ritual as well as theology involved him in controversy, but his significant gift to the church was his example as a pastoral and caring bishop to both clergy and laity.

A Reading from a sermon of Edward King
preached in the year 1893

"Thy gentleness hath made me great." Such was the reflection of the author of this psalm as he looked back over the course of his life. It was not his own natural gifts, not his great valor, not his own cleverness, much less his own goodness, but simply the gentleness of God, by which he would account for his having reached that position in life which had raised him above so many of his fellow-men, and which had been truly great because by it he had been a help and blessing to many.

In the Prayer Book the words of this psalm run: "Thy loving correction hath made me great." This suggests the possibility of improvement, the need of discipline, and a high standard to be reached. The effect of the gentleness or loving correction of God was to raise the natural character of the Psalmist to a higher level than he could otherwise have reached. It should be the same in the application which I have ventured to give to these words this morning.

With the resolve to stand firm and true in the defense of God's truth, remember that the lesson of gentleness implies patience and long-suffering, and waiting for God's good time and for one another. The progress (thank God) of the Church of England has been wonderful in the last fifty years. There is indeed much yet to be done, many prejudices to be put aside, much ignorance to be enlightened, much indifference to be awakened. But we need to remember the words of our text, "Thy gentleness hath made me great." God has waited patiently for us and brought us up to where we are. Let us try to do to others as God has done to us, and by gentleness to lead them on and make them great. While there is life, there is hope: the penitent thief was accepted at the eleventh hour. The grace of God is as strong today as then. Even the end of a wasted life God will not reject if it be offered with a contrite heart, with true faith in the power of the Savior's blood.

Let all impatience, then, all harsh judgements of others, all self-seeking, be put aside, and all love of power and the desire to be first. Rather let us strive to take the lower place, "in honor preferring one another." Then, when all is over, and we are set down at the Supper of the Lamb, and the Bridegroom comes in to see the guests, and the great reversal of human judgements shall take place, and the first shall be last and the last first, may we hope to hear his voice saying to us: "Friend, come up higher."

Meanwhile, "let patience have her perfect work," and let gentleness be the characteristic of your strength.

March 8

Felix

Bishop, Apostle to the East Angles, 647

Born in Burgundy at the beginning of the seventh century, Felix reputedly converted the exiled King Sigbert of the East Angles and, after the King's return to Britain, was consecrated bishop and then persuaded by the king to follow him to effect the conversion of his subjects. He was commissioned by Honorius, Archbishop of Canterbury, to this work and made Dunwich the center of his new See. He established schools and monasteries and ministered in his diocese for seventeen years. He died in the year 647.

A Reading from *A History of the English Church and People* by the Venerable Bede

Not long after King Eorpwold's acceptance of Christianity, he was killed by a pagan named Ricbert, and for three years the province of the East Angles relapsed into heathen ways, until Eorpwold's brother Sigbert came to the throne. Sigbert was a devout Christian and a man of learning. He had been an exile in Gaul during his brother's lifetime, and it was there that he was converted to the Christian faith. As soon as he began his reign, he labored to bring about the conversion of the entire kingdom.

In this enterprise he was nobly assisted by Bishop Felix, who came to Archbishop Honorius from the Burgundian region, where he had been born and ordained. By his own wish, he was sent by the archbishop to preach the word of life to this nation of the Angles. Nor did he fail in his purpose; for, like a good farmer, he reaped an abundant harvest of believers in this spiritual field. He delivered the entire province from its long-lasting wicked ways and unhappiness, brought it to the Christian faith and works of righteousness, and in full accord with the significance of his own name, guided it toward eternal felicity.

He established his episcopal see at Dunwich; and after ruling the province as its bishop for seventeen years, he ended his days there in peace.

March 8

Geoffrey Studdert Kennedy

Priest and Poet, 1929

Born in 1883, Studdert Kennedy was a young vicar in Worcester who became an army chaplain during the First World War. His warm personality soon earned the respect of soldiers, who nicknamed him "Woodbine Willie," after the brand of cigarettes he shared with them. After the First World War, he became a writer and regular preacher, drawing large crowds, who were attracted by his combination of traditional sacramental theology with more unconventional theological views. He worked tirelessly for the Christian Industrial Fellowship, but his frail health gave way and he died (still a young man) on this day in 1929.

A Reading from *The Hardest Part* by
Geoffrey Studdert Kennedy

This is not a theological essay. It is rather a fairly faithful and accurate account of the inner ruminations of an incurably religious man under battle conditions. Battles do not make for carefully balanced thought. There is one main idea in what I have written, but I believe that it is a true idea. We must make clear to ourselves and to the world what we mean when we say: "I believe in God the Father Almighty."

Good people have told me that my writing is crude and brutal. I would remind you that it is not, and it could not be as crude as war, or as brutal as a battle. The brutality of war is literally unutterable. There are no words foul and filthy enough to describe it. Yet I would remind you that this indescribably filthy thing is the commonest thing in history, and that if we believe in a God of love at all, then we must believe in the face of war and all it means. The supreme strength of the Christian faith is that it faces the foulest and filthiest of life's facts in the crude brutality of the cross, and through them sees the glory of God in the face of Jesus Christ.

Thousands of men who have fought out here, and thousands of their womenkind who have waited or mourned for them at home, have dimly felt that the reason and explanation of all this horror was somehow to be found in a crucifix—witness the frequent reproductions of wayside Calvaries in our picture papers and the continual mention of them in our soldiers' letters home. Yet when you talk to soldiers you find that the Calvary appeals to them rather as the summary of their problems than their solution.

The vision of the suffering God revealed in Jesus Christ, and the necessary truth of it, first began to dawn on me in the narrow streets and shadowed homes of an English slum. All that war has done is to batter the essential truth of it deeper in, and cast a fiercer light upon the cross. A battlefield is more striking, but scarcely more really crude and brutal than a slum. Only we have all been suddenly forced to realize war more or less, while it has taken God centuries to make some of us recognize the existence of slums.

In Christ I meet the real God. In him I find no metaphysical abstraction, but God speaking to me in the only language I can understand, which is the human language; God revealed in the only terms I can begin to comprehend which are the terms of perfect human personality. In him I find the truth that human sin and sorrow matter to God, indeed, are matters of life and death to God, as they must be to me. In him I find the truth that the moral struggle of man is a real struggle because God is in it, in it and beyond it too, for in the risen Christ who conquered death and rose again I find the promise and the guarantee that the moral struggle of our race will issue in victory.

March 9

Gregory
Bishop of Nyssa, *c.*394

Gregory of Nyssa was born at Caesarea in what is now Turkey around the year 330, the child of an aristocratic Christian family. Unlike his elder brother Basil, he was academically undistinguished, but ultimately proved to be the most original of the group of theologians known as the Cappadocian Fathers. He was introduced to the spiritual life by his elder sister Macrina who exercised a formative influence upon him, and with whom he maintained close bonds of friendship throughout his life. It was she who, after the death of their father, converted the household into a sort of monastery on one of the family estates. Gregory married a deeply spiritual woman, Theosebia, and at first refused ordination, choosing to pursue a secular career. He was ordained only later in life, and in 372 was chosen to be Bishop of Nyssa. In the year 379 both his brother Basil and his sister Macrina died, and this deeply affected him; but out of this darkness emerged a profound spirituality. For Gregory, God is met not as an object to be understood, but as a mystery to be loved. He died around the year 394.

A Reading from a homily of Gregory of Nyssa

When we look down from the sublime words of the Lord into the ineffable depths of his thoughts, we have an experience similar to that of gazing down from a high cliff into the immense sea below. On the coastline one can often see rocky cliffs where the seaward face has been sliced off sheer from top to bottom, with the tops of the cliffs projecting outwards forming a promontory overhanging the depths. If anyone were to look down from such a lofty height into the sea below they would feel giddy. This is exactly how my soul feels now, as it is raised from the ground by this mighty word of the Lord: "Blessed are the pure in heart, for they shall see God."

God offers himself to the vision of those whose hearts have been purified. And yet, as the great John says: "No one has seen God at any time." And the sublime mind of Paul confirms this opinion when he says that "no one has seen or can see God." God is this slippery, steep crag which yields no footholds for our imagination. Moses too, in his teaching, declares that God is so inaccessible that our mind cannot approach him. He explicitly discourages any attempt to apprehend God, saying: "No one can see the Lord and live." To see the Lord is eternal life, and yet these pillars of the faith, John, Paul and Moses, all declare it to be impossible! What vertigo in the soul this causes! Confronted by the profundity of these words I am confounded.

If God is life, then they who do not see God do not see life. On the other hand, the divinely inspired prophets and apostles assert that it is impossible to see God. Is not all human hope thus destroyed? But the Lord supports our faltering hope, just as he grasped Peter when he was in danger of sinking and stood him on the waves as though it were solid ground. If, then, the hand of the Word is extended to us also, supporting those who are at sea in the midst of conflicting speculations, we can be without fear. We are gripped by the guiding hand of the Word who says to us: "Blessed are the pure in heart, for they shall see God."

Those who see God shall possess in this act of seeing everything that is good: eternal life, eternal incorruption, unending bliss. With these things we shall experience the joy of the eternal kingdom in which happiness is secure; we shall see the true light and hear the delightful voice of the Spirit; we shall rejoice unceasingly in all that is good in the inaccessible glory of God. This is the magnificent consummation of our hope held out to us by the promise of this Beatitude.

March 12

Gregory the Great

Bishop of Rome, 604

Gregory was born in 540, the son of a Roman senator. As a young man he pursued a governmental career, and in 573 was made Prefect of the city of Rome. Following the death of his father, he resigned his office, sold his inheritance, and became a monk. In 579 he was sent by the Pope to Constantinople to be his representative to the Patriarch. He returned to Rome in 586, and was himself elected Pope in 590. At a time of political turmoil, Gregory proved an astute administrator and diplomat, securing peace with the Lombards. He initiated the mission to England, sending Augustine and forty monks from his own monastery to re-found the English Church. His writings were pastorally oriented. His spirituality was animated by a dynamic of love and desire for God. Indeed, he is sometimes called the "Doctor of desire." For Gregory, desire was a metaphor for the journey into God. As Pope, he styled himself "Servant of the servants of God," a title which typified both his personality and ministry. He died in the year 604.

A Reading from a homily of Gregory the Great

The prophet Ezekiel, whom the Lord sent to preach his Word, is described as a watchman. A watchman always selects a high vantage point in order to be able to observe things better. In the same way, whoever is appointed watchman to a people should live on the heights so that he can help his people by having a broad perspective. I find it hard to make such a statement because such words are a reproach to myself. My preaching is mediocre, and my life does not cohere with the values I preach so inadequately. I do not deny that I am guilty, for I recognize in myself lethargy and negligence. Perhaps my very awareness of my failings will gain me pardon from a sympathetic judge.

When I lived in a monastic community I could keep my tongue from idle chatter and devote my mind almost continually to the discipline of prayer. However, since assuming the burden of pastoral care, I find it difficult to keep steadily recollected because my mind is distracted by numerous responsibilities. I am required to deal with matters affecting churches and monasteries, and often I must judge the lives and actions of individuals. One moment I am required to participate in civil life, and the next moment to worry over the incursions of barbarians. I fear these wolves who menace the flock entrusted to my care. At another time I have to exercise political responsibility in order to give support to those who uphold the rule of law; I have to cope with the wickedness of criminals, and the next moment I am asked to confront them, but yet in all charity.

My mind is in chaos, fragmented by the many and serious matters I am required to give attention to. When I try to concentrate and focus my intellectual resources for preaching, how can I do justice to the sacred ministry of the Word? I am often compelled by virtue of my office to socialize with people of the world and sometimes I have to relax the discipline of my speech. I realize that if I were to maintain the inflexible pattern of conversation that my conscience dictates, certain weaker individuals would simply shun my company, with the result that I would never be able to attract them to the goal I desire for them. So inevitably, I find myself listening to their mindless chatter. And because I am weak myself, I find myself gradually being sucked into their idle talk and saying the very things that I recoiled from listening to before. I enjoy lying back where beforehand I was conscious lest I fall myself.

Who am I? What kind of watchman am I? I do not stand on the pinnacle of achievement; I languish in the pit of my frailty. And yet although I am unworthy, the creator and redeemer of us all has given me the grace to see life whole and an ability to speak effectively of it. It is for the love of God that I do not spare myself preaching him.

March 17

Patrick

Bishop and Missionary of Ireland, *c.*461

Patrick was born somewhere on the west coast of Britain around the year 390, and was captured by Irish raiders when he was sixteen years old and taken to Ireland as a slave. After six years, he escaped and seems to have gone to the Continent. He eventually found his way back to his own family, where his previously nominal Christian faith grew and matured. He returned to Gaul and was there trained as a priest and much influenced by the form of monasticism evolving under Martin of Tours. When he was in his early forties, he returned to Ireland as a bishop, and made his base at Armagh, which became the center of his See. He evangelized the people of the land by walking all over the island, gently bringing men and women to a knowledge of Christ. Although he faced fierce opposition and possible persecution, he continued his missionary journeys. Despite being unsuccessful in his attempts to establish the diocesan system he had experienced in Gaul, his monastic foundations proved to be the infrastructure required to maintain the faith after his death, which occurred on this day about the year 461.

A Reading from the *Confession* of Patrick

I was taken captive to Ireland when I was about sixteen years old, together with many thousands of others. At that time I did not know the true God. There I sought him and there I found him. I am convinced that God protected me from all evil through his Spirit who lives and works in me to this very day.

Therefore I give thanks to my God unceasingly who has kept me faithful in times of trial, so that today I offer sacrifice to him confidently, the living sacrifice of my life to Christ my Lord, who has sustained me in all my difficulties. And so I say, "Who am I, Lord, and what is my calling that you should cooperate with me with such a display of divine power? Today, in the midst of heathen peoples, I exalt and magnify your name in all places, not only when things are going well, but also when I am under pressure."

Whether I receive good or ill I always render thanks to God who taught me to trust him unreservedly. His answer to my prayer inspired me in these latter days to undertake this holy and admirable work—in spite of my ignorance—and to imitate those who, as the Lord had foretold, would preach the gospel to all the nations before the end of the world. We have seen it; it has happened. We are indeed witnesses that the gospel has been preached in remote areas, in places beyond which no one has ventured.

How did I come by this wisdom which was not my own, I who knew neither how my life would unfold nor the wisdom of God? What was the source of the gift I was to receive later in my life, the wonderful and rewarding gift of knowing and loving God, even though it meant leaving my homeland and family?

It was the over-powering grace of God at work in me, and no virtue of my own, which enabled all these things. I came to the Irish heathen to preach the gospel. I have had to endure insults from unbelievers; I have heard my mission ridiculed; I have experienced persecution to the point of imprisonment; I have given up my free-born status for the good of others. Should I be worthy, I am even ready to surrender my life, promptly and gladly, for his name; and it is here in Ireland that I wish to spend my remaining days, if the Lord permits me.

In all this I am in debt to God who has given me an abundance of grace with the result that through me many people have been born again in God, and later confirmed, and that clergy have been ordained everywhere. All this was for a people newly come to faith whom the Lord has called from the ends of the earth as he foretold through his prophets: "To you the nations will come from the ends of the earth and will say, 'How false are our idols which our ancestors made for themselves, and how useless they are.' " And again: "I have made you a light for the nations so that you will bring salvation to the ends of the earth."

March 18

Cyril

Bishop of Jerusalem, 386

Born in about the year 315, probably in Caesarea, Cyril became Bishop of Jerusalem when he was about thirty-four years old. There he nurtured both the resident Christian population and the many pilgrims, following the end of the era of persecution, who were beginning to make their way from all over Christendom to the places associated with Christ. Cyril taught the faith in line with the orthodoxy of the Council of Nicaea and the credal statement that became associated with it. Though he found difficulty with the word in that creed which described Jesus as being "of one substance with the Father," nevertheless he took the side of the Nicene party against the Arians, who denied the divinity of Christ. His teaching through his Catechetical Lectures, *intended for those preparing for baptism, show him to have been a man profoundly orthodox and sound. His liturgical innovations to celebrate the observance of Holy Week and Easter are the foundation of Christian practices to this day. He died in the year 386.*

A Reading from the *Catechetical Lectures* of Cyril of Jerusalem

The Church is called catholic because it is spread throughout the whole world, from one end of the earth to the other, and because it teaches in its totality and without any omission every doctrine which ought to be brought to the knowledge of humankind, concerning things both that are seen and unseen, in heaven and on earth. It is called catholic also because it brings into religious obedience every sort of person, rulers and ruled, learned and simple. It also makes available a universal remedy and cure to every kind of sin, whether of soul or body, and possesses within itself every kind of virtue that is named, whether it is expressed in deeds or words or in spiritual graces of every sort.

The Church is well named because it literally calls everyone out, and assembles them together, as the Book of Leviticus records, "Assemble the congregation before the doors of the tabernacle of witness." We should note that this is the first time that the word occurs in Scripture, and it does so in the context where Aaron is appointed high priest. In Deuteronomy also, God says to Moses, "Assemble to me the people, and I will make them hear my words, that they may learn to fear me." But since then the Jews have fallen out of favor because of their plotting against the Lord, so the Savior has built up from among the gentiles a second assembly or Church, our holy Christian Church, and spoke of it to Peter saying: "And upon this rock I will build my Church, and the gates of hell shall not prevail against it."

This is the holy Church which is the mother of us all. She is the bride of our Lord Jesus Christ, the only-begotten Son of God. She is the form and image of the heavenly Jerusalem which is free and the mother of us all. Once she was barren, but now she has many children.

March 19

Saint Joseph

In the Gospel according to Matthew, Joseph is depicted as a good man, a working carpenter, who trusted in God. He received God's messenger who shared with him God's will for him and for Mary, to whom he was engaged to be married. Luke's Gospel describes how Joseph took the newborn child as if he were his own. He was with Mary when, on the fortieth day after the birth, Jesus was presented in the Temple, "where every first-born male is designated as holy to the Lord." The adoption of Jesus by Joseph also established Jesus in the descent of David, to accord with the prophecy that Israel's deliverer would be "of the house and lineage of David."

- A Reading from a sermon of Bernardine of Siena

There is a general rule concerning all special graces given to any human being. Whenever divine grace chooses someone to receive a special grace, or to accept a high vocation, God adorns that person with all the gifts of the Spirit needed to fulfill the task.

This general rule is especially true of that holy man Joseph. He was chosen by the eternal Father to be the faithful guardian and protector of the most precious of all his treasures, namely, his divine Son; and of Mary, who became his wife. This was the task laid upon him which he carried out faithfully right to the end, when he heard the Lord say to him, "Good and faithful servant, enter into the joy of your Lord."

A comparison may be made between Joseph and the whole Church of Christ. Joseph was the specially chosen man through whom and under whom Christ entered the world fittingly and appropriately. Thus, if the whole Church stands in the debt of the Virgin Mary, since it was through her child-bearing that it was able to receive Christ, surely after her, it owes special thanks and honor to Joseph.

For in him the Old Testament finds its fitting close. In him the noble line of patriarchs and prophets comes to its promised fulfillment. What God in his goodness had offered to them as a promise, Joseph held in his arms. Clearly, Christ cannot now deny to him the same intimacy, respect, and high dignity which he gave him on earth, as a son to his father. We should rejoice that in heaven Christ completes and perfects all that he gave to Joseph in Nazareth.

Thus we can understand how the summoning words of the Lord, "Enter into the joy of your Lord," apply so well to this man. In fact, although the joy of eternal happiness enters into our souls, the Lord preferred to say to Joseph, "Enter into joy." In using these words his intention was to alert us to their hidden meaning. They convey not only that this holy man now possesses an inner joy, but also that it surrounds him and enfolds him like the fathomless deep.

March 20

Cuthbert

Bishop of Lindisfarne, 687

Cuthbert was probably born in the Scottish lowlands around the year 640. At the age of eight a prophetic remark from a playmate turned his mind to sober and godly thoughts, and his upbringing as a shepherd gave him ample time for prayer. One night he saw in the sky a dazzling light and angels carrying a soul up to heaven, and resolved to dedicate his life to God. Some years later Cuthbert came to Melrose Abbey asking to be admitted as a monk. It was from here that he began his missionary work, which he continued from Lindisfarne when he became abbot there. Consecrated bishop in 685 he remained an indefatigable traveler and preacher, walking all over his diocese, and spending time as a hermit on Farne Island in between. After only a year however, he felt his end coming and resigned his office, dying on Farne in the company of a few of his monks.

A Reading from *The Life of Cuthbert*
by the Venerable Bede

When Cuthbert came to the church and monastery of Lindisfarne he handed on the monastic rule by teaching and example; moreover, he continued his custom of frequent visits to the common people in the neighborhood, in order to rouse them up to seek and to merit the rewards of heaven.

Some of the monks preferred their old way of life to the rule. He overcame these by patience and forbearance, bringing them round little by little through daily example to a better frame of mind. At chapter meetings he was often worn down by bitter insults, but would put an end to the arguments simply by rising and walking out, calm and unruffled. Next day he would give the same people exactly the same admonitions, as though there had been no unpleasantness the previous day. In this way he gradually won their obedience. He was wonderfully patient and unsurpassed for courage in enduring physical or mental hardship. Though overwhelmed by sorrow at these monks' recalcitrance, he managed to keep a cheerful face. It was clear to everyone that it was the Holy Spirit within giving him strength to smile at attacks from without.

Such was his zeal for prayer that sometimes he would keep vigil for three or four nights at a stretch. Whether he was praying alone in some secret place or saying psalms, he always did manual work to drive away the heaviness of sleep, or else he would do the rounds of the island, kindly inquiring how everything was getting on, relieving the tedium of his long vigils and psalm-singing by walking about.

After many years in the monastery he finally entered with great joy and with the goodwill of the abbot and monks into the remoter solitude he had so long sought, thirsted after, and prayed for. To learn the first steps of the hermit's life he retired to a more secluded place in the outer precincts of the monastery. Not till he had first gained victory over our invisible enemy by solitary prayer and fasting did he take it on himself to seek out a remote battlefield farther away from his fellows. The Inner Farne is an island far out to sea, unlike Lindisfarne which is an island in the strict sense of the word only twice a day, when cut off by the tide. The Inner Farne lies a few miles to the south-east of Lindisfarne, cut off on the landward side by very deep water and facing, on the other side, out toward the limitless ocean. Cuthbert was the first man brave enough to live there alone.

Toward the end of his life this venerable man of God was elected Bishop of Lindisfarne. Following the teaching and practice of the apostles, he adorned his office with good works. He protected the flock committed to him by constant prayer on their behalf, by wholesome admonition and—which is the real way to teach—by example first and precept later.

March 21

Thomas Ken

Bishop of Bath and Wells, 1711

Thomas Ken was born at Berkhampstead in 1637 and educated at New College, Oxford. He was ordained priest in 1662 and worked first in a poor parish in the diocese of Winchester and then at Winchester College for ten years. He served as chaplain to King Charles II for two years and was then consecrated Bishop of Bath and Wells. After the king's death and the accession of the Roman Catholic James II, the new king proposed to rescind the Restoration penal laws, but Thomas and six of his fellow bishops refused to comply with this and were imprisoned on this day in 1688. Such was the integrity of Thomas that, when the king abandoned his throne and fled and the king's Protestant daughter Mary was offered the throne, together with her husband William of Orange, Thomas felt unable in good conscience to forswear his living, anointed monarch. He was deprived of his See, along with many other non-jurors, as they became known, and for a time there was schism in the Anglican fold. Thomas spent his final twenty years in quiet retirement, anxious not to make trouble, and renounced his rights to his bishopric. He wrote many hymns, still much used, and died on March 19, 1711.

A Reading from a letter of Bishop Thomas Ken, to a fellow non-juror, George Hickes, Dean of Worcester, dated March 7, 1700

I wrote to you not long ago to recommend to your serious consideration the schism which has so long continued in our Church; and which I have often lamented to my Brother of Ely, now with God, and concerning which, I have many years had ill abodings. I need not tell you what pernicious consequences it may produce, and I fear has produced already; what advantage it yields to our enemies, what irreligion, the abandoning of the public assemblies may cause in some, and what vexation it creates to tender consciences in the country, where they live banished from the house of God.

I know you concur with me in hearty desires in closing the rupture; and methinks this is a happy juncture for it: the Lower House of Convocation do now worthily affect the rights of the clergy, and I dare say will gladly embrace a reconciliation. The question is, how it may be conscientiously effected? Give me leave to suggest my present thoughts.

If it is not judged advisable for my Brother of Norwich and myself, to resign up our canonical claims, which would be the shortest way, and which I am ready to do for the repose of the flock, having long ago maintained it to justify our character; if, I say, this is not thought advisable, then [I suggest] that a circular letter would be penned and dispersed which should modestly and yet resolutely assist the cause for which we suffer, and declare that our opinion is still the same, in regard to passive obedience, and specify the reasons which induce us to communicate in the public offices, the chiefest of which is to restore the peace of the Church, which is of that importance, that it ought to supersede all ecclesiastical canons, they being only of human, and not divine authority. A letter to this purpose would make our presence at some of the prayers rightly understood to be betraying of our cause; would guard us against any advantage our adversaries may take from our Christian condescension; would relieve fundamental charity, and give a general satisfaction to all well-minded persons.

I offer this with submission, and out of a sincere zeal for the good of the Church, and I beseech the divine goodness to guide both sides into the way of peace, that we may with one mind, and one mouth, glorify God.

alternative reading

A Reading from *An Exposition of the Church Catechism*
by Thomas Ken

O my God, when in any of thy commands a duty is enjoined, love tells me the contrary evil is forbidden; when any evil is forbidden, love tells me the contrary duty is enjoined; O do thou daily increase my love to good, and my antipathy to evil.

Though thy commands and prohibitions, O Lord, are in general terms, yet let thy love direct my particular practice, and teach me, that in one general are implied all the kinds and degrees and occasions and incitements and approaches and allowances, relating to that good or evil which are also commanded or forbidden, and give me grace to pursue or to fly them.

O my God, keep my love always watchful and on its guard that in thy negative precepts I may continually resist evil; keep my love warm with an habitual zeal that in all thy affirmative precepts I may lay hold on all seasons and opportunities of doing good.

Let thy love, O thou that only art worthy to be beloved, make me careful to persuade and engage others to love thee, and to keep thy commandments as well as myself.

None can love thee, and endeavor to keep thy holy commands, but his daily failings in his duty, his frequent involuntary and unavoidable slips, and surreptitions and wanderings, afflict and humble him; the infirmities of lapsed nature create him a kind of perpetual martyrdom because he can love thee no more, because he can so little serve thee.

But thou, O most compassionate Father, in thy covenant of grace dost require sincerity, not perfection; and therefore I praise and love thee.

O my God, though I cannot love and obey thee as much as I desire, I will do it as much as I am able: I will to the utmost of my power, keep all thy commandments with my whole heart and to the end. O accept of my imperfect duty, and supply all the defects of it by the merits and love and obedience of Jesus, thy beloved.

March 22

James DeKoven

Priest and Educator, 1879

A priest and educator born in 1831 in Middletown, Connecticut, James DeKoven served as a member of the faculty at Nashotah House in Wisconsin and as the warden of a church college at Racine. He was best known, however, for his spell-binding oratory as a champion of the "ritualist" cause at the General Conventions of 1871 and 1874, when that controversy was at its height. Though he was elected Bishop of Wisconsin in 1874, opposition to his views was so intense that consents to his election were refused. "You may take away from us, if you will," he said, "every external ceremony; you may take away altars, and super-altars, lights and incense and vestments... but... to adore Christ's person in his sacrament—that is the inalienable privilege of every Christian and every catholic heart. How we do it, the way we do it, the ceremonies with which we do it, are utterly, utterly, indifferent. The thing itself is what we plead for."

A Reading from a sermon by James DeKoven.

I know no sign of life in our own communion as full of hope and promise as the longing prayers and earnest labors, in the midst of reproach and contumely, which go up to Almighty God for the corporate reunion of Christendom. It is, no doubt, the drawing of our own dear Lord. It is the response on earth to his increasing intercession in heaven. It is the answering cry of the members to the gentle voice of their head.... Our prayers, joined unto his prevailing intercession, begin to be answered. Nor does prayer plead alone. Each act of missionary labor, each deed of faith, each bearing of poverty and loss in foreign lands, each act of self-denial, known or unknown, each victory over the world, the flesh, or the devil, each act of self-surrender in any brave young heart, all unions and associations for any Christian work, each offered Eucharist, each sincere confession, each life devoted unto God—these works for Christ join and blend with the prayers, and bring nearer and nearer the day when all shall be at one again, and the kingdoms of the world become the Kingdom of the Lord and of his Christ.

Nor is this all. There are other voices that plead and must be heard by the Judge of all. From those far-off lands where the name of Christ is never named, no prayers are prayed, no sacramental rites are offered—from those who live up to the light and knowledge that they have, and who long for more, from children dying, unstained as yet save by the common burden of us all, a cry of helpless misery and innocence is going up to God. It is louder than the heartless prayers of Christians; it is mightier than the intercession of worldly churches. It pierces the clouds of heaven. It mingles with the ceaseless raptures of the angels. It is caught into the loving bosom of the Savior of men, and wails in its lament, before the throne of the Father of all. Nor yet from heathen lands alone, nor from the toil-worn church, which, with banners torn and weapons blunted, sways to and fro in the agony of the contest, but from that land where all is over, the battle done, and the souls in peace—from the church at rest in paradise, from the company of the elect, from the saints beneath the altar goes up the ceaseless petition, checked by no discord, harmed by no disunion, its power lessened by no sin: "Lord, how long? Lord, how long?" And evermore, above them all and mingling with them all, and making them powerful with a power not their own, the prayer of Jesus, "That they all may be one, as Thou, Father, art in Me, and I in Thee, that the world may believe that Thou hast sent Me."

Soon the day will dawn, soon the New Jerusalem descend, soon the Bride be ready for the Bridegroom. It is not a question of days and months and years. It depends not on the changes of centuries and generations. It is as near at one time as another.

Whenever the mystical number of the elected is completed, whenever that which is behind, of the sufferings of Christ in his body the church, is accomplished, then will he present it to himself a glorious church, no longer torn and divided, but without spot, or wrinkle, or any such thing. Remember, beloved, each offered Eucharist, prayer and fasting, labor and toil, penitence and tears and devotion, giving up all things; and the bearing of persecution and contumely—these bring nearer and nearer the unity that is to be, the conversion of the world which Christ promises, the unending joy of the faithful.

March 23

Gregory the Illuminator

Bishop and Missionary of Armenia, *c.* 332

Born around the year 257, Gregory was carried away from Armenia as a child and brought up as a Christian in Cappadocia. He became known as the Illuminator and the Apostle of the Armenians, returned to Armenia as a young man, and succeeded in converting King Tiridates. With the help of the king, the country was converted and became the first national state to become officially Christian. A cathedral was built in Valarshapat but Gregory centered his work in nearby Echmiadzin, which is still the spiritual center of the Armenian Orthodox Church. Gregory's son, Aristages, was ordained as his successor and attended the Council of Nicaea. The writings attributed to Gregory come from about a century after his time but preserve the spirit of his teaching.

A Reading from *The Teaching of Saint Gregory*

See the sun and moon and stars. So much greater than man they are, yet they stand under God's will, constrained by the requirement of the command. The sun does not linger on its course, nor does the moon cease to wane and wax; the stars do not overstep their paths, nor the mountains change their place. The winds do not cease to blow, nor is the sea, in its confines of deep and furious swells, in its violence of raging and turbulent waves continually amassed, able to pass its fixed boundary and destroy the earth, nor does the earth cease to support and carry all. By his command is all arranged; his holy and heavenly angels stand in ceaseless praising. He made the height of the heavens and the number of the stars, the waters of the sea and the sand of the earth, the balance of the mountains. He raises up the clouds and restrains the winds, and brings back the evening, and makes green the arid dried-up grass, and gathers the raindrops. Concerning him the spirit of prophecy relates: "Who measured with his palm all the waters, and with his span the heavens, and all the earth with his fingers? Who placed the hills in a scale and weighed the plains with measures?" (Isaiah 40:12). Which is the place that holds up him by whose word all creatures are suspended? He knows the paths of the courses of the heavenly bodies, which circle above the air and are not deflected, which spread out and do not go astray. They come and stay as laborers hired for a year, they go out and are relit from day to evening and from evening to day, giving compensation to each other impartially, freely returning to the measure of their times, changing at the four seasons of the year, just as God arranged.

And how do the powers of the stars of the firmament of heaven travel, keeping balance in their paths continuously, without passing over the measure? Or whence come the gusty breezes of violent winds, and whither do they go and die down, and what are the seasons of each one of them? One nourishes the plants with its sweet breeze; another brings on and opens the buds; another weaves garments, decorates the earth with multicolored flowers in diverse hues, clothes the naked trees, and adorns the leafy tops.

Whence come into our ken the cloud-bearing winds in which the rains, born from the sound of thunder, are scattered by the lightning storm? And where the Lord commands them to go, they descend and water the earth, they make the plants to grow and ripen the fruits that fatten the body. From whose womb come the rivers with their sources, unceasing in their course, yet not overflowing in their passage?

Heaven and earth, sun and moon and multitudes of stars, seas and rivers, beasts and animals, reptiles and birds, swimming fishes, created things and things to be, all show their fixed order, following the command to each. Only the will of man has been left independent to do whatever he wills. And he has been constrained in nothing more than what was warned: not to eat the tree (Genesis 2.17), that thereby God might make him worthy to receive greater things in return for lesser, and that by virtue of his having grace for task, he might receive from the Creator, as recompense for lesser deeds, greater grace.

March 25

The Annunciation of our Lord Jesus Christ to the Blessed Virgin Mary

The story of the announcement of the coming of God made flesh in the person of his Son, Jesus the Christ, the Anointed One, is heard in today's proclamation of the good news from the Gospel of Luke. The feast marks the conception of Christ in the womb of Mary and has been celebrated in the Church at least since the late fourth century. The perfect humanity and the complete divinity of Jesus are affirmed, following the controversies around those orthodox assertions, which themselves led to the acknowledgement of Mary as Theotokos, *"the God-bearer," which in the West became translated as "Mother of God." The celebration thus took on strong associations with the person of Mary, and became known in England as "Lady Day." In recent years, the Church has re-affirmed the day as a Feast of our Lord, on which his virgin-mother still has a unique place of honor and veneration.*

A Reading from a sermon of Cyril of Alexandria, preached at the Council of Ephesus in 431, in which he celebrates the special dignity accorded to Mary, the bearer of the Incarnate Word of God

We hail you, O mysterious and Holy Trinity who has gathered us together in council in this church of Holy Mary, the God-bearer.

We hail you, Mary, the God-bearer, sacred treasure of all the universe, the star which never sets, the crown of virginity, the scepter of true law, a temple which cannot be destroyed, the dwelling place of one who cannot be contained.

O Mother and Virgin, we hail you for the sake of the one whom the holy Gospels call "blessed," the one who "comes in the name of the Lord."

We hail you Mary, for in your virginal womb you held the one whom the heavens themselves cannot contain, one through whom the Trinity is glorified and worshipped throughout the world; through whom the heavens exult; through whom angels and archangels rejoice; through whom demons are put to flight; through whom the tempter was thrown out of heaven; through whom fallen creation is raised up to the heavens; through whom the whole world, held captive by idolatry, has now come to know the truth; through whom holy baptism is given to those who believe, anointing them with the "oil of gladness;" through whom churches have been founded throughout the world; through whom the nations have been converted.

What more can I say? It is through you, Mary, that the light of the only-begotten Son of God has shone upon those "who dwell in darkness and the shadow of death." It is through you that prophets have spoken of the future, that the apostles have preached salvation to the nations, that the dead have been raised, that monarchs are reigning in the name of the Trinity.

Is there a single person who can sufficiently set forth the praises of Mary? She is both Mother and Virgin. What a wondrous thing! In fact it is so wonderful that I am overwhelmed by it. Has anyone ever heard of a builder who was stopped from dwelling in the temple he himself had built? Has anyone the right to speak ill of the one who bestowed upon his own servant the title of "mother?" This is why today everyone is rejoicing.

Today, therefore, may we the Church worship and adore the unity, may we worship and honor the undivided Trinity, by singing the praises of Mary ever Virgin, and the praises of her Son and immaculate Spouse, to whom be glory for ever and ever.

alternative reading

A Reading from a sermon of Mark Frank

"Dominus tecum," the Lord Christ's being with Mary, is the chief business the Church commemorates in this day. Her being "blessed," and all our being "blessed," "highly favored," or favored at all, either men or women being so, all our hail, all our health, and peace and joy, all the angels' visits to us, or kind words, all our conferences with heaven, all our titles and honors in heaven and earth, that are worth the naming, come only from it.

For *Dominus tecum* cannot come without them; he cannot come to us but we must be so, must be highly favored in it, and blessed by it. So the incarnation of Christ, and the annunciation of the blessed Virgin, his being incarnate of her, and her blessedness in him with her, make it as well our Lord's as our Lady's day. More his, because his being Lord made her a Lady, else a poor carpenter's wife, God knows; all her worthiness and honor, as all ours, is from him; and we too take heed today, or any day, of parting them; or so remembering her as to forget him; or so blessing her, as to take away any of our blessing him; any of his worship, to give to her.

Let her blessedness, the respect we give her, be among women still; such as is fit and proportionate to weak creatures, not due and proper only to the creator, that *Dominus tecum*, Christ in her be the business: that we take pattern by the angel, to give her no more than is her due, yet to be sure to give her that, and particularly upon this day.

[And yet the day being a day of Lent, seems somewhat strange. It is surely no fasting work, no business or occasion of sadness this. What does it then, or how shall we do it then, in Lent this time of fast and sorrow? Fast and feast too, how can we do it? A feast it is today—a great one, Christ's incarnation—a day of joy, if ever any; and Lent a time of sorrow and repentance, the greatest fast of any. How shall we reconcile them?

Why thus: the news of joy never comes so seasonable as in the midst of sorrow; news of one coming to save us from our sins, can never come more welcome to us than when we are sighing and groaning under them; never can an angel come more acceptably than at such time with such a message. It is the very time to be filled when we are empty; the only time for *Dominus tecum*, for our Lord's being with us when we have most room to entertain him. *Dominus tecum*, Christ is the main business, both of our fasts and feasts; and it is the greatest order to attend his business in the day and way we meet it, be it what it will.]

For from Christ's being with Mary and with us it is that we are blessed. From his incarnation begins the date of all our happiness. If God be not with us all the world cannot make us happy, much less blessed. For God hath exalted the humble and meek, the humble handmaid better than the proudest lady. Blessed the devout affection that is always watching for her Lord in prayer and meditations; none so happy, so blessed, as she; the Lord comes to none so soon as such.

Note: The fourth and fifth paragraphs may be omitted from the above reading if the feast has had to be transferred out of Lent.

alternative reading

A Reading from a poem by Margaret Saunders

Madonna

Black Madonna,
Let me climb on your lap.
Feel my heart
    beating with yours.
Hear your voice
    call me child.
Tell me of the blessing
    of the wise wound
    and the falling blood.
Tell me of the richness
    of my womanhood
    and of the travail
    to bring its darkness to birth.
Tell me of the pain
    and emptiness and loss
    when the sword pierced through your soul also.
Mary
Empty vessel
God-bearer
                and bearer of God's sorrow.

March 27

Charles Henry Brent

Bishop of the Philippines and of Western New York, 1929

Probably no one individual summed up so much in his life of the mission and ministry of the Episcopal Church in the twentieth century as did Charles Henry Brent. Although he was born in Canada in 1862, Brent served first as a mission priest in the slums of Boston and then as the Episcopal Church's first missionary bishop in the Philippine Islands after the Spanish-American War. There he began a crusade against the traffic in opium which led him to preside over an international conference on opium in Shanghai and to represent the United States on the League of

Nations Narcotics Committee. During the First World War Brent became senior chaplain of the American forces in Europe and then accepted election as bishop of Western New York. Concern for Christian unity led him to organize and preside over the first World Conference on Faith and Order, which was held in 1927 in Lausanne, Switzerland. Through all his activity, Brent remained a man grounded in prayer. His prayer for mission is in the 1979 Book of Common Prayer.

A Reading from *Things That Matter*, by Charles Henry Brent

There are but two great realities in the vast universe—the heart of God and the heart of man, and each is ever seeking the other. It is this that makes adventure for God not an experiment, but a certainty. The appeal issuing from man's abysmal need is met by the amplitude of the divine supply.

The thought of God's keeping tryst with us is a winsome thought. When we go to pray, God has already come to the meeting-place. We are never there first. He is indeed more ready to hear than we to pray, more ready to give more than we desire or deserve than we to ask. He comes not with the spirit of toleration but of ardent love. The great thing to remember is that God, being who he is, is more ready to hear than we to pray, more eager to give than we to receive, more active to find us than we to find him. God is ever seeking man: his ear is more sensitive to the words, his heart to the desires, of men than the aspen leaf to the summer breeze, than the compass needle to the call of the poles.

Fellowship with the Divine is as normal as fellowship with man.

Humankind cannot be fairly divided into those who pray and those who do not pray, for everybody prays. Prayer is the universal practice of human nature. There is no commoner form of activity. It is not an artificial part of life, but as instinctive and automatic as breathing. It might be said that the capacity for prayer is the feature that distinguishes man from monkey or dog.

Active or dormant, the instinct of prayer abides, a faithful tenant, in every soul. The instinct to pray may be undeveloped, or paralyzed by violence, or it may lie bedridden in the soul through long neglect; but even so, no benumbed faculty is more readily roused to life and nerved to action than that of prayer. The faculty is there; no one is without it. Whether it expands, and how, is only a question of the will of the person concerned.

Prayer is man's side of converse with God; it is speech Godward. Yes, prayer is speech Godward, and worship is man's whole life of friendship with God, the flowing out, as it were, of all that tide of emotion and service which is love's best speech.

The essence of prayer is desire, forming itself into hope and aspiration, and mounting up into effort, in the direction of the unattained. Prayer is the address made by human personality to that with which it is desired to establish affiliations. It is a movement of the whole being which reaches after the heart's desire.

Prayer is the committal of our way unto the Lord, just as a deed of trust is the committal of our possessions to those who can handle them better than we. By living one day with God, preparation is made for living all days with God.

One may say that the real end of prayer is not so much to get this or that single desire granted, as to put human life into full and joyful conformity with the will of God.

Prayer is love melted into worship.

March 29

John Keble

Priest, Tractarian, Poet, 1866

Born in 1792, the son of a priest, John Keble showed early brilliance as a scholar, becoming a Fellow of Oriel College, Oxford, at the age of nineteen, a few years before his ordination. He won great praise for his collection of poems, The Christian Year, *issued in 1827, and was elected Professor of Poetry in Oxford in 1831. A leader of the Tractarian movement, which protested at the threats to the Church from liberal developments in both politics and theology, he nevertheless did not seek preferment and in 1836 became a parish priest near Winchester, a position he held until his death in 1866. He continued to write scholarly books and was praised for his character and spiritual counsel. Yet he is still best remembered for the Assize Sermon "On National Apostasy" he preached in Oxford, considered by some the beginning of the Oxford Movement, delivered in the year 1833.*

A Reading from the *Assize Sermon*
"On National Apostasy" preached by John Keble
in the University Church of Saint Mary the Virgin, Oxford,
July 14, 1833

What are the symptoms by which one may judge most fairly, whether or not a nation is becoming alienated from God and Christ?

The case is at least possible of a nation, having for centuries acknowledged as an essential part of its theory of government, that as a Christian nation, she is also a part of Christ's Church, and bound in all her legislation and policy, by the fundamental rules of that Church—the case is, I say, conceivable, of a government and people so constituted, deliberately throwing off the restraint which in many respects such a principle would impose on them, disavowing the principle itself; and that, on the plea that other states, as flourishing or more so in regard of wealth and dominion, do well enough without it.

What should be the tenor of their conduct, who find themselves cast on such times of decay and danger? How may a man best reconcile his allegiance to God and his Church with his duty to his country, that country which now by the supposition is fast becoming hostile to the Church, and cannot therefore long be the friend of God?

Should it ever happen (which God avert, but we cannot shut our eyes to the danger) that the Apostolical Church should be forsaken, degraded, nay trampled on and despoiled by the State and people of England, I cannot conceive of a kinder wish for her, on the part of her most affectionate and dutiful children, than that she may consistently act in the spirit of that most noble sentence of the prophet Samuel: "God forbid that I should sin against the Lord in ceasing to pray for you: but I will teach you the good and the right way." In speaking of the Church, I mean, of course, the laity as well as the clergy in their three orders—the whole body of Christians united, according to the will of Jesus Christ, under the successors of the apostles.

The Church would, first of all, have to be constant in intercession. No despiteful usage, no persecution, could warrant her in ceasing to pray, as did her first fathers and patterns, for the State and all who are in authority. That duty once well and cordially performed, all other duties are secured.

Secondly, remonstrance—calm, distinct, and persevering, in public and in private, direct and indirect, by word, look and demeanor, is the unequivocal duty of every Christian, according to his opportunities when the Church's landmarks are being broken down.

Finally, the surest way to uphold or restore our endangered Church, will be for each of her anxious children, in his own place and station, to resign himself more thoroughly to his God and Savior in those duties, public and private, which are not immediately affected by the emergencies of the moment: the daily and hourly duties, I mean, of piety, purity, charity and justice. It will be no unworthy principle, if any man be more circumspect in his behavior, more watchful and fearful of himself, more earnest in his petitions for spiritual aid, from a dread of disparaging the holy name of the English Church, in her hour of peril, by his own personal fault or negligence.

alternative reading

A Reading from a sermon of John Keble preached at Coln St. Aldwyn's, Gloucestershire, in 1829

The thing which hinders us from seeing and feeling things as we ought to do I apprehend to be nothing else than our great carelessness about our Christian calling; our want of faith in the blessings which Jesus Christ provided for us when he received us into his Church. If we had anything like a worthy notion of our near relation to God, adopted as we are by baptism to be his own children in Christ Jesus, we should then understand how very near the same adoption brings us to one another.

But whether we choose to recollect it or no, certain it is that we are all brethren, and as brethren are bound to love and serve one another. By which one consideration, if men would but bear it in mind, a whole host of unkindly thoughts and expressions would at once be silenced and done away with.

Saint Paul's brotherly love, the love he expressed and taught in his epistles, was not merely that he watched for every opportunity of doing good to the Christians among whom he lived; he found leisure to extend his brotherly care and charity to those who were far out of his reach, whom he had never seen, and very likely never might see. Surely we ought to be ashamed, when we compare our brotherly love with his; we who think it a great matter to take some small care of the spiritual good of our nearest relations or children.

And as the term "brotherly love one toward another," shows us how far our kindness to our fellow-Christians should extend, so another expression of Saint Paul shows us in what manner that kindness should be exercised. "Be kindly affectioned one to another with brotherly love." The word literally and properly means, "delighting" in brotherly love, as in an exercise of natural affection; as a mother for instance, delights in showing fondness to her infant or a brother to his sister, or a dutiful child to a tender parent. The love and affection in each of these cases, comes as it were naturally of itself. A mother does not want to be taught that she is to love, and nurse, and watch her child. God has put an instinct into her heart, a silent teacher, which inclines her to perform those duties for her own pleasure. So will brotherly love—love unfeigned toward the meanest of our fellow Christians—arise naturally and without an express call, in the mind of every sincere and practical believer in Jesus Christ. He will be restless and uneasy in mind till he has done, to all within his reach, all the good which lies in his power. His labor will always be fresh, always beginning; and yet he is never over-weary of it, because it is a labor of love.

March 31

John Donne

Priest, Poet, 1631

John Donne was born about the year 1571 and brought up as a Roman Catholic. He was a great-great nephew of Thomas More, although this seems to have had little influence on him because, as a youth, he was skeptical about all religion. He went up to Oxford when he was fourteen, studied further at Cambridge and perhaps on the Continent, and eventually discovered his Christian faith in the Church of England. After much heart-searching, he accepted ordination and later the post of Dean of Saint Paul's Cathedral. Much of his cynicism dissolved and he became a strong advocate for the discerning of Christian vocation, and in particular affirming his own vocation as a priest, loving and loved by the crucified Christ. The people of London flocked to his sermons. He died on this day in the year 1631.

A Reading from a sermon of John Donne, preached at Lincoln's Inn during the Easter Term 1620

I am body and soul, soul and faculties; and as Scripture says, "I shall see God." I, the same man, shall receive the crown of glory which shall not fade. I shall see; but I have had no looking-glass in my grave to see how my body looks in the dissolution; thus I know not how I shall see. I have had no hour-glass in my grave to see how my time passes; thus I know not when I shall see. For when my eyelids are closed in my deathbed, till I see eternity, the Ancient of Days, I shall see no more; but then I shall. Our sensitive faculties have more relation to the soul than to the body; but yet to some purpose, and in some measure, all the senses shall be in our glorified bodies.

"No man ever saw God and lived." And yet, I shall not live till I see God; and when I have seen him I shall never die. What have I ever seen in this world, that hath been truly the same thing that it seemed to me? I have seen marble buildings, and a chip, a crust, a plaster, a face of marble hath pulled off, and I see brick-bowels within. I have seen beauty, and a strong breath from another tells me that that complexion is from without, not from a sound constitution within. I have seen the state of Princes, and all that is but ceremony. As he that fears God, fears nothing else, so he that sees God, sees everything else: when we shall see God, we shall see all things as they are. We shall be no more deluded with outward appearances: for, when this sight, which we intend here comes, there will be no delusory thing to be seen. All that we have made as though we saw in this world, will be vanished, and I shall see nothing but God, and what is in him; and him I shall see in the flesh.

Our flesh, even in the resurrection, cannot be a spectacle, a mere perspective glass to our soul. We shall see the humanity of Christ with our bodily eyes, then glorified; but, that flesh, though glorified, cannot make us see God better, nor clearer than the soul alone hath done all the time from our death to our resurrection. But as an indulgent father, or as a tender mother, when they go to see the king in any solemnity, or any other thing of observation and curiosity, delights to carry their child, which is flesh of their flesh, and bone of their bone, with them, and though the child cannot comprehend it as well as they, they are as glad that the child sees it as that they see it themselves; such a gladness shall my soul have that this flesh, (which she will no longer call her prison, nor her tempter, but her friend, her companion, her wife) that this flesh, that is, I, in the re-union, and re-integration of both parts, shall see God; for then, one principal clause in her rejoicing, and acclamation, shall be, that this flesh is her flesh; "In my flesh I shall see God."

alternative reading

Holy Sonnet

Batter my heart, three person'd God; for you
As yet but knock, breathe, shine, and seek to mend;
That I may rise, and stand, o'erthrow me, and bend
Your force, to break, blow, burn and make me new.
I, like an usurpt town, to another due,
Labor to admit you, but Oh, to no end,
Reason your viceroy in me, me should defend,
But is captiv'd, and proves weak or untrue.
Yet dearly I love you, and would be lov'd fain,
But am betroth'd unto your enemy.
Divorce me, untie, or break that knot again,
Take me to you, imprison me; for I
Except you enthrall me, never shall be free,
Nor ever chaste, except you ravish me.

A Hymn to God the Father

Wilt thou forgive that sin where I begun,
Which is my sin, though it were done before?
Wilt thou forgive those sins through which I run,
And do them still: though still I do deplore?
When thou hast done, thou hast not done,
For, I have more.

Wilt thou forgive that sin by which I won
Others to sin? and, made my sin their door?
Wilt thou forgive that sin which I did shun
A year, or two: but wallowed in, a score?
When thou hast done, thou hast not done,
For, I have more.

I have a sin of fear, that when I have spun
My last thread, I shall perish on the shore;
Swear by thy self, that at my death thy Sun
Shall shine as it shines now, and heretofore;
And, having done that, Thou hast done,
I have no more.

April

April 1

Frederick Denison Maurice
Priest, Teacher of the Faith, 1872

Born into a Unitarian family in 1805, Frederick Maurice became an Anglican in his twenties and was then ordained. He was one of the founders of the Christian Socialist Movement, in which his particular concern was providing education for working men. As a theologian, Maurice's ideas on Anglican comprehensiveness have remained influential. His best-remembered book, The Kingdom of Christ, *demonstrated his philosophical approach to theology. His radicalism was revealed in his attack on traditional concepts of hell in* Theological Essays, *which cost him his Professorship at King's College, London, in 1853. In 1866, however, he was given a chair in Cambridge, which he held until his death on this day in 1872.*

A Reading from a sermon of F. D. Maurice
"On the Lord's Prayer," preached at Lincoln's Inn,
February 13, 1848

The revelation that the God whom we call upon is "Our Father" is grounded upon an act done on behalf of humanity—an act in which all men have a like interest; for if Christ did not take the nature of every rebel and outcast, he did not take the nature of Paul and John. Therefore the first sign that the Church was established upon earth in the name of the Father, and the Son, and the Spirit, was one which showed that it was to consist of men of every tongue and nation; the baptized community was literally to represent mankind. If it be so, the name "Father" loses its significance for us individually, when we will not use it as the members of a family.

God has owned us as spiritual creatures, has claimed us in that character to be his own, to feel that the universe would be a horrible blank without him; that his absence would be infinitely more to us than to all creatures beside; that if he is not, or we cannot find him, consciousness, memory, expectation, existence, must be curses unbearable; but that when the burden of the world and of self is most crushing, we may take refuge from both in him—if at any time such convictions have dawned upon us, let us not hope to keep the blessing of them by our own skill and watchfulness. Let us say: "Our Father, when we least remember thee, fix the thought of thy being deeper than all other thoughts within us; and may we, thy children, dwell in it, and find our home and rest in it, now and for ever."

In the phrase "Our Father" there lies the expression of that fixed eternal relation which Christ's birth and death have established between the littleness of the creature and the majesty of the creator; the one great practical answer to the philosopher who would make heaven clear by making it cold; would assert the dignity of the divine essence, by emptying it of its love, and reducing it into nothingness. "Our Father which art in heaven"—there lies the answer to all the miserable substitutes for faith, by which the invisible has been lowered to the visible; which have insulted the understanding and cheated the heart; which have made united worship impossible, because that can only be when there is one Being, eternal, immortal, invisible, to whom all may look up together, into whose presence a way is opened for all, whose presence is a refuge from the confusions, perplexities and divisions of this world; that home which the spirits of men were ever seeking and could not find till he who had borne their sorrows and died their death, entered within the veil, having obtained eternal redemption for them, till he bade them sit with him in heavenly places.

April 2

James Lloyd Breck
Priest, 1876

In 1835, the Episcopal Church had recovered enough from the Revolutionary War to organize itself for mission. Jackson Kemper was appointed a missionary bishop to plant churches on the frontier and, having become familiar with his jurisdiction, he summoned a group of recent seminary graduates to help him by establishing a seminary at Nashotah, Wisconsin, to prepare priests for mission work on the frontier. Born in the year 1818, James Lloyd Breck was one of those who set out for the West to help with this work. Having established the seminary on a firm foundation, Breck moved on to Minnesota, where he began the church's work among the Chippewa people. By 1867, Breck had moved on to California, where he attempted again to establish a theological school. Though the seminary he founded did not last long, Breck did manage to establish five parishes and bring new strength to the church's work on the West Coast. He died in the year 1876 at the age of fifty-five.

A Reading from a sermon on discipline
by James Lloyd Breck

No word in the gospel is in more common use than *disciple*, and none of so general import, whether for apostle or the humblest follower of the cross. Now, *disciple* is none other than the root derivation of *discipline*, and in consequence it must be, that *discipline* is the government of the disciple. And we find this to be true, from the time that Jesus called unto him the twelve and "ordained them that they should be with him."

If the purpose of the Lord *ended here*, then would *disciple* indeed have a limited meaning; for he chose and ordained apostles for a ministry, not *"to be with him"* only, and afterward, be *"with them to the end of the world"* (which is the true apostolic succession); but he chose them also *"that he might send them forth to preach, and to have power to heal sicknesses, and to cast out devils."* And this commission is *to the laity*, and hence extends the word *discipline*, as it does *disciple*, to every class of mankind without restriction to age or land, for their souls and bodies. From this view of the subject, it will at once be perceived that the American branch of the Catholic church had hitherto embraced, under the head of discipline, the clergy largely to the neglect and oversight and even exclusion of the laity. As though the General Triennial Convention was meant to pass canons for the government, trial, and punishment of bishops of the church, and our diocesan conventions to do the same thing for the clergy, and in no large sense for the due disciplinary education of its laity. And it will appear, I trust, in its just light, to the laity of the church as well as to the clergy, that this is a subject, from its relative point of view as regards principal and practice in the Christian life, worthy of the highest consideration. And one that cannot be dealt with by us as unfairly as regards the laity, for they constitute by our constitution, as an apostolic branch of the church, an integral part of the councils of the church, and nothing in general convention or in diocesan convention can become a law without the concurrent assent of the lay-deputies.

Now, let it be borne in mind that discipline is not to be understood in any obnoxious sense, or in any sense restricted to punishment, with which it is too often been thought to be synonymous. We have already said that *disciple* is the root derivation of *discipline*, and hence that *discipline* is simply the government of the disciple.

It remains with us in the church's council to say whether we shall continue in the past worldly compliance and a worldly policy; weakening before the world the cause, which has martyrs and confessors in its past history, or strengthening the things which remain, so exhibit the church of God to a sinful world, that it shall be as a city set on a hill, known and read of all men, as the way, and the only divinely constituted way, for the salvation of lost mankind.

April 3

Richard

Bishop of Chichester, 1253

Richard de Wych (or of Droitwich as it is now known) was born there in 1197 and worked hard for his yeoman father to restore the family fortunes. Later he studied at Oxford and Paris and then in Bologna as an ecclesiastical lawyer. When he returned to England in 1235, he was made Chancellor of Oxford, and eventually Chancellor to the Archbishop of Canterbury, Edmund of Abingdon. When Richard eventually became Bishop of Chichester, he was seen as a model diocesan bishop: progressing around his diocese on foot, visiting and caring for his clergy and people, generally being accessible to all who needed his ministry. He insisted that the sacraments be administered without payment and with a proper dignity. While on a recruitment campaign for the Crusades, he fell ill at Dover and died there on April 3, 1253. His mortal remains were transferred to Chichester on this day in the year 1276.

A Reading from a contemporary *Life of Saint Richard* by Ralf Bocking

After a life shining with the glory of his miracles and renowned for the purity of his virtues in which, following Christ, blessed Richard learned constantly to bear the cross on which Christ was crucified for the world and the world for Christ, in order to make a glorious end to his life at the foot of the cross in service to and with Christ, he undertook the preaching of the cross for the relief of the Holy Land, a task entrusted to him by the Holy See. And so Christ's glorious priest and preacher set out, seeking to glory not in the commission which he had received from Rome but rather in the wounds of Christ, crying out with the Apostle: "May God forbid that I should glory save in the cross of our Lord Jesus Christ."

During his preaching tour he became very weak. They asked him to eat something and someone said to him, "My Lord, are you having only one dish for supper? Eat as much as you like." But he replied, "It is enough. One dish should suffice for supper." And he added, "Do you know this text? It is what Saint Philip said to Christ, 'Lord, show us the Father and it is sufficient for us.'" For he had already turned his whole mind upon God and could already taste the sweetness of the Lord's presence.

He embraced the image of the Crucified, which he had asked to be brought to him, for he knew that according to St Basil, the honor given to an image belongs to the subject which it represents. He devoutly kissed and tenderly caressed the wounds as if he had just seen them newly inflicted on his Savior's dying body, and cried out: "Thanks be to thee, Lord Jesus Christ, for all the benefits which thou hast granted to me, for all the pains and insults which thou hast suffered for me."

And then he said to his attendants, "Place this wretched body down on the ground." And often repeating the words of the Psalmist, "Into thy hands, O Lord, I commend my spirit," and then turning with both heart and voice to the glorious Virgin, he said: "Mary, mother of grace, mother of mercy, protect us from the enemy now and pray for us at the hour of our death." Thus between the sighs of his pious devotions and the words of his holy prayers, surrounded by monks, priests, clerks and pious laymen, the blessed Richard rendered up his soul to his creator, soon to join those that dwell in the kingdom above. He passed from this world in about the fifty-sixth year of his age, in the ninth year of his episcopate.

April 8

William Augustus Muhlenberg
Priest, 1877

William Augustus Muhlenberg was born in the year 1796. He came into the Episcopal Church from the Lutheran Church because of its use of English, but his ecumenical proposals helped pave the way for the final agreement on intercommunion between the two churches of which he was a member. He submitted a "Memorial" to the General Convention of 1853 that proposed a greater flexibility in the church and an openness to work with others on the basis of the creeds, the Eucharist, Episcopal ordination, and the Reformation doctrine of grace. As revised by others, the Memorial became the Chicago-Lambeth Quadrilateral on the basis of which the Episcopal Church has entered into ecumenical discussions ever since. Ecumenism, however, was only one of a myriad of projects developed by Muhlenberg. He founded the first church in New York City to offer weekly communion and free pews; enriched the church's worship with music, flowers, and color; wrote hymns and compiled hymnals; founded a parish day school and a parish unemployment fund; organized trips to the country for poor children; and worked with Anne Ayres to found Saint Luke's Hospital and to found a religious order for women that became the Community of Saint Mary. He helped reshape the church to minister to the whole of society.

A Reading from *The Weekly Eucharist*
by William Augustus Muhlenberg

The restoration of the weekly Eucharist can seldom, with profit, be a sudden movement in a congregation; it must be viewed in its practical bearings and probable consequences, as well as in its abstract propriety. Now, viewing it thus practically, there are many reflecting persons who have serious doubts of its expediency. This leads me to consider the chief objection to the constant celebration of the Eucharist.

Many devout persons fear that it will impair their feelings of the high sanctity of the ordinance; they fear that the Holy Sacrament will come down from its high and wonted place in their sacred venerations. They look upon it as an extraordinary act of devotion, and this would be to lower it to the rank of an ordinary one. Hence, they fear, too, that the preparation that is now thought so needful in order to ensure a profitable receiving of the sacrament would be gradually laid aside. These are no trifling apprehensions. No one can fear more than I do the habit of coming to the altar, without those previous duties that the best Christian practice has prescribed as most salutary, if not indispensable. We have the mind of our own church on this point. She evidently requires special preparation in her communicants. How earnestly, from time to time, does she there call upon us to "consider the dignity of the Holy mysteries, and the great peril of the unworthy receiving thereof; to search and examine our consciences, and that not lightly and after the manner of dissemblers with God, but so that we may come holy and clean to such an heavenly feast, in the marriage garment required in Holy Scripture; and so be received as worthy partakers of that Holy Table." To follow this counsel, and the more specific directions that the exhortation proceeds to lay down, requires time and thought. To be done well it is a patient work. Self-examination cannot be a hurried performance of a few moments before receiving.

Of course, I would not say that such preliminary duties are invariably necessary, or that there should be no communicating without them, since the requisite fitness consists more in the habitual character and general tenor of life than in any particular state of mind. A good Christian is always fit to partake of the Sacrament; but yet, in order to do it, he will desire to collect himself—to repair himself, as it were—to wipe off the dust and soil of the world, which are forever settling on the soul; just as a good Christian is always prepared to die, while yet he prays against sudden death, in order that he may be actually ready, as well as habitually prepared for the awful change. He would have his lamp not merely burning, but bright, and replenished with oil to light him well as he enters the dark valley. In like manner the communicant, though conscious of having the main qualification for meeting his Lord acceptably at the Holy Table, yet desires to examine it, again and again—to try himself, as the apostle bids him, "whether he be in the faith." Every time he ventures into the presence of the King he endeavors to have his marriage garment cleaner and whiter, more thoroughly purified from the stains of earth. He feels as if he must repent anew—believe anew—love anew—make good resolutions anew; and begin, as it were, his whole Christian life anew. True, the grace which is to enable him to do all this is the very thing he seeks in going to the Eucharist, yet the grace which he obtains is ever in proportion to that with whom he comes. "Whosoever hath, to him more shall be given;

and from him that hath not shall be taken away even that which he hath." So of the grace of which the Eucharist is the means. The more we have to come with, the more we bring away.

April 9

Dietrich Bonhoeffer

Lutheran Pastor, Martyr, 1945

Dietrich Bonhoeffer was born in 1906 into an academic family. Ordained in the Lutheran Church, his theology was influenced by Karl Barth and he became a lecturer: in Spain, the U.S.A. and in 1931 back in Berlin. Opposed to the philosophy of Nazism, he was one of the leaders of the Confessing Church, a movement which broke away from the Nazi-dominated Lutherans in 1934. Banned from teaching, and harassed by Hitler's regime, he bravely returned to Germany at the outbreak of war in 1939, despite being on a lecture tour in the United States at the time. His defiant opposition to the Nazis led to his arrest in 1943. His experiences led him to propose a more radical theology in his later works, which have been influential among post-war theologians. He was murdered by the Nazi police in Flossenburg concentration camp on this day in 1945.

A Reading from a letter of Dietrich Bonhoeffer to his friend Eberhard Bethge, written from Tegel Prison dated July 21, 1944

During the last year or so I've come to know and understand more and more the profound this-worldliness of Christianity. The Christian is not a *homo religiosus*, but simply a human being, as Jesus was human—in contrast, shall we say, to John the Baptist. I don't mean the shallow and banal this-worldliness of the enlightened, the busy, the comfortable, or the lascivious, but the profound this-worldliness, characterized by discipline and the constant knowledge of death and resurrection.

I remember a conversation that I had in America thirteen years ago with a young French pastor. We were asking ourselves quite simply what we wanted to do with our lives. He said he would like to become a saint (and I think it's quite likely that he did become one). At the time I was very impressed, but I disagreed with him, and said, in effect, that I should like to learn to have faith. For a long time I didn't realize the depth of the contrast. I thought I could acquire faith by trying to live a holy life, or something like it. I suppose I wrote *The Cost of Discipleship* as the end of that path. Today I can see the dangers of that book, though I still stand by what I wrote.

I discovered later, and I'm still discovering right up to this moment, that it is only by living completely in this world that one learns to have faith. One must completely abandon any attempt to make something of oneself, whether it be a saint, or a converted sinner, or a churchman (a so-called priestly type!), a righteous person or an unrighteous one, a sick or a healthy one. By this-worldliness I mean living unreservedly in life's duties, problems, successes and failures, experiences and perplexities. In so doing we throw ourselves completely into the arms of God, taking seriously, not our own sufferings, but those of God in the world - watching with Christ in Gethsemane. That, I think, is faith; that is *metanoia*; and that is how one becomes a human being and a Christian. How can success make us arrogant, or failure lead us astray, when we share in God's sufferings through a life of this kind?

I am glad to have been able to learn this, and I know I've been able to do so only along the road that I've traveled. So I'm grateful for the past and present, and content with them. You may be surprised at such a personal letter; but for once I want to say this kind of thing, to whom should I say it?

May God in his mercy lead us through these times; but above all, may he lead us to himself.

alternative reading

A Poem by Dietrich Bonhoeffer, written in Tegel Prison,
and dated July 9, 1944

Who am I?

Who am I? They often tell me
I would step from my cell's confinement
calmly, cheerfully, firmly,
like a squire from his country-house.

Who am I? They often tell me
I would talk to my warders

freely and friendly and clearly,
as though it were mine to command.

Who am I? They also tell me
I would bear the days of misfortune
equably, smilingly, proudly,
like one accustomed to win.

Am I then really all that which others tell of?
Or am I only what I know of myself,
restless and longing and sick, like a bird in a cage,
struggling for breath,
as though hands were compressing my throat,
yearning for colors, for flowers, for the voices of birds,
thirsting for words of kindness, for neighborliness,
trembling with anger at despotisms and petty humiliation,
tossing in expectation of great events,
powerlessly trembling for friends at an infinite distance,
weary and empty at praying, at thinking, at making,
faint, and ready to say farewell to it all?

Who am I? This or the other?
Am I one person today, and tomorrow another?
Am I both at once? A hypocrite before others,
and before myself a contemptibly woebegone weakling?
Or is something within me still like a beaten army,
fleeing in disorder from victory already achieved?

Who am I? They mock me, these lonely questions of mine.
Whoever I am, thou knowest, O God, I am thine.

April 10

William Law

Priest, Spiritual Writer, 1761

Born at Kings Cliffe in Northamptonshire in 1686, William Law was educated at Emmanuel College, Cambridge, and after ordination as a deacon, became a Fellow of the College in 1711. When George I came to the throne in 1714, Law declined to take the Oath of Allegiance, being a member of the Non-Juror party who believed the anointed, but deposed, monarch James II and his heirs should occupy the throne. He lost his fellowship, but in 1728 he was made a priest, and in the same year published A Serious Call to a Devout and Holy Life, *which much influenced such people as Samuel Johnson and John and Charles Wesley. In it he stresses the moral virtues, a personal prayer life and asceticism. He returned to Kings Cliffe in 1740, where he led a life of devotion, simplicity and caring for the poor. He remained there the rest of his life and died on this day in the year 1761.*

A Reading from *A Serious Call to a Devout and Holy Life* by William Law

Devotion signifies a life given or devoted to God. He therefore is the devout man who lives no longer to his own will, or the way and spirit of the world, but to the sole will of God, who considers God in everything, who serves God in everything, who makes all the parts of his common life parts of piety by doing everything in the name of God and under such rules as are conformable to his glory.

We readily acknowledge that God alone is to be the rule and measure of our prayers, that in them we are to look wholly unto him and act wholly for him, that we are only to pray in such a manner for such things and such ends as are suitable to his glory.

Now let anyone but find out the reason why he is to be thus strictly pious in his prayers and he will find the same as strong a reason to be as strictly pious in all the other parts of his life. For there is not the least shadow of a reason why we should make God the rule and measure of our prayers, why we should then look wholly unto him and pray according to his will, but what equally proves it necessary for us to look wholly unto God, and make him the rule and measure of all the other actions of our life. For any of life, any employment of our talents, whether of our parts, our time, or money, that is not strictly according to the will of God, is not for such ends as are suitable to his glory, and are as great absurdities and failings as prayers that are not according to the will of God.

For there is no other reason why our prayers should be according to the will of God, why they should have nothing in them but what is wise, and holy, and heavenly, there is no other reason for this but that our lives may be of the same nature, full of the same wisdom, holiness, and heavenly tempers that we may live unto God in the same spirit that we pray unto him. Were it not our strict duty to live by reason, to devote all the actions of our lives to

God, were it not absolutely necessary to walk before him in wisdom and holiness and all heavenly conversation, doing everything in his name and for his glory, there would be no excellency or wisdom in the most heavenly prayers. Nay, such prayers would be absurdities: they would be like prayers for wings when it was no part of our duty to fly.

As sure, therefore, as there is any wisdom in praying for the Spirit of God, so sure is it that we are to make that Spirit the rule of all our actions; as sure as it is our duty to look wholly unto God in our prayers, so sure is it that it is our duty to live wholly unto God in our lives. But we can no more be said to live unto God unless we live unto him in all the ordinary actions of our life, unless he be the rule and measure of all our ways, than we can be said to pray unto God unless our prayer look wholly unto him. So that unreasonable and absurd ways of life, whether in labor or diversion, whether they consume our time or our money, are like unreasonable and absurd prayers, and are as truly an offence unto God.

alternative reading

A Reading from *The Spirit of Love* by William Law

God always was and always will be the same immutable will to all goodness. So that as certainly as he is the creator, so certainly is he the blesser of every created thing, and can give nothing but blessing, goodness, and happiness from himself because he has in himself nothing else to give. It is much more possible for the sun to give forth darkness than for God to do, or be, or give forth anything but blessing and goodness. Now this is the ground and origin of the spirit of love in the creature; it is and must be a will to all goodness, and you have not the spirit of love till you have this will to all goodness at all times and on all occasions. You may indeed do many works of love and delight in them, especially at such times as they are not inconvenient to you, or contradictory to your state or temper or occurrences in life. But the spirit of love is not in you till it is the spirit of your life, till you live freely, willingly, and universally according to it.

For every spirit acts with freedom and universality according to what it is. It needs no command to live its own life, or be what it is, no more than need bid wrath be wrathful. And therefore when love is the spirit of your life, it will have the freedom and universality of a spirit; it will always live and work in love, not because of this or here or there, but because the spirit of love can only love, wherever it is or goes or whatever is done to it. As the sparks know no motion but that of flying upwards, whether it be in the dark of the night or in the light of the day, so the spirit of love is always in the same course; it knows no difference of time, or persons, but whether it gives or forgives, bears or forbears, it is equally doing its own delightful work, equally blessed from itself. For the spirit of love, wherever it is, is its own blessing and happiness because it is the truth and reality of God in the soul, and therefore is in the same joy of life and is the same good to itself, everywhere and on every occasion.

April 11

George Augustus Selwyn

First Bishop of New Zealand, 1878

George Augustus Selwyn was born in 1809, educated at Cambridge and upon ordination became curate of Windsor. In 1841 he was made the first Bishop of New Zealand and remained there for twenty-seven years, during the first years travelling when few roads or bridges existed. In the wars between colonists and Maoris he stood out heroically for Maori rights, at the cost of fierce attacks from both sides and grave personal danger in his efforts to part the warriors, until later he was revered as one of the founders of New Zealand as well as of its church. He taught himself to navigate and gathered congregations in the Melanesian Islands. His constitution for the New Zealand church influenced the churches of the Anglican Communion and he was a chief founder of the Lambeth Conference of bishops. In 1868 he was persuaded to become the Bishop of Lichfield in England and died there on this day in 1878.

A Reading from a sermon of George Augustus Selwyn delivered before the University of Cambridge in 1854

In the mission-field, schism is an acknowledged evil. We make a rule, therefore, never to introduce controversy among a native people. If the ground has been preoccupied by any other religious body, we forbear to enter. And I can speak from observation, ranging over nearly half the Southern Pacific Ocean, that wherever this law of religious unity is adopted, there the gospel has its full and unchecked power. Missionaries must be ready at a moment to put their lives in their hands and go out to preach the gospel to others, with no weapon but prayer, and with no refuge but in God.

I have visited many of the islands in their days of darkness, and therefore I can rejoice in the light that now bursts upon them, from whatever quarter it may come. I feel that there is an episcopate of love as well as of authority, and that these simple teachers, scattered over the wide ocean, are objects of the same interest to me as Apollos was to Aquila. If in anything they lack knowledge, it seems to be our duty to "expound to them the way of God more perfectly," and to do this as their friend and brother, "not as having dominion over their faith, but as helpers of their joy."

Above all other things, it is our duty to guard against inflicting upon them the curses of our disunion, lest we make every little island in the ocean a counterpart of our own divided and contentious Church. And, further, I would point to the mission-field as the great outlet for the excited and sensitive spirit of the Church at home. There are minds which have placed before them an ideal perfection which can never be realized on earth. They burn with a zeal for God which cannot bear to be confined. Such men would be the very salt of the earth if they would but go out into the mission-field. There are five hundred millions of heathen still waiting for the gospel.

But how, you will ask, shall truth of doctrine be maintained if we tolerate in the mission-field every form of error, and provide no safeguard for the purity of the faith? I answer that, as running water purifies itself, so Christian work is seen to correct its own mistakes. Is it, then, a hope too unreasonable to be entertained, that the power which will heal the divisions of the Church at home may come from her distant fields of missionary work?

And now, my dear friends, I commend you to the grace of God's Holy Spirit. I go from hence if it be the will of God, to the most distant of all countries. There God has planted a standard of the cross, as a signal to his Church to fill up the intervening spaces. Fill up the void. The Spirit of God is ready to be poured out upon all flesh, and some of you are his chosen vessels. Again, I say, offer yourselves to the Primate of our Church. The voice of the Lord is asking, "Whom shall I send, and who will go for us?" May many of you who intend, by God's grace, to dedicate yourselves to the ministry, answer at once: "Here am I; send me."

April 17

Stephen Harding
Abbot of Citeaux, 1134

Robert of Molesme, Alberic and Stephen Harding, along with their companions, are honored as the founders of the New Monastery in 1098 which in a short while came to be called the Abbey of Citeaux. If the title of "founder" of the Cistercian Order can be ascribed to any one man that person would be Stephen Harding, elected abbot in 1101 until his death in 1134. Today, however, the charism of the founder of the Order is more usually located in the group of twenty abbots who assembled for the General Chapter of 1123, among whom most significantly was Bernard of Clairvaux. It was from Abbot Stephen that Bernard received his monastic formation, and if nothing else, Stephen Harding is honored for discernment in recognizing and fostering the outstanding gifts of this young monk. The desire of the Cistercians was to live the Rule of Saint Benedict *more integrally, to rediscover the meaning of the monastic life and to translate their discovery into structures adapted to their age. The white monks were not satisfied with compromises or accommodations. It was essential values that concerned them, not an archaeological reconstruction of a past monastic age.*

A Reading from the *Little Exordium*, one of the foundation documents of the Cistercian Order

The man of God, Alberic, after he had practiced faithfully the regular discipline in the school of Christ for nine and a half years, went home to the Lord, glorious in faith and virtues and deservedly rewarded by God in eternal life.

His successor was a brother by the name of Stephen, an Englishman by nationality, who had also come there with the others from Molesme, a lover of the *Rule* and of the new place. During his time the brethren, together with the abbot, forbade the duke of the country or any other lord to keep court at any time in that monastery as they used to do before at the big festivals.

In order that in the house of God, in which it was their desire to serve God directly day and night, nothing should remain that savored of pride and superfluity or that might eventually corrupt poverty, that safeguard of virtues, which they had chosen of their own free will, they resolved not to keep gold or silver crosses but only painted wooden ones; candelabra only of iron; thuribles only of copper or iron; chasubles only of wool or linen, without silk, gold or silver weave; albs or amices of linen only, also without silk or gold or silver. They eliminated the use of all kinds of elaborate coverings, copes, dalmatics and tunicles. But they retained silver chalices, not golden—though when it could be done, gold plated, as well as the communion tube of silver, gold plated if possible; stoles and maniples were of silk only, without gold or silver. They also ordered that the altar cloths be made of linen and without embroidery, and that the cruets should have nothing in gold or silver on them.

In those days the monastery increased in its possessions of land, vineyards, meadows and farmhouses; they did not decrease, however, in monastic discipline and therefore God visited that place at this time in pouring out his widest mercy over them; for they prayed, cried, and wept before him day and night, groaning long and deep, and had almost come to the brink of despair because they had no successors.

But God's mercy sent to that community many learned clerks as well as laymen who were both powerful and distinguished in the world. Thirty all at once entered with joy into the cells of the novitiate and by bravely combating their own vices and the temptation of evil spirits completed their course. Through their example old and young of every walk of life and from various parts of the world were encouraged when they saw through them that what they had feared impossible, that is the observance of the *Rule*, was in fact possible. So they began to flock together there in order to bow their proud necks under the sweet yoke of Christ, and to love fervently the rigorous and burdensome precepts of the *Rule*, and they began to make the community wonderfully happy and strong.

April 19

Alphege

Archbishop of Canterbury, Martyr, 1012

Alphege became a monk at Deerhurst near Gloucester and withdrew in later life to be a hermit in Somerset. The Archbishop of Canterbury, Dunstan, drew him back to be Abbot of Bath and, in 984, Bishop of Winchester. In 1005, he was made Archbishop of Canterbury, where his austere life and lavish almsgiving made him a revered and much-loved man. In the year 1011, the Danes overran south-east England, taking Alphege prisoner. They put the enormous ransom of £3000 (about $4500) *on his head, but Alphege refused to pay it and forbade anyone from doing so, knowing that it would impoverish the ordinary people even more. He was brutally murdered by his captors at Greenwich on this day in the year 1012.*

A Reading from the *Anglo-Saxon Chronicle*

In the year 1011 the king and his councilors sent to the Danish army and asked for peace, and promised them tribute and provisions on condition that they should cease their ravaging. They had already overrun much of the country. The disasters befell us through bad policy, in that they were never offered tribute in time nor fought against; but when they had done most to our injury, peace and truce were with them; and for all this truce and tribute they journeyed nonetheless in bands everywhere, and harried our wretched people, and plundered and killed them.

Then the Danes besieged the city of Canterbury between the Nativity of Saint Mary and Michaelmas Day, and eventually they got inside the city by treachery, for Aelfmaer, whose life Archbishop Alphege had saved, betrayed it. They captured the archbishop, and the king's reeve Aelfweard, and Abbess Leofrun of Minster-in-Thanet, and Bishop Godwine of Rochester; but they let Abbot Aelfmaer of Saint Augustine's monastery escape. So they took captive there all the ecclesiastics, men and women—it was impossible for any one to tell how many people that was—and they stayed afterwards in that borough as long as they pleased. After they had ransacked the whole burgh, they went to their ships, and took the archbishop with them.

Alphege became a captive, he who had been head of the English people and of Christendom. There could misery be seen where happiness was often seen before, in that wretched city from which first came to us Christianity and happiness in divine and secular things. The Danes kept the archbishop with them till the time when they martyred him.

Next year the Witan assembled at London for Easter, and stayed until the tribute had been paid. Then on the Saturday, the army became greatly incensed against the bishop because he would not promise them any money, and forbade that anything should be paid for him by way of ransom. They were also very drunk, for wine from the south had been brought there. They seized the bishop and brought him to their assembly on April 19, the eve of Low Sunday, and shamefully put him to death there. They pelted him with bones and ox-heads, until one of them struck him on the head with the back of an axe. He sank down with the blow, his holy blood falling on the ground, and he sent his holy soul to God's kingdom.

In the morning, his body was carried from Greenwich to London, and the bishops and citizens received it with all reverence and buried it in Saint Paul's Minster where God now reveals the powers of that holy martyr.

April 21

Anselm

Abbot of Le Bec, Archbishop of Canterbury,
Teacher of the Faith, 1109

Anselm was born in Aosta, northern Italy, in 1033. As a young man, he left home and traveled north, visiting many monasteries and other centers of learning. One such visit was to the abbey of Bec, where he met Lanfranc who advised him to embrace monastic life. Anselm had a powerful and original mind and, during his thirty-four years at Bec (as monk, prior and finally abbot), he taught many others and wrote theological, philosophical and devotional works. When Lanfranc died Anselm was made Archbishop of Canterbury and had to subordinate his scholarly work to the needs of the diocese and nation. Twice he endured exile for championing the rights of the Church against the authority of the king but, despite his stubbornness, intellectual rigor, and personal austerity, he was admired by the Norman nobility as well as loved by his monks. He died in 1109.

A Reading from the *Proslogion* of Anselm

[O my soul, have you found what you were looking for?
I was seeking God,
    and I have found that he is above all things,
    and that than which nothing greater can be thought.
I have found him to be
    life and light, wisdom and goodness,
    eternal blessedness and the bliss of eternity,
    existing everywhere and at all times.
If I have not found my God,
    what is it that I have found and understood
    so truly and certainly?

But if I have found him,
    why do I not experience what I have found?
Lord God, if my soul has found you,
    why has it no experience of you?]

O Lord my God,
    my creator and my re-creator,
    my soul longs for you.
Tell me what you are, beyond what I have seen,
    so that I may see clearly what I desire.
I strive to see more,
    but I see nothing beyond what I have seen,
    except darkness.
Or rather I do not see darkness
    which is no part of you,
    but I see that I cannot see further
    because of my own darkness.

Why is this, Lord?
    Are my eyes darkened by my weakness,
    or dazzled by your glory?
The truth is, I am darkened by myself
    and also dazzled by you.
    I am clouded by my own smallness
    and overwhelmed by your immensity;
    I am restricted by my own narrowness
    and mastered by your wideness.
It is indeed more than a creature can understand!

In truth, Lord, this is the light inaccessible in which you dwell.
Nothing can pierce through it to see you there.
    I cannot look directly into it,
    it is too great for me.
    But whatever I see, I see through it,
    like a weak eye that sees what it does by the light of the sun,
    though it cannot look at the sun itself.
    My understanding cannot take it in,
    it is too bright, I cannot receive it;
    the eye of my soul
    cannot bear to turn toward it for too long.

It is dazzled by its glory,
    mastered by its fullness,
    crushed by its immensity,
    confounded by its extent.

O Light, entire and inaccessible!
    Truth, whole and blessed!
How far you are from me who have come so close to you.
    How remote you are from my sight,
    while I am thus present in your sight.
    Everywhere you are entirely present,
    and I cannot see you.
    In you I move and have my being,
    and I cannot come to you.
    You are within me and around me,
    and I have no experience of you.

My God, I pray that I may so know you and love you
    that I may rejoice in you.
And if I may not do so fully in this life,
    let me go steadily on
    to the day when I come to that fullness.
Let the knowledge of you increase in me here,
    and there let it come to its fullness.
Let your love grow in me here,
    and there let it be fulfilled,
    so that here my joy may be in great hope,
    and there in full reality.

Lord, you have commanded, or rather advised us,
    to ask by your Son,
    and you have promised that we shall receive,
    "that our joy may be full."
That which you counsel
    through our "wonderful counselor"
    is what I am asking for, Lord.
    Let me receive
    that which you promised through your truth,
    "that my joy may be full."

God of truth,
I ask that I may receive
    so that my joy may be full.
Meanwhile let my mind meditate on it,
    let my tongue speak of it,
    let my heart love it,
    let my mouth preach it,
    let my soul hunger for it,
    my flesh thirst for it,
    and my whole being desire it,
    until I enter into the joy of my Lord,
    who is God one and triune, blessed for ever. Amen.

April 23

George

Martyr at Lydda, *c.*304

George was probably a soldier living in Palestine at the beginning of the fourth century. He was martyred at Lydda in about the year 304, the beginning of the Diocletian persecution, and became known throughout the East as "The Great Martyr." The story of his slaying the dragon is probably due to his being mistaken in iconography for Saint Michael, himself usually depicted wearing armor; or it may again be a mistaken identity representing Perseus's slaying of the sea monster, a myth also associated with the area of Lydda. George replaced Edward the Confessor as Patron Saint of England following the Crusades, when returning soldiers brought back with them a renewed cult of Saint George.

A Reading from a sermon of Peter Damian

My dear people, today's feast increases our joy in the glory of Eastertide like a precious jewel whose shining beauty adds to the splendor of the gold in which it is set.

Saint George, whom we commemorate today, moved from one kind of military service to another, exchanging the earthly office of tribune for the ranks of the army of Christ. Like a well disciplined soldier he first jettisoned the burden of his earthly possessions by giving all he had to the poor. Once free and unencumbered, and wearing the breastplate of faith, he was able to advance into the thick of the battle like a valiant soldier of Christ. From this we learn a clear lesson, that we cannot fight properly and boldly for the faith if we are frightened of losing our earthly possessions.

We are told that not only did Saint George fight against an evil king, but burning with the fire of the Holy Spirit and invincibly defended by the banner of the cross, he also defeated the Prince of this evil world in the person of his minion, encouraging the soldiers of Christ to bear themselves valiantly. Clearly, he had at his side the supreme and invisible Judge, who by his free choice allowed the hands of the evil to wreak their violence on Saint George. God gave the body of his martyr over to murderers, while guarding and protecting his soul unceasingly, defended as it was by the unconquerable fortress of faith.

So my dear people, let us not merely admire this soldier of the heavenly army: let us also imitate him. Let us lift our minds to the contemplation of that heavenly reward, fixing our hearts on it, never flinching whether the world smiles on us with its blandishments or menaces us with threats. And following the advice of Saint Paul, let us purify ourselves from every stain whether of body or soul, so that we too may in time be found worthy to enter that temple of blessedness on which our minds are fixed.

For all who wish to sacrifice themselves to God in the tabernacle of Christ, which is the Church, must first be cleansed by washing in the sacred font of baptism, and then be clothed in various garments, by which is meant virtues; as it is written in Scripture: "Let your priests be clothed with righteousness." For those who in baptism are reborn as a new creation in Christ must not put on again the signs of mortality; they have discarded their old humanity and put on the new, and now live in Christ, and will be continually renewed as they strive to live a pure life.

And so, purged of the stain of our old sin and radiant with the brightness of our new way of life, let us celebrate the paschal mystery by truly imitating the example of the blessed martyrs.

alternative reading

A Reading from a commentary on the Psalms
by Ambrose of Milan

Just as there are many kinds of persecution, so there are many forms of martyrdom. You are a witness to Christ every day of your lives.

For example, you are a martyr for Christ when, mindful of the coming judgement of Christ, you maintain a chastity of body and mind in the face of the enticements of sexual promiscuity. You are a witness for Christ when, in the light of God's commandments, you resist the greed that would seize the possessions of a minor or violate the rights of a defenseless widow, and instead of inflicting injury offer them help. Christ wants such witnesses at his side. As Scripture declares: "Defend the orphan, plead for the widow, and come let us reason together, says the Lord." You are a witness for Christ when you resist pride, when on seeing the poor and needy, you tenderly take pity on them, preferring humility to arrogance. In all this you give your testimony not merely with your lips but with your deeds.

Who is a more reliable witness than one who, by observing the precepts of the gospel, "confesses that Jesus Christ has come in the flesh?" For those who hear but who do not act are denying Christ, even though they may confess outwardly with their lips, their deeds repudiate their words. To the many who cry out "Lord, Lord, did we not prophesy in your name, cast out demons and do many mighty deeds?" Christ will reply on that day: "Depart from me, all you workers of evil." A witness is one who testifies to the precepts of the Lord Jesus and supports his deposition by deeds.

Many are martyrs of Christ and confess the Lord Jesus each day in secret. This kind of martyrdom and faithful witnessing to Christ was known to the apostle Paul, who said: "Our boast is this, the testimony of our conscience." How many people have confessed outwardly but denied inwardly? It is said: "Do not trust every spirit, but by their fruits you shall know which ones you should believe."

Therefore my people, in interior persecutions be faithful and strong, so that you may be found worthy in any public persecutions. Even in interior persecutions we encounter kings and governors, judges whose power over us is frightening. You have an example in the temptations which assailed the Lord.

Elsewhere in Scripture we read: "Let not sin reign in your mortal bodies." If a sense of guilt controls you, you will feel as if you are constantly being accused by various kings, governors who are set over sinners. There are as many such kings as there are sins and vices; before these we are brought and before these we stand. These figures have their judgement-seats in our mind. But those who confess Christ, immediately depose them from their throne in the soul, and take them prisoner. For the judgement-seat of the devil cannot remain in place within us when Christ is enthroned.

April 25

Saint Mark the Evangelist

John Mark was a Jew and, according to Paul's Letter to the Colossians, was cousin to Barnabas. He accompanied Barnabas and Paul on their first missionary journey. Afterwards, he went to Cyprus with Barnabas and to Rome with first Paul and then Peter. The Gospel that bears his name is generally regarded as the earliest and was most likely written while he was in Rome. It was probably based as much on Peter's preaching of the good news as on Mark's own memory. Mark's Gospel has a sharpness and an immediacy about it, and he does not spare the disciples in noting their weaknesses and lack of understanding that Jesus the Christ would suffer for the world's redemption. Sharing in the glory of the resurrection means sharing in the giving of self, both in body and spirit, even to death; sharing the gospel was for all, in essence both excessively generous and ultimately sacrificial.

A Reading from the treatise *Against the Heresies*
by Irenaeus

Although the Church is spread throughout the world, even to the ends of the earth, it has received from the apostles and their followers the faith it professes.

It believes in one God, the Father Almighty, the creator of heaven and earth, the sea, and all that is in them; and in one Jesus Christ, the Son of God, who became incarnate for our salvation; and in the Holy Spirit, who announced through the prophets the purposes of God, the advent of our Lord Jesus Christ, his birth from the Virgin, his passion, his resurrection from the dead, and his bodily ascension into heaven, and his future manifestation from heaven in the glory of the Father "to gather up all things in one," and to raise to life all human flesh, in order that in accordance with the will of the invisible Father, "every knee in heaven and earth and under the earth shall bow" before Christ Jesus, our Lord and God, our Savior and our King, and every tongue acknowledge him, and the whole creation be brought to his just judgement. Those who have sinned, be they angels, be they mortals who have renounced their faith, who have behaved profanely or who are unrighteous, shall be condemned to the eternal fire; whereas those who are righteous and holy, who have kept God's commandments faithfully, who have persevered in love whether from the outset of their lives, or by repenting of their evil actions, through the exercise of his grace shall be received into eternal glory.

As I have observed, this is the preaching and the faith which the Church although scattered throughout the world, continues to maintain carefully as if it lived together in one house. The church believes these truths as if it had but one soul, one heart, proclaiming them and teaching them and handing them on to others as if it spoke with one mouth. Although there are many different languages in the world, the content of the tradition is one and the same.

The beliefs of the Church planted in Germany are in accord with those of the Church in Spain and Gaul, the Church in the East, Egypt, Libya and Jerusalem, the center of the world. Just as the sun, that creature of God, is identical wherever it shines throughout the whole world, so too the preaching of the truth shines everywhere, and enlightens all who wish to know the truth.

Someone who is an eloquent speaker among the leaders of the churches will teach nothing different from what I have outlined, for no one is greater than his master; nor will someone less gifted in eloquence be able to diminish the tradition. Our Christian faith is one and the same, and no matter how much you preach, you will never add to it; and no matter how little you say, the tradition will always be bigger than you.

April 28

Peter Chanel

Missionary in the South Pacific, Martyr, 1841

Peter Chanel was born at Cras in France in 1803 and, after ordination, joined the Marist missionary congregation in 1831. In 1836 he was sent to the islands of the South Pacific to preach the faith. Peter and his companions brought healing medicines as well as the gospel and were much loved and respected. On the island of Futuna in the Fiji group, where Peter was living, the chief's son asked for baptism, which so infuriated his father that he dispatched a group of warriors with explicit orders to murder Peter. They attacked him with clubs, axes and knives and he died on this day in the year 1841. Within a year, the whole island was Christian, and Peter became revered throughout the Pacific Islands and Australasia as its protomartyr.

A Reading from *A History of Christian Missions*
by Stephen Neill

The island of New Caledonia in the South Pacific, twice as large as Corsica, was first surveyed by the missionary Society of Mary (Marists) as a mission field in 1843. Four years later the murder of a lay brother led them to withdraw, but in 1851 the work was resumed.

An unexpected set of problems arose when France annexed the island and decided to convert it into a penal settlement. The discovery of the valuable minerals cobalt, chromium, and nickel led to an influx of prospectors and to the commercial exploitation of the islands; the indigenous population tended increasingly to be driven away into the mountainous and less fertile regions. Here was the classic case of the clash between an unsympathetic western civilization and a primitive and helpless people. Christian missions, Protestant as well as Roman Catholic, were the only hope of the New Caledonian people. The struggle was long and arduous, but the ordination of the first New Caledonian priest, a little more than a century after the arrival of the first missionaries, is evidence of the stirring of new life in a people that had been threatened with extinction.

The attempt of the Marists to enter Tonga was for a long time prevented by the solid opposition of the Protestants, headed by the redoubtable King George. Foiled in their first attempt, the Fathers wisely concentrated on two islands in the Fiji group which were still untouched by Protestantism, Wallis and Futuna. Both became wholly Roman Catholic islands.

Peter Chanel was born in France in 1803. As a young priest he worked for three years in a run-down country parish until 1831 when he was accepted as a member by the Marists. In 1836 he was one of a group of missionaries who arrived on the islands. He and two lay brothers were stationed on Futuna, an island where cannibalism had only recently been forbidden by the local ruler, Niuliki. They were at first well received; but, when Peter had learned something of the language and gained the people's confidence, jealousy and fear were aroused in Niuliki. This was aggravated by the conversion and baptism of his son and other young men.

Three years after his arrival, Peter Chanel was set upon by the local ruler's men and clubbed to death on April 28, 1841. When called on to justify his conversion to Christianity, one of Peter's catechumens spoke of him, "He loves us; he does what he teaches; he forgives his enemies. His teaching is good."

Today Peter Chanel is honored as the first martyr of the Pacific Islands, and the patron saint not only of the islands, but of Australasia.

April 29

Catherine of Siena

Teacher of the Faith, 1380

Catherine Benincasa was born in 1347, the second youngest of twenty-five children. Pious from her earliest years, she overcame family opposition to her vocation and became a Dominican tertiary at the age of eighteen. Nourished by a life of contemplative prayer and mystical experience, she devoted herself to active care for the poor and sick. She became increasingly sought after as an adviser on political as well as religious matters and, in 1376, she journeyed to Avignon as an ambassador to the Pope and influenced his decision to return to Rome. She wrote a Dialogue *on the spiritual life as well as numerous letters of counsel and direction, which stressed her devotion to the Precious Blood of Jesus. She suffered a stroke on April 21 and died eight days later, on this day in the year 1380.*

A Reading from *The Dialogue* by Catherine of Siena

Thanks be to you, eternal Father, that you have not despised me, your handiwork, nor turned your face from me, nor made light of my desires. In your light you have given me light. In your wisdom I have come to know the truth; in your mercy I have found your charity and affection for my neighbors. What has compelled you? Not my virtues, but only your charity.

Let this same love compel you to enlighten the eye of my understanding with the light of faith, so that I may know your truth, which you have revealed to me. Let my memory be great enough to hold your favors, and set my will ablaze in your charity's fire. Let that fire burst the seed of my body and bring forth blood; then with that blood, given for love of your blood, and with the key of obedience, let me unlock heaven's gate.

O eternal Trinity! O Godhead! That Godhead, your divine nature, gave the price of your Son's blood its value. You, eternal Trinity, are a deep sea. The more I enter you, the more I discover, and the more I discover, the more I seek you. You are insatiable, you in whose depth the soul is sated yet remains always hungry for you, thirsty for you, eternal Trinity, longing to see you with the light in your light. Just as the deer longs for the fountain of living water, so does my soul long to escape from the prison of my darksome body and see you in truth. O how long will you hide your face from my eyes?

O eternal Trinity, fire and abyss of charity, dissolve this very day the cloud of my body! I am driven to desire, in the knowledge of yourself that you have given me in your truth, to leave behind the weight of this body of mine and give my life for the glory and praise of your name. For by the light of understanding within your light I have tasted and seen your depth, eternal Trinity, and the beauty of your creation. Then, when I considered myself in you, I saw that I am your image. You have gifted me with power from yourself, eternal Father, and my understanding with your wisdom—such wisdom as is proper to your only-begotten Son; and the Holy Spirit, who proceeds from you and from your Son, has given me a will, and so I am able to love.

You, eternal Trinity, are the craftsman; and I your handiwork have come to know that you are in love with the beauty of what you have made, since you made of me a new creation in the blood of your Son.

O abyss! O eternal Godhead! O deep sea! What more could you have given me than the gift of your very self?

MAY

May 1

Saint Philip and Saint James
Apostles

Philip and James appear in the list of the twelve apostles in the first three Gospels, but are frequently confused with other early saints who share their names. In John's Gospel, Philip has a more prominent role, being the third of the apostles to be called by Jesus and then himself bringing his friend Nathanael to the Lord. Philip is presented as the spokesman for the other apostles who are questioning the capacity for feeding the five thousand and, at the Last Supper, enters into a dialogue with Jesus which leads to the "Farewell Discourses" of our Lord. James is said to be the son of Alphæus and is often known as "James the Less" to distinguish him from James the brother of John. He may also be the "James the Younger" who, in Mark's Gospel, is a witness at the Crucifixion. Both apostles are commemorated on the same day because the Church in Rome where their relics rest was dedicated on this day in the year 560.

A Reading from a homily of John Chrysostom

The cross brought conviction to the world and drew the whole world to itself through the work of uneducated people. They succeeded not by preaching trivia, but by speaking of God, of true religion, of a way of living the gospel, and of the coming judgement. It turned peasants and illiterate folk alike into philosophers. See how the foolishness of God is wiser than human wisdom, and his weakness stronger! In what way was it stronger? It was stronger because it turned the world upside down; it gripped people, although countless individuals were busy trying to suppress the name of the Crucified, they only succeeded in promoting its cause. It flourished and grew; by contrast, they perished and withered away. The living who were fighting him who had died proved powerless.

And so, when the Greek tells me that I am a fool, all that he is doing is revealing his own foolishness. He thinks me a fool, but in reality I am wiser than the wise. When he ridicules me as being weak, he only demonstrates his own greater weakness. For by the grace of God, tax collectors and fishermen had the strength to achieve noble things, such things as neither monarchs nor orators nor philosophers, in a word, not the entire world searching in every direction, could even imagine.

Reflecting on this, Paul said: "The weakness of God is stronger than human strength." It is clear from this as well that the gospel is divine. For how else could twelve illiterate men have been inspired to attempt such enormous feats, men who lived on the banks of lakes or rivers, or in deserts? How else could it have occurred to these men, men who had scarcely ventured into a city or the forum, to take on the entire world? It is apparent from the gospel narratives that they were cowardly and timid. The scriptures never attempt to make excuses for them or to cover up their failings. In itself this is compelling evidence of the truth. What then does the gospel say about them? That after the innumerable miracles they had seen Christ perform, when he was arrested, some of them fled, and the one disciple who stayed behind denied him, and he was chief among them!

So then, here we have people who failed to stand up to the Jews when Christ was alive; and yet no sooner was Christ dead and buried, than they take on the whole world. How can this be unless Christ rose from the dead, talked with them and put fresh heart into them? If it were not so, would they have not have said to themselves: "What is all this? If Christ did not have the strength to save himself, how can he protect us? He did not defend himself when he was alive, so will he reach out his hand to defend us now that he is dead? When he was alive he did not conquer a single nation, so how shall we convince the entire world by speaking his name?"

Would it not have been foolish to conceive of such an enterprise, let alone actually to do it? Surely it is obvious that if the disciples had not seen Jesus risen from the dead and received clear evidence of his power, they would never have risked such a gamble.

May 2

Athanasius

Bishop of Alexandria, Teacher of the Faith, 373

Athanasius was born in about the year 296 of Christian parents and educated at the Catechetical School in Alexandria. He was present at the Council of Nicæa as a deacon, accompanying his bishop Alexander, whom he succeeded as Patriarch of Alexandria in 328. Athanasius held firmly to the doctrines of the Church as defined by that Council, and became the leader of those opposed to the teachings of Arianism which denied the divinity of Christ. He was deposed from and restored to his see several times because of his uncompromising faith. In or out of exile, Athanasius continued to write. Ever the proponent of orthodoxy over heterodoxy, he expounded the need for the Church to teach the true doctrines of the faith rather than watered-down versions of it. He was a strong believer in asceticism as a means of restoring the divine image in humanity and thus a supporter of monasticism, which was in its nascent state at that time. He was a friend of Pachomius and wrote the Life of Antony of Egypt, *which portrayed the monastic life as holding a balance between things earthly and heavenly. He died on this day in 373.*

A Reading from the treatise
On the Incarnation of the Word
by Athanasius of Alexandria

The Word of God, incorporeal, incorruptible, and immaterial, entered our world. Yet it was not as if the Word had ever been remote from it. Indeed, there is no part of creation deprived of his presence; together with his Father, he fills everything, everywhere, at all times.

In the loving-kindness of God the Word came to us, and was revealed among us openly. He took pity on the human race and on our weakness; he was moved by our corruption and our impotence to help ourselves; he saw our evil ways, and how little by little we were increasing in evil to an intolerable pitch of self-destruction; and lastly, he realized that he could no longer allow death to rule over us. Had death prevailed, creation would have perished, and the Father's work in fashioning us would have been in vain.

The Word, therefore, took to himself a body no different from our own, for he did not wish to be in just any body or simply to be seen. If he had wanted simply to be seen, he would have chosen another and nobler body. But he took our human body in all its particularity for his own, a body born of a pure and spotless virgin, who had had no sexual relations and who was therefore undefiled. The mighty creator built himself a temple within the Virgin's body, making it an instrument in which to dwell and to reveal himself.

In this way the Word received from human nature a body like our own; and since all are subject to the corruption of death, he surrendered his body to death for us all, and with supreme love offered it to the Father. His purpose in so doing was to destroy the law of corruption which was operating against us, since all humankind may be held to have died in him. This law, which spent its force on the Lord's body, could no longer have any power over those who share his humanity. Furthermore, this was the way in which the Word was able to restore the human race to immortality after it had fallen into corruption, and summon it back to life. As fire consumes straw, so he utterly destroyed the power that death had over us by means of the body he assumed and by the grace of the resurrection.

This was the reason why the Word assumed a mortal body, so that this body, sharing in the Word who is above all, might satisfy death's requirement in place of all. Through the indwelling Word, it would remain incorruptible, and by the grace of the resurrection, it would be freed for ever from corruption. In death the Word made a spotless sacrifice, an oblation of the body he had assumed. By dying for others, he immediately banished death for all humankind.

In this way the Word of God, who is above all, dedicated and offered his temple, the instrument that was his body, for us all, thus paying the debt that was owed. The immortal Son of God, united with all human beings by likeness of nature, fulfilled the requirements of justice, restoring humankind to immortality by the promise of the resurrection. The corruption of death no longer holds any power over men and women because of the Word who has come to dwell among us in his one body.

May 4

Monnica
Mother of Augustine of Hippo, 387

Monnica was born in North Africa of Christian parents in 332. She was married to a pagan, Patricius, whom she converted to Christianity. They had three children of whom the most famous was her eldest child, Augustine. Indeed, Augustine ascribed his conversion to the example and devotion of his mother: "She never left me out of her prayers that you, O God, might say to the widow's son 'Young man, I tell you arise' "—which is why the Gospel of the widow of Nain is customarily read at the Eucharist today as her memorial. Monnica's husband died when she was forty. Her desire had been to be buried alongside him, but this was not to be. She died in Italy, at Ostia, in the year 387 on her way home to North Africa with her two sons.

A Reading from the *Confessions* of Augustine

Monnica was the kind of person she was because she was taught by you, Lord, her inward teacher, in the school of her heart. The day was imminent when she was to depart this life (the day which you knew and we did not). It came about, as I believe by your providence through your hidden ways, that she and I were standing leaning out of a window overlooking a garden. It was at the house where we were staying at Ostia on the Tiber, where, far removed from the crowds, after the exhaustion of a long journey, we were recovering our strength for the voyage.

[Alone with each other, we talked very intimately. "Forgetting the past and reaching forward to what lies ahead," we were searching together in the presence of the truth which is you yourself. We asked what quality of life the eternal life of the saints will have, a life which "neither eye has seen nor ear heard, nor has it entered into the heart of man." But with the mouth of the heart wide open, we drank in the waters flowing from your spring on high, the spring of life which is with you. Sprinkled with this dew to the limit of our capacity, our minds attempted in some degree to reflect on so great a reality. The conversation led us toward the conclusion that the pleasure of the bodily senses, however delightful in the radiant light of this physical world, is seen by comparison with the life of eternity to be not even worth considering.]

As we talked on, my mother said, "My son, as for myself, I now find no pleasure in this life. What I have still to do here and why I am here, I do not know. My hope in this world is already fulfilled. The one reason why I wanted to stay longer in this life was my desire to see you a Catholic Christian before I die. My God has granted this in a way more than I had hoped. For I see you despising this world's success to become his servant. What have I to do here?"

The reply I made to this I do not well recall, for within five days or not much more she fell sick of a fever. While she was ill, on one day she suffered loss of consciousness and gradually became unaware of things around her. We ran to be with her, but she quickly recovered consciousness. She looked at me and my brother standing beside her, and said to us in the manner of someone looking for something, "Where was I?" Then seeing us struck dumb with grief, she said: "Bury your mother here."

I kept silence and fought back my tears. But my brother, as if to cheer her up, said something to the effect that he hoped she would be buried not in a foreign land but in her home country. When she heard that, her face became worried and her eyes looked at him in reproach that he should think that. She looked in my direction and said, "See what he says," and soon said to both of us "Bury my body anywhere you like. Let no anxiety about that disturb you. I have only one request to make of you, that you remember me at the altar of the Lord, wherever you may be." She explained her thought in such words as she could speak, then fell silent as the pain of her sickness became worse. "Nothing," she said, "is distant from God, and there is no ground for fear that he may not acknowledge me at the end of the world and raise me up."

On the ninth day of her illness, when she was aged fifty-six, and I was thirty-three, this religious and devout soul was released from the body.

May 8

Julian of Norwich

Spiritual Writer, *c.*1417

On this day in the year 1373, when she was thirty years old and suffering from what was considered to be a terminal illness, a woman of Norwich, whose own name is unrecorded, experienced a series of sixteen visions, which revealed aspects of the love of God. Following her recovery, she spent the next twenty years of her life pondering their meaning, eventually recording her conclusions in what became the first book written by a woman in English, Revelations of Divine Love. *At an unknown point in her life, she became an anchoress attached to the Church of Saint Julian in Norwich, and it was by this name of Julian that she came to be known to later generations. She died around the year 1417.*

A Reading from the conclusion to the *Revelations of Divine Love* by Julian of Norwich

This book was begun by the gift and grace of God. I do not think it is done yet. We all need to pray God for charity. God is working in us, helping us to thank and trust and enjoy him. Thus does our good Lord will that we should pray. This is what I understood his meaning to be throughout, and in particular when he uttered those sweet, cheering words, "I am the foundation of your praying." I knew truly that the reason why our Lord showed it was that he wants it to be better known than it is. It is by our knowing this that he gives us grace to love and to hold to him. He regards his heavenly treasure on earth with so much love that he wants us to have all the greater light and consolation in the joys of heaven. So he draws our hearts away from the sorry murk in which they live.

From the time these things were first revealed I had often wanted to know what was our Lord's meaning. It was more than fifteen years after that I was answered in my spirit's understanding. "You would know our Lord's meaning in this thing! Know it well. Love was his meaning. Who showed it you? Love. What did he show you? Love. Why did he show you? Love. Why did he show it? For love. Hold on to this and you will know and understand love more and more. But you will not know or learn anything else—ever!"

So it was that I learned that love was our Lord's meaning. And I saw for certain, both here and elsewhere, that before ever he made us, God loved us; and that his love has never slackened, nor ever shall. In this love all his works have been done, and in this love he has made everything serve us; and in this love our life is everlasting. Our beginning was when we were made, but the love in which he made us never had beginning. In it we have our beginning.

All this we shall see in God for ever. May Jesus grant this. Amen.

May 9

Gregory

Bishop of Nazianzus, 389

Gregory of Nazianzus and Basil of Caesarea were two friends bound together by their desire to promote and defend the divinity of Christ as proclaimed in the Nicene Creed. This was against the seemingly overwhelming pressure from both church and state for the establishment of Arianism, which denied Christ's divinity and thus the whole Christian doctrine of the Trinity. Basil was renowned for being headstrong and forceful in comparison to his friend Gregory, who would rather spend his days in prayer and living the simple, ascetic life. Gregory's brilliance in oratory and theological debate meant that a hidden life was virtually impossible and Basil drew him into the forefront of the controversy. Their joint persuasive eloquence convinced the first Council of Constantinople, meeting in 381, that their teaching was the truly orthodox one and the Council ratified the text of the Nicene Creed in the form it is used in the East to this day. Basil died in 379 and Gregory ten years later in 389.

A Reading from an oration "On the Love of the Poor"
by Gregory of Nazianzus

Recognize to whom you owe the fact that you exist, that you breathe, that you understand, that you are wise, and, above all, that you know God and hope for the kingdom of heaven and the vision of glory, now darkly and as in a mirror but then with greater fullness and purity. You have been made a child of God, a co-heir with Christ. Where did you get all this, and from whom?

Now let me turn to what is of less importance: the visible world around us. What benefactor has enabled you to look out upon the beauty of the sky, the sun in its course, the circle of the moon, the countless number of stars, with the harmony and order that are theirs, like the music of a harp? Who has blessed you with rain, with the art of husbandry, with different kinds of food, with the arts, with houses, with laws, with states, with a life of humanity and culture, with friendship and the easy familiarity of kinship?

Who has given you dominion over animals, both those that are tame and those that provide you with food? Who has made you master of everything on earth? In short, who has endowed you with all that makes humankind superior to all other living creatures? Is it not God who asks you now in your turn to show yourself generous above all other creatures and for the sake of all other creatures? Because we have received from God so many wonderful gifts, will we not be ashamed to refuse him this one thing only, our generosity? Though he is God and Lord he is not afraid to be known as our Father. Shall we for our part repudiate those who are our kith and kin?

Friends, let us never allow ourselves to misuse what has been given us by God's gift. If we do, we shall hear Saint Peter say: "Be ashamed of yourselves for holding on to what belongs to someone else. Resolve to imitate God's justice, and no one will be poor." Let us not labor to heap up and hoard riches while others remain in need. If we do, the prophet Amos will speak out against us with sharp and threatening words: "Come now, you that say: When will the new moon be over, so that we may start selling? When will sabbath be over, so that we may start opening our treasures?"

Let us put into practice the supreme and primary law of God. He sends down rain on the righteous and sinful alike, and causes the sun to rise on all without distinction. To all earth's creatures he has given the broad earth, the springs, the rivers and the forests. He has given the air to the birds, and the waters to those who live in water. He has given abundantly to all the basic needs of life, not as a private possession, not restricted by law, not divided by boundaries, but as common to all, amply and in rich measure. His gifts are not deficient in any way, because he wanted to give equality of blessing to equality of worth, and to show the abundance of his generosity.

May 15

Pachomius

Founder of cenobitic monasticism, 346

Pachomius is honored as the first Christian monk who not simply tried to bring hermits together in groups, but actually organized them with a written Rule *and structures of a communal life* (cenobium). *He is said to have been born in Upper Egypt, of pagan parents, and to have been a conscript in the imperial army. Upon discharge he was converted and baptized. He became a disciple of a hermit, and then in about 320, founded a monastery at Tabennisi near the Nile. He used his military experience to organize his growing number of followers, and by the time of his death in 346 he was ruling as abbot-general over nine monasteries for men and two for women. He is honored, therefore, as the founder of cenobitic monasticism.*

A Reading from the *Sarum Lectures* of David Knowles

Monasticism, as its etymology suggests, began with an individual's retirement from the world. Saint Antony the Great, usually known as the first monk, was in fact an anchorite and not the first of that family; but unlike the "pure" hermits, such as Saint Paul of Egypt, he ultimately became the leader of a numerous family to whom he gave instructions and permanent help even when he had retired finally into the desert land near the Red Sea. But in the story of cenobitic monasticism the first name is Pachomius, the father of monks of the common life, who, like Saint Benedict, began as an anchorite but became in 315, as he thought under divine inspiration, the founder of a family of monks living and working together. Recruits came in floods, and when he died he was the father of a large group of monasteries containing possibly five thousand inmates.

Besides writing a Rule, Pachomius also organized every detail of a great institution. When he died, we might almost say that a perfect monastic order was in existence. Not only was all the material framework there—church, refectory, assembly room, cells, enclosure wall—not only was the daily life of prayer and work in all its parts arranged, not only was the spiritual discipline of chastity, poverty and obedience wisely established, but the whole complex was knit together by firm strands of control.

Within each monastery were numerous houses, each containing thirty or forty monks practicing a particular craft. These houses themselves might be thirty or forty in number, making up a settlement of between one and a half and two thousand souls. Within the houses were parties of ten or so under a foreman. Each house was governed by a master, and each monastery by a father or abbot. Pachomius himself remained at the head and lived in the head house of the whole institute.

At every level the superior could direct and transfer his monks and at every level there were regular reunions for spiritual conference and advice. In the monasteries there was, alongside the abbot, a minister who dealt with all economic matters—supplies of food and raw materials, distribution and sale of necessaries and products. Pachomius himself visited all the houses repeatedly, and twice a year there was a general gathering in his monastery. At Easter all came up to celebrate the Pasch and to baptize any catechumens, and at mid-August all the procurators or ministers came up to render an account of the year's workings. It was a remarkable achievement of planning and discipline.

May 19

Dunstan

Archbishop of Canterbury, Restorer of Monastic Life, 988

Dunstan was born near Glastonbury around 910 into a noble family. He received a good education and spent time at the court of the King of Wessex. A saintly uncle urged him to enter the monastic life; he delayed, but followed the advice on recovering from an illness. Returning to Glastonbury, Dunstan lived as a monk, devoting his work time to creative pursuits: illuminating, music, and metalwork. In 943 the new king made him abbot, and this launched a great revival of monastic life in England. Starting with Glastonbury, Dunstan restored discipline to several monasteries and promoted study and teaching. Under two later kings, he rose to political and ecclesiastical eminence, being chief minister and Archbishop of Canterbury under King Edgar. This enabled him and his followers to extend his reforms to the whole English Church. He is reputed to be the author of the coronation oath. In 970, Dunstan fell from political favor but continued as Archbishop of Canterbury, preaching and teaching. He died in the year 988.

A Reading from the earliest *Life of Saint Dunstan*
by an unknown author

Dunstan diligently studied the books of the Irish pilgrims to Glastonbury, meditating on the path of the true faith, and always explored with critical scrutiny the books of other wise men which he perceived from the deep vision of his heart to be confirmed by the assertions of the holy fathers. Thus he controlled his way of life so that, as often as he examined the books of the divine scriptures, God spoke with him. Indeed, as often as he was released from secular cares and delighted with leisure for prayer, he seemed himself to speak with God.

Among his sacred studies of literature he also diligently cultivated the art of writing, that he might be sufficient in all things; and the art of harp-playing, and also skill in painting. He was, so to speak, a skilled investigator of all useful things.

At length when King Athelstan was dead, and the condition of the kingdom changed, the authority of the succeeding king, namely Edmund, ordered the blessed Dunstan, who was of approved way of life and erudite conversation, to appear before him, that he might be chosen and numbered among the royal courtiers and chief men of the palace. Not rashly resisting these orders, but rather remembering the Lord's command, he hastened to render to the king the things that were the king's, and to God the things that were God's.

Throughout his life it was his chief care to occupy himself constantly and frequently in sacred prayers and in the ten-stringed psalmody of David; or to pass the night in vigils, overcoming sweet sleep; or to sweat and labor in the concerns of the Church; or also, when he could see the first light of daybreak, to correct faulty books, erasing the errors of the scribes; or, giving judgement with a keen intelligence between individuals, to distinguish the true from the false; or by calm words to bring to harmony and peace all who were at enmity or quarrelling; or to benefit with his kind support widows, orphans, pilgrims and strangers in their necessities; or to dissolve by just separation foolish or wrongful marriages; or to strengthen by the word of life or by example the whole human order, triply divided in its proper and stable design; or with serene probity to support and enrich the churches of God by just contribution of his own procuring or from other sources; or to season with the celestial salt, that is, with the teaching of wholesome knowledge, the ignorant of both sexes, men and women, whoever he could, by day and night.

Thus it was that the English land was filled with Dunstan's holy teaching, shining before God and mortals alike as the sun and moon. When he resolved to render to Christ the Lord the due hours of his service and celebrations of masses, he so performed and recited them with his whole soul that he seemed to speak face to face with the Lord himself, even though beforehand he may have been much vexed by the agitated disputes of people. And as often as he fitly and splendidly discharged any other duties of his episcopal office, he always did so with a great flow of tears which the invisible indweller, the Holy Spirit, who constantly dwelt in him, mightily drew forth from the rivers of his eyes.

May 20

Alcuin

Deacon, Abbot of Tours, 804

Alcuin was descended from a noble Northumbrian family. Although the date and place of his birth are not known, he was probably born in the year 735 in or near York. He entered the cathedral school there as a child, continued as a scholar and became the Master. In 781, he went to Aachen as adviser to Charlemagne on religious and educational matters, and as Master of the Palace School, where he established an important library. Although not a monk and in deacon's orders, in 796 he became Abbot of Tours, where he died in 804. Alcuin wrote poetry, revised the lectionary, compiled a sacramentary and was involved in other significant liturgical work.

A Reading from a letter of Alcuin to Higbald, Bishop of Lindisfarne and his monks, condoling with them for the sack of Lindisfarne by the Danes on June 8, 793

The intimacy of your love used to rejoice me greatly when I was with you; but conversely, the calamity of your tribulation saddens me greatly every day, though I am absent; when the pagans desecrated the sanctuaries of God, and poured out the blood of saints around the altar, laid waste the house of our hope, trampled on the bodies of saints in the temple of God like dung in the street. What can we say except lament in our soul with you before Christ's altar, and say: "Spare, O Lord, spare your people, and do not give your inheritance to Gentiles, lest the pagan say, 'Where is the God of the Christians?'"

What assurance is there for the churches of Britain, if Saint Cuthbert, with so great a number of saints, defends not his own? Either this is the beginning of greater tribulation, or else the sins of the inhabitants have called it upon them. Truly it has not happened by chance, but is a sign that it was well merited by someone. But now, you who are left, stand manfully, fight bravely, defend the camp of God.

Yet do not be dismayed at this calamity. God chastises every son whom he receives; and thus perhaps he chastised you more harshly because he loved you more. Jerusalem, the city loved by God, perished with the temple of God in the flames of the Chaldeans. Rome, encircled by a crown of holy apostles and innumerable martyrs, was shattered by the ravages of pagans, but by the pity of God soon recovered. Almost the whole of Europe was laid desolated by the fire and sword of the Goths and Huns; but now, by God's mercy, it shines adorned with churches, as the sky with stars, and in them the offices of the Christian religion flourish and increase. Exhort yourselves in turn, saying: "Let us return to the Lord our God, for he is bountiful to forgive, and never deserts them that hope in him."

My brothers, let us love what is eternal, and not what is perishable. Let us esteem true riches, not fleeting ones, eternal, not transitory. Let us acquire praise from God, and not from mortals. Let us do what the saints did whom we praise. Let us follow their footsteps on earth, that we may deserve to be partakers of their glory in the heavens.

May the protection of the divine pity guard you from all adversity, and set you with your fathers in the glory of the celestial kingdom, O dearest brothers.

May 24

Jackson Kemper

First Missionary Bishop in the United States, 1870

The General Convention of 1835 was a turning point in the history of the Episcopal Church; it designated the church as a missionary society and appointed Jackson Kemper as the first missionary bishop. "Go," said Bishop Doane of New Jersey, "bear before a ruined world, the Savior's bleeding Cross. Go, feed, with bread from heaven, the Savior's hungering

Church. Go, thrice beloved, go, and God the Lord go with you." Kemper's first jurisdiction was Indiana and Missouri, but three years later the Church added Iowa and Wisconsin and the Indian Territory, including everything west of Iowa. Some called him the "Bishop of All Outdoors." He traveled more than 300,000 miles riding horseback through driving snowstorms, sleeping on the floors of one-room log cabins, putting vestments on over wet clothes, vesting in the back of wagons or barns. He founded two colleges and a seminary (Nashotah House), laid the foundation of the church's work in at least seven states, and made missionary journeys far beyond those.

A reading from Bishop Kemper's final report
as a missionary bishop

I now with deep emotion tender to the Church my resignation of the office of missionary bishop which, unsought for, and entirely unexpected, was con-ferred upon me twenty-four years ago. Blessed with health, and cheered by the conviction of duty, I have been enabled to travel at all seasons through Indiana, Missouri, Wisconsin, Iowa and Minnesota, and partly through Kansas and Nebraska.

My days must soon be numbered, for in less than three months I will be seventy years old. As age advances, I trust I have an increasing love for our Divine Master, and that Church for which he shed his most precious blood. The adorable Savior's prayer for the unity and peace of his flock is most deeply impressed upon my mind, and truly anxious that we, the members of this branch of his mystical body, should obey his precepts and follow in his steps, I solicit that every effort that is not sanctioned by due authority, either Diocesan or general, be discouraged and abandoned. I rejoice and thank God, that with respect to the foreign field there has been no attempt to interfere or intrude. No true Churchman would even think of it. And why cannot every member of our communion repose with confidence on the ability, judgment, and zeal of the General Convention and its Board of Missions? Let us all, then, throw our contributions for the home field into the Domestic Committee. The amount placed at the disposal of that body is vastly inferior to what it ought to be. There should be thousands of dollars instead of hundreds; we should not rest satisfied until the annual receipts of the treasury are twenty thousand dollars per month. If anyone, perhaps I can realize the immense field of labor and final triumph that is before us. Let our Missionary Bishops be increased—let them be multiplied. The West, the mighty West, demands immediate and thorough attention. Thus far, what we have even attempted, has been but as it were, a drop in the ocean. What ought we not to do for Pike's Peak (soon to be organized into a territory) with its one hundred thousand inhabitants? What for New Mexico, Dacotah, Deseret, and those other vast regions, both South and West, into which the hardy emigrant is pressing, and where, I fear, before we act, there will be a million of people, and among them a goodly number who once enjoyed all the sacred privileges we now possess.

I cannot close this, my last report, without referring to the aborigines of our country, who deserve at our hands, intense and abiding interest; instead of neglect, injury, and destruction. They have immortal souls, precious in the sight of the Redeemer. Their minds are open to the convictions of purity and truth. "Ye have done much," and not altogether in vain, among the Chippewas of Minnesota, and quite a number of their children are now under religious training both at Gull Lake and Faribault. But could the members of the Church have been with me, among the Oneidas, on the 19th September, they would require no arguments to secure an interest in their very heart of hearts for the poor Indian. The day was exceedingly tempestuous. The faithful Missionary and myself had to ride eighteen miles through heavy rains before we were ready for divine Service. The Church was entirely full. The singing, including some good chants, was excellent. The responses were general. The whole of the service was in the Oneida language, excepting the lessons and sermon, which were translated sentence by sentence. Fourteen young persons were presented for confirmation and were earnestly admonished to hold, henceforth, a holy life. The memorials of our dying Saviour's love were received by one hundred communicants at the close of these solemn services which occupied three hours. Every person present, in due order, came up and shook hands with me. Now here were most evidently, courtesy, reverence, worship, and obedience to that Great Spirit, in whose hands are the issues of life. These people had sought the Lord in his appointed ways. Surely they will find Him an all-sufficient and a gracious God. And why should there not be a hundred similar congregations among the red race of this country?

May 25

Bede the Venerable

Monk of Jarrow, Scholar, Historian, 735

Bede was born in Northumbria around the year 670. When he was seven years old, his family gave him to the monastery of Saint Peter and Saint Paul at Wearmouth. He then moved to Jarrow, where he lived as a monk for the rest of his life. Although it seems he never traveled further than York, his monastery (first under Abbot Benedict Biscop and then Abbot Ceolfrith) was a center of learning, and Bede studied extensively. He used all the resources available to write the most complete history of Christian England up to the year 729, as well as commentaries on books of the Bible. He was renowned for his monastic fidelity and his love of teaching, and was fondly remembered by his pupils, including his biographer. He died peacefully in the year 735 and is buried in Durham Cathedral.

A Reading from the conclusion to *A History of the English Church and People* by the Venerable Bede

I, Bede, servant of Christ and priest of the monastery of the blessed apostles Peter and Paul at Wearmouth and Jarrow, have, with the help of God and to the best of my ability, assembled these facts about the history of the Church in Britain, and of the Church of the English in particular, so far as I have been able to ascertain them from ancient documents, from the traditions of our forebears, and from my own personal knowledge.

I was born on the lands of this monastery, and on reaching seven years of age, I was entrusted by my family first to the most reverend Abbot Benedict and later to Abbot Ceolfrid for my education. I have spent all the remainder of my life in this monastery and devoted myself entirely to the study of the Scriptures. Amid the observance of the Rule and the daily task of singing the office in church, my chief delight has always been in study, teaching, and writing.

I was ordained deacon in my nineteenth year, and priest in my thirtieth, receiving both these orders at the hands of the most reverend Bishop John at the direction of Abbot Ceolfrid. From the time of my receiving the priesthood until my fifty-ninth year, I have made it my business, both for my own benefit and that of my brethren, to compile short extracts from the works of the venerable

Fathers on the holy Scriptures, and to comment on their meaning and interpretation.

I pray you, merciful Jesu,
that as you have graciously granted me
joyfully to imbibe the words of your knowledge,
so you will also, of your goodness,
grant that I may come at length to you,
the fount of all wisdom,
and stand before your face for ever.

alternative reading

A Reading from a letter to Cuthwin describing the death of Bede, written by Bede's pupil, Cuthbert the Deacon

On the Tuesday before the feast of the Ascension, his breathing became very much worse, and his feet began to swell. Even so, he spent the whole of that day teaching us, and dictated cheerfully, and among other things said several times: "Be sure to learn your lessons quickly now; for I do not know how much longer I will be with you, or whether my Maker will take me from you very soon now." It seemed clear to us that he knew very well when his end would be.

He spent all that night in thanksgiving, without sleep. When dawn broke that Wednesday, he gave further dictation on the work which we had begun. We were still working at nine o'clock when we went in procession with the relics of the saints, as the custom of that day required. One of us stayed with him, and said to him: "Dear master, there is still one chapter left to be done of that book you were dictating; is it too much trouble if I question you about it?" But he replied "It is not hard at all. Take up your pen and sharpen it, and then write quickly." And so he did.

At three o'clock he said to me: "I have a few valuables in my chest, some pepper, and napkins, and some incense. Run quickly and fetch the priests of our monastery, so that I may share among them these little presents God has given me." I did so in great agitation; and when they were all present, he spoke to all and to each personally, encouraging and pleading with them to offer masses and prayers on his behalf; and they promised they would do this.

But they were very sad, and they all wept, especially when he said that he did not think they would see his face much longer in this world. Yet they rejoiced at one thing that he said: "If it so pleases my Maker, the time has come for me to be released from this body, and to return to the One who formed me out of nothing. I have lived a long time, and the righteous Judge has provided for me well throughout my life. The time for my departure is near, and I long to be dissolved and be with Christ. My soul longs to see Christ my King in all his beauty."

Having said this, and indeed several other things to our great profit, he spent his last day in gladness until the evening. Then Wilberht, the boy whom I mentioned earlier, said once again: "Dear master, there is still one sentence that we have not yet written down." And Bede said: "Then write it quickly." After a little while the boy said: "There, it is written." And he replied: "Good! It is finished; you have spoken the truth. Hold my head in your hands. It would please me much if I could sit opposite the holy place where I used to pray, so that I may call upon my Father sitting up."

And so it happened that as Bede sat upon the floor of his cell, singing "Glory be to the Father and to the Son and to the Holy Spirit" he breathed his last. And we can believe without hesitation that, inasmuch as he always labored in this life to the praise of God, so his soul journeyed to the joys of heaven for which he longed.

May 26

Augustine of Canterbury

First Archbishop of Canterbury, 605

Augustine was prior of the monastery of Saint Andrew in Rome. In 596, at the instigation of Pope Gregory the Great, he was dispatched as the leader of a group of forty monks to re-evangelize the English Church. Augustine appears to have been not a particularly confident person, and in Gaul he wanted to turn back, but Pope Gregory's firm resolution held the group to their mission. The monks finally landed in Kent in the summer of 597 where they were well received by King Ethelbert whose wife, Bertha, was a Christian. Once established, Augustine returned temporarily to Gaul to receive ordination as a bishop. Pope Gregory would have preferred London to have become the primatial see, but in the event Canterbury was chosen, and thus Augustine became the first Archbishop of Canterbury. He died in either the year 604 or 605.

A Reading from *A History of the English Church and People* by the Venerable Bede

King Ethelbert granted Augustine and his companions a dwelling in the city of Canterbury, which was the chief city of his kingdom, and in accordance with his promise he allowed them provisions and did not inhibit their freedom to preach. As soon as they had occupied the house given to them they began to emulate the life of the apostles and the primitive Church. They were constantly at prayer; they fasted and kept vigils; and they preached the word of life to whomsoever they could. They regarded worldly things as of little importance, and accepted only the necessities of life from those they taught. They practiced what they preached, and were willing to endure any hardship, and even to the point of dying for the truths they proclaimed. Before long a number of people, admiring the simplicity of their holy lives and the comfort of their heavenly message, believed and were baptized. On the east side of the city stood an old church, built in honor of Saint Martin during the Roman occupation of Britain, where the queen, who was a Christian, used to pray. Here the monks first assembled to sing psalms, to pray, to celebrate the Eucharist, to preach, and to baptize, until the king's own conversion to the Faith gave them even greater freedom to preach and to build and restore churches everywhere.

At last the king himself, among others, attracted by the pure lives of these holy men and their joyous promises, the truth of which they confirmed by many miracles, believed and was baptized. Thenceforward great numbers gathered each day to hear the word of God, forsaking their heathen worship and entering the unity of Christ's holy Church. While the king was pleased at their faith and conversion, it is said that he would not compel anyone to accept Christianity; for he had learned from his instructors and guides to salvation that the service of Christ must be accepted freely and not under compulsion.

Meanwhile God's servant Augustine visited Arles and, in accordance with the command of the holy father Gregory, was consecrated archbishop of the English nation by Etherius, archbishop of that city.

May 26

Philip Neri

Founder of the Oratorians, Spiritual Guide, 1595

Born in 1515 in Florence, Philip Neri went to Rome when he was eighteen, resolved to give his life to God. He studied hard and led a noticeably austere life and, after a time living the life of a virtual hermit in the Roman catacombs, founded a fraternity to assist pilgrims and the sick. He was ordained in 1551 and he joined a company of priests working in San Girolamo Church, where he soon became a popular confessor and spiritual guide. As many regularly came to the oratory in that church, where he held spiritual conferences, other priests were attracted to his teaching and the Congregation of the Oratory was founded. It finally received papal approval in 1575. Philip was such a popular and revered person in Rome that he was treated almost like a living saint, even instructing the Pope to grant absolution to the French monarch, Henry IV, to prevent a political catastrophe. This kind and gentle priest gave his life for the service of others and died on this day in the year 1595.

A Reading from a letter of Philip Neri to his niece

What a destructive thing is avarice! We have received so much from God. He has given us, besides our being, and all created things from the angels downwards, his own Son. The sweet Christ, the incarnate Word, gave himself to us, without reserve even to the hard and shameful death of the cross. He has given himself to us in a sacrament, as at first he left heaven, humbling himself to become human for us. On the cross he was stripped of his garments, and shed his precious blood, and his soul was separated from his body.

All created things are open-hearted and liberal, and show forth the goodness of their creator; the sun pours abroad light, and fire gives out heat; every tree stretches forth its branches and reaches to us its fruit. The water, the air, and all nature declare the bounty of the creator. And yet we who are his living images do not represent him, but with base degeneracy deny him in our works however much we confess him with our mouths.

Now, if avarice is a monstrous thing in any one, what is it in a religious who has made a vow of poverty, abandoning everything for the love of God! We must, at whatever cost to ourselves, get rid of this foul pestilence of avarice; nor shall we feel the pain if we seriously reflect that as soon as we cast off this sordid garb, our soul is clothed with a regal and imperial garment. I mean not only that we must despise gold and silver and pleasure and all else that is so prized by a blind, deluded world, but that we are to give even the very life we love so much for the honor of God and the salvation of our neighbor. We should have our hearts ever ready to make this sacrifice in the strength of divine grace.

Love greatly holy obedience, and put this before and above every other thing. Never take anything to your own use unless it has been signed and sealed to you with the blessing of your Superior. Together with obedience, cherish love and prayer; but carefully remember that while you love and desire prayer and holy communion with the utmost affection of your heart, you must be always ready to leave either or both at the call of obedience. Regard holy obedience as a true prayer and a real communion; for you must not desire prayer and communion for the sake of the sweetness of devotion you find in them—that would be seeking yourself and not God—but that you may become humble and obedient, gentle and patient. When you find these within you, then you will gather the fruit of prayer and communion, and above all, you will live in peace with all.

May 30

Joan of Arc

Visionary, 1431

Joan of Arc was born at Domrémy in 1412, the daughter of a peasant farmer. She first heard voices of particular saints when she was fourteen years old, telling her to save France, which was caught up in the Hundred Years War with England. Though at first she was dismissed, her credibility increased when some of her predictions began to come true. She managed to identify the disguised Dauphin (who was later to become Charles VII) whose support and approval she gained. Joan persuaded troops to be sent to relieve Orléans and rode at their head, wearing white armor. Their success increased morale and enhanced her reputation. When the Dauphin was crowned king at Rheims, Joan stood at his side. Her voices warned her that her life would be short yet she was dangerously naïve in not seeing the jealousies she was provoking. After some failures in battle, she lost favor and was sold by the Duke of

Burgundy to the English, tried in a court for heresy by the Bishop of Beauvais, and burned at the stake on this day in 1431. Twenty-five years later, the Pope formally declared Joan innocent. She was made second patron of France after her canonization in 1920.

A Reading from the report of the trial of Joan of Arc held at Rouen in 1431, prepared for King Louis XII

Master Jean Estivet, appointed promoter at the trial by Pierre, Bishop of Beauvais, required Jeanne, known as the Pucelle, to be brought and questioned in accordance with the law. She had made a supplication that she might be allowed to hear Mass, but this the bishop refused in view of the crimes of which she was accused, and because she wore man's dress.

The bishop explained that she had been taken within the boundaries of his diocese. And since there was common report of a number of her deeds which were contrary to our faith, not only within the realm of France but in all the states in which they were known and published, and since she was accused of heresy, she had been handed over to him to be tried in a matter of faith.

He told her that she should tell the truth concerning the things which would be asked her, as much for the shortening of her trial as for the unburdening of her conscience, without subterfuge or craft; and that she should swear on the holy Gospels to tell the truth concerning everything she should be asked.

Jeanne answered that concerning her father and mother, and concerning everything she had done since she took the road for France, she would willingly swear. But as for revelations sent her from God, never had she told or revealed them save to Charles, who she said was her king.

She complained of the fetters which she had on her legs. She said also that there is a saying among little children that people are often hanged for telling the truth.

Asked if she knew whether she were in the grace of God, she answered: "If I am not, may God put me there; if I am, may he keep me there." She said further that if she knew she were not in the grace of God, she would be the most miserable person in the world. She said also that if she were in mortal sin, the voices would not come to her. And she would that everyone might hear them as well as she did. She also said that she thought she was thirteen years of age when the voices came to her the first time.

On Wednesday, the penultimate day of May, the trial was concluded and she was condemned as a heretic. After sentence was read, the bishop, the Inquisitor, and many of the judges went away, leaving Jeanne alone upon the scaffold. Then the Bailli of Rouen, an Englishman, ordered that she should be taken to the place where she was to be burned. When Jeanne heard this order given, she began to weep and lament in such a way that all the people present were themselves moved to tears.

And there in the market place of Rouen she was burned and martyred tragically, an act of unparalleled cruelty. And many, both noble and peasant, murmured greatly against the English.

alternative reading

A Reading from a sermon of Ronald Knox

Throughout the history of sanctity you find the persistence of a quality of realizing that what we see and touch and feel are transitory things and unreal, and that the solid things are the things that appear not, a world we only grasp by faith. I think that this is a quality that stands out with quite extraordinary clearness in the life of Saint Joan of Arc: she did really live for a promise, and we know that the promise came true, but she did not—not in this life.

Joan was less than twenty years old when she was burnt at the stake. It is not true that she dressed as a man; she dressed as a boy. When she was only thirteen years old, at the age when the other boys and girls were fidgeting and playing the fool during mass, she could hardly go out of doors without hearing the voices of saints and angels talking to her. And these voices dominated her life; they echoed so loudly in her ears that all the world's noises were drowned for her.

People said: "It is very silly of a small girl like you to think she can go and see the king"—she did not hear them. And the king disguised himself and hid among his courtiers, but she went straight up to him: "I have come to raise the siege of Orleans and crown you king at Rheims." It was no good; the voices had told her about it. And I suppose when she had been appointed Chief of the Army, the General Staff would always be raising military difficulties, but it did not make a bit of difference to her, she always did what the voices told her.

After the first few victories, after the crowning of the king, the people she had come to save contented themselves with a partial conquest, and hung about making treaties and demobilizing troops. But the ingratitude and apathy of the court affected her no more than its honors had done; she simply went on obeying the voices.

And the French lords played her false, and she was taken prisoner. But she endured, as seeing him who is invisible.

And then came the hardest time of all. I do not think she minded being in prison; I do not think she minded the threat of execution; that was not why she tried to escape. No, it was simply that it seemed quite obvious to her she was to deliver France—the voices had told her so—and France was not yet delivered. And so she went to the stake, her hopes still unfulfilled, but never doubting for an instant that the voices were true.

Five years later the king entered Paris; twenty-two years later, England had no possessions left on French soil. She believed that he was faithful who had promised, not having received the promises, but beholding them afar off and saluting them. She could not foresee that her unjust condemnation would be reversed, point by point, twenty-five years after her death.

That, then, is her great witness, that is her capital contribution to our Christian hope—that it is the things of this world that are shams and shadows, and the real things and the solid things are the things we cannot see. Our Savior Christ has ascended up into heaven, and a cloud received him from our sight, but we are not therefore to think of the spiritual world as something far removed from us, only to be reached by a supreme effort of thought. On the contrary, the spiritual world is all about us: the voices are still there, only Saint Joan could hear them and we cannot. But I wonder whose fault that is?

May 31

The Visitation of the Blessed Virgin Mary to Elizabeth

The Church today recalls the visit of Elizabeth to her cousin Mary, as recorded in Luke's Gospel. The celebration of the feast first occurred at a Franciscan Order General Chapter in 1263, but quickly spread throughout Europe. Since it is an event clearly described in the gospel, the Churches of the Reformation were less inclined to proscribe it than they were other Marian feasts, particularly as it was the occasion for Mary to sing her great hymn of praise in the "Magnificat." Luke sees John the Baptist as the last of the prophets of the old covenant, and uses John's leaping in Elizabeth's womb as the first time he bears witness to Christ as the promised Messiah.

A Reading from a sermon of the Venerable Bede

"My soul proclaims the greatness of the Lord, and my spirit rejoices in God my Savior." With these words Mary first acknowledges the special gifts she has been given. Then she recalls God's universal favors, bestowed unceasingly on the human race. When we devote all our thoughts to the praise and service of the Lord, we proclaim the greatness of God. Our observance of God's commands, moreover, shows that we have God's power and greatness always at heart. Our spirit rejoices in God our Savior, and delights in the mere recollection of our creator who gives us hope for eternal salvation.

These words of praise, therefore, may be fittingly uttered by all of God's creatures, but it is especially appropriate that they should be spoken by the blessed Mother of God. She alone was chosen, and she burned with spiritual love for the son she so joyously conceived. Above all other saints, she alone could truly rejoice in Jesus, her Savior, for she knew that he who was the source of eternal salvation would be born in time in her body, in one person both her own son and her Lord.

"For the Almighty has done great things for me, and holy is his name." Mary attributes nothing to her own merits. She refers all her greatness to the gift of the one whose essence is power and whose nature is greatness, for he fills with greatness and strength the small and the weak who believe in him. She did well to add: "and holy is his name," to warn those who heard, and indeed all who would receive his words, that they must believe and call upon his name. For they too can share in everlasting holiness and true salvation according to the words of the prophet: "and it will come to pass, that everyone who calls on the name of the Lord will be saved."

Therefore it is an excellent and fruitful custom of holy Church that we should sing Mary's hymn at the time of evening prayer. By meditating upon the incarnation in this way, our devotion is kindled, and by remembering the example of the Mother of God, we are encouraged to lead a life of virtue.

A Reading from *The Life of our Blessed Lord and Savior Jesus Christ* by Jeremy Taylor

When the eternal God meant to stoop so low as to be fixed in our center, he chose for his mother a holy person and a maid. She received the angel's message with such sublimity of faith that her faith was turned into vision, her hopes into actual possession, and her grace into glory. She who was now full of God, bearing God in her virgin womb, and the Holy Spirit in her heart, arose with haste and gladness to communicate that joy which was designed for all the world; and she found no breast to pour forth the first emanations of her overjoyed heart so fit as her cousin Elizabeth's, for she was to be the mother of the Baptist, who was sent a forerunner "to prepare the way of the Lord" her son.

Let us notice how light and airy was the coming of the Virgin, as she made haste over the mountains; her very little burden which she bore hindered her not but that she might make haste enough; and as her spirit was full of cheerfulness and alacrity, so even her body was made airy and full of life. And there is this excellency in religion that when we carry Christ within us, his presence is neither so peevish as to disturb our health, nor so sad as to discompose our cheerfulness, but he recreates our body by charity and by securing God's providence over us while we are in the pursuit of the heavenly kingdom. For as the Virgin climbed mountains easily, so there is no difficulty in our life so great, but it may be managed by those assistances we receive from the holiest Jesus, when we carry him about us.

It is not easy to imagine what collision of joys was at this blessed meeting; two mothers of two great princes, the one the greatest that was born of woman, and the other his Lord. When these who were made mothers by two miracles came together, they met with joy and mysteriousness. The mother of our Lord went to visit the mother of his servant, and the Holy Ghost made the meeting festival. Never, but in heaven, was there more joy and ecstasy. For these women were not only hallowed, but made pregnant and big with religion, meeting together to compare and unite their joys and their eucharist.

By this God would have us know that when the blessings of God descend upon us, they should be published in the communion of the saints, so that the hopes of others may receive increase, that their faith may receive confirmation, that their charity and eucharist may grow up to become excellent and great, and the praises of God be sung aloud, till the sound strike at heaven and join with the alleluias which the morning stars in their orbs pay to their great creator.

alternative reading

A Reading from the poem *The May Magnificat*
by Gerard Manley Hopkins

May is Mary's month, and I
Muse at that and wonder why:
    Her feasts follow reason,
    Dated due to season—

Candlemas, Lady Day;
But the Lady Month, May,
    Why fasten that upon her,
    With a feasting in her honor?

Is it only its being brighter
Than the most are must delight her?
    Is it opportunest
    And flowers finds soonest?

Ask of her, the mighty mother:
Her reply puts this other
    Question: What is Spring?—
    Growth in everything—

Flesh and fleece, fur and feather
Grass and greenworld all together;
    Star-eyed strawberry-breasted
    Throstle above her nested

Cluster of bugle blue eggs thin
Forms and warms the life within;
    And bird and blossom swell
    In sod or sheath or shell.

All things rising, all things sizing
Mary sees, sympathising
    With that world of good,
    Nature's motherhood.

Their magnifying of each its kind
With delight calls to mind
    How she did in her stored
    Magnify the Lord.

Well but there was more than this:
Spring's universal bliss
    Much, had much to say
    To offering Mary May.

When drop-of-blood-and-foam-dapple
Bloom lights the orchard-apple
    And thicket and thorp are merry
    With silver-surfèd cherry

And azuring-over greybell makes
Wood banks and brakes wash wet like lakes
    And magic cuckoocall
    Caps, clears, and clinches all—

This ecstasy all through mothering earth
Tells Mary her mirth till Christ's birth
    To remember and exultation
    In God who was her salvation.

June

June 1

Justin

Martyr at Rome, *c.* 165

Justin was born at the beginning of the second century in Palestine. As a young man he explored many different philosophies before, at the age of thirty, embracing Christianity. He continued to wear the distinctive dress of a professional philosopher, and taught Christianity as a philosophy first at Ephesus, and later at Rome. He became an outstanding apologist for the Christian faith, and is honored as the first Christian thinker to enter into serious dialogue with the other intellectual disciplines of his day, including Judaism. Justin always sought to reconcile the claims of faith and reason. It was at Rome in about 165 that he and some of his disciples were denounced as Christians, and beheaded. The authentic record of their martyrdom based on an official court report has survived. Traditionally, Justin is often surnamed "Martyr" because of his two-fold witness to Christ, through his apologetic writings and his manner of death.

A Reading from the *First Apology* of Justin

Not only does sound reason direct us to reject the guidance of those who have done or taught what is wrong, but it is incumbent on every lover of truth, at whatever personal cost, even if his own life is at stake, to choose to do and to speak only what is right. I beg you, therefore, my readers, you who are called religious and philosophers, guardians of justice and lovers of learning, pay heed and attend to my address.

You call us Christians "atheists." We confess that we are atheists, in so far as the gods of this world are concerned, but not in respect to the most true God, the Father of righteousness, moderation and all other virtues, who is entirely pure. It is this God, and the Son (who came forth from God and taught us these things, and about the host of other good angels who follow and are made to be like him), and the prophetic Spirit, whom we worship and adore.

When you hear that we are looking for a kingdom, you rashly suppose that we mean something merely human. But we are speaking of a kingdom with God, as must be clear from our confession before you when you bring us to trial, though we know that death is the penalty for such a confession. For if we looked for a human kingdom we would deny our Christ in order to save our lives, and would try to remain in hiding in order to obtain the things we look for. But since we do not place our hopes on the present world, we are not troubled by being put to death, and we know we will have to die one day in any case.

Indeed, of all people we Christians are your best helpers and allies in securing good order, convinced as we are that no wicked person, no covetous person or conspirator (or virtuous person for that matter) can remain hidden from God, and that everyone goes to either eternal punishment or salvation in accordance with the character of their actions. If everyone knew this, nobody would choose vice even for a little time.

What sober-minded person, then, will not admit that we Christians are not atheists, worshipping as we do the creator of this universe, declaring as we have been taught, that God has no need of streams of blood and libations and incense? We praise God to the utmost of our power by prayer, by thanking God for the gift of life itself. We have been taught that the way to honor God is not by burning with fire the very things he has brought into being for our sustenance, but rather to use them for our good and those in need, expressing in psalms and hymns our gratitude to him for our creation, our health, for the sheer richness and diversity of life, for the changing seasons; and laying before him our prayers to live again in incorruption through faith in him.

Our teacher of these things is Jesus Christ, who was crucified under Pontius Pilate, procurator of Judea, in the time of Tiberius Caesar. Him we worship, having learned that he is the Son of the true God, and also the prophetic Spirit. Our detractors proclaim our madness because we honor a crucified man alongside the unchangeable and eternal God, the creator of all. They do not discern the mystery in this, and it is to this mystery that we beg you attend.

June 2

The Martyrs of Lyons
177

The persecution of Christians in the Roman Empire began in the days of Nero and continued intermittently until Constantine's Edict of Toleration published in the year 315. Long periods of peace would be followed by new outbreaks, some of which were quite local in character. Thus it was that a center of Christian activity in southern France came under attack in the year 177. Beginning with social exclusion, then open insults and attacks, the persecution built up over time. Slaves in Christian households were tortured and forced to make accusations of incest and cannibalism which inflamed the mob and created greater violence. At last the governor ordered several days of public torture to take place in which Christians were beaten, burned with hot irons, tossed about by bulls, and finally killed. Among those who bore witness to their faith and died were Pothinus, the elderly bishop; Sanctus, a deacon; Maturus, a recent convert; and Blandina, a slave.

A Reading from the *Church History* of Eusebius

The servants of Christ residing at Vienne and Lyons, in Gaul, to the brethren throughout Asia and Phrygia, who hold the same faith and hope of redemption, peace and grace and glory from God the Father and Christ Jesus our Lord.

The greatness of the tribulation in this region, and the fury of the heathen against the saints, and the sufferings of the blessed witnesses, we cannot recount accurately, nor indeed could they possibly be recorded. For with all his might the adversary fell upon us, giving us a foretaste of his unbridled activity at his future coming. He endeavored in every manner to practice and exercise his servants against the servants of God, not only shutting us out from houses and baths and markets, but forbidding any of us to be seen in any place whatever. But the grace of God led them in the conflict against him, and delivered the weak, and set them as firm pillars, able through patience to endure all the wrath of the Evil One. And they joined battle with him, undergoing all kinds of shame and injury; and regarding their great sufferings as little, they hastened to Christ, manifesting truly that "the sufferings of this present time are not worthy to be compared with the glory that shall be revealed to us." First of all, they endured nobly the injuries heaped upon them by the populace; clamors and blows and draggings and robberies and stonings and imprisonments, and all things that an infuriated mob delight in inflicting on enemies and adversaries. Then, being taken to the forum by the chiliarch and the authorities of the city, they were examined in the presence of the whole multitude and, having confessed, they were imprisoned until the arrival of the governor.

They were also so zealous in their imitation of Christ, "who, being in the form of God, counted it not a prize to be on an equality with God," that, though they had attained such honor, and had borne witness, not once or twice but many times, having been brought back to prison from the wild beasts, covered with burns and scars and wounds, yet they did not proclaim themselves witnesses, nor did they suffer us to address them by this name. If any one of us, in letter or conversation, spoke of them as witnesses, they rebuked him sharply. For they conceded cheerfully the appellation of witness to Christ, "the faithful and true Witness," and "firstborn of the dead," and "prince of the life of God;" and they reminded us of the witnesses who had already departed and said, "They are already witnesses whom Christ has deemed worthy to be taken up in their confession, having sealed their testimony by their departure; but we are lowly and humble confessors." And they besought the brethren with tears that earnest prayers should be offered that they might be made perfect.

For, through the genuineness of their love, their greatest contest with him was that the Beast, being choked, might cast out alive those whom he supposed he had swallowed. For they did not boast over the fallen, but helped them in their need with those things in which they themselves abounded, having the compassion of a mother, and shedding many tears on their account before the Father. They asked for life, and he gave it to them, and they shared it with their neighbors. Victorious over everything, they departed to God. Having always loved peace, and having commended peace to us, they went in peace to God, leaving no sorrow to their mother, nor division or strife to the brethren, but joy and peace and concord and love.

June 3

The Martyrs of Uganda
1886 and 1978

Mwanga, the ruler of Uganda in 1886, wanted boys for his bed and when all the Christian pages began to refuse his advances, he had them put to death. They included Catholics and Anglicans. On their way to the place of execution, these young Christians sang hymns in honor of the Lord and some were still singing when the flames surrounded them. Barely a century later, the peoples of the land were persecuted by a tyrant who put many of the Christian leaders and followers of Christ to death. Anglicans and Roman Catholics unite on this day to remember those who witnessed in Uganda for Christ, even unto death.

A Reading from the homily of Pope Paul VI on the occasion of the canonization of the Ugandan Martyrs

These African martyrs add a new page to that list of victorious men and women that we call the martyrology, in which we find the most magnificent as well as the most tragic stories. The page that they add is worthy to take its place alongside those wonderful stories of ancient Africa, which we who live today, being of little faith, thought we should never see repeated.

We are familiar with the lives of the great saints, martyrs and confessors, of Africa, such as Cyprian, Felicity, and Perpetua, and the great Augustine. Who would have imagined that one day we should be adding to that list those names of Charles Lwanga, Matthias Molumba Kalemba and their twenty companions? Nor should we forget those others of the Anglican Communion who died for the sake of Christ.

These martyrs of Africa have indeed laid the foundation of a new age. We should not dwell on the religious persecutions and conflicts, but rather on the rebirth of Christian and civil life that has begun.

For from the Africa that was sprinkled with the blood of these martyrs, the first of this new age (and, God willing, the last, so sublime, so precious was their sacrifice), there is emerging a free and independent Africa.

June 5

Boniface

Archbishop of Mainz, Apostle of Germany and Martyr, 754

Born at Crediton in Devon about the year 675, Wynfrith took the name Boniface when he entered the monastery in Exeter as a young man. He became a Latin scholar and poet and was ordained when he was thirty years old. He rejected a safe ecclesiastical career in England and, in the year 716, became a missionary to Frisia, following in the steps of Willibrord. He was eventually commissioned by the Pope to work in Hesse and Bavaria where he went after consecration as bishop in the year 722. He courageously felled a sacred oak at Geismar and, since the pagan gods did not come to the rescue, widespread conversion followed. He was the founder of a string of monasteries across southern Germany and made sure that they were places of learning, so that evangelizing could continue. Boniface was made Archbishop of Mainz in 732, where he consecrated many missionary bishops. He worked assiduously for the reform of the Church in France and managed to ensure that the more balanced Rule of Saint Benedict *was adhered to in its monasteries. He crowned Pepin as the Frankish king in 751 but was already very old. While waiting for some new Christians to arrive for confirmation, he was murdered by a band of pagans on this day in the year 754. He has been judged as having a deeper influence on European history than any other Englishman.*

A Reading from a letter of Boniface to Cuthbert, Archbishop of Canterbury, written in 747 on the establishment of the Church in Germany and the obstacles he was encountering

My dear brother, I fear we have undertaken to steer a ship through the waves of an angry sea, and we can neither succeed in our task, nor without sin abandon it. I am reminded of the statement of a certain wise man that "If it is dangerous to be negligent when steering a ship on the open sea, how much more dangerous to let go of the rudder in a storm when the waves are running high. In her voyage across the ocean of this world, the Church is like such a great ship, pounded by the waves of temptation, and it is our duty not to abandon ship, but to control the rudder."

As examples in this we have the early Fathers, Clement and Cornelius and many others in the city of Rome, Cyprian in

Carthage, Athanasius in Alexandria. Living under pagan emperors, they steered the ship of Christ, that is the Church, his most dear spouse, teaching, defending, laboring and suffering, even to the point of shedding their own blood.

In the Church of which I have oversight, I have dug the ground over, manured the soil, but I am conscious that I have failed to guard it. Alas, all my labor seems to me like a dog barking at the approach of thieves and robbers, but because he has no one to help him in his defense, he can only sit there, whining and complaining.

According to the word of God to Ezekiel, when someone is entrusted with preaching the gospel, even though he live a holy life, nevertheless if he is afraid or ashamed to rebuke those who live wickedly, he will perish along with the rest because he remained silent. When I consider the example of such people, and those like them, I am filled with dread. "Fear and trembling come upon me, and the darkness of my sins almost overwhelms me." I would be only too glad to give up the task of guiding the Church which I had accepted, if I could have found some warrant for such a course of action in either the example of the Fathers or in Holy Scripture.

Since this is not to be found, and since although the truth may be attacked it can never be ultimately defeated or falsified, with my tired mind I take refuge in the words of Solomon: "Trust in the Lord with all your heart, and do not rely on your own insights. In all your ways, think on the Lord and he will guide your steps."

Let us stand firm, then, in doing what is right and prepare ourselves to face trials. Let us wait upon the strength of God, and say to him: "Lord, you have been our refuge from one generation to the next." Let us trust in the One who laid this burden upon us. What we cannot bear on our own strength, let us bear with the help of the One who is all-powerful and who said, "My yoke is easy and my burden is light."

Let us never be dogs that do not bark, or silent bystanders, or hired servants who flee at the approach of the wolf. Instead let us be watchful shepherds, guarding the flock of Christ. And as God gives us strength, in season and out of season, let us preach to the powerful and powerless alike, to rich and poor alike, to all people of every rank and of whatever age, the saving purposes of God.

June 6

Philip the Deacon

As the early church grew in numbers, the apostles came to realize that they could not do all the ministry that was needed themselves. Therefore, they called the church together and asked that men be selected to assist them. Seven were chosen and set apart through prayer and the laying on of hands. Traditionally the church has understood this event as the first calling to diaconal ministry, but the only stories told of their work speak of evangelism. In particular, stories are told of Philip: how he proclaimed the word in Samaria (Acts 8:5–8), baptized an Ethiopian eunuch (8:26–39), preached in various towns (8:40), and how Paul stayed with him in Caesarea where Philip is called "the Evangelist." What is clear from these and other stories is that the church very early recognized the need for a variety of ministries. Philip is held up as an example of a recognized ministry other than that of the apostles, and therefore an exemplar for our own day as we seek to revitalize a diversity of ministries by lay people and ordained alike.

A Reading from Tertullian's *Elucidation: On Baptism*

They whose office it is, know that baptism is not rashly to be administered. "Give to every one who begs you," has a reference of its own, appertaining especially to almsgiving. On the contrary, this precept is rather to be looked at carefully: "Give not the holy thing to the dogs, nor cast your pearls before swine;" and, "Lay not hands easily on any; share not other men's sins." If Philip so "easily" baptized the chamberlain, let us reflect that a manifest and conspicuous evidence that the Lord deemed him worthy had been interposed. The Spirit had enjoined Philip to proceed to that road: the eunuch himself, too, was not found idle, nor as one who was suddenly seized with an eager desire to be baptized; but, after going up to the temple for prayer's sake, being intently engaged on the divine Scripture, was thus suitably discovered—to whom God had, unasked, sent an apostle, which one, again, the Spirit bade adjoin himself to the chamberlain's chariot. The Scripture which he was reading falls in opportunely with his faith: Philip, being requested, is taken to sit beside him; the Lord is pointed out; faith lingers not; water needs no waiting for; the work is completed, and the apostle snatched away.

They who are about to enter baptism ought to pray with repeated prayers, fasts, and bendings of the knee, and vigils all the night through, and with the confession of all bygone sins that they may express the meaning even of the baptism of John: "They were baptized" says the Scripture, "confessing their own sins." To us it is matter for thankfulness if we do now publicly confess our iniquities or our turpitudes: for we do at the same time both make satisfaction for our former sins, by mortification of our flesh and spirit and lay beforehand the foundation of defenses against the temptations which will closely follow. "Watch and pray," says the Lord, "lest you fall into temptation." And the reason, I believe, why they were tempted was that they fell asleep; so that they deserted the Lord when apprehended, and he who continued to stand by him, and used the sword even denied him thrice: for the word had gone before, that "no one untempted should attain the celestial kingdoms." The Lord himself forthwith after baptism temptations surrounded, when in forty days he had kept fast. "Then," someone will say, "it becomes us, too, rather to fast after baptism." . . .Thereupon the Lord, driven apart into desert places after baptism, showed, by maintaining a fast of forty days, that the man of God lives "not by bread alone," but "by the word of God" and that temptations incident to fullness or immoderation of appetite are shattered by abstinence.

Therefore, blessed ones, whom the grace of God awaits, when you ascend from that most sacred font of your new birth, and spread your hands for the first time in the house of your mother, together with your brethren, ask from the Father, ask from the Lord, that his own specialties of grace and distributions of gifts may be supplied you. "Ask," says he, "and you shall receive." Well, you *have* asked, and have received; you *have* knocked, and it has been opened to you. Only, I pray that, when you are asking, you be mindful likewise of Tertullian the sinner.

June 9

Columba

Abbot of Iona, Missionary, 597

Born in Ireland in about the year 521, Columba was trained as a monk by Finnian and then founded several monasteries himself, including probably that of Kells, before leaving Ireland to settle off the west coast of Scotland on the isle of Iona. He was accompanied by twelve companions and the number grew as the monastic life became more established and well-known. Columba seems to have been an austere and, at times, harsh man who reputedly mellowed with age. He was concerned with building up both the monastery and its life and of enabling them to be instruments of mission in a heathen land. He converted kings and built churches, Iona becoming a starting point for the expansion of Christianity throughout Scotland. In the last four years of his life, when his health had failed, he spent the time transcribing books of the Gospels for them to be taken out and used. He died on this day in the year 597.

A Reading from *The Life of Columba* by Adomnan, a later abbot of Iona

Saint Columba was born of noble lineage. When he was forty-one he sailed away from Ireland to Britain, choosing to be a pilgrim for Christ. From boyhood he had devoted himself to training in the Christian life, and to the study of wisdom; with God's help, he had kept his body chaste and his mind pure, and shown himself, though placed on earth, fit for the life of heaven. He was like an angel in demeanor, blameless in what he said, godly in what he did, brilliant in intellect and great in counsel. He spent thirty-four years as an island soldier, and could not let even an hour pass without giving himself to praying or reading or writing or some other task. Fasts and vigils he performed day and night with tireless labor and no rest, to such a degree that the burden of even one seemed beyond human endurance. At the same time he was loving to all people, and his face showed a holy gladness because his heart was full of the joy of the Holy Spirit.

When his end was approaching, the venerable man and his faithful servant Diarmait went to bless the nearest barn. As he entered, the saint blessed it and the two heaps of grain stored there.

With a gesture of thankfulness, he said: "I am very glad for the monks of my community, knowing that if I have to go away somewhere you will have bread enough for a year." Hearing this, the servant Diarmait was saddened and said: "Father, this year you make us sad too often as you speak frequently about your passing."

Later that night, when vespers was ended, Columba returned to his lodgings and rested on his bed, where at night instead of straw he had bare rock and a stone for a pillow, which today stands as a memorial beside his grave. There he gave his last commands to the brethren, with only his servant to hear: "I commend to you, my little children, these my last words: Love one another unfeignedly. Peace. If you keep this course according to the example of the holy fathers, God, who strengthens the good, will help you, and I dwelling with him shall intercede for you. He will supply not only enough for the needs of this present life, but also the eternal things that are prepared as a reward for those who keep the Lord's commandments."

As the bell rang out for the midnight office, the saint rose in haste and went to the church, running in ahead of the others and knelt alone in prayer before the altar. In the same moment his servant Diarmait following behind, saw from a distance the whole church filled inside with angelic light around the saint. As he reached the door, the light vanished. The lamps of the brethren had not yet been brought, but feeling his way in the dark he found the saint lying before the altar. Raising him up a little and sitting down at his side, he cradled the holy head on his bosom.

Meanwhile the monks and their lamps had gathered, and they began to lament at the sight of their father dying. Some of those who were present have related how, before his soul left him, the saint opened his eyes and looked about him with a wonderful joy and gladness in his face, for he could see the angels coming to meet him. Diarmait held up the saint's right hand to bless the choir of monks, and he gave up the ghost.

June 10

Ephrem of Edessa

Deacon, Hymn Writer, Teacher of the Faith, 373

Born of Christian parents around 306, Ephrem was baptized as a young man and then ordained deacon. His early years were spent as a teacher in Nisibis in Mesopotamia until the city fell under Persian occupation in 363. Fleeing from his home, he settled in Edessa (Urfa in south-east Turkey) where he established a school of theology. Best known for his Syriac poetry, Ephrem is acclaimed as the greatest poet of the early Christian centuries, described by his contemporaries as the "Harp of the Spirit." His hymns, still used today, have found a place in liturgical traditions outside the East Syrian Church. He died on this day in Edessa in the year 373, ministering to victims of the plague.

A Reading from the *Hymns of Faith* of Ephrem of Edessa

Truth and love are wings that cannot be separated,
for truth without love is unable to fly,
so too love without truth is unable to soar up:
their yoke is one harmony.

Lord, turn me back to your teaching:
I wanted to stand back,
but I saw that I became the poorer.
For the soul does not get any benefit
except through converse with you.

Whenever I have meditated upon you
I have acquired a veritable treasure from you;
Whatever aspect of you I have contemplated,
a stream has flowed from you.
There is no way in which I can contain it.

Your fountain, Lord, is hidden
from the person who does not thirst for you;
Your treasury seems empty
to the person who rejects you.
Love is the treasure of your heavenly store.

June 11

Saint Barnabas the Apostle

Though not listed among the twelve apostles according to the evangelists, Barnabas emerges in the Acts of the Apostles as one of the most significant of their number. He sold his estate and gave the proceeds to the Church, since all things were to be held in common, and clearly became a leader. He is described as a Levite from Cyprus so, like his friend Paul, was from the Greek world rather than that of Palestine, and it was he who introduced Paul to the leaders of the Church in Jerusalem. He was sent to Antioch apparently to guide the Christians there in their relations with non-Jewish converts, promoting the concept of all being one in Christ. He broke with Paul to go to Cyprus and tradition has it that he was martyred there in the year 61.

A Reading from the commentary of Cyril of Alexandria on Saint John's Gospel

Our Lord Jesus Christ has appointed certain people to be guides and teachers of the world and stewards of his divine mysteries. He bids them to shine out like the sun, the moon, and the stars, and to cast their light not only over the land of the Jews, but on every country under the sun and on all people wherever they may be scattered, in whatever distant land they reside.

That person was indeed speaking the truth who said: "No one takes this honor upon himself, but each one is called by God." For our Lord Jesus Christ called his disciples before all others to this most glorious apostolate. These holy disciples became the pillars and buttresses of the truth, and Christ said that he was sending them just as he had been sent by his Father.

By these words he is making clear the dignity of the apostolate and the incomparable glory of the power given to them, but he is also, it would seem, giving them a hint about the methods they are to adopt in their apostolic mission. For if Christ thought it necessary to send out his intimate disciples in this fashion, just as the Father had sent him, then surely it was necessary that they whose mission was to be patterned on that of Jesus should see exactly why the Father had sent the Son. And so Christ interpreted the character of his mission to us in a variety of ways. Once he said: "I have come to call not the righteous but sinners to repentance." And then at another time he said: "I have come down from heaven, not to do my own will, but the will of him who sent me. For God sent his Son into the world, not to condemn the world, but that the world might be saved through him."

Accordingly, in affirming that they are sent as he was sent by the Father, Christ sums up in a few words the approach they themselves should take to their ministry. From what he said they would gather that it was their vocation to call sinners to repentance, to heal those who were sick whether in body or spirit, to seek in all their dealings never to do their own will but the will of him who sent them, and as far as possible to save the world by their teaching.

Surely it is in all these respects that we find his holy disciples striving to excel. To ascertain this is no great labor; a single reading of the Acts of the Apostles or of Saint Paul's writings is enough.

June 12

Enmegahbowh

Priest and Missionary, 1902

Born of a Christian mother in the Ottawa tribe in Canada, John Johnson Enmegahbowh came into the United States as a Methodist missionary in 1832. Becoming discouraged, he decided to abandon missionary work and return across the lake to Canada, but a storm came up and he had a vision in which Jonah addressed him, saying, "Ah, my friend Enmegahbowh, I know you. You are a fugitive. You have sinned and disobeyed God. Instead of going to the city of Ninevah, where God sent you to spread his word to the people, you started to go, and then turned aside." Enmegahbowh turned back to Minnesota and invited the Rev. James Lloyd Breck to work with him in establishing the mission that was eventually moved to White Earth and where he served until his death. Enmegahbowh ("The One Who Stands before His People") is the first recognized Native American priest in the Episcopal Church. Ordained deacon by Bishop Kemper in 1859 and priest by Bishop Whipple in the cathedral at Faribault in 1867, he worked for peace among warring tribes and helped train many others to serve as deacons throughout northern Minnesota.

A Reading from *Enmegahbowh's Story*
by John Johnson Enmegahbowh

I resume to inform you what happened after the meeting with the first chiefs and warriors of the Chippewa nation. These chiefs and warriors were all heathen. They worshipped to wood and stone. They go to meet a man who comes with a different religious spirit, a man who comes to destroy and annihilate their religious faith and worship, the grand medicine faith of our forefathers and great grandfathers. This man, Enmegahbowh, came to teach them a new religion. (Some of these chiefs had heard my teaching before they were removed.) What changed them, and caused them to grasp the Christian teachings?

The first night of our encampment shall never be forgotten. We were talking and talking about our future, what to do and how to live in the new country, White Earth, I was so glad to hear them. I did not at once urge upon them that they all must turn to Christianity. This very point I save until I know the favorable time has arrived. Our encampment four nights were spent talking of our great aim to raise them from their present condition. On the fourth day all left me to go home and bear the message that the poor Enmegahbowh was coming sure, and would be there in two days. And this made no little stir with gladness. But there was one, an educated mixed blood, who was opposed to my coming, and he told the heathen that I was coming to do much injury to them and their new country. The chiefs and warriors gave no heed, and his foolish talking didn't amount to much of anything.

I arrived on Friday. A little comfortable log house had been provided for my dwelling house. Sunday came, and to my great astonishment, chiefs and headmen, women and children, of all grades, came to listen to my teachings. I was moved with compassion to see them seek shelter and strong stockade for shelter, the most impregnable fortress of Christian religion, the only hope of salvation for my unfortunate race.

My greatest aim was to catch all the leading chiefs, and to kill all their little hope that was in them, because when this is done and accomplished, I shall think that my work is truly accomplished. I shall think that my work is truly commenced. This had truly come to pass. I have never seen so much earnestness manifested by these chiefs, talking and talking to their people to receive my instructions, the only hope of our people and of their welfare.

During the winter we used the largest wigwam or our log house, and during the summer I held my public services under the shade of the trees. In the second year I had nearly all the chiefs and the leading men and women under my teachings. I must say, I have lived with my own people from the beginning of my days to the present time. I never saw so large a community of heathen people live so harmoniously and in so great peace.

June 14

Basil the Great

Bishop of Caesarea, 379

Gregory of Nazianzus and Basil of Caesarea were two friends bound together by their desire to promote and defend the divinity of Christ as proclaimed in the Nicene Creed. This was against the seemingly overwhelming pressure from both church and state for the establishment of Arianism, which denied Christ's divinity and thus the whole Christian doctrine of the Trinity. Basil was renowned for being headstrong and forceful in comparison to his friend Gregory, who would rather spend his days in prayer and living the simple, ascetic life. Their joint persuasive eloquence convinced the first Council of Constantinople, meeting in 381, that their teaching was the truly orthodox one and the Council ratified the text of the Nicene Creed in the form used in the East to this day. Basil died in 379 and Gregory ten years later.

A Reading from a letter of Basil the Great to Gregory of Nazianzus, written in about 358 following Basil's move to Pontus in Cappadocia

What I do, day and night, in this remote spot, I am ashamed to write to you about. I have abandoned my career in the city because I am convinced that it will only make me further depressed. Within myself, I am still largely unresolved: I am like a traveler on the ocean who has never been on a voyage before and becomes ill and seasick. Such folk moan because the ship is large and has such an enormous swell, and yet the moment they transfer to a smaller boat or dinghy, they are tossed about even more and become violently ill. Wherever they go, they cannot escape from their nausea and depression. My internal state is something like this. I carry my own problems with me wherever I go and there is no escape.

So in the end, I have got very little out of my solitude. What I ought to have done, what would have helped me to walk securely in the footsteps of Jesus who has led me on the path of salvation, would have been to have come here long ago. Has not our Lord said: "If any would come after me, let them deny themselves, take up their cross and follow me?"

We must strive for a quiet mind. The eye cannot appreciate an object set before it if it is perpetually restless, glancing here, there and everywhere. No more can our mind's eye apprehend the truth with any clarity if it is distracted by a thousand worldly concerns. For just as it is impossible to write upon a wax tablet without first having erased the marks on it, so it is impossible to receive the impress of divine doctrine without unlearning our inherited preconceptions and habitual prejudices. Solitude offers an excellent opportunity in this process because it calms our passions, and creates space for our reason to remove their influence.

Let there be, therefore, places such as this, where we may pursue such spiritual training without interruption, nourishing our souls with thoughts of God. After all, what can be better than to imitate the choirs of angels, to begin a day with prayer, honoring our Creator with hymns and songs? And as the day brightens, to pursue our daily tasks to the accompaniment of prayers, seasoning our labor with hymns as if they were salt? Such soothing melodies compose the mind and establish it in tranquillity.

Our one concern is to flourish in self-control and courage, justice and wisdom, and all those other virtues in their various categories which guide the good person in the proper conduct of life.

alternative reading

A Reading from the eulogy preached in 379 by Gregory of Nazianzus following the death of his life-long friend Basil the Great

Basil and I were at Athens at the time. Like streams of a river, we originated from a common source in our native land, but in going abroad to pursue our studies we had become separated; but now, as if it were planned, as if God had wanted it this way, we found ourselves reunited.

I was not alone during this time in holding my friend, the great Basil, in high regard. I needed no convincing of his seriousness of purpose, his mature and wise conversation, but I sought to persuade others unacquainted with him, to share my regard for him. He was already well respected by many since his reputation had gone before him, with the result that he was accorded the special distinction of being almost the only new student in Athens to escape the treatment generally doled out to newcomers.

This was the prelude to our friendship. This was the kindling of that flame that was to bind us together. We recognized a bond of mutual love. Gradually we were able to admit our affection for one another and to recognize our common ambition to dedicate ourselves to lives of true wisdom. From then on we became inseparable friends, sharing the same lodgings, the same table, the same sentiments, our eyes fixed on the same goal. Our mutual affection grew ever warmer and stronger.

We were driven on by the same hope: the pursuit of learning. This is an area of life notoriously open to jealousy; but between us there was none. Indeed, in some sense rivalry intensified our zeal. For there was indeed a contest between us. But it was not about who should have first place, but about how one could yield it to the other. For each of us regarded the achievement of the other as his own.

We seemed to have a single soul animating two bodies. And, while we could not believe those who claim that "everything is contained in everything," yet in our experience, we were certainly intimately bound up in one another's lives. Our sole object and ambition was virtue and a life so oriented in hope to the blessings that await us, that we severed our attachment to this life before we had to depart it. With this in view we ordered our life and actions, following the guidance of God's law, and at the same time spurred each other on to virtue. And, if it is not too much to say, we were for each other a rule and a pair of scales for discerning good from evil.

Different men have different names, either derived from their ancestors or to do with their jobs and achievements. But our great ambition, the great name we relished, was to be Christian, and to be called Christians.

June 15

Evelyn Underhill
Spiritual Writer, 1941

Born in 1875, Evelyn Underhill was in her thirties before she began to explore religion. At first, she wrote on the mystics, most notably in her book Mysticism, *published in 1911. Her spiritual journey brought her in 1921 back to the Church of England, in which she had been baptized and confirmed. From the mid-1920s, she became highly-regarded as a retreat conductor and an influential spiritual director. Of her many books*

Worship, *published in 1936, embodied her approach to what she saw as the mystery of faith. She died on this day in the year 1941.*

A Reading from *Worship* by Evelyn Underhill

Worship, in all its grades and kinds, is the response of the creature to the eternal: nor need we limit this definition to the human sphere. There is a sense in which we may think of the whole life of the universe, seen and unseen, conscious and unconscious, as an act of worship, glorifying its Origin, Sustainer, and End. Only in some such context, indeed, can we begin to understand the emergence and growth of the spirit of worship in men and women, or the influence which it exerts upon their concrete activities. Thus worship may be overt or direct, unconscious or conscious. Where conscious, its emotional color can range from fear through to self-oblivious love. But whatever its form of expression may be, it is always a subject-object relationship; and its general existence therefore constitutes a damaging criticism of all merely subjective and immanental explanations of reality. For worship is an acknowledgement of transcendence; that is to say, of a reality independent of the worshipper, which is always more or less deeply colored by mystery, and which is there first.

Directly we take this strange thing worship seriously, and give it the status it deserves among the various responses of men to their environment, we find that it obliges us to take up a particular attitude toward that environment. Even in its crudest form, the law of prayer indeed the fact of prayer is already the law of belief; since humanity's universal instinct to worship cannot be accounted for, if naturalism tells the whole truth about life. That instinct means the latent recognition of a metaphysical reality, standing over against physical reality, which human beings are driven to adore, and long to apprehend. In other words it is the implicit, even though unrecognized vision of God that disclosure of the supernatural which is overwhelming, self-giving, and attractive all at once which is the first cause of all worship, from the puzzled upward glance of the primitive to the delighted self-oblation of the saint.

It is possible to regard worship as one of the greatest of humanity's mistakes; a form taken by the fantasy-life, the desperate effort of bewildered creatures to come to terms with the surrounding mystery. Or it may be accepted as the most profound of man's responses to reality; and more than this, the organ of his divine knowledge and the earnest of eternal life.

We are bound to take worship seriously, and ever more seriously with the deepening of our own spiritual sense. Worship points steadily toward the reality of God: gives, expresses, and maintains that which is the essence of all sane religion a theocentric basis to life. The first or central act of religion is *adoration,* the sense of God, his otherness though nearness, his distinctness from all finite beings though not separateness aloofness from them. In this great *sanctus*, all things justify their being and have their place. God alone matters, God alone is creation only matters because of God.

alternative reading

A Prayer of Evelyn Underhill

For Wholeness

O Lord, penetrate those murky corners
where we hide memories and tendencies
on which we do not care to look,
but which we will not disinter
and yield freely up to you,
that you may purify and transmute them:
the persistent buried grudge,
the half-acknowledged enmity
which is still smoldering;
the bitterness of that loss
we have not turned into sacrifice;
the private comfort we cling to;
the secret fear of failure which saps our initiative
and is really inverted pride;
the pessimism which is an insult to your joy, Lord;
we bring all these to you,
and we review them with shame and penitence
in your steadfast light.

June 16

Joseph Butler
Bishop of Durham, Philosopher, 1752

Born in 1692 at Wantage, Joseph Butler was the son of Presbyterian parents and studied at the dissenting academy of Tewkesbury. He abandoned Presbyterianism in 1714 for the Church of England and, after studying at Oxford, was ordained priest in 1718 and began preaching the sermons which won him his fine reputation. He became Bishop of Durham and is ranked among the greatest exponents of natural theology and ethics in England since the Reformation. He died on this day in the year 1752.

A Reading from *The Analogy of Religion*
by Joseph Butler

Whatever account may be given of the strange inattention and disregard in some ages and countries to a matter of such importance as religion, it would, before experience, be incredible that there should be the like disregard in those who have had the moral system of the world laid before them as it is by Christianity, and often inculcated upon them: because this moral system carries in it a good degree of evidence for its truth, upon its being barely proposed to our thoughts. There is no need of abstruse reasonings and distinctions to convince an unprejudiced understanding that there is a God who made and governs the world, and will judge it in righteousness; though they may be necessary to answer abstruse difficulties when once such are raised; when the very meaning of those words which express most intelligibly the general doctrine of religion is pretended to be uncertain; and the clear truth of the thing itself is obscured by the intricacies of speculation.

To an unprejudiced mind, ten thousand thousand instances of design cannot but prove a designer. And it is intuitively manifest that creatures ought to live under a dutiful sense of their Maker; and that justice and charity must be his laws to creatures whom he has made social, and placed in society. Indeed the truth of revealed religion, peculiarly so called, is not self-evident, but requires external proof in order to its being received. Yet inattention among us to revealed religion will be found to imply the same dissolute immoral temper of mind as inattention to natural religion; because, when both are laid before us in the manner they are in Christian countries of liberty, our obligations to inquire into both, and to embrace both upon supposition of their truth, are obligations of the same nature.

For revelation claims to be the voice of God, and our obligation to attend to his voice is surely moral in all cases. And as it is insisted that its evidence is conclusive upon thorough consideration of it, so it offers itself to us with manifest obvious appearances of having something more than human in it, and therefore in all reason requires to have its claims most seriously examined into. It is to be added that though light and knowledge, in what manner soever afforded us, is equally from God, yet a miraculous revelation has a peculiar tendency from the first principles of our nature to awaken mankind, and inspire them with reverence and awe; and this is a peculiar obligation to attend to what claims to be so with such appearances of truth.

It is therefore most certain that our obligations to inquire seriously into the evidence of Christianity, and upon supposition of its truth, to embrace it, are of utmost importance.

June 18

Bernard Mizeki

Apostle of the MaShona, Martyr, 1896

Born in Portuguese East Africa, Bernard Mizeki went to work in Cape Town and there he was converted to the Christian faith by the Cowley Fathers (The Society of Saint John the Evangelist). He then gave his life as a translator and evangelist among the MaShona in what is present day Zimbabwe. He was murdered on this day in 1896 in a tribal uprising and is revered throughout Central Africa as a witness to the gospel of Christ. The site of his martyrdom has become an important place of pilgrimage for many Africans.

A Reading from *Mashonaland Martyr*
by Jean Farrant

June 14, 1896 was a Sunday, a crisp, clear day of the Mashonaland winter. Bernard Mizeki was troubled. Mutwa, his wife, now carried their child in her womb. Had he been right to disobey the orders of the priest in Umtali who had said that all catechists and teachers were to seek safety at Penhalonga? The priest had heard rumors that disturbed him, and feared that any Africans who were associated with the Europeans would be killed.

In his reply, Bernard had written: "Chief Mangwende's people are suffering. The bishop has put me here and told me to remain. Until the bishop returns, here I must stay. I cannot leave my people now in a time of such darkness."

As the hours passed, Bernard's wife became increasingly restless and kept saying that she had "heard things" when she visited Mount Mahopo. She had become almost hysterical when Bernard had cut down the mukute trees and cleared a small plot of ground for growing wheat. She told him the trees were a sacred grove, the abode of the spirits of Chief Mangwende's ancestors. Bernard went out to the newly-cut stumps of the trees, and, thinking it would comfort her, cut a cross in each one saying: "There! I cut the cross. The cross makes us safe from all spirits and sorcerers." But it made no difference to Mutwa who begged him to flee saying that he was in great danger.

Two days later at about midnight, there came a loud knocking at the hut door. "It is Ziute, Mangwende's son," a voice shouted. "Open this door. Mangwende has been killed. European troopers came to the village and shot him. They have beaten the people and driven away our cattle and goats!"

Startled and incredulous, Bernard opened the door. Ziute and another man, Saridjgo, came in. Bernard protested that they were lying or he would have heard news of it before. As he spoke the two men knocked him off balance and dragged him outside the hut where a third man was waiting, armed with a spear. While the two men held him down he drove the spear into Bernard's side.

Believing him to be dead, the attackers fled into the night. As soon as Mutwa was certain they had gone, she crept out of the hut, searching for her husband in the darkness. Eventually she and another woman found Bernard by the water spring where he was trying to wash his wound. He pleaded with the women to leave him, to flee and hide themselves. "Your uncles have attacked me and I am dying," he said to Mutwa. "I wish you to be baptized and the child in your womb. Do not think that because your uncles have killed me the work of the priests and teachers is ended. No, when I am dead there will come many more priests, and one day all your people will be Christian."

Bernard became weak and breathless. Together the two women stole down the hill to the hut to get food and blankets for him. As they began to climb the slope again, they were almost blinded by a great and brilliant white light. The whole of the hillside was lit up and there was a noise "like many wings of great birds." The noise came lower and lower, and as they crouched on the ground, covering their eyes, the women saw through their fingers that in the center of the light where Bernard lay, there was a strange red glow.

After a long time the noise ceased. The light disappeared, but so had Bernard. They crept up the hillside to the rock above the spring. Bernard had gone. They never saw him again and his body was never found.

June 22

Alban

First Martyr of Britain, *c.*250

Alban was a citizen of the Roman city of Verulamium (now St. Alban's in Hertfordshire) who gave shelter to a Christian priest fleeing from persecution, hiding him in his house for several days. Greatly influenced by his devotion to prayer, Alban received instruction from the priest and was converted. When the priest's hidingplace was discovered, Alban dressed himself in the priest's cloak and was arrested in his place. Tortured by the Roman authorities, Alban refused to renounce his faith. He was beheaded on this day, probably in the year 250, and so became the first British martyr. His shrine stands today as a place of pilgrimage in the Cathedral and Abbey Church of Saint Alban.

A Reading from *A History of the English Church and People* by the Venerable Bede

In this country there occurred the suffering of Saint Alban, of whom the priest Fortunatus in his *Praise of the Virgins*, in which he mentions all the blessed martyrs who came to God from every quarter of the globe, says:

In fertile Britain's land
Was illustrious Alban born.

The Emperors Diocletian in the East and Maximianus Heculius in the West had ordered all churches to be destroyed and all Christians to be hunted out and killed. This was the tenth persecution since Nero, and it was more protracted and cruel than almost any that had preceded it. When these unbelieving rulers were issuing violent edicts against the Christians, Alban, though still a pagan at the time, gave shelter to a Christian priest who was fleeing from his persecutors. In the days that followed, Alban observed this man's constant faithfulness in prayer and vigil, and was touched by the grace of God and began to imitate the priest's example of faith and devotion. Little by little, he received instruction in the way of salvation until one day Alban renounced the darkness of idolatry, and wholeheartedly accepted Christ.

But when the priest had lived in his house some days, word came to the ears of the evil ruler that Christ's confessor, whose place of martyrdom had not yet been appointed, was hiding in Alban's house. Accordingly he gave orders to his soldiers to make a thorough search, and when they arrived at the martyr's house, Saint Alban, wearing the priest's long cloak, surrendered himself to the soldiers in the place of his guest and teacher, and was led bound before the judge.

When Alban was brought in, the judge happened to be standing before an altar, offering sacrifice to devils. Seeing Alban, he was furious that he had presumed to put himself in such danger by surrendering himself to the soldiers in place of his guest, and ordered him to be dragged before the idols where he was standing. "Since you have chosen to conceal a sacrilegious rebel," he said, "rather than surrender him to my soldiers to pay the well-deserved penalty for his blasphemy against the gods, you shall undergo all the punishment due to him, if you dare to abandon the practice of our religion."

But Saint Alban, who had freely confessed himself a Christian to the enemies of the faith, was not intimidated by such threats, and armed with spiritual strength, openly refused to obey this order. "What is your family and race?" the judge asked. "Of what concern is my family to you?" replied Alban. "If you wish to know the truth about my religion, know that I am now a Christian, and am ready to do a Christian's duty." The judge said, "I insist on knowing your name. Tell me at once." "My parents named me Alban," he answered, "and I worship and adore the living and true God, who created all things."

Incensed at his reply, the judge ordered God's holy confessor Alban to be flogged by the executioners, declaring that he would shake his constancy of heart by blows, since words had no effect. But Alban bore the most horrible torments patiently and even gladly for Christ's sake. When the judge realized that no torture could break him or make him renounce the worship of Christ, he ordered him to be executed.

And thus it was that Saint Alban suffered on June 22 near the city of Verulamium. Here, when the peace of Christian times was restored, a beautiful church worthy of his martyrdom was built, where sick folk are healed and frequent miracles take place to this day.

June 24

The Nativity of Saint John the Baptist

The Biblical story of John, the son of Elizabeth and Zechariah, begins even before his birth. His leaping in his mother's womb is seen as a great alleluia in anticipation of the birth of his redeemer, and in all four Gospels the good news of Jesus Christ is related as beginning with the emergence of John as the forerunner of Christ. He seemed to have a predestined role akin to that of the Old Testament prophets, particularly in encouraging the people of God to live lives worthy of their calling and in imminent anticipation of the coming of the Anointed One. In the tradition of the early fathers, John was seen as endowed with grace from before his birth, and consequently the Church has always kept the celebration of this day with greater solemnity than that of his death.

A Reading from a sermon of Augustine

The Church observes the birth of John as a holy event. We have no such commemoration for any other of our forebears, and it is significant that we celebrate the birthdays of both John and Jesus. I cannot, therefore, let this day pass without a sermon, and even if my brief words fail to do justice to the dignity of the day, the profundity of the feast will itself give you food for thought.

John's mother was old and barren, while Christ's mother was young and a virgin. The news of John's birth was met with incredulity by his father, and he was struck dumb. The Virgin Mary believed, and Christ was conceived in faith. Such is the subject of our investigation and discourse. But as I have said, if I find myself incapable, either through lack of time or through lack of ability, to plumb the depths of this mystery, I know the Holy Spirit will enlighten you. The voice of the Spirit will make itself heard within you without any help from me, for it is he whom you contemplate in your hearts and minds, and whose temples you have become.

John marks the boundary between the Old and New Testaments. Indeed the Lord speaks of him as a sort of boundary line when he says that "the Law and the prophets are valid until John the Baptist." John is both the representative of the past, and the herald of the new. As a representative of the past, it was fitting that he should have been born of elderly parents; and yet while still in his mother's womb he was declared to be a prophet in recognition of his future role. Although unborn, he leapt in his mother's womb at the arrival of blessed Mary. In the womb he was already designated Christ's precursor before they ever met in the flesh. These divine mysteries transcend the limits of our frail human reasoning. When at last John is born and receives his name, his father's tongue was loosened. Let us reflect on the event.

Zechariah had fallen silent and lost the power of speech until John, the Lord's precursor, is born and restores his voice. Is there not a prophetic dimension to Zechariah's silence, as if there were something hidden, kept secret until Christ could be proclaimed? Zechariah's voice is restored with the birth of John: his speech becomes clear when he is born as was foretold. This restoration can be paralleled to the rending of the veil of the Temple at Christ's crucifixion. If John were announcing his own coming, he could not have restored his father's speech. But Zechariah's tongue was loosened because a voice was born. For when John was preaching the coming of the Lord, he was asked: "Who are you?" And he replied: "I am the voice of one crying in the wilderness." John was indeed a voice, but in the beginning was the Word. John was a voice that lasted only for a time; Christ, who is the Word from the beginning, is eternal.

alternative reading

A Reading from a homily of Rabanus Maurus,
Archbishop of Mainz

Today we celebrate the birth of Saint John the Baptist. It is right that the births of our Lord and Saint John should be celebrated throughout the world because each is a profound mystery worthy of our contemplation. A barren woman gave birth to John, a virgin conceived Christ; in Elizabeth barrenness was overcome, in Blessed Mary the way of human conception was changed. It was through knowing her husband that Elizabeth brought forth a son: Mary believed the angel and conceived a child. Elizabeth conceived a child who was a human being: Mary conceived both God and man.

Great then is John. Indeed, the Savior himself testified to John's greatness when he said that "among those born of woman there has arisen no one greater than John the Baptist." He excels all, each and every one of us. He is greater than the prophets, he is superior to the patriarchs. Everyone born of woman is inferior to John, except the son of the Virgin who is greater still, as John himself said: "He who comes after me ranks before me, and I am not worthy to undo the strap of his sandal."

In the birth of our Lord's forerunner and in the birth of our redeemer there is this mystery: the prophet's birth signifies our humility, but the Lord's birth our ultimate exaltation. John was born as the days began to grow shorter: Christ was born in winter as the days were growing longer, because it was fitting that our status should grow smaller and the glory of God grow greater. John realized this when he said: "I must grow smaller and he must grow greater." John was sent ahead like a voice before a word, a lamp before the sun, a herald before a judge, a servant before his master, the best man before the bridegroom.

We have recognized the blessed forerunner of the Lord as a lamp which went ahead of the true light and who bore witness to the light so that all might believe through him. So let us have recourse to him and attend to his proclamation. Indeed his is the voice announced by the prophet Isaiah: "A voice cries out in the wilderness: 'Prepare the way of the Lord. Make straight his paths. Every valley shall be lifted up, and every mountain and hill be made low; the uneven ground shall become level, and the rough places a plain. And all flesh shall see the salvation of our God.'"

Let us too, therefore, prepare a way for the Lord who is to come into our hearts. Let us remove the barriers of sin by confession and repentance; let us straighten the paths of our life which for too long have been undirected and devious; let us pave the way of true faith with good works. Let us rid ourselves of all arrogance and lift high our fainting hearts. Then, when all is in order, smoothed, and brought into harmony, we shall see the salvation of God as he is, for "his home is in peace and his dwelling in Zion."

alternative reading

A Reading from *God and Man*
by Metropolitan Anthony of Sourozh

When you open Saint Mark's Gospel, you find that John the Baptist is defined as a voice that shouts in the wilderness. He is not even defined as a prophet or a messenger of God. He has got so identified with the message, he has become so one with God's own word which he has got to proclaim and to bring to people that one can no longer see him behind the message, hear the tune of his voice behind the thundering witness of God's own spirit speaking through him.

This is one thing we should learn. Too often when we bring a message, people can perceive us and a message which perhaps comes through us, because we are not sufficiently identified with what we have got to say. In order to be identified we must so read the gospel, make it so much ourselves, and ourselves so much the gospel, that when we speak from within it, in its name, it should be simply whatever words we use. I am not speaking of quota-tions it should be simply the gospel that speaks and we should be like a voice God's voice.

The second thing is that to attain to that state in which John could speak and not be noticed, in which all that people could perceive of him was a man who had been completely transformed into a message, into a vision, into a proclamation, meant that he was a man who consented to lay aside all that was selfish, grasping, all that was delighting selfishly in whatever he wanted to have. He had a pure heart, a clear mind, an unwavering will, a trained body, a complete mastery of self, so that when the message came, fear would not defeat him and make him silent; promises could not beguile him and make him silent, or simply the heaviness of the flesh, the heaviness of the mind, the heaviness of the heart, should not overcome the lightness and the lightening power of the spirit. This is something that is also our task.

June 28

Cyril

Bishop of Alexandria, Teacher of the Faith, 444

Cyril was born in Alexandria and is first heard of as a young priest. He succeeded his uncle as Patriarch in the year 412 and began his great defence of the orthodox doctrines of God the Holy Trinity, and of the Incarnate Christ as a unique, single Person, at once God and human. His chief opponent was Nestorius, the Patriarch of Constantinople, who appears to have taught that there were two separate Persons co-existing in the Incarnate Christ, the one divine and the other human. The Nestorian Party thus rejected the description of Mary as Theotokos, *"the God-bearer," and also rejected the papal ruling that they comply with Cyril's doctrinal position that the union between divinity and humanity in Christ was total and real. The Council of Ephesus was convened in the year 431 to rule on the matter (see reading for March 25) and eventually gave its full support to Cyril, making the term* Theotokos *the touchstone of Christian orthodoxy. Cyril's writings reflect his outstanding qualities as a theologian. They are marked by precision in exposition, accuracy in thought, and skill in reasoning. He died at Alexandria in the year 444.*

A Reading from the commentary of Cyril of Alexandria on Saint John's Gospel

In a plan of surpassing beauty the creator of the universe decreed the renewal of all things in Christ. In his design for restoring human nature to its original condition, he gave a promise that he would pour out on it the Holy Spirit along with his other gifts, for otherwise our nature could not enter once more into the peaceful and secure possession of those gifts.

He therefore appointed a time for the Holy Spirit to come upon us: this was the time of Christ's coming. He gave this promise when he said: "In those days," that is, the days of the Savior, "I will pour out a share of my Spirit on all humanity."

When the time came for this act of unforced generosity, which revealed in our midst the only-begotten Son, clothed with flesh on this earth, born of woman, in accordance with holy Scripture, God the Father gave the Spirit once again. Christ, as the firstfruits of our restored nature, was the first to receive the Spirit. John the Baptist bore witness to this when he said, "I saw the Spirit coming down from heaven, and it rested on him."

Christ "received the Spirit" insofar as he was human, and insofar as a human being could receive the Spirit. He did so in such a way that, though he is the Son of God the Father, begotten of his substance, even before the incarnation, indeed before all ages, yet he was not offended at hearing the Father say to him after he had become human: "You are my Son; today I have begotten you."

The Father says of Christ, who was God, begotten of him before the ages, that he has been "begotten today," for the Father is to accept us in Christ as his adopted children. The whole of our nature is present in Christ, insofar as he is human. So the Father can be said to give the Spirit again to the Son, though the Son possesses the Spirit as his own, in order that we may receive the Spirit in Christ. The Son, therefore, took to himself the seed of Abraham, as Scripture says, and became like us in all things.

The only-begotten Son receives the Spirit, but not for his own advantage, for the Spirit is his, and is given in him and through him, as we have already said. He receives it to renew our nature in its entirety and to make it whole again, for in becoming human he took our entire nature to himself. If we reason correctly, and use also the testimony of Scripture, we can see that Christ did not receive the Spirit for himself, but rather for us in him; for it is also through Christ that all gifts come down to us.

June 28

Irenaeus

Bishop of Lyons, Teacher of the Faith, *c.*200

Irenaeus was probably a native of Smyrna, born about the year 130. As a boy, he had heard Polycarp preach, who had in turn been a disciple of the Apostle John. Irenaeus is thus one of the important connections between the apostolic Church and the second century. He studied at Rome, and later became a priest at Lyons in Gaul, succeeding as bishop upon the martyrdom of his predecessor in 177. He contended against the mythological, unhistorical beliefs of the Gnostics, giving positive value to the full humanity of the Incarnate Christ, and affirmed the public teaching role of the episcopate to combat false doctrine. He is honored as the first great Catholic theologian, one who drew upon the emerging traditions of East and West. Irenaeus died about the year 200.

A Reading from the treatise *Against the Heresies*
by Irenaeus

As those who see light stand within its compass and share its brilliancy, so those who see God are in God, and share his splendor. God's splendor is the source of life, and those who see God are sharing his life. Although beyond human comprehension, incomprehensible and invisible, God has made himself visible, comprehensible and knowable, so that those with faith might see him and live. His greatness is past searching out: his goodness is beyond the bounds of human language. Yet God allows himself to be seen, and in seeing God we come alive. Life is itself a gift, and the means of life is to be found in God alone, so as we come to share the life of God we are also coming to know God and to enjoy his favor.

Those who see God shall live: they will be made immortal by this vision and will be united with God. As Moses declared in Deuteronomy: "Today we have seen that God may speak to someone and that person will live." God sustains the universe in being. His nature and greatness cannot be seen or described by any of his creatures; but this does not mean he is unknowable. We learn from the Word that there is one God and Father who holds everything in being, and gives being to everything. Indeed, it is written in the gospel that "no one has seen God at any time, except his only-begotten Son who is close to the Father's heart who has made him known."

The Son has revealed the Father from the beginning, for he was with the Father in the beginning. He revealed God to the human race through the visions of the prophets, through various gifts, through his own ministry and the glory of the Father, at appropriate times and in order for our benefit. Where there is order, there is harmony; and where harmony exists we can be sure that the time is chosen; and when we know that, we can be sure that what is being revealed is for our benefit.

This is why the Word became the dispenser of the Father's grace for the benefit of humankind, and for our sake made these generous arrangements: revealing God to us, and raising us to God. In raising us to God, he shields the Father from human sight lest we ever undervalue God through familiarity, and also so that we always have something to strive after. On the other hand, he revealed God to us that we would not fall away and as a result, cease to exist. For the glory of God is a human being fully alive, and the life of humanity consists in the vision of God. Thus if the revelation of God in this world gives life to every living thing, how much more will the revelation of the Father by the Word give life to those who see God.

June 29

Saint Peter and Saint Paul
Apostles

Peter has often been called the "Prince of the Apostles" because of the words of Jesus re-naming him Cephas instead of Simon. This name was the Aramaic form of the Greek word Peter, which means "rock." Jesus said that on this rock he would build his Church. According to Saint Matthew, the title was given by Jesus in response to Peter's confession of faith in him as the Christ. Both Peter and Paul came to be honored as having different roles to play within the leadership of the Church: Peter witnessing to the Lordship of Christ, and Paul developing an understanding of its meaning for Christ's followers, Jew and Gentile alike. The two apostles have been remembered jointly on this day from the very early days of the Church, it being honored as the anniversary of their martyrdom in Rome about the year 64.

A Reading from a sermon of Augustine

This day has been made holy by the martyrdom of the blessed apostles Peter and Paul. We are, therefore, not talking about some obscure martyrs. For as Scripture says, "Their voice has gone forth to all the world, and their message to the ends of the earth." These martyrs realized what they taught: they followed the path of integrity, they confessed the truth, and they died for it.

Saint Peter, the foremost of the apostles and a passionate lover of Christ, heard his merits acknowledged when the Lord addressed him: "I say to you that you are Peter." For he had himself said: "You are the Christ, the Son of the living God." Then Christ said: "And I say to you that you are Peter, and on this rock I will build my Church." He meant that "Upon this rock I will build the faith that you now confess, for you have said to me, 'You are the Christ, the Son of the living God.' Therefore, I will build my Church on you, for you are Peter." The name Peter comes from *petra*, the word for rock, just as the word Christian comes from Christ.

In a virtually unique way then, Peter can be said to represent the entire Church. And because of the role which he alone had, he merited to hear the words: "To you I shall give the keys of the kingdom of heaven." It was not an individual who received those keys, but the entire Church considered as one. Now insofar as he represented the unity and universality of the Church, Peter's pre-eminence is clear from the words: "To you I give," for what was given was given to all. But it is clear that it was the Church that received the keys of the kingdom of God from what the Lord says elsewhere to all the apostles after his resurrection: "Receive the Holy Spirit," adding immediately, "whose sins you forgive, they are forgiven, and whose sins you retain, they are retained."

It was logical, therefore, that the Lord after his resurrection should entrust Peter with the care of his sheep. He was not the only disciple who was worthy of this responsibility, but in speaking only to this one man, we should understand that Christ was speaking to all. Peter was addressed because he was foremost among the apostles. Therefore do not be disheartened, Peter; answer once, twice, yes three times. This threefold confession of love is necessary to recover what you lost three times by your fear. Untie by love the knot that you tied about yourself through fear.

Paul emerges out of Saul, the lamb out of the wolf; at first an enemy, he becomes an apostle; at first a persecutor, he becomes the preacher. The Lord showed him the things that he too had to suffer for his name: chains, beatings, imprisonment, shipwrecks. The Lord sustained Paul in his sufferings, and brought him to this day.

Both apostles share the same feast day, for these two were one, even though they were martyred on different days. Peter went ahead, Paul followed. Let our way, then, be made straight in the Lord. It is a narrow, stony, hard road we tread; and yet with so many gone before us, we shall find the way smoother. The Lord himself trod this way, the unshakeable apostles and the holy martyrs likewise. So let us celebrate this feast day made holy by the blood of these two apostles. Let us embrace their faith, their life, their labors, their sufferings, their preaching, and their teaching.

alternative reading

A Reading from a sermon of Leo the Great

The Apostle Paul has taught us that as many as are baptized into Christ have clothed themselves with Christ, for "In Christ Jesus there is no longer Jew or Greek, slave or free, male or female; but all are one. And if you belong to Christ, you are Abraham's offspring, heirs of the promise."

My friends, there can be no doubt that the Son of God took our human nature into so intimate a union with himself that one and the same Christ is present, not only in the firstborn of all creation, but in all his saints as well. The head cannot be separated from the members, nor the members from the head. And although it is true that not in this life, but only in eternity, will "God be all in all," yet even now God dwells, whole and complete in his temple which is the Church. Indeed, this was his promise to us when Christ said: "See, I am with you always, even to the end of the world."

What the Son of God did and taught for the world's reconciliation is for us not simply a matter of past history. It is something we experience here and now through his power at work among us. Born of the Virgin Mother by the action of the Holy Spirit, Christ fertilizes his spotless Church by the inspiration of the same Spirit. In baptism she brings to birth children for God beyond all numbering, of whom it is written: "They are born not of blood, nor of the desire of the flesh, nor of human will, but of God."

In Christ Abraham's posterity is blessed, because in him the whole world is receiving adoption as heirs, and in him the patriarch is becoming the father of all nations through a birth, not from human stock but by faith, of the descendants that were promised to him. From every nation on earth without exception, Christ is forming a single flock of those he has hallowed, daily fulfilling the promise he once made: "I have other sheep, not of this fold, them also I must bring in; and there shall be one flock and one shepherd."

Although it was primarily to Peter that Christ said: "Feed my sheep," yet the one Lord guides all pastors in the discharge of their office and leads to rich and fertile pastures all those who come to the rock. There is no counting the sheep who are nourished by the richness of his love, and who do not hesitate to lay down their lives for the sake of the Good Shepherd who died for them. But it is not only the martyrs who share in Christ's sufferings by their glorious courage; the same is true, by faith, of all of us who are born again in baptism. In our baptism we have renounced the devil and put our faith in God; we have passed from our former way of life and embraced a new life; we have cast off the earthly and been clothed with the heavenly—all these things are images of our dying and rising with Christ. In baptism we are welcomed by Christ and we welcome him into our hearts. We should remember that we are all called to become the flesh of the Crucified.

JULY

July 4

Independence Day

The role of religion in American life is a contentious issue, but only because religion has held a place of such importance. The first continuing settlements in the present United States were not in New England, but the New England settlements were made for religious reasons and they have the primary place in the American mythology. When the Declaration of Independence was drawn up, it cited as "self-evident" the belief that human beings are "endowed by their Creator with certain unalienable rights." If the separation of church and state was enshrined in the Constitution, it was not to diminish the place of religion in American life, but to protect that place against the sort of government control so often established in Europe. Independence Day, then, is not simply a day to celebrate American freedom but a day to reflect on the way in which faith has undergirded that freedom and enriched it with a larger sense of purpose.

A Reading from a sermon of Phillips Brooks

Sometimes there come to us wonderings and questionings when we look at this variety of national character, each nation offering some type of life or some moral quality peculiarly its own—wonderings and questionings which correspond to those with which we ponder on the variety of individual characters which make up the united society in the midst of which we live. A new nation is born like a new man. A nation such as ours comes forth, latest and best equipped, into the light of day. What shall we expect of this last-born of time? Shall we stand by and watch to see what special quality is to be embodied here—whether a new nation of learning, or a new nation of power, or a new nation of wealth, or a new nation of philosophy and religion is going to occupy this continent so long reserved for some one of the last experiments of human life? Does there not sometimes come to us another dream, which is that somehow on this vast latest field the types which elsewhere history has developed may find some kind of union; that here may come a larger national character capable of comprehending all; that here may come wealth, not base, selfish, and vulgar, as wealth is when it lives alone, but pervaded and sanctified by spiritual ambitions and the consciousness of holy uses; that here may come religion, not only as the personal delight and education of the single soul, but also as the organized salvation of humanity; that here Law may learn the lesson of grace and become not merely the restraint but the development of crude and sinful men; that learning here may prove itself a truly moral force and make men better as it makes them wise? Can any thoughtful man look into the future of our country and not dream some such great dream as this? There is something better which must come someday than merely another and another of these partial, one-sided studies of humanity, devoted to the development of some single quality or type of life. Some time the universal nation, like the universal man, must come, in which quality shall blend with quality, each lending the other at once its richness and its restraint, and so the complete nationality, the true Kingdom of God, shall be established.

July 6

Thomas More

Reformation Martyr, 1535

Born in London in 1478, Thomas More studied classics and law, being called to the Bar when he was twenty-three years old. His clear honesty and integrity impressed Henry VIII and he appointed More as his Chancellor. He supported the king in his efforts to reform the clergy but disagreed over Henry's disputes with the papacy, caused by the king's desire to annul his marriage to Catherine of Aragon and to find another queen who might provide him with a male heir. Henry could stand no such act of defiance and imprisoned his Chancellor in the hope that he would renege. Thomas refused to take the Oath of the Act of Succession, which declared the king to be the only protector and supreme head of the Church in England, and was executed for treason on this day in the year 1535, declaring that he died "the king's good servant but God's first."

A Reading from a letter of Thomas More to his daughter, Margaret Roper, written from the Tower of London in 1534

That you fear your own frailty, Margaret, I do not disapprove. God give us both the grace to despair of our own self, and wholly to depend and hang upon the hope and strength of God. The blessed apostle St. Paul found such strength in himself that in his temptation he was thrice to call and cry out to God to take that temptation from him. And yet attained he not his prayer in the manner he required. Of himself never so feeble and faint was he, nor never so likely to fall, yet the grace of God was sufficient to keep him up and make him stand. The more weak that man is, the more is the strength of God in his safeguard declared.

Surely, Meg, a fainter heart than thy frail father hath, canst you not have. And yet I verily trust in the great mercy of God, that he shall of his goodness so stay me with his holy hand that he shall not finally suffer me to fall wretchedly from his favor. And the like trust (dear daughter) in his high goodness I verily conceive of you. And so much the more, in that there is neither of us both, but that if we call his benefits to mind and give him oft thanks for them, we may find tokens many, to give us good hope for all our manifold offences toward him; and that his great mercy, when we will heartily call therefore, shall not be withdrawn from us.

And verily, my dear daughter, in this is my great comfort, that albeit I am of nature so shrinking from pain that I am almost afeard of a cut on my finger, yet in all the agonies that I have had, whereof before my coming hither (as I have showed you ere this) I have had neither small nor few, with heavy fearful heart, forecasting all such perils and painful deaths, as by any manner of possibility might after fall unto me, and in such thought lain long restless and waking, while my wife had thought I was asleep; yet in any such fear and heavy pensiveness (I thank the mighty mercy of God) I never in my mind intended to consent that I would for the enduring of the uttermost do any such thing as I should in mine own conscience (for with other men's consciences I am not a man meet to take upon me to meddle) think to be to myself, such as should damnably cast me in the displeasure of God.

And this is the least point that any man may with his salvation come to, as far as I can see, and is bounden if he see peril to examine his conscience surely by learning and by good counsel and be sure that his conscience be such as it may stand with his salvation, or else reform it. And if the matter be such as both the parties may stand with salvation, then on whither side his conscience fall, he is safe enough before God. But that mine own may stand with my own salvation, thereof I thank our Lord I am very sure. I beseech our Lord bring all parts to his bliss.

It is now, my good daughter, late. And therefore thus I commend you to the Holy Trinity, to guide you, comfort you and direct you with his Holy Spirit, and all ours and my wife with all my children and all our other friends.

July 11

Benedict of Nursia

Abbot of Monte Cassino, Father of Western Monasticism,
Patron of Europe, *c.*550

Benedict was born in Nursia, in central Italy, around the year 480. As a young man he was sent to study in Rome, but appalled by the corruption in society, he withdrew to live as a hermit at Subiaco. He quickly attracted disciples and began to establish small monasteries in the neighborhood. Around the year 525, a disaffected faction tried to poison him, so Benedict moved south to Monte Cassino with a band of monks loyal to him. Later in life, Benedict wrote his Rule for Monks, *based on his own experience of fallible people striving to live out the gospel. He never intended to found an "Order" as such, but his* Rule *proved to be so good and well-balanced that it was disseminated widely, becoming in time the model for all Western monasticism. Benedict died at Monte Cassino in about the year 550.*

A Reading from the prologue to his *Rule for Monks*
by Benedict of Nursia

Listen carefully, my son, to the instructions of your teacher, and attend with the ear of your heart to the advice of a loving father. Welcome it and faithfully put it into practice; so that through the labor of obedience you may return to the God from whom you have drifted through the sloth of disobedience. To you, then, whomever you may be, are my words addressed, that renouncing your own will, and taking up the strong and glorious weapons of obedience, you may do battle in the service of Christ the Lord, our true King.

First of all, whenever you begin a good work, you must pray to God most urgently to bring it to perfection, so that he who has delighted to count us his children, may never be saddened by our evil lives. For we must serve God with the gifts he has given us that he may never as an angry father disinherit us or like some dreaded master, enraged by our sins, hand us over to eternal punishment as worthless servants who have refused to follow him in the way to glory.

Let us then at last arouse ourselves! For the Scriptures challenge us to do so in these words: "Now is the time for us to rise from sleep." Let us open wide our eyes to the light that transfigures, and unstop our ears to the sound of God's voice which daily cries out to us: "O that today you would listen to his voice and harden not your hearts." And again as Scripture says: "You that have ears to hear, listen to what the Spirit is saying to the churches." And what is the Spirit saying? "Come, my children, listen to me and I will teach you the fear of the Lord." "Run while you have the light of life, lest the darkness of death overtake you."

Dear friends, what can be more delightful than this voice of the Lord inviting us? Behold, in his loving mercy, the Lord is showing us the way of life. Clothed then with faith and the performance of good works, and with the gospel as our guide, let us set out on this way of life that we may deserve to see the God "who is calling us in his kingdom."

We propose to establish a school of the Lord's service. In founding this we hope that we shall not make rules that are harsh or burdensome. But if, for the good of all concerned, for the correction of faults or the preservation of charity, there be some strictness of discipline, do not be immediately daunted and run away from the way that leads to salvation. Its entrance is inevitably narrow. But as we progress in this way of life and in faith, our hearts will be enlarged, and we shall run in the way of God's commandments with an inexpressible delight of love. Let us then never swerve from his instructions but rather persevere in God's teaching in the monastery until death. Thus shall we share by patience in the sufferings of Christ, and so deserve to share in his kingdom. Amen.

July 17

William White

Bishop of Pennsylvania, 1836

William White was born in 1747 and was the central figure through the first fifty years of the independent life of the Episcopal Church. Although, like all Anglican clergy at the time, he had been ordained in England and had taken an oath of loyalty to the king, he served as chaplain of the Continental Congress from 1777 until 1789 and then as chaplain of the Senate until 1800. After the war, it was White's proposal to provide bishops for the newly independent church by having them consecrated by priests that galvanized the Connecticut clergy to secure a bishop in apostolic succession from the Scottish church. That, in turn, led the Church of England to obtain new laws permitting ordination of clergy to serve outside British authority and made it possible for White and others to be consecrated in England. When clergy and lay delegates in early gatherings of Episcopalians from the North and South found it difficult to reconcile their views, it was White who provided the moderating influence that kept the church united. Though he himself only once ventured out to visit the western part of his diocese, he ordained some of the most mission-minded bishops and priests of the next generation. John Henry Hobart, Jackson Kemper, and William Augustus Muhlenberg were among those to whom White served as mentor.

A Reading from *A Charge to the Clergy of the Protestant Episcopal Church in the Diocese of Pennsylvania at the Opening of Convention*, May 11, 1825
by the Right Reverend William White

It is sufficiently painful, to be habitually witnesses of the ravages of corrupt passion on the temporal concerns of the commonwealth: but to a religious mind, it ought to be much more painful if, in the concerns of the church, in any instance, there be the same ambition directed to self-exaltation; the same jealousy in the rival claims of competitors, the same envy of merits and of successes; and the same mortification on the defeat of endeavors for celebrity or for advancement. When inconsistencies of this magnitude have diffused themselves over the mass of a religious communion, it may be pertinently asked—is this a branch of the body of the faithful, called in Scripture the "Kingdom of God," his "husbandry" and his "building," "the body and the spouse of Christ," "the city of the living God," "the heavenly Jerusalem," "the general assembly of the church of the first-born whose names are written in heaven;" concerning which body, there is the pledge of the promise, that it will be at last said—"All the kingdoms of the world have become the kingdoms of the Lord and of his Christ," and who are affirmed to have even now in heaven their representatives, casting their crowns before the throne, with the song—"Thou art worthy, O Lord, to receive glory, and honor, and power: for thou hast created all things, and for thy pleasure they are and were created." When we contrast all this with what sometimes passes under our observation, we might reasonably stagger with doubt, were it not that to guard against such an issue, we have been forewarned, that in "the field," there should be "tares" growing with "the wheat;" that in "the net," there should be the difference "of fishes good and bad;" and that the time should come when, in alliance with many dark shades of character, detailed in a long list for our greater caution, there should be "the form, that is, the outward show of "godliness," severed from "the power" of it, meaning over the heart and the life. The profiting by these premonitions must constitute a part of "the faith and patience of the saints" spoken of, although intended of a particular enormity, in the book of Revelation.

If in such feuds as may originate from questions of order, and within spheres subjected to Christian prudence and discretion, there is so much of danger from our frailties they may be more mischievously operative in opposition of opinion, when in one or in both of the opposing parties, it may be thought to involve the essentials of Christian verity.

Let it not be thought that the importance of such discrepancy is here lightly estimated or that under any circumstances, there is supposed to be a dispensation from the duty of "contending earnestly for the faith which was once delivered to the saints," whatever may be the shade or the weight of character of any who may be impliedly censured by such a discharge of duty. But it cannot reasonably be denied that to justify the being an accuser in this respect, the party ought at least to have a perfect understanding of his subject, a correct apprehension of the meaning of those to whom he presents himself as an adversary and, above all, be satisfied that there are no personal feelings operating to their disadvantage. When we consider how much of controversy has arisen from different understanding of the terms made use of, and how much more of it, instead of having any direct authority of Scripture, is metaphysical inference; supposed, perhaps erroneously, to be correctly drawn, we ought, surely, to be guarded in the charge of injury to the foundation of the ecclesiastical building, lest what we are ourselves raising on it should prove the wood, the hay, and the stubble under which the foundation may be scarcely visible.

July 19

Macrina
Teacher of the Faith, 379

Macrina was born at Caesarea in what is now Turkey around the year 327. The child of an aristocratic Christian family, she exercised a formative influence over her distinguished younger brothers Basil and Gregory of Nyssa, introducing them to the spiritual life. As a young woman she had been betrothed to a lawyer, but following his sudden and unexpected death she devoted herself to her family. Following the death of their father, she converted the household into a sort of monastery on one of the family estates on the banks of the river Iris. She died in Pontus in the year 379.

A Reading from the *Life of Macrina* by her brother
Gregory of Nyssa

Barely nine months after the death of our dear brother Basil, a synod of bishops was held in Antioch. Before returning to my diocese I determined to visit my sister, Macrina, whom I had not seen for over eight years.

When I arrived I found her very ill. She was not resting on a couch or in bed, but on the ground, lying on a simple board covered with some coarse material, with another board to support her head. When she saw me standing at the door, she raised herself up on her elbow; her strength was already dissipated by the fever and she was unable to walk. I ran to her, and lifting her head, gently lowered her body to her previous reclining position. She raised her hand to heaven and said, "Thank you Lord, for not depriving me of my desire, and for sending your servant to see your handmaid."

In order not to alarm me, she tried to stifle her pain and gloss over the fact that she was obviously having great difficulty in breathing. We talked about various things, but she longed to hear my news and asked me various questions. As we talked we shared our memories of the great Basil, and immediately my soul was troubled, my face fell and I burst into tears. But dear Macrina, far from being downcast by our grief, made mention of that holy man the starting point for a profound conversation. She always discussed our human predicament, even in misfortune, in the light of the hidden providence of God. And went on to speak of the future life like one inspired by the Holy Spirit. As usual I found my soul lifted up out of the human sphere by her conversation, and under her guidance, I found myself thinking of heavenly realities.

Later, after her rest, I returned to her and she began to tell me the story of her childhood, what she remembered about our parents, what happened before I was born and immediately after my birth. What characterized her own story was the way she always gave thanks to God for all that had happened.

The next day it became clear to me that this was to be her last. The fever had consumed the last vestiges of her strength. As evening came she asked for her couch to be turned toward the east and, drawing our conversation to a close, with her remaining time she gave herself to God in prayer. She said:

> O Lord, you have freed us from the fear of death; you have made the end of life here the beginning of true life for us. For a period you give rest to our bodies in sleep, but then awaken us with the call of the last trumpet. Our earthly body, formed by your hands, you consign in trust to the earth; and then once more you reclaim it, transfiguring with immortality and grace whatever in us is mortal or deformed. You have opened for us the way to resurrection, and given to those who fear you the sign of the holy cross as their emblem, to destroy the enemy and to save our life.
>
> O eternal God, on you I have depended since my mother's womb; you my soul has loved with all its strength; to you I dedicated my body and my soul from childhood. Set by my side an angel of light to lead me to the place of refreshment where there are restful waters in the midst of your holy ones. You have shattered the flaming sword, and in your compassion, you restored the thief who was crucified with you to paradise. Remember me also in your kingdom, for I too have been crucified with you. Let not the terrible abyss of the dead separate me from your chosen ones; let not the accuser bar my way. Forgive me my sins that my soul may be received in your sight, blameless and spotless.

As she ended her prayer she made the sign of the cross upon her eyes and mouth and heart, and little by little, as the fever dried up her tongue, she was no longer able to speak clearly; her voice gave out and only from the trembling of her lips and the motion of her hands did we know that she was continuing to pray. Eventually she breathed a deep breath and with that prayer, her life came to an end.

July 20

Margaret of Antioch

Martyr, 4th century

Margaret, also called Marina, gave her life during the Diocletian persecutions at the beginning of the fourth century. Her preaching before her death is said to have converted many to the Christian faith.

A Reading from a sermon of Leo the Great

Those of you who think that because the persecutions are over there is no struggle against our enemies, I challenge to search the intimate hidden places of your heart. Become discerning inspectors of your soul, explore its byways: check that there lurks no opposing force ready to attack you, no tyrant waiting to dominate the fortress of your mind. I beg you, make no peace with avarice, and despise all wealth gained from unjust practices. Refuse any pact with pride, and fear more to be received in honor than to be walked over in lowliness! Distance yourself from anger, do not allow the thirst for vengeance to awaken in you the torment of envy. Renounce the pursuit of pleasure, turn away from impurity, reject luxury, fly from evil, resist colluding with falsehood. Once you recognize that you too have to wage war on many fronts, then as the martyrs before us, you will secure a glorious victory.

As often as we die to sin, so sin dies in us. "Precious in the sight of the Lord" is even this "death of his saints" for a person is slain to the world, not by the destruction of their mortal frame, but by the destruction of vices. You can only honorably celebrate this solemn day of the martyrs, dear friends, if you stop entering into partnerships with unbelievers, if you stop living sinful lives, if you cease to be controlled by the temptation to indulge every sexual desire.

Therefore, my dearest brothers and sisters, receive what you see with your eyes, and reflect on the example of the martyrs for your own spiritual growth. May each of you so honor this dwelling built by previous generations that you remember that you yourselves are temples of God. Let no one desecrate or weaken the sacred space of their being; but by agreeing with the living and chosen stones through the way you live, you will form an indissoluble bond with those who have gone before us, thus growing into the unity of the Lord's body; and this we shall accomplish with the help of the Cornerstone, Jesus Christ our Lord.

July 20

Sojourner Truth

Liberator and Prophet, 1883

Born in New York State as a slave in either 1797 or 1798, Sojourner Truth spent the first twenty-eight years of her life in several different households into which she was sold. With the help of Quaker friends she escaped and lived first in Philadelphia and then in New York. Joining the African Methodist Episcopal Church, she became a streetcorner evangelist and worked to establish a shelter for homeless women. Later she traveled more widely as an evangelist, using her charismatic presence and imposing six-foot figure to good effect. Though she never learned to read or write, she was able to quote extensively from the Bible from memory. It was at a camp meeting in Ohio, after listening for hours as male preachers attacked women's rights and abolition on the basis of the Bible, that she made her best-known speech, "Ain't I a Woman?"

A Reading from a speech delivered by Sojourner Truth at the Women's Convention in Akron, Ohio, in 1851

Well, children, where there is so much racket there must be something out of kilter. I think that 'twixt the negroes of the South and the women at the North, all talking about rights, the white men will be in a fix pretty soon. But what's all this here talking about?

That man over there says that women need to be helped into carriages, and lifted over ditches, and to have the best place everywhere. Nobody ever helps me into carriages, or over mudpuddles, or gives me any best place! And ain't I a woman? Look at me! Look at my arm! I have ploughed and planted, and gathered into barns, and no man could head me! And ain't I a woman? I could work as much and eat as much as a man—when I could get it—and bear the lash as well! And ain't I a woman? I have borne thirteen children, and seen most all sold off to slavery, and when I cried out with my mother's grief, none but Jesus heard me! And ain't I a woman?

Then they talk about this thing in the head; what's this they call it? [*Member of audience whispers, "Intellect."*] That's it, honey. What's that got to do with women's rights or negroes' rights? If my cup won't hold but a pint, and yours holds a quart, wouldn't you be mean not to let me have my little half measure full?

Then that little man in black there, he says women can't have as much rights as men, 'cause Christ wasn't a woman! Where did your Christ come from? Where did your Christ come from? From God and a woman! Man had nothing to do with him.

If the first woman God ever made was strong enough to turn the world upside down all alone, these women together ought to be able to turn it back, and get it right side up again! And now they is asking to do it, the men better let them.

Obliged to you for hearing me, and now old Sojourner ain't got nothing more to say.

July 20

Amelia Bloomer

Liberator and Prophet, 1894

Born in 1818, and baptized at Trinity Church, Seneca Falls, New York, Amelia Bloomer later moved to Council Bluffs, Iowa, and helped form an Episcopal Church in that community, hosting the first missionaries to come there, Jackson Kemper among them. She was also a lifelong campaigner for justice, first against slavery, then for temperance and women's rights. Because fashion prescribed tight-fitting clothes even for pregnant women, Amelia Bloomer began wearing loose-fitting Turkish trousers, garb that became known as "bloomers." Though she was never able to vote herself, she lived to hear that women had been given the franchise in Colorado and died in the confidence that full emancipation would surely come before much longer.

A Reading from *The Life and Writings of Amelia Bloomer* edited by Dexter C. Bloomer

How any unprejudiced and unbiased mind can read the original account of the Creation and Fall and gather therefrom that the woman committed the greater sin, I cannot understand. When Eve was first asked to eat of the forbidden fruit, she refused, and it was only after her scruples were overcome by promises of great knowledge that she gave way to sin. But how was it with Adam who was with her? He took and ate what she offered him without any scruples of conscience, or promises on her part of great things to follow—certainly showing no superiority of goodness, or intellect, or strength of character fitting him for the headship. The command not to eat of the Tree of Life was given to him before her creation, and he was doubly bound to keep it; yet he not only permitted her to partake of the tree without remonstrating with her against it and warning her of the wrong, but ate it himself without objection or hesitation. And then, when inquired of by God concerning what he had done, instead of standing up like an honorable man and confessing the wrong, he weakly tried to shield himself by throwing the blame on the woman. As the account stands, he showed the greater feebleness of resistance and evinced a pliancy of character and a readiness to yield to temptation that cannot be justly charged to the woman. As the account stands, man has much more to blush for than to boast of.

While we are willing to accept this original account of the Creation and Fall, we are not willing that man should add tenfold to woman's share of sin and put a construction on the whole matter that we believe was never intended by the Creator. Eve had no more to do with bringing sin into the world than had Adam, nor did the Creator charge any more upon her. The punishment inflicted upon them for their transgression was as heavy upon him as upon her. Her sorrows were to be multiplied; and so, too, was he to eat his bread in sorrow and earn it with the sweat of his face amid thorns and thistles. To her, no injunction to labor was given; upon her no toil was imposed, no ground cursed for her sake. The Bible is brought forward to prove the subordination of woman and to show that, because Saint Paul told the ignorant women of his time to keep silent in the churches, the educated, intelligent women of these times must not only occupy the same position in the church and the family but must not aspire to the rights of citizenship. But the same Power that brought the slave out of bondage will, in his own good time and way, bring about the emancipation of woman and make her the equal in dominion that she was in the beginning.

July 20

Elizabeth Cady Stanton

Liberator and Prophet, 1902

With her friend Amelia Bloomer, Elizabeth Cady Stanton was a member of Trinity Church, Seneca Falls, New York, and from that base she traveled widely, preaching the gospel of women's rights. Born in 1815, she studied law in her father's office and learned there of the inequality with which the law treated men and women. In 1848 she circulated petitions that helped gain the passage of a New York state law giving property rights to women. In the same year, she and her friend Amelia Bloomer were among the small group of women that organized the first Women's Rights Convention in Seneca Falls, New York, and which set the goals she would work toward for the rest of her long life. When the Revised Version of the Bible *was published in 1881 by a committee that included no women, Stanton set out to produce her own commentary on Scripture, which she called* The Woman's Bible.

A Reading from *The Woman's Bible*
by Elizabeth Cady Stanton

Here is the sacred historian's first account of the advent of woman; a simultaneous creation of both sexes, in the image of God. It is evident from the language that there was consultation in the Godhead, and that the masculine and feminine elements were equally represented. Scott in his commentaries says, "This consultation of the Gods is the origin of the doctrine of the Trinity." But instead of three male personages, as generally represented, a Heavenly Father, Mother, and Son would seem more rational.

The first step in the elevation of woman to her true position, as an equal factor in human progress, is the cultivation of the religious sentiment in regard to her dignity and equality, the recognition by the rising generation of an ideal Heavenly Mother, to whom their prayers should be addressed, as well as to a Father.

If language has any meaning, we have in these texts a plain declaration of the existence of the feminine element in the Godhead, equal in power and glory with the masculine. The Heavenly Mother and Father! "God created man in his own *image, male and female.*" Thus Scripture, as well as science and philosophy, declares the eternity and equality of sex—the philosophical fact, without which there could have been no perpetuation of creation, no growth or development in the animal, vegetable, or mineral kingdoms, no awakening nor progressing in the world of thought. The masculine and feminine elements, exactly equal and balancing each other, are as essential to the maintenance of the equilibrium of the universe as positive and negative electricity, the centripetal and centrifugal forces, the laws of attraction which bind together all we know of this planet whereon we dwell and of the system in which we revolve.

In the great work of creation the crowning glory was realized, when man and woman were evolved on the sixth day, the masculine and feminine forces in the image of God, that must have existed eternally, in all forms of matter and mind. All the persons in the Godhead are represented in the Elohim, the divine plurality taking counsel in regard to this last and highest form of life. Who were the members of this high council, and whether a duality or a trinity? Verse 27 declares the image of God male and female. How then is it possible to make woman an afterthought? We find in verses 5–16 the pronoun he used. Should it not in harmony with verse 26 be they, a dual pronoun? We may attribute this to the same cause as the use of his in verse 1 instead of it. The fruit tree yielding fruit after "his" kind instead of after "its" kind. The paucity of a language may give rise to many misunderstandings.

The above texts plainly show the simultaneous creation of man and woman, and their equal importance in the development of the race. All those theories based on the assumption that man was prior in the creation have no foundation in Scripture.

As to woman's subjection, on which both the canon and the civil law delight to dwell, it is important to note that equal dominion is given to woman over every living thing, but not one word is said giving man dominion over woman.

Here is the first title deed to this green earth giving alike to the sons and daughters of God. No lesson of woman's subjection can be fairly drawn from the first chapter of the Old Testament.

July 20

Harriet Tubman

Liberator and Prophet, 1913

Born in slavery in the year 1820 on a Maryland plantation, the sixth of eleven children, Harriet Tubman suffered beatings and severe injury but grew up strong and defiant, never appearing to be happy in the presence of her owners. She escaped to Canada when she was about twenty-four years old and began to work with the Quakers to bring other slaves to freedom along the Underground Railway. During the last ten years before the Civil War, Tubman made at least nineteen trips back to Maryland and brought back over three hundred slaves. When war broke out, she joined the Union Army and served as a cook and a nurse and then as a spy and a scout. At one point, as the first black woman to lead American troops in a military action, she led a contingent of black troops on a raid that freed over 350 slaves. After the war, while living in upstate New York and peddling vegetables door to door, she joined the fight for women's rights and worked with Susan B. Anthony and Elizabeth Cady Stanton. When she died in 1913, she was hailed as "the Moses of her people."

A Reading from *Harriet Tubman, Conductor on the Underground Railroad* by Ann Petry

It was as the storyteller, the bard, that Harriet's active years came to a close. She had never learned to read and write. She compensated for this handicap by developing a memory on which was indelibly stamped everything she had ever heard or seen or experienced. She had a highly developed sense of the dramatic, a sense of the comic, and because in her early years she had memorized verses from the Bible, word for word, the surge and sway of the majestic rhythm of the King James version of the Bible was an integral part of her speech. It was these qualities that made her a superb storyteller.

In each house where she stopped, she was given a cup of hot tea with butter in it, which was the way she liked it. As she sipped the buttered tea, she would sometimes tell about the Underground Railroad, and that first trip she made to Canada, and how all of them were ragged, hungry, dirty, cold, and afraid. Hunger worse than cold, the pinching of the stomach, pain in the stomach from hunger. And fear worse than hunger, fear like a paralysis, inhibiting movement, fear so strong it was something they could feel and taste. She, threatening, cajoling, admonishing them: "Go free or die."

She made her listener see the snow in Canada, the trees hung with icicles, see Niagara Falls like frozen music in the winter. And she invariably ended the recital with a note of pride in her voice, as she said: "And I never run my train off the track, and I never lost a single passenger."

She could speak of the death of Lincoln, and epitomize all the sorrow in the world by telling about an old man, at the Contraband Hospital at Fortress Monroe, who, hearing that Lincoln was dead, lifted his tremulous old voice in prayer: "We kneel upon the ground, with our faces in our hands, and our hands in the dust, and cry to Thee for mercy, O Lord, this evening."

Sometimes she talked about Old John Brown, the man with the hawk's face and the white beard, and the fanatic's eyes, cold and hard as granite. She told about the time Old Brown took her to see Wendell Phillips and when he introduced her, he said, "Mr. Phillips, I bring you one of the bravest people on this continent—General Tubman, as we call her."

Sometimes she went even farther back in her memory, to the days of the plantation and the overseer and the master. Then her listener could see a row of sway-backed cabins, smell the smoky smell from the fireplaces, could see a fifteen-year-old girl huddled under a dirty blanket, could see the great hole in her head and blood pouring from what should have been a mortal wound.

As she went farther and farther back in time, she spoke of the old slave ships, and the horror of the Middle Passage, retelling the stories she had heard as a child, stories of whips and chains and branding irons, of a quenchless thirst, and the black smell of death in the hold of a Yankee slaver. The word *freedom* became more than a word, it became a glory over everything.

Whoever heard her talk like that had a deeper understanding of the long hard way she had come, had a deeper understanding of what lay behind Gettysburg and Appomattox.

Despite her work as a nurse, a scout, and a spy in the Civil War, she will be remembered longest as a conductor on the Underground Railroad, the railroad to freedom—a short, indomitable woman, sustained by faith in a living God, inspired by the belief that freedom was a right all men should enjoy, leading bands of trembling fugitives out of Tidewater Maryland.

July 22

Saint Mary Magdalene

All four Gospels give Mary Magdalene a unique place among Jesus' followers. Probably from Magdala by the Sea of Galilee, she is described as having been healed by Jesus before accompanying him during his ministry. Along with other faithful women, she stayed beside the cross during the crucifixion and was the first disciple to discover the empty tomb on Easter morning. She was privileged with the first appearance of the risen Lord, who sent her to take the good news of the resurrection to the other disciples. This commission earned her the title "Apostle to the Apostles" in the early Church.

A Reading from a homily of Gregory the Great

Mary Magdalen had been a "sinner in the city." She loved Jesus, the Truth, and washed away the stain of her wickedness with her tears. In this way the word of truth was fulfilled: "Her many sins have been forgiven her because she has shown great love." Her sins had indeed chilled her heart, but now she was burning inside with an unquenchable love. When she came to the tomb and did not find the Lord's body, she imagined that it had been taken away, and she went and reported it to the disciples. They came, and saw, and they believed that it had actually happened as she had told them. Then the gospel narrative continues: "The disciples went away again to their homes. But Mary stayed behind, standing by the tomb, weeping."

At this point let us pause and reflect upon Mary's state of mind, upon the intense love of this woman who would not leave the Lord's tomb even after the disciples had gone away. She carried on seeking him whom she had not found, weeping as she searched; and ablaze with love, she yearned for him whom she believed had been taken away. Thus it happened that she was alone when she saw Jesus, she who had stayed behind to seek him. From this we learn that at the heart of every good work is to be found the virtue of perseverance. Indeed, the lips of truth itself have said: "Those who persevere to the end will be saved."

"And as she wept, she stooped down and looked into the tomb." Mary had already seen that the tomb was empty and she had told the disciples that the Lord had been taken away; so why did she stoop down again? Why did she want to look a second time? The truth is that it is never enough for a lover to look merely once; the sheer intensity of love will not allow a lover to give up searching. Mary had sought and found nothing. But she persevered, and therefore she found the object of her love.

While she was seeking, her unfulfilled desires grew stronger and stronger until at their most intense moment they were quenched in the embrace of him whom she sought. Holy desires grow with waiting: if they fade through waiting then they cannot be genuine. This must be the quality of love that inflames anyone who reaches out for the truth. It is why David says [in the psalms]: "My soul is thirsting for the living God; when shall I come and behold the face of God?" And the Church says in the Song of Songs: "I am wounded by love," and again, "My soul faints within me."

"Woman, why are you weeping? Whom do you seek?" Mary is asked the cause of her sorrow so that her desire may increase, for as she names the one she seeks, she discovers herself burning with yet greater love for him. "And Jesus said to her: 'Mary.'" First of all he called her "woman," the common address at that time for one of her sex, and she did not recognize him. But now he calls her by her own name, as if to say: "Recognize the one who recognizes you." You will remember that the Lord had said to Moses, "I know you by name." Moses was his own name, and the Lord told him that he knew him by name, as if saying, "I do not know you in some general way, I know you personally." In the same way, addressed by her own name, Mary, too recognized her creator and immediately calls out "Rabboni," that is "teacher." Outwardly, it was he who was the object of her search, but inwardly it was he who was leading her to search for him.

alternative reading

A Reading from a poem by Janet Morley

They have taken away my Lord

It was unfinished.
We stayed there, fixed, until the end,
women waiting for the body that we loved;
and then it was unfinished.
There was no time to cherish, cleanse, anoint;
no time to handle him with love,
no farewell.

Since then, my hands have waited,
aching to touch even his deadness,
smoothe oil into bruises that no longer hurt,
offer his silent flesh my finished act of love.

I came early, as the darkness lifted,
to find the grave ripped open and his body gone;
container of my grief smashed, looted,
leaving my hands still empty.

I turned on the man who came:
"They have taken away my Lord—where is his corpse?
Where is the body that is mine to greet?
He is not gone
I am not ready yet, I am not finished—
I cannot let him go
I am not whole."

And then he spoke, no corpse,
and breathed,
and offered me my name.
My hands rushed to grasp him;
to hold and hug and grip his body close;
to give myself again, to cling to him,
and lose my self in love.
"Don't touch me now."

I stopped, and waited, my rejected passion
hovering between us like some dying thing.
I, Mary, stood and grieved, and then departed.

I have a gospel to proclaim.

July 23

Bridget of Sweden

Abbess of Vadstena, 1373

Bridget's father was governor of Uppland when she was born about the year 1303. She married at the age of fourteen, had eight children and often attended the royal court, where she continued to experience the mystical revelations she had known since childhood. These increased in intensity after her husband's death and, three years later, she responded by founding a monastery for nuns and monks at Vadstena in 1346. Bridget's daughter, Catherine, was the first abbess of the so-called Brigettine Order, which became very influential in northern Europe. After travelling to Rome to obtain the Pope's approval for her plans, Bridget never returned to Sweden but spent the rest of her life as a pilgrim, an adviser to rulers and Church leaders, and a minister to all in need. Her Revelations *were recorded by her confessors before her death, which occurred on this day in the year 1373.*

A Reading from the *Revelations* of Bridget of Sweden

On the day of Pentecost a priest was saying mass in the monastery and when the Body of God was elevated the bride of Christ saw fire come down from heaven over the altar, and behold in the bread in the priest's hands was a living Lamb, and in the Lamb a flaming face.

And she heard a voice speaking to her: "As you see fire descend over the altar, so my Spirit fell over the apostles on a day like this, enflaming their hearts. And the bread becomes through the Word a Living Lamb, that is my Body, and the Face in the Lamb and the Lamb in the Face, just as the Father is in the Son and the Son in the Father, and the Holy Spirit in both." And when the Body of God was again elevated in the priest's hands, she saw a very beautiful young man who said to her: "I bless you who believe, but to those who do not believe I will be a judge."

One day our Lady said to the bride: "Do not be saddened if you must preach the Word of God to those who do not want to listen, because anyone who is slandered or contradicted when doing so but perseveres with patience, is adorning his soul with all beauty. The soul of a person who is thus slandered but refuses to think ill of the slanderer, is clothed with the most beautiful garment which makes her Bridegroom (who is God in Three Persons) long for her to enter the eternal bliss of the Godhead. That is why the friends of God must labor to convert those whose love is pride and avarice more than the love of God, that they may be saved to life, because as it is they are trapped underneath a heavy rock."

"Just as anyone who saw a brother or sister crushed underneath a fallen rock would immediately try to break the rock into smaller pieces in order to remove it, working with all care so as not to inflict further pain, but sometimes of necessity having to make heavy cuts to lessen the weight, and all the time never thinking of themselves and their labors but only of the other person and saving their life, so the friends of God must work for the salvation of souls in peril."

July 24

Thomas à Kempis

Priest and Spiritual Writer, 1471

Toward the end of the fourteenth century, one of the most calamitous in European history, a new order, the Brethren of the Common Life, was founded in the Low Countries with the object of providing for lay and ordained Christians alike a simple, practical, biblical pattern of life. Thomas Hammerken, known as Thomas à Kempis, was born in 1380 and joined this order in 1407, remaining a member until his death in the year 1471. The Imitation of Christ, *which was written out of the experience of this life, has been translated into more languages than any other book than the Bible. It takes the form of a dialogue between God and the aspiring soul and counsels obedience, patience, continence, and poverty, not for their own sake but because they free the spirit for the joy of union with God. It is advice for those who wish to overcome the obstacles placed on their path by the temptations of this world for the sake of what à Kempis calls "the land of everlasting clearness."*

A Reading from *The Imitation of Christ*
by Thomas à Kempis

Lord, what is the trust that I have in this life or what is my greatest solace of all things appearing under heaven? Is it not whether you are my Lord whose mercy is without limit? Where was it well with me without you or when might it be evil, if you are present? I would rather be poor for you than rich without you. I chose rather to be a pilgrim with you in earth than to have heaven without you. Where you are there is heaven: and where you are not there is death and hell. You are my desire and therefore it is necessary to mourn for you, to cry, and to pray. I may fully trust in none that may help me in need except only you, my God.

You are my hope, you are my trust, you are my comfort and most faithful in all things. All others ask and seek their own advantage; you seek only my health and my profit and turn all things into good for me. Yes, though you lay me open to many temptations and adversities, you ordain all that to my profit; you are prone to test your chosen children in thousands of ways. And in that proving you ought no less to be loved and praised than if you fulfilled me with heavenly consolations.

In you, therefore, my Lord God, I put all my hope and all my refuge. In you, therefore, I set all my tribulation and my anguish, for I find whatever I behold outside you is infirm and unstable. For many friends will not avail and no helpers will be able nor many wise counselors give profitable counsel nor books of doctors give comfort nor precious substance of good deliver nor any secret or merry place make sure if you are not helping, comforting, informing, and keeping. For all things that seem to be for the getting of peace and happiness, if you are absent, are not worth nor in truth anything belonging to true felicity.

You therefore are the end of all good, the height of life, the depth of Scriptures; and to hope in you above all is the most mighty solace of your servants. To you my eyes are directed, my God, father of mercies. Bless and sanctify my soul with a heavenly blessing, that it may be your holy dwelling and the seat of your everlasting glory: so that nothing be found in the temple of your dignity that may offend the eyes of your majesty.

Look on me according to the greatness of your goodness and the multitude of your pities and hear the prayer of your servant in exile far off in the region of the shadow of death. Defend and keep the soul of your servant among so many perils of this corruptible life and, your grace going with me, direct me by the way of peace to the country of everlasting clearness. Amen.

July 25

Saint James the Apostle

James, often called "the Great," was a Galilean fisherman who, with his brother John, was one of the first apostles called by Jesus to follow him. The two brothers were with Jesus at his transfiguration and with him again in the garden of Gethsemane. They annoyed the other followers of Jesus by asking "to sit one on his left and the other on his right when he came into his glory" and they were present for the appearances of Christ after the resurrection. James was put to death by the sword on the order of Herod Agrippa, who hoped in vain that, by disposing of the Christian leaders, he could stem the flow of those hearing the good news and becoming followers in the Way. James' martyrdom is believed to have taken place in the year 44.

A Reading from a homily of John Chrysostom

The sons of Zebedee press Christ as follows: "Promise that one of us may sit at your right hand and the other at your left." How does Christ deal with this request? We should note that their demand comes as a response to an earlier question of Christ: "What would you have me do for you?" It is not that Christ was ignorant of what was going through their minds, but that he wanted them to speak their mind, to lay open their wound so that he could apply healing ointment. Furthermore, he wants to show them that it is not a spiritual gift for which they are asking, and that if they knew just what their request involved, they would never dare make it. This is why he says: "You do not know what you are asking," in other words, you do not know what a great and splendid thing it is, and how much beyond the reach even of the heavenly powers.

Then Christ continues: "Can you drink the cup which I must drink and be baptized with the baptism which I must undergo?" He is saying: "You talk of sharing honors and trophies with me, but I must talk of struggle and toil. Now is not the time for rewards or the time for my glory to be revealed. The present time is one of bloodshed, war and danger."

Notice how, by the manner of his questioning, he exhorts and challenges them. He does not say: "Can you face being slaughtered? Are you prepared to shed your blood?" Instead he puts a different question: "Can you drink the cup?" And then he coaxes them, saying: "The cup which I must drink," so that the prospect of sharing it with him may make them more eager. He also calls his suffering a baptism, to show that it will effect a great cleansing of the whole world. The disciples answer him: "We can!" Zeal makes them answer immediately, even though they really do not know what they are saying, but still think they will receive what they ask for.

How does Christ respond to their zealous reply? "You will indeed drink my cup and be baptized with my baptism." He is really prophesying a great blessing for them, since effectively he is telling them: "You will be found worthy of martyrdom; you will suffer what I suffer and end your life with a violent death, thus sharing everything with me. But seats at my right and left side are not mine to give; they belong to those for whom the Father has prepared them." Thus, after lifting their minds to higher goals and preparing them to meet and overcome all that could make them dejected, he corrects their request.

"Then the other ten became angry at the two brothers." See how imperfect all the disciples were: the two who tried to receive preferential treatment over the other ten, and the ten's jealousy of the two disciples. And yet, as I said earlier on, when we look at these two disciples later on in their lives, we observe how free they were of these impulses. In the Acts of the Apostles we read how John, whom here is recorded as the one who asks for preferential treatment, in fact yields to Peter when it comes to preaching and in working miracles. And James, for his part, was not to live long. From the beginning he was inspired by so great a zeal, that setting aside all earthly interests, he rose to such pre-eminence that it was inevitable that he would be killed straight away.

July 26

Anne and Joachim

Parents of the Blessed Virgin Mary

In the Proto-Gospel of James, written in the middle of the second century, the parents of Mary the mother of Jesus are named as Anne and Joachim. The story appears to be based heavily on that of Hannah, the mother of Samuel. The Church maintains their feast day both to emphasize God's plan from the beginning to send his Son, born of a woman, born under the Law, to redeem fallen humanity, and also to show God's faithfulness in keeping his covenant with all generations.

A Reading from an oration of John of Damascus

Anne was to be the mother of the Virgin Mother of God, and hence nature did not dare to anticipate the flowering of grace. Thus nature remained barren, until grace produced its fruit. For she who was to be born had to be a first-born daughter, since she would be the mother of the first-born of all creation, "in whom all things are held together."

Joachim and Anne, how blessed a couple! All creation is indebted to you. For at your hands the creator was offered a gift excelling all other gifts: a chaste mother, who alone was worthy of the creator.

And so rejoice, Anne, O barren one who "has not borne children; break forth into shouts, you who have not given birth."

Rejoice, Joachim, because from your daughter "a child is born for us, a Son is given us, whose name is messenger of great counsel and universal salvation, mighty God." For this child is God.

Joachim and Anne, how blessed and spotless a couple! You will be known by the fruit you have borne, as the Lord says: "By their fruits you will know them." The conduct of your life pleased God and was worthy of your daughter. For by the chaste and holy life you led together, you have fashioned a jewel of virginity: she who remained a virgin before, during and after giving birth. She alone for all time would maintain her virginity in mind and soul, as well as in body.

Joachim and Anne, how chaste a couple! While safeguarding the chastity prescribed by the law of nature, you achieved with God's help something which transcends nature in giving the world the Virgin Mother of God as your daughter. While leading a devout and holy life in your human nature, you gave birth to a daughter nobler than the angels, whose queen she now is. Girl of utter beauty and delight, daughter of Adam and Mother of God, blessed are the loins and blessed is the womb from which you come! Blessed are the arms that carried you, and blessed are your parents' lips.

"Rejoice in God, all the earth. Shout, exult and sing hymns." Raise up your voice, raise it up, and be not afraid.

July 27

William Reed Huntington

Priest, Teacher of the Faith, 1909

William Reed Huntington served as Rector of Grace Church, Manhattan, and for thirty-six years he was a Deputy and leading member of the General Convention. In a time of bitter controversy and division, Huntington worked to set forward his vision for the future and Christian unity was at the center of his vision. In a book called The Church-Idea, *published in 1870, Huntington argued that Christians might unite on the basis of four fundamentals: the Holy Scriptures of the Old and New Testament, the Apostles and Nicene Creeds, the two sacraments of Baptism and Holy Communion, and the historic episcopate. This proposal was adopted by the House of Bishops of the Episcopal Church in 1886 and by the Lambeth Conference of 1888. It continues to shape the Anglican approach to Christian unity. Huntington also worked for the revival of the ancient order of deaconess. The General Convention's adoption of his proposal in 1889 was an important first step toward the full recognition of women in ordained ministry. Huntington also provided leadership in the 1892 revision of the Prayer Book with its significant enrichment and the introduction of a flexibility unknown in previous books. He was known, deservedly, as the "first presbyter of the church."*

A Reading from *The Church-Idea* by William Reed Huntington

Dissatisfaction is the one word that best expresses the state of mind in which Christendom finds itself to-day. There is a wide-spread misgiving that we are on the eve of momentous changes. Unrest is everywhere. The party of the Curia and the party of the Reformation, the party of orthodoxy and the party of liberalism, are all alike agitated by the consciousness that a spirit of change is in the air.

No wonder that many imagine themselves listening to the rumbling of the chariot wheels of the Son of Man. He Himself predicted that "perplexity" should be one of the signs of his coming, and it is certain that the threads of the social order have seldom been more intricately entangled than they now are.

A calmer and perhaps truer inference is that we are about entering upon a new reach of Church history, and that the dissatisfaction and perplexity are only transient. There is always a tumult of waves at the meeting of the waters; but when the streams have mingled, the flow is smooth and still again. The plash and gurgle that we hear may mean something like this.

At all events the time is opportune for a discussion of the Church-Idea; for it is with this, hidden under a hundred disguises, that the world's thoughts are busy. Men have become possessed with an unwonted longing for unity, and yet they are aware that they do not grapple successfully with the practical problem. Somehow they are grown persuaded that union is God's work, and separation devil's work; but the persuasion only breeds the greater discontent. That is what lies at the root of our unquietness. There is a felt want and a felt inability to meet the want; and where these two things coexist there must be heat of friction.

Catholicity is what we are reaching after. But how is Catholicity to be defined? And when we have got our definition, what are we to do with it? The speculative and the practical sides of the question are about equally difficult to meet. The humanitarian scheme would make the Church conterminous with the race; the ultramontane would bound it by the Papal decrees.

Clearly we have come upon a time for the study of first principles, a time to go down and look after the foundations upon which our customary beliefs are built. The more searching the analysis, the more lasting will the synthesis be sure to be.

There are many tokens of a golden morning near at hand. Peoples minds are gradually becoming thoroughly awake to the importance of the subject, and this in itself is a great gain. The first step toward finding a remedy for our ailments is to acknowledge that we are sick. Christendom, with a very querulous voice, is beginning to do just this. Then there is still further encouragement in the fact that all over the world religious thought is concentrating itself more and more every day on the Person of our blessed Lord. Believers and unbelievers are alike agitated with the question, "What think ye of Christ?" This is a sure precursor of renewed efforts after unity. The more clearly our holy religion is seen to have its center in Him whose name it bears, the more will those who love him in sincerity feel that the Church must be one.

At any rate let us who believe in unity hold forth our faith without wavering, well content to rank as fools and mad so long as we are certain that we have the word of Christ and the example of his first missionaries on our side. For be the waves never so angry, the sky never so dark, the forebodings of disaffected friends never so gloomy, if we are confident that the ship's head is right, our only duty is to

"Still bear up and steer right onward."

July 29

Mary and Martha of Bethany

Companions of our Lord Jesus Christ

The Gospels of Luke and John variously describe how Mary, Martha and their brother Lazarus gave Jesus hospitality at their home at Bethany outside Jerusalem. Jesus is said to have loved all three. After Lazarus' death, he wept and was moved by the sisters' grief to bring Lazarus back from the dead. According to John's Gospel, it was Martha who recognized Jesus as the Messiah. On another occasion, Mary was commended by Jesus for her attentiveness to his teaching while Martha served.

A Reading from a sermon of Augustine

The words of our Lord Jesus Christ teach us that there is one goal toward which we should be travelling while we toil among the countless distractions of this world. We make our way like pilgrims on a journey, people of no fixed abode; we are on the road, not yet home; still aiming for our goal, though yet to arrive. So let us press on, never wearying, never giving up, so that one day we may reach our destination.

Martha and Mary were sisters, related not only by blood, but also by a shared desire for holiness. Both were devoted to the Lord, and together served him when he was here among us. Martha welcomed him as a pilgrim would be received. But in her case, the reality was that the servant was receiving her Lord, a sick woman receiving her Savior, the creature receiving her creator. She who was to be fed with the Spirit welcomed him whom she served with bodily food. For it was the will of the Lord to take the form of a servant and while in the form of a servant to be fed by his own servants, for whom it became an honor not a duty. It was an honor that he should present himself to them needing to be fed. He had flesh in which he hungered and became thirsty.

Thus our Lord was received as a guest, who "came to his own home, and his own people received him not. But to all who received him, he gave power to become children of God." He chose servants and raised them to the status of sisters and brothers; he set captives free and made them joint heirs with himself.

Now if any of you happen to say: "How blessed are those who were found worthy to receive Christ into their own homes," do not murmur because you were born in a later age when you no longer see the Lord in the flesh: he has not robbed you of that honor. For he says, "Truly, as you did it to one of the least of these my brothers and sisters, you did it also to me."

You dear Martha, if I may say so, are blessed for your good service; you are seeking the reward of your labors, namely, rest. For the moment you are preoccupied with the demands of service, feeding a mortal body, albeit a holy one. But when you reach your heavenly homeland, will you find a pilgrim to welcome, someone hungry to feed, someone thirsty to whom you may give a drink, someone ill whom you can visit, someone quarrelsome whom you could reconcile, a dead body to bury? Martha, none of these tasks will be there. But what will you find?

You will find what Mary chose. There we shall not have to feed other people: we shall be fed. What Mary chose in this life will on that day be realized in its fullness. She was gathering the crumbs from a rich banquet, the Word of God. And do you wish to know what will happen when we arrive there? The Lord himself tells us when he says of his servants: "Truly, I say to you, he will have them sit at table, and he will come and serve them himself."

alternative reading

A Reading from the treatise *On Spiritual Friendship* by Aelred of Rievaulx

Spiritual friendship should be desired not for consideration of any worldly advantage or for any extrinsic cause, but for the dignity of its own nature and the feelings of the human heart, so that its fruition and reward is nothing other than itself. That is why the Lord in the gospel says: "I have appointed you that you should go, and should bring forth fruit," that is, that you should love one another. For true friendship advances by perfecting itself, and the fruit is derived from experiencing the sweetness of that perfection. Thus spiritual friendship among the righteous is born of a similarity in life, morals, and pursuits, that is, it consists in a mutual conformity in matters human and divine united with generosity and charity.

Have you forgotten that in the Book of Proverbs it says: "He that is a friend loves at all times?" Saint Jerome also, as you may recall, says that "Friendship which can end was never true friendship." That friendship cannot endure without charity has been more than adequately established. Since then in friendship eternity blossoms, truth shines forth, and charity grows sweet, consider whether you ought to separate the name of wisdom from these three things.

And what does all this add up to? Dare I say of friendship what John, the friend of Jesus, says of charity, namely that "God is friendship?"

That would be unusual, to be sure, nor does it have the sanction of the Scriptures. And yet what is true of charity, I surely do not hesitate to grant to friendship, since "those who abide in friendship, abide in God, and God in them."

July 30

William Wilberforce

Social Reformer, 1833

William Wilberforce was born in 1759 in Hull. Converted to an Evangelical piety within the Church of England, Wilberforce decided to serve the faith in Parliament instead of being ordained, becoming a Member of Parliament at the age of twenty-one. He was a supporter of missionary initiatives and helped found The Bible Society. Settling in Clapham in London, he became a leader of the reforming group of Evangelicals known as the "Clapham Sect." Of all the causes for which he fought, he is remembered best for his crusade against slavery. After years of effort, the trade in slaves was made illegal in the British Empire in 1807 and Wilberforce lived to see the complete abolition of slavery, just before his death on this day in the year 1833.

A Reading from a speech of William Wilberforce delivered to the House of Commons in May 1789 on the total abolition of slavery

I mean not to accuse anyone, but to take the shame upon myself, in common indeed with the whole Parliament of Britain, for having suffered this horrid trade of slavery to be carried on under their authority. We are all guilty we ought to all plead guilty, and not to exculpate ourselves by throwing the blame on others.

[In the facts that I have laid before you,] I trust that I have proved that, upon every ground, total abolition ought to take place. I have urged many things which are not my own leading motives for proposing it, since I have wished to show every description of gentlemen, and particularly the West India planters, who deserve every attention, that the abolition is politic upon their own principles. Policy, however, Sir, is not my principle; and I am not ashamed to say it. There is a principle above everything that is politic, and when I reflect on the command which says: "Thou shalt do no murder," believing its authority to be divine, how can I dare to set up any reasonings of my own against it?

Sir, the nature and all the circumstances of this trade are now laid open to us. We can no longer plead ignorance. We cannot evade it. We may spurn it. We may kick it out of the way. But we cannot turn aside so as to avoid seeing it. For it is brought now so directly before our eyes that this House must decide, and must justify to all the world and to its own conscience, the rectitude of all the grounds of its decision.

Let not Parliament be the only body that is insensible to the principles of natural justice. Let us make reparation to Africa, as far as we can, by establishing trade upon true commercial principles, and we shall soon find the rectitude of our conduct rewarded by the benefits of a regular and growing commerce.

July 31

Ignatius of Loyola

Founder of the Society of Jesus, 1556

Born in 1491, the son of a Basque nobleman, Ignatius served as a soldier and was wounded at the siege of Pamplona in 1521. During his convalescence he read a Life of Christ, *was converted and lived a life of prayer and penance, during which he wrote the first draft of his* Spiritual Exercises. *He gathered six disciples, and together they took vows of poverty and chastity and promised to serve the Church either by preaching in Palestine or in other ways that the Pope thought fit. By 1540, Ignatius had won papal approval for his embryonic order and the Society of Jesus was born. For the next sixteen years he directed the work of the Jesuits as it spread around the world, until his sudden death on this day in the year 1556.*

A Reading from the *Spiritual Exercises*
of Ignatius of Loyola,
their "Principle and Foundation"

The human person is created to praise, reverence and serve God Our Lord, and by so doing to save his or her soul. The other things on the face of the earth are created for human beings in order to help them pursue the end for which they are created. It follows from this that one must use other created things in so far as they help toward one's end, and free oneself from them in so far as they are obstacles to one's end. To do this we need to make ourselves indifferent to all created things, provided the matter is subject to our free choice and there is no prohibition. Thus as far as we are concerned, we should not want health more than illness, wealth more than poverty, fame more than disgrace, a long life more than a short one, and similarly for all the rest, but we should desire and choose only what helps us more toward the end for which we are created.

alternative reading

A Reading from the *Reminiscences* or *The Life of Ignatius of Loyola* as heard and recorded by Luis Gonzalez da Camara

Ignatius was badly wounded in battle, with one leg completely shattered. He was carried home to Loyola on a stretcher. Upon arrival it was discovered that the leg had been badly set, and would need to be broken, cut and re-set, and that the pain would be greater than all those he had undergone before. Once the flesh and excess bone had been cut, the concern was to use remedies whereby the leg would not be left so short, applying many ointments to it and stretching it continually with appliances, which on many days were making a martyr of him.

But Our Lord was gradually giving him health, and Ignatius was in such a good state that he was cured in all other respects except that he could not hold himself well on his leg, and thus he was forced to be in bed. And because he was much given to reading worldly and false books, which they normally call "tales of chivalry," he asked, once he was feeling well, that they give him some of these to pass the time. But in that house none of those books which he normally read could be found, and so they gave him a life of Christ and a book of the lives of the saints in Spanish.

Reading through these often, he was becoming rather attached to what he found written there. But, on ceasing to read them, he would stop to think: sometimes about the things he had read, at other times about the things of the world he had been accustomed to think about before. Our Lord was helping him, causing other thoughts, which were born of the things he was reading, to follow these. For, while reading the lives of Our Lord and the saints, he would stop to think, reasoning with himself, "How would it be, if I did this which Saint Francis did, and this which Saint Dominic did?" And thus he used to think over many things which he was finding good, always proposing to himself difficult and laborious things. And as he was proposing these, it seemed to him he was finding in himself an ease as regards putting them into practice. But his whole way of thinking was to say to himself: "Saint

Francis did this, so I must do it; Saint Dominic did this, so I must do it."

These thoughts too used to last a good space, and, after other things in between, the thoughts of the world would follow, and on these too he would stop for a long while. And this succession of such different kinds of thoughts lasted a considerable time for him, with him always dwelling on the thought whose turn it was, whether this was of the former worldly deeds which he wanted to do, or of these latter from God which were occurring to his imagination, until the point came when he would leave them because of tiredness and attend to other things.

Still, there was this difference: that when he was thinking about worldly stuff he would take much delight, but when he left it aside after getting tired, he would find himself dry and discontented. But when about doing the various austerities which the saints had done, not only used he to be consoled while in such thoughts, but he would remain content and happy even after having left them aside. But he wasn't investigating this, nor stopping to ponder this difference, until one time when his eyes were opened a little, and he began to marvel at this difference in kind and to reflect on it, picking it up from experience that from some thoughts he would be left sad and from others happy; and little by little coming to know the difference in kind of spirits that were stirring: the one from the devil, and the other from God.

This was the first reflection he made on the things of God; and later, when he produced the *Spiritual Exercises,* this experience was the starting point for teaching his followers the discernment of spirits.

AUGUST

August 1

Joseph of Arimathea
Missionary

Although there is no clear evidence of the origins of Christianity in the British Isles, there is an ancient tradition that Joseph of Arimathea was a relative of Jesus and that, being involved in the trade between the Cornish tin mines and the eastern Mediterranean, Joseph took Jesus with him on a business trip to Cornwall in the years before Jesus began his public ministry. That part of the tradition is referred to in a poem of William Blake's that asks: "And did those feet in ancient time walk upon England's mountains green? And was the holy Lamb of God on England's pleasant pastures seen?" The tradition is that, after Jesus' resurrection, Joseph returned to England carrying with him two cruets of Jesus' blood that had fallen during the crucifixion and that when Joseph stuck his staff in the ground it budded and grew into a hawthorn tree. The ancient hawthorn at Glastonbury was hewn down by one of Cromwell's soldiers but scions of that tree still exist and one now grows at Glastonbury.

A Reading from *Saint Joseph of Arimathea*
by W. E. C. Baynes

Now, after the Ascension of our Lord, all his disciples became dispersed in different lands, and Saint Philip the Apostle journeyed to Gallia, which is now called France, where he spent many years preaching and converting the people.

And Saint Philip, desiring that the word of God should be spread in Britain, chose twelve of his disciples and sent them to that country, placing at their head his favourite disciple Joseph, together with his son Josephes. So they set out on their journey, and there went with them a great company of those that had been converted. Leaving the shore of France on the eve of our Lord's resurrection, they were miraculously conveyed over the sea, so that they landed on the coast of North Wales on the following morning.

And Joseph with his son Josephes and ten of his companions journeyed from North Wales and came into Britain, where

Arviragus was king, and preached the word of the Lord to him; but he was a pagan and refused to accept the new teaching, being unwilling to change the traditions of his fathers. Nevertheless, seeing that Joseph and his companions had come from a far distant land, and that they were peaceful men, the King allotted them a certain island to dwell in, called by the inhabitants Ynyswytryn, which was covered with trees and brambles and surrounded by marshes.

This island was called by the Britons Ynyswytryn, meaning the Glassy Island, either because of the colour of the water that surrounded it, or because the island abounded in plants of woad from which the Britons made their blue dye. And it was also known as the Isle of Avalon, either from the name of Avalloc, who was an ancient chief of the Britons, or because the island was famed for its apples, which the Britons called "aval." But the Saxons afterwards named the place Glasingbyrig, and it is now called Glastonbury.

And it happened that Joseph stuck his dry staff of thorn into the ground on the hill where they rested, and forthwith it struck root and budded; and afterwards it grew into a great tree with two trunks, and flourished for many ages, budding forth leaves and flowers every year on Christmas Day, in frost or snow or whatever the weather.

But in the days of Queen Elizabeth a zealous puritan, taking offence at the tree, hewed down the biggest of the two trunks, and would have cut down the other also, had he not been miraculously prevented; for while hewing at the tree he cut his leg, and at the same time a chip of wood, flying up to his head, put out one of his eyes. But the trunk that was hewn off, even after it was taken away and cast into a ditch, still flourished and budded as it used to do before.The remaining trunk, which was as great as the ordinary body of a man, was still standing in the year 1633, but it was cut down by another puritan some years later during the Great Rebellion. Even up to the present day trees may be seen which grew from slips taken from the Holy Thorn, and these likewise bud every year on Christmas Day. One of these still stands in the grounds of the Abbey.

August 6

The Transfiguration of our Lord Jesus Christ

The story of the transfiguration of Jesus on the mount is recorded in the Gospels of Matthew, Mark and Luke, and Peter alludes to it in his Second Epistle. Each account makes clear that God's salvation is for all and that Jesus is the Chosen One of God who brings that salvation. Tradition locates the transfiguration on Mount Tabor. The event is significant as showing the testimony of the law and the prophets, represented by the figures of Moses and Elijah, to the messiahship of Jesus. The event is also seen as prefiguring the resurrection, giving a foretaste of the life of glory which is the destiny of all creation. The feast originated in the Eastern Church, not becoming universal until the mid-fifteenth century. It continues to occupy an important place in the spirituality of the Eastern Church.

A Reading from an address on the transfiguration of Christ by Anastasius, Abbot of Saint Catherine's Monastery, Mount Sinai

Upon Mount Tabor, Jesus revealed to his disciples a heavenly mystery. While living among them he had spoken of the kingdom and of his second coming in glory, but to banish from their hearts any possible doubt concerning the kingdom and to confirm their faith in what lay in the future by its prefiguration in the present, he gave them on Mount Tabor a wonderful vision of his glory, a foreshadowing of the kingdom of heaven. It was as if he said to them: As time goes by you may be in danger of losing your faith. To save you from this I tell you now that some standing here listening to me, "will not taste death until they have seen the Son of Man coming in the glory of his Father."

Moreover, in order to assure us that Christ could command such power when he wished, the evangelist continues: "Six days later, Jesus took with him Peter, James and John, and led them up a high mountain where they were alone. There, before their eyes, he was transfigured. His face shone like the sun, and his clothes became as white as light. Then the disciples saw Moses and Elijah appear, and they were talking to Jesus."

These are the divine wonders we celebrate today; this is the saving revelation given us upon the mountain; this is the festival of Christ that has drawn us here. Let us listen, then, to the sacred voice of God so compellingly calling us from on high, from the summit of the mountain, so that with the Lord's chosen disciples we may penetrate the deep meaning of these holy mysteries, so far beyond our capacity to express. Jesus goes before us to show us the way, both up the mountain and into heaven, and—I speak boldly—it is for us now to follow him with all speed, yearning for the heavenly vision that will give us a share in his radiance, renew our spiritual nature and transform us into his own likeness, making us for ever sharers in his Godhead and raising us to heights as yet undreamed of.

Let us run with confidence and joy to enter into the cloud like Moses and Elijah, or like James and John. Let us be caught up like Peter to behold the divine vision and to be transfigured by that glorious transfiguration. Let us retire from the world, stand aloof from the earth, rise above the body, detach ourselves from creatures and turn to the creator, to whom Peter in ecstasy exclaimed: "Lord, it is good for us to be here."

It is indeed good to be here, as you have said, Peter. It is good to be with Jesus and to remain here for ever. What greater happiness or higher honor could we have than to be with God, to be made like him and to live in his light? Therefore, since each of us who possesses God in our heart is being transformed into the divine image, we also should cry out with joy: "It is good for us to be here" here where all things shine with divine radiance, where there is joy and gladness and exultation; where there is nothing in our hearts but peace, serenity and stillness; where God is seen. For here, in our hearts, Christ takes up his abode together with the Father, saying as he enters: "Today salvation has come to this house." With Christ, our hearts receive all the wealth of his eternal blessings, and there where they are stored up for us in him, we see reflected as in a mirror both the firstfruits and the whole of the world to come.

alternative reading

A Reading from the *Spiritual Homilies*
of Pseudo-Macarius

When the soul is counted worthy to enjoy communion with the Spirit of the light of God, and when God shines upon the soul with the beauty of his ineffable glory, preparing her as a throne and dwelling for himself, she becomes all light, all face, all eye. Then there is no part of her that is not full of the spiritual eyes of light.

There is no part of her that is in darkness, but she is transfigured wholly and in every part with light and spirit.

Just as the sun is the same throughout, having neither back nor anything irregular, but is wholly glorified with light and is all light, being transformed in every part; or as fire, with its burning sheath of flame, is constant throughout, having neither a beginning nor an end, being neither larger nor smaller in any part, so also when the soul is perfectly illumined with the ineffable beauty and glory of the light of Christ's countenance, and granted perfect communion with the Holy Spirit and counted worthy to become the dwelling-place and throne of God, then the soul becomes all eye, all light, all face, all glory, all spirit.

alternative reading

A Reading from *Be Still and Know* by Michael Ramsey

In Saint Luke's account of the transfiguration of our Lord, we see his characteristic relating of a scene to prayer and to the mission of Jesus as he moves toward death and glory. Jesus is praying, and the light shines on his face. We do not know that it is a prayer of agony and conflict like the prayer in Gethsemane, but we know that it is a prayer near to the radiance of God and the prayer of one who has chosen the way of death. Luke tells us that the two witnesses, Moses and Elijah, were conversing about the exodus which Jesus would accomplish in Jerusalem: not death alone, but the passing through death to glory, the whole going forth of Jesus as well as the leading forth of the new people of God in the freedom of the new covenant. Luke tells us that after the resurrection Jesus spoke of the witness of Moses and of all the prophets to his suffering and glory.

It was not a glory which the disciples at the time could fathom. No doubt they would have welcomed a glory on the mountain far away from the conflicts which had happened and the conflicts which were going to happen as Jesus sets his face toward Jerusalem. Yet when Jesus went up the mountain to be transfigured he did not leave these conflicts behind, but rather carried them up the mountain so that they were transfigured with him. It was the transfiguration of the whole Christ, from his first obedience in childhood right through to the final obedience of Gethsemane and Calvary.

The disciples could not grasp this at the time, but the writings of the apostolic age were to show that the link between the suffering and the glory came to be understood as belonging to the heart of the Christian message. Glory belongs to the plain as well as to the mountain. The scene on the mount speaks to us today, but we are not allowed to linger there. We are bidden to journey on to Calvary and there learn of the darkness and the desolation which are the cost of the glory. But from Calvary and Easter there comes a Christian hope of immense range: the hope of the transformation not only of mankind but of the cosmos too.

In Eastern Christianity especially there has been the continuing belief that Easter is the beginning of a transformed cosmos. There is a glimpse of this hope in Saint Paul's Letter to the Romans, a hope that the creation itself will be set free from its bondage to decay and obtain "the glorious liberty of the children of God." The bringing of mankind to glory will be the prelude to the bringing of all creation. Is this hope mere fantasy? At its root there is the belief in the divine sovereignty of sacrificial love, a sovereignty made credible only by transfigured lives.

August 7

John Mason Neale

Priest, Hymn Writer, 1866

John Mason Neale was born in 1818 and, while an undergraduate at Cambridge, was influenced by the ideas of the Tractarians. He was a founder of the Cambridge Camden Society, which stimulated interest in ecclesiastical art and which played a part in the revival of Catholic ritual in the Church of England. While Warden of Sackville College, East Grinstead, a post he held from 1846, Neale founded the Society of Saint Margaret, which grew into one of the largest of Anglican women's religious communities. Neale is remembered as an accomplished hymn writer and his influence on Anglican worship has been considerable. He suffered frail health for many years and died on the Feast of the Transfiguration in 1866.

A Reading from a sermon of John Mason Neale preached at Sackville College on All Saints' Day

"In my Father's house are many mansions; if it were not so, I would have told you," says our Lord. A mansion for every one of us, if we really choose to have it. Wishing will not serve the turn; trying a little will not serve the turn; trying a great deal and then leaving off will not serve the turn; but resolving with the grace of the Holy Ghost will.

Great cause have we to rejoice in this Feast of the Saints; good cause have we to think it one of the greatest in the whole year. We keep in memory the saints and righteous persons, known and unknown, not of one nation, not of one kingdom, not of one age, but of every kindred and tongue and people, from just Abel who was slain for the truth, down to the last Christian that has this very day died the death of the righteous. This feast belongs to us.

There is no Christian family so unhappy as not to have some of its ancestors in paradise. Some of you have lost baptized children in infancy. Then we keep them in memory too; seeing that God has embraced them with the arms of his mercy, and made them partakers of everlasting life. Is the day ours in a more particular sense still? Yes, it is: for if of God's great goodness we ever merit to enter into life eternal, the time will come, and not long hence, when we also shall be of the number of the saints. Now we keep others in memory then we shall be kept in memory ourselves: now we celebrate others then others will celebrate us.

This can only be if we walk and live like the saints, thinking no labor too great, no battle too hard, forgetting that there is such a word in the language as "cannot." Cannot has kept many a soul out of heaven. We *can* do all things through Christ who strengthens us. And if we resolve, by the help of the Holy Ghost, to take heaven by violence, and persevere in our resolve, we shall receive from him grace in this life, and in the life to come, the reward of grace which is glory.

August 8

Dominic

Priest, Founder of the Order of Preachers, 1221

Born at Calaruega in Castile, of the ancient Guzman family in 1170, Dominic became an Augustinian or Austin Friar and led a disciplined life of prayer and penance. He became prior in 1201 but three years later, while on a trip to Denmark with his bishop, he passed through France and came across Cathars or Albigenses. They claimed to be Christians but held the heterodox belief that flesh and material things were evil, that the spirit was of God, and that flesh and spirit were therefore in permanent conflict. Dominic formed an Order of Preachers to combat this belief, although he would have nothing to do with the vengeful Crusade that began to be waged against the Albigenses. The Dominican Order spread to many countries in just a few years and did much to maintain the credibility of the orthodox faith in late medieval Europe. Dominic died on this day at Bologna in 1221.

A Reading from selected sources of the history
of the Order of Preachers

Dominic possessed such great integrity and was so strongly motivated by divine love, that without a doubt he proved to be a bearer of honor and grace. He was a man of great serenity, except when moved to compassion and mercy. And since a joyful heart animates the face, he displayed the peaceful composure of a spiritual person in the kindness he manifested outwardly and by the cheerfulness of his countenance.

Wherever he went he showed himself in word and deed to be a follower of the gospel. During the day no one was more community-minded or pleasant toward associates. During the night hours no one was more persistent in every kind of vigil and supplication. Dominic seldom spoke unless it was with God, that is, in prayer, or about God; and in this matter he instructed his brothers.

Frequently Dominic made a special personal petition that God would deign to grant him a genuine charity, effective in caring for and in obtaining the salvation of humankind. For he believed that only then would he be truly a member of Christ, when he had given himself totally for the salvation of all, just as the Lord Jesus, the Savior of all, had offered himself completely for our salvation. So, for this work, after a lengthy period of careful and provident planning, Dominic founded the Order of Friars Preachers.

In his conversations and letters he often urged the brothers of the Order to study constantly the Old and New Testaments. He always carried with him the Gospel according to Matthew and the Epistles of Paul, and so well did he study them that he almost knew them from memory. Two or three times Dominic was chosen bishop, but he always refused, preferring to live with his brothers in poverty.

August 9

Mary Sumner

Founder of the Mothers' Union, 1921

Mary Elizabeth Sumner (née Heywood) was born in 1828 at Swinton. In 1848, she married a young curate, George Henry Sumner, nephew of Archbishop Sumner, who was himself to become Bishop of Guildford in 1888. A mother of three children, Mary called a meeting in 1876 at which the Mothers' Union was founded, providing a forum in which to unite mothers of all classes in the aim of bringing up children in the Christian faith. Baptism and parental example were its two basic principles. At first a parochial organization, it grew steadily into an international concern, encouraging the ideal of a Christian home. Mary died on this day in the year 1921.

A Reading from *Mary Sumner: Her Life and Work* compiled by Mary Porter

It was a heavy task Mary Sumner set herself in the launching of the Mothers' Union. Once or twice she owned that the strain of those first years was sometimes not far from breaking her down. It was her way, however, to constantly relieve the strain of her own efforts by the worship of God's glory. Addressing a group in Winchester she said:

> Let us settle it in our hearts that the greatest work we can do for the nation is to strive to bring the Church into the home; which means Christ himself into hearts and homes. Christ must be in every home, if it is to be in any way a home of peace and love.
>
> God's plans are better than our own, and he has ordained that the training-place for his human creatures should be the *home*; the training-place for *parents* as well as children.
>
> Our task is to restore true family life for it is God's own institution, and therefore a divine thing and to convince all our members that there are these two divine institutions in the world: the Church and the home. The home is God's institution as truly as is the Church: let that be the truth that we proclaim!

In November 1887 the first Diocesan Conference of the Mothers' Union was held in Winchester at which Mary Sumner was able to report a beginning full of promise. At the Conference the following statement was accepted which was to form the basis of the Mothers' Union:

The Principles upon which we would build our work are these:

That the prosperity of a nation springs from the family life of the homes;

That family life is the greatest institution in the world for the formation of the character of children;

That the tone of family life depends in great measure upon the married life of the parents their mutual love, loyalty and faithfulness the one to the other;

That religion is the indispensable foundation of family life, and that the truths of the Christian faith should be taught definitely at home as well as at school;

That parents are themselves responsible for the religious teaching of their children;

That character is formed during the first ten years of life by the example and habits of the home;

That example is stronger than precept, and parents therefore must be themselves what they wish their children to be;

That the history of the world proves the divine power given by God to parents, and to mothers especially, because children are placed in their arms from infancy, in a more intimate and closer relationship with the mother than with the father, and this moreover, during the time when character is formed;

That the training of children is a profession;

That it needs faith, love, patience, method, self-control, and some knowledge of the principles of character-training;

That it is the duty of every mother with her own lips to teach her child that he is God's child, consecrated body and soul in Holy Baptism to be our Lord Jesus Christ's soldier and servant unto his life's end;

That every baptized child should be taught the Creed, the Lord's Prayer and the Ten Commandments and all other things which a Christian ought to know and believe to his soul's health.

August 10

Laurence

Deacon at Rome, Martyr, 258

Early sources of the martyrdom of Laurence are thin on details. It is known that Laurence was one of the seven deacons at Rome and closely associated with Pope Sixtus II, martyred just a few days before him. His examiners insisted he produce the Church treasures. He promptly did so: assembling all the poor, he is reputed to have said, "These are the treasures of the Church." The tradition of his being put to death on a gridiron is probably a later addition to the story. He died on this day in the year 258.

A Reading from a sermon of Leo the Great

No model is more useful in teaching God's people than that of the martyrs. Eloquence may enable intercession, reasoning may succeed in persuading; but in the end examples are always more powerful than words, and teaching communicates better through practice than precept. In this respect, how gloriously powerful is the blessed martyr Laurence whose sufferings we commemorate today. Even his persecutors felt the power of his teaching when they were confronted by his courage, a courage born of love for Christ, which not only refused to yield to them, but actually gave strength to those around him.

When the fury of the pagans was raging against Christ's most chosen members and attacking those especially who were ordained, the wicked persecutor's wrath was vented on Laurence the deacon, who was outstanding not only in the performance of the liturgy, but also in the management of the church's property. The persecutor promised himself a double spoil from this man's capture, reasoning that if once he could force Laurence to surrender the Church's treasures, his action would also discredit him irredeemably. Greedy for money and an enemy to the truth, the persecutor armed himself with a double weapon: with avarice to plunder the gold, and with impiety to carry off Christ.

And so it was that he demanded that the Church's wealth, on which his greedy mind was set, should be brought out to him. The holy deacon then showed him where he had it stored. He pointed to a crowd of holy poor people, in the feeding and clothing of whom, he said, was to be found a treasury of riches which could never be lost, and which was entirely secure because the money had been spent on so holy a cause. At first the plunderer was completely baffled, but then his anger blazed out into hatred for a religion which should put its wealth to such a use. Determined to pillage the Church's treasury, and finding no hoard of money, he resolved then to carry off a still greater prize by carrying off that sacred deposit of faith with which the Church was enriched.

He ordered Laurence to renounce Christ, and prepared to test the deacon's stout courage with terrifying tortures. The deacon's limbs, already torn and wounded by many beatings, were ordered to be roasted alive on an iron grid. The grid was already hot enough to burn anyone, but to prolong his agony and to make his death more lingering, they turned the grid from time to time in the fire so that only one limb at a time was in the flames.

You gain nothing by this, O savage cruelty. When his poor mortal frame is released from your devices, and Laurence departs for heaven, you are vanquished! The flame of Christ's love could not be overcome by your flames, and the fire which burnt outside was weaker than the fire that burnt within Laurence's heart.

August 11

Clare of Assisi

Founder of the Minoresses (Poor Clares), 1253

Born in 1193 in Assisi of a wealthy family, Clare caught the joy of a new vision of the gospel from Francis' preaching. Escaping from home, first to the Benedictines and then to a Béguine-style group, she chose a contemplative way of life when she founded her own community, which lived in corporate poverty understood as dependence on God, with a fresh, democratic lifestyle. Clare became the first woman to write a religious Rule *for women, and in it showed great liberty of spirit in dealing with earlier prescriptions. During the long years after Francis' death, she supported his earlier companions in their desire to remain faithful to his vision, as she did. Some of her last words were: "Blessed be God, for having created me."*

A Reading from the last letter of Clare to Blessed Agnes of Prague, written in 1253 shortly before Clare's death

If I have not written to you as often as your soul and mine well desire and long for, do not wonder or think that the fire of love for you glows less sweetly in the heart of your mother. No, this is the difficulty: the lack of messengers and the obvious dangers of the roads. Now, however, as I write to your love, I rejoice and exult with you in the joy of the Spirit, O bride of Christ, because since you have totally abandoned the vanities of this world, like another most holy virgin, Saint Agnes, you have been marvelously espoused to the spotless Lamb who takes away the sins of the world.

Happy indeed is she to whom it is given to share this banquet, to cling with all her heart to him whose beauty all the heavenly hosts admire unceasingly, whose love inflames our love, whose contemplation is our refreshment, whose graciousness is our joy, whose gentleness fills us to overflowing, whose remembrance brings a gentle light, whose fragrance will revive the dead, whose glorious vision will be the happiness of all the citizens of the heavenly Jerusalem.

Inasmuch as this vision is the splendor of eternal glory, the brilliance of eternal light and the mirror without blemish, look upon that mirror each day, O queen and spouse of Jesus Christ; and continually study your face in it so that you may adorn yourself within and without with beautiful robes, and cover yourself with the flowers and garments of all the virtues as becomes the daughter and most chaste bride of the Most High King. Indeed, blessed poverty, holy humility, and ineffable charity are reflected in that mirror as, by the grace of God, you can contemplate them throughout the entire mirror.

Look at the parameters of the mirror, that is the poverty of him who was placed in a manger and wrapped in swaddling clothes. O marvelous humility! O astonishing poverty! The King of the angels, the Lord of heaven and earth, is laid in a manger! Then, look at the surface of the mirror, dwell on the holy humility, the blessed poverty, the untold labors and burdens which he endured for the redemption of the world. Then, in the depths of this same mirror, contemplate the ineffable charity which led him to suffer on the wood of the cross and to die thereon the most shameful kind of death.

Therefore that mirror, suspended on the wood of the cross, urged those who passed by to reflect, saying, "All you who pass by the way, look and see if there is any suffering like my suffering!" Let us answer his cry with one voice and spirit for he said, "Remembering this over and over leaves my soul downcast within me." In this way, O queen of our heavenly King, let yourself be inflamed more strongly with the fervor of charity.

And as you contemplate further his ineffable delights, his eternal riches and honors, and sigh for them in the great desire and love of your heart, may you cry out in the words of Solomon: "Draw me after you! We will run in the fragrance of your perfumes, O heavenly spouse! I will run and not tire, until you bring me into the wine-cellar, until your left hand is under my head and your right hand will embrace me happily, and you kiss me with the happiest kiss of your mouth."

In this contemplation may you remember your poor mother, knowing that I have inscribed the happy memory of you indelibly on the tablets of my heart, holding you dearer than all the others.

August 13

Jeremy Taylor

Bishop of Down and Connor, Teacher of the Faith, 1667

Jeremy Taylor was born in Cambridge in 1613 and educated there at Gonville and Caius College. He was ordained in 1633 and, as the English Civil War got under way, he became a chaplain with the Royalist forces. He was captured and imprisoned briefly but after his release went to Wales, where the Earl of Carbery gave him refuge. He wrote prolifically while there, notably The Rule and Exercise of Holy Living *in 1650 and of* Holy Dying *the following year. In 1658 he went to Ireland to lecture and two years later was made Bishop of Down and Connor. He found many of his clergy held to Presbyterianism and so ignored him; and the Roman Catholics rejected him as a Protestant. In turn, he treated both sides harshly. His health was worn down by the protracted conflicts and he died on this day in the year 1667.*

A Reading from *Holy Living* by Jeremy Taylor

When religion puts on armor, it may have the power of the sword, but not the power of godliness, and we have no remedy but the fellowship of Christ's sufferings, and the returns of the God of peace. Men are apt to prefer a prosperous error before an afflicted truth; and those few who have no other plot in their religion but to serve God and save their souls, do want such assistance of ghostly counsel as may assist their endeavors in the acquistion of virtues, and relieve their dangers when they are tempted to sin and death; I thought I had reasons enough inviting me to draw into one body those advices: that a collection of holy precepts and the rules for conduct might be committed to a book which they might always have.

A man does certainly belong to God who believes and is baptized into all the articles of the Christian faith, and studies to improve his knowledge in the matters of God, so as may best make him to live a holy life; he that, in obedience to Christ, worships God diligently, frequently, and constantly, with natural religion, that is of prayer, praises, and thanksgiving; he that takes all opportunities to remember Christ's death by a frequent sacrament, as it can be had, or else by inward acts of understanding, will, and memory (which is spiritual communion) supplies the want of the external rite; he that lives chastely; and is merciful; and despises the world, using it as a man, but never suffering it to rifle a duty; and is just in his dealing, and diligent in his calling; he that is humble in spirit; and obedient to government; and is content in his fortune and employment; he that does his duty because he loves God; and especially if after all this he be afflicted, and patient, or prepared to suffer affliction for the cause of God: the man that has these twelve signs of grace does as certainly belong to God, and is his son as surely, as he is his creature.

These are the marks of the Lord Jesus, and the characters of a Christian: this is a good religion; and these things God's grace hath put into our powers, and God's laws have made to be our duty, and the nature of man, and the needs of commonwealths, have made to be necessary.

August 13

Florence Nightingale

Nurse, Social Reformer, 1910

Florence Nightingale was born in 1820 into a wealthy family. In the face of their opposition, she insisted that she wished to train in nursing. In 1853, she finally achieved her wish and headed her own private nursing institute in London. Her efforts at improving conditions for the wounded during the Crimean War won her great acclaim and she devoted the rest of her life to reforming nursing care. Her school at Saint Thomas's Hospital became significant in helping to elevate nursing into a profession. An Anglican, she remained committed to a personal mystical religion which sustained her through many years of poor health until her death in the year 1910.

A Reading from *The Silent Rebellion* by A. M. Allchin

The heroism and ability of Florence Nightingale, and of the nurses who worked with her in the Crimea, caught the imagination of mid-nineteenth century England, and suddenly drew attention to the problem of the position and rights of women in society. A great many difficult questions were raised. Was it right, for instance, for an unmarried lady to make a career for herself in public life? If it were, what professions might she suitably take up? How far, if at all, should the mother of a family engage in activities outside her home? What should be the nature of women's education? These were all issues which had been thought about before 1854, but the events in the Crimea made them the center of widespread and insistent discussion.

It is not easy at this length of time to envisage quite how restricted were the activities of a mid-Victorian lady. The case of Florence Nightingale, because of the outstanding quality of her character, and her exceptional outspokenness, reveals the situation to us in all its difficulty; and although she herself never became a member, or should one say the superior, of a community, her problems are very similar to those of her contemporaries who in fact entered the Anglican sisterhoods. She was facing all the weight of social convention, and the pitch of her feelings is plain in a private note which she wrote in 1851:

> Women don't consider themselves as human beings at all. There is absolutely no God, no country, no duty to them at all, except family. . . . I have known a good deal of convents. And, of course, everyone has talked of the petty tyrannies supposed to be exercised there. But I know nothing like the petty grinding tyranny of a good English family.

or again:

> What I complain of the Evangelical party for, is the degree to which they have raised the claims upon women of "Family"—the idol they have made of it.

This intense dissatisfaction with the Evangelical party was in fact extended to the Church of England as a whole. In a letter written in 1852 she exclaims:

> The Church of England has for men bishoprics, archbishoprics, and a little work. . . . For women she has—what? I had no taste for theological discoveries. I would have given her my head, my hand, my heart. She would not have them. She did not know what to do with them. She told me to go back and do crochet in my mother's drawing room; or, if I were tired of that, to marry and look well at the head of my husband's table. You may go to the Sunday School if you like it, she said. But she gave me no training even for that. She gave me neither work to do for her, nor education for it.

Florence Nightingale was only able to break out of the restrictions of Victorian family life by force of character and exceptional perseverance.

August 14

Maximilian Kolbe

Friar, Martyr, 1941

Maximilian Kolbe was born at Zdunska Wola near Lodz in Poland in 1894. His parents were Franciscan Tertiaries and, beginning his training for ordination in 1907, Maximilian joined the Franciscan novitiate in 1910. He studied at Rome but, suffering from tuberculosis, he returned to Poland and became a lecturer in Church History. After suffering a severe illness, he resolved to publish a magazine for Christian readers and this soon gained a huge circulation. Soon his community was producing daily and weekly journals. After the Nazi invasion of Poland, Maximilian was arrested as an "intellectual" and taken to Auschwitz in May 1941. There he continued his priestly ministry, secretly celebrating the Eucharist. When, after an escape, a prisoner was chosen to forfeit his life as an example, Maximilian stepped forward to take his place and be put to death. Two weeks later he was injected with phenol and died on this day in the year 1941.

A Reading from the homily of Pope John Paul II preached at the canonization of Maximilian Kolbe, October 10, 1982

"How can I repay the Lord for all his goodness to me? I will take up the cup of salvation and call upon the name of the Lord." These are words of thankfulness. Death undergone for love, in place of a brother, is Father Kolbe's heroic act, by which we glorify God at the same time as his saint. For it is from God that the grace of such heroism, the grace of this martyrdom, comes.

Today, then, we glorify the great work of God in this man. Before all of us gathered here, Father Maximilian Kolbe raises his "cup of salvation," in which is brought together the sacrifice of his whole life, sealed by his death as a martyr "for his brother." The world looked at what went on in the camp at Auschwitz. Even if it seemed to some eyes that one of their companions died in torture, even if humanly they could consider his "going from them to be destruction," in reality they were aware that it was not merely death.

Maximilian is not dead, but he has "given his life for his brother." There was in that death, humanly so terrible, all the absolute greatness of the human act and human choice: he, himself, on his very own, had offered himself to death out of love.

And in this human death there was the transparent witness given to Christ: witness given in Christ to the dignity of humanity, to the sanctity of life, and to the saving power of death in which is revealed the strength of love. It is precisely on this account that the death of Maximilian Kolbe has become a sign of victory. It was a victory achieved over a whole system of outrage and hatred toward men and women, and toward what is divine in us, a victory like to that which our Lord Jesus Christ achieved on Calvary.

alternative reading

A Reading from *A Theology of Auschwitz*
by Ulrich Simon

Theology is the science of divine reality. Auschwitz is a place in Poland where millions of human beings were killed between 1942 and 1945. This *Konzentrationslager* occupied about fifteen square miles and consisted of three main and thirty-nine subsidiary camps. The first prisoner arrived on July 14, 1940. The camp was evacuated and for the most part destroyed by January 27, 1945, before Russian troops liberated what was left of it. There were only forty thousand registered prisoners among the millions who perished there without leaving a name.

At first sight theology and Auschwitz have nothing in common. The former articulates a joyful tradition, the latter evokes the memory of untold suffering. Theology speaks of eternal light, Auschwitz perpetuates the horror of darkness. Nevertheless, as light and darkness are complementary in our experience, and as the glory and the shame must be apprehended together, so the momentous outrage of Auschwitz cannot be allowed to stand, as it has done, in an isolation such as the leprous outcast used to inspire in the past. The evils that we do live after us; unless they are understood they may recur.

Such an understanding meets with endless obstacles. It is easy enough to present the documentation of what happened in Auschwitz between 1942 and 1945. The facts are available to all who care to open the files. The lawyers have put us in their debt by enabling us to see the scene of unprecedented crime in as unemotional a light as possible. The pictures of the tormented, the dying, and the dead, as well as of the death factories, have become the exhibits in the many trials which have been held to bring the guilty to justice. The subject has thus been frozen with the unemotional air of the dispassionate procedure of justice. These cases were listed, heard, and concluded under criminal law.

The theologian's enquiry, however, goes beyond the terms of criminal investigation and the sifting of evidence. Unlike the court the theologian is not satisfied by the elucidation of the facts. He must ask the great "Why?" rather than be content to know how and when certain crimes were perpetrated. He extends the "Why?" to the root of the historical drama and to the actors in it. The theologian will compare and contrast his findings with the declared Christian doctrines. How does Auschwitz stand in the light of the Fatherhood of God, the person and work of Christ, and the coming of the Holy Ghost? These norms of Christian theology govern our enquiry and rule out an untidy or hysterical survey. They exclude a morbid fascination with facts which the human eye finds too repulsive to see and which the mind cannot fathom.

Auschwitz belongs to the past, thank God. But its multi-dimensional range of evil extends to the present and throws its shadow over the future. It is the comprehensive and realistic symbol of the greatest possible evil which still threatens humankind. A theology of Auschwitz, therefore, is an attempt to interpret this evil responsibly for the present.

August 14

Jonathan Myrick Daniels
1965

Jonathan Daniels was born in 1939. Uncertain whether to pursue a career in law, medicine, writing, or ministry, he had a profound conversion experience on Easter Day, 1962, at the Church of the Advent in Boston. He enrolled in the Episcopal Theological School and then, in March of 1965, responded to a televised appeal by Martin Luther King, Jr., for volunteers to work that summer in Selma, Alabama. On August 14, he and some companions were arrested and jailed for joining a picket line and then unexpectedly released. Knowing that they were in danger, they walked from the courthouse to a small store. A man with a shotgun appeared and threatened the sixteen-year-old Ruby Sales, who was part of the group. Daniels pulled her to one side and was killed himself by a blast from the gun. His letters and papers speak of the faith that led him to "know in my bones and sinews that I had been truly baptized into the Lord's death and resurrection."

A Reading from an article by Jonathan Myrick Daniels

The disappointments of Holy Week and the bitterness of Easter Communion at St. Paul's forced our eyes back to the inscription over the altar: HE IS NOT HERE. FOR HE IS RISEN. In a dreadful parody of their meaning, the words seemed to tell a grim truth that was not exhausted by their liturgical import.

This is the stuff of which our life is made. There are moments of great joy and moments of sorrow. Almost imperceptibly, some men grow in grace. Some men don't. Christian hope, grounded in the reality of Easter, must never degenerate into optimism. For that is the road to despair. Yet it ought never to conclude that because its proper end is heaven, the church may dally at its work until the end is in sight. The thought of the church is fraught with tension because the life of the church is caught in tension. For the individual Christian and the far-flung congregation alike, that is part of the reality of the Cross.

There are good men here, just as there are bad men. There are competent leaders and a bungler here and there. We have activists who risk their lives to confront a people with the challenge of freedom and a nation with its conscience. We have neutralists who cautiously seek to calm troubled waters. We have men about the work of reconciliation who are willing to reflect upon the cost and pay it. Perhaps at one time or another the two of us are all of these.

Sometimes we take to the streets, sometimes we yawn through interminable meetings. Sometimes we talk with white men in their homes and offices, sometimes we sit out a murderous night with an alcoholic and his family because we love them and cannot stand apart. Sometimes we confront the posse, and sometimes we hold a child. Sometimes we stand with men who have learned to hate, and sometimes we must stand a little apart from them. Our life in Selma is filled with ambiguity, and in that we share with men everywhere. We are beginning to see as we never saw before that we are truly in the world and yet ultimately not of it. For through the bramble bush of doubt and fear and supposed success we are groping our way to the realization that above all else, we are called to be saints. That is the mission of the church everywhere. And in this Selma, Alabama, is like all the world: it needs the life and witness of militant saints.

August 15

Saint Mary the Virgin Mother of Our Lord Jesus Christ

Nothing certain is known of the parentage or the place of birth of the Mother of the Lord. Only her name is known Mary or Miriam (in Hebrew) and that she had an aged relative called Elizabeth. According to the Gospel of Luke, Mary was a young Jewish girl living in Nazareth, engaged to a man called Joseph, when a messenger from the Lord announced that she was to be the bearer of the Son of God to the world. Her response, "Let it be to me according to your word," and her life of obedience and faithfulness have been upheld ever since as a model for all who hear and obey God's word. In Christian tradition Mary is often described as "the second Eve" who offsets Eve's disobedience. Mary was present at the crucifixion of her Son, and was with the apostles and others at Pentecost. According to the Gospel of John, at the time of his death Jesus commended the care of his mother to the beloved disciple, which may explain why in Christian tradition her final years are associated with both Jerusalem and Ephesus. The Church customarily commemorates saints on the day of their death, and although the date and place of Mary's death are unknown, for centuries today has been celebrated as her principal feast. (The Annunciation is seen principally as a feast of

Our Lord.) In the East, today's feast is entitled "The Dormition of the Virgin;" in the Roman Catholic Church, reflecting its distinctive doctrinal emphasis, it is called "The Assumption of the Blessed Virgin Mary."

A Reading from *Revelations of Divine Love*
by Julian of Norwich

With the same cheerful joy our good Lord looked down to his right and thereby brought to mind the place where our Lady was standing during his passion. "Do you want to see her?" he said, saying in effect, "I know quite well you want to see my blessed Mother, for, after myself, she is the greatest joy I can show you, and most like me and worthy of me. Of all my creation, she is the most desirable sight." And because of his great, wonderful, unique love for this sweet maiden, his blessed Mother our Lady Saint Mary, he showed her to be rejoicing greatly. This is the meaning of the sweet words. It was as if he were saying, "Do you want to see how I love her, so that you can rejoice with me in my love for her, and hers for me?"

Here—to understand this word further our Lord God is speaking to all who are going to be saved, as it were to all humankind in the person of one individual. He is saying, "Can you see in her how greatly you are loved? For love of you made her so exalted, so noble, so worthy. This pleases me, and I want it to please you too." For after himself she is the most blessed of all sights.

But, for all that, I am not expected to want to see her physically present here on earth, but rather to see the virtues of her blessed soul, her truth, her wisdom, her charity, so that I can learn to know myself, and reverently fear my God.

When our good Lord had showed me this and said, "Do you want to see her?" I answered, "Yes, good Lord, thank you very much. Yes, good Lord, if it is your will." I prayed this often, and I thought I was going to see her in person. But I did not see her in this way. Jesus, in that word, gave me a spiritual sight of her. Just as I had seen her before, lowly and unaffected, so now he showed her, exalted, noble, glorious, and pleasing to him above all creation.

He wills it to be known that all who delight in him should delight in her too, with the same pleasure he has in her, and she in him. To help understand it better he gave this example. If you love one particular thing above everything else, you will try to make everyone else love and like what it is you love so greatly. When

" I thought it was the nicest
have said, together with the
f her. Except in the case of
ed me no one specially and
ccasion was when she was
nder the cross, and the third
rejoicing.

Blessed Virgin Mary
ingen

e,

beauty,

n:

r saw

ry of God,
h light,
the Virgin

saw

In the fair flower
Born of the sweetest integrity
Of your sealed chastity.
Alleluia!

alternative reading for Roman Catholics

A Reading from *Mary, Mother of God, Mother of the Poor* by Ivone Gebara and Maria Bingemer

Mary's assumption brings a new and promising future for women. Excluded from Jewish initiation rites because of their anatomy, banned from full participation in worship and the synagogue by their menstrual cycles, for a long time women—even in Christianity—subtly or explicitly have been second-class citizens in the world of faith because of the "inferiority" and the "poverty" of their bodies.

Mary's assumption, however, restores and reintegrates woman's bodiliness into the very mystery of God. Starting with Mary, the dignity of women's condition is recognized and safeguarded by the creator of that very bodiliness. In Jesus Christ and Mary the feminine is respectively resurrected and assumed into heaven definitively sharing in the glory of the Trinitarian mystery from which all proceeds and to which all returns.

Her assumption is intimately connected to Jesus' resurrection. Both events of faith are about the same mystery: the triumph of God's justice over human injustice, the victory of grace over sin. Just as proclaiming the resurrection of Jesus means continuing to announce his passion which continues in those who are crucified and suffer injustice in this world, by analogy, believing in Mary's assumption means proclaiming that the woman who gave birth in a stable among animals, whose heart was pierced with a sword of sorrow, who shared in her son's poverty, humiliation, persecution, and violent death, who stood at the foot of the cross, the mother of the condemned, has been exalted. Just as the crucified one is the risen one, so the sorrowing one is the one assumed into heaven, the one in glory. She who, while a disciple herself, shared persecutions, fear and anxiety with other disciples in the early years of the Church, is the same one who, after a death that was certainly humble and anonymous, was raised to heaven. The assumption is the glorious culmination of the mystery of God's preference for what is poor, small, and unprotected in this world, so as to make God's presence and glory shine there.

The virgin of the Magnificat, on whose lips is placed the message that God is exalting the humble and casting down the powerful, finds her life confirmed and glorified by the Father of Jesus. Mary's assumption seen in the light of Jesus' resurrec-tion is hope and promise for the poor of all times and for those who stand in solidarity with them; it is hope and promise that they will share in the final victory of the incarnate God.

August 18

William Porcher DuBose
Priest, 1918

William Porcher DuBose has been called "probably the most original and creative thinker the American Episcopal Church has ever produced," but his work was hardly noticed until he began publishing his writings at the age of fifty-six. He was born in 1836 and studied at the University of Virginia and the Episcopal Seminary in Camden, South Carolina, before being ordained and serving as a chaplain and officer in the Confederate Army. He spent most of the remainder of his life teaching at the University of the South in Sewanee, Tennessee. At a time when the traditional teaching of the Christian church was being challenged by the work of Darwin, Freud, and others who revolutionized human understanding of the world and the place of humanity in it, DuBose worked to synthesize the best of contemporary thought with his own deeply personal understanding of the Christian faith and the catholic tradition.

A Reading from *The Faith of a Christian Today*
by William Porcher DuBose

I never begin the life of Christ without dwelling with a peculiar delight upon the double account which has been called the Gospel of the Infancy—or the Story of the Birth. In the first place there is such a divine charm in the story itself. But what strikes me even more is the background of spiritual—not only height and depth—but inevitable truth in it. And yet I think I can partially understand the difficulty of the present-day mind upon the subject of the miraculous element in the birth record.

Meantime what of my Christian faith: what is honest doubt doing with my Christian conviction as to the person of Christ?

Everything depends upon how—with what eyes—we are looking upon the Virgin Birth. If we are doing so only with the eyes of sense or of science—i.e., of natural vision, if we are assuming that there is nothing of the supernatural in it at all, nothing of the spiritual or the divine—then we are doing something more lowering to our nature and our intelligence than any belittling of mere natural fact or historic truth that we can be guilty of. I beg not to sin against physical fact, but yet more earnestly I pray to be delivered from the more serious offense of spiritual blindness and denial.

The real miracle of the Gospel is the spiritual Jesus. That does not exclude—on the contrary it assumes—all the physical of our common humanity in him. "He was made in all points like unto us—sin only excepted." And that exception was no mere fact of nature; it was an act in the nature (an act at once of faith, of obedience, and of sacrifice) which accomplished and constituted its redemption and salvation. It was the human conquest of the spirit over the flesh. That was a human act, but it was none the less—on the contrary, it was all the more—a divine act. God and man are not mutually exclusive but mutually inclusive: they are most each and both when they are most one. The church from the beginning refused to see in Christ only man. Moreover, it insisted upon seeing in him primarily and causally God in man, and only secondarily and by consequence man in God. The impression produced immediately by Jesus, and left permanently with his church, is best and most fully, in its pure spirituality, portrayed in Saint John, Saint Paul, and the Epistle to the Hebrews. Not one of these refers to the physical features or incidents or explanations of his human genesis or generation. They describe him as having been eternally God's foreknowledge or thought, forepurpose or will of man; as having become in time God's not only revelation or manifestation, but actual accomplishment and fulfillment of man's destiny through the sole process of self-realization in him. We see ourselves now in the mind of God, in the act of God, and in the end or aim of God, and by entering into and uniting ourselves with the divine process as seen in Christ, we attain our own and our only self-realization in eternal life.

August 20

Bernard

Abbot of Clairvaux, Teacher of the Faith, 1153

Bernard was born at Fontaines, near Dijon, in France in the year 1090. He entered the Benedictine abbey at Cîteaux in 1112, taking with him many of his young companions, some of whom were his own brothers. He was a leader of the reform within Benedictinism at this time, and in 1115 was sent to establish a new monastery at a place he named Clairvaux, or "Valley of Light." Though times were hard, he built up the community through his remarkable qualities of leadership. Bernard preached widely and powerfully, and proved himself a theologian of renown. Literally hundreds of houses were founded on the Cîteaux or Cistercian system and Bernard's influence on his own generation and beyond was immense. He died on this day in the year 1153.

A Reading from the treatise *On the Love of God*
by Bernard of Clairvaux

God deserves of us all our love, a love which knows no bounds. This is the first thing to understand. The reason is because God was the first to love. God, who is so great, loves us so much; he loves us freely, poor, pathetic, worthless creatures though we be. This is why I insist that our love for God should know no bounds. And since love given to God is given to the One who is infinite and without boundary, what measure or boundary could we make anyway?

Furthermore, our love is not bestowed for no reason, as God's love is for us: we render it in payment of a debt. God, infinite and eternal, who is love beyond our human capacity to comprehend, whose greatness knows no bounds, whose wisdom has no end, simply *loves.* Should we, for our part then, set limits on our love for God?

"I will love you, O Lord my strength, my strong rock and my defense, my Savior, my sole desire and love." My God, my helper, I will love you with all the power you have given me; not worthily, because that is impossible, but nevertheless to the best of my ability. Do what I will in life, I can never discharge my debt to you, and I can love you only according to the power you have given me. But I will endeavor to love you more and more, as you see fit to enable me to do so; and yet, never, never, as you should be loved. "Your eyes saw my unformed substance." In your book are written all who do the best they can, though they never pay their debt to you in full.

The reason, then, for our loving God *is* God. He is the initiator of our love and its final goal. He is himself the occasion of human love; he gives us the power to love, and brings our desire to consummation. God is loveable in himself, and gives himself to us as the object of our love. He desires that our love for him should bring us happiness, and not be arid and barren. His love for us opens up inside us the way to love, and is the reward of our own reaching out in love. How gently he leads us in love's way, how generously he returns the love we give, how sweet he is to those who wait for him!

God is indeed rich to all who call to him, for he can give them nothing better than to give them himself. He gave himself to be our righteousness, and he keeps himself to be our great reward. He offers himself as refreshment to our souls, and spends himself to set free those in prison. You are good, Lord, to the soul that seeks you. What, then, are you to the soul that finds you? The marvel is, no one can seek you who has not already found you. You want us to find you so that we may seek you, but we can never anticipate your coming, for though we say "Early shall my prayer come before you," a chilly, loveless thing that prayer would be, were it not warmed by your own breath and born of your own Spirit.

August 24

Saint Bartholomew the Apostle

It has long been assumed that Bartholomew is the same as Nathanael though it is not certain. The Gospel according to John speaks of Philip bringing Nathanael to Jesus who calls him "an Israelite worthy of the name." He is also present beside the Sea of Galilee at the resurrection. Although he seems initially a somewhat cynical man, he recognizes Jesus for who he is and proclaims him as Son of God and King of Israel.

A Reading from the treatise *On Prescription against Heresies* by Tertullian

The apostles (whose name means "sent") first bore witness to their faith in Jesus Christ throughout Judea, and established churches there. After this they went out into the rest of the world, proclaiming the same doctrine of the same faith to the nations. In the same way they established churches in every city, from which other churches derived the shoots of faith and the seeds of doctrine, and are still deriving them, in order that they may become churches. It is through this process that these churches are accredited "apostolic," in that they are the offspring of apostolic churches.

Every kind of thing is classified according to its origin. For this reason, the churches, however numerous and significant they are, are ultimately identical with that one primitive church which derives from the apostles, and from which all have their origins. All are primitive and all are apostolic, provided all are one. And this unity is demonstrated by their sharing of peace, by their title of "brother" and "sister," and by a mutual obligation of hospitality. Such rights have no basis other than in the one tradition of a common creed.

It is on this basis, therefore, that we lay down this ruling: if the Lord Jesus Christ sent out the apostles to preach, no preachers other than those which are appointed by Christ are to be received, since "no one knows the Father except the Son and those to whom the Son has revealed him," and the Son appears to have revealed him to no one except the apostles whom he sent to preach what he had revealed to them. What they preached that is, what Christ revealed to them ought, by this ruling, to be verified only by those churches which those apostles founded by their preaching either (as they say) by their living voice, or subsequently through their letters. If this is true, all doctrine which is in agreement with those apostolic churches, the wombs and original sources of the faith, must be reckoned as the truth, since it undoubtedly preserves what the churches received from the apostles, the apostles from Christ, and Christ from God.

On one occasion, it is true, the Lord did say: "I still have many things to say to you, but you cannot bear them now;" but by adding, "when the Spirit of truth comes, he will guide you into all truth," he showed that they would receive the whole truth through the Spirit of truth.

So if there are any heresies that dare to trace their origins back to the apostolic era, so that it might appear that they had been handed down by the apostles because they existed under the apostles, we are able to say: let them declare the origins of their churches; let them declare the list of their bishops, showing that there is indeed a succession from the beginning, that their first bishop had as his precursor and predecessor an apostle or some apostolic man who was closely associated with the apostles. For this is the way that apostolic churches pass on and legitimize their successors. The Church of Smyrna, for example, records that Polycarp was placed in office by the apostle John; the Church of Rome records that Clement was ordained by Peter. In just the same way other churches can show how their current bishops were and are to be regarded as the transmitters of the apostolic seed.

August 25

Louis
King of France, 1270

Born in the year 1214, Louis was crowned King of France at the age of twelve. His reign was marked by a deep personal concern for justice and embodied the highest ideals of medieval kingship. The strong influence of Franciscan asceticism on Louis can be seen both in his public and private works of charity and in his determined effort to live a life of poverty and self-denial in the midst of worldly splendor and power. He spent six years on a crusade in Egypt and Syria with mixed results but on his return built the Sainte-Chapelle, one of the loveliest of Gothic buildings, in Paris as a repository for the Crown of Thorns and other relics that he had brought back. Embarking on a further crusade, he died at Tunis in the year 1270.

A Reading from *The Life of Saint Louis*
by John of Joinville

Once the king called me and said to me, "I hesitate to speak to you of what touches God, for I know the subtlety of your mind; as I wish to ask you a question, I have fetched the two friars you see here." The question was this. "Tell me, Seneschal," he asked, "what sort of a thing is God?" "Sir," I answered, "God is something so good that there cannot be any better." "Indeed," he said, "an excellent answer; for the very words in which you answered are written in this book I hold in my hand."

"But now," he went on, "I have another question: which would you prefer—to be a leper, or to have committed a mortal sin?" I could never tell him a lie, and I answered that I would rather commit thirty mortal sins than become a leper. After the friars had gone he called me by myself and made me sit at his feet and said, "How was it that you gave me that answer yesterday?" When I told him that I was still of the same mind, he said to me, "That is a wild and foolish way of speaking: you should know that there is no leprosy so ugly as being in mortal sin; for the soul that is in mortal sin is in the likeness of the devil, and that is why no leprosy can be more revolting.

"We know well enough that when a man dies he is cured of the leprosy of his body; but when a man who has committed a mortal sin is dying he cannot know for certain that in his lifetime his repentance has been sufficient to win God's pardon: so it is that he must be very afraid that this leprosy will stay with him as long as God is in paradise. Hence I beg you," he said, "with all my strength, to set your heart, for the love of God and for my love, to choosing rather that any evil should befall your body, either from leprosy or from any other sickness, than that mortal sin should enter into your soul."

He asked me whether I washed the feet of the poor on Maundy Thursday. "God forbid, sir!" I answered. "No, I will not wash the feet of those brutes!" "In truth," he said, "that was a poor answer; you should not despise what God did as a lesson to us. I pray you, then, first for God's sake and then for my sake, to make it your habit to wash them."

alternative reading

A Reading from *The Life of Saint Louis*
by John of Joinville

After arriving at Tunis before the castle of Carthage, [the king] succumbed to a dysentery that forced him to take to his bed, with the knowledge that soon he would have to pass from this world to the next.

Then he sent for my Lord Philip, his son, and bade him respect, as he would his will, all the precepts that he bequeathed to him. These precepts, which the king, it is said, wrote out with his own saintly hand, are set out below in the common tongue.

"My dear son, my first precept is to set your heart on the love of God, for without that no man can be saved. Watch that you do not do anything displeasing to God, that is to say, any mortal sin; you should rather suffer any sort of torment than commit a mortal sin.

"If God sends you adversity, accept it with patience and give thanks for it to Our Lord, realizing that you have deserved it and that it will be for your own good. If he gives you prosperity, thank him humbly for it, so that the gift that should improve you may not, through pride or in any other way, make you worse; for one should not use God's gifts to war against him.

"Be frequent in confession, and choose a worthy confessor who can teach you what you should do and what you should avoid; your behavior should be such that your confessor and your friends may not be afraid to reprove you for your misdeeds. Attend devoutly and without irreverence at the service of Holy Church, praying to God with both your heart and your tongue, especially at Mass when the consecration is made. Have a tender and compassionate heart for the poor, for the unhappy and unfortunate, and comfort and help them to the best of your power.

"See to it that you have about you true and worthy men who are not full of covetousness, either religious or laymen, and be constant in consulting them; but fly from and avoid the company of evil men. Listen readily to the word of God and keep it in your heart, and readily seek out prayers and indulgences. Love what will increase your honor and virtue, and hate all evil, wherever it may be.

"Be firm and honest in doing right and justice to your people, turning neither to right nor left, but ever holding a straight course, and uphold the cause of the poor until the truth is manifest; and if any man has an action against you, do not decide the matter until you know the truth of it, for in the light of the truth your councillors will give a freer judgement, either for or against you.

"If you hold anything that belongs to another, either through yourself or through your predecessors, and the matter is certain, give it back without delay; if it is doubtful, have enquiry made by men of sense, quickly and diligently.

"You should strive earnestly that your people and subjects may live in peace and justice under your rule."

August 27

Thomas Gallaudet
1890

Born in 1822, Thomas Hopkins Gallaudet learned the French system of sign language for the deaf and brought it to America. He founded a school to teach the method in Hartford and married a deaf woman. Their son, Thomas Gallaudet, was ordained in the Episcopal Church in 1851 and the next year founded St. Ann's Church, New York, as the first parish for deaf people. In 1959, the congregation purchased a church building as a center for ministry to the deaf. From St. Ann's Church other mission churches were begun in a number of cities and the church's ministry to the deaf was developed.

A Reading from a sermon by Thomas Gallaudet

Mysteries in spiritual matters surround us at every step of our pilgrimage, and it is utterly vain for self-complacent philosophers to attempt to fathom them. Must we not, in our littleness, exclaim, "We know not how," as we behold the amazing work which has gone on since the church of Christ was sent out from the feeble beginning of a grain of mustard seed, on her purifying, elevating mission, leading multitudes from their tendencies toward sin and eternal ruin into that path of life and peace which shines brighter and brighter unto the perfect day? Yes, for the sake of Jesus Christ, none the less the Son of God because he was the son of man, the church of the living God—the pillar and the ground of the truth—has gone on, from the upper room in Jerusalem, where the number of the believing company was about one hundred and twenty—a small grain of mustard seed to plant in this world of sin and misery—has gone on, through successive generations, with its ministry, its preaching, its sacraments, its inspired record of God's dealings with mankind, and its principles of his covenants of mercy—all its holy institutions and godly discipline. It has gone on, through clouds and sunshine, through good report and evil report—withstanding the attacks of myriads issuing from the gates of hell—surviving the onsets of worldlings without and the treachery of hypocrites within. It has grown to be the goodly tree, extending its branches from the river even unto the ends of the earth, proving the instrument of eternal salvation to countless multitudes of Adam's descendants—repenting, believing, obeying—and yet we know not how.

The growth of the spiritual kingdom, as a divinely appointed organization, is a mystery; and the growth of spiritual life in the hearts of each individual member of the spiritual kingdom is a mystery. We behold indications, from time to time, marking the gradual progress of these two kinds of growth: we believe in them, as realities coming to pass, in consequence of Christ's redemption, and yet we know not how. "The wind bloweth where it listeth, and thou hearest the sound thereof, but canst not tell whence it cometh, and whither it goeth: so is every one that is born of the Spirit." Oh! Let those to whom the gospel announcements have come be not faithless, but believing. Beholding the wonderful work which God, through Christ, has wrought for mankind by the mysterious instrumentalities of his infinitely wise appointment, let all become genuine, devout communicants of the organization which has existed, though they know not how, for upward of eighteen hundred years, as the grand regeneration of the human race; and in due time, they shall be the possessors of the peace of God, which passing understanding, is the earnest of the good things to come in the future life, of which it has not entered into the heart of man to conceive. Oh! Let us have entire faith in the Divine arrangements for the growth of spiritual life, although they are to us, in our present condition, unfathomable mysteries.

August 28

Augustine of Hippo

Bishop, Teacher of the Faith, 430

Augustine was born in North Africa in 354. His career as an orator and rhetorician led him from Carthage to Rome, and from there to Milan where the Imperial court at that time resided. By temperament, he was passionate and sensual, and as a young man he rejected Christianity. Gradually, however, under the influence first of Monica, his mother, and then of Ambrose, Bishop of Milan, Augustine began to look afresh at the Scriptures. He was baptized by Ambrose at the Easter Vigil in 387. Not long after returning to North Africa he was ordained priest, and then became Bishop of Hippo. It is difficult to overestimate the influence of Augustine on the subsequent development of European thought. A huge body of his sermons and writings has been preserved, through all of which runs the theme of the sovereignty of the grace of God. He died in the year 430.

A Reading from the *Confessions* of Augustine

With you as my guide I entered into my innermost citadel, and was given power to do so because you had become my helper. I entered and with my soul's eye, such as it was, saw above that same eye of my soul the immutable light higher than my mind—not the light of every day, obvious to anyone, nor a larger version of the same kind which would, as it were, have given out a much brighter light and filled everything with its magnitude. It was not that light, but a different thing, utterly different from all our kinds of light. It transcended my mind, not in the way that oil floats on water, nor as heaven is above earth. It was superior because it made me, and I was inferior because I was made by it. The person who knows the truth knows it, and he who knows it knows eternity. Love knows it.

Eternal truth and true love and beloved eternity: you are my God. To you I sigh "day and night." When I first came to know you, you raised me up to make me see that what I saw is Being, and that I who saw am not yet Being. And you gave a shock to the weakness of my sight by the strong radiance of your rays, and I trembled with love and awe. And I found myself far from you "in the region of dissimilarity," and heard as it were your voice from on high: "I am the food of the fully grown; grow and you will feed on me. And you will not change me into you like the food your flesh eats, but you will be changed into me."

I sought a way to obtain strength enough to enjoy you; but I did not find it until I embraced the mediator between God and man, the man Christ Jesus, who is above all things, God blessed for ever. He called and said "I am the way and the truth and the life." The food which I was too weak to accept he mingled with flesh, in that "The Word was made flesh," so that our infant condition might come to suck milk from your wisdom by which you created all things.

Late have I loved you, beauty so old and so new; late have I loved you. And see, you were within me and I was in the external world and sought you there, and in my unlovely state I plunged into those lovely created things which you made. You were with me, and I was not with you. The lovely things kept me from you, though if they did not have their existence in you, they would have had no existence at all. You called and cried out loud to me and shattered my deafness. You were radiant and resplendent, you put to flight my blindness. You were fragrant, and I drew in my breath and now pant after you. I tasted you, and now I feel nothing but hunger and thirst for you. You touched me, and I am set on fire to attain the peace which is yours.

August 31

Aidan

Abbot, Bishop of Lindisfarne, Missionary, 651

One of Saint Columba's monks from the monastery of Iona, Aidan was sent as a missionary to Northumbria at the request of King Oswald, who was later to become his friend and interpreter. Consecrated Bishop of Lindisfarne in 635, Aidan worked closely with Oswald and became involved with the training of priests. He was able to combine a monastic lifestyle with missionary journeys from the island of Lindisfarne to the mainland where, through his concern for the poor and enthusiasm for preaching, he won popular support. This enabled him to strengthen the Church beyond the boundaries of Northumbria. He died on this day in the year 651.

A Reading from *The History of the English Church and People* by the Venerable Bede

As soon as he came to the throne, King Oswald was anxious that all the people whom he ruled should be filled with the grace of the Christian faith, of which he had had so wonderful an experience in his victory over the heathen. So he sent to the Irish elders among whom he and his companions had received the sacrament of baptism when in exile, asking them to send him a bishop by whose teaching and ministry the English people over whom he now ruled might receive the blessings of the Christian faith and the sacraments. His request was granted without delay, and they sent him Bishop Aidan, a man of outstanding gentleness, holiness, and moderation.

On Aidan's arrival, the king appointed the island of Lindisfarne to be his see at his own request. As the tide ebbs and flows, this place is surrounded by sea twice a day like an island,

and twice a day the sand dries and joins it to the mainland. The king always listened humbly and gladly to Aidan's advice in all things, and diligently set himself to establish and extend the Church of Christ throughout his kingdom. Indeed, when the bishop, who was not fluent in the English language, preached the gospel, it was most beautiful to see the king himself acting as interpreter of the heavenly word for his earldormen and thanes; for he himself had obtained perfect command of Irish during his long exile.

Aidan himself was a monk from the island of Iona. He gave his clergy an inspiring example of self-discipline and continence, and the best recommendation of his teaching to all was that he taught them no other way of life than that which he himself and his followers practiced. He never sought or cared for any worldly possessions, and loved to give away to the poor who chanced to meet him whatever he received from kings or wealthy folk. Whether in town or country, he always traveled on foot unless compelled by urgent necessity to ride; and whatever people he met on his walks, whether rich or poor, he stopped and talked with them. If they were heathen, he invited them to accept the mystery of the faith; if they were Christians, he strengthened their faith, and inspired them by word and deed to live a good life and to be generous to others.

Aidan's life was in marked contrast to the apathy of our own times, for all who walked with him, whether monks or layfolk, were required to meditate, that is, either to read the Scriptures or to learn the psalms by heart. This was their daily occupation wherever they went. If wealthy people did wrong, he never kept silent out of respect or fear, but corrected them publicly. He would never offer money to influential people, but would always offer them food whenever he entertained them. And if the wealthy ever gave him gifts of money, he either distributed it for the needs of the poor, or else used it to ransom any who had unjustly been sold into slavery. In fact, many of those whom he ransomed in this way afterwards became his disciples; and when they had been instructed and trained, he ordained them to the priesthood.

Death came to Aidan when he had completed sixteen years as a bishop while he was staying at a royal residence near Bamburgh. Having a church and cell there, he often used to go and stay at the place, travelling around the surrounding countryside to preach. When he fell ill, a tent was erected for him on the west side of the church, so that the tent was actually attached to the church wall. And so it happened that, as he drew his last breath, he was leaning against a post that buttressed the wall on the outside. He passed away on the last day of August 651, in the seventeenth year of his episcopate, and his body was taken across to Lindisfarne and buried in the monks' cemetery.

SEPTEMBER

September 1

Giles
Hermit, *c.*710

Giles was a hermit who died about the year 710. He founded a monastery at the place now called Saint-Gilles in Provence which became an important place on the pilgrimage routes both to Compostela and to the Holy Land. His care for the wounded and those crippled by disease resulted in his becoming the patron saint of such people, particularly of those with leprosy. Leprosy sufferers were not permitted to enter towns and cities, and therefore often congregated on the outskirts, where churches built to meet their needs were regularly dedicated to Giles.

A Reading from *The Sayings of the Desert Fathers*

Abba Agathon said, "If I could meet a leper, give him my body and take his, I should be very happy." That indeed is perfect charity.

It was also said that going to town one day to sell some small articles, Abba Agathon met a cripple on the roadside, paralyzed in both legs, who asked him where he was going. Abba Agathon replied, "To town in order to sell some things." The other said, "Do me a favor of carrying me there." So he carried him to the town. The cripple said to him, "Put me down where you sell your wares." He did so.

When he had sold an article, the cripple asked, "What did you sell it for?" and he told him the price. The other said, "Buy me a cake," and he bought it. When Abba Agathon had sold a second article, the sick man asked, "How much did you sell it for?" And he told him the price of it. Then the other said, "Buy me this," and he bought it. When Agathon, having sold all his wares, wanted to go, he said to him, "Are you going back?" and he replied "Yes."

Then said he, "Do me the favor of carrying me back to the place where you found me."

Once more picking him up, he carried him back to that place. Then the cripple said, "Agathon, you are filled with divine blessings, in heaven and on earth." Raising his eyes, Agathon saw no one; it was an angel of the Lord, come to try him.

September 1

David Pendleton Oakerhater

1931

Born around 1845 just before the invasion of Oklahoma by white settlers began, David Oakerhater had gained distinction as a spiritual leader and warrior and was therefore seen as a threat by the new authorities. He was arrested with a large group of Plains Indians and taken to Florida as part of a policy of removing native leadership from warlike tribes. They were put in the charge of a Captain Richard Platt, who believed that appropriate treatment and education would do most to provide better relationships between the Native Americans and their captors. The response of Oakerhater and others was so positive that a small group was enrolled in Hampton Normal and Industrial Institute. Four of these, in turn, were taken to central New York State where, in consultation with Bishop Frederick Huntington, they were trained to serve as missionaries. Oakerhater and one other were ordained to the diaconate in 1881 and returned to begin evangelistic work among the Cheyenne. In spite of inadequate support from the church, Oakerhater continued in his ministry of education, service, and pastoral care for fifty years, providing such an example of faithfulness that he became known among the Cheyenne as "God's Warrior."

A Reading from *Journey to Sainthood*
by Alvin D. Turner

When David Pendleton Oakerhater returned to the Cheyenne reservation in 1881, he represented the continuing hope of his people. They responded to his ministry because they admired him and believed his way could become theirs. Twelve years later he was the symbol of what might have been, serving a church and an assimilationist ideal that had not met their needs. He served his people and his church for another thirty-eight years, but national policy, local conditions, and church priorities continued to define the limits of his ministry.

Oakerhater's successes prompted increased attention to the Indian ministry and a priest, David Sanford, was placed in charge of the Indian work in 1895. This action greatly strengthened Oakerhater's efforts but the revitalized ministry soon came into conflict with local Indian agents and changing federal policies. In 1897 the government implemented a policy that was intended to replace boarding schools with day schools on the reservation. In conjunction with this plan, a government day school functioned at the site of Whirlwind's camp near present-day Fay for four years. Oakerhater moved there and initiated a ministry among the school children and others in the area. The school closed four years later because the Cheyenne agent, Charles Shell, believed it contributed to his problems in trying to remove the Indians from a nearby encampment to individual allotments.

Bishop Brooke negotiated permission to establish an Episcopal day school at the site in 1904. This enabled Oakerhater to continue his work with young people in the area, some of whom would later serve the church as lay readers and in other capacities. Various reports confirmed that the Episcopal school did an effective job educating the children over the next few years, but Shell still opposed day schools. His opposition to the school increased in conjunction with a two-year struggle with Sanford that culminated in 1907.

Sanford challenged Shell's handling of lease money due one of the students at the school. Shell then began a campaign that soon involved Bishop Brooke and the commissioner of Indian Affairs. The commissioner wavered between trying to defend the day school concept and Shell's authority and integrity. Brooke finally decided to dismiss Sanford in an effort to resolve the conflict. Shell then moderated his opposition to the school because of strict instructions from the commissioner of Indian Affairs, but Brooke was subsequently unable to find a priest who would stay at the site for more than a year at a time.

Sanford's real successor was Deaconess Harriet Bedell, who moved to Whirlwind in 1911. She labored continuously for six years, enhancing Oakerhater's efforts, enlarging the Cheyenne ministry, and managing the school which received complimentary reviews from county school superintendents and others. Nevertheless, Shell's replacement, W. W. Scott, was happy to see her go. Like Sanford, she had opposed local policies; more importantly, the government had decided that the best policy was to encourage the enrollment of Cheyenne students in public schools.

The new policy effectively mandated the closing of Whirlwind Mission. At the same time, the Episcopal Church abandoned its ministry to the Cheyennes and retired Oakerhater. He moved to Watonga where he continued to preach in his home and other locations until his death in 1931. As he had from the beginning of his ministry, Oakerhater continued to win a few converts even under these conditions. Following his death, the lay readers he had trained struggled to maintain a ministry among the Cheyennes but they abandoned their efforts within five years.

Almost forty years passed before an Episcopal family moved to Watonga and attempted to establish a congregation there. They contacted a priest from Woodward who agreed to assist them and placed an announcement in the Watonga paper inviting interested parties to attend a meeting. Over thirty Cheyennes attended, the remnant of those who had been ministered to by Oakerhater and the lay ministers he had trained. This development eventually triggered a new Indian work by state Episcopalians, chaired by Lois Clark, who then launched the five-year effort that led to national recognition of the sainthood of David Pendleton Oakerhater.

The church rightly honored his faithfulness rather than magnifying his accomplishments. In the end, his achievements did not produce the dramatic results usually associated with saints. They fulfilled neither his hopes, the expectations of his sponsors, nor his own potential and goals. His real legacy was an exemplary life, totally consistent with his understanding of the white man's road and Cheyenne culture. The church's recognition agrees with the opinions of all who knew him, the Cheyenne traditions honoring his memory, and the response of all who admire integrity.

September 2

The Martyrs of Papua New Guinea
1901 and 1942

The Church in Papua New Guinea has been enriched by martyrdom twice in the twentieth century. James Chalmers, Oliver Tomkins and some companions were sent to New Guinea by the London Missionary Society. They met their death by martyrdom in 1901. Forty years later, during the Second World War, New Guinea was occupied by the Imperial Japanese

Army. Christians were severely persecuted, and 333 Church workers of all denominations died for the faith. Among them were twelve Anglicans: two English priests, Vivian Redlich and Bernard Moore, who remained with their people after the invasion of 1942, but were betrayed and killed, eight Australians and two Papuan evangelists, Leslie Gariadi and Lucian Tapiedi.

A Reading from *The White-Robed Army of Martyrs* by David Hand, first Archbishop of Papua New Guinea

As the thrust of the Japanese invasion approached Papua New Guinea in 1942, Bishop Philip Strong broadcast over the radio a message to his staff which has become famous in the annals of missionary history. He said:

> We could never hold up our faces again, if for our own safety, we all forsook him and fled when the shadows of the passion began to gather around him in his spiritual body, the Church in Papua. Our life in the future would be burdened with shame and we could not come back here and face our people again; and we would be conscious always of rejected opportunities. The history of the church tells us that missionaries do not think of themselves in the hour of danger and crisis, but of the Master who called them to give their all, and of the people they have been trusted to serve and love to the uttermost. His watchword is none the less true today, as it was when he gave it to the first disciples: "Whosoever would save his life will lose it, and whosoever will lose his life for my sake and the gospel's shall find it."

We could not leave unless God, who called us, required it of us, and our spiritual instinct tells us he would never require such a thing at such an hour. No, my brothers and sisters, fellow workers in Christ, whatever others may do, we cannot leave. We shall not leave. We shall stand by our trust. We shall stand by our vocation.

Papua is a body, the Church: God will not forsake us. He will uphold us; he will strengthen us and he will guide us and keep us through the days that lie ahead. If we all left, it would take years for the Church to recover from our betrayal of our trust. If we remain — and even if the worst came to the worst and we were all to perish in remaining—the Church will not perish, for there would have been no breach of trust in its walls, but its foundations and structure would have received added strength for the future building by our faithfulness unto death. This, I believe, is the resolution of you all.

I know there are special circumstances which may make it

imperative for one or two to go (if arrangements can be made for them to do so). For the rest of us, we have made our resolution to stay. Let us not shrink from it. Let us trust and not be afraid. To you all I send my blessing. The Lord be with you.

What happened?

To a man and woman, all the bishop's staff stood by their people until it became clear that that course might imperil their people. The Bishop himself was bombed and machine-gunned. He escaped injury, despite travelling freely and fearlessly around his diocese to care for, and encouraged his staff and people, as well as acting as senior chaplain to the military.

Among those who died were the two Gona sisters, teacher Mavis Parkinson and nurse May Hayman. They were handed over to the Japanese, and bayoneted to death at Ururu where an altar-shrine now marks the spot.

Elderly and holy Father Henry Holland, having served in Papua New Guinea for twenty-five years, first as a lay evangelist, and latterly as a priest at Isivita, stacks of whose translations of the Scriptures into the Orokaiva language were scattered and lost when the Japanese looted his station; he and John Duffill, his close colleague, were both killed.

Father Vivian Redlich of Sangara, who refused to abandon his Sunday Mass when warning came that the Japanese arrival at his camp was imminent and Lucian Tapiedi, his devoted teacher-evangelist who had said to his married colleagues: "Take your wives and families to the bush and hide. I am single; I'll stay with the fathers and sisters; it doesn't matter if the Japanese get me;" the Sangara missionary-teachers Lilla Lashmar and Margery Brenchley, who had laid the foundations of the Church's educational work in the Orokaiva area, all perished.

John Barge, recently posted to open up work in a totally unevangelized area, refused to "go bush" with the nearest Roman Catholic priest. Forced to dig his own grave he was then shot into it by Japanese guns.

Many people blamed Bishop Strong for not taking out all his staff to safety. But it was, ultimately, their own choice. To the world, it seemed a waste, a tragedy, a failure like Calvary. But look what God has done with it with their "defeat." He has turned it into victory. Look at the rise of the Martyrs' School in their honor—a living organism, not just a memorial, serving God and the nation. Look at the fruit of martyrdom in the ability of the Orokaiva Church to resurrect after the Lamington eruption. Look at the post-

World War II leap forward into inland Papuan areas, the New Britain Resurrection and the great "putsch" into the New Guinea Highlands.

Yes, "the blood of the martyrs" has once again proved to be "the seed of the Church" here, in this country. Thanks be to God.

September 4

Paul Jones

1941

Paul Jones was born in 1880. By 1918, the United States was deeply involved in the First World War and feelings of patriotism ran high. In Utah, which had only recently been admitted as a state, feelings of patriotism were intensified by the need felt by Mormons to prove their loyalty. Many Episcopalians in the state were embarrassed, therefore, by the fact that their bishop was a pacifist and had publicly stated his belief that "war is un-Christian." The House of Bishops first offered support, but then backed off and asked for his resignation—which he gave. Relieved of Episcopal duties (though he later served for a time as acting bishop of Southern Ohio), Paul Jones spent the next ten years as executive director of the Fellowship of Reconciliation, speaking and writing on behalf of peace. His final years were spent as college chaplain at Antioch College, where he remained active in the peace movement and even ran for governor of Ohio on the Socialist ticket. "Where I serve the church," he said when he resigned his jurisdiction in Utah, "is of small importance, so long as I can make my life count in the cause of Christ."

A Reading from *Christian Loyalty*
by Paul Jones

What should a Christian man do when his country is threatened by another, when long-established rights are invaded, or when some weak nation is ruthlessly oppressed by a hostile power?

There can be only one answer to that question. The Christian man should get to his knees and pray for divine guidance and then go to the sourcebook of Christian teaching, the New Testament, and try earnestly to find out from it what Christ would have him do.

If he tries to answer the question from the point of view of business, expediency, or nationality, he is going to confuse the issue and risk a wrong choice. For the Christian there is but one supreme loyalty and that is to Christ and his gospel. If anything else conflicts with that, so much the worse for that other thing. Duties to country, to home, and to family must always give way to that higher loyalty which alone is capable of taking them up and giving them full significance.

I find it quite impossible to believe that people can be true to the things which he taught and the example which he gave and at the same time take part in war; for war is the organized destruction of our enemies and it is always accompanied by hatred and bitterness, thus necessitating an attitude of mind and course of conduct the opposite of that enjoined by Christ.

As a matter of plain practical conduct fitted to meet a condition and not a theory, I feel perfectly sure that active, aggressive, militant goodwill founded on the example and teaching of Christ is the only power that will effectively preserve real spiritual values in the world.

What can a Christian man do under the present national circumstances? I have gone in search to the sources of our Christian standards, and in the light of what I find there, as I love my country, I must protest against her doing what I would not do myself, because it is contrary to our Lord's teaching. To prosecute war means to kill men, bringing sorrow and suffering upon women and children, and to instill suspicion, fear, and hatred into the hearts of the people on both sides. No matter what principles may appear to be at stake, to deliberately engage in such a course of action that evidently is un-Christian is repugnant to the whole spirit of the gospel.

As a Christian bishop, charged with the responsibility of leadership, I would be deserving only of contempt did I remain silent in the present crisis, when the Christian standards of judgment are apparently being entirely ignored. The day will come when, like slavery, which was once held in good repute, war will be looked upon as thoroughly un-Christian. At present it is recognized as an evil which nobody honestly wants, but not yet has it received its final sentence at the bar of Christian morality. Only when Christian men and women and churches will be brave enough to stand openly for the full truth that their consciences are beginning to recognize, will the terrible anachronism of war between Christian nations be done away.

September 8

The Nativity of the Blessed Virgin Mary

This festival in honor of the birth of the mother of our Lord is celebrated on this day in both the Eastern and the Western Churches. Falling just nine months after the Feast of the Conception of Mary, the feast stands on the boundary between the old and the new covenants, and ushers in the dispensation of grace. Today, with the birth of Mary, "a shrine is built for the creator of the universe."

A Reading from a homily of Andrew of Crete

The law has achieved its goal with Christ, who leads us away from the letter of the law so as to bring us to the spirit. The law is fulfilled because the lawgiver himself has brought it to completion, transforming in his own person the letter into the spirit, summing up all things in himself and living the law of love. He has made law subject to love, and brought love and law into harmony. He has not fused the particular qualities of each, but in a wonderful way has lightened and set on a new foundation what beforehand was experienced by us as burdensome, servile and repressive. For, as the Apostle Paul says, "we are no longer to be enslaved by the elemental spirits of the world" or to be trapped in the yoke of slavery to the letter of the law.

This is the summary of the benefits Christ has secured for us. In Christ the mystery is unveiled, nature is made new, divine and human, and the deification of our human nature is assumed by God. But so radiant, so glorious a visitation of God among mortals required some prelude of joy to introduce to us the great gift of salvation. Today's feast, celebrating the birth of the God-bearer, is that prelude, and the final act is the destined union between the Word and human nature.

Today a virgin is born, suckled and nurtured, and is being made ready to be the God-bearer, the king of all. With justification we should celebrate the mystery of this day, for if we do, our gain will be twofold: we shall be led toward the truth, and we shall be led away from a life of slavery to the letter of the law. How can this be? In the same way that the shadow gives way to the presence of the light, grace introduces freedom in place of the letter of the law. Today's feast stands on the boundary between these two dispensations: it joins us to the truth instead of to signs and figures, and it ushers in the new in place of the old.

Let the whole creation, therefore, sing praise and dance and unite in celebrating the glories of this day. Today let there be one common feast of all in heaven and earth. Let everything that is, in and above the earth, join together in rejoicing. For today a shrine is built for the creator of the universe. The creature is newly ready as a divine dwelling for the creator.

alternative reading

A Reading from the Office for the
Feast of the Nativity of our Most Holy Lady the Theotokos
in the Orthodox Church

What is this sound of feasting that we hear?
Joachim and Anna mystically keep festival.
"O Adam and Eve," they cry, "rejoice with us today:
For if by your transgressions you closed the gates of Paradise
 to those of old,
We have now been given a glorious fruit,
Mary the Child of God
Who opens its entrance to us all."

Thy nativity, O Theotokos,
Has brought joy to all the world:
For from thee has shone forth
The Sun of Righteousness, Christ our God.
He has loosed us from the curse and given the blessing:
He has vanquished death, and bestowed on us eternal life.

By thy holy nativity, O most pure Virgin,
Joachim and Anna were set free from the
 reproach of childlessness,
And Adam and Eve from the corruption of death.
Delivered from the guilt of sin,
Thy people keep the feast and sing:
"The barren woman bears the Theotokos,
 the Sustainer of our life."

Be renewed, O Adam, and be magnified, O Eve;
You prophets, dance with the apostles and the righteous;
Let there be common joy in the world
    among angels and mortals
For the Theotokos is born today of
    righteous Joachim and Anna.

September 9

Constance and her Companions

Religious, 1878

Sister Constance was a member of the Community of Saint Mary who had gone to Memphis at the request of Bishop C. T. Quintard of Tennessee to found a girls' school near St. Mary's Cathedral. When an outbreak of yellow fever occurred in 1878, Sr. Constance was vacationing at her order's mother house in Peekskill, New York, but she returned immediately to Memphis. She found the city in a state of desolation. Over half the citizens had fled and she emerged from the train station to find almost-empty streets sprinkled with lime, mattresses of those who had died burning in the streets, and the only traffic consisting of wagons loaded with coffins. Working with the other sisters and priests of the cathedral staff, Sister Constance went out to find those in need of help. Children whose parents had died were brought into an orphanage they established. Within three weeks Sister Constance had died of the fever herself, as did eventually over a quarter of the remaining population, and three others of the sisters, two of the priests (including the Reverend Charles C. Parsons, cited here), a doctor, and a nurse. Sister Constance was thirty-two years old at her death.

A Reading from a letter of the Reverend Charles C. Parsons to Bishop Quintard of Tennessee

My Dear Bishop:
I have just received your letter of the 28th, addressed to (Dean) Harris. I reply at once. We cannot yet tell how he is, because his case has not yet developed. The doctor promises that it shall be very light, but Sister Constance and I are not so hopeful. He is very quiet and in fact lethargic today, and this alarms us both, as it is not a usual feature of a good case. I telegraphed you today, and shall do so every day until he is decidedly better.

It is almost impossible to find the time to write a detailed account of all our work. Our pastoral duties extend from one end of the city to the other, and include all classes of people. It is incessant. I must hasten this letter to its close, because I have so many visits to make. Sometimes they pass away, or into a final state of unconsciousness, before we can reach them. So poor Tom Darey died yesterday and, at almost the same moment, Walter Oakley also. A large number of those to whom we minister are utter strangers to us until we reach their bedside. Friday I was called to see, at the Whitemore house, a sick family consisting of a mother and two children. I drove there as quickly as possible. They were bringing down stairs the remains of the son. In a little room at the head of the stairs the faithful Mobile nurse had composed the body of the little daughter in death, and on the bed hard by, the mother was breathing her last. The same evening I rode in haste to Mosby Street to communicate a dying girl. You know how short the distance is, and yet before I reached the house there were three instances of persons dying unknown given me, with piteous appeals to procure their immediate interment.

My dear Bishop, the situation is indescribable. Last night when I was trying to give our dear Harris some relief, the message came to me that old Mr. Holt across the street was just dead; that his daughters had been taken over to the sisters, and his son, one of the most devoted of the Howards, was borne from his bedside in a raging fever. I went there as soon as possible, and found that there was scarcely a hope of saving the son, although he is now in the hands of an excellent Charleston nurse. Why, it is a perfect waste of death, and destitution, and desolation all around us here. People constantly send to us, saying, "Telegraph the situation." It is impossible. Go and turn the Destroying Angel loose upon a defenseless city; let him smite whom he will, young and old, rich and poor, the feeble and the strong, and as he will, silent, unseen, and unfelt, until his deadly blow is struck; give him for his dreadful harvest all the days and nights from the burning midsummer sun until the latest heavy frosts, and then you can form some idea of what Memphis and all this valley is, and what they are going to be for the next eight weeks.

The sisters are doing a wonderful work. It is a surprise to see how much these quiet, brave, unshrinking daughters of the Divine Love can accomplish in efforts and results. One of the most exacting and important of their duties henceforth will be to maintain the Asylum for all the destitute children and orphans of the city. In two days, already, thirty-two have been sent to them, and within a short time the number will be named by hundreds. Harris and I were charged by the Citizens' Relief Committee with the duty of organizing this charity, and we took immediate advantage of your authority to locate it in the Canfield Asylum. For our general work we have several excellent nurses in our employ, and for the home and the Asylum one of the best physicians of the city, because we are bound to have fever cases among children taken from infected homes. We need all the contributions we can receive in money, clothing, or provisions.

My dear Bishop, I must close my letter, because there is so much before me for the rest of the day and, perhaps, the night. If Harris gets up this week I shall try to have him go off for a little while. He ought to have thorough repose to gather strength for the rest of his devoted work.

I am well, and strong, and hopeful, and I devoutly thank God that I can say that in every letter.

I beseech your prayers for us, and I am, ever,

Yours faithfully and affectionately,
Charles C. Parsons

alternative reading

A Reading from the last letter of Sister Constance

Dear Bp. Quintard,

I was telegraphed for on Thursday of last week, and on my return, made such arrangements as I could for the safety of the Home, before exposing myself to any possible infection. I have sent Sister Frances to remain at the Home day and night, isolated the House as far as possible, and we *may* get through without any fever cases—but the disease is extremely contagious among children & very fatal this year. The markets are closed—nothing whatever is given to the children in the way of meat, bread, or vegetables—fresh meat cannot be bought, even if we had money—and I fear that there will be real suffering from unproper or insufficient food, and overwork. No servant will do the washing at any ordinary price, and these little girls are really almost ill from their attempts to do it last week. Will you not make a special appeal to the managers—if you know where any of them are? In the universal panic, letters from me would not be at all welcome, even if I had time to write them.

Sister Thecla, Sister Frances, and I are perfectly well, and the anxiety is so great that one has not difficulty in trusting both the present and the future—our nursing and our school—in GOD's hands. You know a great trouble is often easier to bear than a little one! Sister Hughetta is far from well—I have, of course, kept her out of all nursing so far. She sleeps at Colonel Snowden's, but comes in every morning—there are little things which she can do.

I know that we shall have your prayers and your blessing on our work—but we are so helpless for want of means which we cannot yet attempt what we did before.

I see no reason to be more hopeful than we were in 1973—in fact, there are some indications that seem to me to threaten even more serious results, and the form of disease is undoubtedly worse.

We have the daily celebrations, and while we have that, there is nothing that really depresses me.

Yours faithfully in our dear LORD,
Sister Constance S.S.M.

September 10

Alexander Crummell
1898

The struggle against racism in the United States found one of its first and most eloquent champions in the life and ministry of Alexander Crummell. He was born in 1819 in New York City but rejected for admission to the General Theological Seminary. Ordained in Massachusetts, he was excluded from participation in the convention of that diocese. Traveling to England, he was given a degree by Cambridge University and went to Liberia as a missionary. It was his conviction that the unique characteristics of the African people and of the Episcopal Church were especially fitted for each other. A combination of European education and technology with African communal culture and the rational and moral discipline of the Episcopal Church was the vision he espoused. Conversely, when Southern bishops proposed creating a separate missionary jurisdiction for black congregations, Crummell fought against it and created a national convocation to work against the plan. The Union of Black Episcopalians is an outgrowth of that organization. Always Crummell worked to build institutions that would serve his people and provide opportunity for them to develop their gifts for leadership. In spite of repeated discouragement, he held fast the faith that the church transcended racism and could provide a means for black people to express their particular gifts in the service of their Creator.

A Reading from *The Race Problem in America* by Alexander Crummell

Every race of people has its special instincts, carries in its blood its distinctive individuality. This peculiar element is its own and exclusive possession, and is incapable of transference. To seize upon this quality, to give it natural expression, to use it with forceful power, is a spontaneity in men native to the race; but, on the other hand, it is a clumsy and crooked imitation with alien and foreign natures. Out of this springs the strong and urgent need of a Negro ministry, if the church is to work with skill and effect in the Negro race in the United States. The teachers of any race of men must possess the genius of the race; must carry with them the full stuff of the race; must glow with the temperament of the race; and then they become surcharged with power to act upon the reason, to stir the sensibilities, to move the hearts, and to control the affections of their kinsmen; and, further, they are thus fitted and enabled to make the most of the powers and abilities of their people, and to put them to the best uses. This is a conspicuous fact in all human history, discoverable especially in the propagation of the gospel. That gospel is handed over, first of all, by an agency exotic in blood and lineage; but it is made to inhere in a people, as a thing of life and heredity, by an indigenous training and influence.

This racialism is not, be it noticed, simply a matter of language. A missionary may know the language of a people—know it, scientifically, better than the people themselves—but he needs something more than this. He needs the spirit, the sensibilities, the home sympathies, the special desires, the native peculiarities, the crude experiences, the agonized history—nay, even the prejudices—of that people in order to speak to their hearts and to address himself to their needs. There is a vernacular of sympathy as well as a vernacular of speech among all peoples. And it is this vernacular which it is the most difficult of all things for alien blood to acquire.

It is mainly by adherence to this principle of gospel propagation that the church will be able to make progress in her work among the colored people of the land. The principle has already asserted itself, crudely indeed, in the demands of the race. The people wish their children to be taught by men of their own blood. This tendency is a growing one, and it is irresistible. Since emancipation they have demanded colored teachers, colored doctors, colored lawyers, colored editors and newspapers to the number of one hundred, colored colleges and professors, and colored preachers, and they have got them. Such a craving and aspiration of a whole race is neither to be ignored nor despised. It is idle for any man or any organization to suppose they can start a backward revolution which will ever put this whole race, or any large section of them on this soil, under any other than racial training. Whether from weal or woe, the tendency of the black race in the South, in education, in social life, in societies and fraternities, and in religion, is to racial autonomy and racial self-training. It will be well and wise for our church to notice and observe this tendency. If she does not, she may gather under her wings a pitiful brood of black adherents, but the masses will stand aloof from her portals. The great leaders of the race will resort to the fold where the people gather together, and the large black organizations already in existence will use every possible device, through the race feeling, to keep our churches empty and to make our influence a nullity!

September 12

John Henry Hobart

Bishop of New York, 1830

At the end of the American Revolution, Anglicans in the United States were a broken and dispirited body. That the Church of England had been rejected along with the English government seemed obvious to most and it was not until a new generation came into positions of leadership that the Episcopal Church began to revive and grow. Born in 1775, John Henry Hobart served as Bishop of New York, and was a leader in that revival. He traveled by coach and even on foot through the newly opened areas in the western part of the state to plant the church where it had never been. In the seventeen years of his episcopate the number of clergy increased from 27 to 123 and the number of congregations grew from 72 to 163. He founded the General Theological Seminary, the first seminary in the Anglican Communion, to prepare men for the ministry and tirelessly devoted himself to building up the church under the banner of "Evangelical truth, Apostolic Order."

A Reading from a sermon by John Henry Hobart

In uniting us to a visible society, for the purpose of redeeming us from the corruptions of our evil nature and of the world, and for training us for the purity and bliss of a celestial and eternal existence, the Divine Author of our being has not only exercised that sovereign power which makes us in all things dependent on his will, but has mercifully accommodated himself to the social principle which so strongly characterizes us. This, uniform and powerful in its influence, prompts us in *spiritual* as in temporal matters, to mingle with our fellow men our thoughts, our feelings, our pursuits, our hopes. Most conversant as we are, too, with material objects, and most affected by them, what an aid to our conception of spiritual truths, what an excitement to our hopes of spiritual blessings, when they are exhibited as conveyed and pledged by external symbols. Hence the doctrine that the ministrations and ordinances of the church are the means and pledges of salvation to the faithful, to all true believers, is not more enforced by the plainest declarations of sacred writ than it is conformable to a rational and philosophical view of our nature.

That the church is the body of that divine Lord who gave himself for it, that as members of this body true believers are united in him its head, and thus partake of his fullness of mercy and grace, are truths of the divine word too frequently and too strongly set forth to be denied. But though not denied, how much are they neglected! How much decried, how odiously and contemptuously branded are all researches as to the mode by which, in this divine body of the Redeemer, power is to be derived to minister in its holy concerns, to dispense its ordinances! And yet, in this spiritual and divine society, no man can minister unless he be called of God by a commission visibly conferred for that purpose; and there can be no commission which is not derived from that Almighty Head of this mystical body, who only possesses all spiritual power, and who, vesting with his apostles the authority of conferring the right of ministering in holy things, pronounced the infallible promise, that this authority should be perpetuated "even to the end of the world."

The bishop of our church on these subjects may prudently and mildly enforce opinions which boast, in more modern times, of the support of some of the most distinguished names in learning and theology, and which, before papal corruption obscured and deformed them, ranked among their advocates the noble army of martyrs, and the goodly fellowship of apostles. He may enforce them with a spirit which embraces, within the wide-spread arms of charity, the sincere and the pious of every name, and of every nation.

September 13

Cyprian

Bishop of Carthage, Martyr, 258

Born in Carthage in about the year 200, Cyprian was a teacher of rhetoric and a lawyer in the city before his conversion to Christianity. He gave away his pagan library and set his mind to study the sacred Scriptures and the commentaries that were beginning to proliferate. He became a priest and then, in the year 248, was elected Bishop of Carthage by the people of the city, together with the assembled priests and other bishops present. He showed compassion to returning apostates, while always insisting on the need for unity in the Church. During the persecution of Valerian, the Christian clergy were required to participate in pagan worship; Cyprian refused and was first exiled and then condemned to death. He died in the year 258.

A Reading from the letter of Cyprian to Donatus

As I write to you I am aware of the mediocrity of much of my thinking and how shallow a lot of my understanding is. I have gathered a poor harvest. I have little to enrich the soil of your heart. If one is in court, or having to address a public assembly or the senate, a lavish and extravagant eloquence is appropriate. But when speaking of God, our master, the absolute sincerity of what we say will communicate to others not by our eloquence but by the substance of our lives. And so please accept these words that carry conviction rather than charm, and are designed not to win over a popular audience by their cultivated rhetoric, but simply to preach the mercy of God by their unvarnished truth. Accept that which has been sincerely felt rather than merely learned, that which has not been laboriously accumulated over the course of a long apprenticeship, but inhaled in one gulp by a sudden act of grace.

When I was younger I lay in darkness and in the depths of night, tossed to and fro in the waves of this turbulent world, uncertain which path to take, ignorant of my true life and a stranger to the light of truth. At that time, and on account of the life I then led, it seemed difficult to believe what divine mercy promised for my salvation, namely, that it was possible for someone to be born again to a new life by being immersed in the healing waters of baptism. It was difficult to believe that a person though physically the same, could be changed in heart and mind.

How was it possible, I thought, that a change could be great enough to strip us in a single moment of the innate hardness of our nature? How could the bad habits acquired over the course of years disappear, since these are invariably deeply rooted within us? If someone is used to feasting and lavish entertainment, how can they learn the discipline of a simpler lifestyle? If someone is used to dressing ostentatiously in gold and purple, and been admired for their good taste, how can they cast them aside for ordinary clothes? Someone who loves the trappings of public office cannot easily retire into the anonymity of private life. Someone who is surrounded by great crowds of supporters and is honored by an entourage of attendants will consider solitude a punishment. As long as we allow ourselves to be trapped by these outward allurements we will be the more easily seduced by wine, inflated with pride, inflamed by anger, be eaten up with greed, be excited by cruelty, be controlled by ambition, and a prey to our lusts.

These were my frequent thoughts. I was trapped by the past errors of my life from which it seemed impossible to escape. I gave in to my sins which clung fast to me. Since I despaired of improvement I took an indulgent view of my faults and regarded them as if they were permanent occupants in my house.

But after the life-giving water of baptism came to my rescue and washed away the stain of my former years, and the light which comes from above, serene and pure, was poured into my cleansed and reconciled heart, and after the Heavenly Spirit was breathed into me, and I was made a new man by a second birth, then amazingly what I had previously doubted became clear to me. What had been hidden was revealed. What had been in the dark became clear to me. What previously had seemed impossible now seemed possible. What was in me of the guilty flesh I now acknowledged to be earthly. What was made alive in me by God was now animated by the Spirit of holiness.

All our power is of God; I repeat, it is of God. From God we receive the gift of life and strength. By the power derived from God we are able, while still living in this world, to glimpse the things of eternity. But let fear be the guardian of our conscience, so that the Lord, who in his great mercy has infused our hearts abundantly with his grace, may always be honored by the hospitality of a grateful mind, lest the assurance we have received lead us to become careless, and our old enemies creep up on us again.

September 14

Holy Cross Day

The cross on which our Lord was crucified has become the universal symbol for Christianity, replacing the fish symbol of the early Church, though the latter has been revived in recent times. After the end of the persecution era, early in the fourth century, pilgrims began to travel to Jerusalem to visit and pray at the places associated with the life of Jesus. Helena, the mother of the emperor, was a Christian and, while overseeing excavations in the city, is said to have uncovered a cross, which many believed to be the Cross of Christ. A basilica was built on the site of the Holy Sepulchre and dedicated on this day in the year 335.

A Reading from a homily on the
"Exaltation of the Holy Cross" by Andrew of Crete

We are celebrating the feast of the cross which drove away darkness and brought in the light. As we keep this feast, we are lifted up with the crucified Christ, leaving behind us earth and sin so that we may gain the things above. So great and outstanding a possession is the cross that whoever wins it has won a treasure. Rightly could I call this treasure the fairest of all fair things and the costliest, in fact as well as in name, for on it and through it, and for its sake, the riches of salvation that had been lost were restored to us.

Had there been no cross, Christ could not have been crucified. Had there been no cross, life itself could not have been nailed to the tree. And if life had not been nailed to it, there would be no streams of immortality pouring from Christ's side, blood and water for the world's cleansing. The bond of our sin would not be cancelled, we should not have obtained our freedom, we should not have enjoyed the fruit of the tree of life and the gates of paradise would not stand open. Had there been no cross, death would not have been trodden underfoot, nor hell despoiled.

Therefore, the cross is something wonderfully great and honorable. It is great because through the cross the many noble acts of Christ found their consummation very many indeed, for both his miracles and his sufferings were fully rewarded with victory. The cross is honorable because it is both the sign of God's suffering and the trophy of his victory. It stands for his suffering because on it he freely suffered unto death. But it is also his trophy because it was the means by which the devil was wounded and death conquered; the barred gates of hell were smashed, and the cross became the one common salvation of the whole world.

The cross is called Christ's glory; it is saluted as his triumph. We recognize it as the cup he longed to drink and the climax of the sufferings he endured for our sake. As to the cross being Christ's glory, listen to his words: "Now is the Son of Man glorified, and in him God is glorified, and God will glorify him at once." And again, "Father, glorify me with the glory that I had with you before the world came to be." And once more: "Father, glorify your name." Then a voice came from heaven: "I have glorified it and I will glorify it again." Here he speaks of the glory that would accrue to him through the cross. And if you would understand that the cross is Christ's triumph, then hear what he himself also said: "When I am lifted up, then I will draw all people to myself."

Now you can see that the cross is Christ's glory and his triumph.

alternative reading

A Reading from the anonymous Anglo-Saxon poem
The Dream of the Rood

Many years ago the memory abides
I was felled to the ground at the forest's edge,
Severed from my roots. Enemies seized me,
Made of me a mark of scorn for criminals to mount on;
Shoulder-high they carried me and set me on a hill.
Many foes made me fast there. Far off then I saw
The King of all mankind coming in great haste,
With courage keen, eager to climb me.
I did not dare, against my Lord's dictate,
To fold or falter, though I felt a trembling

In the earth's four corners. I could easily
Have felled his foes; yet fixed and firm I stood.
Then the young Warrior it was God Almighty
Strong and steadfast, stripped himself for battle;
He climbed up on the high gallows, constant in his purpose,
Mounted it in sight of many, mankind to ransom.
Horror seized me when the Hero clasped me,
But I dared not bow or bend down to earth,
Nor falter, nor fall; firm I needs must stand.
I was raised up a Rood, a royal King I bore,
The High King of Heaven: hold firm I must.
They drove dark nails through me, the dire wounds still show,
Cruel gaping gashes, yet I dared not give as good.
They taunted the two of us; I was wet with teeming blood,
Streaming from the Warrior's side when he sent forth his spirit.
High upon that hill helpless I suffered
Long hours of torment; I saw the Lord of Hosts
Outstretched in agony; all embracing darkness
Covered with thick clouds the corpse of the world's Ruler;
The bright day was darkened by a deep shadow,
All its colors clouded; the whole creation wept,
Bewailing its King's fall; Christ was on the Rood.

And now I give you bidding, O man beloved,
Reveal this Vision to the children of men,
And clearly tell of the Tree of glory
Whereon God suffered for man's many sins
And the evil that Adam once wrought of old.

September 16

Ninian

Bishop of Galloway, Apostle of the Picts, *c.*432

Ninian was born about the year 360 and was the son of a Cumbrian chieftain who had himself converted to Christianity. It seems he visited Rome in his youth, where he received training in the faith. He was consecrated bishop in the year 394 and returned to Britain, where he set up a community of monks at Candida Casa *(Whithorn) from where they went out on missionary journeys as far as Perth and Sterling. Ninian died in about the year 432.*

A Reading from *The History of the English Church and People* by the Venerable Bede

In the year of our Lord 565, when Justin the Younger succeeded Justinian and ruled as Emperor of Rome, there came from Ireland to Britain a priest and abbot named Columba, a true monk in life no less than habit, to preach the Word of God in the provinces of the Northern Picts, which are separated from those of the Southern Picts by a range of steep and rugged mountains.

The Southern Picts, who live on this side of the mountains, are said to have abandoned the errors of idolatry long before this date and accepted the true faith through the preaching of the Word by Bishop Ninian, a most revered and holy man of British race, who had been regularly instructed in the mysteries of the Christian faith in Rome.

Ninian's own episcopal See, named after St Martin and famous for its stately church, is now held by the English, and it is there that his body and those of many saints lie at rest. The place belongs to the province of Bernicia and is commonly known as *Candida Casa*, the "White House," because he built a church of stone, using a method which was unusual among the Britons.

alternative reading

A Reading from *The Life of Saint Ninian* by Aelred of Rievaulx

As a young man Ninian traveled to Rome, and there the pope placed him in the care of good teachers of the truth to be instructed in the disciplines of the faith and in the meaning of Scripture. The young man, full of God, did not labor in vain or to no purpose. In the course of his studies he came to realize how much of his previous education at the hands of unskilled teachers had been at variance with sound doctrine. Therefore with all eagerness Ninian opened wide the mouth of his soul to receive the word of God. Like a bee which sucks nectar from many different flowers, he formed in his mind honeycombs of wisdom constructed from the arguments he gathered from his various teachers. He stored them in the secret recesses of his heart, preserving them until they had been thoroughly digested, with the result that in later years he could bring forth from his inner person a wisdom that not only nurtured his own soul, but also brought comfort to others. Truly, it was the due reward for one who for the love of truth had been prepared to forsake his native land, wealth and pleasure.

Having lived for many years in the city, it came to the knowledge of the Bishop of Rome that in certain western parts of Britain were yet many who had not received the faith of our Savior, and that some were hearing the word of the gospel from the lips of heretics and those poorly instructed in the law of God. Moved by the Spirit of God, the pope with his own hands therefore ordained the man of God to the episcopate, and having bestowed on him his blessing, appointed him apostle to his native land.

Ninian traveled home via the city of Tours, for at this time the most blessed Martin was its bishop, and he had long been desirous to meet him. There he stayed for a while consulting the holy man. On reaching his native land a great crowd of people went about to meet him. Great was the joy of all, wonderful the devotion; the praise of Christ resounded everywhere, for everyone regarded Ninian as a prophet. Straight away this diligent workman entered upon the field of his Lord, rooting out what had been wrongly planted, scattering what had been wrongly collected, and pulling down that which had been wrongly built. Then, with the minds of his people purged of error, Ninian began to lay in them the foundations of the true faith, building with the gold of wisdom, the silver of knowledge, and the precious stones of good works.

He chose a site for his church at a place which is now called Whithorn. It is situated on the shore of the ocean, the land running far out to sea so that it is enclosed by the sea on three sides, with access only from the north. Here, by the command of the man of God, stone-masons whom he had brought with him from Tours built a church of stone, before which (it is said) no other had ever been built in Britain.

When Blessed Ninian died, perfect in life and full of years, he left this world a happy man, and accompanied by the angels his soul was carried to heaven there to receive his eternal reward.

September 17

Hildegard

Abbess of Bingen, Visionary, 1179

Hildegard was born in 1098 at Böckelheim in Germany. From her earliest years she had a powerful, visionary life, becoming a nun at the age of eighteen, much influenced by her foster-mother, Jutta, who had set up the community and whom she succeeded as abbess in 1136. Her visions of light, which she described as "the reflection of the Living Light," deepened her understanding of God and creation, sin and redemption. They were, however, accompanied by repeated illness and physical weakness. About twenty years later, she moved her sisters to a new Abbey at Bingen. She traveled much in the Rhineland, founding a daughter house and influencing many, including the Emperor Frederick Barbarossa. She was a pastor, a composer and teacher, seeing herself as a "feather on the breath of God." She wrote three visionary works, a natural history and a medical compendium. She died on this day in the year 1179.

A Reading from *The Book of Life's Merits*
by Hildegard of Bingen

Forgetting about God leads to harmful and idle chatter such as: "How can we know about God if we have never seen him? And why should we have any regard for him if we have never set eyes on him?" People who talk like that are no longer mindful of their creator, and their minds are in the darkness of unbelief. For when man fell, darkness fell on the whole of creation. But God had created human beings to be full of light so that they could see the radiance of pure ether and hear the songs of angels. He had clothed them in such radiance that they shone with the splendor of it. But all this was lost when man disobeyed God's commandment and so caused nature to fall with him. Yet the natural elements retained a glimmering of their former pristine position, which human sin could not destroy completely. For which reason people should retain a glimmering of their knowledge of God. They should allow God to return to the center of their lives, recognizing that they owe their very existence to no one else save God alone, who is the creator of all.

alternative reading

A Reading from a letter of Hildegard to Adam,
Abbot of Ebrach, written before 1166

In a true vision of the spirit, my body fully awake, I saw, as it were, a beautiful girl of such great brightness, with so shining a face, that I could hardly gaze upon her. She had a cloak whiter than snow and brighter than the stars, and she had on shoes of the purest gold. And she held the moon and the sun in her right hand, and she embraced them lovingly. On her breast there was an ivory tablet, and on this tablet there was an image of man colored like sapphire. Every creature called this girl sovereign lady. And to the image on her breast, she said: "With thee is the beginning in the day of thy strength: in the brightness of the saints: from the womb before the day-star I begot thee."

And I heard a voice saying to me: This girl that you see is Divine Love, and she has her dwelling place in eternity. For when God wished to create the world, he bent down in sweetest love, and he provided for all necessary things, just as a father prepares the inheritance for his son. Thus it was that in great ardor he established all his works in order." Then all creation in its various kinds and forms acknowledged its creator, for in the beginning divine love was the matrix from which he created all things, when he said, "Let there be, and it was done." Thus every creature was formed through divine love in the twinkling of an eye.

And this figure shines with such great brightness, with so shining a face, that one can scarcely gaze upon her because she displays the fear of the Lord in such pure knowledge that mortal man will never be able to fully realize it. She has a cloak whiter than snow and brighter than the stars because, in pure innocence and without pretence, she embraces all things with the refulgent works of the saints. And she wears shoes of the purest gold, because her paths lead through the best part of God's election. And she holds the sun and the moon in her right hand, embracing them lovingly, because God's right hand embraces all creatures and because divine love is dispersed among the good of all nations and all realms. Moreover, the ivory tablet is on her breast because, in the knowledge of God, the hand of integrity flourished always in the Virgin Mary, so that, in her, the image of man appears colored like sapphire, because the Son of God, in divine love, radiated forth from the ancient of days in divine love.

For when all creation was fulfilled by God's command-ment just as he himself said: "Increase and multiply, and fill the earth" the heat of the true sun descended like dew into the womb of the Virgin and made man from her flesh, just as also he formed Adam's flesh and blood from the mud of the earth. And the Virgin gave birth to him immaculately.

September 18

Edward Bouverie Pusey

Priest, Tractarian, 1882

Edward Pusey was born in 1800 and educated at Oxford, where he became a Fellow of Oriel College in 1823. He became an expert in Biblical languages and criticism and in 1828 he was appointed Regius Professor of Hebrew in Oxford, the same year he was ordained. His patristic studies and firm adherence to a catholic interpretation of doctrine made him one of the leaders of the Oxford Movement. He was significant in encouraging the revival of Religious Life within the Church of England and was a noted preacher. His austere way of life made him much revered by his contemporaries and they founded Pusey House and Library in Oxford in his memory, following his death in the year 1882.

A Reading from a sermon of Edward Bouverie Pusey

Holiness is made for all. It is the end for which we were made; for which we were redeemed; for which God the Holy Ghost is sent down and "shed abroad in the hearts" which will receive him. God willed not to create us as perfect. He willed that we, through grace, should become perfect. We know not why our freewill is so precious in the eyes of God that he waits for us, pleads with us, draws us, allures us, wins us, overpowers us with his love; but he will not force us. He made us to be like him. And what is this but to be holy? "Be ye holy, for I your God am holy."

The mistake of mistakes is to think that holiness consists in great or extraordinary things beyond the reach of ordinary people. It has been well said, "Holiness does not consist in doing uncommon things, but in doing common things uncommonly well." Even in those great saints of God, the things which dazzle us most are not perhaps those which are the most precious in the sight of God. Great was the faith of Joshua, for example, when he said: "Sun, stand thou still upon Gibeon, and thou moon, in the valley of Ajalon." God himself speaks of it that "there was no day before it nor after it, that the Lord hearkened unto the voice of a man." Yet nearer to the heart of God were those words of Joshua's aged love: "As for me and my house, we will serve the Lord."

So too now. It is not by great things, but by great diligence in little everyday things that thou canst show great love for God, and become greatly holy, and a saint of God. Few ever do great things, and the few who can do them can each do but few. But every one can study the will of God and can give great diligence to know it and to do what he knows. Everyone can, by the grace of God, be faithful to what he knows. Your daily round of duty is your daily path to come nearer unto God.

alternative reading

A Reading from a sermon of Edward Bouverie Pusey preached before the University of Oxford at Christ Church in 1851, concerning "The Rule of Faith as maintained by the Fathers and the Church of England"

We acknowledge that Holy Scripture is the source of all saving truth; but it does not therefore follow that everyone, unguided, is to draw for himself the truth out of that living well. This being so, has the Church herself any guide external to herself, except the Holy Scripture as illumined by the light of God's Holy Spirit? Saint Paul writing to Saint Timothy has always been understood to say that she has: "Hold fast the form of sound words which thou hast heard of me, that good thing which was committed unto thee, the good deposit, keep by the Holy Ghost which dwelleth in us."

The word "deposit" became a word set apart to denote the body of the Christian faith, committed to the Church; a sacred deposit to be faithfully guarded and not tampered with, not to be lessened, not to be adulterated, but to be kept for him who left it to her trust. "Keep," Vincentius paraphrases, "that which is committed to thee, not that which is invented of thee: that which thou hast received, not that which thou hast devised; a thing not of wit but of learning: not of private assumption but of public tradition; a thing brought to thee not brought forth of thee; wherein thou must not be an author but a keeper; not a master but a disciple; not a leader but a follower. Keep the deposit. Preserve the talent of the Catholic Faith safe and undiminished; that which is committed to thee, let that remain with thee, and that deliver. Thou hast received gold, render then gold."

The Church of England has, from the Reformation, held implicitly in purpose of heart, all which the ancient Church ever held. The rule of Vincentius was ever held. Discordant voices, as far as they are discordant, cannot be the one voice of truth. One body of truth and faith and morals there can alone be, in which every declaration of Holy Scripture would meet and be combined and fulfilled. It does seem to be a paradox, therefore, when some have put forth that the faith is less faith because not received from a living, infallible authority. Faith is that which rests on him who is the truth—God. Faith is from God to God. It is not gained by man's own toil or search or study, but is given by God.

These are heavy times. Darkly did the last year close; darker has the present begun. Contention has taken the place of love; suspicion of trust. We all desire to know and to teach the Faith; we all believe that we have it; I do trust that if we could understand one another we might meet in one truth. But it cannot be the sound and healthy and normal state of a Church which we have been wont thankfully to call pure and apostolic, that we should be contradicting one another, condemning one another. This is not like the time of the apostles when all "were of one heart and mind." This is not to fulfill the apostolic precept "let the peace of God rule in your hearts to the which also ye are called in one body" when some are ready to cast others out of that body. Instead of this strife, let us rather seek one another, be at pains to understand one another, harmonize what all believe truly, not by abandoning any truth, but by affirming together all which is the truth.

September 19

Theodore of Tarsus

Archbishop of Canterbury, 690

Theodore was born at Tarsus in Cilicia about the year 602. He was an Asiatic Greek and had been educated in Athens before being appointed Archbishop of Canterbury by the Pope. He was raised straight from being a sub-deacon to the archiepiscopal see but proved his worth by immediately undertaking a visitation of the whole of England soon after his arrival. He set about reforming the Church in England with the division of dioceses and summoned the Synod of Hertford on September 24, 673, probably the most important Church council in the land, as it issued canons dealing with the rights and obligations of both clergy and religious: it restricted bishops to working in their own diocese and not intruding on the ministry of their prelate neighbors; it established precedence within the episcopacy; it ensured that monks remained stable to their monastery and obedient to their abbot; and many other matters were dealt with to effect the good order of the church. The canons were based on those of the Council of Chalcedon. Theodore proved to be the first Archbishop of Canterbury to have the willing allegiance of all Anglo-Saxon England. He died on this day in the year 690.

A Reading from *The History of the English Church and People* by the Venerable Bede

Following the death of Deusdedit, the sixth Archbishop of the church at Canterbury, the see of Canterbury was vacant for a considerable time. Egbert, King of Kent, and Oswy, King of Northumbria, jointly sent a priest called Wigheard to Rome, with a request that he might be consecrated archbishop of the English. However, not long after his arrival in Rome, he and almost all of his companions died in a outbreak of the plague.

Pope Vitalian took counsel about the matter and tried hard to find someone worthy to send as archbishop of the English Church. Now there was in Rome at this time a monk named Theodore, a native of Tarsus in Cilicia. He was learned both in sacred and secular literature, in Greek and Latin, of proven integrity, and of the venerable age of sixty-six. Hadrian, a native of Africa and abbot of a monastery near Naples, suggested the name of Theodore to the pope, who agreed to consecrate him on condition that Hadrian himself should accompany Theodore to Britain, since he had already traveled through Gaul twice on various missions and was not only better acquainted with the road, but had sufficient followers of his own available. The pope also ordered Hadrian to give full support to Theodore in his teaching, but to ensure that he did not introduce into the Church which he was to rule any Greek customs which conflicted with the teachings of the true faith.

Theodore arrived in Canterbury on Sunday May 27, in the second year after his consecration, and he held the see for twenty-one years, three months, and twenty-six days. Soon after his arrival, he visited every part of the island occupied by the English peoples, and received a ready welcome and hearing everywhere. He was accompanied and assisted throughout his journey by Hadrian, and he taught the Christian way of life and the canonical method of keeping Easter.

Theodore was the first archbishop whom the entire Church of the English consented to obey. And since, as I have observed, both he and Hadrian were men of learning in sacred and secular literature, they attracted a large number of students, into whose minds they poured the waters of wholesome learning day by day. In addition to instructing them in the holy Scriptures, they also taught their pupils poetry, astronomy and the calculation of the church calendar. In proof of this, some of their students still alive today are as proficient in Latin and Greek as in their native tongue.

Never had there been such happy times as these since the English settled in Britain; for the Christian kings were so strong that they daunted all the barbarous tribes. The people eagerly sought the new-found joys of the kingdom of heaven, and all who wished for instruction in the reading of the Scriptures found teachers ready to hand.

September 20

John Coleridge Patteson and his Companions

First Bishop of Melanesia, Martyrs, 1871

Born in London in 1827, John Coleridge Patteson came under the influence of George Augustus Selwyn while a scholar at Eton. Patteson was ordained and, in 1855 at the age of twenty-eight, left Britain to begin his life's work among the islanders of the South Pacific, becoming their first bishop. His system of evangelization was to train indigenous evangelists in the hope that some would be ordained, and so to equip local people to share the gospel in a way that was within their own culture. This bore fruit and Christianity spread rapidly. Also working in Melanesia were "thief ships" or "blackbirders," essentially European slave-traders who carried off islanders to work in British and other colonies. When Patteson landed alone on the island of Nukapu in the hope of showing that not all white men were deceivers, he was killed, probably in revenge for the stealing of five young men by the blackbirders. His fellow-workers were also attacked in their boat, two of them later dying of tetanus. John Coleridge Patteson gave his life for the gospel on this day in the year 1871.

A Reading from the life of Bishop John Coleridge Patteson
by Margaret Cropper

It had become increasingly clear to Bishop Selwyn that there must be a separate Bishop of Melanesia, and who more suitable than John Patteson, this man of God whom God had given him? Thus it was that on Saint Matthias' Day 1861, John Coleridge Patteson was consecrated first Bishop of Melanesia. Confiding to his diary, he wrote:

> I feel the sense of responsibility deepening on me. I must go out to work without Selwyn, and very anxious I am sometimes, and almost oppressed by it. But strength will come, and it is not one's own work, which is a comfort; and if I fail which is very likely God will place some other man in my position, and the work will go on, whether in my hands or not, and that is the real point.
>
> Indeed I do wonder that I am as calm as I am. When I look at the map, the countless islands overwhelm me. Where to begin? How to decide on the best method of teaching? I must try to be patient, and be content with very small beginnings, and endings too, perhaps.

Later, in a letter to his cousin, he recorded impressions of his work:

> I see everywhere signs of a really extraordinary change in the last few years. I know of twenty or thirty or perhaps forty places where a year ago, no white man could land without some little uncertainty as to his reception, but where I can feel confident now of meeting with friends. I can walk inland, a thing never dreamt of in the old days, sleep ashore, and put myself entirely in their hands and meet with a return of confidence on their part.

Mota was the language that Patteson had chosen for the translations from the Gospels and parts of the Prayer Book, the product of his genius and devotion. But in the wake of the Church's mission to Melanesia, there came traders, and worse, slave traders. "Thief ships" the islanders called them. Some of the people even asked one of the bishop's staff: "How was it that you and the bishop came first and then the slaughterers? Did you send them?"

On September 20, 1871 Patteson and four companions went ashore the island of Nu Kapu. As he stepped ashore, the group was attacked by islanders. Later the ship's crew discovered the body of the bishop with five wounds, inflicted with club and arrow; only his face was untouched. Across his breast his murderers had laid a palm branch with five knots in the leaves which led the Melanesians to believe that his death was an act of vengeance for five men whom the traders had killed. He was buried at sea. Later two of his companions also died from the effects of poisoned arrows received in the attack.

One of the Melanesians wrote: "The Bishop did nothing for himself alone, but always sought what he might keep others with, and the reason was his pity and his love. He never despised anyone, or rejected anyone with scorn, whether it was a white person or a black person. He thought of them all as one, and treated them all alike." Patteson's murder was brutal, but it proved to be the seed of the Melanesian Church which grew and continues to grow from strength to strength.

September 21

Saint Matthew

Apostle and Evangelist

Matthew appears in the list of the twelve apostles of Jesus and, according to the Gospel written under his name, was a tax collector. Mark and Luke called the tax collector Levi, and it has been assumed that they are one and the same person. This occupation was despised by his fellow Jews as a betrayal to the occupying Roman force, but Christ showed that judging by outward appearance was not what he was about. He ate with Matthew and with his friends, scandalizing those around him.

A Reading from a homily of the Venerable Bede

"Jesus saw a man called Matthew sitting at the tax office, and he said to him: 'Follow me'." Jesus saw Matthew, not merely in the usual sense, but more significantly with his merciful understanding of humankind. He saw the tax collector and, because he saw him through the eyes of mercy and chose him, he said to him: "Follow me." This following meant imitating the pattern of his life—not just walking after him. Saint John tells us: "Whoever says he abides in Christ ought to walk in the same way in which he walked."

"And he rose and followed him." There is no reason for surprise that the tax collector abandoned earthly wealth as soon as the Lord commanded him. Nor should one be amazed that neglecting his wealth, he joined a band whose leader had, on Matthew's assessment, no riches at all. Our Lord summoned Matthew by speaking to him in words. By an invisible, interior impulse flooding his mind with the light of grace, he instructed him to walk in his footsteps. In this way Matthew could understand that Christ, who was summoning him away from earthly possessions, had incorruptible treasures of heaven in his gift.

"And as he sat at table in the house, behold many tax collectors and sinners came and sat down with Jesus and his disciples." The conversion of one tax collector provided many, those from his own profession and other sinners, with an example of repentance and pardon. Notice also the happy and true anticipation of his future status as apostle and teacher of the nations. No sooner was he converted than Matthew drew after him a whole crowd of sinners along the same road to salvation. He took up his appointed duties while still taking his first steps in the faith, and from that he fulfilled his obligation, and thus grew in merit.

To see a deeper understanding of the great celebration Matthew held at his house, we must realize that he not only gave a banquet for the Lord at his earthly residence, but far more pleasing was the banquet set in his own heart which he provided through faith and love. Our Savior attests to this: "Behold I stand at the door and knock; if any hear my voice and open the door, I will come in to them and eat with them, and they with me."

On hearing Christ's voice, we open the door to receive him, as it were, when we freely assent to his prompting and when we give ourselves over to doing what must be done. Christ, since he dwells in the hearts of his chosen ones through the grace of his love, enters so that he might eat with us and we with him. He ever refreshes us by the light of his presence insofar as we progress in our devotion to and longing for the things of heaven. He himself is delighted by such a pleasing banquet.

September 25

Sergei of Radonezh

Russian Monastic Reformer, Teacher of the Faith, 1392

Born in Rostov in 1314, Sergei (Sergius) founded, together with his brother Stephen, the famous monastery of the Holy Trinity, near Moscow, which re-established the community life that had been lost in Russia through the Tartar invasion. Sergei had great influence and stopped civil wars between Russian princes and inspired Prince Dimitri to resist another invasion from the Tartars in 1380. Two years before that, he had been elected metropolitan but had refused the office. Altogether, he founded forty monasteries and is regarded as the greatest of the Russian saints and is patron of all Russia. He died on this day in the year 1392.

A Reading from *A Life of Saint Sergius* compiled by his disciple Epiphanius

One day a Christian from a nearby village, who had never seen the saint, came to visit him. The abbot was digging in the garden. The visitor looked about and asked, "Where is Sergius? Where is the wonderful and famous man?" A brother replied, "In the garden, digging; wait a while until he comes in."

The visitor, growing impatient, peeped through an aperture, and perceived the saint wearing attire shabby, patched, in holes, his face covered with sweat; and he could not believe that this was he of whom he had heard. When the saint came from the garden, the monks informed him, "This is he whom you wish to see."

But the visitor turned away from the saint and mocked at him; "I came to a prophet and you point out to me a needy looking beggar. I see no glory, no majesty and honor about him. He wears no fine and rich apparel; he has no attendants, no trained servants; he is but a needy, indigent beggar."

The brethren, reporting to the abbot, said, "This man has been discourteous and disrespectful about you, reproaches us, and will not listen to us."

The holy man, fixing his eyes on the brethren and seeing their confusion, said to them, "Do not send him away, brethren, for he did not come to see you. He came to visit me." He went toward him, humbly bowing low to the ground before him, and blessed and praised him for his right judgement. Then, taking him by the hand, the saint sat him down at his right hand, and bade him partake of food and drink. The visitor expressed his regret at not seeing Sergius, whom he had taken the trouble to come and visit; and his wish had not been fulfilled. The saint remarked, "Be not sad about it, for such is God's grace that no one ever leaves this place with a heavy heart."

As he spoke a neighboring prince arrived at the monastery, with great pomp, accompanied by a retinue of boyars, servants and attendants. The prince then advanced and, from a distance, made a low obeisance to Sergius. The saint gave him his blessing and, after bestowing a kiss on him, they both sat down. The visitor thrust his way back through the crowd, and going up to one of those standing by, asked, "Who is that monk sitting on the prince's right hand, tell me?"

A man turned to him and said, "Are you then a stranger here? Have you indeed not heard of blessed father Sergius? It is he who is speaking with the prince." Upon hearing this the visitor was overcome with remorse, and after the prince's departure, came before the abbot and said, "Father, I am but a sinner and a great offender. Forgive me and help my unbelief."

The saint readily forgave, and with his blessing and some words of comfort, he took leave of him. From henceforth, and to the end of his days, this man held a true, firm faith in the Holy Trinity and in Saint Sergius. He left his village a few years later, and came to the monastery where he became a monk, and there spent several years in repentance and amendment of life before he passed away to God.

September 26

Lancelot Andrewes

Bishop of Winchester, 1626

Born in 1555 in Barking, Lancelot Andrewes studied at Merchant Taylors' School and Pembroke Hall (now Pembroke College), Cambridge. After ordination, he held several posts before accepting appointments as Bishop, first of Chichester, then of Ely and finally of Winchester in 1619. Andrewes was present at the Hampton Court Conference in 1604, which furthered the reform of the Church of England, and he was also a translator of much of the Old Testament of what is known as the "Authorized Version" of the Bible. His preaching and his writings proved highly influential and his holiness of life and gentle nature endeared him to all who met him. He died in the year 1626 and his remains lie in a church that was then in his diocese of Winchester but now is the cathedral for the diocese of Southwark.

A Reading from the *Private Devotions* of Lancelot Andrewes

Let the preacher labor to be heard intelligently, willingly, obediently. And let him not doubt that he will accomplish this rather by the piety of his prayers than by the eloquence of his speech. By praying for himself, and those whom he is to address, let him be their beadsman before he becomes their teacher; and approaching God with devotion, let him first raise to him a thirsting heart before he speaks of him with his tongue; that he may speak what he hath been taught and pour out what hath been poured in.

I cease not therefore to ask from our Lord and Master, that he may, either by the communication of his Scriptures or the conversations of my brethren, or the internal and sweeter doctrine of his own inspiration, deign to teach me things so to be set forth and asserted, that in what is set forth and asserted I may ever hold me fast to the truth; from this very truth I desire to be taught the many things I know not, by him from whom I have received the few I know.

I beseech this truth, that loving kindness preventing and following me, he would teach me the wholesome things that I know not; keep me in the true things I know; correct me wherein I am (which is human) in error, confirm me wherein I waver; preserve me from false and noxious things, and make that to proceed from my mouth which, as it shall be chiefly pleasing to the truth itself, so it may be accepted by all the faithful, through Jesus Christ our Lord. Amen.

alternative reading

A Reading from a biography of Lancelot Andrewes
by his pupil and friend Henry Isaacson

The virtues and good parts of this honorable prelate were so many, and those so translucent, that to do him right, a large volume would be but sufficient which I shall leave to some of better abilities to perform, which I shall, by way of epitome, only point a finger at in what follows.

His first and principal virtue was his singular zeal and piety which showed itself not only in his private and secret devotions between God and himself, in which they that were about him well perceived that he daily spent many hours, yea, and the greatest part of his life in holy prayers, and abundant tears; but also in his exemplary public prayers with his family in his chapel wherein he behaved himself so humbly, devoutly, and reverently, that it could not but move others to follow his example. His chapel in which he had monthly communions was so decently and reverently adorned, and God served there with so holy and reverent behavior of himself and his family, that the souls of many were very much elated.

The whole Christian world took especial notice of his profound and deep learning, yet was he so far from acknowledging it in himself that he would often complain of his defects, even to the extenuating, yea vilifying of his own worth and abilities; professing many times, that he was but a useless servant, nay, a useless lump. Insomuch that being preferred by King James to the Bishopric of Chichester, and pretending his own imperfections and insufficiency to undergo such a charge, as also that he might have not only his clergy, but all others to take notice thereof, he caused to be engraven about the seal of his Bishopric those words of St Paul, "And who is sufficient for these things?"

His indefatigability in study cannot be paralleled, if we consider him from his childhood to his old age. Never any man took such pains, or at least spent so much time in study, as this reverend prelate; from the hour he arose, his private devotions finished, to the time he was called to dinner, which, by his own order, was not till twelve at noon at the soonest, he kept close at his book, and would not be interrupted by any that came to speak with him, or upon any occasion, public prayer excepted. Insomuch that he would be so displeased with scholars that attempted to speak with him in a morning, that he would say "he doubted they were no true scholars that came to speak with him before noon."

Of the fruit of this seed-time, the world, especially this land, hath reaped a plentiful harvest in his sermons and writings. Never went any beyond him in the first of these, his preaching, wherein he had such a dexterity, that some would say of him, that he was quick again as soon as delivered; and in this faculty he hath left a pattern unimitable. So that he was truly styled, "an angel in the pulpit."

September 27

Vincent de Paul

Founder of the Congregation of the Mission (Lazarists), 1660

Born in 1581 at Ranquine in Gascony, Vincent was educated by the Franciscans and was ordained at the age of nineteen. He was something of a token priest until his conversion in 1609, when he resolved to devote himself and all he owned to works of charity. He founded communities for men and, with Louise de Marillac, helped to begin the Sisters of Charity, the first community of women not to be enclosed and which was devoted to caring for the poor and sick. Vincent worked for the relief of galley slaves, victims of war, convicts, and many other groups of needy people. He became a legend in his own lifetime and died on this day in the year 1660.

A Reading from a letter of Vincent de Paul

We should not judge the poor by their clothes and their outward appearance nor by their mental capacity, since they are often ignorant and uncouth. On the contrary, if you consider the poor in the light of faith, then you will see that they take the place of God the Son who chose to be poor. Indeed, in his passion, having lost even his basic human dignity, regarded as foolishness by the Gentiles and a scandal by the Jews, he showed he was to preach the gospel to the poor in these words: "He has sent me to preach good news to the poor." Therefore we should be of the same mind and should imitate what Christ did, caring for the poor, consoling them, helping them and guiding them.

Christ chose to be born in poverty and called his disciples from among the ranks of the poor; he himself became the servant of the poor and so shared their condition that whatever good or harm was done to the poor, he said he would consider done to himself. Since God loves the poor, he also loves the lovers of the poor: when you love another person, you also love those who love or serve that person as well. So we too hope that God will love us on account of the poor. We visit them then, we strive to concern ourselves with the weak and needy, we so share their sufferings that with the Apostle Paul we feel we have become all things to all people. Therefore we must strive to be deeply involved in the cares and sorrows of our neighbor and pray to God to inspire us with compassion and pity, filling our hearts and keeping them full.

The service of the poor is to be preferred to all else, and to be performed without delay. If at a time set aside for prayer, medicine or help has to be brought to some poor person, go and do what has to be done with an easy mind, offering it up to God as a prayer. Do not be put out by uneasiness or a sense of sin because of prayers interrupted by the service of the poor: for God is not neglected if prayers are put aside, if the work of God is interrupted, in order that another such work may be completed.

Therefore, when you leave prayer to help some poor remember this that the work has been done for God. Charity takes precedence over all rules, everything ought to tend to it since it is itself a great lady: what it orders should be carried out. Let us show our service to the poor, then, with renewed ardor in our hearts, seeking out in particular any destitute people, since they are given to us as lords and patrons.

September 29

Saint Michael and all Angels

Michael, Gabriel, and Raphael are the three named Biblical angels, depicted as the belovèd messengers of God. Michael, which means "Who is like God," is portrayed as protector of Israel and leader of the armies of God, and is perhaps best known as the slayer of the dragon in the Revelation to John. Michael thus came to be regarded as the protector of Christians from the devil, particularly those at the hour of death. Gabriel, which means "The Strength of God," is the one, according to the Gospel of Luke, who is sent by God to Mary to announce the birth of Christ. Raphael, which means "The Healing of God," is depicted in the Book of Tobit as the one who restores sight to Tobit's eyes. A basilica near Rome was dedicated in the fifth century in honor of Michael on September 30, with celebrations beginning on the eve of that day, with the result that September 29 came to be observed as a feast in honor of Michael and all Angels throughout the Western Church.

A Reading from a sermon of Gregory the Great

You should be aware that the word "angel" denotes a function rather than a nature. Those holy spirits of heaven have indeed always been spirits, but they are only called angels when they deliver some divine message. Moreover, in Scripture those who deliver messages of lesser importance are called angels; whereas those who proclaim messages of supreme importance are called archangels.

Thus it was that not merely an angel but the archangel Gabriel was sent to the Virgin Mary. It was only fitting that the highest angel should come to announce the greatest of all messages.

Some angels are given proper names to denote the service they are empowered to perform. In that holy city, where perfect knowledge flows from the vision of almighty God, those who have no names may easily be known. But personal names are assigned to some, not because they could not be known without them, but rather to denote their ministry when they come among us. Thus, Michael means "Who is like God;" Gabriel is "The Strength of God" and Raphael is "The Healing of God."

Whenever some act of wondrous power must be performed, Michael is sent, so that action and name may make it clear that no one can do what God does by his own superior power. So also our ancient foe desired in pride to be like God, saying: "I will ascend into heaven; I will exalt my throne above the stars of heaven; I will be like the Most High." Satan will be allowed to remain in power until the end of the world when he will be destroyed in the final punishment. Then, he will fight with the archangel Michael, as we are told by John in the Revelation: "And there arose war in heaven, and a battle was fought with Michael the archangel."

So too Gabriel, who is called God's strength, was sent to Mary. Gabriel came to announce the One who appeared in humility to quell the cosmic powers. Thus God's strength announced the coming of the Lord of the heavenly powers, mighty in battle.

Raphael means, as I have said, the healing of God, for when this angel touched Tobit's eyes in order to cure him, Raphael banished the darkness of his blindness. Thus, since this angel is to heal, Raphael is rightly called the healing of God.

alternative reading

A Reading from a sermon of Bernard of Clairvaux

Today we observe the feast of the angels, and you wish me to preach to you a sermon worthy of the occasion. But how can we poor earthworms speak worthily of angelic spirits? Most certainly we believe that they who stand in the presence and sight of God enjoy the good things of the Lord for all eternity. But concerning those good things as Scripture says "neither has eye seen, nor has ear heard, nor have they entered into the human heart." So how can a mere mortal speak of them to other mortals given that we have neither knowledge to speak of them nor the ability to understand?

The mouth speaks from the overflowing of the heart; if the tongue is silent, it is from lack of thoughts. But even if the splendor and glory of the holy angels before God is beyond our comprehension, we can at least reflect upon the loving-kindness they show us. For there is in these heavenly spirits a generosity that merits our love, as well as an honor that evokes our wonder. It is only right that we who cannot comprehend their glory should all the more embrace their loving-kindness in which, as we know, the members of the household of God, the citizens of heaven, the heirs of paradise, are so exceedingly rich. As the Apostle says, "They are all ministering spirits, sent out in the divine service for the sake of those who are to inherit salvation."

So let nobody think this incredible, given that the creator and King of angels himself came not to be served but to serve, and to give his life for many. It would be strange to reject the idea of the angels' service, when he whom they serve in heaven himself leads the way in serving us! One of the prophets saw them serving God in heaven, and declared: "Thousands of thousands served him, and ten thousand times a hundred thousand stood before him." And another prophet when speaking of the Son says: "You have made him a little lower than the angels." So indeed it was that the One who surpassed all in majesty, chose to conquer through humility: superior to the angels, he chose to be made inferior to them in their service.

You may ask, "Why does his coming to serve us make him lower than the angels when they too are sent to serve?" The answer is that he is lower in that he not only served us, but allowed us to serve him. Also, the angels render service out of that which is not theirs, presenting to God our works, not their own and bringing to us his grace. That is why when Scripture says "the smoke of the incense ascended before God out of the angel's hand," it carefully tells us that there was *given* to him much incense. In other words, it is our labors and tears that the angels are offering to God, not their own; and it his gifts and not their own that they are bringing back to us. Thus the Servant who presented himself as a sacrifice of praise, and in offering his life to the Father, still gives us his flesh today, is both lower than all others, but also much higher.

So let us avoid everything that might grieve the holy angels, and instead, if we would enjoy their intimacy, cultivate those things that would please them. There are indeed many things that would please them; for example, being moderate, being chaste, giving up things voluntarily, praying with sighs and tears and with a heart full of loving ardor. But more than these things the angels of peace desire in us unity and peace, for these are things that characterize their own commonwealth, and when they see such things produced in us, they marvel at the birth of the new Jerusalem on earth.

alternative reading

A Reading from an ancient Celtic poem in praise of Michael the Archangel

Thou Michael the victorious,
I make my circuit under thy shield,
Thou Michael of the white steed,
And of the bright brilliant blades,
Conqueror of the dragon,
Be thou at my back,
Thou ranger of the heavens,
Thou warrior of the King of all,
O Michael the victorious,
My pride and my guide
O Michael the victorious,
The glory of mine eye.

I make my circuit
In the fellowship of my saint,
On the machair, on the meadow,
On the cold heathery hill;
Though I should travel oceans
And the hard globe of the world
No harm can e'er befall me
'Neath the shelter of thy shield;
O Michael the victorious,
Jewel of my heart,
O Michael the victorious,
God's shepherd thou art.

Be the sacred Three of Glory
Aye at peace with me,
With my horses, with my cattle,
With my woolly sheep in flocks.
With the crops growing in the field
Or ripening in the sheaf,
On the machair, on the moor,
In cole, in heap, or stack.

Every thing on high or low,
Every furnishing and flock,
Belong to the holy Triune of glory,
And to Michael the victorious.

September 30

Jerome
Priest and Monk of Bethlehem, 420

Jerome was born at Strido near Aquileia on the Adriatic coast of Dalmatia, in about the year 342. He studied at Rome, where he was baptized. He tried the life of a monk for a time, but unsuccessfully. Following a dream in which he stood before the judgement seat of God and was condemned for his faith in classics rather than Christ, he learned Hebrew the better to study the Scriptures. This, with his polished skills in rhetoric and mastery of Greek, enabled him to begin his life's work of translating the newly-canonized Bible into Latin which became the standard version for the Western Church for more thaner a thousand years. He eventually settled at Bethlehem, where he founded a monastery and devoted the rest of his life to study. He died on this day in the year 420.

A Reading from a letter of Jerome to a young priest written in the year 394

Read the Holy Scriptures constantly. Indeed, never let the sacred volume be out of your hand. Learn what you have to teach. As Scripture itself says: "Have a firm grasp of the word that is trustworthy in accordance with the teaching, so that you may be able both to preach with sound doctrine and to refute those who contradict it." "Continue in the things that you have learned and that have been entrusted to you, knowing from whom you learned it"; and be always "ready to give an answer to anyone who asks you a reason for the hope that is in you."

Do not let your deeds contradict your words, lest when you speak in church someone may be saying to themselves: "Why does not this man practice what he preaches? Look at the hypocrite! His stomach is bloated with rich food and he stands here preaching to us about fasting! A thief might just as well accuse others of avarice." In a Christian priest, mouth, mind and hand should all be in harmony.

When you are teaching in church, try not to seek applause but lamentation. Let the tears of your hearers be your glory. A presbyter's words ought to be seasoned by the reading of Scripture. Do not declaim or rant, gabbling your words without rhyme or reason, but rather show yourself learned in deep things, versed in the mysteries of God. To let forth a stream of words in order to impress an uneducated audience is mark of conceit. The fact that you have a deep conviction will communicate to your hearers, and become authoritative. I learned this from my own teacher, Gregory of Nazianzus. Certainly, there is nothing so cheap as deceiving an uneducated audience by sheer force of words. Such people admire what they are failing to understand.

Many people are building churches nowadays, with walls and pillars of glowing marble, ceilings glittering with gold, and altars encrusted with jewels. Yet little thought is given in the selection of Christ's ministers. Let no one try to contradict me by reference to the ancient temple of the Jews, with its altar, lamps, censers, dishes, cups, spoons, and the rest of its golden vessels. If such things enjoyed the Lord's approval it was because they corresponded to the time when the priests had to offer sacrifices, and when the blood of sheep was redemptive of sins. They were merely figures pointing to a new order. But now our Lord by his own poverty has consecrated the poverty of his house. Let us, therefore, think only of his cross and count worldly riches as refuse.

Finally, would you know what sort of apparel the Lord requires you to wear? Prudence, justice, moderation, courage. These are four virtues which should fill your horizon. Think of them as a four-horse team bearing you, Christ's charioteer, along at full speed to your goal. No necklace can be more precious than these; no gems could create a brighter galaxy. So let them be the decoration you bear and with which you clothe yourself, for they will protect you on every side. They are your defense and your glory; for each of these gems God turns into a shield.

October

October 1

Remigius
Bishop of Rheims, *c.*530

Born about the year 438, the son of the Count of Laon, Remigius studied at Rheims and was elected bishop and metropolitan of the city when he was only twenty-two years old. In the year 496, he baptized Clovis I, King of the Franks, and about three thousand of his subjects. Under the king's protection, Remigius preached the gospel, created dioceses, built churches and baptized many more Christians. His name is linked to the ampulla of chrism oil used at the coronation of French monarchs, together with the gift of healing. He died on January 13, around the year 530 and his mortal remains were transferred to the abbey of Saint Remi on this day in the year 1049.

A Reading from *The History of the Franks*
by Gregory of Tours

Queen Clothild ordered holy Remigius, Bishop of Rheims, to be summoned secretly, begging him to impart the word of salvation to the king. The bishop asked to meet King Clovis in private, and began to urge him to believe in the true God, the maker of heaven and earth, and to forsake all idols which were powerless to help him or his people.

The king replied: "I have listened to you willingly, holy father; but there remains one obstacle. The people who follow me will never agree to forsake their gods. I will go and reason with them according to what you have said to me." King Clovis arranged a meeting with his people, but God in his power had gone before him, and before he could say a word all those present shouted with one voice: "We will give up worshipping our mortal gods, O gracious king, and we are prepared to follow the immortal God whom Remigius preaches."

News of this was reported to the bishop. He was greatly pleased and he ordered the baptismal font to be made ready. The public squares were draped with colored hangings, the churches were adorned with white hangings, the baptistery was prepared, the smoke of incense spread in clouds, scented candles gleamed bright, and the holy place of baptism was filled with divine fragrance. God filled the hearts of all present with such grace that they imagined themselves to have been transported to some paradise.

King Clovis asked that he might be baptized first by the bishop. Like some new Constantine he stepped forward to the water, to wash away the sores of his former leprosy and to be cleansed in the flowing water of the sordid stains he had borne so long. As he came forward for baptism, the holy man of God addressed him in these pregnant words: "Meekly bow your head. Worship what you have burnt; and burn what you have been worshipping." For holy Remigius was a bishop of immense learning, and above all a great scholar, exemplary in holiness.

Thus it was that King Clovis confessed his belief in God Almighty, three in one, and was baptized in the name of the Father, and of the Son, and of the Holy Spirit, anointed with holy chrism with the sign of the cross of Christ. And more than three thousand of his army were baptized with him that day.

October 1

Thérèse of Lisieux

Carmelite nun, 1897

Thérèse was born at Alenon in France in the year 1873. At the age of fifteen she entered the Carmelite Convent at Lisieux in Normandy where two of her sisters were already nuns. Poor health prevented her from following the full rigor of the Rule *of her Order, and she died nine years later after much suffering from tuberculosis. Outwardly her life was undistinguished, but she pioneered her "little way" fidelity in small things, simple trust, and complete self-surrender to God. Her autobiography, a work undertaken at the request of her elder sister Pauline who was Prioress of the convent, was published after her death under the title* The Story of a Soul. *Its success was sensational perhaps because it demonstrated to ordinary people that holiness is open to everyone by the faithful doing of small things, the routine duties of daily life performed in the spirit of the love of God.*

A Reading from the autobiography of
Thérèse of Lisieux

The retreat before my profession brought no consolation with it, only complete dryness and almost a sense of dereliction. Once more, our Lord was asleep on the boat; how few souls there are that let him have his sleep out! He can't be always doing all the work, responding to all the calls made upon him; so for my own part I am content to have him undisturbed. I dare say he won't make his presence felt till I start out on the great retreat of eternity; I don't complain of that, I want it to happen. It shows, of course, that there's nothing of the saint about me; I suppose I ought to put down this dryness in prayer to my own fault, my own lukewarmness and want of fidelity. What excuse have I, after seven years in religion, for going through all my prayers and my thanksgivings as mechanically as if I, too, were asleep?

Anyhow, my profession retreat, like all the retreats I've made since, was a time of great dryness; and yet I felt that all the time, without my knowing it, God was showing me the right way to do his will and to reach a high degree of holiness. You know, I always have the feeling that our Lord doesn't supply me with provisions for my journey, he just gives me food unexpectedly when and as I need it; I find it there without knowing how it got there. It simply comes to this, that our Lord dwells unseen in the depths of my miserable soul, and so works upon me by grace that I can always find out what he wants me to do at this particular moment.

When the great day came, my wedding-day, there was no cloud on my horizon; on the eve of it, my soul had been in such tumult as I had never before experienced. Till then, I'd never known what it was to have a doubt about my vocation, and this was the ordeal I now had to face. That evening, as I made the Stations of the Cross after Matins, my vocation seemed to me a mere dream, a mere illusion; I still saw life at Carmel as a desirable thing, but the devil gave me the clear impression that it wasn't for me; I should only be deceiving my superiors if I tried to persevere in a way of life I wasn't called to. Darkness everywhere; I could see nothing and think of nothing beyond this one fact, that I'd no vocation. I was in an agony of mind; I even feared (so foolishly that I might have known it was a temptation of the devil's) that if told my Novice-mistress about it she'd prevent me taking my vows. And yet I did want to do God's will, even if it meant going back to the world; that would be better than doing my own will by staying at Carmel.

On the morning of my profession I seemed to be carried along on a tide of interior peace; and this sense of peace "which surpasses all our thinking" accompanied the taking of my vows. This wedding of my soul to our Lord was not heralded by the thunders and lightning of Mount Sinai, rather by that "whisper of a gentle breeze" which our father Elijah heard there. I offered myself to our Lord, asking him to accomplish his will in me and never let any creature come between us.

October 4

Francis of Assisi

Friar, 1226

Francis was born in Assisi in central Italy either in 1181 or the following year. He was baptized Giovanni but given the name Francesco by his father, a cloth merchant who traded in France and had married a French wife. There was an expectation that he would eventually take over his father's business but Francis had a rebellious youth and a difficult relationship with his father. After suffering the ignominy of imprisonment following capture while at war with the local city of Perugia, he returned a changed man. He took to caring for disused churches and for the poor, particularly those suffering from leprosy. While praying in the semi-derelict church of Saint Damian, he distinctly heard the words: "Go and repair my church, which you see is falling down." Others joined him and he prepared a simple, gospel-based Rule *for them all to live by. As the Order grew, it witnessed to Christ through preaching the gospel of repentance, emphasizing the poverty of Christ as an example for his followers. Two years before his death, his life being so closely linked with that of his crucified Savior, Francis received the stigmata, the marks of the wounds of Christ, on his body. At his death, on the evening of October 3, 1226, his Order had spread throughout Western Christendom.*

A Reading from the *Earlier Rule* of 1209 of Francis of Assisi

This is the life of the gospel of Jesus Christ which Brother Francis asked the Lord Pope to be granted and confirmed for him; and he granted and confirmed it for him and his brothers present and to come. Brother Francis and whoever will be the head of this Order promises obedience and reverence to the Lord Pope Innocent and to his successors. And all the other brothers are bound to obey Brother Francis and his successors.

The rule and life of these brothers is this: to live in obedience, in chastity, and without anything of their own, and to follow the teaching and the footprints of our Lord Jesus Christ, who says: "If you wish to be perfect, go and sell everything you have and give it to the poor, and you will have treasure in heaven; and come, follow me." And again, "If any wish to come after me, let them deny themselves and take up their cross and follow me." And again, "If anyone wishes to come to me and does not hate father and mother and wife and children and brothers and sisters, and even his own life, he cannot be my disciple." Or again, "Everyone who has left father or mother, brothers or sisters, wife or children, houses or lands because of me, shall receive a hundredfold and shall possess eternal life."

If anyone, desiring by divine inspiration to accept this life, should come to our brothers, let him be received by them with kindness. And if he is determined to accept our life, the brothers should take great care not to become involved in his temporal affairs; but let them present him to their minister as quickly as possible. The minister on his part should receive him with kindness and encourage him and diligently explain to him the tenor of our life. When this has been done, the aforesaid person—if he wishes and is able to do so spiritually and without any impediment—should sell all his possessions and strive to give them all to the poor.

The brothers and the minister of the brothers should take care not to become involved in any way in his temporal affairs; nor should they accept any money either themselves or through an intermediary. However, if they are in need, the brothers can accept instead of money other things needed for the body like other poor people. And when he has returned, let the minister give him the clothes of probation for a whole year, namely, two tunics without a hood, a cord and trousers, and a small cape reaching to the cord. When the year and term of probation has ended, let him be received into obedience. Afterward he will not be allowed to join another Order or to "wander outside obedience" according to the decree of the Lord Pope and according to the gospel; for no one "who puts his hand to the plough and looks back is fit for the kingdom of God."

But if someone should come who cannot give away his possessions without an impediment and yet has the spiritual desire [to do so], let him leave those things behind; and this suffices for him. No one should be accepted contrary to the form and the prescription of the holy Church. The brothers should wear poor clothes, and they can patch them with sackcloth and other pieces with the blessing of God; for the Lord says in the gospel: "Those who wear costly clothes and live in luxury and who dress in soft garments are in the houses of kings." And although they may be called hypocrites, nonetheless they should not cease doing good nor should they seek costly clothing in this world, so that they may have a garment in the kingdom of heaven.

alternative reading

A Reading from *The Canticle of Brother Sun*
by Francis of Assisi

Most High, all powerful, good Lord,
to you be praise, glory, honor and all blessing.
To you alone, Most High, do they belong,
and no one is worthy to call upon your name.

Praised be you, my Lord, with all your creatures,
especially by Brother Sun,
who makes the day and through whom you give us light.
He is beautiful and radiant with great splendor,
like you, O Most High.

Praised be you, my Lord,
by Sister Moon and the stars,
who shine clear and precious and beautiful
in the heaven you formed.

Praised be you, my Lord,
by Brother Wind, and by air and clouds,
clear skies and all weathers,
through which you give sustenance to your creatures.
Praised be you, my Lord,
by Sister Water,
who is very useful and humble and precious and chaste.

Praised be you, my Lord,
by Brother Fire, by whom you lighten the night.
He is beautiful and cheerful, powerful and strong.

Praised be you, my Lord,
by our Sister, Mother Earth, who sustains and governs us,
and who produces various fruits, colored flowers, and herbs.

Praised be you, my Lord,
by those who forgive for love of you,
and who bear infirmity and tribulation.
Blessed are those who endure in peace,
for by you, Most High, they shall be crowned.

Praised be you, my Lord,
by our Sister Death, from whom no one living can escape.
Woe to those who die in mortal sin.
Blessed are those whom death finds doing your most holy will,
for the second death shall do them no harm.

Praise and bless my Lord and give him thanks,
and serve him with great humility.

6 October

William Tyndale

Priest, 1536

Born in Gloucestershire about the year 1494, William Tyndale studied first at Magdalen Hall (now Magdalen College), Oxford, and then at Cambridge. He became determined to translate the Scriptures from Greek directly into contemporary English but was thwarted in this by the Bishop of London. So he settled in Hamburg in 1524, never returning to

England. When the first copies of his translation arrived in England in 1526, it was bitterly attacked as subversive by the ecclesial authorities. He spent much of the rest of his life making revisions to his translation, but also writing many theological works. His life's-work proved good enough to be the basic working text for those who, at the beginning of the following century, were to produce what became known as the Authorized Version of the Bible. He was eventually arrested in 1535 and imprisoned in Brussels on charges of heresy. He was first strangled and then burnt at the stake on this day in 1536. His last words were, "Lord, open the King of England's eyes."

A Reading from William Tyndale's *Epistle to the Reader* which he included in his first published version of the New Testament in 1526

Give diligence, reader, I exhort thee, that thou come with a pure mind, and as the scripture saith, with a single eye unto the words of health and of eternal life; by the which, if we repent and believe them, we are born anew, created afresh, and enjoy the fruits of the blood of Christ: which blood crieth not for vengeance, as the blood of Abel, but hath purchased life, love, favor, grace, blessing, and whatsoever is promised in the scriptures to them that believe and obey God; and standeth between us and wrath, vengeance, curse, and whatsoever the scripture threateneth against the unbelievers and disobedient, which resist and consent not in their hearts to the law of God, that it is right, holy, just, and ought so to be.

Mark the plain and manifest places of the Scriptures, and in doubtful places see thou add no interpretations contrary to them; but (as Paul saith) let all be conformable and agreeing to the faith. Note the difference of the law and of the gospel. The one asketh and requireth, the other pardoneth and forgiveth. The one threateneth, the other promiseth all good things to them that set their trust in Christ only. The gospel signifieth glad tidings, and is nothing but the promises of good things. All is not gospel that is written in the gospel-book: for if the law were away, thou couldest not know what the gospel meant; even as thou couldest not see pardon and grace, except the law rebuked thee, and declared unto thee thy sin, misdeed, and trespass. Repent and believe the gospel, as saith Christ in the first of Mark. Apply alway the law to thy deeds, whether thou find lust in thine heart to the law-ward; and so shalt thou no doubt repent, and feel in thyself a certain sorrow, pain, and grief to thine heart, because thou canst not with full lust do the deeds of the law. Apply the gospel, that is to say the promises, unto the deserving of Christ, and to the mercy of God and his truth, and so shalt thou not despair; but shalt feel God as a kind and merciful Father. And his Spirit shall dwell in thee, and shall be strong in thee, and the promises shall be given thee at the last, (though not by and by, lest thou shouldst forget thyself and be negligent) and all threatenings shall be forgiven thee for Christ's blood's sake, to whom commit thyself altogether, without respect either of thy good deeds, or of thy bad.

Them that are learned christianly I beseech, forasmuch as I am sure, and my conscience beareth me record, that of a pure intent, singly and faithfully, I have interpreted it, as far forth as God gave me the gift of knowledge and understanding, that the rudeness of the work now at the first time offend them not; but that they consider how that I had no man to counterfeit, neither was helped with English of any that had interpreted the same or such like thing in the scripture beforetime.

alternative reading

A Reading from *The Obedience of a Christian Man*
by William Tyndale, published in 1528

The kings ought to remember that they are in God's stead, and ordained of God, not for themselves, but for the wealth of their subjects. Let them remember that their subjects are their brethren, their flesh and blood, members of their own body, and even their own selves in Christ. Therefore ought they to pity them, and to rid them from such wily tyranny, which increaseth more and more daily. And though that the kings, by the falsehood of the bishops and abbots, be sworn to defend such liberties; yet ought they not to keep their oaths, but to break them; forasmuch as they are upright and clean against God's ordinance, and even but cruel oppression, contrary unto brotherly love and charity.

And let the kings put down some of their tyranny, and turn some unto a common wealth. If the tenth part of such tyranny were given the king yearly, and laid up in the shire-towns, against the realm had need, what would it grow to in certain years? Moreover one king, one law, is God's ordinance in every realm. Therefore ought not the king to suffer them to have a several law by themselves, and to draw his subjects thither. It is not meet, will they say, that a spiritual man should be judged of a worldly or temporal man. O abomination! see how they divide and separate themselves: if the lay-man be of the world, so is he not of God! If he believe in Christ, then is he a member of Christ, Christ's brother, Christ's flesh, Christ's blood, Christ's spouse, co-heir with Christ, and hath his Spirit in earnest, and is also spiritual. Because thou art put in office to preach God's word, art thou therefore no more one of the brethren?

If any question arise about the faith of the Scripture, let them judge by the manifest and open Scriptures, not excluding the lay-men: for there are many found among the lay-men which are as wise as the spiritual officers. Or else, when the officer dieth, how could we put another in his room? Wilt thou teach twenty, thirty, forty, or fifty years, that no man shall have knowledge or judgement in God's word save thou only? Is it not a shame that we Christians come so oft to church in vain, when he of fourscore years old knoweth no more than he that was born yesterday?

October 6

Bruno

Founder of the Carthusian Order, 1101

Bruno was born at Cologne in about 1032. He was gifted intellectually and became rector of the cathedral school at Rheims where the quality of his lectures won for him respect and admiration among his pupils, among them the future Pope Urban II. After eighteen years, however, Bruno felt drawn to the monastic life. He and six companions received permission and encouragement from the Bishop of Grenoble to establish themselves at La Chartreuse in 1084. Its ethos was fostered by the ideals of primitive Christian monasticism when, during the third and fourth centuries in the Egyptian desert, solitaries lived in individual houses or cells, but near enough to one another for mutual support. "Christ's poor men who dwell in the desert of the Chartreuse for the love of the name of Jesus" was how Bruno and his companions described themselves. Silence, austerity, solitude and total renunciation of the world were and are the hallmarks of Carthusian spirituality. Bruno died in the year 1301.

A Reading from a meditation on solitude by Guigo II, ninth prior of La Chartreuse

"Woe to the lonely one" when you alone, my good Jesus, are not with him or her. How many in a crowd are alone because you are not with them? Be always with me, so that I may never be alone! I am in no one's company, and yet I am not alone. I myself am a crowd. My wild beasts are with me, those whom I have nourished in my heart from my childhood. There they have made their lairs which they love so much that even in my loneliness they will not leave me. How often have I protested to them: "Go away from me, wicked ones, so that I may search out the commandments of my God." It is as though frogs were croaking in my entrails, as if Egypt's plague of flies were blinding my eyes.

Let one sit alone, the Scripture says; and indeed, unless one sits and rests, one will not be alone. So it is good to be humbled, Lord, and to bear your burden. By carrying your burden the proud learn meekness. And you say to those who take up your burden: "Learn from me, for I am meek and humble of heart." The one who is mounted on pride does not know how to sit still. But your throne is humility and peace. And now I see that no one can be at peace until they have become humble. Humility and peace: how good it is for a man or woman to be humbled so that they can attain to peace. Then indeed will one sit alone and be silent. The one who is not alone cannot be silent. And the one who is not silent cannot hear you when you speak to him or her.

Scripture says: "The words of the wise are as a goad" to those who listen to them in silence. Let all my world be silent in your presence, Lord, so that I may hear what the Lord God may say in my heart. Your words are so softly spoken that no one can hear them except in a deep silence. But to hear them lifts the one who sits alone and in silence completely above his or her natural powers, because the one who humbles himself will be lifted up. The one who sits alone and listens will be raised above himself. But where? This surely does not mean a lifting up of the body? No: it means of the heart. But how can one's heart be above one's self? It can because one forgets one's self, does not love one's self, thinks nothing of one's self. Of what then does one think? Of that which is above one, one's highest good, one's God. And the more one sees and loves God, the more one sees and loves one's self.

October 9

Denys and his Companions

Bishop of Paris, Martyrs, *c.*250

Denys, also called Dionysius, was born in Italy at the beginning of the third century and was sent to convert the peoples of Gaul, along with five other bishops. On reaching Paris, he established there a Christian church on an island in the Seine. He and others were martyred in about the year 250 and an abbey was later built over their tombs, dedicated to Denys. The church became the burial place of French monarchs and Denys has long been regarded as patron saint of France.

A Reading from a sermon of Augustine

The Lord Jesus Christ not only instructed his martyrs through his teaching, he strengthened them through his own example. In order that those who would suffer for him might have an example to follow, he first suffered for them. He showed the way and became it.

When we talk of death, we speak in terms of the body and the soul. In one sense, the soul cannot die, but in another it can. It cannot die inasmuch as the awareness of itself endures; yet it can die if it loses God. For just as the soul is the life of the body, so God is the life of the soul. The body perishes when the soul that is its life departs: the soul perishes when God casts it away. So lest God cast our souls away, let us always live in faith. Only so will we not fear to die for God, and not die abandoned by God.

The death of the body will always remain a fear. And yet Christ the Lord has made his martyrs a counter-balance to our fear. Why worry about the safety of limbs when we have been reassured that the hairs on our head are secure? Does not Scripture say that "the very hairs on your head are numbered?" Why should our human frailty cause us to be so frightened when the truth has spoken thus?

Blessed indeed then, are the saints whose memory we commemorate on the day of their passion. In surrendering their security in this world, they received an eternal crown and immortality without end. As we gather to remember them in prayer, their example sends us messages of encouragement. When we hear how the martyrs suffered, we rejoice and glorify God in them. We do not grieve because they died. If they had not died, do you think they would still be alive today? Their confession of faith served to consummate what sickness would one day also have brought about.

Therefore, my dear friends, let us rejoice in their commemoration. Let us pray to God that we may follow in the steps of his martyrs. They were mortal like you: their manner of birth no different from yours. They had bodies no different from your own.

We are all descended from Adam: we should all seek to return to Christ.

Honor the martyrs; praise, love, preach and honor them. But remember, worship only the God of the martyrs.

October 9

Robert Grosseteste

Bishop of Lincoln, 1253

Robert Grosseteste (meaning "large-head") was born at Stradbroke in Suffolk in about 1175. He studied at Oxford and Paris and held various posts until, after a grave illness, he returned to Oxford, where he taught at the Franciscan house of studies. He became Bishop of Lincoln in 1235, then the largest English diocese, which received from him a thorough visitation soon after his arrival. He met opposition in his attempts at vigorous reforms in the shape of his Dean and Chapter in the cathedral at Lincoln, who saw themselves as beyond his jurisdiction. The affair was settled in 1245 when the Pope issued a bull giving the bishop full power over the Chapter. Robert attended the Council of Lyons that year and also traveled to Rome a few years later. His wide-ranging interests covered mathematics, optics and many of the sciences; he translated large numbers of theological works from Greek and wrote his own theological commentaries and philosophical works. He died on this day in the year 1253.

A Reading from the *Memorial* of Bishop Grosseteste addressed and delivered to Pope Innocent IV before the Papal Court at Lyons on May 13, 1250, concerning abuses affecting the life of the Church in England

What is the cause of this hopeless fall of the Church? Unquestionably the diminution in the number of good shepherds of souls, the increase of wicked shepherds, and the circumscription of pastoral authority and power. Bad pastors are everywhere the cause of unbelief, division, heresy and vice. It is they who scatter the flock of Christ, who lay waste the vineyard of the Lord, and desecrate the earth. No wonder, for they preach not the gospel of Christ with that living word which comes forth from living zeal for the salvation of souls, and is confirmed by an example worthy of Jesus Christ.

And what is the cause of this evil? I tremble to speak of it, and yet I dare not keep silence. The cause and source of it is the *Curia* itself! Not only because it fails to put a stop to these evils as it can and should, but still more, because by its dispensations, provisions and collations, it appoints evil shepherds, thinking only of the income it yields for a person, and for the sake of it, handing over many thousands of souls to eternal death. And all this comes from him who is the representative of Christ! He who so sacrifices the pastoral office is a persecutor of Christ in his members. And since the doings of the *Curia* are a lesson to the world, such a manner of appointment to the cure of souls, on its part, teaches and encourages those who exercise the rights of patrons to make pastoral appointments of a similar nature, as a return for services rendered to themselves, or to please those in power, and thus destroy the sheep of Christ.

The cure of souls consists not only in the dispensation of the sacraments, in singing of the hours, and reading of masses, but in the true teaching of the word of life, in rebuking and correcting vice; and besides all this, in feeding the hungry, giving drink to the thirsty, clothing the naked, housing the strangers, visiting the sick and prisoners—especially those who are the parish priest's own parishioners. By such deeds of charity, a priest will instruct his people in the holy exercises of daily life.

The end of the evils of which I speak is not the upbuilding, but the destruction of the Church.

October 10

Paulinus

Bishop of York, Missionary, 644

Born in the latter part of the sixth century, probably in Italy, Paulinus was among the second group of monks sent by Pope Gregory to England to assist Augustine in his work. He was among the party that accompanied Ethelburga to Northumbria, where she was to marry the king, Edwin, who subsequently took his wife's Christian faith as his own. Paulinus built the first church in York in about 627 and was its first bishop. He traveled much, north and south of the Humber, building churches and baptizing new Christians. He had to flee for his life, however, when Edwin was killed in battle by the pagan king, Penda of Mercia, and Paulinus became Bishop of Rochester. He died on this day in the year 644.

A Reading from *The History of the English Church and People* by the Venerable Bede

On learning from Bishop Augustine that the harvest was rich but that the laborers to help him gather it were few, Pope Gregory sent with his envoys several colleagues and ministers of the word, of whom the principal and most outstanding were Mellitus, Justus, Paulinus, and Rufinianus.

Paulinus was a tall man with a slight stoop. He had black hair, an ascetic face, a thin hooked nose, and a venerable and awe-inspiring presence. He was consecrated bishop by Archbishop Justus on July 21, in the year of our Lord 625, and came to King Edwin of Northumbria with Princess Ethelberga, a daughter of King Ethelbert. She had been betrothed to Edwin, and Paulinus was to act as her chaplain and spiritual counselor. He was determined to bring the nation to which he was sent to the knowledge of the truth. His desire in the words of the apostle was "to espouse her to one husband, that he might present her as a chaste virgin to Christ."

Therefore, directly he entered the province he set to work vigorously. His goal was not only, with God's help, to maintain the faith of his companions without them lapsing, but if possible to bring some of the heathen to grace and faith by his teaching. He labored long, but, as the apostle says, "the god of this world blinded the minds of those who did not believe, lest the light of the glorious gospel of Christ should shine upon them."

Although Paulinus found it difficult to bring the king's proud mind to accept the humility of the way of salvation or to accept the mystery of the life-giving cross, he nevertheless continued, by words of exhortation addressed to the people, and by words of supplication addressed to the divine compassion, to strive for the conversion of the king and his nation.

King Edwin hesitated to accept the word of God which Paulinus preached, and used to sit alone for hours at a time, debating within himself what he should do and what religion he should follow. On one of these occasions, the man of God came to him and, laying his right hand on his head, enquired whether he remembered this sign. The king trembled and would have fallen at his feet; but Paulinus raised him and said in a friendly voice: "God has helped you to escape from the hands of the enemies whom you feared, and it is through his bounty that you have received the kingdom that you desired. Remember now your own promise that you made, and hesitate no longer. Accept the faith and keep the commandments of the God who has delivered you from all your earthly troubles and raised you to the glory of an earthly kingdom. If you will henceforth obey his will, which he reveals to you through me, he will save you likewise from the everlasting doom of the wicked and give you a place in his eternal kingdom in heaven."

So it was that King Edwin, with all the nobility of his kingdom and a large number of humbler folk, finally accepted the faith and were washed in the cleansing waters of baptism in the eleventh year of his reign, that is in the year of our Lord 627, and about 180 years after the first arrival of the English in Britain. The king's baptism took place in York on Easter Day in the church of Blessed Peter the Apostle which the king had hastily built of wood during the time of his instruction and preparation for baptism; and in this city he established the episcopal see of Paulinus, his teacher and bishop. Soon after his baptism, at Paulinus' suggestion, the king gave orders to build on the same site a larger and more noble basilica of stone which was to enclose the little oratory he had built previously.

Thenceforward for six years, until the close of Edwin's reign, Paulinus preached the word in that province with the king's full consent and approval, and as many as were predestined to eternal life believed and were baptized.

October 10

Thomas Traherne

Poet, Spiritual Writer, 1674

Thomas Traherne was born in Hereford in about 1636. After studying in Oxford and being a parish priest for ten years, he became private chaplain to the Lord Keeper of the Seals of Charles II. He was one of the English Metaphysical poets and yet, in his lifetime, only one of his works was ever printed. It was at the beginning of the twentieth century that his poems, until then in manuscript, were published and he took on the mantle of an Anglican Divine. His poetry is probably the most celebratory among his fellow Metaphysical poets, with little mention of sin and suffering and concentrating more on the glory of creation, so that some regard his writings as on the verge of pantheism. He died on this day in the year 1674.

A Reading from *Centuries of Meditation* by Thomas Traherne

Adam in Paradise had not more sweet and curious apprehensions of the world than I when I was a child. All appeared new and strange at first, inexpressibly rare and delightful and beautiful. I was a little stranger, which at my entrance into the world was saluted and surrounded with innumerable joys. I was entertained like an angel with the works of God in their splendor and glory, I saw all in the peace of Eden; heaven and earth did sing my Creator's praises, and could not make more melody to Adam than to me. All time was eternity and a perpetual Sabbath. Is it not strange, that an infant should be heir of the whole world, and see those mysteries which the books of the learned never unfold?

The corn was orient and immortal wheat which never should be reaped, nor was ever sown. I thought it had stood from everlasting to everlasting. The dust and stones of the street were as precious as gold: the gates were at first the end of the world. The green trees when I saw them first through one of the gates, transported and ravished me, their sweetness and unusual beauty made my heart to leap, and almost mad with ecstasy, they were such strange and wonderful things. The people! O what venerable and reverend creatures did the aged seem! Immortal cherubims! And young men glittering and sparkling angels, and maids strange seraphic pieces of life and beauty! Boys and girls tumbling in the street, and playing, were moving jewels. I knew not that they were born or should die; but all things abided eternally as they were in their proper places.

Eternity was manifest in the light of the day, and something infinite behind everything appeared which talked with my expectation and moved my desire. The city seemed to stand in Eden, or to be built in heaven. The streets were mine, the temple was mine, the people were mine, their clothes and gold and silver were mine, as much as their sparkling eyes, fair skins and ruddy faces. The skies were mine, and so were the sun and moon and stars, and all the world was mine; and I the only spectator and enjoyer of it. I knew no churlish proprieties, nor bounds, nor divisions: but all proprieties and divisions were mine: all treasures and the possessors of them. So that with much ado I was corrupted, and made to learn the dirty devices of this world which now I unlearn, and become, as it were, a little child again, that I may enter into the Kingdom of God.

October 12

Wilfrid

Bishop of Ripon, Missionary, 709

Wilfrid, or Wilfrith, was born in Northumbria about the year 633. He was educated at the monastery on Lindisfarne, but disapproved of what he judged to be their Celtic insularity. He journeyed to Canterbury and then to Rome. He spent three years at Lyons where he was admitted as a monk. He was appointed Abbot of Ripon and took with him the Roman monastic system and Benedictine Rule, which he immediately introduced. At the Synod of Whitby, his dominance was largely responsible for the victory of the Roman party over the Celts and, when he was elected Bishop of York, he went to Compiègne to be consecrated by twelve Frankish bishops rather than risk any doubt of schism by being ordained by Celtic bishops. There were upsets first with Chad and then with Archbishop Theodore of Canterbury, but the Roman authorities took his side and he was eventually restored to his See. After further disputes, he resigned the See of York and became Bishop of Hexham, spending his remaining years at Ripon. His gift to the English Church was to make it more clearly a part of the church universal, but his manner and methods were not such as to draw people close to him at a personal level. He died on this day in the year 709, and was buried at Ripon.

A Reading from *The History of the English Church and People* by the Venerable Bede

As a boy, Wilfrid was of a good disposition and behaved well for his age, always bearing himself modestly and thoughtfully, so that he was deservedly loved, admired, and welcomed by his elders as though he were one of themselves. When he reached the age of fourteen, he chose monastic life rather than secular. He informed his father of his desire, for his mother was dead, and he readily consented to his son's godly desires and aspirations, encouraging him to persevere in such a laudable undertaking. Wilfrid therefore went to the island of Lindisfarne and offered himself for the service of the monks, diligently setting himself to learn and practice all that conduces to monastic purity and devotion. Having a quick mind, he very soon learned the psalter by heart and certain other books. Even before he was tonsured, he already exhibited a maturity of monastic outlook in humility and obedience which is more important than any outward tonsure. This naturally endeared him to the older monks as well as to his contemporaries.

When he had served God in that monastery for some years, being a thoughtful youth, he gradually came to realize that the way of life taught by the Irish was by no means perfect; so he decided to visit Rome and see what ecclesiastical and monastic customs were in use at the apostolic see.

On his return to Britain, he was admitted to the friendship of King Alchfrid, who had learned to love and follow the Catholic laws of the Church. When he found Wilfrid to be a Catholic, the king gave him ten hides of land at a place called Stanford, and not long afterwards, a monastery with thirty hides of land at Ripon. It was at this time that the king sent Wilfrid to Gaul, asking that he might be consecrated his bishop, Wilfrid being about thirty years of age.

But Wilfrid remained overseas for some time, as a result of which a holy man named Chad was consecrated Bishop of York at the orders of King Oswy. Chad, having ruled the Church very ably for three years, eventually resigned the see and retired to his monastery at Lastingham, with the result that Wilfrid then became bishop of the whole province of the Northumbrians. Wilfrid died in the year 709 in the district of Oundle after forty-five years as a bishop. The coffin containing his body was later carried back by the brothers to his own monastery at Ripon, where he was buried in the church of the blessed Apostle Peter close to the altar on the south side.

October 13

Edward the Confessor

King of England, 1066

Edward was born in 1002, the son of the English King Ethelred and his Norman wife Emma. Living in exile during the Danish supremacy, he was invited back to England in 1042 to become king, and was heartily welcomed as a descendant of the old royal line. However, his reign was a balancing act between the influences of stronger characters at his court or overseas, sustained by Edward's diplomacy and determination. Edward's reputation for sanctity was built on his personal, more than his political, qualities. He was concerned to maintain peace and justice in his realm, to avoid foreign wars, and to put his faith into practice. He was generous to the poor, hospitable to strangers, but no mere pietist. Having vowed as a young man to go on pilgrimage to Rome should his family fortunes ever be restored, he later felt it irresponsible to leave his kingdom, and was permitted instead to found or endow a monastery dedicated to Saint Peter. Edward chose the abbey on Thorney Island, by the river Thames, thus beginning the royal patronage of Westminster Abbey. He died on January 5, 1066 and his remains were translated to the Abbey on this day in the year 1162.

A Reading from *The Life of King Edward who rests at Westminster,* attributed to a monk of Saint Bertin

When the one thousand and sixty-fifth year of the Lord's incarnation approached, the zeal of the house of God took possession of King Edward's mind even more warmly, and fired him to the marrow to celebrate the marriage of the heavenly King and his new bride. For it was not the royal scepter which aroused this love of justice: he found it hidden within him. And so, while the building of the church dedicated to Saint Peter the Prince of the Apostles at Westminster rose into a lofty structure, the glorious king began with duteous zeal to devote himself to the business of this important consecration. He had also become aware of the approaching end of his mortal life and was drawn to the execution of his good purpose before he should reach life's bourn.

At that time the days of the Lord's nativity were approaching, and those men for whom throughout the kingdom the heralds of this great dedication were sounding, had added the joys of the one festival to the other. But on the very night on which the Virgin in childbed gave the light of heavenly glory to those who had been darkened by the shadow of death, and, unstained, brought forth without travail the King of Ages, the glorious King Edward was afflicted with an indisposition, and in the palace the day's rejoicing was checked by a fresh calamity. The holy man disguised his sickness more than his strength warranted, and for three days he was able to produce a serene countenance. He sat at table clad in a festal robe, but had no stomach for the delicacies which were served. He showed a cheerful face to the bystanders, although an unbearable weakness oppressed him. But after the banquet he sought the privacy of his inner bedchamber, and bore with patience a distress which grew severer day by day. The close ranks of his vassals surrounded him, and the queen herself was there, in her mourning foretelling future grief. When that celebrated day, which the blessed passion of the Holy Innocents adorns, had come, the excellent prince ordered them to hasten on with the dedication of the church and no more to put it off to another time.

When he was sick unto death and his men stood and wept bitterly, King Edward said, "Do not weep, but intercede with God for my soul and give me leave to go to him. For he will not pardon me so that I shall not die who would not pardon himself so that he should not die." [Then he addressed his last words to Edith, his Queen, who was sitting at his feet, in this wise: "May God be gracious to this my wife for the zealous solicitude of her service. For she has served me devotedly, and has always stood close by my side like a beloved daughter." And stretching forth his hand to his governor, her brother, Harold, he said: "I commend this woman and all the kingdom to your protection.... Let the grave for my burial be prepared in the Minster in the place which shall be assigned. I ask that you do not conceal my death, but announce it promptly in all parts, so that all the faithful can beseech the mercy of Almighty God on me, a sinner."] Now and then he also comforted the queen, who ceased not from lamenting, to ease her natural grief. "Fear not," he said, "I shall not die now, but by God's mercy regain my strength." Nor did he mislead the attentive, least of all himself, by these words, for he has not died, but has passed from death to life, to live with Christ.

And so, coming with these and like words to his last hour, he took the viaticum from the table of heavenly life and gave up his spirit to God the creator on the fourth of January. They bore his holy remains from his palace home into the house of God, and offered up prayers and sighs and psalms all that day and the following night. And before the altar of Saint Peter the Apostle, the body, washed by his country's tears, was laid up in the sight of God.

A Reading from a sermon of Ronald Knox

When we venerate Saint Edward, we venerate a failure. We do so advisedly. Not because success in life necessarily falls to the grasping and the unscrupulous, so that success itself should be mistrusted by Christians as a sign of rascality. Not that there have not been great saints who were also great kings, great statesmen, great warriors Saint Oswald, Saint Dunstan, Saint Joan of Arc. But because we will not let ourselves be blinded by the lure of worldly success so as to forget that the true statesmanship is exercized in the council chamber, and the true warfare fought on the battlefield of the human soul.

Ask yourself which you would rather have been in life, of all those great dead who lie in Westminster Abbey, and you will find it a difficult question to answer: there is so much that dazzles, so much that captivates the imagination. Would you rather have written this, have painted that, have built that, have discovered that, have won this triumph or have carried that enactment? You can hardly say. But ask yourself which of those great dead you would rather be now; your body there, your soul far away—is there any Christian who would not ask to change places with the Confessor? Who would not choose his resting-place, there to wait for the opening of the great Doomsday Book, in which nothing is recorded of men and women but whether they meant good or evil, whether they loved or neglected God?

Many of those who sleep in King Edward's Abbey were devoted servants of their kind, who left the world better for their passing. But this is certain, that true satisfaction came to them and true success crowned them only so far as their ambitions were for a cause, not for a party; for others, not for themselves. Our happiness lies in devoting ourselves; success lies in the offering we can make. And our Confessor was a successful man, yes, even in this world, because in his simple piety, in the unaffected generosity of his nature, he set himself to serve his people by easing their burdens, by relieving their necessities, by confirming them in their allegiance to the faith. Great opportunities passed him by, and he never marked them; he might have altered the dynastic history of England, have left us different manners and a different political constitution, if he had been other than he was. Instead, he left all these things to God's providence; and God's providence, using the ambitions of human agents as its puppets, molded our history beyond expectation. And what do they mean to us now, those human agents? The Conqueror, who diverted the stream of history, went to his grave disappointed and lies there an historical memory. The Confessor, whose ambitions could be satisfied by finding a poor man his dinner, saw no corruption in death, and lives the patron of his fellow countrymen.

One task only he set before himself that had any external magnificence about it, and that was characteristic of him. It was no fortress, no royal palace, no court of justice that he planned: the House of God lay waste, and he must rebuild it. And, as if it were a symbol of the life he lived, built together from little acts of kindness and little sacrifices of self, stone by stone and arch by arch rose the Abbey Church of Westminster, which for all the additions and the restorations that have altered it in the course of the centuries, we still call his church.

October 14

Samuel Isaac Joseph Schereschewsky

Bishop of Shanghai, 1906

Born in 1831 of Jewish parents in Lithuania, Samuel Isaac Joseph Schereschewsky began studying to be a rabbi but became interested in Christianity while doing graduate studies in Germany. He emigrated to the United Sates in 1854 and entered the Presbyterian seminary in Pittsburgh. Unable to accept the Calvinist doctrine of predestination, Schereschewsky transferred to the General Theological Seminary in New York and was ordained in the Episcopal Church. Responding to a call for missionaries to serve in China, he learned to write Chinese on the voyage out and became involved almost immediately in projects to translate the Bible into Chinese. Reluctantly he accepted election as Bishop of Shanghai in 1877 and established Saint John's University, but a stroke six years later forced his resignation. Although he was limited to typing with the middle finger of his partially paralyzed right hand, he completed translations of the Bible both into the literary language and the spoken language of China before his death in 1906. He said to a visitor a few years before his death, "I have sat in this chair for over twenty years. It seemed very hard at first. But God knew best. He kept me for the work for which I am best fitted."

A Reading from " An Appeal for Establishing a Missionary College in China," by Samuel Isaac Joseph Schereschewsky

From the earliest days of the church, education has been an important agent in the propagation of Christianity. During the Middle Ages education was one of the chief instrumentalities by which Christianity was introduced among European nations. Rome has always availed herself of this power, both to extend her dominion and to regain lost ground. And if education has been an element of such importance in establishing Christianity in the West, have we any reason to believe that it will be a less powerful agent in establishing Christianity in the East? Not only so, but it seems to me that our endeavor to propagate the Christian religion *among* such a people as the Chinese (without it), would be most unwise, for among heathen nations there are few where literature is so identified with the national life. It is only necessary as a proof of this to refer to the vastness of their literature, and the profound respect that is accorded to the pursuit of learning and literary men. A "literary degree" is the "open sesame" to all avenues of distinc-tion in China, and in that land above all others the influence of such an institution as the one proposed could hardly fail to produce results exceeding perhaps our most sanguine expectations.

Again, the better one is acquainted with the state of things in China, and the more one studies the Chinese people with an heartfelt desire for their speedy conversion to Christianity, the more strongly one is convinced that the most effective agency that can be employed in carrying on the great work of evangelizing that nation must be thoroughly trained native ministers, who shall go forth to proclaim the gospel with the might and power which only a native ministry can possess. A college such as the one proposed would be undoubtedly the most efficient means of attracting Chinese young men from all parts of the empire, and bringing them under the influences of our Christian religion and Christian civilization.

And from these young men, with God's blessing, we might look for constant accessions to the ranks of a native ministry, and for hearty and efficient co-workers in carrying on the work of the Church in China.

Having thus briefly stated the pressing need of a missionary college in China, and having indicated the importance of such an institution in carrying on our missionary work there, it remains to be considered whether the establishment of such a college as the one proposed is a practical undertaking. Certainly so if the church can only be aroused to the importance of the enterprise, and provide the means to carry it out. China, long hermetically sealed from intercourse with Christian nations, is now thrown open to missionary enterprise, and there is nothing to hinder the establishment of such a college in any part of China where missionaries have found free scope for carrying on their work.

That our church may be willing to give to China a missionary college as an enduring testimony of our love to our Lord and Master is my earnest prayer.

October 15

Teresa of Avila

Carmelite nun, 1582

Teresa was born into an aristocratic Spanish family in 1515. Following her mother's death, she was educated by Augustinian nuns and then ran away from home to enter a Carmelite convent when she was twenty-one. After initial difficulties in prayer, her intense mystical experiences attracted many disciples. She was inspired to reform the Carmelite rule and, assisted by Saint John of the Cross, she traveled throughout Spain founding many new religious houses for men as well as women. Her writings about her own spiritual life and progress in prayer toward union with God include The Way of Perfection *and* The Interior Castle, *which are still acclaimed. She knew great physical suffering and died of exhaustion on October 4, 1582. Her feast is observed on October 15 because the very day after her death the reformed calendar was adopted and eleven days were omitted from October that year.*

A Reading from *The Way of Perfection*
by Teresa of Avila

It seems very easy to say that we will surrender our will to someone, until we try it and realize that it is the hardest thing we can do if we carry it out as we should. The Lord knows what each of us can bear, and, when he sees that one of us is strong, he does not hesitate to fulfill his will in him.

Do not fear that he will give you riches or pleasures or honors or any such earthly things; his love for you is not so poor as that.

And he sets a very high value on what you can give him and desires to recompense you for it since he gives you his kingdom while you are still alive. Would you like to see how he treats those who make the prayer "Your will be done" from their hearts? Ask his glorious Son, who made it thus in the Garden. Think with what resolution and fullness of desire he prayed; and consider if the will of God was not perfectly fulfilled in him through the trials, sufferings, insults and persecutions which he gave him until at last his life ended with death on a cross.

So you see what God gave to his best beloved, and from this you can understand what his will is. These, then, are his gifts in this world. He gives them in proportion to the love which he bears us. He gives more to those whom he loves most, and less to those he loves least; and he gives in accordance with the courage which he sees that each of us has and the love we bear to his majesty. When he sees a soul who loves him greatly, he knows that soul can suffer much for him, whereas one who loves him little will suffer little. For my own part, I believe that love is the measure of our ability to bear crosses, whether great or small. So if you have this love, try not to let the prayers you make to so great a Lord be words of mere politeness, but brace yourselves to suffer what his majesty desires. For if you give him your will in any other way, you are just showing him a jewel, making as if to give it to him and begging him to take it, and then, when he puts out his hand to do so, taking it back and holding on to it tightly.

Such mockery is no fit treatment for One who endured so much for us. If for no other reason than this, it would not be right to mock him so often—and it is by no means seldom that we say these words to him in the "Our Father." Let us give him once and for all the jewel which we have so often undertaken to give him. For the truth is that he gives it to us first so that we may give it back to him.

Unless we make a total surrender of our will to the Lord, so that he may do in all things what is best for us in accordance with his will, he will never allow us to drink of the fountain of living water.

A Reading from *Teresa of Avila* by Shirley du Boulay

They say in Spain that to understand Saint Teresa one must look at Castile. Its windswept plains, its granite boulders, its bitter winters and sun-scorched summers were the womb that nourished the "undaunted daughter of desires" of Richard Crashaw's poem. A gentler landscape would not have produced a woman of such courage and determination.

Teresa entered the Convent of the Incarnation at Avila in 1536 when she was twenty-one years old. Life in the Convent was largely uneventful. Apart from the social life of the parlor, meals and recreational periods, most of the day was spent in church. It was a demanding day and, many would say, a boring routine, though Teresa never complained or even referred to it.

Though Teresa was, for the most part, able to appear calm, even cheerful, beneath the surface she lived in torment. Her writings show clearly that her inner life was deeply troubled and difficult. In fact she describes the first twenty years at the Convent of the Incarnation as a time when she constantly failed God and was buffeted on "that stormy sea, often falling in this way, each time rising again, but to little purpose, as I would only fall once more."

She was generous and scrupulously honest in her writing, and it is this first-hand knowledge of her inner life, particularly during this period, which enables us to identify with her as a fellow human being and as a woman. She experienced spiritual apathy, aridity in prayer and a sense of failure common to so many. Had we only known her as the recipient of extraordinary experiences, as a mystic as gifted in prayer as was Rembrandt in art, Beethoven in music or Shakespeare in literature, we would not be able to identify with her so closely, nor would she have touched so many lives.

The stormy sea on which she was tossed was not only the sea of prayer, fraught with problems and highlighting her sense of sin, but also of her richly complex personality. In her, to a rare extent, the opposites met, fought out their various differences and were eventually reconciled. Though part of Teresa's appeal is the extent to which she was in many ways such an ordinary woman, loving and longing to be loved, motherly, practical and skilled in the feminine arts around the house, blessed with down-to-earth common sense, she also had the independence of mind, efficiency and capability in those days normally associated with men.

The contradictions in her nature ranged across all human characteristics; she epitomized the conflicts that tear many apart. Delighting in human relationships she yearned to abandon herself solely to God; commending poverty, she was fastidious; loving and gregarious, she needed solitude; concerned with the things of God, her upbringing would never let her forget worldly etiquette and honor; and wanting nothing more than to be alone with God, she knew she had practical tasks on earth. She knew that virtues have their corresponding vices, and her own moods vacillated between joy and torment. The conflict which obsessed her for twenty years was that she was torn between God and the world.

Anyone who has ever tried to pray will have experienced difficulties; yet there tends to be an unspoken assumption that for saints and mystics prayer is easy. The open and totally honest way in which Teresa admits to her own problems in prayer is one of her most valuable legacies; that she, too, found prayer difficult is not only endearing but also immensely reassuring. She writes of her trials:

> Over a period of several years, I was more occupied in wishing my hour of prayer were over, and in listening whenever the clock struck, than in thinking of things that were good. Again and again I would rather have done any severe penance that might have been given me than practice recollection as a preliminary to prayer. Whenever I entered the oratory I used to feel so depressed that I had to summon up all my courage to make myself pray at all.

She felt imprisoned and alone, unable to believe her confessors, who treated so lightly the shortcomings in her prayer life which she knew, in her heart, were a failure in her obligation to God. But one of the ways in which she is set apart from most people is in the courage and determination with which she persevered; she battled and fought against her problems in prayer as fiercely as any soldier fights his enemy. Through her twenties and thirties she endured boredom, aridity, frustration, disappointment and an acute sense of failure. This period, too often glossed over, was the soil from which the flower of her mysticism was to grow. It should never be forgotten that it lasted from her novitiate until she was about forty years old.

October 16

Nicholas Ridley and Hugh Latimer
Bishops, 1555

Born into a wealthy Northumbrian family in about the year 1500, Nicholas Ridley studied at Cambridge, the Sorbonne and in Louvain. He was Chaplain to Thomas Cranmer and Master of Pembroke Hall in Cambridge before being made Bishop of Rochester in 1547. He had been clearly drawing closer to the Reformers as early as 1535 and, at the accession of King Edward VI, declared himself a Protestant. He assisted Cranmer in preparing the first Book of Common Prayer *and was made Bishop of London in 1550. On the death of Edward, he supported the claims of Lady Jane Grey and was thus deprived of his See on the accession of Mary Tudor. He was excommunicated and executed in 1555.*

Hugh Latimer was a Leicestershire man, also educated at Cambridge but fifteen years older than Nicholas Ridley. He was articulate and yet homely in his style of preaching, which made him very popular in the university, and he received its commission to preach anywhere in England. He became a close adviser of King Henry VIII after the latter's rift with the papacy and was appointed Bishop of Worcester in 1535. He lost the king's favor in 1540, over his refusal to sign Henry's "Six Articles," designed to prevent the spread of Reformation doctrines, and resigned his see. He returned to favor on the accession of Edward VI but was imprisoned in the Tower of London when Queen Mary ascended the throne in 1553. He refused to recant any of his avowedly reformist views and was burned at the stake, together with Nicholas Ridley, on this day in the year 1555.

A Reading from a letter of Nicholas Ridley to John Hooper, Bishop of Gloucester, written from prison on January 18, 1555

My dearly beloved brother and fellow Elder, whom I reverence in the Lord, pardon me, I beseech you, that hitherto, since your captivity and mine, I have not saluted you by my letters; whereas, I do indeed confess, I have received from you (such was your gentleness) two letters at sundry times, but yet at such times as I could not be suffered to write unto you again; or, if I might have written, yet was I greatly in doubt lest my letters should not safely come unto your hands. But now, my dear brother, forasmuch as I understand by your works, which I have yet but superficially seen, that we thoroughly agree and wholly consent together in those things which are the grounds and substantial points of our religion, against the which the world so furiously rageth in these days, howsoever in time past in smaller matters and circumstances of religion your wisdom and my simplicity (I confess) have in some points varied; now, I say, be you assured, that even with my whole heart (God is my witness) in the bowels of Christ, I love you, and in truth, for the truth's sake which abideth in us, and (as I am persuaded) shall by the grace of God abide with us for evermore.

And because the world, as I perceive, brother, ceaseth not to play his pageant, and busily conspireth against Christ our Savior with all possible force and power, exalting high things against the knowledge of God, let us join hands together in Christ; and if we cannot overthrow, yet to our power, and as much as in us lieth, let us shake those high things, not with carnal, but with spiritual weapons; and withal, brother, let us prepare ourselves to the day of our dissolution; whereby after the short time of this bodily affliction, by the grace of our Lord Jesus Christ, we shall triumph together with him in eternal glory.

alternative reading

A Reading from a sermon of Hugh Latimer,
preached at Cambridge in 1529

Evermore bestow the greatest part of thy goods in works of mercy, and the less part in voluntary works. Voluntary works be called all manner of offering in the church, except your four offering-days, and your tithes: setting up candles, gilding and painting, building of churches, giving of ornaments, going on pilgrimages, making of highways, and such other, be called voluntary works; which works be of themselves marvelous good, and convenient to be done.

Necessary works, and works of mercy, are called the commandments, the four offering-days, your tithes, and such other that belong to the commandments; and works of mercy consist in relieving and visiting thy poor neighbors. Now then, if men be so foolish of themselves, that they will bestow the most part of their goods in voluntary works, which they be not bound to keep, but willingly and by their devotion; and leave the necessary works undone, which they are bound to do; they and all their voluntary works are like to go unto everlasting damnation. And I promise you, if you build a hundred churches, give as much as you can make to gilding of saints, and honoring of the church; and if thou go as many pilgrimages as thy body can well suffer, and offer as great candles as oaks; if thou leave the works of mercy and the commandments undone, these works shall nothing avail thee.

No doubt the voluntary works be good and ought to be done; but yet they must be so done, that by their occasion the necessary works and the works of mercy be not decayed and forgotten. If you will build a glorious church unto God, see first yourselves to be in charity with your neighbors, and suffer not them to be offended by your works. Then, when ye come into your parish church, you bring with you the holy temple of God; as Saint Paul saith, "You yourselves be the very holy temples of God," and Christ saith by his prophet, "In you will I rest, and intend to make my mansion and abiding-place."

Again, if you list to gild and paint Christ in your churches, and honor him in vestments, see that before your eyes the poor people die not for lack of meat, drink, and clothing. Then do you deck the very true temple of God, and honor him in rich vestures that will never be worn, and so forth use yourselves according unto the commandments: and then, finally, set up candles, and they will report what a glorious light remaineth in your hearts; for it is not fitting to see a dead man light candles. Then, I say, go your pilgrimages, build your material churches, do all your voluntary works; and they will then represent you unto God, and testify with you, that you have provided him a glorious place in your hearts.

October 16

Thomas Cranmer

Archbishop of Canterbury, 1556

Born in Aslockton in Nottinghamshire in 1489, Thomas Cranmer, from an unspectacular Cambridge academic career, was recruited for diplomatic service in 1527. Two years later he joined the team working to annul Henry VIII's marriage to Catherine of Aragon. He was made Archbishop of Canterbury in 1533 and duly pronounced the Aragon marriage annulled. By now a convinced church reformer, he married in 1532 while clerical marriage was still illegal in England. He worked closely with Thomas Cromwell to further reformation, but survived Henry's final, unpredictable years to become a chief architect of Edwardian religious change, constructing two editions of The Book of Common Prayer *in 1549 and 1552, the Ordinal in 1550, and the original version of the later Thirty-Nine Articles. Cranmer acquiesced in the unsuccessful attempt to make Lady Jane Grey Queen of England. Queen Mary's regime convicted him of treason in 1553 and of heresy in 1554. Demoralized by imprisonment, he signed six recantations, but was still condemned to the stake at Oxford. Struggling with his conscience, he made a final, bold statement of Protestant faith. Perhaps too fair-minded and cautious to be a ready-made hero in Reformation disputes, he was an impressively learned scholar, and his genius for formal prose has left a lasting mark on Anglican liturgy. He was burned at the stake in the year 1556.*

A Reading from the Preface to *The First Prayer Book of King Edward VI* published in 1549

There was never anything by the wit of man so well devised, or so surely established, which in continuance of time hath not been corrupted, as (among other things) it may plainly appear by the common prayers in the Church, commonly called divine service: the first and original ground whereof, if a man would search out by the ancient fathers, he shall find that the same was not ordained, but of good purpose, and for a great advancement of godliness. For they so ordered the matter that the whole Bible (or the greatest part thereof) should be read over once in the year, intending thereby, that the clergy (and specially such as were ministers of the congregation) should by often reading and meditation of God's word be stirred up to godliness themselves, and be more able to exhort others by wholesome doctrine, and to confute them that were adversaries to the truth. And further, that the people by daily hearing of holy Scripture read in the Church should continually profit more and more in the knowledge of God, and be the more inflamed with the love of his true religion.

But these many years past, this godly and decent order of the ancient fathers hath been so altered, broken, and neglected, by planting in uncertain stories, legends, responds, verses, vain repetitions, commemorations, and synodals, that commonly when any book of the Bible was begun, before three or four chapters were read out, all the rest were unread. And in this sort the Book of Isaiah was begun in Advent, and the book of Genesis in Septuagesima; but they were only begun and never read through. After a like sort were other books of holy Scripture used.

And moreover, whereas Saint Paul would have such language spoken to the people in the church as they might understand and have profit by hearing the same, the service in this Church of England (these many years) hath been read in Latin to the people, which they understand not; so that they have heard with their ears only; and their hearts, spirit and mind have not been edified thereby. Moreover the number and hardness of the rules, the manifold changings of the service, was the cause that to turn to the book was so hard and intricate a matter, that many times there was more business to find out what should be read, than to read it when it was found out.

These inconveniences therefore considered: here is set such an order, whereby the same shall be redressed. Furthermore by this order, the curates shall need none other books for their public service but this book and the Bible: by the means whereof the people shall not be at so great charge for books as in time past they have been.

And where heretofore, there hath been great diversity in saying and singing in churches within this realm, some following Salisbury use, some Hereford use, some the use of Bangor, some of York, and some of Lincoln: now from henceforth, all the whole realm shall have but one use.

alternative reading

A Reading from *A Defense of the True and Catholic Doctrine of the Sacrament of the Body and Blood of our Savior Christ* by Thomas Cranmer

As meat and drink do comfort the hungry body, so doth the death of Christ's body and the shedding of his blood comfort the soul, when she is after her sort hungry. There is no kind of meat that is comfortable to the soul, but only the death of Christ's blessed body; nor no kind of drink can quench her thirst, but only the blood-shedding of our Savior Christ, which was shed for her offences.

For as there is a carnal generation and a carnal feeding and nourishment, so is there also a spiritual generation and a spiritual feeding. And as every man, by carnal generation of father and mother, is carnally begotten and born into this mortal life, so is every good Christian spiritually born by Christ unto eternal life. And as every man is carnally fed and nourished in his body by meat and drink, even so is every good Christian man spiritually fed and nourished in his soul by the flesh and blood of our Savior Christ.

And although our carnal generation and our carnal nourishment be known to all men by daily experience and by our common senses; yet this our spiritual generation and our spiritual nutrition be so obscure and hid unto us, that we cannot attain to the true and perfect knowledge and feeling of them but only by faith, which must be grounded upon God's most holy word and sacraments.

And for this consideration our Savior Christ hath not only set forth these things most plainly in his holy word, that we may hear them with our ears; but he hath also ordained one visible sacrament of spiritual regeneration in water, and another visible sacrament of spiritual nourishment in bread and wine, to the intent that, as much as is possible for man, we may see Christ with our eyes, smell him at our noses, taste him with our mouths, grope him with our hands, and perceive him with all our senses. For as the word of God preached putteth Christ into our ears, so likewise these elements of water, bread, and wine, joined to God's word, do after a sacramental manner put Christ into our eyes, mouths, hands, and all our senses.

October 17

Ignatius of Antioch

Bishop of Antioch, Martyr, *c.*115

Ignatius was born probably in Syria in about the year 35 and was either the second or third Bishop of Antioch, the third largest city in the Roman Empire. Nothing is known of his life except his final journey under armed escort to Rome where he was martyred about the year 115. In the course of this journey, he met Polycarp in Smyrna, and wrote a number of letters to various Christian congregations that are among the greatest treasures of the primitive Church. In the face of persecution he appealed to his fellow Christians to maintain unity with their bishop at all costs. His letters reveal his passionate commitment to Christ, and how he longed "to imitate the passion of my God."

A Reading from a letter of Ignatius of Antioch to the Church in Rome as he prepared for his forthcoming death

My prayer that I might live to see you all face to face has been granted. In fact, I have been given more than I asked for, since I now hope to greet you in the chains of a prisoner of Christ Jesus, if his will finds me worthy to reach my journey's end.

One thing only I beg of you: allow me to be a libation poured out to God, while there is still an altar ready for me. Then you can form a choir of love around it and sing hymns of praise to the Father in Christ Jesus for allowing Syria's bishop, summoned from the realms of the rising sun, to have reached the land of its setting. How good it is to be sinking down below the world's horizon toward God that I may rise again into the dawn of his presence!

I am writing to all the churches and assuring them that I am truly in earnest about dying for God, provided you put no obstacles in the way. I beg you to do me no such untimely kindness. Let me be a meal for the beasts, for it is they who can provide my way to God. I am God's wheat, to be ground fine by the teeth of lions so that I become the purest bread for Christ. Intercede with him on my behalf, that by their instrumentality I may be made a sacrifice to God.

All the ends of the earth and all the kingdoms of this world would profit me nothing. As far as I am concerned, to die in Christ Jesus is better than to be king of earth's widest bounds. I seek only him who for our sake died; my whole desire is for him who rose again for us. The pangs of birth are upon me. Have patience with me, my brothers and sisters, and do not shut me out from life, do not wish me to be stillborn. Do not make a present to the world again of one who longs only to be God's; do not try to deceive him with material things. Allow me rather to attain to light, light pure and undefiled; for only when I am come to the light shall I become truly human. Allow me to imitate the passion of my God. If any of you have God within you, let them understand my longings and sympathize with me, because they will know the forces by which I am constrained.

It is the hope of the prince of this world to get hold of me and undermine my resolve, set as it is upon God. Let none of you lend him any assistance, but take my part instead, for indeed it is the part of God. Do not have Jesus Christ on your lips, and the world in your heart; do not cherish thoughts of grudging me my fate. Even if I were to come and beg you in person, do not yield to my pleading; keep your mind focused on this written resolve. Here and now, as I write in the fullness of life, I am longing for death with all the passion of a lover. Earthly longings have been crucified; there is no spark of desire for mundane things left within me, but only a murmur of living water that whispers within me, "Come to the Father."

October 18

Saint Luke the Evangelist

Luke was a dear friend of the Apostle Paul, and is mentioned by him three times in his Letters. Paul describes him as "the beloved physician" and, in his Second Letter to Timothy, as his only companion in prison. He is believed to be the author of the Gospel that bears his name, and that of the Acts of the Apostles. Luke's narrative of the life of Christ has a pictorial quality and shows the sequential pattern from the nativity through to the death and resurrection. The developed sense of theology that comes over in Paul's writings is virtually unknown in those of Luke but, as a Gentile, Luke makes clear that the good news of salvation is for all, regardless of gender, social position or nationality. Traditionally, Luke is said to have written his Gospel in Greece and to have died in Boeotia at the age of eighty-four.

A Reading from a homily of Gregory the Great

Our Lord and Savior teaches us sometimes through what he says, and sometimes through what he does. For his deeds are teachings in themselves, because when he does something, even without commenting on it, he is showing us what we ought to do. For example, according to Luke, he sent out his disciples to preach in pairs, because the precepts of charity are two-fold: to love God and to love our neighbor. Charity cannot exist except between two persons: love is only possible when we reach out to another.

Our Lord sent out his disciples to preach in pairs, thereby implying that someone who has no love for people should never take on the task of preaching. Very significant too is the statement that he "sent them ahead of him into every city and place where he himself was to come." For our Lord follows in the wake of those who preach him. Preaching paves the way, and then our Lord himself comes to make his home in our souls. Initially we hear words to challenge us, and through their agency our minds become receptive to the truth. It was for this reason that through the mouth of Isaiah preachers are commanded to: "Prepare the way of the Lord; make straight in the desert the paths of our God."

But now listen to what our Lord has to say after sending out those who are to preach: "The harvest is plentiful but the laborers are few. Pray therefore the Lord of the harvest to send out laborers into his harvest." There are only a few laborers for so huge a harvest, something we cannot mention without sadness, because, although there are many who crave to hear the good news, there are few to preach it. The world is full of priests, and yet it is rare that you find one of them at work in God's harvest. We accept the role, but refuse the hard work.

But as for you, my dear brothers and sisters, ponder well the Lord's command. Pray indeed the Lord of the harvest to send out laborers into his harvest. And pray for us that we may be able to serve you as you deserve, that our tongue may never grow tired of exhorting you, lest having undertaken this office of preaching, our silence condemn us in the sight of our just judge.

October 19

Henry Martyn

Priest, and Missionary to India and Persia, 1812

Born in Truro in 1781, Henry Martyn went to Cambridge at the age of sixteen. He became an avowed evangelical and his friendship with Charles Simeon led to his interest in missionary work. In 1805, he left for Calcutta as a chaplain to the East India Company. The expectation was that he would minister to the British expatriate community, not to the indigenous peoples; in fact, there was a constant fear of insurrection and even the recitation of the Magnificat at Evensong was forbidden, lest "putting down the mighty from their seats" should incite the natives. Henry set about learning the local languages and then supervised the translation of the New Testament first into Hindustani and then into Persian and Arabic, as well as preaching and teaching in mission schools. He went to Persia to continue the work but, suffering from tuberculosis, he died in Armenia on this day in 1812.

A Reading from the *Indian Journal* of Henry Martyn

January 1, 1807—Dinapore
Seven years have passed away since I was first called of God. Before the conclusion of another seven years, how probable is it that these hands will have moldered into dust! But be it so: my soul through grace hath received the assurance of eternal life, and I see the days of my pilgrimage shortening without a wish to add to their number. But oh, may I be stirred up to a faithful discharge of my high and awful work; and laying aside as much as may be,

because the Lord has brought me safely to India and permitted me to begin, in one sense, my missionary work.

My trials in it have been very few; everything has turned out better than I expected; loving-kindness and tender-mercies have attended me at every step: therefore here will I sing his praise. I have been an unprofitable servant, but the Lord hath not cut me off: I have been wayward and perverse, yet he has brought me further on the way to Zion. Here, then, with sevenfold gratitude and affection would I stop and devote myself to the blissful service of my adorable Lord. May he continue his patience, his grace, his direction, his spiritual influences, and I shall at last surely come off conqueror! May he speedily open my mouth, to make known the mysteries of the gospel, and in great mercy grant that the heathen may receive it and live.

February 18—Buxar

My birthday—twenty-six. With all the numerous occasions for deep humiliation, I have cause for praise in recollecting the promising openings and important changes which have occurred since my last birthday. The Lord, in love, makes me wax stronger and stronger.

Walked after breakfast to a pagoda within the fort at Buxar where a Brahmin read and expounded. It was a scene, I suppose, descriptive of the ancient times of Hindu glory. The Brahmin sat under the shade of a large banyan tree near the pagoda; his hair and beard were white, and his head most gracefully crowned with a garland of flowers. A servant of the Rajah sat on his right hand, at right angles; and the venerable man then sung the Sanskrit verses of the Huribuns, and explained them to him without turning his head, but only his eyes, which had a very dignified effect. I waited for the first pause to ask some questions, which led to a long conversation; and this ended by my attempting to give them a history of redemption. The Rajah's servant was a very modest, pensive man, but did not seem to understand what I said so well as did the old Brahmin who expressed his surprise and pleasure, as well as the other, at finding a Sahib who cared anything about religion. I afterwards sent a copy of the Nagree Gospels to the servant, desiring that it might be given to the Rajah if he would accept it.

I rose at four and left Buxar, and at nine in the evening reached Dinapore again in safety, blessed be God! May my life, thus preserved by God's unceasing providence, be his willing sacrifice.

October 23

Saint James of Jerusalem

Brother of Our Lord Jesus Christ, and Martyr, *c.* 62

Although the gospels speak of opposition to Jesus by the members of his family, the Acts of the Apostles speaks of a James who was "brother of the Lord" and a leader in the church in Jerusalem. It remains unclear whether James was truly a "brother" or half-brother or cousin, but it is clear that his leadership was quickly accepted. Paul's Epistle to the Corinthians speaks of a post-resurrection appearance of the Lord to James (15:7). Tradition names James the first bishop of Jerusalem and Paul speaks of a council at which James seems to have presided and to have summed up the council's conclusions on the church's ministry among Gentiles (15:19).

A Reading from Hegesippus

James, the brother of the Lord, succeeded to the government of the church in conjunction with the apostles. He has been universally called the Just, from the days of the Lord down to the present time. For many bore the name of James; but this one was holy from his mother's womb. He drank no wine or other intoxicating liquor, nor did he eat flesh; no razor came upon his head; he did not anoint himself with oil, nor make use of the bath. He alone was permitted to enter the holy place; for he did not wear any woolen garment, but fine linen only. He alone, I say, was accustomed to go into the temple: and he used to be found kneeling upon his knees, begging forgiveness for the people—so that the skin of his knees became hard like that of a camel's, because of his constantly bending the knee in adoration to God, and begging forgiveness for the people. Therefore, because of his pre-eminent justice, he was called the Just, and Oblias, which signifies in Greek "Defense of the people" and "Justice," in accordance with what the prophets declare concerning him.

Now some persons belonging to the seven sects existing among the people, which have been described by me in the Notes, asked him, "What is the door of Jesus?" And he replied that he was the Savior. Because of this answer, some believed that Jesus is the Christ. But the sects mentioned before did not believe, either in a resurrection or in the coming of One to repay every man according to his works. But those who did believe did so on account of James. So, when many even of the ruling class believed, there was a commotion among the Jews and scribes and Pharisees, who said: " A little more, and we shall have all the people looking for Jesus as the Christ."

They came, therefore, in a body to James, and said, "We entreat you, restrain the people; for they have gone astray in their opinions about Jesus, as if he were the Christ. We entreat thee you to persuade all who have come here for the day of the Passover concerning Jesus. For we all listen to your persuasion, since we, as well as all the people, bear testimony that you are just, and bear partiality to none. Therefore, persuade the people not to entertain erroneous opinions concerning Jesus: for all the people, and we also, listen to your persuasion. Take your stand, then, upon the summit of the Temple, that from that high position you may be clearly seen, and that your words may be plainly audible to all the people. For all the tribes, with the Gentiles also, are come together on account of the Passover."

The aforesaid scribes and Pharisees therefore placed James upon the summit of the temple, and cried aloud to him and said: "O just one, whom we are all bound to obey, because all the people are in error and follow Jesus the crucified, tell us, what is the door of Jesus." And he answered with a loud voice, "Why do you ask me concerning Jesus, the Son of Man? He himself sits in heaven at the right hand of the Great Power, and will come on the clouds of heaven."

And, when many were fully convinced by these words, and offered praise for the testimony of' James, and said, "Hosanna to the Son of David," then again the same Pharisees and scribes said to one another, "We have not done well in procuring this testimony to Jesus. But let us go up and throw him down, that they may be afraid and not believe him." And they cried aloud, and said, "Oh! Oh! The just man himself is in error." Thus they fulfillled the Scripture written in Isaiah, "Let us away with the just man, because he is troublesome to us: therefore they shall eat the fruit of their doings." So they went up and threw down the just man, and said to one another, "Let us stone James the Just." And they began to stone him, for he was not killed by the fall; but he turned, and kneeled down, and said, "I beseech you, Lord God our Father, forgive them, for they know not what they do."

And while they were thus stoning him to death, one of the priests, the sons of Rechab, the son of Rechabim, to whom testimony is borne by Jeremiah the prophet, began to cry aloud, saying, "Cease, what are you doing? The just man is praying for us." But one among them, one of the fullers, took the staff with which he was accustomed to wring out the garments he dyed, and hurled it at the head of the just man. And so he suffered martyrdom: and they buried him on the spot, and the pillar erected to his memory still remains. This man was a true witness to both Jews and Greeks that Jesus is the Christ.

October 26

Alfred the Great

King of the West Saxons, 899

Born in the year 849, Alfred was the King of the West Saxons who effectively brought to an end the constant threat of Danish dominion in the British Isles. He came to the throne at the age of twenty-two and, after establishing peace, set about bringing stability to both church and state. He gave half of his income to founding religious houses, which themselves acted as Christian centers for education, care of the sick and poor and respite for travelers. He was a daily attender at Mass and himself translated many works into the vernacular, an example of which is offered as a reading here. He evolved a legal code based on common sense and Christian mercy. His whole life was marked by the compassion of Christ. He died on this day in the year 899.

A Reading from the *Prose Preface* from King Alfred's translation of Gregory the Great's *Pastoral Care*

I would have it known that very often it has come to my mind what men of learning there were formerly throughout England; both in religious and secular orders; and how there were happy times then throughout England; and how the kings, who had authority over this people, obeyed God and his messengers; and how they not only maintained their peace, morality, and authority at home but also extended their territory outside; and how they succeeded both in warfare and in wisdom; and also how eager were the religious orders both in teaching and in learning as well as in all the holy services which it was their duty to perform for God; and how people from abroad sought wisdom and instruction in this country; and how nowadays, if we wished to acquire these things, we would have to seek them outside.

Learning had declined so thoroughly in England that there were very few on this side of the Humber who could understand their divine services in English, or even translate a single letter from Latin into English: and I suppose that there were not many beyond the Humber either. There were so few of them that I cannot recollect even a single one south of the Thames when I succeeded to the kingdom. Thanks be to God almighty that we now have any supply of teachers at all! Therefore I beseech you to do as I believe you are willing to do: as often as you can, free yourself from worldly affairs so that you may apply that wisdom which God gave you wherever you can. Remember what punishments befell us in this world when we ourselves did not cherish learning nor transmit it to others. We were Christians in name alone, and very few of us possessed Christian virtues.

When I reflected on all this, I recollected how before everything was ransacked and burned the churches throughout England stood filled with treasures and books. Similarly, there was a great multitude of those serving God. And they derived very little benefit from those books, because they could understand nothing of them, since they were not written in their own language. It is as if they had said: "Our ancestors, who formerly maintained these places, loved wisdom, and through it they obtained wealth and passed it on to us. Here one can still see their track, but we cannot follow it." Therefore we have now lost the wealth as well as the wisdom, because we did not wish to set our minds to the track.

Therefore it seems better to me that we too should turn into the language that we can all understand certain books which are the most necessary for all to know, and accomplish this, as with God's help we may very easily do provided we have peace enough, so that all the free-born young men now in England who have the means to apply themselves to it, may be set to learning (as long as they are not useful for some other employment) until the time that they can read English writings properly. Thereafter one may instruct in Latin those whom one wishes to teach further and wishes to advance to holy orders.

A Reading from *The Life of King Alfred*
by Bishop Asser

In the year of the Lord's Incarnation 849, Alfred, King of the Anglo-Saxons, was born at the royal estate called Wantage, in the district known as Berkshire. In 853, King Ethelwulf sent his son Alfred to Rome in state, accompanied by a great number of both nobles and commoners. At this time the lord Pope Leo was ruling the apostolic see; he anointed the child Alfred as king, ordaining him properly, received him as an adoptive son and confirmed him.

Now Alfred was greatly loved, more than all his brothers, by his father and mother and indeed by everybody with a universal and profound love, and he was always brought up in the royal court and nowhere else. In spite of all the demands of the present life, it was the desire for wisdom, more than anything else, together with the nobility of his birth, which characterized the nature of his noble mind; but alas, by the shameful negligence of his parents and tutors, Alfred remained ignorant of letters until his twelfth year, or even longer. However, he was a careful listener, by day and night, to English poems, most frequently hearing them recited by others, and he readily retained them in his memory.

He learned by heart the "daily round," that is, the services of the hours, and then certain psalms and prayers; these he collected in a single book, which he kept by him day and night, as I have seen for myself; amid all the affairs of the present life he took it around with him everywhere for the sake of prayer, and was inseparable from it. But alas, he could not satisfy his craving for what he desired the most, namely the liberal arts; for, as he used to say, there were no good scholars in the entire kingdom of the West Saxons at that time.

He used to affirm with repeated complaints and sighing from the depths of his heart, that among all the difficulties and burdens of his present life this had become the greatest: namely, that at the time when he was of the right age and had the leisure and the capacity for learning, he did not have the teachers. For when he was older, and more incessantly preoccupied day and night or rather harassed by all kinds of illnesses unknown to the physicians of this island, as well as by the cares (both domestic and foreign) of the royal office, and also by the incursions of the Vikings by land and sea, he had the teachers and scribes to some extent, but he was unable to study.

He similarly applied himself attentively to charity and distribution of alms to the native population and to foreign visitors of all races, showing immense and incomparable kindness and generosity to all, as well as to the investigation of things unknown. Wherefore many Franks, Frisians, Gauls, Vikings, Welshmen, Irishmen and Bretons subjected themselves willingly to his lordship, nobles and commoners alike; and, as befitted his royal status, he ruled, loved, honored, and enriched them all with wealth and authority, just as he did his own people.

October 28

Saint Simon and Saint Jude

Apostles

Simon and Jude were named among the twelve apostles in the Gospels of Matthew, Mark and Luke. Simon is called "the Zealot," probably because he belonged to a nationalist resistance movement opposing the Roman occupation forces. There is no indication in the Gospels whether Simon moved from the Zealot party to be a follower of Christ or, on the other hand, if after the resurrection he became a supporter of that group, seeing it as a response to God's call to proclaim the kingdom. Luke describes Jude as the son of James, while the Letter of Jude has him as the brother of James, neither of which negates the other. It seems he was the same person as Thaddaeus, which may have been a last name. Owing to the similarity of his name to that of Judas Iscariot, Jude was rarely invoked in prayer and it seems likely that because of this, interceding through him was seen as a final resort when all else failed. He became known, therefore, as the patron saint of lost causes! The two apostles are joined together on October 28 because a church, which recently had acquired their relics, was dedicated to their memory in Rome on this day in the seventh century.

A Reading from the homilies of Origen
on the Book of Joshua

All of us who believe in Christ Jesus are said to be living stones, according to the words of Scripture: "Like living stones, let yourselves be built into a spiritual house, to be a holy priesthood, to offer spiritual sacrifices acceptable to God through Jesus Christ."

When we look at the construction of earthly buildings, we can see how the largest and strongest stones are always set in the foundations, so that the weight of the whole building can rest securely on them. In the same way you should understand how some of the living stones referred to by Scripture have become the foundations of a spiritual building. And who are those foundation stones? The apostles and the prophets. This is what Paul himself declares in his teaching: "You are built upon the foundation of the apostles and prophets, Christ Jesus himself being the cornerstone."

You should learn that Christ himself is also the foundation of the building we are describing, so that you may more eagerly prepare yourselves for the construction, and be found to be one of those stones strong enough to be laid close to the foundation. For these are the words of Paul the Apostle, "No other foundation can anyone lay than that which is laid, namely Christ Jesus." Blessed are those, therefore, who will be found to have constructed sacred and religious buildings upon such a glorious foundation!

But in this building of the Church there must also be an altar. From this I conclude that those of you who are ready and prepared to give up your time to prayer, to offer petitions and sacrifices of supplication to God day and night, such people I say will be the living stones out of which Jesus will build his altar.

Reflect upon the praise that is lavished upon these stones of the altar. "Moses the lawgiver," Joshua said, "ordered that an altar be built out of unhewn stones, untouched by a chisel." Who now are these unhewn stones? Perhaps these unhewn, undefiled stones could be said to be the holy apostles, who together make one altar by reason of their harmony and unity. For Scripture tells that, as the apostles prayed together with one accord they opened their mouths and said, "You, Lord, know the hearts of all."

These then, who were able to pray with one mind, with one voice and in one spirit, are perhaps worthy of being employed together to form an altar upon which Jesus may offer his sacrifice to the Father.

But let us too strive to be of one mind among ourselves, and to speak with one heart and voice. Let us never act out of anger or vainglory, but united in belief and purpose, let us hope that God may find us stones fit for his altar.

October 29

James Hannington
Bishop of Eastern Equatorial Africa, and his Companions, Martyrs, 1885

James Hannington was born in 1847 of a Congregationalist family but he became an Anglican before going to Oxford. He was ordained and, after serving a curacy for five years, went with the Church Missionary Society to Uganda. He was consecrated bishop for that part of Africa in 1884 and a year later began a safari inland from Mombasa, together with other European and indigenous Christians. He (or his guides) made the mistake of attempting to enter Uganda from the east, through Busoga, the traditional approach of the enemy. The King of the Buganda, Mwanga, who was already suspicious of white men, also despised Christians because they refused to condone his moral turpitude. He seized the whole party, tortured them for several days and then had them butchered to death on this day in the year1885.

A Reading from the Last Journals of James Hannington

Every morning during that hard-fought journey James Hannington greeted the sunrise with his travelling psalm, saying: "I will lift up mine eyes unto the hills, from whence cometh my help." He often encouraged his companions in times of doubt and difficulty with the words: "Never be disappointed, only praise." His last journals record his anxiety that his travelling companions, in spite of repeated reassurances to the contrary, were in fact uncertain of the path they were taking. On Wednesday October 21, 1885 he and his retainers were taken prisoner by Chief Mwanga's men. The last disjointed entries in his journal read as follows:

Friday, October 23
I woke full of pain and weak, so that with the utmost difficulty I crawled outside and sat in a chair, and yet they guard every move as if I were a giant. My nerves too have received such a shock that, after some loud yells and war cries arising outside the prison fence, I expected to be murdered, and simply turned over and said: "Let the Lord do as he sees fit; I shall not make the slightest resistance."

Seeing how bad I am, they have sent for my tent for me to use in the daytime. Going outside I fell to the ground exhausted, and had to be helped back inside in a poor condition to my bed. I don't see how I can stand all this, and yet I don't want to give in, but it almost seems as if Uganda itself is going to be forbidden ground to me.

Wednesday, October 28
A terrible night, first with noisy drunken guards, and secondly with vermin which have found out my tent and swarm. I don't think I got one hour's sound sleep, and woke with fever fast developing. O Lord, do have mercy upon me and release me. I am quite broken down and brought low. Comforted by reading Psalm twenty-seven.

In an hour or two fever has developed quite rapidly. My tent is so stuffy that am obliged to go inside the filthy hut. Delirious.

Thursday, October 29
I hear no news, but was much upheld by Psalm thirty which came to me with great power. A hyena howled near me last night, smelling a sick man, but I hope it is not to have me yet.

These are the last words in his little pocket-diary. According to a boy called Ukutu, one of Bishop Hannington's porters who escaped the general massacre of his party, later that morning the guards came and bound the bishop. As they led him off to the spot where he was to be murdered, he sang hymns nearly all the way. The only English word the African boy recognized in what the Bishop sang was one that recurred frequently: Jesus.

alternative reading

A Reading from *A History of Christian Missions*
by Stephen Neill

When the Churches of the West were rich and their countries powerful, when the missionary impulse reawoke after 1790, it was natural for Western Churches to be "sending" churches and the other countries to be only on the receiving end. It could not have been otherwise. With the existence of a universal Church a new period dawned. The terms "sending" and "receiving" lost much of their meaning. Quickly the terms "older churches" and "younger churches" grew out of date. At the Second Vatican Council the black bishops of Africa contributed to the debates with mellow wisdom. Christians everywhere had the same work: to present Christian faith and life in the world, Western, Eastern, or Southern, which has its doubts, hostilities, and rival philosophies of life.

The age of missions ended. The age of mission began.

It was still different in different societies. To be a Christian in a half-Christian or post-Christian society, even in an officially anti-Christian but formerly Christian society, is not the same task as to be a Christian in an area which has never heard the gospel before, in a speech which was never used there before, in a society where the organization was never touched by Christian principles. A third of the people in the world, perhaps, have not yet heard the name of Jesus Christ, and another third, perhaps, have never heard the gospel presented in such a way as both to be intelligible and to make a claim on their personal lives. There is plenty still to be done.

In this narration we have not tried at any point to conceal the weakness of human endeavor—the sinfulness and pettiness of the agents, the blind selfishness of the Churches, the niggardliness of the support that they have given to the work of the gospel, the mistakes that have been made, the treacheries, the catastrophes, the crimes by which the record is sullied. And yet the Church is there today, the Body of Christ in every land, the great miracle of history, in which the living God himself through his Holy Spirit is pleased to dwell.

NOVEMBER

November 1

All Saints' Day

From its earliest days, the church has recognized as its foundation stones those heroes of the faith whose lives have excited others to holiness and have assumed a communion with the church on earth and the church in heaven. Celebrating the Feast of All Saints began in the fourth century. At first, it was observed on the Sunday after the Feast of Pentecost; this was to link the disciples who received the gift of the Holy Spirit at Pentecost, the foundation of the church, with those who were martyrs, giving their lives as witnesses for tshe faith. In the eighth century, a pope dedicated a chapel to All Saints in Saint Peter's at Rome on November 1, and within a century this day was being observed in England and Ireland as "All Saints' Day."

A Reading from a sermon of Bernard of Clairvaux

Why should our praise and glorification, or even our celebration of this feast day, mean anything to the saint? What do they care about earthly honors when their heavenly Father honors them by fulfilling the faithful promise of his Son? What does our commemoration mean to them? The saints have no need of honor from us; neither does our devotion add the slightest thing to what is already theirs. Clearly, when we venerate their memory, it is serving us, not them. But I tell you, when I think of them, I feel myself inflamed by a tremendous longing to be with them.

Calling the saints to mind inspires, or rather arouses in us, above all else, a longing to enjoy their company which is desirable in itself. We long to share in the citizenship of heaven, to dwell with the spirits of the blessed, to join the assembly of patriarchs, the ranks of the prophets, the council of apostles, the great host of martyrs, the noble company of confessors and the choir of virgins. In short, we long to be united in happiness with all the saints. But our dispositions change. The church of all the first followers of Christ awaits us, but we do nothing about it. The saints want us to be with them, and we are indifferent. The souls of the just await us, and we ignore them.

Come, let us at length spur ourselves on. We must rise again with Christ, we must seek the world which is above and set our mind on the things of heaven. Let us long for those who are longing for us, hasten to those who are waiting for us, and ask those who look for our coming to intercede for us. We should not only want to be with the saints, we should also hope to possess their happiness. While we desire to be in their company, we must also earnestly seek to share in their glory. Do not imagine that there is anything harmful in such an ambition as this; there is no danger in setting our hearts on such glory.

When we commemorate the saints we are inflamed with another yearning: that Christ our life may also appear to us as he appeared to them and that we may one day share in his glory. Until then we see him, not as he is, but as he became for our sake. He is our head, crowned, not with glory, but with the thorns of our sins. As members of that head, crowned with thorns, we should be ashamed to live in luxury; his purple robes are a mockery rather than an honor. When Christ comes again, his death shall no longer be proclaimed, and we shall know that we also have died, and that our life is hidden with him. The glorious head of the Church will appear and his glorified members will shine in splendor with him, when he transforms this lowly body anew into such glory as belongs to himself, its head.

Therefore, we should aim at attaining this glory with a wholehearted and prudent desire. That we may rightly hope and strive for such blessedness, we must above all seek the prayers of the saints, that what is beyond our own efforts to obtain may be granted through their intercession.

alternative reading

A Reading from a treatise by Hugh Latimer

As touching the saints in heaven, they be not our mediators by way of redemption; for so Christ alone is our mediator and theirs both: so that the blood of martyrs hath nothing to do by way of redemption; the blood of Christ is enough for a thousand worlds. But by way of intercession, so saints in heaven may be mediators, and pray for us: as I think they do when we call not upon them; for they be charitable, and need no spurs.

We have no open bidding of God in Scripture to call upon them, as we have to call upon God, nor yet we may call upon them without any diffidence or mistrust in God; for God is more charitable, more merciful, more able, more ready to help than them all. So that, though we may desire the saints in heaven to pray God for us, yet it is not so necessary to be done, but that we may pray to God ourselves, without making suit first to them, and obtain of him whatsoever we need, if we continue in prayer; so that, whatsoever we ask the Father in the name of Christ his Son, the Father will give it us. For saints can give nothing without him, but he can without them; as he did give to them. Scripture doth set saints that be departed before our eyes for examples; so that the chiefest and most principal worship and honoring of them is to know their holy living, and to follow them, as they followed Christ.

God biddeth us come to him with prayer; and to do his bidding is no presuming. It is rather presuming to leave it undone, to do that which he biddeth us not do. We must have saints in reverent memory; and learn at God's goodness toward them to trust in God; and mark well their faith toward God and his word, their charity toward their neighbor, their patience in all adversity; and pray to God which gave them grace so to do, that we may do likewise, for which like doings we shall have like speedings: they be well honored when God is well pleased. The saints were not saints by praying to saints, but by believing in him that made them saints; and as they were saints, so may we be saints also.

alternative reading

A Reading from *The Vision of God* by Kenneth Kirk

Although Jesus spoke little about "seeing God," he brought God more vividly before the spiritual eyes of his contemporaries than any other person has ever done. He gave a vision of God where others could only speak of it. It is worth while to consider for a moment the importance of this factor in his teaching.

There must be both ethics and doctrine in every gospel we present to the world. But the moment ethics predominates over doctrine the moment, that is, that the thought of man ousts the thought of God from the place of primary honor the whole purpose of a gospel is undone, whether the gospel be Christian or any other. Ethics, or teaching about man and the conduct proper to him, centers a person's thoughts upon himself; and the end of self-centerlines is unethical and unevangelical alike. It is bound to result as Saint Paul so clearly showed either in spiritual pride or in spiritual despair: and by neither of these roads can we find our true destiny. The path of purity, humility, and self-sacrifice is only possible to those who can *forget* themselves, can disinfect themselves from egoism; where the mind is centered not upon self, but at least upon one's fellows and their needs, and at most and at best upon God and our neighbors seen through the eyes of God. We cannot by thinking add a cubit to our stature: still less can we, by thinking about ourselves and our conduct, achieve that self-forgetfulness or self-sacrifice which is the hall-mark of the saints.

It would be absurd to say that self-criticism and self-examination play no part in the making of saintliness. But the essential fact about religion in its relation to ethics is this that self-examination and self-criticism are dangerous in the highest degree unless the soul is already reaching out in self-forgetfulness to something higher and better than itself. Self-centerlines, even in the morally earnest, is the greatest snare in life: "God-centerlines" the only true salvation. This throws a flood of light upon the whole of the New Testament. It makes it clear why Jesus spoke first and foremost of God, and only in the second place of man and human conduct. And it gives a reason why the Church fixed upon the single text in the beatitudes "Blessed are the pure in heart, for they shall see God" and elevated it into the summary of all that it had to give to the world.

Where the best Christian thought about the vision of God has differed from non-Christian aspiration is in its emphasis upon the *attitude* rather than upon the *experiences* of worship. What matters is that we should look toward God, rather than that we should here and now receive the vision. But that there is such a vision, and that it is attainable, theology no less than experience affirms. Not only do the saints see God in heaven not only has the Church seen him in the face of Jesus Christ on earth; for the inspiration and renewal of the individual it has been insisted that the pure in heart shall from time to time have personal experience of God and intercourse with him, both in their prayers and even in the ordinary activities of life.

A Reading from *New Seeds of Contemplation*
by Thomas Merton

The forms and individual characters of living and growing things, of inanimate beings, of animals and flowers and all nature, constitute their holiness in the sight of God. Their inscape is their sanctity. It is the imprint of his wisdom and his reality in them.

The special clumsy beauty of this particular colt on this April day in this field under these clouds is a holiness consecrated to God by his own creative wisdom and it declares the glory of God. The pale flowers of the dogwood outside this window are saints. The little yellow flowers that nobody notices on the edge of that road are saints looking up into the face of God. This leaf has its own texture and its own pattern of veins and its own holy shape, and the bass and trout hiding in the deep pools of the river are canonized by their beauty and their strength. The lakes hidden among the hills are saints, and the sea too is a saint who praises God without interruption in her majestic dance. The great, gashed, half-naked mountain is another of God's saints. There is no other like him. He is alone in his own character; nothing else in the world ever did or ever will imitate God in quite the same way. That is his sanctity.

But what about you? What about me? Unlike the animals and the trees, it is not enough to be what our nature intends. It is not enough for us to be individuals. For us, holiness is more than humanity. If we are never anything but people, we will not be saints and we will not be able to offer to God the worship of our imitation, which is sanctity.

It is true to say that for me sanctity consists in being *myself*, and for you sanctity consists in being *yourself* and that, in the last analysis, your sanctity will never be mine and mine will never be yours, except in the communism of charity and grace.

For me to be a saint means to be myself. Therefore the problem of sanctity and salvation is in fact the problem of finding out who I am and of discovering my true self. Trees and animals have no problem. God makes them what they are without consulting them, and they are perfectly satisfied.

With us it is different. God leaves us free to be whatever we like. We can be ourselves or not, as we please. We are at liberty to be real, or to be unreal. We may be true or false, the choice is ours. We may wear now one mask and now another, and never, if we so desire, appear with our own true face. But we cannot make these choices with impunity. Causes have effects, and if we lie to ourselves and to others, then we cannot expect to find truth and reality whenever we happen to want them. If we have chosen the way of falsity we must not be surprised that truth eludes us when we finally come to need it!

Our vocation is not simply to be, but to work together with God in the creation of our own life, our own identity, our own destiny. We are free beings and children of God. This means to say that we should not passively exist, but actively participate in his creative freedom, in our own lives, and in the lives of others, by choosing the truth. To put it better, we are even called to share with God the work of *creating* the truth of our identity.

We do not know clearly beforehand what the result of this work will be. The secret of my full identity is hidden in God. He alone can make me who I am, or rather who I will be when at last I fully begin to be. But unless I desire this identity and work to find it with God and in God, the work will never be done.

November 2

All Faithful Departed

The commemoration of all the faithful departed (commonly known as All Souls' Day) on the day following All Saints' Day began as a monastic custom at the great abbey of Cluny. Under the influence of Abbot Odilo, who in 998 ordered its observance in all Cluniac houses, the custom gradually spread until by the thirteenth century it was universal throughout the Western Church. The medieval rite contained the famous sequence Dies Irae. *Although the observance did not survive the liturgical changes of the Reformation, it was restored in the proposed English* 1928 Book of Common Prayer, *largely in response to the huge weight of grief following the First World War. In recent years it has become increasingly customary to hold a service (either this day or at this season) for the bereaved. In a society that has largely abandoned traditional patterns of mourning, the opportunity to express grief continues to have a valued place in the ministry of the Church. Various readings from the Church's tradition are offered here which acknowledge the hard and painful reality of death in the "sure and certain hope of the resurrection to eternal life." In the words of the Anglican-Roman Catholic International Commission:*

"The believer's pilgrimage of faith is lived out with the mutual support of all the people of God. In Christ all the faithful, both living and departed, are bound together in a communion of prayer."

A Reading from an oration of Gregory of Nazianzus

"What are human beings that you should be mindful of us, mere mortals that you should care for us?" What is this new mystery confronting me? I am both small and great, both lowly and exalted, mortal and immortal, earthly and heavenly. I am to be buried with Christ and to rise again with him, to become a co-heir with him, a son of God, and indeed God himself.

This is what the great mystery means for us; this is why God became human and became poor for our sake: it was to raise up our flesh, to recover the divine image in us, to re-create humankind, so that all of us might become one in Christ who perfectly became in us everything that he is himself. So we are no longer to be "male and female, barbarian and Scythian, slave and free" distinctions deriving from the flesh but to bear within ourselves only the seal of God, by whom and for which we were created. We are to be so formed and molded by him that we are recognized as belonging to his one family.

If only we could be now what we hope to be, by the great kindness of our generous God! He asks so little and gives so much in this life and in the next, to those who love him sincerely. In a spirit of hope and out of love for God, let us then "bear and endure all things" and give thanks for everything that befalls us, since even reason can often recognize these things as weapons to win salvation. Meanwhile let us commend to God our own souls and the souls of those who, being more ready for it, have reached the place of rest before us although they walked the same road as we do now.

Lord and creator of all, and especially of your human creatures, you are the God and Father and ruler of your children; you are the Lord of life and death; you are the guardian and benefactor of our souls. You fashion and transform all things in their due season through your creative Word, as you know to be best in your deep wisdom and providence. Receive this day those who have gone ahead of us in our journey from this life.

And receive us too at the proper time, when you have guided us in our bodily life as long as may be profitable for us. Receive us prepared indeed by fear of you, but not troubled, not shrinking back on the day of our death or uprooted by force like those who are lovers of the world and the flesh. Instead, may we set out eagerly for that eternal and blessed life which is in Christ Jesus our Lord. To him be the glory for ever and ever.

alternative reading

A Reading from a treatise by Hugh Latimer

The faithful departed have charity in such surety that they cannot lose it, so that they cannot murmur nor grudge against God; cannot be displeased with God; cannot be dissevered from God; cannot die, nor be in peril of death; cannot be damned, nor be in peril of damnation; cannot be but in surety of salvation.

They be members of the mystical body of Christ as we be, and in more surety than we be. They love us charitably. Charity is not idle: if it be, it worketh and sheweth itself: and therefore I say, they wish us well and pray for us. They need not cry loud to God: they be in Christ, and Christ in them. They be in Christ, and Christ with them. They joy in their Lord Christ always, taking thankfully whatsoever God doth with them; ever giving thanks to their Lord God; ever lauding and praising him in all things that he doth; discontent with nothing that he doth.

And forasmuch as they be always in charity, and when they pray for us, they pray always in charity, and be always God's friends, God's children, brothers and sisters to our Savior Christ, even in God's favor, even have Christ with them to offer their prayer to the Father of heaven, to whom they pray in the name of the Son; and we many times for lack of charity, having malice and envy, rancor, hatred, one toward another, be the children of the devil, inheritors of hell, adversaries to Christ, hated of God, his angels and all his saints; they in their state may do us more good with their prayers, than we in this state. And they do us alway good, unless the lack and impediment be in us: for prayer said in charity is more faithful to them that it is said for, and more acceptable to God, than that which is said out of [lack of] charity. For God looketh not to the work of praying, but to the heart of the prayer.

Thus we may well pray for the departed, and they much better for us: which they will do of their charity, [even] though we desire them not.

alternative reading

A Reading from the *Holy Sonnets* of John Donne

Death be not proud, though some have called thee
Mighty and dreadful, for, thou art not so,
For, those, whom thou think'st, thou dost overthrow,
Die not, poor death, nor yet canst thou kill me;
From rest and sleep, which but thy pictures be,
Much pleasure, then from thee, much more must flow,
And soonest our best men with thee do go,
Rest of their bones, and soul's delivery.
Thou art slave to fate, chance, kings, and desperate men,
And dost with poison, war, and sickness dwell,
And poppy, or charms can make us sleep as well,
And better than thy stroke; why swell'st thou then?
One short sleep past, we wake eternally,
And death shall be no more: Death thou shalt die.

alternative reading

A Reading from a sermon preached in All Souls College, Oxford, by Austin Farrer

"May they rest in peace, and may light perpetual shine upon them"—those millions among whom our friends are lost, those millions for whom we cannot choose but pray; because prayer is a sharing in the love of the heart of God, and the love of God is earnestly set toward the salvation of his spiritual creatures, by, through and out of the fire that purifies them.

The arithmetic of death perplexes our brains. What can we do but throw ourselves upon the infinity of God? It is only to a finite mind that number is an obstacle, or multiplicity a distraction. Our mind is like a box of limited content, out of which one thing must be emptied before another can find a place. The universe of creatures is queuing for a turn of our attention, and no appreciable part of the queue will ever get a turn. But no queue forms before the throne of everlasting mercy, because the nature of an infinite mind is to be simply aware of everything that is.

Everything is simply present to an infinite mind, because it exists; or rather, exists because it is present to that making mind.

And though by some process of averaging and calculation I should compute the grains of sand, it would be like the arithmetic of the departed souls, an empty sum; I could not tell them as they are told in the infinity of God's counsels, each one separately present as what it is, and simply because it is.

The thought God gives to any of his creatures is not measured by the attention he can spare, but by the object for consideration they can supply. God is not divided; it is God, not a part of God, who applies himself to the falling sparrow, and to the crucified Lord. But there is more in the beloved Son than in the sparrow, to be observed and loved and saved by God. So every soul that has passed out of this visible world, as well as every soul remaining within it, is caught and held in the unwavering beam of divine care. And we may comfort ourselves for our own inability to tell the grains of sand, or to reckon the thousands of millions of the departed.

And yet we cannot altogether escape so; for our religion is not a simple relation of every soul separately to God, it is a mystical body in which we are all members one of another. And in this mystical body it does not suffice that every soul should be embraced by the thoughts of God; it has also to be that every soul should, in its thought, embrace the other souls. For apart from this mutual embracing, it would be unintelligible why we should pray at all, either for the living or for the departed. Such prayer is nothing but the exercising of our membership in the body of Christ. God is not content to care for us each severally, unless he can also, by his Holy Spirit in each one of us, care through and in us for all the rest. Every one of us is to be a focus of that divine life of which the attractive power holds the body together in one.

So even in the darkness and blindness of our present existence, our thought ranges abroad and spreads out toward the confines of the mystical Christ, remembering the whole Church of Christ, as well militant on earth as triumphant in heaven; invoking angels, archangels and all the spiritual host.

November 3

Richard Hooker

Priest, 1600

Born in Heavitree in Exeter in about 1554, Richard Hooker came under the influence of John Jewel, Bishop of Salisbury, in his formative years and through that influence went up to Corpus Christi College, Oxford, where he became a Fellow. He was ordained and then married, becoming a parish priest and, in 1585, Master of the Temple in London. Hooker became one of the strongest advocates of the position of the Church of England and defended its "middle way" between puritanism and papalism. Perhaps his greatest work was Of the Laws of Ecclesiastical Polity *which he wrote as the result of engaging in controversial debates. He showed Anglicanism as rooted firmly in Scripture as well as tradition, affirming its continuity with the pre-Reformation* Ecclesia Anglicana, *but now both catholic and reformed. Hooker became a parish priest again near Canterbury and died there on this day in the year 1600.*

A Reading from *The Laws of Ecclesiastical Polity*
by Richard Hooker

We are in God through Christ eternally according to that intent and purpose whereby we were chosen to be made his in this present world before the world itself was made. We are in God through the knowledge which is had of us, and the love which is borne toward us from everlasting. For his Church he knoweth and loveth, so that they which are in the Church are thereby known to be in him.

For in Christ we are by our actual incorporation into that society which hath him for their head, and doth make together with him one body, he and they in that respect having one name; by virtue of this mystical conjunction, we are of him and in him even as though our very flesh and bones should be made continuate with his. We are in Christ because he knoweth and loveth us even as parts of himself. No man is in him but they in whom he actually is. For he which hath not the Son of God hath not life. "I am the vine and you are the branches: he which abideth in me and I in him the same bringeth forth much fruit"; but the branch severed from the vine withereth. We are, therefore, adopted sons of God to eternal life by participation of the only-begotten Son of God, whose life is the wellspring and cause of ours.

It is too cold an interpretation, whereby some men expound our being in Christ to import nothing else, but only that the selfsame nature which maketh us to be men, is in him, and maketh him man as we are. For what man in the world is there which hath not so far forth communion with Jesus Christ? It is not this that can sustain the weight of such sentences as speak of the mystery of our coherence with Jesus Christ. The Church is in Christ as Eve was in Adam. Yea by grace we are every of us in Christ and in his Church, as by nature we are in those our first parents. God made Eve of the rib of Adam. And his Church he frameth out of the very flesh, the very wounded and bleeding side of the Son of Man. His body crucified and his blood shed for the life of the world, are the true elements of that heavenly being which maketh us such as himself is of whom we come. For which cause the words of Adam may be fitly the words of Christ concerning his Church, "flesh of my flesh, and bone of my bones," a true native extract out of mine own body. So that in him even according to his manhood we according to our heavenly being are as branches in that root out of which they grow.

November 3

Martin de Porres

Friar, 1639

Born in Lima in Peru in 1579, Martin de Porres was the illegitimate son of a Spanish knight and a black, Panamanian freewoman. He joined the Third Order of the Dominicans when he was fifteen years old and was later received as a lay brother into the First Order, mainly because of his reputation for caring for the poor and needy. As the friary almoner, he was responsible for the daily distribution to the poor and he had a particular care for the many African slaves, whose lives were a dreadful indictment of the Christian conquistadores. De Porres became sought after for spiritual counsel, unusual for a lay brother at that time. His care for all God's creatures led many to love and revere him, and his own brothers chose him as their spiritual leader. He died of a violent fever on this day in the year 1639 and, because of his care for all, regardless of class or color, is seen as the patron saint of race relations.

A Reading from a homily of Pope John XXIII following the canonization of Martin de Porres on June 3, 1962

Three passions burned in the heart of Brother Martin of Porres: charity, particularly with regard to the poor and the sick, the most rigorous penance, which he regarded as "the price of love," and the humility which fed these virtues. Allow us to dwell particularly on this last, humility, and to contemplate it in Brother Martin's transparent soul.

Humility brings the vision that one has of oneself within the true limits marked out by human reason. It brings to its perfection the gift of the fear of God, by which the Christian, aware that the sovereign good and its authentic greatness are found only in God, offers him a unique and supreme respect, and avoids sin, the only evil which can separate the soul from him. This is the key to the practical wisdom which governs the life of those who are prudent and discreet. "The fear of God is the school of wisdom" we are told in the holy book.

Martin de Porres was the angel of Lima. The novices turned to him in their difficulties, the most important of the Fathers sought advice from him. He reconciled households, healed the most refractory diseases, brought enmities to an end, resolved theological disputes, and gave his decisive opinion on the most difficult of matters. What an abundance of wisdom, balance and goodness was found in his heart! He was not a learned man, but he possessed that true knowledge which ennobles the spirit, the "inner light in the heart" which God gives to those who fear him, that "light of discernment" of which Saint Catherine of Siena speaks. In his soul there reigned the holy fear of God, the foundation of all upbringing, of true spiritual progress, and, in the last analysis, of civilization itself. "The fear of God is the beginning of wisdom."

When we see him raised to the honors of the altar, we admire Martin de Porres with the delight of one who gazes upon a magnificent panorama from the top of a mountain. But it must not be forgotten that humility is the way which leads to these heights: "Humility goes before glory." The higher the building, the deeper must be the foundations. As Saint Augustine wrote: "Before the building is raised, it must go down: before putting on the roof, the foundations must be dug." Martin teaches us the same lesson.

May the light of his life guide all people on the path of Christian social justice and of universal love without distinction of color or race.

November 6

Leonard

Hermit, 6th century

According to an eleventh-century Life, *Leonard was a sixth-century Frankish nobleman who refused a bishopric to become first a monk, then a hermit, at Noblac (now Saint-Léonard) near Limoges. The miracles attributed to him, both during his lifetime and after his death, caused a widespread cultus throughout Europe and, in England alone, over a hundred and seventy churches are dedicated to him. His popularity in England may also be due in part to the enthusiasm of returning crusaders, who looked to him as the patron saint of prisoners.*

A Reading from *Pastoral Care* by Gregory the Great

A leader should be exemplary in conduct, so that his manner of life may itself indicate the way of life to his people, and the flock, following the teaching and conduct of its shepherd, will fare better because it is nourished on example and not mere words. For it is clear that by the nature of his role, a leader is bound to set forth the highest ideals, and must therefore live by them himself. His words will permeate the hearts of his hearers more effectively if his way of life commends what he preaches. What he promotes in words, he will enable to be fulfilled by example.

In the prophecy of Isaiah it is written: "Get you up to a high mountain, O Zion, herald of good tidings." In other words, those who preach the things of heaven must themselves have abandoned the lower things of earth, and be already scaling the heights. From such a height, a leader will the more readily draw his people, for the integrity of his life will sound forth to all below.

Through active sympathy a leader should seek to be a neighbor to all his people, and through contemplation seek to maintain a clear perspective, so that through his heart of compassion he can transfer to himself the infirmities of others, and through the heights of contemplation transcend the seen in pursuit of what is unseen. This balance is vital, otherwise he may so preoccupy himself with lofty aspirations that he despises the infirmities of his neighbors, or else become so enmeshed in their problems that he ceases to seek the things that are above.

Thus it was that the apostle Paul speaks of being led into paradise and being caught up into the third heaven, and yet, though exalted by the contemplation of what is unseen, was able to recall his mind to the needs of daily life. Paul was united by a bond of love with highest and lowest alike, caught up by the power of the Spirit, but content in his compassion for others to share their weakness. That is why he said, "Who is weak, and I am not weak? Who is hurt, and I do not burn with indignation?" And again, "To the Jews, I became as a Jew." He did so, not by abandoning his faith, but by expanding his compassion for others. By transfiguring the person of the unbeliever into himself, he wanted to learn personally how to care for others, giving to them in the same way as he himself would like to receive, were their positions in life to be reversed.

So let not the shepherd of the sheep ever be afraid; for under God, who balances all things, he will be more easily rescued from his own temptations the more he allows himself to feel the temptations that assail others.

November 6

William Temple
Archbishop of Canterbury, 1944

William Temple was born in 1881 and baptized on this day in Exeter Cathedral. His father was Bishop of Exeter and later Archbishop of Canterbury. Temple excelled in academic studies and developed into a philosopher and theologian of significance. After ordination, he quickly made a mark in the Church and at forty became a bishop. Within a decade, he was Archbishop of York. He is especially remembered for his ecumenical efforts and also for his concern with social issues, contributing notably to the debate which led to the creation of state welfare provision after the Second World War. He died in 1944, only two years after his translation to the See of Canterbury.

A Reading from *Christianity and Social Order*
by William Temple

The claim of the Christian Church to make its voice heard in matters of politics and economics is very widely resented, even by those who are Christian in personal belief and in devotional practice. It is commonly assumed that religion is one department of life, like art or science, and that it is playing the part of a busybody when it lays down principles for the guidance of other departments, whether art and science or business and politics.

In an age when it is tacitly assumed that the Church is concerned with another world than this, and in this with nothing but individual conduct as bearing on prospects in that other world, hardly anyone reads the history of the Church in its exercise of political influence. It is assumed that the Church exercises little influence and ought to exercise none; it is further assumed that this assumption is self-evident and has always been made by reasonable people.

A survey of history, however, shows that the claim of the Church today to be heard in relation to political and economic problems is no new usurpation, but a reassertion of a right once universally admitted and widely regarded. But it also shows that this right may be compromised by injudicious exercise, especially when the autonomy of technique in the various departments of life is ignored. Religion may rightly censure the use of artistic talents for making money out of people's baser tastes, but it cannot lay down laws about perspective or the use of a paintbrush. It may insist that scientific inquiry be prompted by a pure love of truth and not distorted (as in Nazi Germany) by political considerations. It may declare the proper relation of the economic to other activities, but it cannot claim to know what will be the purely economic effect of particular proposals. It is, however, entitled to say that some economic gains ought not to be sought because of the injuries involved to interests higher than economic; and this principle of the subordination of the whole economic sphere is not yet generally accepted.

The primary principle of Christian ethics and Christian politics must be respect for every person simply as a person. If each man and woman is a child of God, whom God loves and for whom Christ died, then there is in each a worth absolutely independent of all usefulness to society. The person is primary, not the society; the State existed for the citizen, not the citizen for the state. The first aim of social progress must be to give the fullest possible scope for the exercise of all powers and qualities which are distinctly personal; and of those the most fundamental is deliberate choice. Consequently society must be so arranged as to give to every citizen the maximum opportunity for making deliberate choices and the best possible training for the use of that opportunity. Freedom must be freedom *for* something as well as freedom *from* something. It must be the actual ability to form and carry out a purpose.

Finally, I should give a false impression of my own convictions if I did not state that there is no hope of establishing a more Christian social order except through the labor and sacrifice of those in whom the Spirit of Christ is active, and that the first necessity for progress is more and better Christians taking full responsibility as citizens for the political, social, and economic system under which they and their fellows live.

November 7

Willibrord

Archbishop of Utrecht, Missionary to Frisia, 739

Willibrord was born in Northumbria and educated at Ripon but the main part of his life was dedicated to his missionary work in Frisia and northern Germany. He built many churches, inaugurated bishoprics and consecrated cathedrals. The Cathedral of Utrecht, with a diocesan organization based on that of Canterbury, is his best known foundation. Together with his younger contemporary, Boniface, he began a century of English Christian influence on continental Christianity. Alcuin described him as venerable, gracious, and full of joy, and his ministry as based on energetic preaching informed by prayer and sacred reading. He died on this day in the year 739 and was buried at Echternach monastery in Luxembourg, which he founded. He is the patron saint of Holland.

A Reading from *The History of the English Church and People* by the Venerable Bede

The venerable servant of Christ, Bishop Egbert, planned to bring blessings to more people by undertaking the apostolic task of carrying the Word of God, through the preaching of the gospel, to some of the nations who had not heard it. He had learned that there were many peoples in Germany, of whose stock came the Angles or Saxons now settled in Britain.

Egbert realized that he was not permitted to go and preach to the heathen himself, being needed for some other purpose by holy Church, so he attempted to send other holy and industrious men for the work of preaching, among whom the outstanding figure by his priestly rank and his merit was one named Willibrord.

When he and his twelve companions arrived, they made a detour to visit Peppin, Duke of the Franks, by whom they were graciously received. Since Peppin had recently conquered Nearer Frisia and driven out King Radbod, he dispatched them to preach there, supporting them with his imperial authority so that no one should interfere with their preaching, and granting many favors to those who wished to embrace the faith. Consequently, aided by God's grace, they converted many folk in a short while from idolatry to faith in Christ.

When those who had come over had taught in Frisia for a number of years, Peppin with their unanimous consent dispatched the venerable Willibrord to Rome, where Sergius was still pope, with the request that he might be consecrated archbishop of the Frisians. His request was carried out in the year of our Lord 696, and Willibrord was consecrated in the church of the holy martyr Cecilia on her feast day, when the pope gave him the name of Clement. He was sent back to his bishopric without delay, fourteen days after his arrival in the city.

Peppin assigned him a place for his see in his own famous fortress, which is known in the ancient language of that people as Wiltaburg, that is, the Town of the Wilti; but it is known in the Gallic tongue as Utrecht. Having built a church here, the most reverend bishop preached the word of faith far and wide, recalling many from their errors and establishing several churches and a number of monasteries in those parts.

November 9

Margery Kempe

Mystic, *c.*1440

Margery Kempe was born in Lynn in Norfolk in the late fourteenth century, a contemporary of Julian of Norwich. She received many visions, several of them of the Holy Family, one of the most regular being of the crucifixion. She also had conversations with the saints. She was much sought after as a visionary, was endlessly in trouble with the Church, rebuked by the Archbishop of York, and was more than once imprisoned. Following the messages in her visions, she undertook pilgrimages to many holy places, including Walsingham, Canterbury, Compostela, Rome and Jerusalem, often setting out penniless. She was blessed with the gift of tears and seems to have been favored with singular signs of Christ's love, whereby for long periods she enjoyed consciousness of a close communion with him and developed a strong compassion for the sinful world. Her autobiography, The Book of Margery Kempe, *recounts her remarkable life. She died toward the middle of the fifteenth century.*

A Reading from *The Book of Margery Kempe*

In this extract Margery Kempe is brought before the court of the Archbishop of York, her outspoken opinions having led her detractors to level the charge of heresy against her.

At last the archbishop came into the chapel with his clerics, and he said to her abruptly, "Why do you go about in white clothes? Are you a virgin?" She, kneeling before him, said, "No, sir, I am no virgin; I am a married woman."

Speaking to her very roughly, the archbishop asked, "Why do you weep so, woman?" She answering said, "Sir, you shall wish some day that you had wept as sorely as I."

And then, after the archbishop had put to her the Articles of our Faith to which God gave her grace to answer well, truly and readily, without much having to stop and think, so that he could not criticize her he said to the clerics, "She knows her faith well enough. What shall I do with her?"

The clerics said, "We know very well that she knows the Articles of the Faith, but we will not allow her to dwell among us, because the people have great faith in her talk, and perhaps she might lead some of them astray." Then the archbishop said to her: "I am told very bad things about you. I hear it said that you are a very wicked woman." And she replied, "Sir, I also hear it said that you are a wicked man. And if you are as wicked as people say, you will never get to heaven, unless you amend while you are here."

Then he said very roughly, "Why you! What do people say about me?" She answered, "Other people, sir, can tell you well enough." Then the archbishop said to her, "You shall swear that you will not teach people or call them to account in my diocese."

"No, sir, I will not swear." she said, "for I shall speak of God and rebuke those who swear great oaths wherever I go, until such time that the pope and holy Church have ordained that nobody shall be so bold as to speak of God, for God almighty does not forbid, sir, that we should speak of him. And also the gospel mentions that, when the woman had heard our Lord preach, she came before him and said in a loud voice, 'Blessed be the womb that bore you, and the teats that gave you suck.' Then our Lord replied to her, 'In truth, so are they blessed who hear the word of God and keep it.' And therefore, sir, I think that the gospel gives me leave to speak of God."

"Ah, sir," said the clerics, "here we know that she has a devil in her, for she speaks of the Gospel." A great cleric quickly produced a book and quoted Saint Paul for his part against her, that no woman should preach. She, answering to this, said, "I do not preach, sir; I do not go into any pulpit, I use only conversation and good words, and that I will do while I live."

When the archbishop heard her defense he commended her for her honesty. And she, kneeling down on her knees, asked his blessing. He, asking her to pray for him, blessed her and let her go.

Then she, going back again to York, was received by many people, and by very worthy clerics who rejoiced in our Lord who had given her uneducated as she was the wit and wisdom to answer so many learned men without shame or blame.

November 10

Leo the Great

Bishop of Rome, 461

Leo the Great became Bishop of Rome in the year 440 and twice proved his bravery in saving the citizens of Rome from the invading barbarians. He was an eloquent and wise preacher, using simple gospel texts to proclaim the Christian faith. His administrative skills were unrivalled and he used the resources of the Church for the good of the people. Rather than further confuse Christians by entering into the controversy over the person of Christ, Leo spoke simply of the humility of Christ who was divine and human in his compassion, uniting Biblical images in prayer rather than dividing in debate. Leo died on this day in the year 461.

A Reading from a letter of Leo the Great, Bishop of Rome,
to Flavian, Bishop of Constantinople, dated
June 13, 449; also known as *The Tome of Leo*

We could not overcome the author of sin and death, unless Christ had taken our nature and made it his own, he whom sin could not defile or death imprison. He was conceived of the Holy Spirit within the womb of his Virgin Mother, whose virginity remained undefiled in his birth as in his conception.

That birth, uniquely marvelous and marvelously unique, should not be understood in such a way as to suggest that the distinctive characteristics of our humanity were excluded by this process of new creation. For while it is true that the Holy Spirit made the Virgin fertile, it is equally true that Christ received a real body from her body.

In this way the characteristics of each nature and being were completely preserved in Christ, coming together in his one person. Humility was assumed by majesty, weakness by strength, mortality by eternity; and to pay the debt that we had incurred, an inviolable nature was united to a nature that can suffer. To fulfill the conditions of our inner healing, the man Jesus Christ, one and the same mediator between humankind and God, was able to die in respect of one nature, and unable to die in respect of the other. Thus in the whole and perfect nature of a human being, true God was born, complete in what pertained to his divine nature, and complete in what pertained to ours.

By "ours" I mean only what the creator formed in us from the beginning, which Christ assumed in order to repair. In our Savior there was no trace of those characteristics which the Deceiver introduced to humanity, and which we, being deceived, allowed to enter into our common inheritance. Christ did not participate in sin simply because he entered into fellowship with our human frailty. He assumed the form of a servant without any trace of sin, thereby enhancing our humanity, but without detracting from his divinity. For that "emptying of himself" whereby the invisible God made himself visible, and the creator and Lord of all willed to become mortal, was a reaching out in compassion, not a failure of power.

Accordingly, he who made humanity, while remaining in the form of God, was himself made human in the form of a servant. Each nature preserves its own characteristics without diminution, so that the form of a servant does not detract from the form of God.

November 11

Martin

Bishop of Tours, *c.*397

Born in about the year 316 in Pannonia (in modern-day Hungary), Martin was a soldier in the Roman army and a Christian. He found the two roles conflicted and, under the influence of Hilary, Bishop of Poitiers, he founded a monastery in Hilary's diocese in the year 360, the first such foundation in Gaul. The religious house was a center for missionary work in the local countryside, setting a new example where, previously, all Christian activity had been centered in cities and undertaken from the cathedral there. In 372, Martin was elected Bishop of Tours by popular acclaim and he continued his monastic lifestyle as a bishop, remaining in that ministry until his death on this day in the year 397.

A Reading from *The Life of Saint Martin*
by Sulpicius Severus

During the three years before his baptism, Martin was a professional soldier, but managed to keep himself free from the vices in which so often soldiers indulge. He was extremely kind toward his fellow-soldiers, and held them in great affection; while his patience and humility surpassed what seemed possible for human nature to sustain. His self-denial needs no praise. It was evident even at this date. In fact, many regarded him not so much a soldier as a monk. By these qualities he so endeared himself to his comrades that they held him not simply in high esteem, but truly loved him.

Although not yet made a new creation in Christ, by his good works Martin was already a candidate for baptism. He regularly came to the help of those in trouble, giving practical help to the destitute, supporting the needy, clothing the naked, and from his military pay would keep back only what he needed for his daily needs. He was already complying with the gospel precept to "take no thought for tomorrow."

One day, during a particularly severe winter, a winter so extreme that many of the populace were dying of the cold, Martin was out on duty. He was wearing his soldier's uniform and was armed. He met in the gateway of the city of Amiens a poor man who was destitute of clothing. He was begging for help, but all passed by the poor man without even acknowledging his presence. When Martin, that man full of God, saw the poor man whom no one pitied, he questioned himself about what was best do. He had nothing left save the cloak he was wearing, having already given away the rest of his clothes to the destitute. Unsheathing his sword, he cut his cloak in two, giving one half to the poor man, and wrapping the remaining half round himself.

At this, some of the bystanders started laughing because Martin looked so peculiar. He stood out from the other soldiers, being only partly dressed. Other people of more sensitive understanding, however, were deeply moved by his action, ashamed that they had done nothing themselves. They felt this particularly, having more than Martin they could have clothed the poor man without reducing themselves to nakedness if they had wanted to.

The following night, Martin fell into a deep sleep, and as he slept he had a vision of Christ arrayed in part of the cloak with which he had clothed the poor man. He contemplated the sight of the Lord with wonder, and was told to clothe himself with the robe he had given. He heard Jesus speaking to him quite distinctly, "Martin, you may be still a catechumen, but you have clothed me with this robe." The Lord, mindful of his own words while on earth, (when he said "Inasmuch as you have done this to the least of my brothers and sisters, you have done it to me") revealed that he himself had been clothed in that poor man. After this vision the holy man was not puffed up with his own importance, but acknowledging the goodness of God in what had happened, presented himself without further delay for baptism. He was twenty years of age.

[Not long after this the barbarians launched an attack on the two divisions stationed in Gaul. Julian Caesar summoned the army and, in preparation for battle, began to issue each soldier with his pay. Judging this a suitable opportunity for seeking discharge—for he did not think it right to receive pay if he intended to leave the army—Martin addressed Caesar: "Until now I have served you as a soldier. Give me leave to become a soldier for God. Let the men who are to serve you in the army receive their due pay: I am a soldier of Christ, and it is not right that I should fight."

The tyrant stormed at Martin on hearing this, declaring that it was from no religious conviction that he was withdrawing from military service, but from fear of the forthcoming battle. But Martin, very courageously and resolute in the face of personal danger, replied: "If my conduct is ascribed to cowardice, and not to faith, then allow me to take my place in the front-line of battle tomorrow unarmed, and in the name of the Lord Jesus, protected by the sign of the cross rather than by shield or helmet, I will safely penetrate the ranks of the enemy." Caesar ordered Martin to be put in prison and to put his words to the test the next day.

The following morning, however, the enemy sent ambassadors to Caesar to sue for peace, surrendering both themselves and their possessions. In such circumstances, who can doubt that the victory was due to this saintly man? For Christ has no wish to secure any victory for his soldiers than that an enemy should be subdued without bloodshed, and that no one should be killed.]

alternative reading

A Reading from *The Life of Saint Martin*
by Sulpicius Severus

It is beyond my powers to set forth adequately how Martin distinguished himself in the discharge of his duties as Bishop of Tours. He remained just the same as he had been before his ordination. There was the same humility in his heart, and the same unpretentious clothing. He always maintained his role as bishop with true dignity and courtesy, without ever setting aside the life and virtues of a monk.

For a long time he made use of a cell connected to the church, but increasingly this became impracticable with the vast numbers of people visiting him. So he established a monastery two miles outside the city. This exact spot he kept secret and away from people, so that he could enjoy the solitude of a hermit. On one side, his hermitage was bordered by a precipitous rock face of a high mountain, while on the other side, the river Loire cut off the land from the rest of the valley with the result that the place could only be approached one person at a time along a very narrow passage. Here then, Martin constructed for himself a wooden cell.

Many of the other monks also built for themselves hermitages, but most of these were hollowed out caves on the mountainside. Altogether there were eighty disciples who followed the discipline of their saintly master. No one kept anything as his own; everything was held in common. No one bought or sold anything for himself, as is monastic custom. No craft was practiced there except that of transcribing texts, and this task was allocated to the younger brothers, leaving the seniors free to devote themselves to prayer. Rarely did one of the brothers go beyond his cell, unless it was to assemble for corporate prayer. They ate communally, once their daily fast was completed; no one drank wine, except in illness; and most of brothers wore simple, rough garments. Softer material was frowned upon which was quite remarkable given that a number of the monks were drawn from the nobility. Although from different backgrounds, all were united in observing a common observance of humility and patient endurance. A number of the monks were subsequently made bishops. For what city or church would not covet as its priests those trained in the monastery of Martin?

November 12

Charles Simeon

Priest, 1836

Born in Reading in England in 1759, Charles Simeon was educated at Cambridge University and spent the rest of his life in that city. He became a Fellow of King's College in 1782 and was ordained priest the following year, when he became Vicar of Holy Trinity Church nearby. He had Evangelical leanings as a boy but it was while preparing for holy communion on his entrance to college that he became aware of the redeeming love of God, an experience he regarded as the turning point in his life. Many of the parishioners of Holy Trinity Church did not welcome him, since he had been appointed through his own family links, but his patent care and love for them all overcame their antipathy and his preaching greatly increased the congregation. Charles had carved on the inside of the pulpit in Holy Trinity Church, where only the preacher could see, the words from John 12:21, when Philip brought the Greeks to our Lord, and they said, "Sir, we would see Jesus." These words were a constant reminder to him that people came not to gaze on a great preacher or to admire his eloquence, but to seek Jesus. Simeon became a leading evangelical influence in the church and was one of the founders of the Church Missionary Society. He also set up the Simeon Trust which made appointments to parishes of fellow evangelicals. He remained Vicar of Holy Trinity until his death in the year 1836.

A Reading from "Evangelic and Pharisaic Righteousness Compared," being a sermon delivered by Charles Simeon before the University of Cambridge in November 1809

There is a kind of religion which is held in esteem by mankind at large. An outward reverence for the ordinances of religion, together with habits of temperance, justice, chastity, and benevolence, constitute what the world considers a perfect character. The description which Saint Paul gives of himself previous to his conversion is so congenial with their sentiments of perfection that they would not hesitate to rest the salvation of their souls on his attainments. But what said he of his state when once he came to view it aright? "What things were gain to me, those I counted loss for Christ. Yea doubtless, and I count all things but loss for the excellency of the knowledge of Christ Jesus my Lord." He saw that brokenness of heart for sin, a humble affiance in the Lord Jesus Christ, and an unreserved devotedness of heart to his service, were indispensable to the salvation of the soul. He saw that, without these, no attainments would be of any avail. Yes, a man might have all the biblical learning of the scribes, and all the sanctified habits of the Pharisees, and yet never be approved of the Lord in this world, nor ever be accepted of him in the world to come.

Is it not then desirable that those who are in repute for wisdom and piety among us should pause and inquire whether their righteousness really exceeds that of the scribes and Pharisees? Would they not do well to study the account which St Paul gives of himself previous to his conversion, and to examine wherein they surpass him? Alas! alas! we are exceedingly averse to being undeceived; but I would entreat every one of my hearers to consider deeply what our blessed Lord has spoken of such characters: "You are those who justify yourselves before men; but God knows your hearts: for that which is highly esteemed among men is abomination in the sight of God."

Lastly, we would suggest some profitable considerations to those who profess to have attained that superior righteousness spoken of in our text. You need not be told that the examples of Christ and his apostles, and indeed of all the primitive Christians, were offensive, rather than pleasing, to the pharisee of old. The same disapprobation of real piety still lurks in the hearts of those who occupy the seat of Moses. You must not wonder, therefore, if your contrition be called gloom; your faith in Christ, presumption; your delight in his ways, enthusiasm; and your devotion to his service, preciseness of hypocrisy. Well, if it must be so, console yourselves with this, that you share the fate of all the saints that have gone before you, and that your state, with all the obloquy that attends it, is infinitely better than that of your revilers and persecutors. You may well be content to be despised by men while you are conscious of the favor and approbation of God.

November 14

Consecration of Samuel Seabury

First Anglican Bishop in North America, 1796

Samuel Seabury was born in Connecticut in 1729 and, after graduating from Yale, was ordained priest in England and assigned by the Society for the Propagation of the Gospel to a church in New Brunswick, New Jersey. During the American War of Independence, he remained faithful to the British Crown, serving as a chaplain in the British army. At a secret meeting of the clergy in Connecticut, Seabury was chosen to seek consecration as bishop but, after a year of fruitless negotiation with the Church of England, he was ordained bishop by the non-juring bishops in the Scottish Episcopal Church on this day in 1784. Returning to America, he held his first Convention in Connecticut the following August and took part in the first General Convention of the American Episcopal Church in 1789. There, they adopted some aspects of the Scottish eucharistic rite and a similar name to the Church which had proved itself their friend. Samuel died on February 25, in the year 1796.

A Reading from the *Concordat* established between the Scottish bishops and Dr. Samuel Seabury, presbyter in Connecticut, November 15, 1784

The wise and gracious providence of merciful God, having put into the hearts of the Christians of the Episcopal persuasion in Connecticut in North America, to desire that the blessings of a free, valid, and purely ecclesiastical episcopacy might be communicated to them, and a Church regularly formed in that part of the western world upon the most ancient and primitive model:

And application having been made for this purpose by the Reverend Dr. Samuel Seabury, presbyter in Connecticut, to the Right Reverend the Bishops of the Church in Scotland:

The said bishops having taken this proposal into their serious consideration, most heartily concurred to promote and encourage the same, so far as lay in their power; and accordingly, began the pious and good work recommended to them by complying with the request of the clergy in Connecticut and advancing the said Dr. Samuel Seabury to the high order of the episcopate; at the same time earnestly praying that this work of the Lord, thus happily begun, might prosper in his hands, till it should please the great and glorious head of the Church to increase the number of bishops in America and send forth more laborers into that part of his harvest.

Animated with this pious hope and earnestly desirous to establish a bond of peace and holy communion between the two Churches, the bishops of the Church in Scotland, whose names are underwritten, having had full and free conference with Bishop Seabury after his consecration and advancement as aforesaid, agreed with him on the following articles, which are to serve as a concordat or bond of union, between the Catholic remainder of the ancient Church of Scotland and the now rising Church in the State of Connecticut.

They agree in thankfully receiving and humbly and heartily embracing the whole doctrine of the gospel as revealed and set forth in the holy Scriptures;

They agree in believing this Church to be the mystical body of Christ, of which he alone is the head and supreme governor; and that under him the chief ministers or managers of the affairs of this spiritual society are those called bishops, whose exercise of their sacred office being independent of all lay powers, it follows of consequence that their spiritual authority and jurisdiction cannot be affected by any lay deprivation.

They agree in desiring that there may be as near a conformity in worship and discipline established between the two Churches as is consistent with the different circumstances and customs of nations.

As the celebration of the Holy Eucharist, or administration of the sacrament of the body and blood of Christ, is the principal bond of union among Christians, as well as the most solemn act of worship in the Christian Church, the bishops aforesaid agree in desiring that there be as little variance here as possible. And though the Scottish bishops are very far from prescribing to their brethren in this matter, they cannot help ardently wishing that Bishop Seabury would endeavor all he can, consistently with peace and prudence, to make the celebration of this venerable mystery conformable to the most primitive doctrine and practice in that respect. Which is the pattern the [Episcopal] Church of Scotland has copied after in her Communion Office; and which it has been the wish of some of the most eminent divines of the Church of England, that she also had more closely followed than she seems to have done since she gave up her first reformed liturgy used in the reign of King Edward VI—between which and the form of the [Episcopal] Church of Scotland there is no difference in any point which the primitive Church reckoned essential to the right ministration of the Holy Eucharist.

The bishops aforesaid do hereby jointly declare, in the most solemn manner, that in the whole of this transaction they have nothing else in view but the glory of God and the good of his Church.

November 16

Margaret of Scotland

Queen of Scotland, Philanthropist, Reformer of the Church, 1093

Born in the year 1046, Margaret was the daughter of the Anglo-Saxon royal house of England but educated in Hungary, where her family lived in exile during the reign of Danish kings in England. After the Norman invasion in 1066, when her royal person was still a threat to the new monarchy, she was welcomed in the royal court of Malcolm III of Scotland and soon afterwards married him in 1069. Theirs was a happy and fruitful union and Margaret proved to be both a civilizing and a holy presence. She instituted many church reforms and founded many monasteries, churches and pilgrim hostels. She was a woman of prayer as well as good works who seemed to influence for good all with whom she came into contact. She died on this day in the year 1093.

A Reading from *The Life of Saint Margaret, Queen of Scotland,* by Turgot, Bishop of St. Andrews

Many people derive their names from a quality of mind, so that a correspondence is revealed between the sense of their name and the grace they have received. The same is true of this virtuous woman, in whom the fairness indicated by her name was surpassed by the exceeding beauty of her soul. She was called Margaret, that is, "a pearl," and in the sight of God she was esteemed a lovely pearl by reason of her faith and good works. She was a pearl to her children, to me, to us all, even to Christ; and because she was Christ's, she is all the more ours now that she has left us and is taken to the Lord.

In the Queen's presence no one ventured to do anything wrong, or even utter an unseemly word, for repressing all evil in herself, there was great gravity in her joy and something noble in her anger. Her conversation was seasoned with the salt of wisdom: her silence was filled with good thoughts. She would often call her children to her, and, as far as their age would allow, instruct them concerning Christ and the faith of Christ, and carefully endeavor to admonish them to always fear him.

We need not wonder then, that the Queen ruled herself and her household wisely, since she was always guided by the most wise counsel of the holy Scriptures. What I used frequently to admire in her was that amid the distraction of lawsuits and the countless affairs of the kingdom, she gave herself with wonderful diligence to the reading of the word of God, concerning which she used to ask profound questions of the scholars who were sitting near her.

To the excellent gifts of prayer and fasting, she joined the gifts of mercy. For what could be more compassionate than her heart? Who more gentle to the needy? It was her custom as soon as dawn had broken, to rise from bed, and to continue a long time in prayer and reading the psalms, and as she read she performed this work of mercy. Nine little orphan children who were utterly destitute, she had brought into her at the first hour of the day so that she could feed them. She ordered soft food such as little children delight in, to be prepared for them daily; and when the little ones were brought to her, she did not think it beneath her to pick them up and sit them on her knee, and feed them herself with the spoons from her own table.

Thus Queen Margaret, honored by all the people, performed for Christ's sake the office of a most devoted servant and mother.

November 16

Gertrude of Helfta

Mystic, *c.*1302

Gertrude was born in 1256. At the age of five she was given by her parents to be brought up by the Benedictine nuns of Helfta in Thuringia. She was a gifted child and received a good education at their hands. At the age of twenty-five she experienced a profound conversion in consequence of a vision of Christ, and for the rest of her life she led a life of contemplation. Of the so-called Revelations of Gertrude, *only* The Herald of Divine Love *is genuinely hers, written partly from her notes or dictation, and partly by herself. She is sometimes called "Gertrude the Great" to distinguish her from Gertrude of Hackeborn who was Abbess of Helfta when she was brought there as a child. Gertrude was one of the first exponents of devotion to the Sacred Heart.*

A Reading from *The Herald of Divine Love* by Gertrude of Helfta

One day, wearied by the consideration of earthly pleasures, she said to the Lord: "I can find no pleasure in anything on earth save in yourself alone, my sweetest Lord!" To which the Lord in his turn replied: "And in the same way, I find nothing in heaven or on earth which could please me without you, because I associate you in love with all that pleases me, and so I always find in love all that gives me pleasure. The greater these pleasures are for me, the greater will be the profit for you."

That she was assiduous in prayers and vigils is clear from the fact that she never neglected to observe any of the canonical hours unless she lay sick in bed with some infirmity or was engaged in some charitable work for the glory of God or the salvation of others. And because the Lord never failed to gladden her prayers with the blissful consolation of his presence, she prolonged her spiritual exercises long after her strength would have been exhausted by any other occupation. She observed so lovingly all the statutes of her Order concerning assistance at Choir, fasting and manual work, that she never omitted any of them without feeling grievous dissatisfaction. Saint Bernard says: "If you have once been inebriated by the taste of charity, soon every labor and sorrow is made mirthful."

The freedom of her spirit was so great that she could not tolerate for an instant anything that went against her conscience. The Lord himself bore witness to this, because when someone asked him in devout prayer what it was that pleased him most in his chosen one, he replied: "Her freedom of heart." This person, most astonished and, so to speak, considering this an inadequate answer, said: "I should have thought, Lord, that by your grace she would have attained to a higher knowledge of your mysteries and a greater fervor of love." To which the Lord answered: "Yes, indeed, it is as you think. And this is the result of the grace of the freedom of her heart which is so great a good that it leads directly to the highest perfection. I have always found her ready to receive my gifts, for she permits nothing to remain in her heart which might impede my action."

November 17

Hugh

Bishop of Lincoln, 1200

Hugh was born at Avalon in Burgundy in 1140 and at first made his profession with the Augustinian canons but, when he was twenty-five, he became a monk at Grande Chartreuse. In about 1175, he was invited by the English king, Henry II, to become Prior of his Charterhouse foundation at Witham in Somerset, badly in need of reform even though it had been only recently founded. In 1186, Hugh was persuaded to accept the See of Lincoln, then the largest diocese in the land. He brought huge energy to the diocese and, together with discerning appointments to key posts, he revived the Lincoln schools, repaired and enlarged the cathedral, visited the See extensively, drew together the clergy to meet in synod and generally brought an efficiency and stability to the church, which was to be much emulated. Hugh also showed great compassion for the poor and the oppressed, ensuring that sufferers of leprosy were cared for and that Jews were not persecuted. He both supported his monarch and also held out against any royal measures he felt to be extreme, yet managing not to make an enemy of the king. He died in London on this day in the year 1200.

A Reading from *Magna Vita: The Life of Saint Hugh of Lincoln*, by Adam, monk of Eynsham

With the help of many gifted men as his counselors and members of his household, the new Bishop of Lincoln immediately transformed his diocese. He preached the word of God with vigor, and zealously carried out its commandments following a text of Scripture: "Where the spirit of the Lord is there is liberty." He rebuked sinners sternly, with no undue consideration for persons of importance.

The worst abuse in the kingdom, under which countryfolk groaned, was the tyranny of the foresters. For them violence took the place of law, extortion was praiseworthy, justice was an abomination and innocence a crime. When in their usual way the foresters maltreated his people, in defiance of the liberties of the Church, Hugh excommunicated the chief forester. This news aroused the king to great indignation.

It is impossible adequately to record among the other marks of his devotion, his great compassion and tenderness toward the sick, and even to those afflicted with leprosy. He used to wash and dry their feet and kiss them affectionately, and having refreshed them with food and drink, gave them alms on a lavish scale. There were hospitals on certain of the episcopal manors, where many men and women afflicted by this disease were maintained. He made a practice of giving gifts of many different kinds to these in addition to the revenue already assigned to them by his predecessors, and frequently visited them himself with a few of his more God-fearing and devout retainers. He would sit in their midst in a small inner room and would comfort their souls by his kindly words, relieving their sorrow by his motherly tenderness, and encouraging those who were so desolate and afflicted in this life to hope for an eternal reward, combining with amazing gentleness words of consolation and exhortations to good conduct. Also if he noticed any tendency to wrong-doing, he would exhort them not to give way to it, and if they had done so to repent, and from henceforth neither to dare nor desire to do wrong. Before his address the women withdrew at his command and he went to kiss the men one by one, bending over each of them and giving a longer and more tender embrace to those whom he saw worse marked by the disease.

Have pity, sweet Jesus, on the unhappy soul of the narrator! I cannot conceal, would that it were concealed from your vengeance, how much I shuddered not merely to touch but even to behold those swollen and livid, diseased and deformed faces with the eyes either distorted or hollowed out and the lips eaten away! To an eye darkened by arrogance the pearl of God did not gleam in the mire. But your servant Hugh, whose eyes you had completely blinded to external superficiality, saw clearly their internal splendor, and therefore those seemed to him the more beautiful who outwardly were the most horribly diseased.

The openly expressed feeling of this saintly man for the divine healer of our wounds, and his words and acts concerning his sick members show plainly how afire Hugh was with love for God and his neighbor. He gave so lavishly to those who were in need that it is estimated that at least a third of his annual income was devoted to almsgiving.

November 18

Hilda

Abbess of Whitby, 680

Hilda was born in the year 614 of the royal house of Northumbria and was baptized in York at the age of twelve by Paulinus. Encouraged by Aidan of Lindisfarne, she become a Religious at the age of thirty-three. She established monasteries first at Hartlepool, and two years later at Whitby. This house became a great center of learning and was the meeting-place for the important Synod of Whitby in the year 664 at which it was decided to adopt the Roman tradition in preference to Celtic customs. Although herself a Celt in religious formation, Hilda played a crucial rôle in reconciling others of that tradition to the decision of the Synod. She is also remembered as a great educator, exemplified in her nurturing of Caedmon's gift of vernacular song. She died on November 17, in the year 680.

A Reading from *The History of the English Church and People* by the Venerable Bede

In the year of our Lord 680, Hilda, abbess of the monastery of Whitby, a most devoted servant of Christ, after an earthly life given to the work of heaven passed away to receive the rewards of a heavenly life on the seventeenth of November at the age of sixty-six. Her life on earth fell into two equal parts: for she spent thirty-three years most nobly in secular occupations, and dedicated an equal number of years still more nobly to the Lord in the monastic life.

She was of noble birth, being the daughter of Hereric, the nephew of King Edwin. With Edwin she received the faith and sacraments of Christ through the preaching of Paulinus of blessed memory, the first bishop of the Northumbrians, and she preserved this faith inviolate until she was found worthy to see her Master in heaven.

When she decided to abandon the secular life and serve God alone, she went to the province of the East Angles, whose king was her relation, with the intention of going abroad. However, she was recalled home by Bishop Aidan and was granted one hide of land on the north bank of the river Wear, where she observed the monastic rule with a handful of companions for another year.

After this she was made abbess of the monastery at Hartlepool which had been founded not long before, and from there she moved to Tadcaster. When she had ruled this monastery for some years, constantly occupied in establishing a *Rule* of life, Hilda further undertook to found or organize a monastery at a place known as Whitby, and carried out this appointed task with great energy. She established the same *Rule* of life as in her former monastery, and taught the observance of righteousness, mercy, purity, and other virtues, but especially of peace and charity. After the example of the primitive church, no one there was rich, no one was needy, for everything was held in common, and nothing was considered to be anyone's personal property. So great was her prudence that not only ordinary folk, but kings and princes used to come and ask her advice in their difficulties. Those under her direction were required to make a thorough study of the holy Scriptures and occupy themselves in good works, to such good effect that many were found fitted for holy orders and the service of God's altar.

All who knew Abbess Hilda, the handmaid of Christ, called her mother because of her wonderful devotion and grace. She was not only an example of holy life to members of her own community; she also brought about an opportunity for salvation and repentance to many living at a distance, who heard the inspiring story of her industry and goodness.

November 19

Elizabeth

Princess of Hungary, 1231

Elizabeth was born in 1207, the daughter of a king of Hungary, and was given in marriage to Louis IV, Landgrave of Thuringia, with whom she had three children. Theirs was a happy marriage but her husband of four years died of the plague. Elizabeth was driven from the court and she settled in Marburg. There she had a confessor, Conrad of Marburg, whose domineering and almost sadistic ways exemplified one who had himself been a successful inquisitor of heretics. She suffered mental and physical abuse from him, in the name of religious austerity, but bore it all humbly. Elizabeth became a member of the Franciscan Third Order, which reflected her life of caring for the poor, even cooking and cleaning for them. Due to the severe regime under which she lived, her weakened body gave way under the pressure and she died on this day, just twenty-four years old, in the year 1231.

A Reading from the deposition of Isentrude, companion of Elizabeth of Hungary, to the Papal Commission concerning her canonization

While her husband King Ludwig was away on imperial business, there was a general famine, and blessed Elizabeth caused the reserves of corn in the king's granaries to be expended to satisfy the needs of the poor, each day as much as was necessary. Beneath the high castle of the Wartburg there was a large building which she filled with a number of sick people for whom the general almsgiving could not suffice; and despite the long steep hill she visited them several times a day, consoling them and encouraging them to patience, and she sold her own jewels in order to satisfy their needs. She paid no heed to the fetid air and to the stench of corruption made worse by the summer heat, which her attendants only bore with much murmuring.

Once there were in this hospital a number of poor children for whom she provided everything and with much gentleness and kindness kept them near her; and as many as came ran to her calling her "mother." She paid the most loving care to the worst cases among these children, the deformed, the dirtiest, the weakest, those suffering from the most repulsive illnesses, and would take them tenderly into her arms.

These sick people shared in her general almsgiving, but besides this blessed Elizabeth chose the poorest and weakest and lodged them in a dwelling outside the castle where she could feed them from her own table with her own hands, denying herself and her attendants many things in order to give them to the poor.

alternative reading

A Reading from a homily of John Chrysostom

Do you want to honor the body of Christ? Then do not despise his nakedness. Do not honor him here in church clothed in silk vestments and then ignore him, naked and frozen in the street. Always remember that he who said, "This is my body," and gave effect to his word, also said, "I was hungry and you gave me no food," and "inasmuch as you did not do it to one of these, you did not do it to me." The body of Christ needs no clothing in the first sense but only the worship of a pure heart. But in the second case it needs clothing and all the care we can lavish upon it.

It is vital, therefore, that we become discerning Christians and learn to honor Christ appropriately in ways of which he approves. When someone is honored, the form of honor bestowed is appropriate to the person receiving it, not the donor. Peter thought he was honoring the Lord when he tried to prevent him from washing his feet, but in reality this was far from the case. In the same way, give God the honor he seeks and give your money generously to the poor. God does not need golden cups but he does need golden hearts.

I am not saying that you should not donate golden chalices, but I am insisting that there is no substitute for almsgiving. The Lord will not refuse your gift but he prefers almsgiving; and inevitably so, because in the former case only you, the donor, benefits, whereas in the latter case the poor benefit. The gift of a chalice may be extravagant; the giving of alms is sincere kindness which shows love for our fellow men and women.

What is the point of weighing down Christ's table with golden chalices while he himself is starving? Feed the hungry and then, if you have any money left over, lavish his table. Will you fashion a cup of gold and withhold a cup of water? What use is it to adorn his table with hangings of cloth of gold but refuse Christ a coat for his back? What gain is to be had from such behavior?

Answer me this question: if you saw someone starving and refused to give them any food but instead spent your money on covering Christ's table with gold, would Christ thank you for it? Would he not rather be furious with you? Or again, if you saw someone in rags and frozen stiff, and then instead of giving them clothing you went and erected golden columns in Christ's honor, would not Christ say that you were mocking and ridiculing him? Imagine that Christ is that tramp, that stranger who comes to you in need of a bed for the night. You turn him away and then start laying carpets on the floor, draping the walls, hanging lamps on silver chains from the capitals of the columns. Meanwhile the tramp is arrested and put in prison, but you never give him a second thought.

Let me repeat, I am not condemning generosity; but I am urging you to care for the poor; indeed, to give the poor priority. No one was ever condemned for not beautifying Christ's house, but those who neglect their neighbor were threatened with hell fire and eternal punishment with devils. Beautify this house if that is what you want to do, but never neglect your brother or sister in need. They are temples of infinitely greater value.

November 19

Mechtild

Beguine of Magdeburg, Mystic, 1280

Mechtild was born in about the year 1210. The writings for which she is known speak of her experience of the love of God as it was revealed to her. This experience began when she was twelve years old. She responded to it by joining a community of Béguines at the age of about eighteen. After forty years, she moved to the Cistercian convent of Helfta and in about 1270 completed her writings there. Helfta was a remarkable center of learning at that time with other outstanding personalities in the community. She wrote with poetic sensitivity in direct and simple language of the exchange of love with God. She died on this day in the year 1280.

A Reading from *The Revelations of Mechtild of Magdeburg*,
also known as
The Flowing Light of the Godhead

I was warned about my book and told by many people
That it should not be preserved
But rather should be thrown in the fire.
Then I did what from childhood I have always done
When trouble overtakes me:
I resorted to prayer.
I bowed myself before my Love and said:
"Lord, I am deeply troubled.
Must I always walk devoid of comfort
For the sake of your glory?
You have tricked me
For you yourself told me to write this book!"

But holding my book in his right hand, the Lord said:
"Beloved, do not be hard on yourself.
No one can burn truth.
Those who wish to rip this book out of my hand
Must be stronger than I!
This book has three parts
And it concerns me alone.
The parchment here before me
Speaks of my pure, righteous and wise humanity
Which suffered death for you.
Your words speak of my glorious godhead
Which flows from hour to hour
Into your receptive soul from my heavenly mouth.
Your words speak with my living Spirit
And embody in themselves the living truth.
So behold in all these words
How graciously they proclaim my holiness
And do not doubt your worth."

"But, Lord, were I a learned priest,
And had you worked your wonders in a man,
Then you would have derived endless honor
From such writings.
But how will any believe me
This unworthy soil
On which you have deigned to raise up a golden dwelling

Wherein dwells your mother
And all creation
And all the heavenly host?
Lord, I can find no earthly wisdom in your ways!"

"My daughter, many a wise man has lost precious gold
Through carelessness on the highway of life
Along which he thought he traveled to higher realms;
Leaving others to find the way.
Whenever I have bestowed my special grace
I have always searched
For the poorest, the smallest and most hidden.
The proud mountains cannot receive
The revelations of my grace,
For the flood of my Holy Spirit
By nature flows down into the lowliest valleys.
There are many so-called wise writers
Who, in my eyes, are fools.
And I tell you more,
It greatly honors me
And greatly strengthens holy Church
That your unlearned lips should teach
The learned tongues the things of my Holy Spirit."

November 20

Edmund

King of East Anglia, Martyr, 870

Born about the year 840, Edmund was nominated as king while still a boy. He was crowned King of Norfolk in 855 and of Suffolk the following year. As king, he won the hearts of his subjects by his care of the poor and his steady suppression of wrong-doing. When attacked by the Danes, he refused to give over his kingdom or to renounce his faith in Christ. He was tied to a tree, shot with arrows, and finally beheaded on this day in the year 870.

A Reading from *The Lives of the Saints*
by Aelfric of Eynsham

Blessed Edmund, King of the East Angles, was a wise and honorable man, and by his excellent conduct always gave glory to almighty God. He was humble and devout, and of such steadfast faith that throughout his life he never yielded to any shameful behavior. He was unswerving in his duties, refusing to compromise his integrity, mindful of the counsel that if you should be made a chief, never exalt yourself, but rather always be among your people as one of them. He was generous to the poor and widows, and like a father gently guided his people toward righteousness, controlling the violent in the land, and allowing people to live securely in the true faith.

Eventually the Danes came with a great fleet of ships, harrying and killing the populace over a wide area. They landed first of all in Northumbria, wasted the land and slew the people. Hingwar, one of their leaders, sent a threatening message to King Edmund, who undismayed turned to the messenger and said, "Truly you deserve to die, but I will not defile my clean hands with your foul blood, because I follow Christ who has given us an example. Go now quickly, and say to your lord: Edmund the king will never bow in this life to Hingwar the heathen leader, unless he will in faith first bow in this land to Jesus Christ." The messenger left quickly, and meeting the bloodthirsty Hingwar and his army who were already on their way to confront Edmund, told that wicked man how he had been answered. Hingwar then arrogantly ordered his troops to take the king who despised his command and arrest him.

Edmund stood within his hall and, mindful of the Savior, threw down his weapons, desiring to imitate the example of Christ who forbade Peter to fight with weapons against the bloodthirsty soldiers. Then those wicked men bound Edmund, insulted him shamefully, and beat him with clubs. Then they led the faithful king to a tree, tied him to it with hard ropes, and scourged him, while with true faith he called between the blows on Jesus Christ. The heathen were mad with rage because he called upon Christ to help him, and made him a target for their arrows, shooting at him as if for amusement, until he was covered with arrows as with a porcupine's bristles, as Sebastian was. When Hingwar, the wicked tyrant, saw that the noble king would not deny Christ and with steadfast faith continued to call upon him, he ordered his men to behead him. While he was still calling upon Christ, the heathen murdered the saint and with one blow struck off his head; and so his soul departed joyfully to Christ.

November 22

Cecilia

Martyr at Rome, *c.*230

Cecilia was one of the most revered martyrs of the Roman Church, but the only thing known for certain is that, at some point in the second or third century, a woman called Cecilia allowed the Church to meet in her house in Trastevere in the city of Rome and that subsequently the church erected on that site bore her name. She was remembered as a brave woman who risked giving hospitality to the Christian Church when to do so was to court censure and possibly death. According to a tradition that can be dated no earlier than the fifth century, she converted her pagan husband and his brother to the faith, both of whom were martyred before her. She is honored as the patron saint of musicians.

A Reading from an *Exposition of the Psalms*
by Augustine

"Praise the Lord with the lyre; make melody to him with the harp of ten strings! O sing to God a new song!" My friends, you have learned the new song: so now forget the old one. We are a new humanity, we have a new covenant with God; so let our song be new; new songs do not emerge from an old humanity. Only a new humanity can learn it, human beings whose old nature has been made new by the grace of God, men and women who enjoy a new covenant which is nothing less than the kingdom of heaven. Our hearts yearn for it. So let us sing our new song not with our lips but with our lives.

"Sing to God a new song. Sing to him with joyful melody." You ask me in what way each of us is to sing the praises of God. Well, sing to God, but not out of tune. God does not want his ears assaulted by discordant noise: sing in harmony, dear sisters and brothers.

Imagine you are asked to entertain some fine musician with a song. "Sing a song to please him," you are asked. There you are, quite untrained in music, anxious and afraid lest you irritate this skilled musician because what might pass unnoticed by an untrained ear will be criticized by a great artist. By the same token, no one is going to rush forward, thinking to please God (even if they think they have a beautiful voice) because God who will listen to that singer, and who will give his verdict on the performance, knows everything in us. Do you think you will command an art so polished that you need never fear singing a jarring note on that discerning listener's ear?

But God himself has provided you with a way of singing. You do not have to bother to search for the right words as if you needed to find a lyric to please God. Simply praise God with "songs of joy." It is fine praise of God when you sing with real joy. You ask, how is this done? It means realizing that words are not enough to express what we are singing to God in our hearts. At harvest time, both in the fields and the vineyard, the laborers work incredibly hard, and they always begin their day with songs whose words express their joy. But when their joy brims over and words are not enough, they abandon even this coherence and give themselves up to the sheer delight of singing.

What is this joy I speak of, this singing exultantly? It is an inner melody that means our hearts are bursting with feeling that words cannot contain. And to whom does such joy belong if not to the God who is beyond language? When words will not come, and you cannot keep silent, what else can you do but let the melody soar? What else can you do when the rejoicing heart runs out of words and the intensity of your joy will not be imprisoned by language? What else can you do but to sing out to God with "songs of joy?"

November 23

Clement

Bishop of Rome, *c.*100

Clement was active as an elder in the church in Rome toward the end of the first century and was reputed to have been a disciple of the apostles. He wrote a letter to the Corinthians which focused on ministry in the church and dealt with controversial issues relating to authority and duty. The letter clearly reveals an exercise of authority on the part of one senior presbyter intervening in a conflict in another church, and as such it provides valuable information about the history of the developing church and its ministry at this time. Clement's hierarchical view of church order set a future pattern for episcopal practice and ministry. He seems to have been president of a council of presbyters that governed the church in Rome and he appears to be writing on their behalf. A fourth-century document states that Clement was exiled to the Crimea where he was then put to death by being thrown into the sea with an anchor around his neck.

A Reading from a letter of Clement of Rome
to the Church in Corinth

How blessed and wonderful are the gifts of God, my friends! Some of them we can already comprehend—the life that knows no death, the splendor of righteousness, the liberating power of truth, the faith that is perfect assurance, the holiness of living chastely—but what of the things God has prepared for those who wait for him? Only the creator and Father of eternity knows their greatness and their beauty. Let us strive then, to be found among those who wait for him, that we too may share in these promised gifts. And how is this to be done, my friends? By fixing our minds on God; by finding out what would be pleasing and acceptable to him; by doing what is in harmony with his perfect will; and by following the way of truth. Thus injustice, wrongdoing of every kind, greed, covetousness, quarrelling, malice, and fraud should all be renounced.

This is the way, dear friends, that we find our salvation, even Jesus Christ, the high priest by whom our gifts are offered, and the defender by whom our weakness is aided. Through him we can gaze into the highest heaven and see the reflection of God's perfect and pure face. Through him the eyes of our hearts are opened, and our dim and darkened understanding unfolds like a flower in the sunlight; for through him the Lord has willed us to taste the wisdom of eternity. As it is written in Scripture: "He is the splendor of the majesty of God, and is as much greater than the angels as the title he has inherited is more excellent than theirs."

So my dear friends, let us serve resolutely in the army of the Lord, never swerving from his unerring commands. In the case of our physical bodies, the head is nothing without the feet, and our feet are useless without the head. Even the seemingly insignificant parts of our bodies are necessary and valued for the good working of the whole, each part working co-operatively, all united by a common subordination to maintain the integrity of the body.

In the same way let this corporate body of ours in Christ Jesus be maintained in integrity. Each of us should give precedence to the other according to his or her spiritual gifts. The strong are not to despise the weak, and the weak are to respect the strong. The rich should provide for the poor out of their resources, and the poor for their part should thank God for giving them somebody who can meet their needs. If you are wise, then display your wisdom by good deeds; and if you are modest, let others speak of your modesty instead of proclaiming the fact yourself.

To God we owe everything, and therefore on every count we are under obligation to thank him. Glory be to him for ever and ever. Amen.

November 25

James Otis Sargent Huntington

James Otis Sargent Huntington was born in 1854. While engaged in a ministry to immigrants on New York City's Lower East Side, he received a call to the monastic life and founded the first indigenous monastic order for men in the Episcopal Church, making his life vows on November 25, 1884. The Order of the Holy Cross grew slowly at first but finally settled at West Park, New York, and became one of the Church's best known monastic orders. Father Huntington served as superior of the order several times and continued an active ministry of preaching, teaching, and spiritual direction until his death in 1935. Huntington also continued to be deeply involved in the social issues of the time and did much to develop the commitment of the Episcopal Church to social ministries.

A Reading from *Bargainers and Beggars*
by J. O. S. Huntington

It belongs to God to give; it is our part to receive. That is a very simple and primary truth. Let us not on that account despise it. It is the truth with which our Lord began in teaching his disciples, that is, in teaching the world, including ourselves. Let us not think that we know better than he what we need to learn. "It belongs to God to give; it is ours to receive." Plain people, the poor, little children, know that, and are happy in knowing it. They make no secret of their weakness, their dependence, their need. They breathe, instinctively as it were, the universal prayer, "Give us this day our daily bread." They find it good to "hold fast by God," to "put their trust in the Lord God."

But what is clear as the light to the simple-hearted may be dim and obscure to the sophisticated and world-beguiled. How can it be otherwise when we find intelligent men, trained in habits of scientific accuracy, talking about the "gifts of Nature"? A moment's reflection ought to disclose the absurdity of the phrase, if taken as anything but a highly poetical expression. The gifts of Nature! But not only is it true that "the gift without the giver is bare," there can be no "gift" at all without a "giver." For giving is a moral act. It implies a will to impart—a "will to love," not merely a "will to live." If behind "Nature" is the personal will of God, then we can speak of the sunshine and the rain, the revolving seasons, and the fruits of the earth that they bring with them as "gifts." Otherwise the word has no real significance. One does not take off one's hat to a penny-in-the-slot machine, or express gratitude to an automat.

But if God gives us all we have, then he is giving continually. He is, in very deed, the giver. In him alone do we find the full realization of *bestowal*, of *donation*. For only his own love prompts him to give existence to his creatures, and to continue to endow them with what they have, or are, or ever can become. The very nature and being of a God as the only possessor and dispenser of any life there is in the universe imply that he must every moment communicate to every creature the power by which it exists. And just as this is the very place and nature of God, to be unceasingly the supplier of every want in the creature, so the very place and nature of the creature is nothing but this—to wait upon God, and receive from him what he alone can give, what he delights to give. The more distinct and clear-cut is our sense that what we have and are is a gift, the more vivid will be our sense of a direct and abiding relation with God, a consciousness that we are only because he is.

November 25

Catherine of Alexandria

Martyr, 4th century

Tradition has it that Catherine was a girl of a noble family who, because of her Christian faith, refused marriage with the emperor as she was already a "bride of Christ." She is said to have disputed with fifty philosophers whose job it was to convince her of her error, and she proved superior in argument to them all. She was then tortured by being splayed on a wheel and finally beheaded.

A Reading from a hymn "In Praise of Virginity"
by Ephrem of Edessa

Blessed are you, virgin, with whom
the comely name of virginity grows old.
In your branches chastity built a nest;
may your womb be a nest for her dwelling place.
May the power of mercy preserve your temple.

Blessed are you, heavenly sparrow
whose nest was on the cross of light.
You did not want to build a nest on earth
lest the serpent enter and destroy your offspring.

Blessed are your wings that were able to fly.
May you come with the holy eagles
that took flight and soared from the earth below
to the bridal couch of delights.

Blessed are you, O shoot that Truth cultivated;
He engrafted your medicine into the Tree of Life.
Your fruit exults and rejoices at all times
to drink the drink of the Book of Life.
Blessed are your branches.

Blessed are you, O bride, espoused to the Living One,
you who do not long for a mortal man.
Foolish is the bride who is proud
of the ephemeral crown that will be gone tomorrow.

Blessed is your heart, captivated by love
of a beauty portrayed in your mind.
You have exchanged the transitory bridal couch
for the bridal couch whose blessings are unceasing.

Blessed are you, free woman, who sold yourself
to the Lord who became a servant for your sake!

November 25

Isaac Watts

Hymn Writer, 1748

Born in Southampton in 1674, Isaac Watts was educated at the local grammar school and had the opportunity to go on to university, but declined because he preferred the dissenting academy at Stoke Newington. He received there an education of high academic standard and went on to become pastor to the Independent (or Congregationalist) Church at Mark Lane in London. Because of deteriorating health, he resigned this post in 1712 and retired to Stoke Newington. Seven years later, he opposed the imposition of the doctrine of the Trinity on his fellow dissenting ministers, which led to the belief that he had become a Unitarian. Isaac wrote several collections of hymns many of which are still used in worship. He died at Stoke Newington on this day in the year 1748.

A Reading from the poetry of Isaac Watts

When I survey the wondrous cross

When I survey the wondrous cross,
Where the young Prince of glory died,
My richest gain I count but loss,
And pour contempt on all my pride.

Forbid it, Lord, that I should boast
Save in the death of Christ my God;
All the vain things that charm me most,
I sacrifice them to his blood.

See from his head, his hands, his feet,
Sorrow and love flow mingled down;
Did e'er such love and sorrow meet,
Or thorns compose so rich a crown?

His dying crimson like a robe,
Spreads o'er his body on the tree;
Then am I dead to all the globe,
And all the globe is dead to me.

Were the whole realm of nature mine,
That were a present far too small;
Love so amazing, so divine,
Demands my soul, my life, my all.

The Day of Judgement

When the fierce North-wind with his airy forces
Rears up the Baltic to a foaming fury;
And the red lightning with a storm of hail comes
Rushing amain down;

How the poor sailors stand amazed and tremble,
While the hoarse thunder, like a bloody trumpet,
Roars a loud onset to the gaping waters,
Quick to devour them.

Such shall the noise be, and the wild disorder
(If things eternal may be like these earthly),
Such the dire terror when the great Archangel
Shakes the creation;

Tears the strong pillars of the vault of Heaven,
Breaks up old marble, the repose of princes;
See the graves open, and the bones arising,
Flames all around them.

Hark, the shrill outcries of the guilty wretches!
Lively bright horror and amazing anguish
Stare through their eyelids, while the living worm lies
Gnawing within them.

Thoughts, like old vultures, prey upon their heart-strings,
And the smart twinges, when their eye beholds the
Lofty Judge frowning, and a flood of vengeance
Rolling afore him.

Hopeless immortals! how they scream and shiver,
While devils push them to the pit wide-yawning,
Hideous and gloomy, to receive them headlong
Down to the center!

Stop here, my fancy: (all away, ye horrid
Doleful ideas!) come, arise to Jesus,
How he sits God-like! and the saints around him
Throned, yet adoring!

O may I sit there when he comes triumphant,
Dooming the nations! then ascend to glory,
While our Hosannas all along the passage
Shout the Redeemer!

November 28

Kamehameha & Emma

King and Queen of Hawaii, 1834 and 1885

Kamehameha became king of Hawaii at the age of twenty and worked with his wife Emma to establish the Anglican Church in the islands. The king had been upset by an experience of racism in the United States when he was taken for a servant during a visit, but he had been deeply impressed by the beauty and dignity of Anglican liturgy during a visit to England. He translated The Book of Common Prayer *and much of the hymnal into Hawaiian. The influx of Americans and Europeans into Hawaii had brought with it diseases that ravaged the native population and Kamehameha and Emma worked to establish hospitals. The king went door-to-door with a notebook soliciting pledges for the establishment of Queen's Hospital, still the largest civilian hospital in Hawaii. After the king's early death, Emma continued to devote herself to acts of charity and was deeply involved in the creation of Saint Andrew's Priory school for girls and Iolani College.*

A Reading from a letter of Queen Emma
(also known as Kaleleonalani)

My Dear Hoapili,

Your letter of the 17th arrived this morning and I am glad to hear that both of you are well & once more at your old place. I rejoice to hear Kiliwehi as far as appearances can tell is trying to be herself again; how grateful ought we to be more especially here to our ever loving Father in Heaven for his patience with her shortcomings & weaknesses. I have frequently thought of her lately. She needs much love though they be our pleading intercessory prayers as well as her own to the God of Mercy whose all seeing eye can fathom the yearnings of a contrite heart. How appropriately the teachings of our dear church through her *Book of Common Prayer* comes home to us in our sorrows to comfort & lift us up. I like very much that little sentence from Scripture which the young sailor boys of the Clio used to chant at the commencement of our Sunday services on board that ship "I will arise & go to my Father & will say unto him, 'Father I have sinned against heaven & before thee & am no more worthy to be called thy son.'" I have taught my household to chant it & my little boys sing it tolerably well. Besides the pleasure of hearing their young voices lifted up in prayer to their Maker it carries me back to the midst of that mariner congregation on the Clio out on the wide boundless sea. One of the essential parts of our creed, "I believe in the communion of saints" certainly is clear in moments like that. At least we know that every Sunday we & they & our friends scattered over this world as well as those gone before are all gathered before his throne breathing the one wish, to me who have all that is dear taken to the world of spirits it is a consoling knowledge to know that we are only separated by this mortal body. If we would but say with earnest truth at our daily prayers "Vouchsafe O Lord to keep us this day without sin & act accordingly it would be well for us."

Good bye
Kaleleonalani

alternative reading

A Reading from King Kamehameha's Preface to the
Hawaiian Book of Common Prayer
translated by Kamehameha

If we are Christians according to the teaching of the Holy Scriptures, we cannot withhold our belief in the Holy Catholic Church established on earth by Christ Jesus our Lord. There are branches of this church in every land. How the church has come down from the times of the Apostles to these days in which we live is not a matter about which the generality of men are ignorant. It were useless perhaps to set forth how she has taken root sooner or later all over the world. She is planted in America, in Asia, in

Europe, in Africa, in the islands which stud the ocean, and now, behold! She is here with us in these islands of our own.

Let us see how she felt her way and reached us at last. Our ancient idols had been dethroned, the sexes ate together, and the prohibition upon certain articles of food was held in derision by the females to whom it had been a law; the temples were demolished, the *kapu* had become no more than a memory of something that was hateful before, and the priests had no longer any rites to perform—indeed, there were no priests, for their office had died out. These changes came no doubt by the inspiration of the Holy Spirit, acting through blind, unsuspecting agents. These revolutions were greatly furthered and helped along by those devout and devoted men who first brought here and translated into our mother-tongue God's Holy Word; and we, while these lines are being written, see the complete fulfillment of what the Bible enjoins in the establishment here of Christ's church complete in all her functions.

The church is established here in Hawaii through the breathings of the Holy Spirit and by the agency of the chiefs. Vancouver, long ago, was requested to send us the True God; Iolani (Liholiho, the king who, as Kamehameha II, died in London in 1824) then your King, went to a distant and powerful country to hasten the advent of that which our eyes now see and the spirit within us acknowledges, the very church, here planted in Hawaii—but how long we had waited! It is true that the representatives of the various forms of worship had come here, and there had been many controversies, one side generally denying what some other sect had laid most stress on. Now we have grounds to rejoice, and now we may hold fast to the hope that the true Church of God has verily taken root here. In this *Book of Common Prayer* we see all that she prescribes; we see what she rules and enforces; what her offices, her creeds, her system, her support in life, her promises in death; what things we ought to do and leave undone; which things being constantly before our eyes and dutifully followed, we may humbly hope to be indeed her children, and be strengthened to fulfill all the commandments of our blessed Lord, the one Head of the One Church, which we now gladly behold and gratefully acknowledge.

November 30

Saint Andrew the Apostle

Andrew appears to have been one of the first four disciples called by Jesus, and in the Gospels of Matthew, Mark, and Luke, is described as a fisherman in partnership with his brother Simon Peter and the brothers James and John. It is in the Gospel according to John, however, that most is learned about him. According to John, all four were disciples of John the Baptist before Jesus summoned them. The two traditions are not irreconcilable. Andrew is honored as the first "missionary" because it was he who went off to bring his brother Simon Peter to meet Jesus. Andrew seems to have remained with Jesus until the very end. He was there at the feeding of the five thousand and then later, when some Greeks in Jerusalem wanted to see Jesus, Philip brought them to Andrew who told Jesus of their desire. Tradition has him travelling on several missionary journeys in Scythia, and eventually being martyred by being crucified on an X-shaped cross. He became the patron saint of Scotland because of a legend that his relics had been brought there in the eighth century. The Church in the East also honors him as the founder of the Patriarchal See of Constantinople.

A Reading from *The Cost of Discipleship*
by Dietrich Bonhoeffer

The call of Jesus goes forth, and is at once followed by the response of obedience. The response of the disciples is an act of obedience, not a confession of faith in Jesus. How could the call immediately evoke obedience?

The story of the call of the first disciples is a stumbling-block to our natural reason, and it is no wonder that frantic attempts have been made to separate the two events. By hook or by crook a bridge must be found between them. Something must have happened in between, some psychological or historical event. Thus we get the stupid question: Surely the disciples must have known Jesus before, and that previous acquaintance explains their readiness to hear the Master's call. Unfortunately our text is ruthlessly silent on this point, and in fact it regards the immediate sequence of call and response as a matter of crucial importance. It displays not the slightest interest in the psychological reasons for a person's religious decisions. And why? For the simple reason that the cause behind the immediate following of call by response is Jesus Christ himself. It is Jesus who calls, and because it is Jesus, the disciple follows at once.

This encounter is a testimony to the absolute, direct, and unaccountable authority of Jesus. There is no need of any preliminaries, and no other consequence but obedience to the call. Because Jesus is the Christ, he has the authority to call and to demand obedience to his word. Jesus summons us to follow him not as a teacher of a pattern of the good life, but as the Christ, the Son of God. In this short text, Jesus Christ and his claim are proclaimed to the world. Not a word of praise is given to the disciple for his decision for Christ. We are not expected to contemplate the disciple, but only him who calls, and his absolute authority. According to our text, there is no road to faith or discipleship, no other road only obedience to the call of Jesus.

And what does the text inform us about the content of discipleship? Follow me, run along behind me! That is all. To follow in Christ's steps is something which is void of all content. It gives us no intelligible program for a way of life, no goal or ideal to strive after. When we are called to follow Christ, we are summoned to an exclusive attachment to his person. The grace of his call bursts all the bonds of legalism. It is a gracious call, a gracious commandment. It transcends the difference between the law and the gospel. Christ calls, the disciple follows; that is grace and commandment in one.

alternative reading

A Reading from a sermon by Mark Frank

Jesus came first and walked by the sea. He looked upon Andrew and Peter and spake to them. And what then? They straightway followed and who but Jesus?

Let us always think, when we hear Christ calling us to his service, that we cannot make too much haste to follow him. It may be he has called his last, and will call no more; or he will be gone if we make not haste. It is not safe to loiter by the way for fear of temptations that may prevent our good purposes and quite overthrow our holy resolutions. It is an unworthy usage and unmannerly to stand talking to anyone else when God is speaking to us to come to him. Christ would have Andrew and Peter do his business quickly: for in the midst of their work he called them, and in the midst they leave: away with nets, come Christ; fish who will, for them they will follow Christ, not so much as stay to draw up their nets, be what will in them, they care not; let all go, so they may catch him.

And alas what have we, the best, the richest of us as highly as we think of ourselves and ours, more than Andrew and his brother: a few old broken nets? What are all our honors but old nets to catch the breath of the world? What are our estates but nets to entangle us? What are all our ways and devices of thriving but so many several nets to catch a little yellow sand and mud? What are all those fine catching ways of eloquence, knowledge, good parts of mind and body, but so many nets and snares to catch others with? The rational soul itself we too often make but a net to catch flies, petty, buzzing knowledges only; few solid sober thoughts. And our life itself, what is it but a few rotten threads knit together into veins and sinews, its construction so fragile that the least stick or stone can unloose it or break all to pieces?

O blessed saint of this day, that we could but leave these nets as thou didst thine; that nothing might any longer entangle us or keep us from our Master's service! Follow we Saint Andrew as he did Christ; follow him to Christ, cheerfully and without delay, and while it is today, begin our course. Cast off the networks, the catching desires of the flesh and the world, and so you also may be said to have left your nets. And having so weaned your souls from inordinate affection to things below, let Christ be your business, his life your pattern, his commands your law.

Be followers of Christ, and let Saint Andrew this day lead you after him into all universal obedience, ready, pure, sincere. You may well throw away your nets, having caught him in whom you have caught glory and immortality and eternal life; and by following him shall undoubtedly come at last out of this sea of toil and misery into the port and haven of everlasting rest, and joys, and happiness.

DECEMBER

December 1

Nicholas Ferrar

Deacon, Founder of the Little Gidding Community, 1637

Born in London in 1592, Nicholas Ferrar was educated at Clare Hall (now Clare College), Cambridge and elected a Fellow there in 1610. After 1613, he traveled on the Continent for five years, trying his hand as a businessman and then as a parliamentarian on his return. In 1625, he moved to Little Gidding in Huntingdonshire, where he was joined by his brother and sister and their families and by his mother. They established together a community life of prayer, using The Book of Common Prayer, *and developing a life of charitable works in the locality. He was ordained to the diaconate by William Laud the year after they arrived. He wrote to his niece in 1631, "I purpose and hope by God's grace to be to you not as a master but as a partner and fellow student." This indicates the depth and feeling of the community life Nicholas and his family strove to maintain. After the death of Nicholas on this day in 1637, the community was broken up in 1646 by the Puritans, who were suspicious of it and referred to it as the "Arminian Nunnery." They feared it would promote the return of Romish practices in England, and so all Nicholas's manuscripts were burned.*

A Reading from *The Life of Mr. George Herbert*
by Isaac Walton

Mr. Nicholas Ferrar (who got the reputation of being called "Saint Nicholas" at the age of six years) was born in London. At an early age he was made Fellow of Clare Hall in Cambridge where he continued to be eminent for his piety, temperance, and learning. About the twenty-sixth year of his age, he betook himself to travel, in which he added to his Latin and Greek, a perfect knowledge of all the languages spoken in the western parts of our Christian world; and understood well the principles of their religion and of their manner and the reasons of their worship. In this his travel he met with many persuasions to come into a communion with that Church which calls itself Catholic, but he returned from his travels as he went, eminent for his obedience to his mother, the Church of England.

In his absence from England, Mr. Ferrar's father (who was a merchant) allowed him a liberal maintenance; and, not long after his return into England, Mr. Ferrar had by the death of his father, or an elder brother, or both, an estate left him that enabled him to purchase land to the value of four or five hundred pounds a year, the greatest part of which land was at Little Gidding, four or six miles from Huntingdon and about eighteen from Cambridge; which place he chose for the privacy of it, and for the hall, which had the parish-church, or chapel, belonging and adjoining near to it. For Mr. Ferrar, having seen the manners and vanities of the world and found them to be, as Mr. Herbert says, "a nothing between two dishes," did so condemn it, that he resolved to spend the remainder of his life in mortifications and in devotion and charity, and to be always prepared for death.

He and his family, which were about thirty in number, were like a little college. About the year 1630, he did betake himself to a constant and methodical service of God, and it was in this manner. He, being accompanied with most of his family, did himself use to read the Common Prayers (for he was a deacon) every day at the appointed hours of ten and four in the parish-church, which was very near his house and which he had both repaired and adorned for it was fallen into a great ruin by reason of a depopulation of the village before Mr. Ferrar bought the manor.

And he did also constantly read the Matins every morning at the hour of six, either in the church, or in an oratory which was within his own house. And many of the family did there continue with him after the prayers were ended, and there they spent some hours in singing hymns or anthems, sometimes in the church, and often to an organ in the oratory. And there they sometimes betook themselves to meditate, or to pray privately, or to read part of the New Testament to themselves, or to continue praying or reading the psalms. And it is to be noted that in this continued serving of God, the Psalter was in every four and twenty hours sung or read over, from the first to the last verse; and this was done as constantly as the sun runs his circle every day about the world, and then begins again the same instant that it ended.

Thus did Mr. Ferrar and his happy family serve God day and night. And this course of piety and great liberality to his poor neighbors, Mr. Ferrar maintained till his death, which was in the year 1637.

December 2

Channing Moore Williams

Missionary Bishop in China and Japan, 1910

Channing Moore Williams was born in 1829. When Japan was opened at last to Western businesses and missionaries, he was serving in China, and was sent from there to Nagasaki, beginning work there in 1859. Believing in the importance of a slow and careful approach, Williams waited nine years before baptizing his first convert. In that same year, Williams was consecrated bishop for the church's mission in China and Japan but after two years decided to concentrate his efforts in Japan. In 1874, Williams established a divinity school that eventuality became Saint Paul's (Rikkyo) University, still one of Japan's best known colleges. In 1887, Williams helped bring together the English and American missions to form the Nippon Seikokai, the Holy Catholic Church of Japan. The new church had fewer than a thousand members at the time but now includes eleven dioceses. Williams resigned his jurisdiction in 1889 but stayed in Japan for nearly twenty years after that, assisting his successor and helping to establish new congregations.

A Reading from a letter of Channing Moore Williams

In a former journal, I mentioned that Mr. Liggins and myself had determined on making an attempt to establish a new mission station at Tá-Tsong. We made the effort, but failed, as no one was disposed to incur the wrath from the Mandarin for renting us a house. We returned to Shanghai at the time, much discouraged at our want of success, but now that we are established at a place in nearly every respect superior, we rejoice at our failure. We can now look back and recognize "the hand of our God which was good upon us," leading us by a way that we knew not, and opening a wide and, I trust, effectual door for preaching the blessed gospel of our Lord Jesus Christ. After our return to Shanghai, I met at Dzang-Zok several boatmen, whose accounts at Dzang-Zok were such that it was proposed that we should visit it before making another attempt at Tá-Tsong. We accordingly came here, about the Chinese New Year, and were so delighted with the place and the people—the seeming readiness with which they listened to the message of salvation—the eagerness with which they received books—their bearing toward ourselves, and the absence, in a great measure, of those offensive epithets, so generally applied to foreigners in China—that we were not many days in coming to the determination that, if possible, we would make Dzang-Zok our future home....

Melanchthon, in the ardor of his first love, thought it would be only necessary to tell sinners of the gracious Savior he had found, and numbers would immediately flee unto him, to hide them from the wrath of an offended God. But Luther replied, "Old Satan is too strong for young Melanchthon." This is a lesson it might be well for some to learn, who seem to think that so soon as the gospel is made known to the heathen, they will see it so infinitely superior to their own false and foolish systems—that it possesses such beauty, and such suitableness to their wants, they will forthwith close with its offers of mercy. But it is not to be expected that Satan will give up China thus easily. He considers it the fairest portion of his dominions. Here he rules with undisputed sway over the hearts of 360 million people—a third of our race. Here he has entrenched himself for ages behind the most effectual barriers—not the least formidable of which is an overweening pride, and a system of morality, second only to that taught in the Bible the practice of which he persuades them is possible, and restores them to that state of holiness of heart, which they think all have at birth. Now, the missionary who comes, and the church which sends the missionary, must make up their minds that there will be a long and desperate struggle before Satan is expelled. Every inch of ground will have to be contested. That he shall be driven from China none can doubt. The heathen have been given to the Son of God for his inheritance, and the uttermost parts of the earth for his possession. We should therefore labor and faint not. Because we do not meet with immediate success, we have no *right* to be discouraged and relax our efforts. This is too much like dictating to God. It is almost as if we should say to him, because you do not give success in the manner, the measure, and at the time we wish, we work no longer. God's ways are not as man's ways, and we must labor untiringly *when* and *where* he directs. He will see to the rest.

I know you will rejoice with us. God has been before us and made our path plain. Oh, that his presence may continue with us, and prepare the hearts of many of this people to receive the engrafted word, which is able to save their souls. The encouragement we have met, I doubt not will be found at other places. We greatly need more missionaries to occupy these posts. But where are the men? Are there none who will come over and help us? May the Lord of the harvest put it into the hearts of many to come to China to gather sheaves into his garner.

December 3

Francis Xavier

Missionary, Apostle of the Indies, 1552

Francis was born at the castle of Xavier in Spanish Navarre in 1506. He was educated in Paris and, with Ignatius of Loyola, became one of the group of seven who took vows as the first members of the Society of Jesus, or Jesuits. Since preaching the gospel overseas was an integral part of the Jesuit vocation, Francis sailed for Goa, on the west coast of India, in 1541. He traveled all over the East Indies, evangelizing and establishing the Church in Ceylon, Malacca, Malaya and notably in Japan, where he left behind two thousand converts. He had just reached China when he died on board ship in December in the year 1552.

A Reading from two letters of Francis Xavier to Ignatius of Loyola, written while working in India between 1542 and 1544

We have visited the villages of the new converts who accepted the Christian religion a few years ago. No Portuguese live here the country is so utterly barren and poor. The native Christians have no priests. They know only that they are Christians. There is nobody to say Mass for them; nobody to teach them the Creed, the Our Father, the Hail Mary, and the Commandments of God's Law.

I have not stopped since the day I arrived. I have conscientiously made the rounds of the villages. I bathed in the sacred waters [of baptism] all the children who had not yet been baptized. This means that I have purified a very large number of children so young that, as the saying goes, they could not tell their right hand from their left. The older children would not let me say my Office or eat or sleep until I had taught them one prayer or another. Then I began to understand: "The kingdom of heaven belongs to such as these."

I could not refuse so devout a request without failing in devotion myself. I taught them first the confession of faith in the Father, the Son, and the Holy Spirit; then the Apostles' Creed, the Our Father, and Hail Mary. I noticed among them persons of great intelligence. If only someone could educate them in the Christian way of life, I have no doubt that they would make excellent Christians.

Many, many people hereabouts are not becoming Christians for one reason only: there is nobody to make them Christians. Again and again I have thought of going round the universities of Europe, especially Paris, and everywhere crying out like a madman, riveting the attention of those with more learning than charity: "What a tragedy! How many souls are being shut out of heaven and falling into hell, thanks to you!" I wish they would work as hard at this as they do at their books, and so settle their account with God for their learning and the talents entrusted to them.

This thought would certainly stir most of them to meditate on spiritual realities, to listen actively to what God is saying to them. They would forget their own desires, their human affairs, and give themselves over entirely to God's will and his choice. They would cry out with all their heart: "Lord, I am here! What do you want me to do? Send me anywhere you like even to India!"

December 4

John of Damascus

Monk, Teacher of the Faith, *c.*760

John was born in Damascus about the year 675. The city by this date was Muslim. John's father, although a Christian, was Chief of the Revenue, and the principal representative of the Christians in the city. In 716, John, by then well-educated in science and theology, became a monk at the monastic settlement of Mar Saba near Jerusalem and later was ordained priest there. He became a prolific writer of theological works and of hymns. His summary of the teachings of the Greek Fathers, called De Fide Orthodoxa, *proved an immense influence in the Church in the following centuries, in both East and West. He died on this day about the year 760.*

A Reading from a treatise
On the Incarnation and the Holy Icons
by John of Damascus

In former times God, who is without form or body, could never be depicted. But now that God has appeared in the flesh and dwelt among us, I make an image of God in so far as he has become visible. I do not venerate matter; but I venerate the creator of matter who became matter for my sake, who willed to make his dwelling in matter; who worked out my salvation through matter. I shall never cease, therefore, to venerate the matter which wrought my salvation. Do not insult matter, for it is honorable. Nothing is without honor that God has made.

How could God be born out of material things which have no existence in themselves? God's body is God because he joined it to his person by a union which shall never pass away. The divine nature remains the same; the flesh created in time is henceforth quickened by reason-endowed soul. Because of this I salute all matter with reverence because God has filled it with his grace and power. Through it my salvation has come to me. Was not the thrice-happy and thrice-blessed wood of the cross matter? Was not the holy and exalted mount of Calvary matter? Was not the life-bearing rock, the holy and life-giving tomb, the fountain of our resurrection, was it not matter? Is not the ink in the most holy book of the Gospels matter? Is not the life-giving altar matter? Do we not receive from it the bread of life? Are not gold and silver matter? From them we make crosses, patens, chalices! And over and above all these things, is not the Body and Blood of our Lord matter?

Thus either do away with the honor and veneration all these material things deserve, or accept the tradition of the Church and the veneration of icons. Learn to reverence God and his friends; follow the inspiration of the Holy Spirit. Never despise matter, for matter is not despicable. God has made nothing despicable. Rather, contemplate the glory of the Lord, for his face has been unveiled.

December 5

Clement of Alexandria

Priest, *c.*217

Clement was born in Athens of pagan parents in about the year 153. The apostles and their immediate successors laid the foundation on which, toward the end of the second century, Clement of Alexandria and others began to create a sophisticated literature, drawing on the Greek philosophical tradition and able to dismiss paganism as an outworn creed, no longer worthy of serious attention. Having absorbed the best the Greek philosophers had to offer, Clement turned to Christianity and traveled extensively to learn from the best teachers of his day. Coming to Alexandria in 190, he became the head of the catechetical school in that city and produced an impressive body of writing that drew extensively on both pagan and Christian writings and was centered on the idea of Christ, the Logos, as both the source of all human reason and the unique interpreter of God to humanity. Clement was forced to flee Alexandria by an outbreak of persecution in 202 and is supposed to have died as a martyr in about the year 217.

A Reading from *An Exhortation to the Greeks*
by Clement of Alexandria

Let us haste, let us run, my fellow-men, us, who are God-loving and God-like images of the Word. Let us haste, let us run, let us take his yoke, let us receive, to conduct us to immortality, the good charioteer of men. Let us love Christ. He led the colt with its parent; and having yoked the team of humanity to God, directs his chariot to immortality, hastening clearly to fulfill, by driving now into heaven, what he shadowed forth before by riding into Jerusalem. A spectacle most beautiful to the Father is the eternal Son crowned with victory. Let us aspire, then, after what is good; let us become God-loving men, and obtain the greatest of all things that are incapable of being harmed—God and life. Our helper is the Word; let us put confidence in him; and never let us be visited with such a craving for silver and gold, and glory, as for the Word of truth himself. For it will not, it will not be pleasing to God himself if we value least those things that are worth most, and hold in the highest estimation the manifest enormities and the utter impiety of folly, and ignorance, and thoughtlessness, and idolatry. For not improperly the sons of the philosophers consider that the foolish are guilty of profanity and impiety in whatever they do; and describing ignorance itself as a species of madness, allege that the multitude are nothing but madmen. There is therefore no room to doubt, the Word will say, whether it is better to be sane or insane; but holding on to truth with our teeth, we must with all our might follow God, and in the exercise of wisdom regard all things to be, as they are, his; and besides, having learned that we are the most excellent of his possessions, let us commit ourselves to God, loving the Lord God, and regarding this as our business all our life long. And if what belongs to friends be reckoned common property, and man be the friend of God—for through the mediation of the Word has he been made the friend of God—then accordingly all things become man's, because all things are God's, and the common property of both the friends, God and man.

It is time, then, for us to say that the pious Christian alone is rich and wise, and of noble birth, and thus call and believe him to be God's image, and also his likeness, having become righteous and holy and wise by Jesus Christ, and so far already like God. Accordingly this grace is indicated by the prophet when he says, "I said that you are gods, and all sons of the Highest." For us, yes for us, he has adopted, and wishes to be called the Father of us alone, not of the unbelieving. Such is then our position who are the attendants of Christ.

As are men's wishes, so are their words;
As are their words, so are their deeds;
And as their works, such is their life.
Good is the whole life of those who have known Christ.

Enough, I think, of words, though, impelled by love to man, I might have gone on to pour out what I had from God, that I might exhort to what is the greatest of blessings—salvation. For discourses concerning the life that has no end are not readily brought to the end of their disclosures. To you still remains this conclusion, to choose which will profit you most—judgment or grace. For I do not think there is even room for doubt which of these is the better; nor is it allowable to compare life with destruction.

December 6

Nicholas
Bishop of Myra, *c.*342

Nicholas was a fourth-century bishop of Myra in Asia Minor (southern Turkey). His reputation as a worker of wonders was enhanced by a ninth-century author of his hagiography and he is now best known through these stories. Many of them concern his love and care for children, how he fed the hungry, healed the sick, and cared for the oppressed. He saved three girls from a life of prostitution by providing them with dowries and so developed the tradition of bearing gifts to children on his feast day, a practice appropriated by the Christmas celebrations. Nicholas is also one of the patron saints of Russia.

A Reading from a homily of Gregory the Great

Our Lord said to his disciples: "See, I am sending you out like lambs among wolves." There are many people, when put in positions of authority, who become hard and severe, relishing the chance to tear their subordinates to pieces, and using their power to terrify and hurt those whom they are called to serve. There is no love in their hearts because they always need to be in control: they forget that they are called to nurture their people as a parent. They exchange humility for pride in the positions they occupy, and though outwardly they may sometimes appear indulgent, inwardly they are full of anger. It is of them that in another place in the Gospels our Lord says: "They come to you in sheep's clothing, but inwardly they are ravenous wolves."

My friends, we should remember that we are sent as lambs among wolves, and must therefore guard our innocence lest malice overtake us. Those who undertake any pastoral office should never be the cause of evil, and should actually be prepared to have to endure it. By gentleness they must soften the anger of the violent: wounded ourselves by ill treatment, we can bring healing to other sinners. If on a particular occasion a zeal for justice requires a display of severity, then let severity have its source in love and not brutality. In this way, authority is demonstrated outwardly, and inwardly we experience a true parental love for those in our care. This is what our blessed Master was teaching us when he himself demonstrated that his was no selfish love, being unconcerned with worldly honor or ambition.

Our Lord continues: "Take neither purse, nor bag for the journey, nor sandals, and greet no one along the way." We should have such confidence in God that though we have no material security, we will never lack the necessities of life. Such confidence obviates the necessity of spending time in the pursuit of temporal goods when we should be securing eternal goods for others. We have no leisure for idle conversation in our calling; rather we must hurry along the path of preaching.

December 7

Ambrose

Bishop of Milan, 397

Born in Trier in 339, Ambrose was of an aristocratic family and was Governor of northern Italy, with his headquarters in Milan. While trying to bring peace to the Christian community, with Arianism and orthodoxy each trying to gain the election of its man as bishop, Ambrose, known and respected by all, though not yet baptized, found himself being urged to accept the role of bishop himself, the gathered Christian populace taking up the cry, "Ambrose for bishop." He finally accepted and was baptized and consecrated on this day in the year 374. Ambrose proved his worth, becoming a teacher and preacher of great renown, promoting the essential divinity of Christ as being at the center of Christian faith. He is credited with being the first person to introduce hymns into Western worship, and wrote several hymns himself which gave a clear understanding of orthodox teaching. He came up against the Imperial powers and, with the support of the whole community, stood firm against the interference of the state in church affairs and matters of faith. He also baptized the future Saint Augustine. Ambrose died on Good Friday, April 4, in the year 397.

A Reading from a treatise *On Penitence* by Ambrose

Show your wound to the Physician so that he may heal it. Though you refuse to expose it to his gaze, Christ still knows it: he is waiting to hear your voice. Wash away the scars of your sins by your tears. That is what the woman in the gospel did. She wiped away the decaying smell of her sin: she washed away her faults when she washed the feet of Jesus with her tears.

Lord Jesus, allow me to wash the stains from your feet which you have contracted since you walked within me. O that you would allow me to wash the steps before you of my faults! But where could I ever obtain the living water with which to wash them? And yet, though I have no living water within me, I can at least offer you my tears, trusting that while I wash your feet with them, I am cleansing myself.

But where do I find the grace of hearing what you said to her: "Her sins, which are many, are forgiven, for she loved much?" I have to confess, Lord, my debts are greater. The sins that have been forgiven me are more numerous because I have come to the priesthood from the uproar of the law courts and the burden of public life. I am afraid that I may be found ungrateful, if I, to whom more has been forgiven, should be found to have loved less.

And yet if we are unable to equal this woman, the Lord Jesus knows how to help the weak. He himself comes to the tomb to release us. O Lord, I beg you come to my tomb, wash me with your tears for my hardened, dry eyes do not possess tears sufficient to wash me. But if you will weep for me, I shall indeed be saved. As you once called forth your servant Lazarus from the tomb, call forth me. I find myself bound down with the chains of my sins, my feet fettered, my hands tied. I am buried in dead thoughts and works. Yet at your voice I shall walk free, and shall be found worthy to sit at your feast in your house.

Those whom you set free, you also guard. Guard, therefore, your work Lord; guard in me the grace you have given me, in spite of my flight from you. I knew that I was not worthy to be called to the episcopate because I had devoted myself to secular affairs, and yet by your grace I am what I am. Indeed, I am the least of all bishops, the lowest in merit of the bishops. But since you have granted me to work for your Church, guard the fruits of my labor. You called me to the priesthood when I was a lost child. Let me not lose myself in my priesthood.

Above all give me the grace of compassion. Grant me the ability to have compassion on sinners from the depth of my heart: for that is of supreme importance. Give me compassion every time I witness the fall of a sinner. Let me never arrogantly admonish such a person, but let me suffer with him and weep with him. And when I weep for my neighbor, make me weep for myself as well. This is vital, for he who rejoices at the downfall of another is rejoicing at the victory of the devil. Let us rather mourn when we hear that one of us for whom Christ died, has perished, for Christ despises no one.

December 8

The Conception of the Blessed Virgin Mary

This festival in honor of the Conception of the Mother of our Lord is celebrated on this day in both the Eastern and the Western Church. This feast, which dates from the seventh century, marks the dawn of the New Covenant, celebrating the gracious preparation by God of his people to receive their Savior and Lord, putting "heaven in ordinary" and showing that mortal flesh can indeed bring Christ to the world.

A Reading from the discourses of Anselm of Canterbury

Sky, stars, earth, rivers, day, night, and all things that are meant to serve us and be for our good rejoice because of you, blessed Lady. Through you they have in a way come back to life, enriched with a new grace that words cannot describe. When they lost the noble purpose of their nature for which they had been made, of serving and helping those who praise God, they were like dead things. They were crushed, disfigured, and abused by idol worshippers for whom they had not been made. They rejoice now as if they had come to life again. Now they are made beautiful because they serve and are used by those who believe in God.

A new and priceless grace has made them almost leap for joy. They have not merely felt God himself, their creator, ruling them invisibly from above, but they have seen him visibly within themselves using them in his work of sanctification. These immense benefits have come through the blessed fruit of the blessed womb of the blessed Mary.

Through the fullness of your grace, the things in the lower world rejoice in the gift of freedom and the things above the world are gladdened by being renewed. Through the one glorious Son of your glorious virginity all the just who died before his life-giving death rejoice that their captivity has been ended, and the angels delight that their half-ruined city is restored.

O woman, full and more than full of grace, all creation has received of the overflow of your fullness and its youth has been renewed! O blessed and more than blessed Virgin, through your blessing all creation is blessed. Not only is creation blessed by the creator, but creation blesses its creator.

God gave to Mary his Son, the only-begotten of his heart, equal to himself, whom he loved as himself. From Mary he fashioned himself a Son, not another one but the same, so that by nature there would be one and the same Son both of God and of Mary. Every nature is created by God, and God is born of Mary. God created all things and Mary gave birth to God. God himself, who made all things, made himself from Mary. In this way he remade all that he had made. He who was able to make all things out of nothing, when they had been defaced would not remake them without Mary's help.

God is, then, Father of all created things and Mary is mother of all that has been recreated. God is Father of the institution of all things and Mary is mother of the restitution of all things. God begot him through whom all things were made and Mary gave birth to him through whom all things were saved. God begot him without whom nothing at all exists and Mary gave birth to him without whom nothing that exists is good.

The Lord is indeed with you, Mary. For he granted to you that all nature should owe so great a debt to you jointly with himself.

alternative reading

A Reading from *Mary, Mother of God, Mother of the Poor*
by Ivone Gebara and Maria Bingemer

Today's feast must be understood in connection with the people of which Mary is both figure and symbol, and in relation to God in whom she believes and who chooses her and gives her a particular vocation and mission within salvation history.

As "Daughter of Zion" Mary is to be understood as the incarnation of the Jewish people from which she descends and to which she is closely connected. With her the journey of this people on the way toward the Messiah who is the fullness of time comes to its destination. Israel, God's chosen people, is more particularly that people in whose midst God resides and dwells by means of the temple. Jerusalem, the holy city which after the trials of exile once more takes on and represents the community of the chosen people, is the beloved spouse of Yahweh her husband. All her infidelities are redeemed by this God, whose love is more powerful than anything else. Her afflictions are turned into joy by the presence of the husband. Mary personifies and sums up the ancient Zion-Jerusalem. In her the process of renewal and purification of the whole people of God a process that has as its goal that the people will live the alliance with God more fully finds a model begin-ning. Wholly belonging to God, Mary is the prototype of what the people is called to be, chosen "in him before the world began, to be holy and blameless."

The full identity of the people, given by God in creation and election, and lost in the people's infidelity and exile, is restored by God in a "new creation," as it were, with the advent of new heavens and a new earth. In Mary this new creation actually takes place. She is the figure of the re-created people, filled and overflowing with the glory and power of Yahweh, pregnant with the promised Messiah who has now been sent. The time in which God's presence and holiness were restricted to the stone temple in Jerusalem is drawing to a close. Now, in the fullness of time, human flesh is God's temple. It is in the flesh of the woman Mary, full of grace, pregnant with the man Jesus, that the fullness of divine holiness is found in the world. It is in the flesh of every man and every woman who belong to the same race as Jesus and Mary that God must be sought, respected, venerated, and adored.

Today's feast of the conception of Mary rehabilitates woman's bodiliness, which in Genesis is denounced as the cause of original sin, laying on women a blemish and a burden that were difficult to bear. It is this body animated by the divine Spirit that is proclaimed blessed. In it God works the fullness of God's wonders.

December 12

Jane Frances de Chantal

Foundress of the Order of the Visitation, 1641

Jane Frances de Chantal was born at Dijon in France in 1572. As a young woman she married happily, and had four children. In 1601, however, her husband was killed in an accident. In her widowhood she resolved to give herself more profoundly to the spiritual life, and took a vow of chastity. In 1604 she met Francis de Sales, and placed herself under his spiritual direction. The correspondence between them which has survived reveals a quite remarkable friendship. In 1610, while still maintaining her duties as a mother, she founded the first convent of the Visitation at Annecy in Savoy for women and widows unsuited to the severe ascetic life of many religious congregations. She devoted the remainder of her life to visiting the sick and the poor, and fostering the Order. She had considerable administrative ability, and by the time of her death in 1641 a further sixty-four convents had been founded. Vincent de Paul, who knew her personally and well, said that she was "one of the holiest people I have ever met on this earth."

A Reading from a letter of Jane Frances de Chantal to the Sisters of the Visitation at Annecy, written from Paris on September 30, 1619

Since our Lord, in his goodness, has gathered our hearts into one, allow me, my dearest sisters, to greet you all, as a community and individually; for this same Lord will not allow me to greet you in any other way. But what a greeting it is! The very one that our great and worthy Father [Francis] taught us: LIVE JESUS! Yes, my beloved sisters and daughters, I say the words with intense delight: LIVE JESUS in our memory, in our will, and in our actions! Have in your thoughts only Jesus, in your will have only the longing for his love, and in your actions have only obedience and submission to his good pleasure by an exact observance of the Rule, not only in externals, but much more, in your interior spirit: a spirit of gentle cordiality toward one another, a spirit of recollection of your whole being before our divine Master, and that true, sincere humility which makes us as simple and gentle as lambs. Finally, strive for that loving union of hearts which brings about a holy peace and the kind of blessing we should desire to have in the house of God and his holy Mother.

All this is what I want from you, my dearest daughters, and I urge you to have great devotion to our Lady to whom I beg you to pray for me. Every day of my life I offer all of you to her maternal care. Good-bye, my very dearest sisters; pray for my needs. Live joyously and serenely with whatever our Lord will do with you and for you. I am yours with all my love.

December 13

Lucy

Martyr at Syracuse, 304

Lucy was a native of Syracuse in Sicily. She lived at the beginning of the fourth century, when the Roman authorities were attempting to re-establish the worship of gods they approved. The emperor himself was the focus of one of the cults. Tradition has it that Lucy, as a young Christian, gave away her goods to the poor and was betrayed to the authorities by her angry betrothed, who felt that they should have become his property. She was put to death for her faith in the year 304. Her name in Latin means Light and, as her feastday fell in December, she became associated with the one true Light who was coming as the redeemer of the world, the Light that would lighten the nations, the Light that would banish darkness and let the eyes of all behold Truth incarnate.

A Reading from *An Exhortation to the Greeks* by Clement of Alexandria

"The commandment of the Lord shines clearly, giving light to the eyes." Receive Christ, receive power to see, receive light that you may recognize in him both God and man. "More delightful than gold and precious stones, more desirable than honey from the honeycomb" is the Word that has given us light. How could he not be desirable, he who illumined minds buried in darkness, and endowed with clarity of vision the light-bearing eyes of our souls?

In spite of the countless stars, if it were not for the sun our world would be plunged in darkness. In the same way, were it not for the Word that has given us light, we too would have been no better than poultry, reared in the dark, fattened up for the killing. So let us open ourselves to the light, and thus to God. Let us open ourselves to the light, and become disciples of the Lord. For he promised his Father, saying: "I will make known your name among the nations, and praise you in the assembly."

Sing your Father's praises, then, Lord, and make him who is God known to me. Your words will save me; your song will instruct me. Until now I have gone astray in my search for God, but you are light for my path, and in you I find God; in you I receive the Father; in you I become a fellow heir, for you are not ashamed to call me your brother.

Let us all cast off all half-truths; let us cast off the mists of ignorance and the darkness that dims our inner vision, and let us contemplate the true God. Let us raise our hearts in praise to him, singing "Hail, O Light!" For upon us poor creatures, buried in darkness, imprisoned in the shadow of death, a heavenly light has shone, a light of such clarity that it surpasses the sun's, and of such sweetness that exceeds anything this world can offer us. The light of which I speak is eternal life, and those who receive it will live. The night, by contrast, is terrified of the light, melting away in fear at the approach of the day of the Lord. A light that can never fail has penetrated everywhere: sunset has turned into dawn. This is the meaning of "new creation;" for the Sun of Righteousness, pursuing his course through the universe, visits all alike, in imitation of his Father who makes his sun rise on all, and rains down his truth upon everyone.

He it is who has transformed sunset into dawn, death into life, and has done so through his crucifixion. He rescued the human race from perdition and exalted us to the skies. He is God's gardener, transplanting what was corruptible to new soil where it would grow incorruptible, transforming earth into heaven. He points out the way of growth, prompting his people to good works, encouraging us to live by the truth, and bestowing upon us a divine inheritance from his Father of which no one can rob us. He makes us divine by his heavenly teaching, instilling into our minds his laws, and writing them on the pages of our hearts. And what are the laws that he prescribes? That all, irrespective of class or status, shall know God.

December 14

John of the Cross

Poet, Teacher of the Faith, 1591

Born to an impoverished noble family near Avila in Spain in 1542, Juan de Yepes was brought up by his widowed mother and went to a charity school. He worked as a nurse and received further education from the Jesuits before entering the Carmelite Order when he was twenty-one. Having distinguished himself at Salamanca University, he was ordained in 1567 and met Teresa of Avila soon afterwards. He made a great impression on her and she persuaded him to help with her reform of the Carmelite Order. His labors brought him into conflict with the religious authorities, and he was even imprisoned for a period, yet these experiences prompted some of his finest poetry and mystical writing. In particular, he described the "dark night" of the soul as it is purified in its approach toward God. After ten years as superior to several different houses, he again fell out of favor and was banished to Andalusia in southern Spain, where he died after a severe illness on this day in the year 1591.

A Reading from *The Spiritual Canticle* of John of the Cross

However numerous the mysteries and marvels which holy doctors and saintly souls have understood in this earthly life, there is always more to be said and understood. There are great depths to be fathomed in Christ, for he is like a rich mine with many recesses containing treasures, so that however deep you dig, you never reach their end, but rather in each recess you find new veins with new riches everywhere.

On this account Saint Paul said of Christ: "In Christ are hidden all the treasures of wisdom and knowledge." But the soul cannot enter these caverns or reach these treasures if it does not first pass over to the divine wisdom through the thicket of exterior and interior suffering. For even that degree of these mysteries of Christ to which a soul may attain in this life cannot be reached without great suffering, without having received from God the grace of many gifts for the mind and the senses, and without having undergone much spiritual discipline. But note that all such gifts are of a lower order to the wisdom that comes from the mysteries of Christ. They serve merely as preparations for coming to this wisdom.

Oh, if we could fully understand how a soul cannot reach the thicket of the wisdom and riches of God, which are of many kinds, without entering the thicket of many kinds of suffering, finding in this its delight and consolation. A soul with an authentic desire for divine wisdom first desires suffering in order to enter this wisdom by the thicket of the cross.

For this reason Saint Paul exhorted the Ephesians not to grow faint in tribulations, but to be very strong, and rooted in charity, in order to comprehend with all the saints what is the breadth and height and depth, and to know also the surpassing love of the knowledge of Christ, so as to be filled with all the fullness of God. For the gate whereby we may enter into these riches of his wisdom is the cross, which is narrow. Many desire the delights to which that gate leads, but few are prepared to pass through it.

alternative reading

A Reading from a poem entitled
"Song of the Soul that is glad to know God by faith"
by John of the Cross

How well I know that fountain's rushing flow
Although by night

Its deathless spring is hidden. Even so
Full well I guess from whence its sources flow
Though it be night.

Its origin (since it has none) none knows:
But that all origin from it arose
Although by night.

I know there is no other thing so fair
And earth and heaven drink refreshment there
Although by night.

Full well I know its depth no one can sound
And that no ford to cross it can be found
Though it be night.

Its clarity unclouded still shall be:
Out of it comes the light by which we see
Though it be night.

Flush with its banks the stream so proudly swells;
I know it waters nations, heavens, and hells
Though it be night.

The current that is nourished by this source
I know to be omnipotent in force
Although by night.

From source and current a new current swells
Which neither of the other twain excels
Though it be night.

The eternal source hides in the Living Bread
That we with life eternal may be fed
Though it be night.

Here to all creatures it is crying, hark!
That they should drink their fill though in the dark,
For it is night.

This living fount which is to me so dear
Within the bread of life I see it clear
Though it be night.

December 21

Saint Thomas the Apostle

Thomas is mentioned among the number of the apostles in the Gospels of Matthew, Mark, and Luke; but it is in John's Gospel that his significance is revealed. First, he is heard encouraging the other disciples to go to Judea with Jesus; then, not knowing what Jesus meant when he talked about where he was to go, elicited the answer that Jesus was himself the Way. But most famously he was the apostle notably unconvinced by reports of the resurrection of Jesus, causing Jesus to show him the marks in his hands and feet and side. Thomas then proclaims the words that have been described as the great climax to John's Gospel by saying to Jesus, "My Lord and my God!"

A Reading from a homily of Gregory the Great

"Thomas, called the Twin, who was one of the twelve, was not with them when Jesus came." Thomas was the only disciple missing. When he returned and heard what had happened, he refused to believe what he heard. The Lord came again and offered his side to his skeptical disciple to touch. He showed his hands; and by showing the scars of his wounds he healed the wound of Thomas' unbelief.

What conclusion, dear sisters and brothers, do you draw from this? Do you think it was by chance that this chosen disciple was absent? Or that on his return he heard, that hearing he doubted, that doubting he touched, and touching he believed? This did not happen by chance, but by the providence of God. Divine mercy brought it about most wonderfully, so that when that doubting disciple touched his Master's wounded flesh he healed the wound of our unbelief as well as his own. Thomas' skepticism was more advantageous to us than was the faith of the other disciples who believed. When he was led to faith by actually touching Jesus, our hearts were relieved of all doubt, for our faith is made whole.

After his resurrection Jesus allowed this disciple to doubt, and he did not desert him in his doubt. He became a witness to the reality of the resurrection. Thomas touched him and cried out: "My Lord and my God." Jesus said to him: "Because you have seen me, Thomas, you have believed." When the apostle Paul says that "faith is the guarantee of the blessings that we hope for, the proof of the realities that are unseen," it is clear that faith provides the proof of those things that are not evident; visible things do not require faith, they command recognition. Why, when Thomas saw and touched him, did Jesus say: "Because you have seen me, you have believed?" What Thomas saw was one thing; what he believed, was another. A mortal could not have seen God. Thomas saw a human being, but by his words, "My Lord and my God," he acknowledged his divinity. It was by seeing that he believed. He recognized the reality of the man and testified that he was the invisible God.

Let us rejoice at what follows: "Blessed are they who have not seen and have believed." This expression makes special reference to us for we have not seen him in the flesh but know him in the mind. The reference is for us, but only if we follow up our faith with good works. Those who give expression to their faith are the genuine believers.

December 25

The Nativity of Our Lord and Savior Jesus Christ

A Reading from a Christmas sermon
by Lancelot Andrewes

I know not why it is that when we hear of saving or of a Savior, our mind is carried to the saving of our skin, and other saving we think not of. But there is another life not to be forgotten, and the dangers and destruction there are more to be feared than those here, and it would be well sometimes to remember that. Besides our skin and flesh we have a soul, and that is our better part by far, and also has need of a Savior. It has a destruction out of which and a destroyer from which it should be saved, and this should be thought of. Indeed, our chief thought and care should be for that: how to escape the destruction to come, to which our sins will certainly bring us.

Sin it is which will destroy us all, and there is no person on earth who has so much need of a Savior as does a sinner. There is nothing so dangerous, so deadly to us, as the sin in our hearts; nothing from which we have so much need to be saved, whatever account we make of it. From it comes all the evil of this life and of the life to come. In comparison of that last, the evil here is not worth speaking of. Above all, then, we need a Savior for our souls, and from our sins, and from the everlasting destruction which sin will bring on us in the other life, which is not far from us, not even from the one who thinks it furthest away.

Then if it is good tidings to hear of a Savior when it is only a matter of the loss of earth, or of this life here, what is it when it comes to the loss of heaven, to the danger of hell, when our soul is at the stake and the welfare or destruction of it forever? One who could save our souls from that destroyer—would not the birth of such a one be good news? Is not such a Savior worth listening to? Is he not? Is it then because we lack that sense of our souls and the dangers of them that we have of our bodies, nor that fear of our spiritual enemies, nor that awareness of the eternal torments of that place, and how near we are to it, nothing being between us and it but this poor puff of breath which is in our nostrils. Our bodies are living and sensitive, our spirit is dead and dull. We lack the feeling of our sins that we have of our sickness. If we had, we would hear this news with greater cheerfulness and hold this day of the birth of such a Savior with joy indeed. We cannot conceive it yet. This destruction is not near enough to affect us. But in the end, when the destroyer shall come and we shall want a Savior, we shall plainly understand and value this benefit and the joy of it as we ought, and find there is no joy on earth like the joy of a Savior.

alternative reading

A Reading from a Christmas sermon by
the Reverend Martin Luther King, Jr.

This Christmas season finds us a rather bewildered human race. We have neither peace within nor peace without. Everywhere paralyzing fears harrow people by day and haunt them by night. Our world is sick with war; everywhere we turn we see its ominous possibilities. And yet, my friends, the Christmas hope for peace and goodwill toward all men can no longer be dismissed as a kind of pious dream of some utopian. If we don't have goodwill toward men in this world, we will destroy ourselves by the misuse of our own instruments and our own power. Wisdom born of experience should tell us that war is obsolete. There may have been a time when war served as a negative good by preventing the spread and growth of an evil force, but the very destructive power of modern weapons of warfare eliminates even the possibility that war may any longer serve as a negative good. And so, if we assume that life is worth living, if we assume that mankind has a right to survive, then we must find an alternative to war—and so let us this morning explore the conditions for peace. Let us this morning think anew on the meaning of that Christmas hope: "Peace on Earth, Good Will toward Men." And as we explore these conditions, I would like to suggest that modern man really go all out to study the meaning of nonviolence, its philosophy, and its strategy.

I have a dream that one day men will rise up and come to see that they are made to live together as brothers. I still have a dream this morning that one day every Negro in this country, every colored person in the world, will be judged on the basis of the content of his character rather than the color of his skin, and every man will respect the dignity and worth of human personality. I still have a dream that one day the idle industries of Appalachia will be revitalized, and the empty stomachs of Mississippi will be filled, and brotherhood will be more than a few words at the end of a prayer, but rather the first order of business on every legislative agenda. I still have a dream today that one day justice will roll down like water, and righteousness like a mighty stream. I still have a dream today that in all of our state houses and city halls men will be elected to go there who will do justly and love mercy and walk humbly with their God. I still have a dream today that one day war will come to an end, that men will beat their swords into plowshares and their spears into pruning hooks, that nations will no longer rise up against nations, neither will they study war any more. I still have a dream today that one day the lamb and the lion will lie down together and every man will sit under his own vine and fig tree and none shall be afraid. I still have a dream today that one day every valley shall be exalted and every mountain and hill will be made low, the rough places will be made smooth and the crooked places straight, and the glory of the Lord shall be revealed, and all flesh shall see it together. I still have a dream that with this faith we will be able to adjourn the councils of despair and bring new light into the dark chambers of pessimism. With this faith we will be able to speed up the day when there will be peace on earth and good will toward men. It will be a glorious day, the morning stars will sing together, and the sons of God will shout for joy.

alternative reading

A Reading from a sermon for the Nativity of Christ
by Julian of Vezelay

"While gentle silence enveloped the whole earth, and night was halfway through its course, your all-powerful Word, O Lord, leaped down from your royal throne in the heavens." In this ancient text of Scripture, the most sacred moment of time is made known to us, the moment when God's all-powerful Word would leave the tender embrace of the Father and come down into his mother's womb, bringing us the news of salvation. For, as it says elsewhere in Scripture, "God spoke to our ancestors in many and various ways by the prophets, but in these last days he has spoken to us by a Son," declaring: "This is my beloved Son in whom I am well pleased." And so from his royal throne the Word of God has come to us, humbling himself in order to raise us on high, becoming poor himself in order to make us rich, becoming human in order to make us divine.

So lost and so profoundly unhappy was the human race, that it could only trust in a word that was all-powerful. Anything less would have inspired in us nothing more than the feeblest of hopes in being set free from sin and its power. Therefore, to give poor lost humanity a categorical assurance of being saved, the Word that came to save us was called all-powerful. And see how truly all-powerful that Word was! When neither heaven nor anything under the heavens as yet had existence, the Word spoke, and they came into being, created out of nothing. He spoke the command, "Let there be earth," and the earth came into being, and when he decreed, "Let there be human beings," human beings were created.

But the Word of God did not remake his creatures as easily as he had made them. He had made them by issuing a command; he remade them by dying. He made them by commanding; he remade them by suffering. "You have burdened me," he told them, "with your sinning. To direct and govern the whole fabric of the world is no effort for me, for I have power to reach from one end of the world to the other, and to order all things as I please. It is only humanity, with its obstinate disregard for the law I have given, which has caused me distress by their sins. That is why I have come down from my royal throne; that is why I have not shrunk from enclosing myself in the Virgin's womb nor from entering into a personal union with poor lost humanity. See, I lie in a manger, a newly born baby wrapped in swaddling bands, since the Creator of the world could find no room in the inn."

And so there came a deep silence and the whole earth was still. The voices of prophets and apostles were hushed, for the prophets had delivered their message, whereas the time for the apostles' preaching was yet to come. Between these two proclamations a period of silence intervened, and in the midst of this silence the Father's all-powerful Word leaped down from his royal throne. In this movement is great beauty: in the ensuing silence the mediator between God and man intervened, coming as a human being among human beings, as a mortal among mortals, to save the dead from death.

I pray that the Word of the Lord may come again this night to those who wait in silence, and that we may hear what the Lord God is saying to us in our hearts. Let us, therefore, still the desires and cravings of the flesh, the roving fantasies of our imaginations, so that we can attend to what the Spirit is saying.

alternative reading

A Reading from an oration of Gregory of Nazianzus

Christ is born: let us glorify him. Christ comes down from heaven: let us go out to meet him. Christ descends to earth: let us be raised on high. Let all the world sing to the Lord: let the heavens rejoice and let the earth be glad, for his sake who was first in heaven and then on earth. Christ is here in the flesh: let us exult with fear and joy with fear, because of our sins; with joy, because of the hope that he brings us.

Once more the darkness is dispersed; once more the light is created. Let the people that sat in the darkness of ignorance now look upon the light of knowledge. The things of old have passed away; behold, all things are made new. He who has no mother in heaven is now born without a father on earth. The laws of nature are overthrown, for the upper world must be filled with citizens. He who is without flesh becomes incarnate; the Word puts on a body; the invisible makes itself seen; the intangible can be touched; the timeless has a beginning; the Son of God becomes the Son of Man, Jesus Christ, the same yesterday, today and for ever.

Light from light, the Word of the Father comes to his own image in the human race. For the sake of my flesh he takes flesh; for the sake of my soul he is united to a rational soul, purifying like by like. In every way he becomes human, except for sin. O strange conjunction! The self-existent comes into being; the uncreated is created. He shares in the poverty of my flesh that I may share in the riches of his Godhead.

This is the solemnity we are celebrating today: the arrival of God among us, so that we might go to God or more precisely, return to God. So that stripping off our old humanity we might put on the new; for as in Adam we were dead, so in Christ we become alive: we are born with him, and we rise again with him.

A miracle, not of creation, but of re-creation. For this the feast of my being made whole, my returning to the condition God designed for me, to the original Adam. So let us revere the nativity which releases us from the chains of evil. Let us honor this tiny Bethlehem which restores us to paradise. Let us reverence this crib because from it we, who were deprived of self-understanding, are fed by the divine understanding, the Word of God himself.

alternative reading

A Reading from a treatise *Against Heresies*
by Irenaeus

Just as it is possible for a mother to give her infant strong food but choose not to do so because her child is not able yet to receive such bodily nourishment; so it was possible for God on his part to have given human beings the fullness of perfection right from the beginning, but we were not capable of receiving so great a gift being mere children. In these last days, however, when our Lord summed up all things in himself, he came to us, not as he could have done, but as we were capable of beholding him. He could, indeed, have come to us in the radiance of his glory, but we were not capable of bearing it. So, as to infants, the perfect Bread of the Father gave himself to us under the form of milk he came to us as a human being in order that we might be fed, so to speak, at the breast by his incarnation, and by this diet of milk become accustomed to eating and drinking the Word of God. In this way we might be enabled to keep within us the Bread of Immortality which is the Spirit of the Father.

alternative reading

A Reading from a sermon of Leo the Great

Dearly beloved, today our Savior was born; let us rejoice! This is no season for sadness it is the birthday of Life! It is a life that annihilates the fear of death; a life that brings us joy with the promise of eternal happiness.

Nobody is an outsider to this happiness; we all have common cause for rejoicing. Our Lord, the victor over sin and death, finding no one free from guilt, has come to free us all. Let the saint exult for the palm of victory is at hand. Let the sinner be glad in receiving the offer of forgiveness. Let the gentile take courage on being summoned to life.

In the fullness of time, chosen in the unfathomable depths of God's wisdom, the Son of God took on himself our human nature in order to reconcile us with our Creator. He came to overthrow the devil, the origin of death, in that very nature by which the devil had overthrown humankind. In this conflict undertaken for us, a war has been waged on the mighty and highest principles of justice. The almighty Lord has gone into battle against our cruel enemy clothed not in his own majesty, but in our weakness. In Christ majesty has taken on humility, strength has taken on weakness, eternity has taken on mortality, and all in order to settle the debt we owe for our condition.

That is why at the birth of our Lord the angels sang for joy: "Glory to God in the highest," and proclaimed the message "peace to his people on earth." For they see the heavenly Jerusalem being constructed out of all the nations of the world. How greatly then should we mere mortals rejoice when the angels on high are so exultant at this mysterious undertaking of divine love!

Let us, then, dearly beloved, give thanks to God the Father, through his Son, in the Holy Spirit, because in his great love for us he has taken pity on us, "and when we were dead in our sins he brought us to life with Christ," so that in him we might be a new creation, a new work of his hands. Let us throw off our old nature and all its habits and, as we have come to birth in Christ, let us renounce the works of the flesh.

Christian, acknowledge your own dignity; and now that you share in God's own nature, do not return by sin to your former base condition. Bear in mind who is your head and of whose body you are a member. Remember that "you have been rescued from the power of darkness and brought into the light of God's kingdom." Through the sacrament of baptism you have become a temple of the Holy Spirit. Do not drive away so great a guest by evil conduct and become again a slave to the devil, for your liberty was bought at the price of Christ's blood.

alternative reading

A Reading from a poem by Robert Southwell

The Nativity of Christ

Behold the father is his daughter's son,
The bird that built the nest is hatched therein,
The old of years an hour hath not outrun,
Eternal life to live doth now begin,
The Word is dumb, the mirth of heaven doth weep,
Might feeble is, and force doth faintly creep.

O dying souls, behold your living spring;
O dazzled eyes, behold your sun of grace;
Dull ears, attend what word this Word doth bring;
Up, heavy hearts, with joy your joy embrace.
From death, from dark, from deafness, from despairs,
This life, this light, this Word, this joy repairs.

Gift better than himself God doth not know;
Gift better than his God no man can see.
This gift doth here the giver given bestow;
Gift to this gift let each receiver be.
God is my gift, himself he freely gave me;
God's gift am I, and none but God shall have me.

Man altered was by sin from man to beast;
Beast's food is hay, hay is all mortal flesh.
Now God is flesh and lies in manger pressed
As hay, the brutest sinner to refresh.
O happy field wherein this fodder grew,
Whose taste doth us from beasts to men renew.

December 26

Saint Stephen

Deacon and First Martyr

In the book of the Acts of the Apostles, Stephen is described as one of the seven deacons whose job it is to care for the widows in the early Church in Jerusalem. His eloquent speech before the Sanhedrin, in which he shows the great sweep of Jewish history as leading to the birth of Jesus, the long-expected Messiah, and his impassioned plea that all might hear the good news of Jesus, leads to his inevitable martyrdom by being stoned to death. As the author of Acts, Luke's description of Stephen bears direct parallels to that of Christ: for example, the passion; being filled with the Holy Spirit; seeing the Son of God at the right hand of God, as Jesus promised he would be; commending his spirit to Jesus, as Jesus commended his to the Father; kneeling as Jesus did in Gethsemane and asking forgiveness for his persecutors. Witnessing to Jesus by acting like Jesus in every way is seen by Luke as of the essence of the Christian life.

A Reading from a sermon of Fulgentius, Bishop of Ruspe

Yesterday we celebrated the birth in time of our eternal King. Today we celebrate the triumphant suffering of his soldier. Yesterday our king, clothed in his robe of flesh, left his place in the virgin's womb and graciously visited the world. Today his soldier leaves the tabernacle of his body and goes triumphantly to heaven.

Our king, despite his exalted majesty, came in humility for our sake; yet he did not come empty-handed. He brought his soldiers a great gift that not only enriched them but also made them unconquerable in battle, for it was the gift of love, which was to bring us to share in his divinity. He gave of his bounty, yet without any loss to himself. In a marvelous way he changed into wealth the poverty of his faithful followers while remaining in full possession of his own inexhaustible riches.

And so the love that brought Christ from heaven to earth raised Stephen from earth to heaven; shown first in the king, it later shone forth in his soldier. Love was Stephen's weapon by which he gained every battle, and so won the crown signified by his name. His love of God kept him from yielding to the ferocious mob; his love for his neighbor made him pray for those who were stoning him. Love inspired him to reprove those who erred, to make them amend; love led him to pray for those who stoned him to save them from punishment. Strengthened by the power of his love, he overcame the raging cruelty of Saul and won the persecutor on earth as his companion in heaven. In his holy and tireless love he longed to gain by prayer those whom he could not convert by admonition.

Now at last, Paul rejoices with Stephen, with Stephen he delights in the glory of Christ, with Stephen he exalts, with Stephen he reigns. Stephen went first, slain by the stones thrown by Paul; but Paul followed after, helped by the prayer of Stephen. This, surely, is the true life, beloved, a life in which Paul feels no shame because of Stephen's death, and Stephen delights in Paul's companionship, for love fills them both with joy. It was Stephen's love that prevailed over the cruelty of the mob, and it was Paul's love that covered the multitude of his sins; it was love that won for both of them the kingdom of heaven.

Love, indeed, is the source of all good things; it is an impregnable defense, and the way that leads to heaven. Whoever walks in love can neither go astray nor be afraid: love guides, protects, and brings the one who loves to the journey's end.

Christ made love the stairway that would enable all Christians to climb to heaven. Hold fast to it, therefore, in all sincerity, give one another practical proof of it, and by your progress in it, make your ascent together.

December 27

Saint John
Apostle and Evangelist

Whether or not John the Apostle and John the Evangelist are one and the same, the Church honors on this day the one who proclaims Jesus as "the Word made flesh" and who is "the disciple whom Jesus loved." The Gospel narratives speak of John as one of the sons of Zebedee who followed Jesus. He was present at the transfiguration of Jesus on the holy mountain; he was there with Jesus at the last supper; he was there with Jesus in his agony in the garden; he was there with Jesus and his mother, standing at the foot of the cross; he was there with Jesus as a witness of his resurrection and "he saw and believed." According to tradition, John died at Ephesus in advanced old age.

A Reading from the commentary of Augustine
on the First Letter of John

"Our message is the Word of life. We announce what existed from the beginning, what we have heard, what we have seen with our own eyes, what we have touched with our own hands."

Who could touch the Word with his hands unless "the Word was made flesh and lived among us?" Now this Word, whose flesh was so real that he could be touched by human hands, began to be flesh in the Virgin Mary's womb; but he did not begin to exist at that moment. We know this from what John says: "What existed from the beginning." Notice how John's Letter bears witness to his Gospel: "In the beginning was the Word, and the Word was with God."

Someone might interpret the phrase "the Word of life" to mean a word about Christ, rather than Christ's body itself which was touched by human hands. But consider what comes next: "and life itself was revealed." Christ, therefore, is himself the Word of life.

And how was this life revealed? It existed from the beginning, but was not revealed to mortals, only to angels, who looked upon it and feasted upon it as their own spiritual bread. But what does Scripture say? "Humans ate the bread of angels."

Life itself was therefore revealed in the flesh. In this way what was visible to the heart alone could become visible also to the eye, and so heal human hearts. For the Word is visible to the heart alone, while flesh is visible to bodily eyes as well. We already possessed the means to see the flesh, but we had no means of seeing the Word. The Word was made flesh so that we could see it, to heal the part of us by which we could see the Word.

John continues: "And we are witnesses and we proclaim to you that eternal life which was with the Father and has been revealed among us" one might say more simply "revealed to us." "We proclaim to you what we have heard and seen." Make sure that you grasp the meaning of these words. The disciples saw our Lord in the flesh, face to face; they heard the words he spoke, and in turn they proclaimed the message to us. So we also have heard, although we have not seen.

Are we then less favored than those who both saw and heard? If that were so, why should John add: "so that you too may have fellowship with us?" They saw, and we have not seen; yet we have fellowship with them, because we and they share the same faith.

"And our fellowship is with God the Father and Jesus Christ his Son. And we write this to you to make your joy complete" complete in that fellowship, in that love and in that unity.

December 28

The Holy Innocents

Herod "the Great" was appointed King of the Jews by the Roman authorities in Palestine and he proved to be ruthlessly efficient in his thirty-three years of dealing with his subjects. In the Gospel according to Matthew, Herod tried to persuade the Magi, to whom he played host on their journey seeking the one "who has been born king of the Jews," to bring word to him once they had found the child. His desire was to eliminate Jesus and, when he realized that the Magi had tricked him and left the country, Herod killed all the children under the age of two in and around Bethlehem. These were God's "innocent" ones. The incident has significant parallels with the story of the birth of Moses who was to lead the people of Israel out of slavery, and his miraculous survival during the slaughter of the Hebrew children in Egypt by Pharaoh.

A Reading from a sermon of Quodvultdeus,
Bishop of Carthage

A tiny child is born who is a great king. Wise men are led to him from afar. They come to adore one who lies in a manger and yet reigns in heaven and on earth. When they tell of one who is born a king, Herod is disturbed. To save his kingdom he resolves to kill him, though if he would have faith in the child, he himself would reign in peace in this life and for ever in the life to come.

Why are you afraid, Herod, when you hear of the birth of a king? He does not come to drive you out, but to conquer the devil. But because you do not understand this you are disturbed and in a rage, and to destroy one child whom you seek, you show your cruelty in the death of so many children.

You are not restrained by the love of weeping mothers or fathers mourning the deaths of their little ones, nor by the cries and sobs of the children. You destroy those who are tiny in body because fear is destroying your heart. You imagine that if you accomplish your desire you can prolong your own life, though you are seeking to kill Life himself.

Yet your throne is threatened by the source of grace so small, and yet so great who is lying in the manger. He is using you, all unaware of it, to work out his own purposes in freeing souls from captivity to the devil. He has taken up the children of the enemy into the ranks of God's adopted children.

The children die for Christ, though they do not know it. The parents mourn for the death of martyrs. The children make of those as yet unable to speak fit witnesses to themselves. See the kind of kingdom that is his, coming as he did in order to be this kind of king. See how the deliverer is already working deliverance, the Savior already working salvation.

But you, Herod, do not know this and are disturbed and furious. While you vent your fury against the children, you are already paying them homage, and you do not know it. How great a gift of grace is here! To what merits of their own do the children owe this kind of victory? They cannot speak, yet they bear witness to Christ. They cannot use their little limbs to engage in battle, yet already they bear off the palm of victory.

A Reading from the conclusion to *Evil and the God of Love* by John Hick

The only permissible theodicy is one that sees moral and natural evil as necessary features of the present stage of God's creating of perfected finite persons. Thus the ultimate responsibility for the existence of evil belongs to the creator; and Christianity also believes that, in his total awareness of the history of his creation, God bears with us the pains of the creative process.

What is the greatest difficulty in the way of such a theodicy? It is, I think, the stark question whether all the pain and suffering, cruelty and wickedness of human life can be rendered acceptable by an end-state, however good. Dostoievsky unforgettably presented the negative case in his novel *The Brothers Karamazov* when Ivan engages his brother Alyosha in a long and agonized discussion of the suffering of innocent children. He concludes thus:

> ["It's the defenselessness of children that tempts their torturers, the angelic trustfulness of the child who has nowhere to go and no one to run to for protection it is this that inflames the evil blood of the torturer. In every man a wild beast is hidden the wild beast of irascibility, the wild beast of sensuous intoxication from the screams of the tortured victim.
>
> "People tell me that without such suffering man could not even have existed on earth, for he would not have known good and evil. But why? To me, the whole world's knowledge isn't worth a child's tear to her "dear and kind God!" I'm not talking of the sufferings of grown-up people, for they have eaten the apple and to hell with them but these little ones!
>
> "If the sufferings of children go to make up the sum of sufferings which is necessary for the purchase of truth, then I say beforehand that the entire truth is not worth such a price. Too high a price has been placed on harmony.]
>
> "I challenge you answer. Imagine that you are creating a fabric of human destiny with the object of making people happy in the end,
>
> giving them peace and rest at last, but that it was essential and inevitable to torture to death only one tiny creature a baby beating its breast with

> its fist, for instance and to found that edifice on its unavenged tears, would you consent to be architect on those conditions? Tell me the truth."
>
> "No, I wouldn't consent," said Alyosha softly.

The implication, of course, is that if there is a God, in the sense of One who is responsible for the world, and ultimately therefore for the existence of evil within it, then that God cannot be good and cannot properly be worshipped as such.

In face of this gravest of all challenges to a Christian faith in God I can well understand and sympathize with the negative response which Dostoievsky has so powerfully articulated. But we believe or disbelieve, ultimately, out of our own experience and must be faithful to the witness of that experience; and together with very many others, I find that the realities of human goodness and human happiness make it a credible possibility that this life with its baffling mixture of good and evil, and including both its dark miseries and its shining joys, including both man's malevolence and his self-forgetting love, is indeed part of a long and slow pilgrim's progress toward the Celestial City. If so, the journey must have many stages beyond the present one; and the end must be good beyond our present imagining and must be far more positive than the mere "peace and rest at last" of which Dostoievsky speaks. And in the meantime the fact that the process does not declare its own nature but remains mysteriously ambiguous is a necessary aspect of a soul-making or person-making history.

I therefore end by formulating this ultimate question: can there be a future good so great as to render acceptable, in retrospect, the whole human experience, with all its wickedness and suffering as well as all its sanctity and happiness? I think that perhaps there can, and indeed that perhaps there is.

December 29

Thomas Becket

Archbishop of Canterbury, Martyr, 1170

Thomas was born in London in 1118, of a family of merchants. After a good education he served as clerk to another burgess then entered the service of Archbishop Theobald of Canterbury. Thomas proved himself an excellent administrator and skilled diplomat. In 1155, he was appointed chancellor by King Henry II. For several years, king and chancellor worked harmoniously together in mutual admiration and personal friendship. As a result, the king nominated Thomas as Archbishop of Canterbury to succeed Theobald in 1161. From the start there was friction, with Thomas insisting on every privilege of the Church. The conflict worsened until 1164 when Thomas fled to France. Encouraged by the Pope he pursued his arguments from exile, sending letters and pronouncing excommunications. Three efforts at mediation failed before an apparent reconciliation brought him back triumphant to Canterbury in 1170. But the nobility still opposed him, and words of anger at court led four knights to journey to Canterbury where they finally chased Thomas into the cathedral, and murdered him on this day in the year 1170. Thomas was undoubtedly a proud and stubborn man, for all his gifts, and his personal austerities as archbishop were probably an attempt at self-discipline after years of ostentatious luxury. His conflict with King Henry stemmed from their equal personal ambitions, exacerbated by the increasingly international claims of the papacy, played out in the inevitable tension between church and state.

A Reading from a contemporary account of the murder of Thomas Becket, Archbishop of Canterbury, by Edward Grim, an eye-witness

[On the fifth day after the Nativity of Christ, the hour of dinner being over, the saint had already withdrawn with some of his household into an inner chamber to transact some business. The four knights with an attendant forced their way in. They were received with respect as servants of the king and well known to the archbishop's household. For a long time they sat in silence and neither saluted the archbishop nor spoke to him.

William FitzUrse, who seemed to be their leader, breathing fury, broke out in these words: "We have something to say to you by the king's command: that you depart with all your men from the kingdom and the lands which own his dominion; for from this day forth there can be no peace betwixt him and you or any of yours, for you have broken the peace."

To this the archbishop answered: "Cease your threats and still your brawling. I put my trust in the King of Heaven who for his own suffered on the cross; for from this day forth no one shall see the sea between me and my church. I have not come back to England to flee again; here shall he who wants me find me."

Confounded by these words, the knights sprang to their feet, for they could no longer bear the firmness of his answers. Coming up close to him they said: "We declare to you that you have spoken in peril of your head." As they retired amidst tumult and insults, the man of God followed them to the door and cried out after them, "Here, here will you find me."

Terrified by the noise and uproar, almost all the clerks and the servants were scattered hither and thither like sheep before wolves. Those who remained cried out to the archbishop to flee to the church; but he, mindful of his former promise that he would not through fear of death flee from those who kill the body, rejected flight. But the monks still pressed him, saying that it was not becoming for him to absent himself from vespers.

The monks hastened to ward off the foe from the slaughter of their shepherd by fastening the bolts of the folding doors giving access to the church. But Christ's doughty champion turned to them and ordered the doors to be thrown open, saying: "It is not meet to make a fortress of the house of prayer, the Church of Christ, which, even if it be not closed, affords sufficient protection to its children. By suffering rather than by fighting shall we triumph over the enemy; for we are come to suffer, not to resist."]

Straightway those sacrilegious men, with drawn swords, entered the house of peace and reconciliation. In a spirit of mad fury the knights called out: "Where is Thomas Becket, traitor to the king and the realm?" When he returned no answer, they cried out the more loudly and insistently: "Where is the archbishop?" At this quite undaunted, the archbishop descended from the steps whither he had been dragged by the monks through their fear of the knights. In a perfectly clear voice he answered: "Lo! here I am, no traitor to the king, but a priest. What do you seek from me?"

Having said thus, he turned aside to the right, under a pillar. "Absolve," they cried, "and restore to communion those whom you have excommunicated." But he answered, "There has been no satisfaction made, and I will not absolve them." "Then you shall die this instant," they cried.

"I am ready to die for my Lord, that in my blood the Church may obtain peace and liberty; but in the name of almighty God I forbid you to harm any of my men, whether clerk or lay."

Then they made a rush at him and laid sacrilegious hands upon him, pulling him and dragging him roughly and violently across the floor. Then the unconquered martyr understood that his hour had come. Inclining his head as one in prayer and joining his hands together and uplifting them, he commended his cause and that of the Church to God and Saint Mary and the blessed martyr Saint Denys. Scarce had he uttered these words than the wicked knight leapt suddenly upon him and wounded the sacrificial lamb of God in the head, cutting off the top of the crown which the unction of the sacred chrism had dedicated to God, and by the same stroke he almost cut off the arm of him who tells this story.

The archbishop then received a second blow on the head, but still he stood firm and immovable. At the third blow he fell on his knees and elbows, offering himself to God a living sacrifice. The third knight inflicted a terrible wound as he lay prostrate, in such a way that the blood white with the brain, and the brain no less red from the blood, dyed the floor of the cathedral with the white of the lily and the red of the rose, the colors of the Virgin and Mother, and of the life and death of the martyr and confessor.

Neither with hand nor robe, as is the manner of human frailty, did the archbishop oppose the fatal stroke. Bespattered with blood and brains, as though in an attitude of prayer, his body lay prone on the pavement, while his soul rested in Abraham's bosom.

Selected Holy Days Collects from The Book of Common Prayer

Conversion of Saint Paul
January 25
O God, by the preaching of your apostle Paul you have caused the light of the Gospel to shine throughout the world: Grant, we pray, that we, having his wonderful conversion in remembrance, may show ourselves thankful to you by following his holy teaching; through Jesus Christ our Lord, who lives and reigns with you, in the unity of the Holy Spirit, one God, now and for ever. Amen.

The Presentation
February 2
Almighty and everliving God, we humbly pray that, as your only-begotten Son was this day presented in the temple, so we may be presented to you with pure and clean hearts by Jesus Christ our Lord; who lives and reigns with you and the Holy Spirit, one God, now and for ever. Amen.

The Annunciation
March 25
Pour your grace into our hearts, O Lord, that we who have known the incarnation of your Son Jesus Christ, announced by an angel to the Virgin Mary, may by his cross and passion be brought to the glory of his resurrection; who lives and reigns with you, in the unity of the Holy Spirit, one God, now and for ever. Amen.

Saint Mark
April 25
Almighty God, by the hand of Mark the evangelist you have given to your Church the Gospel of Jesus Christ the Son of God: We thank you for this witness, and pray that we may be firmly grounded in its truth; through Jesus Christ our Lord, who lives and reigns with you and the Holy Spirit, one God, for ever and ever. Amen.

The Visitation
May 31
Father in heaven, by your grace the virgin mother of your incarnate Son was blessed in bearing him, but still more blessed in keeping your word: Grant us who honor the exaltation of her lowliness to follow the example of her devotion to your will; through Jesus Christ our Lord, who lives and reigns with you and the Holy Spirit, one God, for ever and ever. Amen.

The Nativity of Saint John the Baptist
June 24
Almighty God, by whose providence your servant John the Baptist was wonderfully born, and sent to prepare the way of your Son our Savior by preaching repentance: Make us so to follow his teaching and holy life, that we may truly repent according to his preaching; and, following his example, constantly speak the truth, boldly rebuke vice, and patiently suffer for the truth's sake; through Jesus Christ your Son our Lord, who lives and reigns with you and the Holy Spirit, one God, for ever and ever. Amen.

Saint Mary Magdalene
July 22
Almighty God, whose blessed Son restored Mary Magdalene to health of body and of mind, and called her to be a witness of his resurrection: Mercifully grant that by your grace we may be healed from all our infirmities and know you in the power of his unending life; who with you and the Holy Spirit lives and reigns, one God, now and for ever. Amen.

The Transfiguration
August 6
O God, who on the holy mount revealed to chosen witnesses your well-beloved Son, wonderfully transfigured, in raiment white and glistening: Mercifully grant that we, being delivered from the disquietude of this world, may by faith behold the King in his beauty; who with you, O Father, and you, O Holy Spirit, lives and reigns, one God, for ever and ever. Amen.

Saint Matthew
September 21
We thank you, heavenly Father, for the witness of your apostle and evangelist Matthew to the Gospel of your Son our Savior; and we pray that, after his example, we may with ready wills and hearts obey the calling of our Lord to follow him; through Jesus Christ our Lord, who lives and reigns with you and the Holy Spirit, one God, now and for ever. Amen.

Saint Luke
October 18
Almighty God, who inspired your servant Luke the physician to set forth in the Gospel the love and healing power of your Son: Graciously continue in your Church this love and power to heal, to the praise and glory of your Name; through Jesus Christ our Lord, who lives and reigns with you, in the unity of the Holy Spirit, one God, now and for ever. Amen.

All Saints' Day
November 1
Almighty God, you have knit together your elect in one communion and fellowship in the mystical body of your Son Christ our Lord: Give us grace so to follow your blessed saints in all virtuous and godly living, that we may come to those ineffable joys that you have prepared for those who truly love you; through Jesus Christ our Lord, who with you and the Holy Spirit lives and reigns, one God, in glory everlasting. Amen.

Saint John
December 27
Shed upon your Church, O Lord, the brightness of your light, that we, being illumined by the teaching of your apostle and evangelist John, may so walk in the light of your truth, that at length we may attain to the fullness of eternal life; through Jesus Christ our Lord, who lives and reigns with you and the Holy Spirit, one God, for ever and ever. Amen.

ABBREVIATIONS

ACW Ancient Christian Writers: The Works of the Fathers in Translation; ed. J. Quasten and J. C. Plumpe, New York & Mahwah, New Jersey, 1946.

ANF The Ante-Nicene Fathers, general editors Roberts and Donaldson, Edinburgh, 1867; reprinted Grand Rapids, Michigan, 1978.

BEH *Ecclesiastical History of the English People* by the Venerable Bede, critical edition of Latin text by B. Colgrave & R. A. B. Mynors, Oxford, 1969.

CCSL *Corpus Christianorum: Series Latina*, Turnhout, Belgium, 1953.

CSEL *Corpus Scriptorum Ecclesiasticorum Latinorum,* Vienna, 1866.

CWS Classics of Western Spirituality, New York & Mahwah, New Jersey, 1978.

ET English translation

ICEL *The Roman Catholic Liturgy of the Hours,* 1974, American edition; ET of non-biblical readings by the International Commission for English in the Liturgy.

LACT Library of Anglo-Catholic Theology, Oxford, 1841.

LCC The Library of Christian Classics, Philadelphia & London, 1953-6.

Loeb The Loeb Classical Library, Cambridge, Massachusetts & London, 1923.

NPNF The Nicene and Post-Nicene Fathers, series 1 & 2, general editors Schaff and Wace, New York, 1887-92; Oxford, 1890-1900; reprinted Grand Rapids, Michigan, 1976-9.

PG *Patrologiae cursus completus: Series Graeca,* 161 vols, ed. J. P. Migne, Paris, 1857-66.

PL *Patrologiae cursus completus: Series Latina,* 221 vols, ed. J. P. Migne, Paris, 1844-64.

SC *Sources Chrétiennes,* Paris, 1940.

Notes and Sources

The figure in **BOLD** on the left indicates the day in the month, *not* the page number. Where a number of saints are commemorated in the calendar on the same day, the references below are printed in the order they appear in the anthology.

Where no source for an ET is cited, the English version is that of the author. If this has been based on an existing (often nineteenth-century translation) it is acknowledged in the notes.

January

1 a. William of St. Thierry, *On Contemplating God,* 9; ET by Penelope Lawson CSMV in *The Works of William of St. Thierry I,* Spencer, Massachusetts, 1971, p.38.
b. Mark Frank, sermon 17; *Sermons by Dr. Mark Frank,* LACT, Oxford, 1849; vol. 1, pp.258-72 (abridged).

2 *A Treasury of Russian Spirituality,* vol. 2, ed. & ET by George P. Fedotov, London, 1950, pp.267-9 (abridged).

2 Constance M. Millington, *An Ecumenical Venture: The History of Nandyal Diocese in Andhra Pradesh (1947-1990),* Bangalore, 1993, pp.2-20 (abridged).

6 a. Peter Chrysologus, *Sermon* 160; PL 52, cols 620-2; ET by ICEL.
b. Ephrem of Syria, *Hymns "On the Nativity",* 23:1, 3, 10; ET by Kathleen E. McVey, *Ephrem the Syrian,* New York & Mahwah, New Jersey, 1989, pp.187-9.
c. Lancelot Andrewes, *Sermon* 14; *The Works of Bishop Lancelot Andrewes,* Oxford, 1841, vol. 1, pp.238-49 (abridged).
d. "The Divine Image" by William Blake.
e. "Journey of the Magi" by T. S. Eliot.

9 Margaret A. Tomes, "Words of Appreciation," *The Woman's Auxiliary to the National Council of the Episcopal Church 1924*; Boston, Mass., 1924.

10 William Laud, *Works*, ed. G. W. Scott & James Bliss, 8 vols, LACT, Oxford, 1847-60; vol. IV, pp.430-7 (abridged).

11 Richard Symonds, *Far Above Rubies: The Women Uncommemorated by the Church of England,* Leominster, 1993, pp.215, 222-3 (abridged).

12 a. Aelred, *Pastoral Prayer,* 6; ET by Penelope Lawson CSMV in *The Works of Aelred of Rievaulx I,* Spencer, Massachusetts, 1971, pp.112-3.
b. Aelred, *Spiritual Friendship,* II, 11-14; ET by Mary Eugenia Laker SSND, Spencer, Massachusetts, 1977, pp.72-3.
NB The "Wise Man" Aelred refers to is the author of Sirach 6:16.

13 Hilary of Poitiers, *On the Trinity,* I, 1-7, 10-12; CCSL 62A, pp.1-7, 9-12; ET based on NPNF vol. IX, pp.40-3.
NB The text Hilary refers to is Wisdom 13:5.

15 Martin Luther King, Jr., *A Testament of Hope: the Essential Writings of Martin Luther King, Jr.*, ed., James Melvin Washington, San Francisco, 1986, pp. 219–20.

17 Athanasius, *The Life of Antony,* 1-4; ET by Robert Gregg, New York & Mahwah, New Jersey, 1980, pp.30-3.

18 *Acts of the Holy Apostles Peter and Paul,* ANF, 8, pp. 484–5.

19 William of Malmesbury, *The Life of St Wulfstan,* I, 14, III, 20; critical ed. by R. R. Darlington, Camden Society, 3rd series, vol. XL, London, 1928.
NB William's Latin *Vita Wulstani* is itself a version (made between 1124 and 1143) of an earlier English *Life* by the monk Coleman, Wulfstan's friend and chaplain, who wrote it after Wulfstan's death in 1095. No copy of Coleman's work is known to have survived.

20 *The Epistles of Pope Fabian*, ANF, 8, pp. 630–1.

21 Ambrose, *On Virginity* I, 2, 5, 7-9; PL 16, cols 197-9.

22 Augustine, *Sermon* 274; PL 38, col. 1254.

23 Phillips Brooks, *The Light of the World and Other Sermons*, New York, 1890, pp. 14–5.

24 Francis de Sales, *Introduction to the Devout Life,* part I, 2-3.

25 a. John Chrysostom, *Homily 2 "In Praise of Saint Paul;"* PG 50, cols. 477-80; ET by ICEL.
b. Augustine, *Sermon* 278, 1-2, 5; PL 38, cols 1268-70.

26 John Chrysostom, *Homily 1 on the Second Letter to Timothy,* 1-2 (abridged); PG 11, cols. 600-1.

27 John Chrysostom, *Homily before His Exile*, 1-3; PG 52, cols. 427-30.

28 Thomas Aquinas, *Summa Theologiae,* foreword, part I, i, 8.

30 *The Letters, Speeches and Proclamations of King Charles I,* ed. Charles Petrie, London, 1935, pp.263-73.

31 John Bosco, *Letter 4,* 201-5; ET based on G. Bonetti, *St. John Bosco's Early Apostolate,* London, 1934.

FEBRUARY

1 Cogitosus, *The Life of St. Brigid;* PL 72, cols. 775, 782-3.

2 a. Sophronius, *Sermon 3 "On the Presentation of Christ in the Temple,"* 6-7; PG 87, 3, cols. 3291-3.
b. Ephrem of Edessa, *Hymns "On the Nativity,"* 6: 12-16; ET by Kathleen E. McVey, *Ephrem the Syrian,* New York & Mahwah, New Jersey, 1989, pp.112-3.
c. Guerric of Igny, Sermon 1 "On the Presentation of Christ in the Temple", 2, 3, 5; PL 185, cols. 64-7.

3 Rimbert, *The Life of St. Anskar*; text in *Scriptores Rerum Germanicarum*, ed. G. Waitz, Hanover, 1884; ET based on that by Charles H. Robinson, *Anskar: Apostle of the North 801-865*, London, 1921.

4 Cyril of Jerusalem, *Catechetical Lecture,* LCC, 4, pp. 120–5.

5 a. Luis Froes, *Historia XXVI Crucifixorum in Japon,* 14; *Acta Sanctorum: Februarium* I, col. 769; ET by ICEL.
NB There are several contemporary (or near contemporary) accounts of the martyrs of Japan. The most important (quoted here) is that by Luis Froes, a

Jesuit, who witnessed the events he recorded, and supplies us with the names of those who died.

b. Lactantius, *The Epitome of the Divine Institutes,* 54-5; PL 6, cols. 1061-2.

10 Gregory the Great, *Dialogues,* II, 33 & 34; ed. U. Moricca, Rome, 1924; ET by O. Zimmermann and Benedict Avery, Collegeville, Minnesota, 1981.
NB In the ancient world, it was commonly believed that at death, a person's soul left their body in the form of a bird. See also the death of Polycarp (23 February).

13 Absalom Jones, *Thanksgiving Sermon Preached January 1, 1808, in St. Thomas's Church, or the African Episcopal Church, Philadelphia, on Account of the Abolition of the African Slave Trade on that day by the Congress of the United States*, Philadelphia, 1808.

14 *The Life of Constantine,* 18; ET by ICEL.
NB Constantine adopted the name Cyril upon taking monastic vows on his deathbed. He was a deacon; it is uncertain if he was ever ordained priest. Methodius, however, was certainly a monk before he went to Moravia, and probably also a deacon. He was consecrated bishop by Pope Hadrian II in 870. For further background, see J. M. Hussey, *The Orthodox Church in the Byzantine Empire,* Oxford, 1986, pp.90-101.

14 a. Cyprian, *Letter* 58, 8-9, 11; CSEL 3, ii, pp.663-6.
b. George Herbert, "Love", first published in 1633 in *The Temple: Sacred Poems and Private Ejaculations.*

15 Thomas Bray, *Apostolick Charity, its Nature and Excellence Consider'd in a Discourse upon Daniel 12:3*; London, 1698, pp.19-20, 25-7.
NB This sermon was preached at the ordination of clergy to be sent to work in the colonies.

17 a. Margaret Ford, *Janani,* London, 1978, p.75.
b. Homily of Pope Paul VI, October 18, 1964.

18 Martin Luther, *Preface to the first volume of Latin Writings,* 1545; critical edition, Weimar, 1938, vol. 54, pp.185-6; ET by Lewis Spitz, *The Protestant Reformation,* ed. Hans J. Hillerbrand, London, 1968, pp.1-3.

23 *The Martyrdom of Polycarp,* 9-10, 13-16, 18-19; *Apostolic Fathers* II, Loeb 25, pp.307-46.
NB In the ancient world, it was commonly believed that at death, a person's soul left their body in the form of a bird. See also the death of Scholastica (10 February).

24 John Chrysostom, *Homilies on the Acts of the Apostles,* 3, 1-3.

27 a. George Herbert, *The Country Parson,* VI; *The Works of George Herbert,* ed. F. E. Hutchinson, Oxford, 1941, p.231; spelling modernized.
b. George Herbert, "Aaron," first published in 1633 in *The Temple: Sacred Poems and Private Ejaculations.*

MARCH

1 Rhigyfarch the Wise, *The Life of Saint David,* 1, 56, 63, 65; critical ed. and ET by J. W. James, *Rhigyfarch's Life of Saint David,* Cardiff, 1967, pp.29, 46-8.

2 Bede, *A History of the English Church and People,* III, 28; IV, 2 & 3; BEH pp.316, 334-6.

3 a. *The Journal of John Wesley.*
b. Charles Wesley, verses from "Wrestling with Jacob;" full text *The Faber Book of Religious Verse,* ed., Helen Gardner, London, 1972, pp.207-10.

7 *The Martyrdom of St Perpetua and St Felicity,* 1, 18-21 (abridged).
NB The account of the death of the martyrs in the amphitheater of Carthage consists of an introduction, Perpetua's own narration of their imprisonment and her dreams, and the continuation of the story of their deaths by another writer. Although anonymous, it is possible that this may have been written by Tertullian.

8 Edward King, *The Love and Wisdom of God,* ed. B. W. Randolph, London, 1910, pp.277-83 (abridged).
NB Edward King loved to preach on this text, Psalm 108:36, preferring the Authorized Version.

8 Bede, *A History of the English Church and People,* II, 15; BEH, p.190.

8 Geoffrey Studdert Kennedy, *The Hardest Part,* London, 1918, pp.189-201 (abridged).

9 Gregory of Nyssa, *Homily 6 "On the Beatitudes."*

12 Gregory the Great, *Commentary on Ezekiel,* I, 11, 4-6; PL 76, cols 907-8.

17 Patrick, *Confession,* 1, 34, 37, 38; critical edition by Bieler, *Libri Epistolarum Sancti Patricii Episcopi,* part 1, Dublin, 1952.

18 Cyril of Jerusalem, *Catechetical Lecture* XVIII, 23-6 (abridged); PG 33, cols 1044-8.

19 Bernadine of Siena, *Second Sermon on Saint Joseph*; *Opera S. Bernardini,* VII, 1627-30.

20 Bede, *The Life of Cuthbert,* 16, 17, 21; ET by J. F. Webb, *Lives of the Saints,* London, 1965, pp.92-4, 105.

21 a. *The Prose Works of the Right Reverend Father in God Thomas Ken,* ed. J. T. Round, London, 1938, pp.48-9.
NB Bishop Ken refers first of all to Francis Turner, Bishop of Ely from 1684; and William Lloyd, Bishop of Norwich from 1690. All three had been deprived of their sees for refusing to swear the oath of allegiance to William and Mary, following the deposition of James II. Turner had just died when Ken wrote the letter.
b. Ken, *op. cit.,* pp.144-6.

22 James DeKoven, *Sermons Preached on Various Occasions*, New York, 1880, pp. 120–2.

23 *The Teaching of Saint Gregory*, ed., Robert W. Thomson, Cambridge, Massachusetts, 1970.

25 a. Cyril of Alexandria, "Sermon at the Council of Ephesus 431," *Homily 4;* PG 77, col. 991.

NB Cyril uses the title *Theotokos* of Mary, literally "Bearer of God." In the Latin West this was rendered *Mater Dei*, "Mother of God." At the Council this title was formally endorsed as being appropriate for the mother of Jesus Christ, thereby underscoring the reality of the Incarnation.
b. Mark Frank, Sermon 30; LACT, *Sermons by Dr Mark Frank*, Oxford, 1849; vol. 2, pp. 34-5, 48-50 (abridged).
c. "Madonna" by Margaret Saunders - an unpublished poem.

27 Charles H. Brent, *Things that Matter; The best of the writings of Bishop Brent*, ed., with biographical sketch by Frederick Ward Kates, New York, 1949, pp. 44–6.

31 a. *The Sermons of John Donne*, ed. George R. Potter & Evelyn Simpson (10 vols.) Berkeley & Cambridge, 1957, vol. 3, sermon 3, pp. 110-12.
b. John Donne, *Poems*, 1633.

APRIL

1 F. D. Maurice, *Sermons "On the Lord's Prayer,"* I, 2-4; London, 1880, pp. 286-92 (abridged).

2 James Lloyd Breck, *"On Discipline:" A Sermon Delivered in Trinity Church, San Francisco, California, before the Diocesan Convention, May 3, 1871*; San Francisco, 1871.

3 Ralf Bocking, *The Life of Saint Richard*, I, 48; ET by Duncan J. Jones, in Sussex Record Society, vol. 79, Lewes, Sussex, 1995, pp.211, 213.
NB The so-called "Prayer of Saint Richard of Chichester" goes back at least as far as the thirteenth century, and appears both here in Bocking's *Life* and in a sermon of Odo of Châteauroux. The second part of the prayer was composed in the early twentieth century.

8 William Augustus Muhlenberg, "The Weekly Eucharist," *Pastoral Tracts*, New York, 1848, pp. 10–4.

9 a. Dietrich Bonhoeffer, *Letters and Papers from Prison*, ed. Eberhard Bethge, 2nd ed., London, 1971, p.369.
b. Bonhoeffer, *op. cit.*, p.347-8.

10 a. William Law, *A Serious Call to a Devout and Holy Life*, 1.
b. William Law, *The Spirit of Love*, I.

11 George Augustus Selwyn, *Four Sermons on the Work of Christ in the World*, IV; G. H. Curteis, *Bishop Selwyn of New Zealand and Lichfield*, 3rd ed., London, 1889, pp.150-2.

17 *Little Exordium*, 17.
NB The *fistula* was a metal tube through which the laity occasionally received from the chalice at the Eucharist during the Middle Ages.

19 *Anglo-Saxon Chronicle*, 1011-1012; *English Historical Documents* vol. 1 (*c.*500-1042), ed. Dorothy Whitelock, 2nd ed., London, 1979, pp.244-5.
NB Alphege's body was translated from London to Canterbury in 1023.

21 Anselm, *Proslogion*, 14, 16, 26 (abridged); ET by Benedicta Ward SLG, *The Prayers and Meditations of Saint Anselm*, London, 1973, pp.255-8, 266-7.

23 a. Peter Damian, *Sermon 13 "On Saint George;"* PL 144, cols. 567-8.
b. Ambrose, *Exposition of Psalm 118*, 20, 47-50; CSEL 62.

25 Irenaeus, *Against the Heresies,* I, 10, 1-2; SC 100; ET based on those by John Keble, London, 1872, and Dominic Unger, ACW 55, New York & Mahwah, New Jersey, 1992.

28 Stephen Neill, *A History of Christian Missions,* London, 2nd ed., 1986, pp.353-4; last two paragraphs, Donald Attwater, *The Penguin Dictionary of Saints,* London, 1965, pp.277-8, (adapted).

29 Catherine of Siena, *The Dialogue,* 167; ET by Suzanne Noffke OP, New York & Mahwah, New Jersey, 1980, pp.364-5.

MAY

1 John Chrysostom, *Homilies on the First Letter to the Corinthians*, 3, 4; PG 61, cols. 34-6.

2 Athanasius, *On the Incarnation of the Word,* 8-9; PG 25, cols. 80-3.

4 Augustine, *Confessions,* IX, x-xi; ET by Henry Chadwick, Oxford, 1991, pp.170-4.

8 Julian of Norwich, *Revelations of Divine Love*, 86; ET by Clifton Walters, London, 1966, pp.211-12.

9 Gregory of Nazianzus, *Oration 14, "On the Love of the Poor,"* 23-5; PG 35, cols. 887-90; ET by ICEL.

15 David Knowles, *The Sarum Lectures*, 1964.

19 *The Life of Saint Dunstan*, 11-13, 37; *English Historical Documents* vol. 1 (*c*.500-1042), ed. Dorothy Whitelock, 2nd ed., London, 1979, pp.898, 902-3.

20 Alcuin, Letter 193; *English Historical Documents* vol. 1 (*c*.500-1042), ed. Dorothy Whitelock, 2nd ed., London, 1979, pp.845-6 (abridged).

24 Jackson Kemper, "Report of the Rt. Rev. Jackson Kemper, D.D., Missionary Bishop for the Northwest," *The Spirit of Mission,* 1859; Edward Rochie Hardy, Jr., "Kemper's Missionary Episcopate: 1835-1859," *The Historical Magazine of the Episcopal Church,* September 1935, vol. 4, no. 3.

25 a. Bede, *A History of the English Church and People*, conclusion; BEH pp.566, 570.
b. Cuthbert, *Letter on the Death of Bede*; BEH pp.580-6.

26 Bede, *A History of the English Church and People,* I, 25-7; BEH pp.72-8.

26 Philip Neri, Letter to his Niece; A. Capecelatro, *The Life of Saint Philip Neri*, ET by T. A. Pope, London, 1926, pp.345-6 (adapted).

30 a. The Trial of Joan of Arc; ET of the Orl—ans manuscript by W. S. Scott, London, 1956; reprinted *The Trial of Joan of Arc*, with introduction by Marina Warner, Evesham, 1996, pp.41, 42, 56, 163.
b. *Occasional Sermons of Ronald A. Knox*, ed. Philip Caraman, London, 1960, pp.58-9.
NB "Jeanne la Pucelle" or "Joan the Maid" seems to have been her nickname. The bishop referred to was Pierre Cauchon, Bishop of Beauvais; the inquisitor was Brother Jean le Maitre.

31 a. Bede, *Homily* 1, 4; CCSL 122, pp.25-6, 30; ET by ICEL (adapted).
b. Jeremy Taylor, *The Life of our Blessed Lord and Savior Jesus Christ,* Part I, sections 1 & 2; *The Works of Bishop Jeremy Taylor*, ed. Charles Eden, London, 1847, vol. II, pp.53-9 (abridged).
c. Gerard Manley Hopkins, "The May Magnificat."

JUNE

1 Justin, *First Apology*, 2, 6, 11-12; PG 6, cols. 329, 336, 337, 341-4.
2 Eusebius, *Church History*, NPNF, 1, pp. 212–8.
3 Homily of Pope Paul VI, 18 October 1964.
5 Boniface, *Letter* 78; *Monumenta Germaniae Historica* III, pp. 352-4 (abridged).
NB The "wise person" to whom Boniface refers is Julianus Pomerius, *De vita contemplativa*, PL 59, col. 431.
6 Tertullian, *On Baptism*, ANF, 3, pp. 677–79.
9 Adomnan, *The Life of Columba*, Preface II and Book III, 23; ET by Richard Sharpe, *Adomnan's Life of St. Columba*, London, 1995, pp. 105-6, 226-9 (abridged).
NB *peregrinatio pro Dei amore* "choosing to be a pilgrim for Christ." The language of pilgrimage and exile is Biblical in origin (*cf.* Hebrews 11:13-16), and is a recurrent theme in monastic Celtic literature (e.g. *The Confession of Patrick*). The monk was representative of fallen humanity, a wandering exile for the love of God, seeking his heavenly homeland. *Cf.* also Sharpe, *op. cit.*, p. 248.
10 Ephrem of Syria, *Hymns of Faith,* 20:12, 32:1-3; ET by Sebastian Brock, *The Luminous Eye: The Spiritual World Vision of Saint Ephrem the Syrian,* Spencer, Massachusetts, 1985, pp.43-4.
11 Cyril of Alexandria, *Commentary on Saint John's Gospel,* 12, 1; PG 74, cols. 707-10; ET by ICEL.
12 John Johnson, *Enmegahbowh's Story: An Account of the Disturbances of the Chippewa Indians at Gull Lake in 1857 and 1862 and Their Removal in 1868*, Women's Auxiliary, Saint Barnabas Hospital, Minneapolis (Reprinted by Brainerd, Minnesota, in 1985).
14 a. Basil the Great, *Letter* 2, 1-2; Loeb (4 vols.) ed. Roy Deferrari, 1926; ET based on Deferrari, vol. 1, pp. 7-11.
b. Gregory of Nazianzus, *Oration 43 "In praise of Basil the Great,"* 15-17, 19-21; PG 36, cols. 514-23.
15 a. Evelyn Underhill, *Worship,* London, 1936, pp. 3-5 (abridged).
b. Source unknown.
16 Joseph Butler, *The Analogy of Religion,* 1736; conclusion to part 2.
18 Jean Farrant, *Mashonaland Martyr: Bernard Mizeki and the Pioneer Church,* Oxford & Johannesburg, 1966, pp.107-20 (abridged).
22 Bede, *A History of the English Church and People,* I, 6-7; BEH pp. 28-34.
24 a. Augustine, *Sermon* 293, 1-3; PL 38, cols. 1327-28.
b. Rabanus Maurus, *Homilies on Feasts* 26; PL 110, cols. 51-2.
c. Metropolitan Anthony of Sourozh (Anthony Bloom), *God and Man,* London, 1971.
27 Cyril of Alexandria, *Commentary on Saint John's Gospel,* 5, 2; PG 73, cols. 751-4; ET by ICEL.
28 Irenaeus, *Against the Heresies,* IV, 20, 5-6; SC 100; ET based on those by John Keble, London 1872, and Dominic Unger, ACW 55, New York & Mahwah, New Jersey, 1992.
29 a. Augustine, *Sermon* 295, 1-8 (abridged); PL 38, cols 1348-52.

b. Leo the Great, *Sermon 12 "On the Lord's Passion,"* 2-3, 6-7; PL 54, cols. 355-7; ET based on NPNF vol. XII, pp. 176-7.

JULY

4 Phillips Brooks, *The Spiritual Man and Other Sermons*, London, 1895, pp. 3–4.

6 Thomas More, Letter 61 "To Mistress Roper;" *Saint Thomas More: Selected Letters*; ed. Elizabeth Frances Rogers, New Haven, 1961, pp. 241-2.

11 Benedict, *Rule,* prologue.
NB In some churches the Feast of St Benedict is observed on March 21, the day of his death. This date continues to be observed by monastic communities, but in the wider Church, in part because this date invariably falls in Lent, and in part to honor Benedict as patron of Europe, it has become customary to observe his feast on July 11.

14 a. John Keble, *The Assize Sermon* "On National Apostasy," July 14, 1833, (abridged).
b. John Keble, *Sermons, Occasional and Parochial,* Oxford & London, 1868, pp. 262-5 (abridged).

15 Bonaventure, *The Soul's Journey into God,* VII, 1, 2, 4-6; English paraphrase based on ICEL and CWS.

17 William White, "A Charge to the Clergy of the Protestant Episcopal Church in the Diocese of Pennsylvania at the Opening of Convention," delivered May 11, 1825.

19 Gregory of Nyssa, *The Life of Macrina,* 7-10 (abridged); for full text see Virginia Woods Callahan, *Ascetical Works,* Washington DC, 1967, pp. 163-91.
NB Macrina was the oldest of ten children. Gregory tells the story of her life and death (at which he was present). He revered her as the holiest and strongest member of their family. The eight years Gregory refers to is the time he spent in exile having been deposed from his see by the strong Arian faction in the diocese. In 378, following the death of the Emperor Valens, who had supported Arianism, Gregory was allowed to return to Nyssa, and was immediately hailed as a champion of othodoxy.

20 Leo the Great, *Sermon* 97, 2-4; PL 54, cols. 458-60.

20 Sojourner Truth, "Ain't I A Woman?", a speech delivered in December, 1851, at the Women's Convention in Akron, Ohio.

20 Dexter C. Bloomer, *The Life and Writings of Amelia Bloomer,* St. Clair Shores, Michigan, 1895.

20 Elizabeth Cady Stanton, *The Woman's Bible*, Salem, New Hampshire, 1988.

20 Ann Petry, *Harriet Tubman: Conductor on the Underground Railroad*, New York, 1955, pp. 236–41.

22 a. Gregory the Great, *Homily 25 "On the Gospels,"* 1-5; PL 76, cols. 1189-93.
NB In his portrayal of Mary Magdalene, Gregory conflates three separate figures: the sinful woman of Luke 7:36-50; the woman who anointed Jesus in Matthew 26:7 & Mark 14:3, who is called "Mary" in John 12:3; and Mary Magdalene herself.

b. Janet Morley, *All Desires Known,* London, 1992, p.104.

23 Bridget of Sweden: *Revelations,* VI, 86; VI, 47; ET by Sr Marianne Sodorstrom.

24 Thomas à Kempis, *The Imitation of Christ,* ET in *The Consolation of Philosophy*, New York, 1943, pp. 278–9.

25 John Chrysostom, *Homilies on St Matthew's Gospel,* 65, 2-4; PG 58, cols. 619-22.

26 John of Damascus, *Oration 6 "On the Nativity of the Blessed Virgin Mary,"* 2, 4, 5, 6; PG 96, cols. 663, 667, 670; ET by ICEL.

27 William Reed Huntington, *The Church Idea*, New York, 1869.

29 a. Augustine, *Sermon* 103, 1-2; PL 38, cols. 613-15.
b. Aelred, *Spiritual Friendship,* I, 45, 69-70; ET by Mary Eugenia Laker SSND, Spencer, Massachusetts, 1977, pp.60-1, 65-6.

30 As quoted by Garth Lean, *God's Politician: William Wilberforce's Struggle,* London, 1980, pp. 48-50.

31 a. Ignatius of Loyola, *The Spiritual Exercises,* 23; ET by Joseph Munitiz & Philip Endean, London, 1996, p. 289.
b. *Reminiscences* or *The Life of Ignatius of Loyola,* I, 4-8; ET by Munitiz & Endean, *op. cit.*, pp. 14-5.

AUGUST

1 W. E. C. Baynes, *St. Joseph of Arimathea: the Glastonbury Legend*, London.

6 a. Anastasius of Sinai, *Conferences,* 6-10; ET by ICEL.
b. Pseudo-Macarius, *Spiritual Homilies,* Alphabetical Collection "H," 1, 2; *Coptic Apophthegms,* Paris, 1894.
c. A. M. Ramsey, *Be Still and Know,* London, 1982, pp.64-5, 70.

7 John Mason Neale, *Sermon* 111; J. M. Neale, *Sermons* (3 vols), London, 1875; vol. 2, pp. 340-1.
NB No year is given for the date of this sermon.

8 The reading represents a compilation of testimonies from various followers of Dominic which were submitted during hearings for his canonization process in 1233: *Acta canonisationis Sancti Dominici: Monumenta OP Mist.* 16, Rome, 1935, pp. 30, 146-7; ET by ICEL.

9 Mary Porter, *Mary Sumner: Her Life and Work*, Winchester, 1921, pp.29-31.

10 Leo the Great, *Sermon* 85, 1-4; PL 54, cols. 435-7; ET based on NPNF (2nd series) 12, Oxford, 1895, pp. 197-8.

11 *The Fourth Letter of Clare to Blessed Agnes of Prague*, 4-33; ET by R. J. Armstrong & Ignatius Brady, *Francis and Clare: The Complete Works,* New York & Mahwah, New Jersey, 1982, pp. 203-5.

13 Jeremy Taylor, *Holy Living,* 1650, preface.

13 A. M. Allchin, *The Silent Rebellion,* London, 1958, pp. 114-5.

14 a. Pope John Paul II, *Homily for the Canonization of Maximilian Kolbe,* 10 October 1982.
b. Ulrich Simon, *A Theology of Auschwitz,* London, 1967, pp. 9-12 (abridged).

14 Jonathan Myrick Daniels, "The Burning Bush," *The New Hampshire Churchman*, June, 1965, vol. 7, no. 9.

15 a. Julian of Norwich, *Revelations of Divine Love,* 25; ET by Clifton Walters, London, 1966, pp. 101-2.
b. Hildegard of Bingen, *A Responsory and Alleluia for the Blessed Virgin Mary;* ET by Robert Carver, *Hildegard of Bingen: An Anthology,* edited by Fiona Bowie & Oliver Davies, London, 1990, pp.116-7.
c. Ivone Gebara & Maria Clara Bingemer, *Mary, Mother of God, Mother of the Poor*, ET by Phillip Berryman, London & New York, 1989, pp. 119-21 (abridged).

18 William DuBose, "The Faith of a Christian Today," *A DuBose Reader: Selections from the Writings of William Porcer DuBose*, ed., Donald S. Armentrout, 1984, pp. 204–5.

20 Bernard of Clairvaux, *On the Love of God,* 6-7; PL 182, cols 983-5; ET based on that by "A Religious CSMV," London & Oxford, 1950.

24 Tertullian, *On Prescription against Heresies,* 20-22, 32; SC 46, pp.112-15, 130.

25 John of Joinville, *The Life of St. Louis*, ET by René Hague, London, 1955, pp. 25–6, 213–5.

27 Thomas Gallaudet, "A Sermon delivered upon the occasion of Saint Ann's Church for Deaf-Mutes commencing its services, August 7, 1859," New York, 1859.

28 Augustine, *Confessions,* VII, x, xviii; X, xxvii; ET by Henry Chadwick, Oxford, 1991, pp. 123-4, 128, 201.

31 Bede, *A History of the English Church and People,* III, 3, 5, 17; BEH pp. 218-220, 226-8, 262-4.

SEPTEMBER

1 *The Sayings of the Desert Fathers,* Agathon 26 & 30; ET by Benedicta Ward SLG, Oxford, 1975, pp. 20-1.

1 Alvin O. Turner, "Journey to Sainthood: David Pendleton Oakerhater's Better Way," *The Chronicles of Oklahoma*, LXX, no. 2, 1992, pp. 116–40.

2 David Hand, "The White-Robed Army of Martyrs," *Papua New Guinea Church Partnership* (abridged); an account written for the centenary celebrations of the Church, London, 1991.
NB Lucian Tapiedi is one of the ten twentieth-century martyrs whose statues have recently been carved for the west front of Westminster Abbey.

4 Paul Jones, "Christian Loyalty," in John Howard Melish, *Bishop Paul Jones: Witness for Peace,* Cincinnati, Ohio, 1992, pp. 50–4.

8 a. Andrew of Crete, *Oration 1 "On the Nativity of the Blessed Virgin Mary;"* PG 97, cols. 805-9.
b. *The Festal Menaion;* ET by Mother Mary and Archimandrite Kallistos Ware, London, 1969, pp. 105, 107, 119, 125.
NB For use of term *Theotokos* see above March 25.

9 Anonymous, *The Sisters of Saint Mary at Memphis with the Acts and Sufferings of the Priests and Others who were with them during the Yellow Fever Season of 1878*, printed but not published, New York, 1879.

10 Alexander Crummell, "The Race-Problem in America," ed. J. R. Oldfield, *Civilization and Black Progress: Selected Writings of Alexander Crummell on the South,* Charlottesville, 1995.

12 John Henry Hobart, *The Christian Bishop approving himself unto God in reference to the Present State of the Protestant Episcopal Church in the United States of America*, Philadelphia, 1827.

13 Cyprian, *Letter 1 "To Donatus,"* 2-4; PL 4, cols. 197-202.

14 a. Andrew of Crete, *Oration 10 "On the Exaltation of the Holy Cross;"* PG 97, cols. 1018-9, 1022-3; ET by ICEL.
b. Anonymous, *The Dream of the Rood,* vv. 27-56, 96-100.

16 a. Bede, *A History of the English Church and People,* III, 4; BEH pp. 220-2.
NB Over the centuries "White House" became Whithorn.
b. Aelred of Rievaulx, *The Life of Saint Ninian*, 2, 11; ET based on W. M. Metcalfe, *Pinkerton's Lives of the Scottish Saints,* Paisley, 1895 (reprinted 1998), vol. 1, pp. 8-10, 24.

17 a. Hildegard, *The Book of Life's Merits,* IV, 67; ET by Robert Carver, *Hildegard of Bingen: An Anthology,* edited by Fiona Bowie & Oliver Davies, London, 1990, p. 87.
b. Hildegard, *Letter* 85r/a; *The Letters of Hildegard of Bingen*, ET by Joseph L. Baird & Radd K. Ehrman, Oxford & New York, 1994, vol. 1, pp. 192-3.

18 a. E. B. Pusey, *Parochial and Cathedral Sermons,* Oxford, 1882; sermon 12 entitled "Saintliness of Christians," pp. 167-70.
NB No year is given for this but it was preached at Hursley on the Feast of the Annunciation (March 25).
b. E. B. Pusey, *University Sermons,* Oxford, 1879; sermon 6, pp. 4, 6-8, 42, 60, 61.
NB The Vincentius Pusey refers to is Vincent of L—rins (d. before 450) who emphasized the role of tradition in guarding against innovations in the doctrine of the Church. He is credited with the so-called "Vincentian canon" or "rule of faith" that "we hold that which has been believed everywhere, always, and by all people" (*quod ubique, quod semper, quod ab omnibus creditum est*).

19 Bede, *A History of the English Church and People,* IV, 1-2; BEH pp. 328-34.

20 Margaret Cropper, *Shining Lights: Six Anglican Saints of the Nineteenth Century,* London, 1963, pp. 50-67 (abridged).

21 Bede, *Homily* 21; CCSL 122, pp.149-51; ET by ICEL.

25 *A Treasury of Russian Spirituality,* vol. 2, edited & ET by George P. Fedotov, London, 1950, pp. 69-70.

26 a. Lancelot Andrewes, "A Caution before Preaching after the example of Saint Fulgentius," *Preces Privatae*; originally composed in Greek and Latin, and published posthumously in 1648.
b. Henry Isaacson, *The Life of Bishop Andrewes,* London, 1650; LACT, *The Works of Bishop Andrewes,* ed. James Bliss, 1854, pp. xii-xiii, xxiv-xxvi.

27 Vincent de Paul, *Letter* 2546; ET based on J. Leonard, *St Vincent de Paul: Selected Letters and Addresses,* London, 1925.

29 a. Gregory the Great, *Homily 34 "On the Gospels,"* 8-9; PL 76, cols. 1250-51.

b. Bernard of Clairvaux, *Sermon 1 "For the Feast of Saint Michael,"* 1-3, 5; PL 183, cols. 447-50.
NB Bernard when quoting from Hebrews 1:14 shares the assumption of his contemporaries that the Apostle Paul was the author of the epistle.
c. *Carmina Gadelica,* I, no.77; ET by Alexander Carmichael, 2nd ed. Edinburgh, 1928.
NB In the Celtic tradition, the Feast of Michaelmas is of special significance. Michael is patron saint of the sea, of coastal regions, boats and horses. This accounts for the numerous dedications to him around the Celtic coast, such as Mont St. Michel in Brittany, and St. Michael's Mount in Cornwall. On land, he is often portrayed as riding a milk-white steed, an image also associated with Saint George. Michael the Archangel is also seen as the one whose duty it is to convey the souls of the departed to paradise. These various ideas are reflected in the imagery of the poem quoted here.

30 Jerome, *Letter* 52, 7-8, 10, 13; CSEL 54, pp. 426-35; ET based on NPNF (2nd series), vol. 6, Oxford, 1893, pp. 92-5.

OCTOBER

1 Gregory of Tours, *The History of the Franks,* II, 31; ET based on O. M. Dalton, Oxford, 1927.

1 Th—rℵse of Lisieux, *The Story of a Soul;* ET by Ronald Knox, *The Autobiography of a Saint,* London, 1958, pp. 198-9, 201 (abridged).

4 a. "The Earlier Rule of 1209," prologue, 1-2; ET by R. J. .Armstrong & Ignatius Brady, *Francis and Clare: The Complete Works,* New York & Mahwah, New Jersey, 1982, pp. 109-11.
b. Francis of Assisi, *The Canticle of Brother Sun.*

6 a. William Tyndale, *Epistle to the Reader*, included in his first published version of the New Testament in 1526; *The Doctrinal Treatises of William Tyndale,* Cambridge, 1848, pp. 389-90.
b. William Tyndale, "Of Antichrist," *The Obedience of a Christian Man,* 1528; *op. cit.,* pp. 239-40.

6 Guigo II, *The Ladder of Monks and Twelve Meditations,* meditation 1; ET by Edmund Colledge OSA & James Walsh SJ, London, 1978, pp. 104-5.

9 Augustine, *Sermon* 273, 1; PL 38.

9 Robert Grosseteste, *Memorial to Pope Innocent IV*; in G. Lecher, *John Wyclif and his English Precursors;* ET by P. Lorimer, London, 1884, pp. 32-3 (abridged).
NB Not long before his death, Bishop Grosseteste traveled to Lyons to see the Pope and his *curia,* in order personally to deliver his "memorial" concerning abuses affecting the life and stability of the Church in England, including the impotence of the bishops to remove corrupt clergy, and certain abuses emanating from Rome itself. His petition succeeded, and his personal integrity was vindicated.

10 Bede, *A History of the English Church and People,* I, 29; II, 9, 12, 14, 16; BEH pp. 104, 164, 176, 180-2, 186, 192.

10 Thomas Traherne, *Centuries of Meditation,* III, 1-3.

12 Bede, *A History of the English Church and People,* V, 19; BEH pp. 516-24, 528.

13 a. *The Life of King Edward who rests at Westminster,* attributed to a monk of Saint Bertin, II, 9, 11; edited and ET by Frank Barlow, 2nd ed., Oxford, 1992, pp. 111-13, 123-5.
NB The date when Edward began to be called "the Confessor" has not been established; but the intention presumably was to distinguish him from his uncle and namesake, Edward, king and martyr, whose feast day is celebrated on March 18. The anonymous *Life* quoted here pre-dates that by Osbert of Clare who used and "improved" it. It was probably written soon after the Conquest (see Barlow). The text, however, is damaged and incomplete, and in parts has had to be reconstructed with interpolations from the later work of Osbert of Clare.
b. *Occasional Sermons of Ronald A. Knox,* ed. Philip Caraman, London, 1960, pp.26, 28.

14 Samuel Isaac Joseph Schereschewsky, "An Appeal for Establishing a Missionary College in China," Philadelphia, 1877.

15 a. Teresa of Avila, *The Way of Perfection,* 32; ET by E. Allison Peers, London, 1946, pp. 136-8 (abridged).
b. Shirley du Boulay, *Teresa of Avila,* London, 1991, pp. 1, 29-35 (abridged).

16 a. *The Works of Bishop Ridley,* Cambridge, 1843, pp. 355-8.
b. "The Second Sermon on the Card," *Sermons of Bishop Latimer,* Cambridge, 1844, pp. 23-4.

16 a. *The First Prayer Book of King Edward VI*, 1549, Preface.
b. Thomas Cranmer, *A Defence of the True and Catholic Doctrine of the Sacrament of the Body and Blood of our Savior Christ,* 1551, I, 10, 12; *The Remains of Thomas Cranmer,* Oxford, 1833, vol. 2, pp. 300-2.

17 Ignatius of Antioch, *The Letter to the Romans,* 1, 2, 4, 6-7; Loeb 24, *Apostolic Fathers I;* ET based on Kirsopp Lake, London, 1912, pp. 227-35.

18 Gregory the Great, *Homily 17 "On the Gospels,"* 1-3; PL 76, cols. 1139-40.

19 John Sargent, *The Life and Letters of the Reverend Henry Martyn*, London, 1862; 10th ed. 1885, pp. 187, 196-7.

23 Hegesippus, *Fragments from his Five Books of Commentaries on the Acts of the Apostles*, ANF, 8, p. 206.

26 a. Alfred the Great, *Prose Preface to his translation of Gregory the Great's "Pastoral Care;"* ET by Simon Keynes & Michael Lapidge, *Alfred the Great,* London, 1983, pp. 124-6.
NB This was probably the earliest of the translations undertaken by the king himself, and may date as early as 890. Gregory the Great was concerned principally with ecclesiastical leadership and government, but his language was equally applicable to holders of secular office; hence the appeal to the king. In the prose preface, King Alfred explains why he has translated the work and it is therefore a cardinal document for understanding his mind.
b. Asser, *The Life of King Alfred,* 1, 8, 22, 24, 25, 76; ET by Keynes & Lapidge, *op. cit.,* pp. 67-9, 74-6, 90.

28 Origen, *Homilies on Joshua,* 9, 1-2; SC 71, pp. 244-6.

29 a. *The Last Journals of James Hannington,* ed. by E. C. Dawson, London, 1888, pp. 213-8 (abridged).

b. Stephen Neill, *A History of Christian Missions,* London, 1964; 2nd ed. 1986, pp. 477-8.

NOVEMBER

1 a. Bernard of Clairvaux, *Sermon* 2; *S. Bernardi Opera,* ed. J. Leclercq and H. Rochais, vol. V, 1968, pp. 364-8; ET by ICEL (adapted).
b. Hugh Latimer, "Articles untruly, falsely, uncharitably imputed to me by Dr Powell of Salisbury," *Sermons and Remains of Bishop Hugh Latimer,* Cambridge, 1844, pp. 234-5.
c. Kenneth Kirk, *The Vision of God,* Oxford, 1931, abridged ed. 1934, pp. 46-7.
d. Thomas Merton, *New Seeds of Contemplation,* London, 1961, pp. 24-6.

2 a. Gregory of Nazianzus, *Oration* 7, 23-4; PG 35, cols. 786-7; ET by ICEL.
b. Hugh Latimer, "Articles untruly, falsely, uncharitably imputed to me by Dr Powell of Salisbury," *Sermons and Remains of Bishop Hugh Latimer,* Cambridge, 1844, pp. 236-7.
c. John Donne, *Holy Sonnets: Divine Meditations,* 6.
d. Austin Farrer, *Said or Sung,* London, 1960, pp.133-4 (abridged).

3 Richard Hooker, *The Laws of Ecclesiastical Polity,* V, lvi, 7.

3 Pope John XXIII, *Homily following the Canonization of Martin de Porres,* June 3, 1962.

6 Gregory the Great, *Pastoral Care,* II, 3, 5; PL 77, cols 28-32; ET based on NPNF (2nd series) 12, Oxford, 1895, pp. 10, 13.
NB It is likely that in this book Gregory intended to provide secular clergy with a spiritual counterpart to the *Rule of Saint Benedict.* Throughout he uses the term *rector* which is more correctly translated in English as "ruler" but which has been rendered here by the less hierarchical term "leader." Gregory was writing primarily for the episcopate, but the term *rector* could and did include "secular" as well as ecclesiastical leaders.

6 William Temple, *Christianity and Social Order,* London, 1942; quotation from 1976 reprint, pp. 28, 31, 32, 67.

7 Bede, *A History of the English Church and People,* V, 9-11; BEH pp. 476, 480, 486.

9 *The Book of Margery Kempe,* I, 52; ET by B. A. Windeatt, London, 1985, pp. 162-7 (abridged).

10 Leo the Great, *Letter 28 "To Flavian,"* 2-3; ET based on NPNF (2nd series) 12, Oxford, 1895, pp. 39-40.

11 a. Sulpicius Severus, *The Life of St Martin,* 2-4 (abridged); PL 20, cols. 160ff. ET based on NPNF (2nd series) 11, Oxford, 1895, pp. 5-6.
b. Sulpicius Severus, *The Life of St Martin,* 10; PL 20, col. 166; ET based on *op. cit.,* pp. 8-9.
NB Martin was the first non-martyr saint to be commemorated in the Western Church. The medieval Office hymn *Iste confessor* ("He who bore witness by a good confession" *New English Hymnal* 220) was almost certainly written in his honor and later adopted, with much else from the office of this saint, as part of the office of Bishops, and is therefore most

appropriately sung today. Modern English translations regrettably omit the original third verse which commemorates Martin's healing miracle. See *Hymns of the Roman Liturgy,* ed. J. Connelly, London, 1957, p. 151.

12 Charles Simeon, "Evangelic and Pharisaic Righteousness Compared," *University Sermons*; *Let Wisdom Judge: University Addresses and Sermon Outlines by Charles Simeon,* ed. Arthur Pollard, London, 1959, pp. 87-8.

14 E. Edwards Beardsley, *The Life and Correspondence of the Right Reverend Samuel Seabury,* Boston, 1881, pp. 150-3.

16 Turgot, *The Life of Saint Margaret, Queen of Scotland,* 1-3 (abridged); ET based on W. M. Metcalfe, *Pinkerton's Lives of the Scottish Saints,* Paisley, 1895 (reprinted 1998), vol. 2, pp. 298-310.

16 Gertrude of Helfta, *The Herald of Divine Love,* I, 11; ET by Margaret Winkworth, New York & Mahwah, New Jersey, 1993, pp.72-3.

17 Adam of Eynsham, *Magna Vita: The Life of Saint Hugh of Lincoln,* III, 9; IV, 3; critical ed. and ET by D. L. Douie and David Farmer, 2nd ed. Oxford, 1985, (2 vols.) vol. 1 pp. 112-14, vol. 2 pp. 12-15.

18 Bede, *A History of the English Church and People,* IV, 23; BEH pp.404-10.

19 a. Depositions to the Commission of Pope Gregory IX, 1232; ET by Nesta De Robeck, *Saint Elizabeth of Hungary,* Milwaukee, 1954, pp. 162-3.
b. John Chrysostom, *Homilies on Saint Matthew's Gospel,* 50, 4.

19 Mechtild of Magdeburg, *Revelations: The Flowing Light of the Godhead,* II, 26; ET based on Lucy Menzies, London, 1953, pp. 58-9.
NB Mechtild's writing is characterized by strong, fresh images, and by dialogues between the soul and God. She was the first mystic to write in her own vernacular (German) rather than Latin.

20 Aelfric of Eynsham, *The Lives of the Saints;* vol. II ed. W. Skeat, London, 1881, pp.315-34.
NB The "great Viking fleet" referred to by both Aelfric and Asser (biographer of King Alfred) arrived toward the end of 865 and spent the winter of 865-6 in East Anglia. According to the chronicler Aethelweard, the Viking force was led by "the tyrant Igwar" (Hingwar), though other sources mention Ubbe. From later Scandinavian tradition "Hingwar" or "Igwar" could be Ivar the Boneless. For further discussion see Simon Keynes & Michael Lapidge, *Alfred the Great,* London, 1983, pp. 238-9, n.44, & p. 241, n.61. See also Dorothy Whitelock, "Fact and Fiction in the Legend of Saint Edmund," *Proceedings of the Suffolk Institute of Archaelogy,* 31, 1969, pp. 217-33.

22 Augustine, *First Exposition of Psalm 32* (Hebrew: Psalm 33), 7-8; CCSL 38, pp. 253-4.

23 Clement of Rome, *Letter to the Corinthians,* 35-8; Loeb 24, *Apostolic Fathers I*; ET based on Kirsopp Lake, London, 1912, pp. 67-75.

25 James Otis Sargent Huntington, *Bargainers and Beggars*, West Park, New York, 1919, pp. 31–4.

25 Ephrem of Edessa, *Hymns on Virginity,* 24, 1-5, 13; ET by Kathleen E. McVey, *Ephrem the Syrian,* New York & Mahwah, New Jersey, 1989, pp. 365-8.

25 Isaac Watts, *Horae Lyricae,* 1706 & 1709.

28 a. Bishop Museum Archives—Ms HC Box 1 (letter A-J).

b. Kamehameha, Preface to the *Book of Common Prayer* in Hawaiian, Honolulu, 1863.

30 a. Dietrich Bonhoeffer, *The Cost of Discipleship;* ET by R. H. Fuller, London, 1959, pp. 48-9.
b. Mark Frank, Sermon 50; LACT, *Sermons by Dr Mark Frank,* Oxford, 1849; vol. 2, pp. 382-3 (abridged).

DECEMBER

1 Isaac Walton, *The Life of Mr. George Herbert;* 3rd ed., York, 1817, pp. 106-11.
NB Clare Hall was subsequently raised to collegiate status, and should not be confused with the current institution of that name in Cambridge.

2 Channing Moore Williams, "A Letter from Dzang-Zok," June 25, 1858; Gene Lehman and Beverley D. Tucker, *History of Rikkyo (Saint Paul's) University and Schools,* Tokyo, 2000.

3 Francis Xavier, *Letter* 4 (1542) and *Letter* 5 (1544); text H. Tursellini, *Vita Francisci Xaverii,* Rome, 1956, Book IV; ET by ICEL.

4 John of Damascus, *On the Incarnation and the Holy Icons,* I, 16; PG 94, col. 1245.

5 Clement of Alexandria, *An Exhortation to the Greeks (Heathen)*, ANF, 2, p. 206.

6 Gregory the Great, *Homily 17 "On the Gospels,"* 4-5; PL 76, cols. 1140-1.

7 Ambrose, *On Penitence,* II, 66, 67, 70-3, 78; PL 16, col. 431; ET based on NPNF (2nd series) 10, Oxford, 1895, pp. 353-5.

8 a. Anselm, *Oration* 52; ET by ICEL.
b. Ivone Gebara & Maria Clara Bingemer, *Mary, Mother of God, Mother of the Poor*, ET by Phillip Berryman, London & New York, 1989, pp. 111-3 (abridged).

12 Jane de Chantal, *Letter* 178; ET by Peronne Marie Thibert VHM, *Francis de Sales, Jane de Chantal: Letters of Spiritual Direction,* New York & Mahwah, New Jersey, 1988, pp. 239-40.
NB At the head of each of the letters she wrote, and throughout the writings of Francis de Sales, appears the words "Live Jesus!" "*Vive Jesus!*" became the motto of the Visitation of Holy Mary, the congregation founded by Francis de Sales and Jane de Chantal. It was expressive of the particular vision of the Christian life that they sought to bring to birth in their own persons.

13 Clement of Alexandria, *An Exhortation to the Greeks,* 11; SC 2, pp. 181-3.

14 a. John of the Cross, *The Spiritual Canticle,* second redaction, stanza 37, 4, stanza 36, 13; ET by E. Allison Peers, *The Complete Works of Saint John of the Cross,* London, 1935, pp.363, 365-6 (from three volumes in one edition).
b. John of the Cross, "Song of the Soul that is glad to know God by faith," *The Poems of Saint John of the Cross*; ET by Roy Campbell, London, 1966, pp. 61-2.

21 Gregory the Great, *Homily 26 "On the Gospels,"* 7-9; PL 76, cols. 1201-2.

25 a. Lancelot Andrewes, *Sermons on the Nativity,* Grand Rapids, Michigan, 1955, pp. 73–4.

b. Martin Luther King, Jr., *A Testament of Hope: the Essential Writings of Martin Luther King, Jr.*, ed. James Melvin Washington, San Francisco, 1986, pp. 257–8.

c. Julian of Vezelay, *Sermon 1 'On the Nativity';* SC 192, pp.45, 52, 60. NB The text of Scripture Julian refers to is Wisdom 18:14 which formed the medieval Latin introit at Christmas.

d. Gregory of Nazianzus, *Oration 38 'For Christmas'*; PG 36, cols. 311-4.

e. Irenaeus, *Against Heresies,* IV, 38, 1; SC 100, p. 946; ET based on NPNF vol. I, p. 521

f. Leo the Great, *Sermon 1 'On the Nativity',* 1-3; PL 54, cols. 190-3; ET based on NPNF vol. XII, pp. 128-9.

g. Robert Southwell, *The Nativity of Christ.*

26 Fulgentius of Ruspe, *Sermon* 3, 1-3, 5-6; CCSL 91A, pp. 905-9; ET by ICEL.

27 Augustine, *Commentary on the First Letter of John,* 1, 3; PL 35, cols. 1978-80; ET by ICEL.

28 a. Quodvultdeus, *Sermon 2 On the Creed;* PL 40, col. 655; ET by ICEL.

b. John Hick, *Evil and the God of Love,* 2nd ed., London & New York, 1985, pp. 385-6.

NB Hick is quoting from Dostoyevsky, *The Brothers Karamazov,* Part II, Bk. 5, chapter 4; ET by David Magarshack, London, 1958, p. 287. The whole chapter of Dostoyevsky, however, is worth reading for background to Hick's argument. The section of the quotation from Dostoyevsky (*op. cit.,* pp.282-3) printed in square brackets is additional to that originally quoted by Hick, and is included here, with permission, for its appropriateness to Holy Innocents' Day.

29 Edward Grim, *"The Narrative of the Murder of Thomas Becket;" English Historical Documents,* vol. 2 (1042-1189), ed. David Douglas & George Greenaway, London, 1968, pp. 761-8 (abridged).

NB Of the five contemporary biographers of Thomas Becket, each of whom includes an account of the martyrdom, the eye-witness account by Edward Grim is regarded by scholars as the most detached and impartial. His presence was entirely accidental: he was a stranger only lately come to Canterbury for the purpose of seeing the archbishop. The fact that he himself was wounded in the attack is corroborated by nearly all the other biographers and eye-witnesses. It is part of his account, therefore, that is included here (*op. cit.,* pp. 761, 767 n.3).

Index of Saints' Days

Aelred	*January 12*
Agnes	*January 21*
Aidan	*August 31*
Alban	*June 22*
Alcuin	*May 20*
Alfred	*October 26*
All Saints' Day	*November 1*
All Souls' Day	*November 2*
Alphege	*April 19*
Ambrose	*December 7*
Andrew	*November 30*
Andrewes, Lancelot	*September 26*
Anne	*July 26*
Anselm	*April 21*
Anskar	*February 3*
Antony of Egypt	*January 17*
Aquinas, Thomas	*January 28*
Athanasius	*May 2*
Augustine of Canterbury	*May 26*
Augustine of Hippo	*August 28*
Azariah, Samuel Vedanayagam	*January 2*
Barnabas	*June 11*
Bartholomew the Apostle	*August 24*
Basil the Great	*June 14*
Becket, Thomas	*December 29*
Bede, the Venerable	*May 25*
Benedict,	*July 11*
Bernard of Clairvaux	*August 20*
Bloom, Amelia	*July 20*
Bonaventure	*July 15*
Bonhoeffer, Dietrich	*April 9*
Boniface	*June 5*
Bray, Thomas	*February 15*
Breck, James Lloyd	*April 2*
Brent, Charles Henry	*March 27*
Bridget of Sweden	*July 23*
Brigid of Kildare (Bride)	*February 1*
Brooks, Phillips	*January 23*

Bruno *October 6*
Butler, Joseph *June 16*

Catherine of Alexandria *November 25*
Catherine of Siena *April 29*
Cecilia *November 22*
Chad *March 2*
Chanel, Peter *April 28*
Chantal, Jane Frances de *December 12*
Charles *January 30*
Chrysostom, John *January 27*
Clare *August 11*
Clement of Alexandria *December 5*
Clement of Rome *November 23*
Columba *June 9*
Constance *September 9*
Cornelius, The Centurion *February 4*
Cranmer, Thomas *October 16*
Crummell, Alexander *September 10*
Cuthbert *March 20*
Cyprian *September 15*
Cyril of Alexandria *June 27*
Cyril of Jerusalem *March 18*
Cyril & Methodius *February 14*

Daniels, Jonathan Myrick *August 14*
David *March 1*
DeKoven, James *March 22*
Denys *October 9*
Dominic *August 8*
Donne, John *March 31*
DuBose, William Porcher *August 18*
Dunstan *May 19*

Edmund *November 20*
Edward the Confessor *October 13*
Elizabeth of Hungary *November 19*
Emery, Julia Chester *January 9*
Enmegahbowh *June 12*
Ephrem of Edessa (Syria) *June 9*

Fabian *January 20*
Faithful Departed, Commemoration of *November 2*

Felicity	*March 7*
Felix	*March 8*
Ferrar, Nicholas	*December 1*
Francis of Assisi	*October 4*
Francis de Sales	*January 24*
Francis Xavier	*December 3*
Gallaudet, Thomas	*August 27*
George	*April 23*
Gertrude of Helfta	*November 16*
Giles	*September 1*
Gregory the Great	*March 12*
Gregory the Illuminator	*March 23*
Gregory of Nazianzus	*January 2*
Gregory of Nyssa	*March 9*
Grosseteste, Robert	*October 9*
Hannington, James	*October 29*
Harding, Stephen	*April 17*
Herbert, George	*February 27*
Hilary	*January 13*
Hilda	*November 19*
Hildegard	*September 17*
Hobart, John Henry	*September 12*
Holy Innocents	*December 28*
Hooker, Richard	*November 3*
Hugh	*November 17*
Huntingdon, William Reed	*July 27*
Ignatius of Antioch	*October 17*
Ignatius of Loyola	*July 31*
Innocents, The Holy	*December 28*
Irenaeus	*June 28*
James of Jerusalem	*October 23*
James the Apostle	*May 1*
James the Deacon	*October 11*
James the Great	*July 25*
Jane Frances de Chantal	*December 12*
Japan, The Martyrs of	*February 6*
Jerome	*September 30*
Joachim	*July 26*
Joan of Arc	*May 30*

John of the Cross *December 14*
John of Damascus *December 4*
John the Baptist, Birth of *June 24*
John the Evangelist *December 27*
John Chrysostom *January 27*
Jones, Absolom *February 13*
Jones, Paul *September 4*
Joseph of Arimathea *August 1*
Joseph of Nazareth *March 19*
Jude the Apostle *October 28*
Julian of Norwich *May 8*
Justin *June 1*

Keble, John *March 29*
Kempe, Margery *November 9*
Kemper, Jackson *May 24*
Kempis, Thomas à *July 24*
Ken, Thomas *March 21*
King, Edward *March 8*
King, Martin Luther, Jr. *January 15*
Kolbe, Maximilian *August 14*

Latimer, Hugh *October 16*
Laud, William *January 10*
Laurence *August 10*
Law, William *April 10*
Leo the Great *November 10*
Leonard *November 6*
Louis *August 25*
Lucy *December 13*
Luke the Evangelist *October 18*
Luther, Martin *February 18*
Luwum, Janani *February 17*
Lyons, The Martyrs of *June 2*

Macrina *July 19*
Margaret of Antioch *July 20*
Margaret of Scotland *November 16*
Mark the Evangelist *April 25*
Martha *July 29*
Martin de Porres *November 3*
Martin of Tours *November 11*

Mary, The Blessed Virgin	*August 15*
Annunciation to	*March 25*
Birth	*September 8*
Conception	*December 8*
Visit to Elizabeth	*Mary 31*
Mary & Martha of Bethany	*July 29*
Mary Magdalene	*July 22*
Maurice, Frederick Denison	*April 1*
Mechtild	*November 19*
Methodius	*February 14*
Michael & All Angels	*September 29*
Miki, Paul and his companions	*February 6*
Mizeki, Bernard	*June 18*
Monnica	*May 4*
More, Thomas	*July 6*
Muhlenberg, William Augustus	*April 8*
Nathanael (see Bartholomew)	*August 24*
Neale, John Mason	*August 7*
Neri, Philip	*May 26*
Nicholas	*December 6*
Nightingale, Florence	*August 13*
Ninian	*September 16*
Oakerhater, David Pendleton	*September 1*
Pachomius	*May 15*
Papua New Guinea, Martyrs of	*September 2*
Patrick	*March 17*
Patteson, John Coleridge	*September 20*
Paul (and Peter)	*June 29*
Paul, The Conversion of	*January 25*
Paul, Vincent de	*September 27*
Paulinus	*October 10*
Perpetua and her companions	*March 7*
Peter the Apostle	*June 29*
Peter, The Confession of	*January 18*
Philip (and James)	*May 1*
Philip the Deacon	*June 6*
Polycarp	*February 23*
Porres, Martin de	*November 3*
Pusey, Edward Bouverie	*September 18*

Remigius	*October 1*
Richard of Chichester	*April 3*
Ridley, Nicholas	*October 16*
Robert Grosseteste	*October 9*
Sales, Francis de	*January 24*
Schereschewsky, S. I. J.	*October 14*
Scholastica	*February 10*
Seabury, Samuel	*November 14*
Selwyn, George Augustus	*April 11*
Seraphim of Sarov	*January 2*
Sergei of Radonezh	*September 25*
Simeon, Charles	*November 12*
Simon (and Jude)	*October 28*
Slessor, Mary	*January 11*
Stanton, Elizabeth Cady	*July 20*
Stephen, protomartyr	*December 26*
Stephen Harding	*April 17*
Stuart, Charles (Charles I)	*January 30*
Studdert Kennedy, Geoffrey	*March 8*
Sumner, Mary	*August 9*
Taylor, Jeremy	*August 13*
Temple, William	*November 6*
Teresa of Avila	*October 15*
Thaddaeus (see Jude)	*October 28*
Theodore of Tarsus	*September 19*
Th—rℵse of Lisieux	*October 1*
Thomas the Apostle	*December 21*
Thomas Aquinas	*January 28*
Thomas Becket	*December 29*
Timothy	*January 26*
Titus	*January 26*
Traherne, Thomas	*October 10*
Truth, Sojourner	*July 20*
Tubman, Harriet	*July 20*
Tyndale, William	*October 6*
Uganda, Martyrs of	*June 3*
Underhill, Evelyn	*June 15*
Valentine	*February 14*
Vedanayagam, Samuel Azariah	*January 2*

Vincent de Paul *September 27*
Vincent of Saragossa *January 22*

Watts, Isaac *November 25*
Wesley, John and Charles *March 3*
White, William *July 17*
Wilberforce, William *July 30*
Wilfrid *October 12*
Williams, Channing Moore *December 2*
Willibrord *November 7*
Wulfstan *January 19*

Xavier, Francis *December 3*

Feasts of our Lord

Annunciation *March 25*
Epiphany *January 6*
Holy Cross Day *September 14*
Naming & Circumcision *January 1*
Nativity (Christmas Day) *December 25*
Presentation in the Temple *February 2*
Transfiguration *August 6*

Biographical Notes

The following are biographical sketches of ancient authors not listed in the Calendar of Saints whose writings have been used in this anthology.

Adomnan (*c.*625-704)
Adomnan was probably a native of County Donegal in Ireland. He became a novice at Iona and was elected abbot in 679. He was one of the greatest scholars that Iona produced and wrote *The Life of Saint Columba* some time between 688 and 692. He visited Ireland at least three times in his life and was instrumental in getting a law passed forbidding women and children to be made prisoners of war.

Aelfric (*c.*955-*c.*1020)
Aelfric, known as "The Grammarian," entered monastic life at Winchester and became in due course the greatest scholar of the English Benedictine revival, promoting the ideals of Saint Dunstan. In 1005 he was appointed Abbot of Eynsham in Oxfordshire. Among his many writings was a series of writings on the *Lives of the Saints*, among which was a biography of Edmund, King of East Anglia.

Anastasius of Sinai (d. 599)
Anastasius was a Palestinian monk and later abbot of Saint Catherine's Monastery, Mount Sinai. He was a strong supporter of orthodoxy, and much of his literary output was directed against all forms of heresy. In 559 he was made Patriarch of Antioch.

Andrew of Crete (*c.*660-740)
Andrew was a native of Damascus. He was a monk of Jerusalem for many years, and in around 692 became Archbishop of Gortyna in Crete. He was a celebrated theologian and hymn writer. He is said to have been the first writer of the compositions called "canons." His "Great Canon," a penitential hymn for Lent, is still sung in the Byzantine liturgy. He was an eloquent preacher and a number of his sermons have survived.

Asser (d. 909)
Asser was a Welshman from St. David's. His name, however, is not Welsh but Hebrew, and was evidently adopted from Asher, the eighth son of Jacob. The custom of adopting Biblical names was common in medieval Wales. He was a scholar and adviser to Alfred the Great. He was made Bishop of Sherborne some time between 892 and 900.

Bernardine of Siena (1380-1444)
Bernardine became a Franciscan Friar at the age of twenty-two. He was responsible for moral reforms in many cities throughout Italy. He was a renowned preacher of great elegance and a promoter of devotion to the Holy Name of Jesus.

Caesarius of Arles (*c.*470-543)
Caesarius was born in France. In 489 he entered monastic life at L—rins. So outstanding was he that he was made Archbishop of Arles. He was deeply influenced by the teaching of Augustine on grace, and was a celebrated preacher.

Cogitosus (early sixth century)
Cogitosus was the monastic biographer of Saint Brigid of Kildare.

Frank, Mark (*c.*1612-64)
Mark Frank was born in Buckinghamshire, and went up to Pembroke Hall (College), Cambridge in 1627, becoming a Fellow in 1634. He was a friend of Nicholas Ferrar at Little Gidding, and possibly, therefore, of Ferrar's other close friend, George Herbert. He was primarily a scholar and preacher who enjoyed the patronage of Charles I. Stylistically, Frank was influenced by Andrewes, but he is more accessible. In his preaching he stands mid-way between the elegant, highly-wrought sermons of Andrewes, and the plain moralistic preaching that came later. His *Course of Sermons* was published in 1642. In 1644, because of his Royalist and Arminian sympathies, he was ejected by the Parliamentary visitors from his fellowship and had to leave Cambridge. On the restoration of the monarchy, he was reinstated, and in 1662 elected Master of Pembroke. He was at the same time Chaplain to Archbishop Sheldon.

Froes, Luis (dates unknown)
Luis Froes was a Jesuit who was in Japan at the time of the martyrdom of Paul Miki and his companions. He was an eye-witness of the events he recorded, and it is from him that we know the names of those who died.

Fulgentius of Ruspe (*c.*462-527)
Fulgentius was a Roman civil servant who became Bishop of Ruspe in North Africa around 502. He was of a scholarly disposition and knew some Greek. He was a strong supporter of the theology of Augustine. Some eighty or so sermons by him have survived.

Gregory of Tours (*c.*540-94)
Gregory was elected Bishop of Tours in 573. In about 576 he began his *History of the Franks* without which the early history of France would be largely unknown. He was a well-informed (if unreflective) historian who had access to original documents.

Guerric of Igny (*c.*1070-1157)
Little is known of Guerric's early life. He seems to have lived a life of prayer and study at or near the cathedral of Tournai. At some point he became a Cistercian novice, and in 1138 was made Abbot of Igny, near Rheims. A number of his sermons have survived.

Guigo II (dates unknown)
Guigo II was the ninth Prior of La Grande Chartreuse.

Hippolytus of Rome (*c.*170-*c.*236)
A leading theologian of the third century, Hippolytus wrote in Greek at a time when Latin was coming to prevail in the Christian community at Rome. His *Apostolic Tradition* was a code of regulations and discipline in the Church which includes eucharistic prayers which are the oldest known in the Roman Church. Theologically and socially, he was very conservative.

Lactantius (*c.*240-*c.*320)
Before his conversion to Christianity, Lactantius was a teacher of rhetoric. He became a notable Latin Christian apologist, especially remembered for his *Divine Institutes* which was intended to demonstrate the cultural and intellectual credibility of Christianity. The Emperor Constantine made him tutor to his son Crispus.

Origen (*c.*185-*c.*254)
Origen was born in Egypt and became a leading representative of the Alexandrian school of theology. He was the most powerful mind of early Christianity, primarily a Biblical scholar who recognized a three-fold meaning to Scripture: literal, moral and allegorical. He edited the text of the Old Testament in six columns (the *Hexapala*) comparing the Hebrew text with various Greek translations. In his theological treatise *On Principles* he outlines the basic principles of the Christian concept of the world. He was a mystic, and wrote two key ascetical works *On Prayer* and *An Exhortation to Martyrdom*, both of which were read widely. Sadly, the Greek originals of many of his works, including his extensive Biblical commentaries, have been lost. Some are known only now in fragmentary (poor) Latin translation.

Osbert of Clare (*c.*1090-*c.*1155)
Osbert was a monk of Westminster who enjoyed a chequered monastic career. From *c.*1129-33 he was banished from the monastery. In 1136, however, he was elected Prior, and subsequently in 1141 sent to Rome to advocate the canonization of Edward the Confessor. However, he was expelled from the monastery a second time. He wrote the lives of various saints, most notably that

of Edward the Confessor, perhaps making use of an earlier anonymous *Life* which some have attributed to a monk of St. Bertin.

Peter Chrysologus (*c.*400-50)
Peter Chrysologus was born in Italy, and became Bishop of Ravenna. He was a faithful pastor, many of whose sermons have been preserved. He was named "Chrysologus" (Greek meaning "golden-worded") to make him a Western counterpart of John "Chrysostom" ("golden-mouthed") in the East.

Peter Damian (1007-72)
Peter Damian was born in Ravenna of poor parents. In 1035 he entered the Benedictine hermitage at Fonte Avella, and in 1043 became Prior. He founded many new monasteries and reformed existing ones. He was famous as an uncompromising preacher against the worldliness and corrupt practices of the clergy. He became Cardinal Bishop of Ostia in 1057.

Quodvultdeus (d. *c.*453)
As a young man Quodvultdeus knew and corresponded with Augustine who was bishop in the neighbouring town of Hippo Regis. He was elected Bishop of Carthage, the most important see in North Africa, at the time of the Barbarian invasions. He ended his days in Naples where he had been exiled. A number of his sermons have survived.

Rabanus Maurus (776 or 784-856)
Rabanus Maurus was one of the greatest theologians of his age, and known as the "Teacher of Germany." He was educated at the monastery of Fulda and later at Tours under the direction of Alcuin. He was ordained priest in 814, and elected abbot in 822. He resigned the abbacy in 842 to lead a life of prayer and study, but in 847 was made Archbishop of Mainz. He carried forward the evangelization of Germany and wrote many commentaries on Scripture, often with a mystical interpretation.

Rhigyfarch the Wise (eleventh century)
Rhigyfarch was a monk of St. David's at the end of the eleventh century. He claims to have based his *Life of David* on earlier manuscripts. In its present form it may well have been written to further the metropolitical claims of the see of St David's.

Rimbert (dates unknown)
Rimbert was a disciple of Anskar and a fellow missionary, who succeeded him as Bishop of Bremen in 865. He wrote his *Life of Saint Anskar* a few years after the saint's death, and it is regarded as one of the best hagiographies of its time.

Sophronius (*c.*560-638)
Sophronius was born in Damascus. He became a monk first of all in Egypt, later near the Jordan, and finally (from 619) in Jerusalem. In 634 he was elected Patriarch of Jerusalem where he was concerned to promulgate the teaching of the Council of Chalcedon about the two natures in Christ. Some of his sermons and poems have survived, many of which reflect the liturgical customs of the Jerusalem Church. Just before he died he witnessed the capture of Jerusalem by the Saracens under Caliph Omar in 637.

Sulpicius Severus (*c.*360-*c.*420)
Sulpicius Severus trained as a lawyer. Following his wife's death, he became an ascetic and disciple of Martin of Tours. As far as Martin had personal friends, Sulpicius could be numbered among them, and Martin would talk to him freely. As a result of this friendship he wrote his *Life*, portraying Martin as a man of God whose authenticity was attested by God through miracles and visions. His work was highly influential on later hagiography.

Tertullian (*c.*160-*c.*225)
Tertullian was the first major figure in Latin theology. He was born in Carthage of pagan parents, trained as a lawyer, and became a Christian in about 193. It is uncertain whether or not he was ever ordained. He produced a series of significant controversial and apologetic writings. He is particularly noted for his ability to coin new Latin terms to translate the emerging theological vocabulary of the Greek-speaking Eastern Church. He was a man of passionate feeling, full of paradox, with a tendency to extremes. This led him in about 207 to espouse Montanism - a charismatic movement that claimed to be inaugurating the age of the Spirit.

Turgot (*c.*1060-*c.*1120)
Turgot was a Saxon from Lincolnshire who was confessor to Queen Margaret of Scotland. He left her court to become part of the monastic community at Durham, subsequently becoming Prior. In 1109 the last Celtic Bishop of St. Andrews died, and King Alexander I appointed Turgot as the first "Roman" Bishop of St. Andrews.

Walton, Isaac (1593-1683)
Isaac Walton was born in Staffordshire, but as a young man traveled to London and became an ironmonger. There he came under the influence of John Donne. He was a strong High Churchman and a Royalist, and after the Battle of Marston Moor in 1644 retired from business. In retirement he wrote not only the *Compleat Angler* (1653) for which he is justly famous, but also his *Lives* of Dr. John Donne (1640), Sir Henry Wotton (1651), Mr. Richard Hooker (1665), Mr. George Herbert (1670) which also contains a pen-portrait of Herbert's friend Nicholas

Ferrar, and Dr. Robert Sanderson (1678). Based on personal knowledge and remarkable for the beauty of their language, they represent valuable contemporary documents of the period.

William of Malmesbury (*c.*1090-*c.*1143)

William was the chief English historian of his generation. He was a monk of Malmesbury where he was offered, but declined, the abbacy in 1140. His two most important works were the *Annals of the English Kings* (1120) and the *Annals of the English Prelates* (1125) which dealt with respectively secular and ecclesiastical English history. He also wrote a *Life of Saint Dunstan* and a *Life of Saint Wulfstan.*

William of St. Thierry (*c.*1085-1148)

William was born at Li—ge. He entered the Benedictine Abbey of Rheims in 1113, and in 1119 or 1120 was elected Abbot of St. Thierry nearby. Before his election as abbot, he had already made the acquaintance of Bernard of Clairvaux, and in 1135 he resigned his abbacy and went to join a group of Cistercian monks from Igny. He wrote a number of influential treatises, including several expositions of the Song of Songs. His last years were devoted to a synthesis of his doctrine and experience, known as *The Golden Epistle*.

ACKNOWLEDGEMENTS

A. BIOGRAPHIES

The biographical sketches of the saints are largely reproduced from *Exciting Holiness,* edited by Br. Tristam Holland SSF, Canterbury: SCM Press, 1997. The Authors are grateful for his permission to reproduce material to provide continuity between volumes.

The contributions of individual authors are acknowledged as follows:

Reverend Robert Atwell for Augustine of Canterbury, Augustine of Hippo, Cecilia, Cyril of Alexandria, Gertrude the Great, Cyril & Methodius, Gregory of Nyssa, Macrina, Gregory the Great, Ignatius of Antioch, Irenaeus, Jane Frances de Chantal, John Chrysostom, Justin, The Blessed Virgin Mary, Pachomius, Thérèse of Lisieux, All Souls Day, and Stephen Harding;
Sister Catherine OHP for Hilda;
Reverend Professor Owen Chadwick for George Augustus Selwyn;
Dr. Petà Dunstan for Dietrich Bonhoeffer, John Keble, Edward King, Frederick Denison Maurice, John Mason Neale, Florence Nightingale, Edward Bouverie Pusey, Mary Slessor, Geoffrey Studdert Kennedy, Mary Sumner, William Temple, Evelyn Underhill, and William Wilberforce;
Reverend Claire Farley for Hildegard of Bingen;
Sister Gillian Claire OSC for Clare;
Reverend Dr. Donald Gray for Alcuin;
Brother Tristam Holland SSF for approximately one hundred and forty biographies;
Reverend Dr. Simon Jones for Aidan, Alban, and Ephrem;
Reverend Dr. Diarmaid MacCulloch for Thomas Cranmer;
Very Reverend Michael Perham and the Norwich Diocesan Liturgical Committee for Edmund of East Anglia, Julian of Norwich and Margery Kempe;
Brother Thomas Quin OSB for Anselm, Bede, Benedict, Cuthbert, Dunstan, Edward the Confessor, Scholastica and Thomas Becket;
Reverend Bernard Schunemann for Willibrord;
Reverend Philip Sheldrake for George Herbert;
Sister Marianne Sodorstrom for Anskar;
Reverend Dr. Jo Spreadbury for Bridget of Sweden, Catherine of Siena, John of the Cross, Mary Magdalene, Mary & Martha, and Teresa of Avila;
Christopher L. Webber for those biographies unique to the American edition.

B. COPYRIGHT MATERIAL

The Authors and Publishers are grateful for permission to reproduce material under copyright. They are grateful in particular for the cooperation of:

The International Committee for English in the Liturgy Inc. (ICEL), for permission to reproduce the English translation of the non-biblical readings from the *Roman Catholic Liturgy of the Hours,* American Edition; © 1974; all rights reserved; adapted with permission;
and
The Church Hymnal Corporation of the Episcopal Church of the United States of America, for permission to adopt the modifications in the ICEL texts employed by J. Robert Wright in *Readings for the Daily Office from the Early Church,* New York, 1991 and *They Still Speak,* New York, 1993, to accord with Anglican usage (see Wright, *Readings for the Daily Office from the Early Church,* pp. 515-23).

Every effort has been made to trace the copyright owners of material included in this book. The Authors and Publishers would be grateful if any omissions or inaccuracies in these acknowledgements could be brought to their attention for correction in any future edition. They are grateful to the following copyright holders:

Addison Wesley Longman, for an extract from *The Vision of God,* by Kenneth Kirk, 1931.
Bruce Publishing Company (Milwaukee), for an extract from *Saint Elizabeth of Hungary: A Story of Twenty-four Years,* by Nesta De Robeck, 1954.
Burns & Oates Ltd, for extracts from *Charles de Foucauld: Meditations of a Hermit,* translated by Charlotte Balfour, 1930; *The Complete Works of Saint John of the Cross,* translated by Allison Peers, 1935; *New Seeds of Contemplation* by Thomas Merton, 1961, used with permission of the Thomas Merton Legacy Trust; *Mary, Mother of God, Mother of the Poor*, by Ivone Gebara & Maria Clara Bingemer, translated by Phillip Berryman, 1989.
The estate of Roy Campbell, for an extract from his translation of *The Poems of Saint John of the Cross,* 1966.
Cistercian Publications Inc., Kalamazoo, Michigan, for extracts from *The Works of Aelred of Rievaulx I,* translated by Penelope Lawson CSMV, 1971; *The Works of William of St. Thierry I,* also translated by Penelope Lawson CSMV, 1971; *The Sayings of the Desert Fathers,* translated by Benedicta Ward SLG, 1975/1983; *The Luminous Eye: The Spiritual*

World Vision of Saint Ephrem the Syrian, translated by Sebastian Brock, 1985.
Darton Longman & Todd Ltd, for an extract from *God and Man,* by Metropolitan Anthony of Sourozh (Anthony Bloom), 1971.
Eagle of Inter-Publishing Service (IPS) Ltd, for an extract from *Worship,* by Evelyn Underhill, 1936.
Episcopal Diocese of New Hampshire, *The New Hampshire Episcopal News* for use of " The Burning Bush," by Johathan Myrick Daniels, June, 1965, Vol. 7, No. 9.
William B. Eerdmans Publishing Co., Grand Rapids, Michigan, for an extract from "Exhortation to the Greeks," by Clement of Alexandria, *The Ante-Nicene Fathers*, vol. 2, eds. Alexander Roberts and James Donaldson; for an extract from "On Baptism," by Tertullian, *The Ante-Nicene Fathers*, vol. 3, eds. Alexander Roberts and James Donaldson; for an extract from "Acts of the Holy Apostles Peter and Paul," an extract from "Fragments from His Five Books of Commentaries on the Acts of the Apostles," by Hegesippus, and an extract from "The Epistles of Pope Fabian," *The Ante-Nicene Fathers*, vol. 8, eds. Alexander Roberts and James Donaldson, Grand Rapids, Michigan, all reprinted 1977;and for an extract from "The Church History of Eusebius," *The Nicene and Post-Nicene Fathers*, Second Series, vol. 1, eds. Philip Schaff and Henry Wace, reprinted 1970.
Faber and Faber Ltd, in association with the estate of T. S. Eliot, for an extract from *Murder in the Cathedral,* by T. S. Eliot, and for the poem "Journey of the Magi" from *T. S. Eliot: Collected Poems 1909-1962.*
Jean Farrant, for an extract from her book *Mashonaland Martyr: Bernard Mizeki and the Pioneer Church,* 1966.
The Folio Society Ltd, for an extract from *The Trial of Joan of Arc,* translated by W. S. Scott, 1956.
Victor Gollancz, for an extract from *The Theology of Auschwitz* by Ulrich Simon, 1967.
Grow Forward Movement Publications, for an extract from "Christian Loyalty," by Paul Jones, in *Bishop Paul Jones, Witness for Peace*, by John Howard Melish, ed. Peter Eaton, Cincinnati, Ohio, 1992.
HarperCollins Publishers Ltd, for an extract from *Be Still and Know,* by Michael Ramsey, 1982.
Harper & Row, Publishers, Inc. Copyright 1949; Copyright © renewed 1977 by Frederick Ward Kates; reprinted by permission of HarperCollins Publishers, Inc. for an extract from *Things that Matter: The Best of the Writings of Bishop Brent* by Frederick Ward Kates.
Hodder & Stoughton, an imprint of Hodder Headline PLC, for an extract from *Teresa of Avila,* by Shirley du Boulay, 1991.

David Jones in association with the Sussex Record Society, for an extract from Ralf Bocking's *The Life of Saint Richard,* translated by David Jones, 1995.
The Heirs to the Estate of Martin Luther King, Jr., c/o Writers House, Inc., as agent for the Proprietor; copyright 1963 by Martin Luther King, Jr., renewed 1991 by Coretta Scott King, for an extract from "I have a Dream."
The Liturgical Press, St. John's Collegeville, for extracts from the *The Life and Miracles of Saint Benedict,* translated by O. Zimmermann & B. R. Avery.
Macmillan Publishing Company, a division of Macmillan Inc., for extracts from *The Protestant Reformation,* edited by Hans J. Hillerbrand, 1968.
Macmillan Press Ltd, for an extract from *Evil and the God of Love,* by John Hick (2nd edition) 1985, altered with permission.
Marshall, Morgan & Scott Ltd, for an extract from *Janani,* by Margaret Ford, 1978.
Constance Millington in association with the Asian Trading Corporation, for an extract from *An Ecumenical Venture: The History of Nandyal Diocese in Andhra Pradesh.*
Mowbray, an imprint of Cassell plc, (last known copyright holders) for an extract from *The Ladder of Monks and Twelve Meditations,* translated by Edmund Colledge OSA and James Walsh SJ, 1978.
New Directions Publishing Corporation for an except from *New Seeds of Contemplation* by Thomas Merton, 1961.
Oklahoma Historical Society, for an extract from "Journey to Sainthood: David Pendleton Oakerhater's Better Way," by Alvin O. Turner, *The Chronicles of Oklahoma*, vol. LXX, no. 2, 1992.
The Order of the Holy Cross, on behalf of Holy Cross Press, for an extract from *Bargainers and Beggars*, by James Otis Sargent Huntington, West Park, New York, 1919.
Oxford University Press UK, for extracts from *The Confessions of Saint Augustine,* translated by Henry Chadwick, 1991; *Magna Vita: A Life of Saint Hugh of Lincoln by Adam, Monk of Eynsham Abbey,* translated by D. L. Doule & David Farmer, 1985; *The Life of King Edward who rests at Westminster,* attributed to a monk of St. Bertin, edited and translated by Frank Barlow, 2nd edition, 1992.
Oxford University Press, New York, for an extract from *The Letters of Hildegard of Bingen*, translated by Joseph L. Baird & Radd K. Ehrman, 1994.
Papua New Guinea Church Partnership, for an extract from *The White-Robed Army of Martyrs,* by Bishop David Hand.

Paulist Press, Mahwah, New Jersey, for extracts from *Athanasius: The Life Of Antony,* translated by Robert Gregg, 1980; *Catherine of Siena: Dialogue,* translated by Suzanne Noffke OP, 1980; *Francis and Clare: The Complete Works,* translated by R. J. Armstrong and Ignatius Brady, 1982; *Gertrude of Helfta: Herald of Divine Love*, translated by Margaret Winkworth, 1993; *Ephrem of Syria: Hymns*, translated by Kathleen E. McVey, 1989; *Francis de Sales & Jane de Chantal: Letters of Spiritual Direction,* translated by Peronne Marie Thibert VHM, 1988. In the above, all translations are © their translators.

Penguin Books Ltd., for extracts from *The Lives of the Saints,* translated by J. F. Webb, 1965; *The Prayers and Meditations of Saint Anselm,* translated by Benedicta Ward SLG, 1973; *Revelations of Divine Love* by Julian of Norwich, translated by Clifton Walters, 1966; *Alfred the Great*, selected and translated by Simon Keynes and Michael Lappidge, 1983; *The Life of Saint Columba,* by Adomnan, translated by Richard Sharpe, 1995; *Saint Ignatius of Loyola: Personal Writings,* translated by Joseph Munitiz and Philip Endean, 1996; *A History of Christian Missions,* by Stephen Neill, 2nd edition 1986; *The Book of Margery Kempe,* translated by B. A. Windeatt, 1985; Donald Attwater, *The Penguin Dictionary of Saints,* 1965.

Russell & Volkening as agents for the author. *Harriet Tubman: Conductor of the Underground Railroad.* Copyright © 1955 by Ann Petry, renewed in 1983 by Ann Petry. Reprinted by permission.

Saint Vladimir's Seminary Press, Crestwood, New York, for the use of a passage from the publication *God and Man* by Metropolitan Anthony of Sourozh (Anthony Bloom, 1971.

SCM Press, for extracts from *Letters and Papers from Prison,* by Dietrich Bonhoeffer, translated by E. Bethge, 2nd enlarged edition, 1971; *The Cost of Discipleship,* by Dietrich Bonhoeffer, translated by R. H. Fuller, 1959; *The Silent Rebellion,* by A. M. Allchin, 1958; *Said or Sung,* by Austin Farrer, 1960.

Sheed & Ward Ltd., for extracts from *The Way of Perfection,* by Teresa of Avila, translated and edited by E. Allison Peers, 1946; *A Treasury of Russian Spirituality,* edited by George P. Fedotov, 1950.

Simon & Schuster, Inc. New York, New York, for use of an excerpt from the book *The Cost of Discipleship* by Dietrich Bonhoeffer, translated by R.H. Fuller.

SPCK, for extracts from *Christianity and Social Order,* by William Temple, 1942 & re-prints; *Hildegard of Bingen: An Anthology,* translated by Robert Carver, and edited by Fiona Bowie & Oliver Davies, 1990; Janet Morley, *All Desires Known,* 1992; used by permission of Morehouse Publishing.

Tessa Sayle Agency, for the prayer of Evelyn Underhill entitled "For Wholeness."
University of the South Press, for an extract from "The Faith of a Christian Today," by William Porcer DuBose, *A DuBose Reader: Selections from the Writings of William Porcer DuBose*, ed., Armentrout, Donald S., 1984.
University Press of Virginia for an extract from "The Race-Problem in America," *Civilization and Black Progress: Selected Writings of Alexander Crummell on the South*, ed. J. R. Oldfield, Charlottesville, 1995.
University of Wales Press, for an extract from *Rhigyfarch's Life of Saint David,* translated by J. W. James, 1967.
A. P. Watt Ltd and the Estate of Ronald Knox, for extracts from *Occasional Sermons* by Msgr. R. A. Knox, published by Burns & Oates, 1960; and for an extract from *Autobiography of a Saint,* published by Harvill Press, 1958.
The Westminster Press, for extracts from *The Library of Christian Classics*, vol. IV, Philadelphia, 1953.

C. OTHER MATERIAL

Many individuals, societies and friends have offered their advice and help in the selection of extracts. The Author is grateful to the following in particular:

Sister Tessa Debney SLG for the extracts of and about Teresa of Avila;
Professor Ann Loades of Durham University, for information and advice on various saints;
Christine Luxton, secretary to the Papua New Guinea Church Partnership, for information relating to the PNG martyrs;
Reverend Margaret Saunders for allowing me to include a poem of hers, hitherto unpublished;
Sister Marianne Sodorstrom of Alisike Kloster, Sweden, for selecting and translating the extracts for Bridget of Sweden and Anskar;